CRIME IN A COMPLEX SOCIETY
An introduction to criminology

THE DORSEY SERIES IN ANTHROPOLOGY AND SOCIOLOGY

EDITOR ROBIN M. WILLIAMS, JR. *Cornell University*

Crime
in a
complex society

An introduction to criminology

RICHARD D. KNUDTEN
Chairman, Department of Sociology
Valparaiso University

1970

The
Dorsey
Press HOMEWOOD, ILLINOIS
IRWIN-DORSEY LIMITED, GEORGETOWN, ONTARIO

FIRST PRINTING, JUNE, 1970

Library of Congress Catalog Card No. 78–119808
Printed in the United States of America

To
Mary, Stephen, David, Thomas, and *Susan*

PREFACE

The decade of the 1960's found the attention of the American public centered upon the problem of crime, a product related to the general growth of the population which posed a major threat to the stability of the emergent urban community. It was not until the latter part of that decade, however, that the first serious steps were undertaken to complete a major evaluation of delinquency and crime problems, to make additional financial and personnel commitments to often-neglected law enforcement agencies, and to renew the system of justice in its entirety. While the process of renewal gained new momentum in the early 1970's, a fresh optimism, tempered by a realistic recognition that crime may well be a by-product of modern culture, characterizes the current response. But because delinquency and crime are not expressed in a single form, renewal promises to be a slow process. Part of the crime problem is due to the fact that apprehension of offenders is uncertain, their conviction problematic, and their treatment marginal. Also, society is somewhat ambivalent about the existence of crime, despite its loud protestations and fears regarding "crime in the streets."

The commonness and diversity of criminal deviance make it extremely hard to detect and to control. At any given point the total volume of reported crime is merely a sample of the total volume of delinquent or criminal acts. Many events are never detected or, if detected, are never reported and/or prosecuted. This is especially true in the area of delinquency where public policy fluctuates between a desire to control deviant activity and a wish to give the juvenile offender a second chance to lead a "legitimate" life.

All is not well with the current systems of enforcement and justice. Police officers are being attacked by radicals who claim the police are nothing more than "pigs" and agents of the establishment. They in turn often express their hostility by overt action against these protagonists. In many jurisdictions the prosecutor remains a part-time public official who gives priority to his own legal practice over his public duties, a situation which tends to encourage plea bargaining at the possible expense of justice. Even the person of the judge is under attack, as his trial objectivity, general judicial fairness, and financial and ethical dealings are being increasingly questioned. But the challenge does not end even there. The training and capability of probation and parole personnel and correctional officers and administrators are openly criticized. Claims that prisons actually assist the growth of homosexuality and professional criminality fill the air. In short, the total system of social control and criminal justice has been laid bare both in its weaknesses and in its hopes.

Crime in a Complex Society examines these problems. In Part One, subtitled "Crime, Criminology, and the Twentieth Century," the reader is introduced to the context of criminal deviance, the relationship of crime and criminal law, statistics concerning the prevalence and distribution of crime, and the criminological approach to deviance analysis. In Part Two, "Differential Criminal Expressions," he reviews the scope of property crimes and their participants, criminal violations against the person, the context of juvenile delinquency, special forms of female criminality, and organized and white-collar crime.

Part Three deals with historical and current physio-psychological, socioenvironmental and sociocultural, and social-psychological explanations of crime causation in a series of four chapters. The last of these, Chapter 14, introduces the student of criminology to the general theoretical contributions of Talcott Parsons, Robert Merton, George Homans, and Leon Festinger, and presents the author's middle-range *theory of relativity,* a new conceptual explanation of delinquency and crime causation. Contrary to the many *ad hoc* theories of the past, the *theory of relativity* integrates known criminological knowledge in a manner that reveals the complexity of criminal and deviant behavior and the relationship of cultural, social, small group, and personality factors to such forms of deviance.

Part Four, focusing on the "Formal Systems of Social Control," probes the system of law enforcement and the roles of the prosecuting and defense attornies. Part Five, on the other hand, examines the multiple facets of the systems of justice. The functions of the juvenile court, the adult criminal court, the military tribunal, and the appellate and Supreme courts in the development and control of delinquency and crime problems are reviewed. In Part Six attention is directed to the system of sentencing and probation, and the nature and operations of juvenile institutions, the various approaches to the imprisonment of adults, and the inevitable question of the death penalty. Part Seven examines the problems associated with the offender's return to recidivism, and the issues of delinquency and crime prediction. Part Eight closes the volume with a discussion of the prevention of delinquent and criminal conduct.

From its conception, *Crime in a Complex Society* has been designed to cover the entire scope of the social control and justice systems. Possessing a cross-cultural perspective, the volume reveals the commonality of delinquent and criminal behavior and the wide diversity of legal, enforcement, and correctional practice. In a unique way it focuses special attention upon the roles and actions of the prosecuting and defense attorneys, the military tribunal, the appellate and Supreme courts, the incarceration of adults, and the problems of community reentry, recidivism, and prediction.

Crime in a Complex Society is a NOW book. The history of delinquency and crime has consciously been minimized in order to emphasize the behavioral subtleties of the modern situation. Special attention has been given to contemporary data which reveal the vast deficiencies and challenges of current procedures. Written from a social system point of view, this work reveals the interrelatedness and interactional quality of the delinquency and crime problem. Throughout it recognizes that delinquent-criminal behavior is human behavior, that such forms of deviance are common to a large proportion of any population, and that the current legal conception of crime is incomplete and refers primarily to those crimes that are committed by an individual or a group of individuals against another person or his property.

Although the work is the author's, many hands have left their imprint on these pages. Vernon Fox (Florida State); Daniel Glaser (Southern California); George Homans (Harvard); Stephen Schafer (Northeastern); William Cross, LeRoy Martinson, and Nancy Sederberg (Valparaiso); and the undergraduate students in my criminology, penology, and sociology-of-religion seminars during the fall of 1969 contributed to the final version of the author's new middle-range *theory of relativity*. Colleen Casey, Linda Crowell, Barbara Gerken, Beverly McCray, Beverly McCollum, and Nathalie Rayder relieved the author of much of the tedious work of manuscript preparation. Each receives special thanks.

Valparaiso University   RICHARD D. KNUDTEN
May, 1970

CONTENTS

Part TWO
Differential criminal expressions

Part THREE
Theoretical origins of delinquent and
criminal behavior

ment. Enter Ferri. Enter Garofalo. The phrenological explanation. The examination of physical types: Goring and Hooten. Studies of the Jukes and Kallikak families. The growth of experimental psychology: The investigation of mental disorders and deficiencies. Sheldon and somatotypes. The Gluecks. The rise of the psychoanalytic approach. Modifications in psychoanalytic theory. Other interpretations.

Part SIX
The disposition of offenders

Part SEVEN
The return to the community

Part EIGHT
The prevention of delinquency and crime

Appendix

INTRODUCTION

The post-World War II era has been marked by a variety of social conditions which have heavily influenced the nature and scope of delinquency and crime. The large general increase in population has also enlarged the numbers of juveniles in the delinquency-prone age ranges. The concern for social justice, particularly among the young, has led many to be arrested for civil disobedience. The quest for world peace has been expressed by some in forms of violence in the name of peace. That the older formal definitions of delinquency and crime are inadequate is now clear. As never before, the public has become aroused and concerned about "crime" of environmental pollution. Organized crime is being attacked with renewed determination and vigor. While the shortcomings of the total system of social control are being eagerly discussed, and vigorously protested, the system is being modified only slowly.

Nowhere are the challenges of our times more evident than in the areas of juvenile delinquency and adult criminality. While the traditional concern for harms against the person (for example, murder or forcible rape) or against property (burglary and theft) still remains, the scope of criminal deviance has passed well beyond these traditional levels. Today it includes refusal to register for the draft, burning draft cards, and rejection of the validity of laws against the use of marihuana. But the new definitions and forms of crime do not stop there. Crimes against the public good are hesitatingly being incorporated into the body of criminal law. Attempts were made to eliminate electrical company price-fixing in the early 1960's through the trial process. In the 1970 trials of the "Chicago Seven," new criminal definitions of conspiracy to incite riots and crossing state lines to incite riots have been put to the test. Private arms collections and resistance to police by the Black Panthers

1

have created new tensions and controversies. New ways have been found to prosecute members of organized crime syndicates.

Delinquency and crime have become more diversified. The automobile has made mobility fully possible. Mass existence in urban complexes have forced modifications of the processes of social control. Adaptation evolution, and even revolution have been encouraged by basic changes in living patterns. The development of newer crime forms and the intensification of the older ones are only facets of the process of change.

But behind these situations is the quest for delinquency-crime causation. What causes these expressions? How can they be explained? Sigmund Freud found the causes of many deviant acts in the relationships of id, ego, and superego and particularly in the effects of repression into the unconscious of antisocial desires which nevertheless continue to affect behavior. Karl Marx, on the other hand, saw criminal deviance as the result of poverty and the defects of the economic system. Edwin H. Sutherland viewed nonnormative behavior as a product of learning processes and of the dynamics of associational relationships. Albert H. Cohen suggests that adolescent male delinquency is encouraged by delinquent subcultures. David Matza relates the deviant's offenses to a condition of drift. While many other theorists have attempted to explain the causes of delinquency and crime, most fail to offer an explanation that covers all forms of delinquent and criminal conduct.

A THEORY OF RELATIVITY: RICHARD D. KNUDTEN

The author's theory of relativity, presented in its entirety in Chapter 14 and here in a shortened version, is designed to present a broad explanation of delinquent and criminal conduct and to bring known criminological data into a coherent middle-range theoretical explanation of delinquency and crime causation. Conceived in a series of 39 propositions together with an introductory and concluding statement, the theory in shortened form suggests that *the definition, character, and incidence of delinquency and crime are relative to the cultural, social, small-group, and personality factors which produce and shape them.*

I. Relativity and culture

1. The definition, character, and incidence of delinquency and crime, while often similar in a number of other cultures, are relative.
2. Because delinquency and crime are by definition violations of some normative legal code, they are relative to normative social definitions.

3. The distinction between serious and less serious offenses is relative.
4. Although young adult and adult crimes are specific violations of the criminal code, delinquent offenses, while also specified in law, are generally more extensive and cover behavior often permitted adults.
5. The number of delinquent and criminal offenses known to the police are only a fraction of the total volume of such violations.
6. Every cultural system is composed of multiple normative and deviant subsystems.
7. For some persons within a social or cultural system, crime is a functional act for attaining major social and cultural goals.
8. Delinquency is often a product of social roles provided and supported within a subculture of delinquency.
9. Subcultures of deviance may be of different types.
10. Where delinquent and criminal conduct are more a product of cultural than of personality factors, decreased functioning of normative social controls, increased value conflicts, and greater social disorganization are likely to exist.
11. Some delinquent behavior is an anticipated outcome of "normal" adolescent socialization.
12. Because the totality of culture is always greater than the individual or group's ability to comprehend and command that culture, delinquent and criminal groups will reveal distinct patterns which are not found to the same degree among the more norm-maintaining elements of society.
13. Social factors act selectively upon delinquents who possess or are excessively exposed to certain personal traits and/or who belong to certain stigmatized ascriptive categories.
14. Male juveniles often engage in "conspicuous masculinity," attempting to prove their manhood by malicious and destructive acts.
15. As the distance between classes narrows, forms of class delinquency and crime will become less well defined.
16. The volume of delinquency and crime will tend to increase in direct relationship to a variety of factors listed below.

II. Relativity and social organization

17. While the social functions of a deviant organization help to determine the structure of that organization, the structure helps to determine the eventual effectiveness of the deviant functions of that organization.
18. Some delinquency and crime functions are manifest (intended)

and others are latent (unintended) consequences of a completed action.

19. Social structures frequently exert pressures upon some person, especially the poorly socialized, to participate in nonconforming rather than conforming actions.

20. Deviant and normative social structures are composed of role relationships which include role transactions and sequences of role bargains.

21. Each actor is located within the delinquent-criminal group in terms of status-roles.

22. The stability and the orderly development of the delinquent-criminal social system depend upon the meeting of a minimum number of needs for a majority of actors, the maintenance of a minimum of control over potentially disruptive behavior, and the continued internalization of a personality level adequate for one's participation within that system.

23. Delinquency and crime are potential status equalizers in a competitive society.

24. As individuals, delinquents and criminals reveal a tendency to seek immediate gratification and an inability or unwillingness to defer their desires for fulfillment.

25. The basic delinquent-criminal interests of the juvenile or adult offender are determined in large degree by whether he is pursuing his own private interest or one which he shares with others.

III. Relativity and the small group

26. Socialization to delinquency and crime generally occurs in small groups which share a dynamic social equilibrium and possess true uniformities in activity (what group members do), interaction (relation of one member to another) and sentiment (sum of interior feelings or codes of behavior which groups adopt).

27. Each delinquent or criminal group participates within an external system (relationship between group and environment) and an internal system (group sentiments to another which have implications for behavior).

28. When men interact within a delinquent or criminal group or system, they are more likely to hold similar norms, believe themselves to be be distinct from other persons or subgroups, and participate in similar activities.

29. The size and nature of the delinquent or criminal group are variable and relative.

30. Although inherited physical characteristics are the raw material

from which personality is formed through a process of socialization in multiple social groups, most crimes are products of all the processes involved in learning.

IV. Relativity and the individual

31. *Some* delinquency or crime may be a substitute or symbolic expression of a repressed personality structure and may be a product of guilt or anxiety resulting from a conflict in the unconscious mind.
32. The processes of stigmatization and alienation play an important part in the development of delinquent or criminal personalities.
33. Deviating behavior in the form of delinquency and crime may also be a product of dissociation between culturally prescribed aspirations and socially structured avenues for realizing these aspirations.
34. Because delinquents and criminals are unable to accept continued tension and/or conflict throughout their lives, they will make every effort to reduce dissonance (inconsistency).
35. The move to lessen dissonance (inconsistency) and achieve consonance (consistency) will include attempts by the delinquent or criminal to avoid situations or information which produce or increase dissonance and to unify one's cognition about one's self, one's behavior, and one's environment.
36. Because the delinquent or criminal's sense of reality will bring pressures to bear upon his person to bring appropriate cognitive elements into line, the situations which are real in their consequences will be those which persons define as real.
37. Delinquents or criminals who become personally demoralized or socially deinstitutionalized may adapt to their social context through innovation, ritualism, retreatism or withdrawal, isolation, and rebellion or aggression.
38. Although the greater number of juveniles overcome delinquent tendencies, many continue into adult crime.
39. The violator's success or failure in overcoming delinquency and crime depends in large degree upon his ability to bargain and upon his assets in the interactional negotiated exchange process.

Delinquency and crime are relative and depend upon the situation in which criminal norms and action are located as defined by the cultural environment, the person's tendency to ignore or to neutralize limits placed upon his actions by his social class and social status, his ability to resist pressures which call for violation placed upon him by his group roles, and his tendency toward action as determined by his individual personality.

CONCLUDING COMMENTS

No theory has complete meaning without an understanding of the data upon which it is based. This theory of relativity is no exception. What follows in these pages represents the core data and knowledge which this theory presumes. The reader's quest for criminological understanding begins in the next chapter with an introduction to the context of criminal deviance.

Part ONE

Crime, criminology, and
the twentieth century

Chapter 1

THE SOCIAL CONTEXT
OF CRIMINAL DEVIANCE

Crime is varied and complex, possessing no single face and limited to no one particular social group. Whether national or international, crime results from natural human interaction as persons act within cultural systems, react to social conditions, and respond to existing opportunities. Fear has gripped many Americans as criminal activity has increased in volume. The rise of criminal deviance has not been restricted to the United States; crime has been increasing internationally, partly as a result of expanded opportunity, greater urbanization, and ready access to mass-produced goods. Since crime is a product of the social system, each person becomes its perpetuator and yet its victim.

THE AMERICAN CONTEXT

The precise volume of American crime is unknown, since crime, insofar as possible, is an activity of stealth and secrecy. Although existing crime indexes, especially the Federal Bureau of Investigation's *Uniform Crime Reports,* suggest that increased criminal activity poses a substantial threat to social mores and urban security, the exact dimensions of the challenge are yet unclear. While the traditional crimes of assault, robbery, burglary, and larceny are well documented in these indexes, the newer types of white-collar and organized crime, made possible by modern technology, are largely ignored.

Most citizens believe that crime is simply a product of deviant groups (such as professional criminals, juvenile delinquents, black rioters, or hippie students), and they ignore or excuse their own forms of disrespect for or violation of the law. Ironically, many persons who openly chal-

√**TABLE 1-1**

Number and rate of arrests for the 10 most frequent offenses, 1968
(4,812 agencies reporting; total population 145,306,000)

Rank	Offense	Number	Rate (Per 100,000 Population)	Percent of Total Arrests
1	Drunkenness	1,415,961	974.5	25.6
2	Disorderly conduct	593,104	408.2	10.7
3	Larceny	463,924	319.3	8.4
4	Driving under the influence	307,231	211.4	5.5
5	Burglary	256,216	176.3	4.6
6	Simple (other) assault	239,918	165.1	4.3
7	Liquor laws	215,376	148.2	3.9
8	Runaways	149,052	102.6	2.7
9	Motor vehicle theft	125,263	86.2	2.3
10	Vandalism	110,182	75.8	2.0
	Total, 10 most frequent offenses	3,876,227	2,667.6	70.0
	Arrests for all offenses*	5,526,853	3,803.6	100.0

* Does not include arrests for traffic offenses.

Source: *Uniform Crime Reports—1968* (Washington, D.C.: U.S. Department of Justice, 1969), pp. 110-11.

lenge modern Supreme Court decisions undermine the honor and prestige of law by their own arguments and vociferousness. Policemen, frustrated by low salaries, poor citizen support, and pressures for increased efficiency in the face of a crime volume increase, periodically erupt with biased statements that undermine public respect for impartial law enforcement. Even those who suggested that the former Chief Justice of the U.S. Supreme Court, Earl Warren, should be hanged rather than impeached in order to preserve freedom and to guarantee law and order did little to establish confidence in the American legal system which they claimed to uphold. They only heightened the public sense of fear and uncertainty.

While crime indexes suggest that crime is increasing in volume, so is the population. Drunkenness and disorderly conduct are the most common crimes (*see* Table 1-1). Since most forms of crime are activities of youth, any increase in the teen-age or young adult population inevitably generates a proportional increase in criminal activity. However, the increasing crime rate cannot be explained away by a simple recognition of an enlarged population of youth. For example, robbery, a theft involving the use of threat or force, whether in the form of a mugging, stickup, bank robbery, or even violent purse snatching, has increased at a faster proportional rate than the youth population. Three hundred and twenty-six robberies, one robbery for every 1,630 Americans, occurred each day during 1965. Although 118,916 robberies were reported and recorded as *known to the police*, the majority were not cleared from police files by the formal *arrest* of the offender. The actual number of additional robberies, of course, is unknown.[1] Some of the reported crime increase may be a function of better crime reporting.

Americans fear crime more than they fear the risks of simple living. Conditioned by newspaper reporting which emphasizes the sensationalism of a local murder, the average citizen believes that the murder threat is universal and immediate, even in his neighborhood. And yet data show that less than 13,648 willful homicides (including deaths by nonnegligent manslaughter) took place among an approximate 1968 population of 210 million Americans, a fractional amount.[2] At the same time, the citizen ignores the approximate 50,000 automobile deaths, five times the homicide volume, which occurred during the same period. Although slightly more than 140 serious assaults for every 100,000 persons took place during 1968, more than 12,000 home accidents per 100,000 persons occurred during the same interval.

The fear of street attack has caused many Americans to become over-fearful about travel to and from areas of supposed risk. Most fail to recognize that nearly two thirds of all cases of willful homicide and aggravated assaults occur between criminals and victims, often members of the same family, who have previously known each other. A woman, in fact, is more likely to be murdered by her husband than she is by someone attacking her on the street. Even if raped, she is not likely to be killed. While women especially fear physical attack in the form of rape or murder, robbery offers the principal source of violence from strangers. Where violence does occur in the commission of a robbery, it may be triggered by the panic of the victim rather than by the intended action of the robber, since the victim in most robberies, it has been found, frequently initiates the action that results in the infliction of physical harm against his person (*i.e.*, lunges at an armed robber and is shot in response). As a result, the person's fears often encourage that type of crime which the individual fears the most. The fear of traveling the streets, for example, actually encourages greater urban criminal activity, since the elimination of public traffic merely serves to deliver street control to those with enough courage to prowl the darkness.

Although the FBI's *Uniform Crime Reports* record the yearly volume of illegal acts occurring in 29 crime categories, seven serious crimes—

[1] The President's Commission on Law Enforcement and Administration of Justice, *The Challenge of Crime in a Free Society* (Washington, D.C.: U.S. Government Printing Office, 1967), p. 1. The difficulties in comparing international delinquency rates are examined by I. Richard Perlman, "Antisocial Behavior of the Minor in the U.S.," *Federal Probation*, Vol. 28, No. 4 (December, 1964), p. 23.

[2] *Uniform Crime Reports—1968* (Washington, D.C.: U.S. Department of Justice, 1969), p. 58.

willful homicide, forcible rape, aggravated assault, robbery, burglary, theft of $50 or over, and motor vehicle theft—are reported in a special quarterly evaluation of *Index Crimes*. The greater criminal incidence, however, takes place in the less severe crime categories.[3] Slightly more than 1 million of a total of 5.5 million arrests recorded in the 1968 *Uniform Crime Reports* were for serious index offenses. Nearly half of the total arrests involved crimes without direct victims (for example, narcotic addiction, juvenile curfew violations, gambling, prostitution, disorderly conduct, drunkenness, and vagrancy).

Although most people commonly agree that homicide, rape, and aggravated assault are serious crimes, the exact seriousness of auto theft, on the other hand, is open to question. While auto theft, the President's Commission of Law Enforcement and Administration of Justice assumes, may be the first step to a criminal career, its seriousness often rests with the value of the stolen car (average monetary value of $991 in 1968), rather than with the actual social threat of the act; actually most automobiles are stolen by youths under 21 who abandon them after joyriding. As long as teen-age status is determined in part by having "wheels," male teen-agers will continue to "borrow" available cars for personal use. Therefore, defining teen-age status behavior as a major criminal act may simply encourage the development of later criminality. In addition, the arbitrary definition of crimes involving $50 or more as serious crimes leads to the inclusion of greater numbers of small offenders in the more serious categories, due to inflation and the corresponding increase in the monetary value of the stolen object.

Since most criminals attempt to operate in secrecy, meaningful analysis of the crime problem depends upon the discovery of criminal activity and the tabulation of accurate data. While the *Uniform Crime Reports* offer the best American crime statistics, they are no better than the statistical integrity of the reporting public and the recording police departments from which these reports are drawn. The *Reports* indicate that the volume of individual crime has risen at a faster rate than the increase of the population in the last decade. The greatest growth has occurred in crimes against property, a not-too-surprising conclusion when one recognizes that most law enforcement agencies are content with a near 20 percent property crime *clearance rate* (normally, when an offender is identified, charged and taken into custody by the police).[4]

---

[3] Less serious crimes include: other assaults; arson; forgery and counterfeiting; fraud; embezzlement; illegal buying, receiving or possessing stolen property; vandalism; illegal carrying or possession of weapons; prostitution or commercialized vice; sex offenses; narcotic drug law violations; gambling; offenses against family and children; driving under the influence of alcohol; violation of liquor laws; drunkenness; disorderly conduct; vagrancy; other offenses; suspicion; curfew and loitering violations by juveniles; and juvenile runaways.

[4] *Uniform Crime Reports—1968* (Washington, D.C.: U.S. Department of Justice,

Since this implies that more than 75 percent of all known national property crime *never* results in an arrest, much of the crime increase, we may assume, is due to the fact that property crime is profitable. As long as the public remains satisfied with the status quo and refuses to assume its responsibility for inadequate modern law enforcement and judicial systems, legal deterrence is readily offset by property crime profit.

The public, police agencies, and courts, however, can do little to control criminal deviance in certain instances. The threat of punishment, for example, is insufficient to control spontaneous or planned assaults on or murders of relatives or acquaintances arising out of emotional involvement. Although more than 85 percent of all murders are cleared by arrest, the homicide rate continues near the same level each year despite continued community sanctions and an increased use of diagnostic and mental health centers. Punishment, for example, hardly deters the potential rapist who possesses the biological capability of committing multiple rapes in a period of a few hours. Since his problem is a form of fundamental psychological maladjustment, not readily subject to control through self-discipline, the rapist's sexual deviance is clearly difficult to anticipate or to regulate.

Crime conditions cannot be divorced from social situations. The increase in juvenile delinquency has paralleled the elimination of effective juvenile economic roles. Even though more than one half of willful homicides and armed robberies and nearly one fifth of all aggravated assaults involve the use of guns, firearms control legislation has been opposed by a significant proportion of the American population. The acquisitive character of modern society, too, is evident in the fact that 87 percent of the reported 1968 index crimes involved thefts of automobiles, goods, and money, while the remaining 13 percent were crimes of violence.[5] The American fear of crime is based, however, upon the perceived increase in crimes of violence rather than on the actual growth of crimes against property.

The public regards impersonal, organized, large-scale criminal activity as being beyond individual control. Although the Cosa Nostra, one of several confederations or syndicates of loosely organized criminals and itself a composite of 24 "families" coordinating their activities through the "Commissione," offers services under monopoly conditions to reputable citizens, its power to corrupt law enforcement and political officials far exceeds that of the common criminal. Operating in marginal areas of gambling, narcotics, prostitution, labor racketeering, and usury (also

---

1969), pp. 100–103. In some instances, crimes are cleared without actual placing of charges if victim refuses to assist prosecution or prosecutor declines to prosecute. One arrest may clear multiple crimes which the offender has committed.

[5] *Uniform Crime Reports—1968*, p. 4.

FIGURE 1–1

A general view of the criminal justice system*

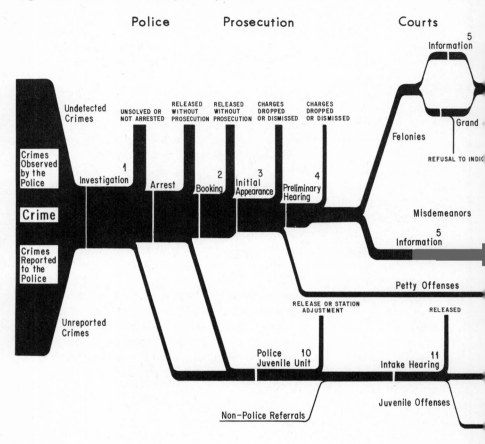

* Note:

This chart seeks to present a simple yet comprehensive view of the movement of cases through the criminal justice system. Procedures in individual jurisdictions may vary from the pattern shown here. The differing weights of line indicate the relative volumes of cases disposed of at various points in the system, but this is only suggestive since no nationwide data of this sort exists.

   [1] May continue until trial.

   [2] Administrative record of arrest. First step at which temporary release on bail may be available.

   [3] Before magistrate, commissioner, or justice of peace. Formal notice of charge, advice of rights. Bail set. Summary trials for petty offenses usually conducted here without further processing.

   [4] Preliminary testing of evidence against defendant. Charge may be reduced. No separate preliminary hearing for misdemeanors in some systems.

   [5] Charge filed by prosecutor on basis of information submitted by police or citizens. Alternative to grand jury indictment; often used in felonies, almost always in misdemeanors.

   [6] Reviews whether government evidence sufficient to justify trial. Some states have no grand jury system; others seldom use it.

   [7] Appearance for plea; defendant elects trial by judge or jury (if available); counsel for indigent usually appointed here in felonies. Often not at all in other cases.

   [8] Charge may be reduced at any time prior to trial in return for plea of guilty or for other reasons.

   [9] Challenge on constitutional grounds to legality of detention. May be sought at any point in process.

   [10] Police often hold informal hearings, dismiss or adjust many cases without further processing.

   [11] Probation officer decides desirability of further court action.

   [12] Welfare agency, social services, counseling, medical care, etc., for cases where adjudicatory handling not needed.

   Source: The President's Commission on Law Enforcement and Administration of Justice, *The Challenge of Crime in a Free Society* (Washington, D.C.: U.S. Government Printing Office, 1967), pp. 8–9.

FIGURE 1–1 (*Continued*)

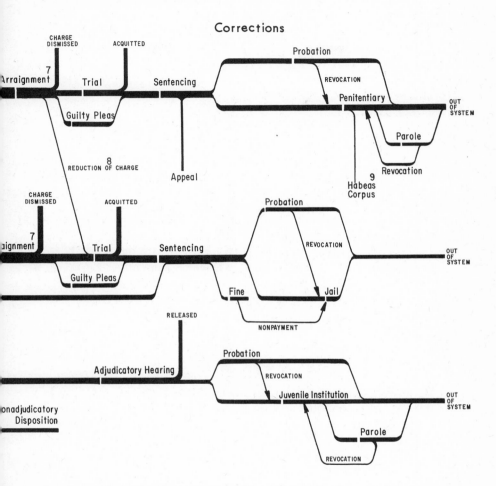

known as loan-sharking or "juice"), organized crime seeks to maximize profits while minimizing risks, serving a significant minority of the so-called "legitimate" population.[6] Although this type of crime is largely beyond individual control and hence tends to be disregarded, the more typical and historic criminal forms do provoke public emotion. Nearly 70 percent of all index crime arrests in 1968 involved persons under 25 years of age.[7] Fifteen- and sixteen-year-old youths were arrested for more index crimes than any other age category, although seventeen-

---

[6] A detailed discussion of the nature and structure of organized crime appears in The President's Commission on Law Enforcement and Administration of Justice, *Task Force Report: Organized Crime* (Washington, D.C.: U.S. Government Printing Office, 1967) and in Chapter 9 of this volume.

[7] *Uniform Crime Reports—1968,* pp. 115–16.

year-olds were a close second. At the same time, however, these youths were more likely to be treated under the supervision of the noncriminal juvenile courts which may have jurisdiction up to the age of 18.

Crime is not merely an activity of youth, however. Current data suggest its major urban orientation. Approximately 3,375,000 index offenses known to the police took place in cities during 1968, while an additional 857,000 and 197,000 violations occurred in suburban and rural areas. The rural crime rate reached 878.7 and the suburban rate neared 1,708.6 violations per 100,000 residents; the 1968 urban rate exceeded 2,870.9 offenses known to police.[8] Urban disorganization, encouraged by war, changes in female roles, deferred births, lags in economic adjustment to the needs of the expanding population, and demands for greater technological skills as prerequisites for employment, have taken their toll upon 15- to 24-year-olds, who represent the most crime-prone group in modern society.

The crime problem cannot be divorced from the American system of criminal justice (see Figure 1–1). Because the judicial system attempts to serve municipal, county, state, and federal political interests, it lacks the integrated legal coherency evident in England and other European states. Since the United States has jealously guarded the right of the individual and the local community to control their own destiny, the American system of criminal justice has remained relatively unintegrated and overlapping. Each hamlet, village, town, county, and state, as well as the federal government, possesses its own system of law enforcement and criminal justice. Although designed to guarantee local or community autonomy and to protect the individual from governmental power, the system of justice suffers from a lack of common definition of crimes and sentences, uncoordinated enforcement, and an imbalance in the structure and distribution of courts.[9] The shortage of police well trained in the commensurate skills required of a sophisticated age compounds the problem. Antiquated criminal and penal philosophy which assumes that criminal tendencies can be counteracted by simply isolating the offender in a prison so that he can meditate upon his crime and change his behavior, although a basic failure, continues to dominate contemporary penal efforts. Dominated by an excessive concern for the incorrigible 10 to 15 percent of the criminal population, legislatures have been slow to integrate recent behavioral discoveries into the formal structures of enforcement, justice, and treatment.[10]

---

[8] *Uniform Crime Reports—1968*, pp. 96–97.

[9] The problems of the criminal courts are discussed in The President's Commission on Law Enforcement and Administration of Justice, *Task Force Report: The Courts* (Washington, D.C.: U.S. Government Printing Office, 1967).

[10] See The President's Commission on Law Enforcement and Administration of Justice, *Task Force Report: Corrections* (Washington, D.C.: U.S. Government Printing Office, 1967), for a valuable analysis of the treatment problem.

CRIME FOCUS: AN AMERICAN CITY

The scope of the crime problem, however, is better understood when examined in relationship to a particular urban environment. Crime is not evenly distributed throughout a city or even a nation. Murder, forcible rape, robbery, aggravated assault, and burglary, crimes provoking the greatest public concern, most frequently occur in large-city slums. Victims and offenders are reported most often from the poorest, most deteriorated, and most disorganized urban areas. Crime-prone individuals are often attracted to these communities, and community history suggests that such areas tend to encourage the increase of deviance. Low income, ethnic hopelessness, unstable family life, unemployment, overproportion of single males, substandard and overcrowded housing, high rates of infant mortality and disease, mixed land use, high population density, and low rates of home ownership frequently stimulate criminal activity. However, many slum inhabitants, bound together by an intense social and cultural solidarity, have been able to overcome these limitations and to create meaningful lives. Nevertheless, urban crime generally reaches its highest point where social disorganization rather than group cohesion is the rule. Although American crime rates tend to be highest in the inner city and to decrease as one travels from the central city, the suburban community, believed to be more stable, has also known an increase in delinquency and crime in recent years.[11]

Ghetto riots, largely centered in marginal urban areas, are extralegal reactions to coercive urban disorganization. While oppressive institutions or persons, whether loan companies, policemen, or white businessmen, have most often been the principal objects of attack, nonoppressive institutions (for example, schools, churches, and libraries) have been largely exempt from collective action. Ghetto rioters, largely young Negro males, represent a cross-section of the Black community. Their actions serve to protest alleged police misconduct, commercial and economic deprivation or exploitation, and *de facto* racial discrimination. Urban riots, therefore, are symptomatic expressions of wider social problems rather than merely actions of traditional criminality.[12]

A clearer indication of the distribution of traditional American urban crime is available in the yearly report of the Chicago Crime Commission.

---

[11] The President's Commission on Law Enforcement and Administration of Justice, *Task Force Report: Juvenile Delinquency* (Washington, D.C.: U.S. Government Printing Office, 1967) offers specific insight into suburban delinquency problem.

[12] For a professional policeman's viewpoint, see O. W. Wilson, "Civil Disturbances and the Rule of the Law," *Journal of Criminal Law, Criminology, and Police Science,* Vol. 58, No. 2 (1967), pp. 155–59.

TABLE 1–2
Major offenses reported in Chicago, 1967–68

	1967	1968	Percentage Change + or −
Murder and nonnegligent manslaughter....	552	647	+17.0
Forcible rape.........................	1,403	1,237	−11.8
Robbery..............................	18,456	18,997	+ 2.9
Aggravated assault....................	12,417	12,320	− 0.8
Burglary.............................	31,354	34,344	+ 8.9
Larceny—$50 and over................	18,509	18,927	+ 2.3
Auto theft...........................	32,268	33,251	+ 3.0
Total...........................	114,959	119,723	+ 4.1

Source: Virgil W. Peterson, *A Report on Chicago Crime for 1968* (Chicago: Chicago Crime Commission, 1969), p. 6.

Chicago crime, as noted in Table 1–2, rose by 4.1 percent between 1967 and 1968,[13] although it decreased in volume during 1969 (see Table 1–3).[14] The total 1969 volume was less than that reported in 1968. The decrease amounted to minus 2 murders and nonnegligent manslaughters; minus 11 forcible rapes; minus 8 aggravated assaults; minus 200 burglaries; minus 72 larcenies $50 and over; and minus 484 auto thefts. Robberies were plus 10. Although Chicago police reported a net 1968 increase of 4,764 crimes (a 4.1 percent increase), the 1969 total (118,966) barely exceeded the 1964 volume (117,266) by 1,700 serious crimes. A more revealing insight into the urban crime problem, however, appears in the analysis of yearly *arrest* data (*offenses cleared by arrest*) for the six-year period between 1964 and 1968 (see Table 1–4).[15] While 114,959 serious crimes were reported to Chicago police during 1967,

TABLE 1–3
Major offenses reported in Chicago, January 4, 1968
through January 1, 1969
(Chicago Police Department 13-period year)

Murder and nonnegligent manslaughter........	645
Forcible rape.............................	1,226
Robbery..................................	19,007
Aggravated assault........................	12,312
Burglary.................................	34,144
Larceny—$50 and over....................	18,855
Auto theft...............................	32,777
Total..............................	118,966

Source: Peterson, *A Report on Chicago Crime for 1968*, p. 6.

[13] See Virgil W. Peterson, *A Report on Chicago Crime for 1968* (Chicago: Chicago Crime Commission, 1969), p. 6.
[14] Also note *ibid.*, p. 6.
[15] *Ibid.*, p. 11.

TABLE 1–4
Index offenses cleared by arrest, 1964–68, Chicago, Illinois

	1964	1965	1966	1967	1968
Murder and nonnegligent manslaughter.............	377	371	448	503	616
Forcible rape...............	842	773	860	1,016	743
Robbery...................	8,052	6,524	6,612	7,681	7,084
Aggravated assault..........	8,709	7,541	8,259	8,813	7,926
Burglary...................	12,094	10,687	10,121	10,587	10,328
Larceny—$50 and over.......	7,352	4,609	4,605	4,994	4,556
Auto theft.................	9,443	9,721	9,476	8,703	5,951
Total...............	46,869	40,226	40,381	42,297	37,204

Source: Peterson, *A Report on Chicago Crime for 1968*, p. 10.

only 42,297 arrests were completed, many for violations which had occurred in previous years. The situation was even worse in 1968 when police accomplished only 37,204 arrests while receiving notification of 119,723 violations.[16]

Thirty-seven percent of the 1968 Chicago serious crime volume was committed in 5 of the 21 Chicago police districts: Fillmore (11th), Wabash (2d), Marquette (10th), East Chicago (18th), and Englewood (7th) (see Figure 1–2). The actual distribution of serious offenses in Chicago is given in Table 1–5. Fifty-three percent of the 1968 Chicago murder and nonnegligent manslaughter offenses (willful homicides) occurred in five districts: the Second (99), Third (72), Seventh (67), Eleventh (54), and Tenth (50).[17] Similar trends were also found for other major offenses. Nearly 52 percent of the 12,312 reported aggravated assaults, 53 percent of the 1,226 forcible rapes, and nearly 49 percent of the 19,007 robberies occurred in five police districts of the city.[18]

A special urban focus

Although crime statistics look ominous in themselves, a more detailed investigation of one particular police district more adequately illustrates the diversity of the crime problem. Chicago's North Side Nineteenth (Town Hall) district, composed of less affluent ethnic groups (Puerto Ricans, Indians, Appalachian whites, some Orientals, and a few Negroes) and of upper-income families living in high-rise apartments near Lake

---

[16] Since the same person may actually commit more than one offense, an arrest may result in the clearance of multiple previous violations which were reported to police several months or years earlier.

[17] Peterson, *op. cit.*, p. 8.

[18] *Ibid.*, p. 9.

Michigan, reflects a wide variety of economic, cultural, and ethnic tensions. Some 50 of the 365 crimes reported to the police during the week of October 27 to November 2, 1966, proved to be *unfounded*. Eighteen of 86 reported burglaries, ten of 33 reported car thefts, four of 43 reported assaults, two of 9 reported robberies, and one of 32 reported thefts of over $50 could *not* be verified. One murder and two attempted

FIGURE 1–2
Chicago Police District map

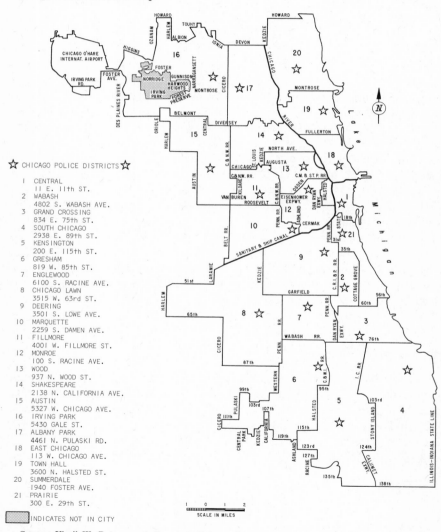

☆ CHICAGO POLICE DISTRICTS ☆

    1 CENTRAL
       11 E. 11th ST.
    2 WABASH
       4802 S. WABASH AVE.
    3 GRAND CROSSING
       834 E. 75th ST.
    4 SOUTH CHICAGO
       2938 E. 89th ST.
    5 KENSINGTON
       200 E. 115th ST.
    6 GRESHAM
       819 W. 85th ST.
    7 ENGLEWOOD
       6100 S. RACINE AVE.
    8 CHICAGO LAWN
       3515 W. 63rd ST.
    9 DEERING
       3501 S. LOWE AVE.
   10 MARQUETTE
       2259 S. DAMEN AVE.
   11 FILLMORE
       4001 W. FILLMORE ST.
   12 MONROE
       100 S. RACINE AVE.
   13 WOOD
       937 N. WOOD ST.
   14 SHAKESPEARE
       2138 N. CALIFORNIA AVE.
   15 AUSTIN
       5327 W. CHICAGO AVE.
   16 IRVING PARK
       5430 GALE ST.
   17 ALBANY PARK
       4461 N. PULASKI RD.
   18 EAST CHICAGO
       113 W. CHICAGO AVE.
   19 TOWN HALL
       3600 N. HALSTED ST.
   20 SUMMERDALE
       1940 FOSTER AVE.
   21 PRAIRIE
       300 E. 29th ST.

▨ INDICATES NOT IN CITY

1 0 1 2
SCALE IN MILES

Source: Virgil W. Peterson, *A Report on Chicago Crime for 1965*, (Chicago: Chicago Crime Commission, 1966), p. 2.

TABLE 1-5
Major offenses—Chicago by police districts, 1968

District	Number	Murder and Nonnegligent Manslaughter	Forcible Rape	Robbery	Aggravated Assault	Burglary	Theft—$50 and Over	Auto Theft	Total
						Offenses			
Central	1st	14	17	525	200	353	1,523	805	3,437
Wabash	2d	99	181	2,836	1,898	2,117	892	2,009	10,032
Grand Crossing	3d	72	117	1,314	769	2,243	599	2,273	7,387
South Chicago	4th	11	21	378	156	861	337	1,364	3,128
Kensington	5th	18	44	587	195	1,195	368	1,840	4,247
Gresham	6th	15	44	401	176	1,151	351	1,319	3,457
Englewood	7th	67	114	1,161	1,174	2,378	801	2,182	7,877
Chicago Lawn	8th	6	13	220	156	899	510	1,213	3,017
Deering	9th	19	12	312	296	767	539	1,097	3,042
Marquette	10th	50	106	1,492	1,042	3,117	795	1,951	8,553
Fillmore	11th	54	126	1,882	1,331	3,668	955	2,171	10,187
Monroe	12th	37	36	1,477	730	1,452	1,189	1,290	6,211
Wood	13th	41	68	1,143	950	2,351	1,116	1,941	7,610
Shakespeare	14th	13	17	415	326	1,261	754	1,336	4,122
Austin	15th	15	58	627	301	1,808	542	1,713	5,064
Jefferson Park	16th	2	7	120	72	806	697	904	2,608
Albany Park	17th	7	9	160	103	872	822	941	2,914
East Chicago	18th	24	83	1,591	808	1,615	2,090	1,929	8,140
Town Hall	19th	14	38	482	445	1,785	1,344	1,589	5,697
Foster	20th	22	36	559	532	1,964	1,909	1,486	6,508
Prairie	21st	45	79	1,325	652	1,481	722	1,424	5,728
Total		645	1,226	19,007	12,312	34,144	18,855	32,777	118,966

Source: Peterson, *A Report on Chicago Crime for 1968*, p. 7.

rapes occurred during the week, while the police made five additional arrests for narcotic violations, one for gambling and one for prostitution. One woman reported herself a victim of a confidence game, while a gypsy woman was reported for fortune-telling. Several reports of indecent exposure and lewd telephone calls added variety to the 48 reports of theft and the 65 reports of vandalism.[19]

The majority of Town Hall assaults involved alcoholism or romantic difficulties. The excessive dependence of Appalachian whites upon knives or force as a means to settle community arguments was reflected in the criminal statistics. Evaluating the Town Hall data, The President's Commission on Law Enforcement and the Administration of Justice concluded:

What the crimes of that week in Town Hall strongly suggest is that, although there is always some danger in the city of being robbed and perhaps injured on the street and a considerable danger of being burglarized, what people have to fear most from crime is in themselves: their own carelessness or bravado; their attitudes toward the people they work for or who work for them; their appetites for drugs and liquor and sex; their own eccentricities; their own perversities; their own passions.[20]

Town Hall, a community of 6 square miles containing some 200,000 persons, merely depicts, the Commission concluded, a normal week of crime in a normal police district.

CRIME FOCUS: CALIFORNIA—AN AMERICAN STATE

Although California crime rates are higher than those found in most other states, this is probably due to the more exacting state reporting system. Since California law requires that all crime and arrest data be reported to a central recording agency, the analysis of the State Bureau of Criminal Statistics is believed to offer the most complete crime data of any state in the United States. Because California, however, defines burglary as an entering of certain structures with intent to commit a larceny or any felony, many offenses nationally defined in less serious categories and not subject to review in the FBI's serious crime index are classified as serious crimes in the California reports. Although the state population increased about 4 percent during 1965, California crimes of personal violence grew by 4,000 to a total of 51,672, and property crimes rose by 36,000 to 335,036.[21]

---

[19] See The President's Commission on Law Enforcement and Administration of Justice *Task Force* and *Research Reports.*

[20] *Ibid.*

[21] Department of Justice of the State of California, *Crime and Delinquency in California, 1965* (Sacramento: Bureau of Criminal Statistics, 1966), p. 15. Colonel Houser Garrison, Jr., "The Crime Problem in Texas," *American Criminal Law Quarterly,* Vol. 4, No. 2 (Winter, 1966), pp. 95–102, gives insight into the Texas problem.

FIGURE 1–3
California felony crime rates, 1960–65
(seven major offense groups)

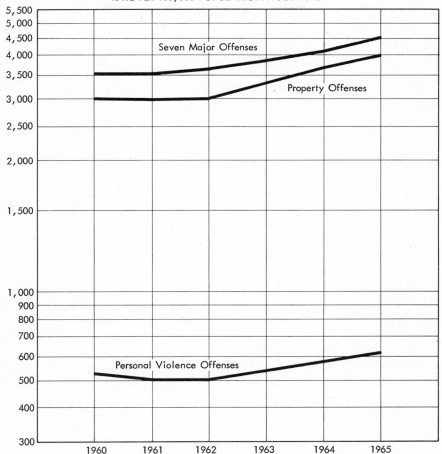

RATE PER 100,000 POPULATION AGED 10–29

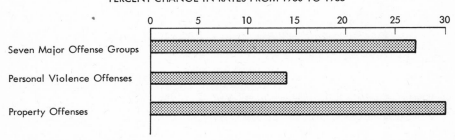

PERCENT CHANGE IN RATES FROM 1960 TO 1965

Source: Department of Justice of the State of California, *Crime and Delinquency in California, 1965* (Sacramento: Bureau of Criminal Statistics, 1966), p. 17.

TABLE 1-6

Statewise clearance rates for each of the seven major offense groups, 1960-65

	Personal Violence Offenses				Property Offenses		
Year	Homicide	Robbery	Aggravated Assault	Forcible Rape	Burglary	Grand Theft	Auto Theft
1960.................	90.0	45.9	74.9	68.0	31.6	25.6	33.4
1961.................	90.8	47.3	77.5	64.0	32.8	28.6	31.3
1962.................	85.2	39.5	73.4	62.9	25.2	24.9	27.9
1963.................	89.3	38.1	71.8	60.7	24.2	22.0	27.0
1964.................	83.9	33.1	69.0	56.4	22.5	20.3	26.6
1965.................	84.2	33.7	67.3	56.1	21.7	19.1	23.8
Percentage change in rate 1964 and 1965 over 1960 and 1961...	−7.0	−28.3	−10.6	−14.8	−31.4	−27.3	−22.1

Source: State of California, *Crime and Delinquency in California*, 1965, p. 18.

While California felony crimes have increased each year since 1960 (see Figure 1-3), clearance by arrest rates of reported crimes have declined each year. Although critics may readily conclude that California policing practices have become less efficient, a more realistic appraisal suggests that more marginal and serious crimes are being reported to the police than ever before in history. The decline in statewide clearance rates (see Tables 1-6 and 1-7), however, reveals the radical changes necessary in public attitudes, law enforcement, and judicial procedure if crime is ever to be controlled effectively. California law enforcement agencies, like police units throughout the country, are operating with a minimal number of enforcement personnel. Unable to respond to all criminal violations, California police, therefore, tend to respond to selective crimes, giving less serious crimes lower priority (see Figure 1-4). Even then, however, 45 to 50 percent of all adult felony arrests fail

TABLE 1-7

Total arrests reported, 1964 and 1965

	Total		Adult		Juvenile	
Type	1964	1965	1964	1965	1964	1965
Total.................	975,168	1,017,198	705,584	739,549	269,584	277,649
Felony.....................	146,888	154,817	100,690	108,559	46,198	46,258
Misdemeanor..............	660,381	686,621	604,894	630,990	55,487	55,631
Delinquent tendencies........	167,899	175,760	..	..	167,899	175,760

Source: State of California, *Crime and Delinquency in California*, 1965, p. 18.

FIGURE 1–4

Felony arrest rates, 1960–65

(rates are arrests per 100,000 population aged 10–39 years)

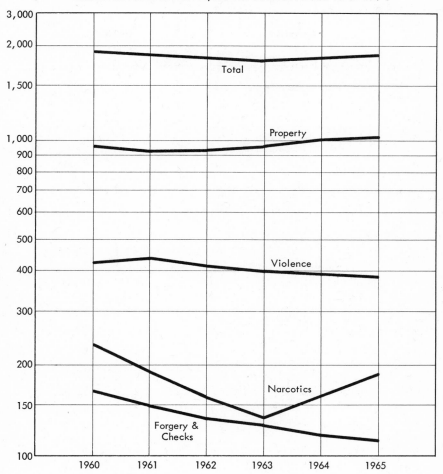

RATES ARE ARRESTS PER 100,000 POPULATION AGED 10-39 YR.

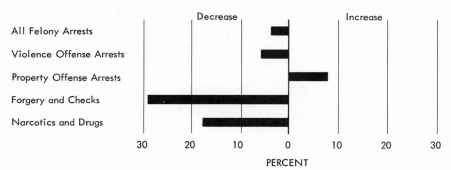

PERCENT CHANGE 1960-1965 IN FELONY ARREST RATES

Source: State of California, *Crime and Delinquency in California, 1965*, p. 22.

FIGURE 1–5
Percent distribution of adult felony arrests
BY TYPE OF FINAL DISPOSITION 1960–1965

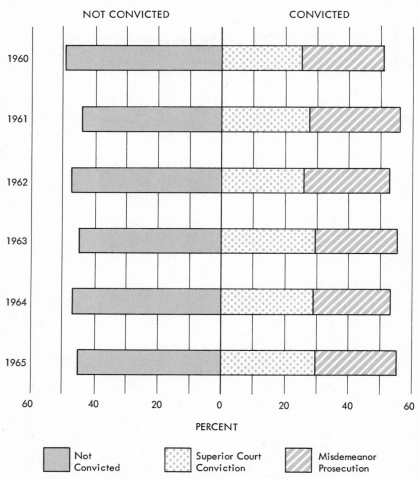

Source: State of California, *Crime and Delinquency in California, 1965*, p. 25.

to result in convictions (see Figure 1–5). Other serious crimes, too, may have been downgraded to less serious misdemeanor offenses in order to gain convictions.

CRIME FOCUS: AREAS OF FEDERAL JURISDICTION

Although the crime problem in areas of federal jurisdiction differs somewhat from that of cities and states, due to the interstate jurisdiction and regional isolation of many of its areas of responsibility, it is yet similar in scope. However, federal crimes represent only a small percentage of all criminal offenses observed in the United States. Since more than 50 percent of all federal crimes in territorial or maritime jurisdictions directly subject to federal control are also state offenses (for example, bank robberies which are recorded in the *Uniform Crime Reports*), federal reports usually exclude these violations. The special dimensions of the federal crime problem, however, are evident in Table 1–8. Immigration law abuses, federal income tax evasion, and antitrust

TABLE 1–8
Selected federal crimes
(cases filed in court—1966)

Antitrust.	7
Food and drug.	350
Income tax evasion.	863
Liquor revenue violations.	2,729
Narcotics.	2,293
Immigration.	3,188

Source: The President's Commission on Law Enforcement and Administration of Justice, *The Challenge of Crime in a Free Society*, p. 20.

violations are almost exclusively federal crimes. When compared with the greater diversity of state and local crime, federal crimes appear minor and insignificant. At the time of President Kennedy's assassination, for example, the murderer of the President could only be charged under Texas criminal code, since no federal laws dealt with the issue.

However, federal criminal jurisdiction is not simply restricted to violations of interstate commerce, national taxation, or interstate narcotics laws. Jurisdiction also extends to territories under federal protection which are subject to criminal codes formulated under the supervision of the federal government. Washington, D.C., a major urban community indirectly governed by Congress, has not been spared the international crime increase. Serious crimes increased by 59 percent in the District of Columbia between 1950 and 1965 (from 20,163 to 32,053), and major felonies increased by 8 percent in 1966 to a total reported crime volume of 34,765 violations (see Table 1–9). The greatest increase occurred in petit larcenies (thefts) of property valued at less than $100 (see Table 1–10). Forty-four percent of all major offenses and forty-nine percent of all major felonies between 1961 and 1965 were centered in four Washington, D.C., police precincts. Only two precincts, on the other hand, remained relatively free of crime.[22]

---

[22] President's Commission on Crime in the District of Columbia, *Report of the President's Commission* (Washington, D.C.: U.S. Government Printing Office, 1966), p. 20. For a condensed summary of the report see "An investigation of Crime in Washington—The C. C. Crime Commission Report," *D. C. Bar Journal*, Vol. 34, No. 1 (January, 1967), pp. 34–47.

The District of Columbia Crime Commission's data reveal that while young Negro males are most often the serious crime offenders, blacks generally are the primary victims of serious crimes committed by blacks, except in cases of robbery and commercial housebreaking. Of all persons arrested for serious offenses between 1950 and 1965, 80 percent were black and more than 30 percent were juveniles under 18. The popular belief that Washington, D.C., one of the few American cities with a majority Negro population, is the most criminal city in the United States

TABLE 1–9
Part I—Total offenses, District of Columbia,
1950–66

Year	Felonies	Misdemeanors	Total
1950	12,229	7,934	20,163
1951	12,156	8,034	20,190
1952	14,066	8,525	22,591
1953	15,251	8,667	23,918
1954	11,917	8,113	20,030
1955	11,488	7,422	18,910
1956	10,048	7,562	17,610
1957	9,155	6,399	15,554
1958	9,895	7,152	17,047
1959	10,193	7,322	17,515
1960	11,714	8,215	19,929
1961	12,948	8,854	21,802
1962	13,274	8,260	21,534
1963	15,191	8,003	23,194
1964	19,693	8,776	28,469
1965	23,174	8,879	32,053
1966	23,089	11,676	34,765

Source: President's Commission on Crime in the District of Columbia, *Report of the President's Commission* (Washington, D.C.: U.S. Government Printing office, 1966), p. 24.

is not supported by recent FBI data. During 1968, more serious crimes were reported to the police in proportion to the population in such diverse Standard Metropolitan Statistical Areas as Atlantic City (N.J.), Baltimore (Md.), Detroit (Mich.), Fresno (Calif.), Jacksonville (Fla.), Los Angeles (Calif.), Miami (Fla.), Newark (N.J.), New York (N.Y.), San Francisco (Calif.), Stockton (Calif.), and Tampa (Fla.) than in the District of Columbia.[23] Persons 15 years or under accounted for 36 percent of housebreaking and 31 percent of robbery and auto theft arrests in 1965. Most murders and aggravated assaults, however, were

[23] *Uniform Crime Reports—1968* (Washington, D.C.: U.S. Department of Justice, 1969), pp. 76–90.

TABLE 1–10
Part I—Types of offenses District of Columbia, 1965–66

Offense	1965 Frequency	1966 Frequency	Change
Murder......................	155	146	−9
Manslaughter..................	8	11	+3
Negligent homicide.............	14	14	......
Rape.........................	132	169	+37
Attempted rape................	27	27	......
Robbery......................	3,663	3,531	−132
Attempted robbery.............	282	266	−16
Aggravated assault.............	2,474	2,823	+349
Housebreaking.................	9,076	8,920	−156
Attempted housebreaking.......	233	301	+68
Grand larceny.................	1,621	1,901	+280
Petit larceny..................	8,632	11,361	+2,729
Auto theft....................	5,736	5,295	−441
Total....................	32,053	34,765	+2,712

Source: President's Commission on Crime in the District of Columbia, *Report of the President's Commission*, p. 24.

committed by persons over 29 years of age. Homicide, rape, and aggravated assault victims, the D.C. Crime Commission found, were generally related to, or acquainted with, their assailants. Since many personal crimes occurred indoors, police prevention and control remained largely impossible.[24]

THE INTERNATIONAL CONTEXT

Available international crime statistics suggest wide cultural divergences in forms of criminal activity and in crime rates. Although the homicide rate seems abnormally high to the U.S. citizen, a comparative analysis suggests that it is only a fraction of the rate evidenced in South Africa, Mexico, and Colombia (see Table 1–11). While other data indicate that international property offenses continue to increase, most other nations do not present any definite pattern of growth in violent crime. Property crime rates have increased more than 200 percent in West Germany, the Netherlands, Sweden, and Finland, and more than 100 percent in France, Wales, Italy, England, and Norway since 1955, but property crime indexes have remained relatively stable in Denmark, Belgium, and Switzerland. A further comparison of West Germany and North Central U.S. rates, however, indicates that the highly industrialized Federal Republic (including West Berlin) maintained a murder

---

[24] President's Commission on Crime in the District of Columbia, *op. cit.*, p. 21.

TABLE 1–11
Homicide rates for selected countries
(per 100,000 population)

Country	Rate	Year Reported
Colombia.........................	36.5	1962
Mexico...........................	31.9	1960
South Africa......................	21.8	1960
United States.....................	4.8	1962
Japan............................	1.5	1962
France...........................	1.5	1962
Canada...........................	1.4	1962
Federal Republic of Germany..........	1.2	1961
England/Wales....................	0.7	1962
Ireland...........................	0.4	1962

Source: President's Commission, *The Challenge of Crime in a Free Society*, p. 30.

rate of 0.8 murders per 100,000 inhabitants during 1964, while the comparable North Central U.S. rate was 3.5 homicides. Rape rates, on the other hand, were nearly equal (10.6 in the Federal Republic and 10.5 in the United States). The North Central United States nevertheless maintained a higher robbery rate (76.2 to 12.4 robberies per 100,000 population), although West Germany led in larcenies (1,628.2 versus 1,337.2 per 100,000 population). The United States dominated the category of auto thefts, 234.7 to 78.2 per 100,000 population, during the same period.[25] Much of this variation in rates is due to cultural and ethnic factors, differences in national economic policies, public attitudes and practices regarding criminal deviance, the context of criminal law and the location and size of the country.

A. Great Britain

Although the English murder rate only increased by less than one murder per million inhabitants aged eight or over between 1930 and 1960 (see Table 1–12),[26] the major increase in the English indictable woundings (from 46 to 372 reported offenses per million inhabitants) during the 30-year period indicates that many victims of inflicted violence are now saved from death by modern medicine. Although the

---

[25] President's Commission on Law Enforcement and Administration of Justice, *The Challenge of Crime in a Free Society*, p. 30.
[26] Nigel Walker, *Crime and Punishment in Britain*, (Edinburgh: University Press, 1966), p. 19.

rate of recorded murders increased about 20 percent, the rate for recorded attempts, both successful and unsuccessful, increased by 60 percent. Even though the 1960 indictable wounding rate was almost eight times as high the rate given in the 1930–39 index, a major portion of the increase, English criminologist Nigel Walker analyzes, was directly due to changes in police reporting and recording methods.

More recent data suggest that Londoners, living in a dense metropolitan area, are no more prone to violence than are other Englishmen. Although rates in other large English cities are somewhat higher than in London, the rates in southern England generally remain lower than those found in the northern part of the country. Young adults between 17 and 21 evidence the greatest tendency to violence. One third of

TABLE 1–12
Annual average numbers of reported offenses in England (per million inhabitants aged eight or older)

Years	Murder*	Attempted Murder	Indictable Woundings
1930–39	3.6	2.2	46
1950–54	3.7	4.0	152
1955–59	4.2	4.2	243
1960–61	4.4	4.8	372

* Including murder reduced to manslaughter by reason of diminished responsibility.
Source: Nigel Walker, *Crime and Punishment in England* (Edinburgh: University Press, 1966), p. 19.

the London violent crimes resulted from street attacks; another third occurred as an aftermath of a domestic quarrel. One fifth took place in public houses and cafes; one eighth involved direct attacks on the police. Seven percent of the violent crimes involved knives, razors, or firearms deliberately carried for the violent purposes. Fists and feet, on the other hand, were the only available "weapons" in more than 50 percent of the cases. Eighty percent of the offenders had not been previously convicted of a violent crime, although nearly one half of the offenders had earlier convictions for other types of offenses, generally larceny. Unskilled manual workers were overrepresented among violent offenses, larceny, and burglary. Ninety percent of all violent crimes, however, could be traced to the offender, since the victim usually knew the identity of his assailant.[27]

---

[27] *Ibid.*, pp. 20–21.

English murders often resulted from domestic disputes. While nearly 30 percent of all adult male victims and over one half of the adult female victims were killed by their spouse or relatives, nearly 75 percent of the victims under the age of 16 were murdered by their own parents or relatives. A majority of English murderers, Evelyn Gibson found, suffered from either severe mental strain or a diagnosable mental disorder. One third committed suicide before their arrest; another third evidenced insanity; and although the remaining third constituted a "mentally normal" group, many persons in the category were later found to be psychologically disordered. The "sane" murderer, differentiated from other rational men who commit bodily violence only by the fact that his victim dies as a result of his attack, committed less than one third of all yearly British murders.[28]

TABLE 1–13
Trends in sexual offenses in England
(annual average numbers of reported offenses per million inhabitants [figures in brackets show the extent of the increase, treating the annual average for 1930–39 as a base of 100])

Years	Rape and Indecent Assault*	Intercourse with Girls under 16 or 13	Incest	Homosexual Offenses†
1930–39	60 (100)	14 (100)	2.5 (100)	26 (100)
1950–54	198	36	6.3	140
1955–59	226	60	7.4	153
1960–61	248 (414)	99 (709)	7.7 (308)	134 (515)

* Rape, attempted rape, and indecent assault on a female are grouped together because an act, which in one place or year is charged as one of these, might elsewhere or at another time have been charged as one of the other offenses.
† For similar reasons, buggery, attempted buggery, and gross indecency between males are grouped together. Nonindictable offenses are excluded.
Source: Walker, *Crime and Punishment in England*, p. 25.

Although British heterosexual and homosexual offenses increased at a marked rate following World War II, the rate of sexual offenses has become more stable in recent years. However, when compared with prewar rates, reported incest has increased threefold; indecent assault, fourfold; homosexual offenses, fivefold; and intercourse with girls under 16, fivefold (see Table 1–13). While no more than 5 percent of all illegal sexual misconduct, English criminologist Leon Radzinowicz assumes, was ever reported previously, freer sexual attitudes, evidenced both in

[28] *Ibid.*, p. 21. See also Pauline Callard, "Crime and Criminology in England," Joseph S. Roucek (ed.), *The Sociology of Crime* (New York: Philosophical Library, 1961), p. 377.

public discussion and social practice, may have stimulated the rise of complaints to police. When the British government authorized the Wolfenden Committee to survey homosexual behavior, reported homosexuality in 1955 reached a peak of 170 violations per million inhabitants. The reported rate sharply declined, however, when the Committee recommended the legalization of homosexual acts between consenting adults in 1957.

English crimes of larceny, burglary, robbery and fraud have likewise increased since 1930. In the 10 years between 1950 and 1960, larceny alone showed almost a 50 percent increase, and burglary evidenced a 70 percent rise in volume (see Table 14–4). Although the robbery

TABLE 1–14
Trends in property offenses in England
(annual average numbers of reported offenses per million inhabitants aged eight or older)

Years	Larceny	Burglary	Robbery, etc.	Fraud
1930–39.......	4,441 (100)	1,086 (100)	6 (100)	432 (100)
1950–54.......	8,320	2,359	24	702
1955–59.......	9,267	2,681	33	686
1960–61.......	12,631 (284)	3,915 (278)	54 (900)	937 (217)

Source: Walker, *Crime and Punishment in England*, p. 28.

rate more than doubled, it remained at close to 2,000 robberies per year. Fraud, however, showed the lowest percentage increase during the 10-year period. While property theft reached its highest incidence among 14-year-old males, crimes of violence were most common among 20-year-old men. Juvenile criminal activity reached its peak one year before the legal end of British public education (at 14 years in 1937 and 15 years in 1956), suggesting the general inadequacy of public education and the problem of poor student motivation (see Figure 1–6).

Murder, crimes of violence and sexual offenses are currently among the least frequent British forms of criminal activity, although they elicit greater public concern than other crimes, in Great Britain just as in the United States. "Murder," Nigel Walker summarizes, "is numerically as insignificant in the criminal statistics as death from anthrax is among this country's diseases."[29] Nearly two thirds of all persons found guilty in English courts are traffic offenders. The remaining third consists largely of property offenders, since British sexual and violence offenders

[29] *Ibid.*, p. 36.

FIGURE 1–6
The peak age of offenses in England

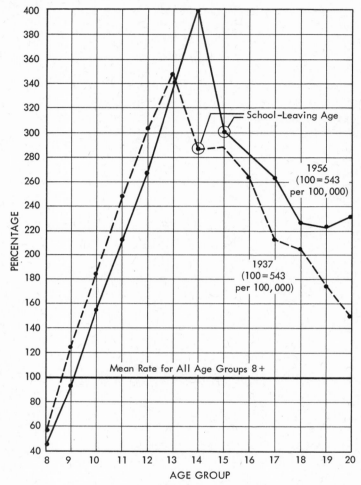

Note: Rates at which young males of different ages were found guilty of indictable offenses in 1937 and 1956, shown as percentages of the mean rate for all age
groups in the year (England and Wales).
Source: Walker, *Crime and Punishment in England*, p. 30.

accounted for only 3 percent of those found guilty in English courts
during 1961 (see Table 1–15).

B. Other Western European countries

Western European crime has followed similar trends, although reflecting unique political as well as social causes. Although *Spanish* prisoners,

for example, numbered less than 19,500 in 1933, the prison population reached nearly 100,000 persons in 1939 following the Spanish civil war. While more than 270,000 prisoners were reported in 1940, their number declined to approximately 93,000 by 1943. In *Italy,* however, crimes of personal violence increased from 119,000 in 1939 to nearly 168,000 in 1949, while theft rose from 230,000 to 312,000. Although *Belgium* showed a marked crime growth due to large numbers of Nazi collaborators prosecuted following World War II, conventional criminal convictions dropped from 11,800 per 100,000 by 1950. On the other hand, *Luxemburg,* possessing a population of 300,000, barely knew major

TABLE 1–15
English offenses in perspective
(percentage of persons found guilty in English courts in 1961)

Traffic offenses	61.3
Breaking and entering (3.2) receiving (0.8) and larceny (9.3)	13.3
Drunkenness	7.0
Murder (.001) and other nonsexual violence* (1.999)	2.0
Sexual offenses†	1.0
Revenue evasions	2.5
Railway offenses	1.8
Breaches of local bylaws and similar regulations	2.2
Malicious damage to property	1.6
Miscellaneous	7.3
Total 1,152,397‡ =	100

* Including nonindictable assaults.
† Including soliciting, indecent exposure, and other nonindictable offenses.
‡ This total represents appearances in court at which a finding of guilt was recorded, and since an unknown number of persons were involved in such appearances more than once in the same year, the figure does *not* indicate the number of individuals involved.
Source: Walker, *Crime and Punishment in England,* p. 37.

crime, as evidenced by its constant prison population of a mere 300 to 400 persons.

European criminal activity, however, varies widely (see Table 1–16).[30] The lower *Swedish* and *French* rate sharply contrasts with the higher *Italian* and *English* indexes. Juvenile crime has followed a similar trend (see Table 1–17). The significant decline in 1931 *German* and 1951 *French* delinquency rates, American criminologist Vernon Fox observes, was due to changed definitions of delinquency brought about by new legislation.

---

[30] Vernon Fox, "Criminality and Corrections in Western Europe," in Joseph S. Roucek (ed.), *The Sociology of Crime* (New York: Philosophical Library, 1961), pp. 401–23. Added data may be gained from James B. McWhinnie, *Denmark—A New Look at Crime* (London: Institute for the Study and Treatment of Delinquency, 1961).

TABLE 1–16

Criminal indices for selected European countries for the first half of the 20th century (in thousands)

Country	Rates	1901	1911	1921	1931	1936	1941	1946	1951
England...........	Population	38,700	42,700	44,400	46,100	47,000	48,200	49,200	50,600
	Crimes	82	98	105	290	283	358	472	524
	Criminal index	2.1	2.3	2.3	6.2	6.0	7.4	9.5	10.3
France...........	Population	38,900	39,600	39,200	41,800	41,900	38,800	40,500	42,100
	Crimes	202	240	254	255	238	385	355	254
	Criminal index	5.1	6.1	6.4	6.1	5.6	9.9	8.7	6.0
Germany........	Population	56,367	64,900	59,170	63,000	65,200	70,200	43,900	48,100
	Crimes	579	693	797	680	(not available)	292	538	469
	Criminal index	10.2	10.6	13.4			·	12.2	9.7
Italy...........	Population	32,400	34,600	38,000	41,200	43,200	43,900	44,900	46,200
	Crimes	510	542	654	511	506	624	1,042	658
	Criminal index	15.7	15.7	17.2	12.4	11.7	14.2	23.2	14.2
Sweden........	Population	5,100	5,500	5,900	6,100	6,270	6,380	6,700	7,070
	Crimes	15	14	9	12	12	15	18	20
	Criminal index	2.8	2.5	1.6	1.9	1.9	2.3	2.7	2.8

Source: Vernon Fox, "Criminality and Corrections in Western Europe," in Joseph S. Roucek (ed.), *The Sociology of Crime* (New York: Philosophical Library, 1961), p. 411.

TABLE 1–17
Juvenile delinquents in Europe from 1911 to 1951
(in thousands)

Country	1911	1921	1931	1936	1941	1946	1951
England........	44	43	74	46	64	71	85
France..........	40	43	35	24	42	31	15
Germany........	51	77	23	..*	21	28	30
Italy............	16	15	12	..*	..*	24	20
Sweden..........	..*	..*	..*	1	2	2	2

* Not available.
Source: Fox, "Criminality and Corrections in Western Europe," p. 412.

C. The Orient: Japan and Korea

More than 1,026,000 crimes were reported to Japanese police, who made more than 860,000 arrests in 1940. The crime and arrest rates, however, declined during World War II, evidencing a 30 percent reduction to 711,000 reported offenses and 472,000 arrests.[31] Crimes, however, far outstripped the ability of the police to deter their occurrence during the immediate years of postwar recovery. In the decade between 1955 and 1964, major Japanese crime convictions increased by 67.2 percent from 186,000 to 311,000. And yet, Tokyo, a major city of more than 11 million persons, has failed to reflect the criminal patterns found in most American cities. During 1966, Tokyo recorded only 183 murders, 658 robberies, 4,103 cases of blackmail, 9,172 swindles, 2,030 embezzlements, 32 kidnappings, and 565 sex assaults. The low Tokyo crime rate, however, is encouraged by a police ratio of one officer for every 376 residents, a stringent gun control law threatening sentences up to 10 years imprisonment, and a strict record system which carefully records the lifetime activity of each resident.[32] The sharp rise in *Korean* crime, on the other hand, reflects the various factors at work in the urban complex. As the urban population increased from 11.6 percent in 1940 to 31.3 percent during 1955 in the Republic of Korea, serious crimes also rose from 2,154 in 1953 to 18,576 during 1957. The social disorganization caused by the Korean War and the continuing urbanization of the population contributed to the growth.[33]

THE PARADOX OF CRIME IN THE COMPLEX SOCIETY

Many myths, uncertainties, and ambiguities dominate the popular attitude toward the crime problem. Although most citizens fear crimes

---

[31] Walter A. Lunden, *Crimes and Criminals* (Ames, Iowa: Iowa State University Press, 1967), p. 91.
[32] *The New York Times*, August 1, 1967. See also, Akira Masaki, *Reminiscences of a Japanese Penologist* (Tokyo, 1965).
[33] Lunden, *op. cit.*, p. 67.

of violence, they evidence greater tolerance for crimes against property which they are *more likely* to experience in their lifetime. While expressing a near pathological fear of criminal violence, the average citizen tends to exempt the shoplifter, embezzler, or white-collar offender from the ranks of what he personally defines as "criminal." Ignoring that most murders and assaults are committed by persons known to the victim, whether relative, friend, or acquaintance, the average citizen ascribes violence to strangers or other imaginary persons. In his fear of attack, he ignores the fact that suicides are twice as common as all forms of homicide. Although he fears the increase in crime, the citizen fails to recognize that increased apprehension may well be the prelude to greater community safety. While deploring mass murders by a sniper in Austin, Texas, he may temper his fear long enough to excuse his opposition to gun legislation with a rationalization which assumes that no legislation could have possibly controlled the Texas incident. As he demands community security and strict police enforcement, he may actually hinder its realization by opposing taxes needed to modernize the police force and pay higher salaries.

The general population tends to ignore its responsibility in crime control. And yet, the rise in crime has been directly influenced by the unwillingness of responsible citizens to demand increased police and court efficiency and to support the needed urban reforms which might attack the basic sources of the crime problem. The need to enter a new age of community reintegration and institutional cooperation is obvious from an evaluation of the data presented in this volume. The current crime problem is directly related to the rapid growth of urban communities, the uneven assimilation of ethnic minorities, the inadequate provisions made for human existence, and the failure to provide training opportunities commensurate to the *needs* of the present day. Crime is not a result of chance; it is a logical and continuing result of factors put into operation within the social system through processes of human interaction.[34]

A multitude of factors are involved in the general international increase in criminality, and the exact causal relationship of each factor in the development of the crime problem is unclear. Modern data, however, suggest that crime is a likely by-product of a highly industrialized and urbanized state and is closely related to evident urban disorganization and existing subcultural attitudes. Although primitive and rural societies evidenced lower crime rates and greater social stability, they were also identified by limited social progress. Societies possessing homogeneous cultural and ethnic components possess lower crime rates

---

[34] An interesting analysis is presented by Evelle J. Younger, "Crime in the Space Age," *American Criminal Law Quarterly*, Vol. 4, No. 3 (Spring, 1966), pp. 130–36.

than heterogeneous communities, and societies identified by vertical and horizontal mobility tend to show major crime increases.[35] Since the crime rise is related to rapid social change which tends to shatter former communal or national isolation, crime control depends upon the successful reintegration of diverse groups within the modern social system.

The historical redefinition of social functions and the reformation of social structures have also given rise to increased criminality. As wars and revolutions take their toll, existing social stability and group integration are often replaced by insecurity and disorganization. A general breakdown of authority, especially among defeated nations, is quickly evidenced in the rise of deviance. And yet, floods, earthquakes, explosions, or other disasters which obviate normal controls also yield increased criminal activity. Contractual societies (*Gesellschaft*), however, evidence higher crime rates than those dominated by primary and familial commitment (*Gemeinschaft*). Marked class differences, too, also tend to encourage high crime rates. Crime rates tend to remain higher in societies identified with a high degree of *anomie* (rootlessness, normlessness); affluent nations tend to evidence higher crime rates than poorer nations. Criminal violations, therefore, tend to be greater in societies in which conflicting value systems undermine a single normative system and in which legal codes conflict with established mores and other general norms.[36]

---

[35] See Arthur S. Riffenbaugh, "Cultural influences and Crime Among Indian-Americans of the Southwest," *Federal Probation*, Vol. 20, No. 3 (September, 1964), p. 38.
[36] H. L. A. Hart, *Law, Liberty, and Morality* (Stanford, Calif.: Stanford University Press 1963), gives added insight into the problems of law and ethics.

Chapter 2

CRIME AND CRIMINAL LAW

Modern criminal codes emerged from centuries of human interaction and refinement of group customs. The crimes of primitive societies, anthropologist Bronislaw Malinowski generalizes from his study of Trobriand Islanders, were occasional breaches of custom rather than violations of formal laws. Possessing no precise rules, primitive societies failed to provide general enforcement mechanisms. Although flagrant crime was generally punished by specific group activity designed to purge the violator or the violation, the Melanesian tradition worked to prevent antitribal frictions by coordinating individual and tribal behavior through tradition enforced by manners, customs, and definitions of acceptable private and public behavior. The sanction of tribal punishment, due as Malinowski believes, to a community reaction of anger and indignation, safeguarded human life, property, personal honor, exogamy, rank, marriage, and even chieftainship.[1]

Although the Trobriand community formally failed to differentiate civil and criminal law, it functionally applied sanctions for actions violating flexible, and often relative, community standards. *General norms,* regulating personal relations, economic activity, exercise of power and magic, and relationships of husband and wife, were community rules corresponding to modern *civil law.* The *fundamental rules,* safeguarding life, property, and personality, on the other hand, were comparable to the modern forms of *criminal law.* As a result, common limitations,

---

[1] Bronislaw Malinowski, *Crime and Custom in Savage Society* (Totowa, N.J.: Littlefield, Adams & Co., 1964), p. 66. Some anthropologists question Malinowski's generalizations and point out that precise rules and general enforcement mechanisms are not uncommon in primitive societies.

defined by generations of action and reaction, influenced and governed the social relations of the Trobriand Islanders. The concept of mother-right, which assumed that a child is bodily related and morally committed by kinship to its mother, governed inheritance, class mobility, power, social status, economic inheritance, local citizenship, membership in the totemic clan, and even the person's right to the soil. The laws of marriage, the social constitution of a village community, the position of the head man in his village and the chief in his district, and the privileges and duties of the public magician represented independent noninstitutionalized legal systems. The principles of Trobriand justice, although highly vague, were enacted to eliminate illegal or intolerable social situations and to restore community equilibrium. However, Trobriand punishment, Malinowski discovered, was governed more by chance and personal passion than by any systematic legal procedures.[2]

THE MODERN CONTEXT OF CRIMINAL LAW: THE UNITED STATES

Modern complex societies have advanced well beyond the flexible interpretations evident in Malinowski's general picture of the Trobriand Islands. American criminal law, including three subfields of substantive criminal law, criminal procedure, and special problems in the administration and enforcement of criminal justice, defines a crime as *any defined social harm made punishable by law.*[3] Social harm, however, may be divided into offenses against a person, against a habitation, against property, against morality and decency, against the public peace, and against the administration of government.[4] Although the earlier common law, emerging from centuries of custom and practice, divided crime into the three major forms of felony, misdemeanor, and treason, the modern American criminal code divides offenses into misdemeanors and felonies, including the felony of treason. The *misdemeanor*, a less serious criminal violation, is usually penalized with a fine and/or imprisonment in a municipal or county institution for less than one year. A more serious *felony*, however, is usually punished by a term of imprisonment served in a state or federal institution for a period longer than one year, al-

---

[2] *Ibid.*, p. 99. See Ronald L. Akers, "Toward a Comparative Definition of Law," *Journal of Criminal Law, Criminology, and Police Science*, Vol. 56, No. 3 (September, 1965), pp. 301–6. This general picture, too, has been questioned by Malinowski's critics.

[3] Rollin M. Perkins, *Cases on Criminal Law and Procedure* (Mineola, N.Y.: Foundation Press, Inc., 1966), p. 1. See also Richard C. Donnelly, *Criminal Law* (New York: Free Press, 1962).

[4] Rollin M. Perkins, *Perkins on Criminal Law* (Brooklyn: Foundation Press, 1957), p. 21. For a short survey of the American setting, see Frank E. Hartung, *Crime, Law, and Society* (Detroit: Wayne State University Press, 1966).

though this arbitrary distinction is not evenly enforced.[5] While conviction in cases of exceptional felonies may potentially command a death sentence, capital punishment has become increasingly rare in the United States.

The concepts of law, crime, and punishment are central to the essential nature of criminal law. They are, however, incomplete without the added clarification of such concepts and ideas as *mens rea* (guilty mind), the act or effort, harm, causation, punishment, and legality.[6] Since the modern concept of crime assumes the rational ability of the particular violator to undertake an act designed to harm either an individual or property, legal punishment can only be enacted against the violator if his action was *intended* and *apparent* to his mind. While intent presupposes that the individual desires to complete whatever act he originates, *mens rea* assumes that the intent was knowledgeable and intelligible to the person as he undertook his particular action.[7]

Modern criminal law had its birth in early common law, a system of rules, principles, concepts, and standards which became a form of legal custom enforced by the court.[8] Based upon the authority inherent in common practice and acceptance, common law, however, was later codified by legislation designed to give structural stability to the emerging mass society. While a modern legal statute frequently restates an aspect of common law, it establishes a *specific* definition of expected behavior which is continually interpreted by the courts within the context of social practice and public intention. Criminal law, as a result, now reflects the composite blend of legislative enactment, public attitudes, and judicial interpretation.

Crimes may be procedurally divided into *major* crimes and *petty* offenses, a practice originating in English common law in order to expedite judgments in less complex or less serious cases. While the category of major crimes may include all *felonies* and *serious misdemeanors,* petty offenses are generally limited to *minor* misdemeanors. This distinction, however, is rather arbitrary, since most simple offenses may easily become major crimes through chance or accident. A person failing to stop at a posted intersection may be ticketed for a traffic violation (misdemeanor), but he may be charged with a major crime (felony) if he kills another person due to his failure to stop.

---

[5] Perkins, *Cases,* p. 5.

[6] Jerome Hall, *General Principles of Criminal Law* (Indianapolis: Bobbs-Merrill Co., Inc., 1960), p. 18. See also Richard W. Nice, *Crime and Responsibility* (Tallahassee, Fla.: Dixie Press, 1962).

[7] Hall, *op. cit.,* p. 18. See also Sol Rubin, *Psychiatry and Criminal Law* (New York: Oceana Publications, Inc., 1965) and H. L. A. Hart, *Punishment and the Elimination of Responsibility* (New York: Oxford University Press, Inc., 1962).

[8] Perkins, *Perkins on Criminal Law,* p. 22. See Morris Ginsberg, *On Justice in Society* (Baltimore, Md.: Penguin Books, Inc., 1965), for a philosophical discussion of the nature and problem of justice.

Offenses *against the person* generally include homicide, assault and battery, abduction, abortion, and use of contraceptives, rape and carnal knowledge of a child, false imprisonment, kidnapping, and other special offenses against the individual, including mayhem, dueling, robbery, and larceny from the person. Offenses *against a habitation* are evident in definitions of burglary and arson. Offenses *against property* encompass larceny, robbery, embezzlement, false pretenses, theft, receiving stolen property, malicious mischief, forgery, counterfeiting, and extortion. Adultery, fornication, illicit cohabitation, bigamy, incest, seduction, sodomy, prostitution, obscenity, blasphemy, and mistreatment of dead bodies are included in offenses *against morality and decency*. Offenses *against the public peace* may include breach of the peace, fighting, unlawful assembly or riot, disturbance of public assembly, disorderly house, forcible entry and detainer, libel, and carrying of weapons. Offenses *against the administration of government or sovereignty* range from treason to perjury and subornation. Bribery, misconduct of office, counterfeiting, obstruction of justice, escape, contempt, and other similar acts are also prohibited by the American criminal code.

Although most people believe criminal law is a steady, stable, and unchanging codification of expected and prohibited behavior, law is far from being immutable. It is continually changing as social changes force the reevaluation of previous custom and earlier legislative enactments. Originating as a pragmatic solution to the conditions of the day, a specific law becomes codified through political legitimation and public acceptance. Reflecting the emotional and rational concerns of the community, criminal law emerges in an uneven and semi-integrated development. While periodic revisions of the penal code are designed to standardize legislation and to coordinate judicial interpretation, the actual application of the law to a particular trial situation is interpreted against the backdrop of community mores and previous local traditions. Community influence in the interpretation of a particular impartial law, for example, is apparent in the obvious differences in justice shown blacks in Mississippi and New York.

The growth of the penal code is illustrated in the formulation of the crime of abduction. Criminal abduction was unknown in early English common law. The first criminal statute appeared in the late 1400's, when a felony statute was enacted to protect the young heiress from those seeking her fortune. Its eventual form included the taking of any female against her will, providing the woman had substance in land and/or goods or was the heir apparent. Later applications, however, extended this statute to prohibit the unlawful taking, whether in the form of enticing or detaining, of a girl under a specified age from her parent or guardian with the intent of depriving the parent or guardian of her lawful custody. Other jurisdictions expanded the offense of abduction to include the enticement of any unmarried female under a prescribed age for the purposes of prostitution, sexual intercourse, or concubinage.[9]

Rape laws evidence a similar evolution, having been defined in common law as the unlawful carnal knowledge of a woman without her consent, except if she is the *man's* lawful wife. Assuming that sexual intercourse is a fundamental part of marriage, common law, in effect, favored male initiative in the marital sexual relationship. A husband who aided *another male* to commit rape upon his wife, however, faced rape charges in spite of his marital status. The attempt to protect young girls eventually resulted in statutory rape legislation which progressed beyond earlier common-law definitions. Defined as the unlawful knowledge of a young girl under the age of consent, the law sought to make the male responsible for any sexual relations with an underaged female, *with* or *without* her consent. Although the early English statute protected the young girl to the age of 12, modern American statutes normally guarantee protection until the age of 18. Current rates of teen-age illegitimate births, however, suggest that only a fraction of the existing statutory rape violations are ever prosecuted.

THE MODERN CONTEXT OF CRIMINAL LAW: GREAT BRITAIN

The distinction between civil and criminal law is not as sharp in Great Britain as it is in the United States. Although a judge may hear both civil and criminal cases in the same week, he applies a consistent body of rules to the violations brought before his bench.[10] Since the private person, while able to report a criminal violation, does not initiate action against the violator, criminal prosecution generally rests with the public prosecutor, who initiates action on behalf of the victim and the state. As a result, the public prosecutor, English criminologist Nigel Walker claims, is more competent, less susceptible to bribery or intimidation, and more effective in the use of his time. He is able to work independently and is not dependent upon the victim's signed complaint. While British law allows the simultaneous prosecution of the offender in both civil and criminal courts, few civil compensation suits for loss of stolen property or for personal injury are filed. Although English criminal courts, as also American criminal courts, enact sanctions against the criminal violators, they ignore the plight of the victim. Even though Parliament adopted a program of victim compensation in 1965, reim-

---

[9] Perkins, *Cases*, p. 86. See also W. Friedman, *Law in a Changing Society* (Baltimore, Md.: Penguin Books, Inc., 1964), and Howard Jones, *Crime in a Changing Society* (Baltimore, Md.: Penguin Books, Inc., 1965).

[10] Nigel Walker, *Crime and Punishment in Britain* (Edinburgh: University Press, 1965), p. 4.

bursement is sporadic and is not coordinated with a consistent philosophy of criminal justice.

The differential separation of criminal and civil law is directly related to cultural traditions and variations in penal evolution. While the British penal law, together with other primitive and civilized codes, prohibits homicide, unjustifiable violence, rape, theft, and the intended destruction of personal property, marginal types of behavior are defined differentially in accordance with local mores and customs. While adultery, the extra-marital intercourse of a married person with someone *other than* his or her spouse, is not defined as a criminal offense in Britain, it is a ground for divorce and civil action against the corespondent (the adultery participant). Adultery by the wife, however, is regarded as a crime in France and Italy, while the same activity by the husband is largely ignored under the local moral double standard. A French husband who cohabits with his mistress in the marital home can be convicted of concubinage, a concept foreign to the United States. American law, on the other hand, contains a distinct puritanical emphasis which prohibits fornication (extramarital intercourse between unmarried persons) and adultery (extramarital intercourse between a married person and someone other than the spouse), although these acts are seldom prosecuted.

Modern criminal codes also reflect the differences in social attitudes and mores regarding homosexuality and prostitution. While Britain, most states of the United States, and Germany have traditionally defined male homosexuality as a criminal offense, Britain exempted female homosexuality (lesbianism) from the criminal code. The 1957 report of the English Wolfenden Committee, however, recommended that homosexual acts between consenting adults, if committed in private with a male above a prescribed age, be exempted from the criminal prosecution.[11] While this recommendation was endorsed by the British Parliament in 1967, it has not found similar support in the United States or Germany. Prostitution, on the other hand, has received state sanction in parts of Germany, while continuing to be viewed in the United States as a cardinal legal violation when finally prosecuted. Although prostitution is not regarded as a crime in Britain, street soliciting, brothel keeping, and self-support through prostitution are criminal offenses. A proposal by the archbishop of Canterbury to prosecute the client of the prostitute has received little parliamentary support.

Abortion laws continue to reflect variations in cultural values. The artificial termination of pregnancy generally is a crime in Britain, the United States (with the exception of North Carolina, Colorado, and California in certain instances), and the Catholic countries, although

---

[11] *Ibid.*, p. 6. See also Leon Radzinowicz, *A History of English Criminal Law* (New York: Macmillan Co., 1948), Vols. I–III.

abortion is permitted in England if it is necessary to save the life of the mother. While Soviet Russia evidences a greater permissiveness, abortion is a criminal offense unless performed at an official state clinic. Sweden allows abortion without criminal sanctions when recommended by a liberal reviewing board of medical examiners. As part of its population control program, Japan allows the termination of pregnancy on demand for as little as $8.[12]

Some crimes, however, possess even greater social marginality. While attempted suicide was prosecuted as a criminal offense in England from 1854 until 1961, the same violation resulted in a simple breach-of-the-peace charge in Scotland. The 1961 Suicide Act finally omitted attempted suicide from the British criminal code. While the injury to another caused by negligence can lead to a current criminal conviction in Canada, a case of negligent death or injury to a second party is procedurally prosecuted in Britain along several alternate lines. If the injury is fatal but is not due to gross negligence, the violator may be charged with manslaughter. If it has been caused by a moving vehicle, the driver may be charged with careless or dangerous driving. A person who negligently cripples another while demolishing a building or trimming a tree, on the other hand, cannot be charged with a crime in Britain; although he can be sued for civil damages.

Although almost all civilized criminal codes contain laws against incest, euthanasia, bigamy, and traffic violations, pressures to remove these acts from the criminal code have been growing in Britain. While incest was strongly discouraged by social pressures and was held punishable under ecclesiastical law until 1857, it was not made a criminal offense in Britain until 1908. Modern opponents to incest laws assume that the protection of children against incestuous adults is already guaranteed by other statutes and that incest by consenting adults in private, as with homosexuality, is not a proper concern of criminal law. On the other hand, euthanasia, known also as mercy killing, has been commonly defined as a form of murder. Although the deliberate termination of life finds little support among civilized criminal codes, even in instances of severe pain or incurable disease, modern English critics of euthanasia laws argue that sane adults desiring death for legitimate reasons should be allowed their choice without the application of sanctions against those who would aid them in reaching this goal.

Although bigamy, made a felony in Britain in 1603, no longer carries

---

[12] For additional discussion of the relationships of sex and the law, see James E. Bates and Edward S. Zawadski, *Criminal Abortion* (Springfield, Ill.: Charles C. Thomas, Publisher, 1964), and Ralph Slovenko, *Sexual Behavior and the Law* (Springfield, Ill.: Charles C. Thomas, Publisher, 1965). The controversial nature of the abortion question is discussed in Richard D. Knudten, *Criminological Controversies* (New York: Appleton-Century-Crofts, 1968).

the death penalty, critics of bigamy laws suggest other legal modifications. Under British law a married man living with another woman commits only a matrimonial offense, although his cohabitation, if certified by a ceremony of marriage, is punishable with imprisonment for seven years, even if the man believes himself to be divorced or if his cohabiting "wife" is aware of his previous marriage. He is only exempt from bigamy prosecution if he marries during the lifetime of his wife while believing himself a widower. British critic Granville Williams, however, thinks these laws are outmoded, arguing that the only antisocial consequences of bigamy are the falsification of records and the waste of the time of the minister or registrar.[13]

Proposals to eliminate automobile or traffic offenses from criminal law have centered in the argument that erratic or dangerous drivers are not morally culpable but lack adequate driving skills to function properly in modern traffic. The public, traffic critic P. J. Fitzgerald argues, should be protected by the disqualifying of bad drivers from driving rather than by punishing supposed traffic criminals with fines or imprisonment.[14]

In the final analysis, British criminal law is a composite of the practices, feelings, and mores of the community. Resulting from the expansion of the common law in response to the demands of the public, clergy, police, and government, English criminal law represents both the intelligence and emotion of the nation. Since law attempts to define desired behavior, to structure the social system, and to offer the foundation for social cohesion and legal commonality, it reflects its physical and cultural environment. Like all law codes, British criminal law includes a variety of goals in the actual stipulations of the code. Primary, of course, are:

1. The protection of the person (for example, against intentional violence or cruelty).
2. The protection of the person against particular forms of unintended harm (for example, food poisoning and traffic accident).
3. The protection of the easily susceptible against personal or property exploitation (for example, the young and feebleminded).
4. The prevention of unnatural acts (such as incest, homosexuality, and bestiality).
5. The prevention of shocking acts (such as obscenity, blasphemy, nakedness, and heterosexual public copulation).
6. The discouragement of behavior which might provoke disorder (for example, personal insults, inciting to riot).

---

[13] Walker, *op. cit.*, p. 8.
[14] *Ibid.*, p. 8.

7. The protection of property (for example, against larceny, arson, or forgery).
8. The prevention of inconvenience (for example, road obstruction, falsification of records).
9. The collection of revenue (as through licensing of automobiles, dogs, radio, or television).
10. The defense of the realm or community (as against espionage).
11. The enforcement of justice (through outlawing perjury or resisting arrest).[15]

Naturally, inconsistencies arise when such a multitude of goals are sought simultaneously.

THE MODERN CONTEXT OF CRIMINAL LAW: NORWAY

The Norwegian penal code has undergone many revisions since its original adoption on May 22, 1902. Although a 1927 amendment to the code established a high minimum punishment for serious sexual offenses, its provisions, although demanded by the public, soon proved to be inadequate. The excessive punishment of the offender led quickly to the increased use of the pardon and a parallel rise of acquittals.[16] The world tensions of the early 1950's, in turn, stimulated the revision of code sections dealing with treason and other felonies against the state.

The modern Norwegian penal code is divided into three parts. The general part defines the scope of Norwegian penal law, correctional procedures, self-defense and defense of others and property, *mens rea* (guilty mind), and responsibility. The second part defines the nature of felonies, and the third part details misdemeanors. Since only acts committed intentionally or by negligence are punishable in Norwegian law, factors of intent and mental responsibility take on added importance. A person committing an act while insane or unconscious may not be punished. If an offender was insane at the time of the offense, the community, the code assumes, must protect itself by means other than punishment.[17] Acts committed while under the influence of alcohol, however, are not included within the definition of unconsciousness, a distinction reflecting the general Norwegian legal antagonism to alcohol. Since each *expert* medical witness is a court-appointed witness subject to the supervision of a National Commission of Legal Medicine, the level of forensic psychiatry remains high. Although the Norwegian penal

---

[15] *Ibid.,* p. 10.
[16] Harold Schjoldager, *The Norwegian Penal Code* (South Hackensack, N.J.: Fred B. Rothman & Co., 1961), p. 2.
[17] *Ibid.,* p. 6.

code does not legalize the death penalty, the military penal code of 1902 allows capital punishment for treasonous acts committed during wartime or in time of national emergency. Misdemeanors are largely punished by fines, but the presiding judge possesses wide discretionary power to determine the exact fine in proportion to the offender's economic situation.

THE MODERN CONTEXT OF CRIMINAL LAW: FRANCE

The current French penal code evolved from the ancient European Common Law of Crimes operative in France until the completion of the post–French Revolution (1789) legal revision. Composed of elements of Roman law, canon law, and customary law, common law evidenced a general uniformity throughout the European continent. Characterized by a concept of expiation of guilt together with the possibility of severe corporal punishments and torture, it allowed the judge unlimited judicial power to define an act as criminal and to pronounce appropriate punishment.[18] Beccaria, Montesquieu, Voltaire, and Rousseau, 18th-century critics of the common law, attacked the code and pressed for the reorganization of society on the principles of legality and human rights. While agreeing that written (statutory) law should remain the expression of the general will, they demanded a legal revision which would delineate specific crimes and restrict unlimited punishments. Arguing that punishments are invalid if laws prohibiting the punishable act do not exist at the time of the particular act, the legal reformers demanded that punishments be made identical for each crime and for each crime actor. Collaterally, they demanded that the individual violator be held singly accountable for his guilt without extending the guilt to his parents or members of his extended family in a form of collective punishment as had the former practice.

The July, 1791, promulgation of the misdemeanor and penal code, including provisions for the adjudication (judgment) of cases by jury courts, became the first major step in French legal reform emerging from legislative action completed during the French Revolution. By 1810, however, a revised code of criminal procedure and a modified penal code were enacted under Napoleon I.[19]

Although periodic revisions were undertaken in the decades that followed, the Napoleonic revision, reflecting the French social revolution, gave form to the modern French penal code. The 1810 penal code, as amended in 1859, divided legal punishment into three categories:

---

[18] Gerhard O. W. Mueller and Jean F. Moreau, *The French Penal Code* (South Hackensack, N. J.: Fred B. Rothman & Co., 1960), pp. 1–2.
[19] *Ibid.*, p. 4.

a violation, a misdemeanor, a felony. Violations, punishable by jailing for no more than one month, could be defined by administrative rather than legislative action. Misdemeanor and felony offenses, however, could only be codified through legislative action. Based upon the concept of *mens rea,* the individual's ability to form a rational intent or to understand his action and thereby to possess a guilty mind, the penal code attempted to ascertain whether an act was rationally conceived or was merely an act of ignorance.[20] The code, however, held that every attempt to commit a felony assumes the completion of the felony unless the interrupted attempt was unsuccessful because of circumstances which were independent of the perpetrator's will. Restricting the previous discretionary authority of the courts, the code stipulated that no violation, misdemeanor, or felony could be punished by punishments not provided by law prior to the commission of the crime and that only the most severe of all applicable punishments could be imposed upon the offender when convicted of several felonies and misdemeanors.

Felony punishments, however, could be either deprivational and infamous or simply infamous. Deprivational and infamous punishments included death, hard labor for life, transportation (criminals sent to another country as cheap labor), hard labor for a limited time, imprisonment, and solitary confinement. Less serious infamous punishments, however, included banishment and loss of civil rights. Punishments for less serious misdemeanors under the French criminal code included jailing or imprisonment for a limited time in a house of correction, loss of specific civil, personal, and family rights for a limited period, or monetary fine.[21]

THE MODERN CONTEXT OF CRIMINAL LAW: GERMANY

The contemporary German penal code, closely allied with the French code, was adopted in the German Reich in 1871. Although it has since undergone many changes, the code's structure is similar to that of other European model codes. Although divided into general and special parts, the German code, following the principles of the French *Code Pénal,* differentiates between felonies, gross misdemeanors, and petty misdemeanors.[22] Since punishment can only be inflicted when the criminal offender has voluntarily violated a written law, the actual infliction of punishment is limited to the violations and conditions prescribed by the penal code. *Ex post facto* penal laws, while prohibited, may be applied to a particular case if it benefits the defendant. Because punish-

---

[20] *Ibid.,* p. 7.
[21] *Ibid.,* p. 18.
[22] Gerhard O. W. Mueller, *The German Penal Code of 1871* (South Hackensack, N.J.: Fred B. Rothman & Co., 1961), p. 3.

ment may be enacted only upon confirmation of the violator's guilt, the criminal's capacity for incurring guilt must be proved.

Since the German penal code has abolished capital punishment, deprivation of liberty has become the most severe penalty enacted for criminal behavior. Confinement to a penitentiary for felony violations, imprisonment for gross misdemeanors, and confinement in jail for petty misdemeanors are common punishments.[23] The exact application of punishment depends upon the gravity of the offense, the degree of unlawfulness of the act, and the nature of the guilt of the perpetrator. Although the German code represents punishment as a form of group retribution, it also anticipates the secondary goals of protection of the community and the resocialization of the violator.

THE MODERN CONTEXT OF CRIMINAL LAW: KOREA

The Korean penal code was the first major Korean code enacted since the mythical founding of the nation in 2333 B.C. Although a semi-hybrid criminal code which merged traditional Chinese and Japanese legal variations, it was soon replaced in 1908 by the Japanese criminal code, itself patterned after the German code of 1871. Anti-Japanese sentiment fostered by the post–World War II reaction, however, resulted in the first autonomous modern Korean criminal code in October, 1953. Although it betrays the influence of Chinese classicism and Anglo-American and German criminal law, the code's *general provisions,* stipulated in Part I, include sections on territorial jurisdiction, general principles concerning elements of crime, specifics pertaining to punishments, and more recently, provisions for the suspension of sentence.[24] The *specific provisions,* discussed in Part II, delineate three basic dimensions of specific crimes: state interests, social interests, and individual interests. Crimes violating state interests include false accusations, crimes against the national flag, nonperformance of wartime contracts, obstruction of police or public prosecutor's function, organization of criminal groups, impersonation of public officials, and abandonment of official duties. Crimes against social interests, on the other hand, deal with acts against deceased persons and prohibitions against arson and fire caused by negligence, opium, drinking water, currency, documents and seals, morals, gambling and lotteries.[25] Provisions protecting individual interests include laws against pandering, infanticide, abandoning a baby, cruelty, delivery of a child for employment at hard labor, sexual intercourse

---

[23] *Ibid.,* p. 9.
[24] Paul Ryu and Gerhard O. W. Mueller, *The Korean Criminal Code* (South Hackensack, N.J.: Fred B. Rothman & Co., 1960), pp. 1–2.
[25] *Ibid.,* p. viii.

under the pretext of marriage, unjustifiable acquisition of profit by taking advantage of another person's state of necessity, receiving stolen property, and trespassing upon a boundary.

Although the Korean code has been influenced by Anglo-American and German criminal law, distinct cultural influences are still apparent. The teachings of Confucius and Mencius, evidenced in the belief that human beings are born good rather than evil and that society is composed of differentiated statuses which enable the nobleman to rule the common man, have limited the development of trial by jury and the functional use of Korean law as a means of social control. Gradations of crime, unknown in Western legal tradition, are additionally evident in the Korean criminal code. The presence of an "evil motive," a Korean moral idea, may make a simple crime an aggravated offense. The subtle distinctions between simple and malicious perjury or the suppression of evidence and the harboring of criminals are based upon the presence of an evil motive which, if present, demands the infliction of a greater penalty for the more serious crimes of malicious perjury and harboring of criminals.[26]

Following the principles of the German criminal code, the Korean code makes a clear distinction between intent and general negligence. Although it defines certain acts as criminal only if committed through gross negligence, the code rejects the traditional Anglo-American view that the ignorance of the law is no excuse for violation of the law. The Korean penal code waives potential punishment when a man commits a crime in the belief that his conduct does not constitute a crime, provided he can offer a plausible explanation for his mistakes.[27] On the other hand, the Korean code, as with most other legal codes, allows the punishment of individuals who fail to perform required duties. Although the criminal code gives some support to individual rights, its primary emphasis remains the protection of state interests.[28]

THE MODERN CONTEXT OF CRIMINAL LAW: SOVIET RUSSIA

The overthrow of the czars and the establishment of the Russian Socialist Federated Soviet Republic (RSFSR) led to the formation of the 1918 Soviet Constitution, which omitted any systematic statements

---

[26] *Ibid.*, p. 5.
[27] *Ibid.*, p. 9.
[28] *Ibid.*, p. 21. Refer to "Crime and Aggression in Changing Ceylon," *Transactions of the American Philosophical Society*, Vol. 51, No. 8 (1961); S. N. Bagga, *The Indian Penal Code* (Allahabad, India: Law Book Co., 1958), and Edwin D. Driver, "Interaction and Criminal Homicide in India," *Social Forces*, Vol. 40 (December, 1961), p. 153.

on criminal law. A 1919 statement on principles of criminal legislation issued by the People's Commissariat of Justice later defined basic rules concerning crime and punishment, stages of commissions of crimes, types of punishment, and other items pertinent to criminal procedure and law in a series of 27 articles.[29] Early post-Revolutionary confusion was further reduced with the promulgation of the 1924 Constitution of the Union of Soviet Socialist Republics (U.S.S.R.), which delegated the specific codification of criminal and civil law to the individual republics while retaining primary responsibility for the definition of fundamental legal principles central to the maintenance of the larger Soviet Union. Periodic attempts to reform the criminal code were stymied during the lifetime of Josef Stalin. Reactions to Stalin's abuses, however, led to the 1958 and 1960 reforms in criminal law.[30]

Although the 1926 criminal code subjected any "socially dangerous" act to judicial-correctional, medical, or medico-educational penalties, the 1960 revision of the criminal code held that a specific violation of the code must be committed before punishment may be applied. In effect, the 1960 code rejected the earlier inclusive definition of crime as a socially dangerous act in favor of an explicit definition which was limited to the violation of a specific law. While the 1926 criminal code prescribed a variety of punishments for acts or struggles against the worker class (counterrevolutionary activity), the 1960 code, reflecting the new stability of the Soviet state, redefined both the threat and the treatment of the offender. Enforced social control through the power of the state, necessary in the early stages following the Revolution, gave way to a greater leniency evident in the 1960 code. The maximum period of deprivation of freedom for any crime was reduced from 25 years to 15 years, although the latter could be supplemented with an additional 5-year banishment or exile. General penalties, however, were also reduced.

The control of many minor offenses, previously punished under the formal provisions of the criminal code, was transferred to social organizations and associations, which now applied informal social control mechanisms (for example, warning, reprimand, or small fine) to encourage acceptable social behavior.[31] New definitions of individual rights were codified in the definition of the new crimes of obstruction of the exercise of equal rights for women, violation of secrecy or correspondence, and

[29] Harold J. Berman, *Soviet Criminal Law and Procedure* (Cambridge, Mass.: Harvard University Press, 1966), p. 19. See also Joseph Roucek, *The Sociology of Crime* (New York: Philosophical Library, 1961), pp. 453–87.

[30] Berman, *op. cit.*, p. 23.

[31] *Ibid.*, p. 56. See also George H. Hanna, *Fundamentals of Soviet Criminal Legislation, the Judicial System, and Criminal Court Procedure* (Foreign Languages Publishing House, 1960).

intrusion upon a citizen's dwelling place. The liberal tendency of the 1960 criminal code, however, was modified in the 1961 and 1962 revisions, which increased the penalties for the more serious crimes while introducing a new series of official crimes, economic crimes, and crimes against the system and administration of the state and Socialist property.[32]

Although the 1960 RSFSR criminal code and code of criminal procedure remain a distinct advance over their early predecessors, they lack many of the specific guarantees evidenced in the Western tradition. Under their provisions, a suspect may be held for 10 days without presentation of charges, and an accused may be held up to nine months without being allowed to consult a lawyer or other persons. Although recent revisions have attempted to clarify the specific rights of the citizen in greater detail, the Soviet code still bears the scars of the Bolshevik Revolution and its aftermath. While the protection of the Soviet state still remains a primary function of the criminal code, the mere social danger of a person or his act is no longer enough to justify the imposition of criminal punishment. Criminal sanctions and punishment can only be applied when a crime, a violation of a specific provision of a special part of the criminal code, exists.

THE CULTURAL CONTEXT OF CRIMINAL LAW

The American legal code makes an arbitrary division between *crimes* (violations of penal law) and *torts* (violations of civil or private law). Both may involve public injury or action harmful to the public interest. Crimes offer a greater theoretical threat to the state. Torts, on the other hand, are regarded as actions of one person or group against another person or group in a civil court, which acts as a social arbiter in order to maintain public order and minimize social friction. The distinction between real crimes and public torts has been largely based upon the evolving legal distinction between *mala in se* (a heinous act or true crime) and *mala prohibita* (an undesired act prohibited by definition).[33] Modern criminal law, therefore, defines specific crimes and specific punishments. *Specificity,* a central ingredient in the definition of a crime, limits punishment to acts which are either committed when prohibited or omitted when demanded by law.

Law represents a codified behavioral standard defined by persons possessing access to the legislative process, but individual behavior varies

---

[32] *Ibid.,* p. 64. See also Vladimir Gsovski, "Reform of Criminal Law in the Soviet Union," *Social Problems,* Vol. 7 (Spring, 1960), p. 315.

[33] Hall, *op. cit.,* p. 201. Refer also to Jerome Hall, *Studies in Jurisprudence and Criminal Theory* (New York: Oceana Publications Inc., 1958).

widely. Since the social variables of age, sex, education, income, religion, and social class influence individual behavior, a person's response to a specific law may not coincide with the prescribed legal standards. While law is specific, its specificity is somewhat relative. Legal definitions vary from time to time and from place to place. Polygamy, for example, defined as a criminal act in the United States, finds acceptance in some African and Oriental countries. Parricide (killing of one's father), subject to special laws in Russia and France, is simply included in the prohibition against murder in the Americas. The prohibition of alcoholic beverages, ineffectively legislated during the early 1900's, was unenforceable in American cities. Attempts to legalize abortion and the use of marijuana today challenge legislative restrictions which several generations previously believed were valid institutionalized norms.

Although many definitions of crime, however, change as the cultural context of the crime changes, crimes of physical violence, whether in the form of homicide or assault, are universally held to be criminal acts. Crimes of treason, incest, and theft, challenges to personal and state security, are also judged criminal violations in nearly all nations. International penal codes, however, prescribe variable punishments which reflect the variations of culture and legitimating power of particular social groups. Even murder, universally defined as a criminal act, is often legitimized in particular cultural circumstances. The murder of a seducer, acceptable in Sicily in order to defend the honor of the seduced, finds immediate prosecution in the United States.[34] An American policeman, on the other hand, possesses the right to kill a suspected but fleeing felon even though the law suggests that every man is innocent until proven guilty by the state. The cultural redefinition of murder is even more apparent in social attitudes toward war, in which mass homicide is defined as a legitimate goal of the state.

Although criminal definitions may originate in a relative manner within a particular culture, they pass beyond a relative definition, becoming codified supports for the entire social system. The emergence of new social and economic systems results in collateral changes in the total culture. As a result, modern technology, accompanied by the social changes of the Industrial Revolution, has given birth to new norms, new behaviors, and new crimes. A coherent and stable social system has given way to patterns of high mobility and change, replacing an agrarian society with industrial specialization. Consequently, new crimes and new criminals have been created, as the state has attempted to create a rational structure for the reintegration of social change. Deviant conduct, formerly governed by informal local controls, has become the object of special legislation designed to constrain antisocial behavior,

---

[34] Hall, *Studies*, p. 205.

as the local group has become quickly subordinated to the demands of the mass society.[35]

Although legal standards are rational constructs, they are not devoid of emotional overtones. Congressional legislation designed to control the interstate travel of persons engaged in incitement to riot, for example, ignores the fact that no man can readily provoke a riot if cultural conditions or subgroups do not support the grievances which the riot ultimately expresses. Although such a law is a rational-emotional attempt to limit the perceived source of present urban discontent, it reflects the presuppositions, beliefs, and biases of those defining desired behavior and acceptable social values.

Changes in American society, we may hypothesize, will ultimately lead to the formulation of new laws designed to meet current needs. Rising consumer power, for example, will undoubtedly be expressed in laws against criminal fraud and questionable business practices. The formation of new legislation, however, will eventually create a new group of criminals who may be simply carrying out the same activity which was formerly tolerated before the passage of consumer-dominated legislation. Embezzlement, for example, recognized as a modern middle-class offense, was legally undefined in England until 1799. Although similar behavior occurred previously, it was commonly treated as a mere breach of trust. The major increase of untrustworthiness which accompanied the growth of the banking profession eventually led to the definition of criminal embezzlement.[36] American crimes of cattle rustling, bootlegging, horse stealing, and racketeering show a similar evolution within the American cultural context. Criminal laws against blasphemy, Sabbath degradation, idleness, witchcraft, religious minorities, and polygamy are direct reflections of American social history and values.

Although laws may include the legitimate or illegitimate bias of those possessing the legitimating power, they still represent structured attempts to form a functional social system. Incorporating new advances, discoveries, inventions, and corresponding changes occurring within the cultural system, penal law prescribes the exact limits of social tolerance at a particular point in history. Some laws, however, pass beyond local, community, or state limitations. The growth of international law has been marked by attempts to find common legal standards. The Nazi extermination of the Jews during World War II gave birth to new laws against genocide, the attempted extermination of a particular human group. Although no law prohibiting mass extermination previously existed, international repulsion to the mass executions of some 4 million

[35] *Ibid.*, p. 207. For a discussion of another dimension of the problem see Arthur E. Bonfield, "The Abrogation of Penal Statutes by Nonenforcement," *American Criminal Law Quarterly*, Vol. 2, No. 4 (Summer, 1964), pp. 178–90.

[36] *Ibid.*, p. 208.

Jews led to the ex post facto Nuremburg and Tokyo War Crimes trials, which were justified on the grounds that the defendants had committed crimes against humanity. While some states have held that the trials were nothing more than trials of the vanquished by the victors, others maintain that they represent the foundation of future international attempts to control war and mass homicide. Since legal categories, however, are attempts to define desired behavior, they usually emerge from observed violations in actual behavior. A time lag necessarily exists, therefore, between the behavior which challenges the society and the enactment of laws designed to limit this behavior.

While American criminal law assumes that each violator is responsible for his action, criminologists readily recognize that a wide variety of motivations and behaviors are involved in the development of criminal activity. Personal values, achieved education, economic conditions, variable contexts of human interaction, living conditions, and marital status are among the many variables which affect an individual's choices and actions within the total social complex. Many crimes depend upon the ultimate cooperation of the actual victim. The confidence man, for example, depends upon the greed of the "pigeon." Modern merchandising techniques which capitalize on impulsive purchasing encourage the shoplifter, who may be simply engaging in a form of impulsive "buying without paying." Since crime involves a variety of behaviors, interactions, and codes, any attempt to ascribe all crimes to the person's free will or free choice fails to consider a major dimension of the crime problem. Crime is a social action—a social product. And yet, it is subject to individual control and discipline. Criminal law faces the dilemma that it cannot assume a flexible standard of behavior which might vary for each person by age, sex, education, occupation, or religion, although the person's attitudes and behavior are structured by his general social environment and position. Since criminal law is a social common denominator, it is necessarily applied equally to all persons. Because criminal law must remain impartial, a basic statement of social attitude and practice, it must assume that each person who violates the prescribed legal standard does so for good and sufficient reason. But yet, it must allow enough tolerance to compensate for special cases which the criminal code is unable to anticipate in either its early formation or later revision.[37]

---

[37] *Ibid.*, pp. 212–14. See W. Owen Keller, *Criminal Procedure: History of the Criminal Code* (Kentucky Legislative Research Commission, Research Publication Number 69), for the development of Kentucky's legal code. See also Donald S. Leonard, "The Changing Faces of Criminal Law," *Journal of Criminal Law, Criminology, and Police Science,* Vol. 56 (1965), pp. 517–22.

Chapter 3

THE PREVALENCE AND DISTRIBUTION OF CRIME

Valid crime statistics concerning the more than 2,800 federal crimes and the uncounted state and local violations are difficult to obtain. Available data, submitted voluntarily by enforcement, prosecution, and judicial agencies, are unevenly reported and tabulated. Since the *exact* crime volume is never fully revealed, the announced statistics can only *suggest* the full dimension of the crime problem. Dominated by definitions of traditional crime (such as theft, burglary, and murder), the reports tend to neglect the vast areas of organized crime and white-collar criminality (crimes of respectable citizens) which may threaten social consequences even greater than those entailed by the traditional crimes.

DATA SOURCES

Although characterized by these statistical shortcomings, the *Uniform Crime Reports* of the Federal Bureau of Investigation provide tabulations of the most comprehensive data available on American crime. Published annually since 1930, the *Uniform Crime Reports* survey the American crime scene, recording arrest data in 29 crime categories ranging from the more serious criminal homicide to the less important juvenile runaway. The total volume of known criminal activity recorded under the title *offenses known to the police* represents the composite crime volume as reported by local officers, prosecuting attorneys, court officials, and the general public. Since the *Uniform Crime Reports* depend upon the voluntary submission of crime information, the validity of the *Re-

ports ultimately rests with the accuracy of law enforcement statistical procedures. Because the police are more likely to know of a murder than a successful theft, data concerning the violent offenses, more likely to be reported to the police, are believed to hold greater accuracy and validity. Less serious crimes, such as curfew and loitering law violations, offer less accurate statistics and information.

The seven most serious crimes of murder and nonnegligent manslaughter, forcible rape, robbery, aggravated assault, burglary (breaking or entering), larceny $50 and over, and auto theft, reported in an additional separate quarterly report by the FBI, constitute a special category of *Index Crimes* (see Figure 3–1).[1] Based upon the assumption that the extreme nature of the offense will lead the victim to report an attack or major theft to the police, the FBI presumes that these data are the most accurate index of criminality trends. Such an assumption, however, may be far from the truth. The estimated rape volume is almost three times the rate recorded in the *known-to-police* index of crime. Since the crime index only records the number of alleged but unproven offenses, the sharp recent increase in the volume of recorded crimes may partially be due to a greater public willingness to report alleged or actual criminal acts to the police. Although the *Uniform Crime Reports* possess other statistical limitations, due to variations in state criminal statistics and in reporting procedures, they presently represent the best source of data concerning American criminality.

The establishment of the National Crime Information Center in January, 1967, offers hope that more valuable information concerning crime will be made available through the use of principles of computerized information system in analyses of data. Even then, the final value of the received and analyzed data will continue to depend upon the accuracy of the reports submitted *to* and *by* the local police. Periodically, as in New York[2] and Chicago in the past, local precincts have minimized the actual volume of crime in the police district in the attempt to present a strong enforcement image. Although reporting procedures are being increasingly tightened, the FBI still is unable to fully validate the data in the *Uniform Crime Reports*.[3]

[1] The President's Commission on Law Enforcement and Administration of Justice, *The Challenge of Crime in a Free Society* (Washington, D.C.: U.S. Government Printing Office, 1967), p. 18. See also Ronald H. Beattie, "Criminal Statistics in the United States—1960," *Journal of Criminal Law, Criminology and Police Science,* Vol. 51 (1960), p. 61.

[2] *The New York Times,* February 21, 1967.

[3] *Uniform Crime Reports—1968* (Washington, D.C.: U.S. Department of Justice, 1969), pp. 53–54. The procedures of data gathering and analysis are examined on pages 51–56. For a more critical evaluation, see Norman E. Issacs, "The Crime of Present Day Crime Reporting," *Journal of Criminal Law, Criminology, and Police Science,* Vol. 52 (1961), pp. 405–10.

FIGURE 3–1
Estimated number and percentage of index offenses, 1968
(5,706 agencies; 199,861,000 estimated population)

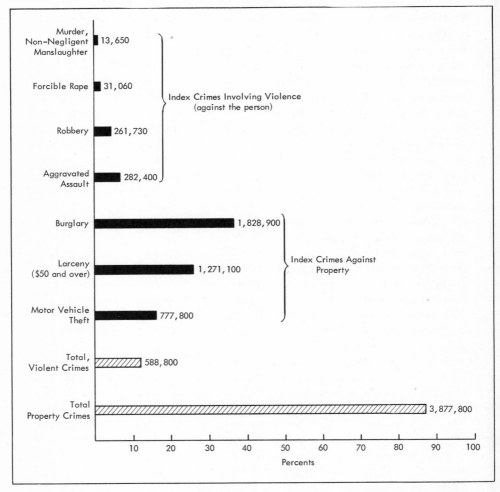

Source: *Uniform Crime Reports—1968* (Washington, D.C.: U.S. Department of Justice, 1969), p. 57.

Court statistics offer a second source of information concerning criminal activity. Although most state and local courts fail to follow a common procedure in recording prosecutions, dismissals, acquittals, convictions, prison sentences, penalties, and probations, the Administrative Office of the United States Courts compiles such detailed information for the federal courts. Since the disposition of the actual court case, however, dominates their focus, the full dimensions of the crime problem are not revealed in the Administrative Office data. *Institutional crime statistics,* a third source of criminality data, suffer from similar deficiencies. Periodic reports of the U.S. Bureau of the Census and the Federal Bureau of Prisons only superficially survey the local, state, and federal prisoner population. Local or state penal summaries are no better, presenting only a cursory overview of the inmate population and a continuing plea for added public support. Other sporadic data secured from irregular or yearly *crime surveys* and *commission reports* provide special insights concerning problems of the local community. The reports of the Chicago Crime Commission and the American Bankers' Association, for example, focus upon the specific characteristics of organized crime and robberies in Chicago effected against member banks. The localized nature of these surveys, however, limit their value in obtaining an overview of the crime problem.

Information concerning *juvenile delinquency* is available in the arrest statistics of the *Uniform Crime Reports,* the juvenile court statistics of the U.S. Children's Bureau, the special and decennial reports of sentences served by juvenile delinquents in correctional institutions issued by the U.S. Bureau of Census, and other local data available through specific community sources. The volume of hidden delinquency, however, never appears in these sources, since these cases, if detected, may simply be handled in an informal manner by individual or local agencies. Detection, however, is not assured. State variations in juvenile laws and court jurisdiction further hinder the gathering of national juvenile delinquency data.

UNDETECTED AND UNREPORTED CRIME

Since criminals seek secrecy, a large volume of crime is never detected. James Wallerstein and Kenneth Wylie reported in 1947 that 99 percent of 1,698 respondents admitted having committed one or more criminal offenses, from the 49 violations listed on their questionnaire, without having ever been arrested. The average number of violations committed by 1,020 men was 18, while women laborers alone admitted 9.8 offenses after age 16. Females reported a mean number of 11 offenses. Almost two thirds of the males and nearly one third of the females admitted their guilt to one or more of the 14 listed serious felonies.[4]

Although their act may have been recorded in the *UCR's crimes known to the police* summary, they may also have succeeded in avoiding detection. Many of these offenders, the researchers found, were part

---

[4] Marvin Wolfgang, *Crime and Race: Conceptions and Misconceptions* (New York: Institute of Human Relations Press, 1964), pp. 21–22.

of a hidden criminal population which once participated in crime but later rejected criminal deviance as a life pattern as the individuals succeeded in legitimate social channels. The most likely traditional offenders, Wallerstein and Wylie concluded, were persons from the lowest social and economic groups who had an inferior education, a disproportionate amount of unemployment, and a prior criminal record, and who were single or had an abnormal home life (divorce, broken home).[5]

TABLE 3–1
Unreported crime: Comparison of survey and *UCR* rates
(per 100,000 population)

		UCR Rate	
Index Crimes	NORC Survey 1965–66	For Individuals 1965*	For Individuals and Organizations 1965*
Willful homicide...............	3.0	5.1	5.1
Forcible rape..................	42.5	11.6	11.6
Robbery.......................	94.0	61.4	61.4
Aggravated assault..............	218.3	106.6	106.6
Burglary......................	949.1	299.6	605.3
Larceny ($50 and over)..........	606.5	267.4	393.3
Motor vehicle theft.............	206.2	226.0	251.0
Total Violence............	357.8	184.7	184.7
Total Property............	1,761.8	793.0	1,249.6

* *Uniform Crime Reports—1965*, p. 51. The *UCR* national totals do not distinguish crimes committed against individuals or households from those committed against businesses or other organizations. The *UCR* rate for individuals is the published national rate adjusted to eliminate burglaries, larcenies and vehicle thefts not committed against individuals or households. No adjustment was made for robbery.
Source: The President's Commission on Law Enforcement and Administration of Justice, *The Challenge of Crime in a Free Society* (Washington, D.C.: U.S. Government Printing Office, 1967), p. 21.

Other studies during the period supported this picture. Edward E. Schwartz, for example, found that only 43 percent of all known juvenile delinquency cases were ever handled by the Washington, D.C., juvenile court during the early 1940's.[6] A 1945–46 study of 101 Cambridge and Somerville (Massachusetts) boys, involving 6,416 offenses, revealed that 1.5 percent of their total offenses ever resulted in an official court hearing over the five year period. Fourteen hundred infractions of city ordinances were never processed to the complaint level. Only 27 of 4,400 minor offenses, six tenths of 1 percent, were finally prosecuted. Sixty-eight

---

[5] President's Commission, *op. cit.*, p. 44.
[6] Edward E. Schwartz, "A Community Experiment in the Measuring of Delinquency," *National Probation and Parole Association Yearbook, 1945*, pp. 157–81.

of 616 serious offenses, 11 percent, resulted in punishment.[7] More recent evidence suggests that middle- and upper-class delinquency rates may be considerably higher than those reflected in local delinquency statistics. The higher delinquency rates of the lower class, in fact, may be due to their larger number, their higher probability of discovery, and their greater vulnerability to court processes.

FIGURE 3–2
Estimated rates of offense*; comparison of police† and Bureau of Social Science Research Survey data (three Washington, D.C. precincts; rates per 1,000 residents 18 years or over)

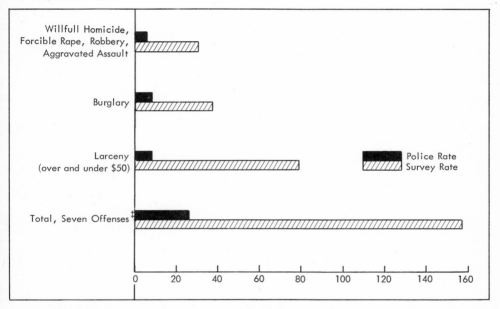

* Incidents involving more than one victim adjusted to count as only one offense. A victimization rate would count the incidence for each individual.
   † Police statistics adjusted to eliminate nonresident and commercial victims and victims under 18 years of age.
   ‡ Willful homicide, forcible rape, robbery, aggravated assault, burglary, larceny (over and under $50), and motor vehicle theft.
   Source: President's Commission, *The Challenge of Crime in a Free Society*, p. 21.

The clearest insight into the degree of *unreported* crime emerged from a 1965 National Opinion Research Center survey of 10,000 households. While asking whether the person questioned or any member of the household had been a criminal victim during the year, the NORC survey revealed that the respondents knew of fewer murders (3.0 per

---
   [7] Fred J. Murphy, Mary Shirley, and Helen Witmer, "The Incidence of Hidden Delinquency," *American Journal of Orthopsychiatry*, Vol. 16 (1946), pp. 686–96.

TABLE 3–2
Victims' most important reason for not notifying police*
(in percentages)

Crimes	Percent of Cases in Which Police Not Notified	Reasons for not notifying police				
		Felt It Was Private Matter or Did Not Want to Harm Offender	Police Could Not Be Effective or Would Not Want to Be Bothered	Did Not Want to Take Time	Too Confused or Did Not Know How to Report	Fear of Reprisal
Robbery	35	27	45	9	18	0
Aggravated assault	35	50	25	4	8	13
Simple assault	54	50	35	4	4	7
Burglary	42	30	63	4	2	2
Larceny ($50 and over)	40	23	62	7	7	0
Larceny (under $50)	63	31	58	7	3	(‡)
Auto theft	11	20†	60†	0†	0†	20†
Malicious mischief	62	23	68	5	2	2
Consumer fraud	90	50	40	0	10	0
Other fraud (bad checks, swindling, etc.)	74	41	35	16	8	0
Sex offenses (other than forcible rape)	49	40	50	0	5	5
Family crimes (desertion, nonsupport, etc.)	50	65	17	10	0	7

* Willful homicide, forcible rape, and a few other crimes had too few cases to be statistically useful, and they are therefore excluded.
† There were only five instances in which auto theft was not reported.
‡ Less than 0.5 percent.
Source: President's Commission, *The Challenge of Crime in a Free Society*, p. 22.

100,000 persons) than were known to the police (5.1).[8] Forcible rapes, robberies, aggravated assaults, burglaries, and larcenies $50 and over, however, were more commonly known to those surveyed than to enforcement agencies (see Table 3–1). Personal injury crime, NORC reported, was almost twice the *UCR* rate, while property crime was *more than* twice the rate reported by the *UCR* for individuals.

Other research studies of victimization undertaken in Washington, Boston, and Chicago illustrate the clear disparity between reported and unreported crimes. A survey of three Washington precincts, reported in Figure 3–2, suggests that the actual crime volume is hidden below the surface like an iceberg. Citizen unwillingness to report known crimes to the police, the surveyors found, was motivated by the belief that the crime was beyond police control or that any report would only cause public embarrassment and personal inconvenience.[9] Police aid was sought least often in cases of consumer fraud (10 percent), although auto thefts stimulated an 89 percent report rate (see Table 3–2)

THE KNOWN CRIME VOLUME

Crime increased during the seven-year period between 1960 and 1968 (see Table 3–3). The slightly more than 2 million reports of 1960 index crimes rose to more than 4,466,600 in 1968. The population increased from 179 million to an approximate 200 million persons during the same period. The crime rate grew from nearly 1,123 to 2,234 alleged criminal violations per 100,000 inhabitants. While murder and nonnegligent manslaughter increased 51.7 percent, the increase reflected 4,650 additional murders and a population growth of some 20.5 million persons. Forcible rapes, increased in volume by 84.3 percent (16,860 to 31,060). However, when compared with the increase in population, the 21.4 percent volume increase in murder and nonnegligent manslaughter becomes a smaller 36 percent increase, while forcible rape, representing a 84.3 percent increase in volume, reaches a lesser 64.9 percent growth for the same nine-year period.[10] Other index crime categories, represented in Table 3–4, evidence similar trends. The greatest number of reported incidents, both in number of offenses and generally in rates per 100,000 inhabitants, occurred in the property crimes of burglary, larceny ($50 and over), and auto theft.

---

[8] President's Commission, *op. cit.*, p. 21.

[9] *Ibid.*, p. 22. The late Dean Joseph D. Lohman, School of Criminology, University of California (Berkeley) suggests that the current approach to crime automatically writes off human resources on a vast scale.

[10] *Uniform Crime Reports—1968*, p. 105. Ronald H. Beattie and John P. Kennedy, "Aggressive Crimes," *The Annals*, Vol. 364 (March, 1966), pp. 73–85, present an analysis of violence trends.

TABLE 3–3

Index of crime, United States, 1960 to 1968 (known to the police)

Population*	Total Crime Index	Violent† Crime	Property† Crime	Murder and Non-negligent Man-slaughter	Forcible Rape	Robbery	Aggravated Assault	Burglary	Larceny $50 and Over	Auto Theft
Number of offenses:										
1960—179,323,175	2,014,600	285,200	1,729,400	9,000	16,860	107,390	152,000	897,400	506,200	325,700
1961—182,953,000	2,082,400	286,100	1,796,300	8,630	16,890	106,210	154,400	934,200	528,500	333,500
1962—185,822,000	2,213,600	298,200	1,915,400	8,430	17,210	110,390	162,100	978,200	573,100	364,100
1963—188,531,000	2,435,900	313,400	2,122,500	8,530	17,310	115,980	171,600	1,068,800	648,500	405,200
1964—191,334,000	2,755,000	360,100	2,395,000	9,250	21,020	129,830	200,000	1,193,600	732,000	469,300
1965—193,818,000	2,930,200	383,100	2,547,200	9,850	22,970	138,100	212,100	1,261,800	792,300	493,100
1966—195,857,000	3,264,200	425,400	2,838,800	10,920	25,330	157,320	231,800	1,387,200	894,600	557,000
1967—197,864,000	3,802,300	494,600	3,307,700	12,090	27,100	202,050	253,300	1,605,700	1,047,100	654,900
1968—199,861,000	4,466,600	588,800	3,877,700	13,650	31,060	261,730	282,400	1,828,900	1,271,100	777,800
Percent change 1960–68‡	+121.7	+106.5	+124.2	+51.7	+84.3	+143.7	+85.8	+103.8	+151.1	+138.8
Rate per 100,000 inhabitants‡										
1960	1,123.4	159.0	964.4	5.0	9.4	59.9	84.7	500.5	282.3	181.6
1961	1,138.2	156.4	981.8	4.7	9.2	58.1	84.4	510.6	288.9	182.3
1962	1,191.2	160.5	1,030.8	4.5	9.3	59.4	87.3	526.4	308.4	196.0
1963	1,292.0	166.2	1,125.8	4.5	9.2	61.5	91.0	566.9	344.0	214.9
1964	1,439.9	188.2	1,251.7	4.8	11.0	67.9	104.5	623.8	382.6	245.3
1965	1,511.9	197.6	1,314.2	5.1	11.9	71.3	109.5	651.0	408.8	254.4
1966	1,666.6	217.2	1,449.4	5.6	12.9	80.3	118.4	708.3	456.8	284.4
1967	1,921.7	250.0	1,671.7	6.1	13.7	102.1	128.0	811.5	529.2	331.0
1968	2,234.8	294.6	1,940.2	6.8	15.5	131.0	141.3	915.1	636.0	389.1
Percent change 1960–68‡	+98.9	+85.3	+101.2	+36.0	+64.9	+118.7	+66.8	+82.8	+125.3	+114.3

* Population is Bureau of the Census provisional estimates as of July 1, except April 1, 1960, census.
† Violent crime is offenses of murder, forcible rape, robbery, and aggravated assault. Property crime is offenses of burglary, larceny $50 and over, and auto theft.
‡ Percent change and crime rates calculated prior to rounding number of offenses. Revised estimates and rates based on changes in reporting practices.
Source: *Uniform Crime Reports—1968*, p. 59.

Crimes *known* to the police, however, do not automatically result in clearance of the crime by the *arrest* of a particular offender. Arrests, in like manner, do not necessarily produce formal criminal charges, court hearings, or criminal judgments. In fact, a gradual shrinkage in the total known crime volume occurs at each stage of the enforcement, adjudication, and incarceration process, reducing the number of convicted offenders to a mere fraction of the total population committing some known crime. Murder and nonnegligent manslaughter offer the highest crime *clearance* of crimes solved or concluded by police arrest and charge of offender. While nearly 86 percent of known murders and nonnegligent manslaughters are cleared by arrest, only 56.6 percent of the reported forcible rapes ever result in an arrest of an alleged offender. Aggravated assault, another visible crime against the person, also exhibits a high clearance rate, since a large proportion of the victims and offenders are known to each other. Robbery, on the other hand, is largely successful. Only 27.3 percent of all known robberies were cleared by the arrest of an alleged offender in 1968. The low rates of burglary, larceny, and auto theft clearance suggest that these forms of crime are even more potentially successful (see Table 3–4).[11]

Each of the seven index crime categories showed a similar percent of 1968 arrests which resulted in an eventual charge (14.6 to 90.0 percent). Adult acquittals and dismissals ranged from 10.8 percent for auto theft to 4.6 percent for manslaughter by negligence. The juvenile tendency to commit unsophisticated robberies, burglaries, larcenies, and auto thefts, eventuated in a disproportionate number of juvenile arrests. However, the greatest number of property offenders, whether adult or juvenile, are never arrested (see Fig. 3–3). Although popular fiction suggests that crime does not pay, this is not true for those with the necessary skills and contacts to make larceny and burglary a profitable undertaking.

The highest conviction rate, as noted in Table A–1 (see Appendix, page 723), occurred in the crime category of drunkenness (86.8 percent), while the lowest was reported for arson (15.1 percent of those formally charged by the police). Nearly 45.5 percent of all persons charged for tabulated index offenses in 1968 were eventually referred to the juvenile court, while 34.2 percent of index crime violators were judged guilty as charged. Juvenile referrals for all reported crimes, however, declined to less than 18 percent. The greatest crime volume occurred in crimes of drunkenness, the inclusive category of "all other offenses," disorderly conduct, larceny, driving under the influence, other assaults, and other miscellaneous crimes of lesser volume.[12]

---

[11] *Ibid.*
[12] *Ibid.*

TABLE 3-4

Offenses known, cleared; persons arrested, charged and disposed of in 1968 (2,530 cities; 1968 estimated population 63,163,000)

Type	Total	Murder and Nonnegligent Manslaughter	Forcible Rape	Robbery	Aggravated Assault	Burglary—Breaking or Entering	Larceny-Theft	Auto Theft
Offenses known	2,476,720	4,073	9,534	80,722	82,285	616,459	1,384,865	298,782
Offenses cleared	505,731	3,496	5,395	22,066	56,695	121,736	237,855	58,488
Percent cleared	20.4	85.8	56.6	27.3	68.9	19.7	17.2	19.6
TOTAL ARRESTS	**491,882**	**3,940**	**5,019**	**26,511**	**42,816**	**109,397**	**244,902**	**59,297**
Per 100 offenses	19.9	96.7	52.6	32.8	52.0	17.7	17.7	19.8
Arrests under 18	263,390	378	1,098	8,807	7,120	64,897	141,528	39,562
Per 100 offenses	10.6	9.3	11.5	10.9	8.7	10.5	10.2	13.2
Persons charged	422,859	3,664	4,758	23,331	40,041	95,999	202,629	52,437
Per 100 offenses	17.1	90.0	49.9	28.9	48.7	15.6	14.6	17.6
Persons guilty as charged	124,781	976	1,147	5,588	13,253	19,950	75,045	8,822
Per 100 offenses	5.0	24.0	12.0	6.9	16.1	3.2	5.4	3.0
Persons guilty of lesser offenses	20,226	443	448	1,690	3,893	5,790	5,604	2,358
Per 100 offenses	0.8	10.9	4.7	2.1	4.7	0.9	0.4	0.8
Persons acquitted or dismissed	56,508	867	1,277	3,794	9,771	10,139	25,384	5,276
Per 100 offenses	2.3	21.3	13.4	4.7	11.9	1.6	1.8	1.8
Juveniles referred to juvenile court	172,955	234	871	7,109	5,375	50,284	77,974	31,108
Per 100 offenses	7.0	5.7	9.1	8.8	6.5	8.2	5.6	10.4

Source: *Uniform Crime Reports—1968*, p. 105.

FIGURE 3–3
Crimes cleared by arrest, 1968

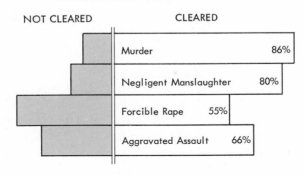

AGAINST THE PERSON

| NOT CLEARED | CLEARED |

Murder	86%
Negligent Manslaughter	80%
Forcible Rape	55%
Aggravated Assault	66%

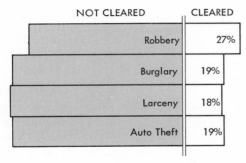

AGAINST PROPERTY

| NOT CLEARED | CLEARED |

Robbery	27%
Burglary	19%
Larceny	18%
Auto Theft	19%

Source: *Uniform Crime Reports—1968*, p. 31.

AGE AS A DETERMINANT

Juvenile delinquency is generally a forerunner of adult crime. The earlier a juvenile's arrest and contact with the juvenile court, the more likely will be his participation in serious adult criminal activity. The more serious his first offense, the greater his likelihood to continue serious crimes, especially crimes against property. The more frequently he is processed by the police, the juvenile court, and the correctional system, the greater is the likelihood that he will be eventually arrested, charged, convicted, and imprisoned as an adult. Although he may start with petty stealing or more serious theft (for example, auto theft), he is most likely to progress to more serious property offenses as an adult.[13]

Persons under 25 accounted for more than one half of all persons

---

[13] President's Commission, *op. cit.*, p. 45.

arrested in 1968. Juveniles under 15 were arrested for nearly 49 percent of vandalism, 43 percent of arson, 40 percent of runaways, 29 percent of larcenies, 27 percent of burglaries, 25 percent of curfew and loitering violations, and lesser percents in all remaining crime categories. The majority of persons arrested for arson (69.3 percent), auto theft (60.7 percent), larceny (54.0 percent), burglary (54.7 percent), curfew or loitering law violations (100 percent), and runaways (100 percent) were juveniles under 18 years of age. The greatest 1960–68 increase in arrests occurred among persons under 18 years of age, reflecting the problems of juvenile adjustment to a complex society (see Table A–2).[14]

Although educational and occupational data concerning arrested and incarcerated criminals are incomplete, the 1960 Census of Population indicated that state and federal prisoners completed a median schooling of 8.6 years. The general American population, on the other hand, finished an educational equivalent of 10.6 years.[15] Only 5.8 percent of the 1960 offender population were gainfully employed in professional, technical, managerial, official, proprietor, or other high-status occupations at the time of their incarceration, although the general population reported 20.6 percent in these advantaged occupations.

THE VARIABLE OF SEX

Although males are arrested nearly seven times as frequently as females for all seven index offenses and larceny under $50, the differential between male and female arrest rates is declining as females commit crimes at a faster rate. While the male arrest rate increased 18 percent between 1960 and 1965, the female rate increased by a substantial 62 percent (from 10 to 164 female arrests per 100,000 women). The high 1960–65 female increase, however, was due to the 81 percent growth in female larceny arrests. Aggravated assault, the next highest female arrest category, increased only 4 percent. Although women are most likely to be arrested for prostitution and commercialized vice, this category may also include male arrests (see Table A–3). During 1968, nearly 50 percent of the teen-age runaways were female. Major female crimes included larceny (24.4 percent), murder and nonnegligent manslaughter (16.1 percent), and aggravated assault (12.4 percent). Nearly one fifth of all 1968 violators arrested for forgery and counterfeiting, fraud, embezzlement, and curfew and loitering law violations were female. Females, however, only accounted for 12.9 percent of all persons arrested during the year. Female crime and arrest rates, however, may not be

---

[14] *Uniform Crime Reports—1968*, p. 112.
[15] President's Commission, *op. cit.*, p. 45.

accurate indicators of female criminal activity, since American society tends to protect women.

Male crimes far outnumbered female. Males committed more than 75 percent of all crimes in *all* categories with the exception of prostitution—commercialized vice and runaways. They were responsible for more than 90 percent of all robberies, burglaries, auto thefts, arsons, possessions of illegal property, vandalism, illegal weapons offenses, gambling, offenses against family and children, driving under the influence of alcohol, and drunkenness. The highest percentage of all male arrests occurred for drunkenness (25.2), disorderly conduct (10.6), and all other miscellaneous offenses (11.5). Male arrests in more serious categories, however, were smaller, by comparison. Approximately 7.2 percent of all 1968 male arrests were for larceny, while burglary (5.0), auto theft (2.4), aggravated assault (1.9), and robbery (1.3) represented a smaller volume of male crime.[16] The higher rate of male delinquency and criminality is due to such factors as general male aggressiveness, the public tendency to protect women, variations in male roles and skills, lessened parental supervision of males, and greater likelihood of males to be arrested than females.

THE VARIABLE OF RACE

Although white Americans dominate the yearly arrest figures, black Americans evidence a significantly higher arrest rate in every general crime category with the exception of offenses against public order and against morals. The 1965 Negro rate for all index offenses plus larceny under $50 was four times the rate of the white population (1,696 to 419 per 100,000 persons).[17] The disproportionate black arrest rate, however, was partially due to the lesser tolerance shown to Negroes by the police and the prejudiced public.

While the black arrest rate for murder was 24.1 in 1965, the comparable white arrest rate reached only 2.5 per 100,000 persons. Burglary arrests, however, were less extreme, although blacks evidenced a 1965 rate that was more than three times greater than the rate of the whites (378 to 107 arrests per 100,000 inhabitants). Although blacks accounted for approximately 11 percent of the American population, black youth under 18 were arrested three times as often as white (1,689 to 591 arrests per 100,000 persons). Blacks 18 and over evidenced a rate approximately five times the white rate (1,684 to 325).

---

[16] *Uniform Crime Reports—1968,* p. 118. Also refer to Clinton T. Duffy *et. al., Sex and Crime* (New York: Doubleday & Co., Inc., 1965).
[17] President's Commission, *op. cit.,* p. 44.

The black arrest rate for murder, rape, and aggravated assault increased by only 5 percent between 1960 and 1965; the white rate, on the other hand, increased by 27 percent. The reverse was true in the crime of robbery, where the white rate rose by 3 percent while the Negro rate increased by 24 percent. Factors of unemployment, poor housing, and limited education, however, influence the disproportionate black rate. Blacks composed 78 percent of a sample of 932 felons convicted during 1964 and 1965 in Washington, D.C., although the District of Columbia possessed an estimated Negro population of 61 percent at that time. Eighty percent of the felons had previous adult criminal records. Fifty-two percent had six or more prior arrests, while 65 percent had faced previous confinement in some type of juvenile or adult facility.[18] Blacks were arrested for more 1968 murders and nonnegligent manslaughters than whites in both the below-18 and the 18-and-above categories (see Table A–7).

American Indian juveniles under 18 were most frequently arrested for larceny, drunkenness, and runaway in 1968. Adult Indians, on the other hand, were predominantly arrested for drunkenness, although facing arrest in lesser volume for disorderly conduct, driving under the influence, liquor violations, vagrancy, general assaults, and larceny. Chinese youth under 18 were arrested most frequently for larceny, while adult Chinese were apprehended most frequently for gambling, drunkenness, and larceny. Juveniles of Japanese ancestry faced arrest most often for larceny, auto theft, curfew and loitering law violations, burglary, and runaway. Adult Japanese-Americans evidenced their largest number of arrests in the categories of drunkenness, gambling, driving under the influence, and larceny.[19]

A Chicago Police Department study of 13,713 cases of non-homicide assaultive crimes found that the Black male and female were the most likely victims of crimes against the person. Although the Black Chicago male was the victim nearly 6 times as often as the white male, the Negro woman became the victim almost 8 times as often as the white female.[20] Blacks, the Chicago Police found, were most likely to assault blacks, whites to assault whites (see Table 3–5). Similar racial relationships were uncovered in a 1966 survey by the District of Columbia Crime Commission. Less than 7 percent (12 of 172) murders and 20 percent of Washington rapes were interracial in character. Robbery represented the only crime of violence in which the majority of the victims (56 percent) were white.

---

[18] *Ibid.*, p. 45.
[19] *Uniform Crime Reports—1968,* pp. 121–22.
[20] President's Commission, *op. cit.*, p. 40.

TABLE 3–5
Victim-offender relationships by race and sex in assaultive crimes against the person (except homicide)

	Offenses by Type of Offender				
	Whites		*Negroes*		
	Male	*Female*	*Male*	*Female*	*All Types*
Victim rate for each 100,000:*					
White males................	201	9	129	4	342
White females..............	108	14	46	6	175
Negro males................	58	3	1,636	256	1,953
Negro females..............	21	3	1,202	157	1,382
Total population*...........	130	10	350	45	535

* The rates are based only on persons 14 years of age or older in each race-sex category. The "total population" category in addition excludes persons from racial groups other than Negro or white.
Source: President's Commission, *The Challenge of Crime in a Free Society*, p. 40.

THE ECOLOGICAL FACTOR

Although the 1968 rural crime rate was less than one third the rate recorded in the urban Standard Metropolitan Statistical Areas, it approximated one half the rate of other smaller American cities (see Table 3–6). While rural communities generally maintained a lower overall crime rate in proportion to population, rural murder or nonnegligent manslaughter and forcible rape were proportionally higher than those found in the smaller "other cities." The rural murder rate nearly approximated the SMSA rate (6.3 to 7.5 per 100,000 population). On the other hand, rural forcible rape rates fell far short of the urban rate (8.8 to 19.1), although they remained at a higher level than evidenced in smaller urban cities (6.7 per 100,000 inhabitants). Rural index crime rates, however, remained proportionately lower in all other crime categories.

Robberies were 14 times more common in Standard Metropolitan Statistical Areas than in rural territories. Rural aggravated assault rates, however, were nearly one half the rate of SMSA communities. Burglary and larceny ($50 and over) rates, on the other hand, were greatest in the large SMSA cities.[21]

Recent crime data also show that criminal activity varies by geographic region. The highly urbanized northeastern states possessed the lowest 1968 murder arrest rate, while the more rural southern states maintained a rate more than two times that of the northeastern states (see Table 3–7). The western states, nearly midway between murder

---

[21] *Uniform Crime Reports—1968*, p. 58.

TABLE 3–6

Index of crime, United States, 1968

Area	Population*	Total Crime Index	Violent† crime	Property† crime	Murder and non-negligent manslaughter	Forceible rape	Robbery	Aggravated assault	Burglary	Larceny $50 and over	Auto theft
United States Total............	199,861,000	4,466,573	588,837	3,877,736	13,648	31,057	261,728	282,404	1,828,911	1,271,070	777,755
Rate per 100,000 inhabitants......	......	2,234.8	294.6	1,940.2	6.8	15.5	131.0	141.3	915.1	636.0	389.1
Standard Metropolitan Statistical Area	**136,385,000**	......	......	......	......	......	......	......	......	......	......
Area actually reporting‡......	97.2 %	3,764,260	507,189	3,257,071	10,047	25,571	249,018	222,553	1,507,904	1,046,243	702,924
Estimated total......	100.0 %	3,822,920	512,811	3,310,109	10,211	25,989	250,543	226,068	1,532,909	1,065,455	711,745
Rate per 100,000 inhabitants......	......	2,803.0	376.0	2,427.0	7.5	19.1	183.7	165.8	1,124.0	781.2	521.9
Other Cities............	**25,730,000**										
Area actually reporting......	88.6 %	313,587	30,530	283,057	909	1,543	5,931	22,147	134,377	111,786	36,894
Estimated total......	100.0 %	349,349	35,114	314,235	1,071	1,736	6,582	25,725	149,843	123,567	40,825
Rate per 100,000 inhabitants......	......	1,357.8	136.5	1,221.3	4.2	6.7	25.6	100.0	582.4	480.2	158.7
Rural............	**37,746,000**										
Area actually reporting......	75.3 %	230,234	27,144	203,090	1,569	2,463	3,301	19,811	117,893	65,358	19,839
Estimated total......	100.0 %	294,304	40,912	253,392	2,366	3,332	4,603	30,611	146,159	82,048	25,185
Rate per 100,000 inhabitants......	......	779.7	108.4	671.3	6.3	8.8	12.2	81.1	387.2	217.4	66.7

* Population is Bureau of the Census provisional estimates as of July 1, 1968.

† Violent Crime is offenses of murder, forcible rape, robbery and aggravated assault; property crime is offenses of burglary, larceny $50 and over, and auto theft.

‡ The percentage representing area actually reporting will not coincide with the ratio between reported and estimated crime totals since these data represent the sum of the calculations for individual states which have varying populations, portions reporting and crime rates.

Source: *Uniform Crime Reports—1968*, p. 58.

extremes, led in forcible rape arrests. Robbery, lower in the southern states (40.4 per 100,000 persons), was nearly 53 percent higher during 1968 in the western states (64.3). The southern states dominated the category of aggravated assault (107.3 per 100,000 inhabitants).

Regional burglary arrests ranged from 129.2 in the northeastern states to 265.1 per 100,000 inhabitants in the western region. Western larceny arrests were more than two times the rate of the northeastern region. The western region, in addition, led in the greatest number of auto thefts (137.9) and dominated the overall crime index total, outnumbering the arrest volume of the northeastern states alone by 504.7 arrests per 100,000 inhabitants.[22]

TABLE 3–7
Arrests by region, 1968
(rate per 100,000 inhabitants)

Offense	Northeastern States	North Central States	Southern States	Western States
Murder...............	5.2	6.7	10.7	6.3
Forcible rape............	7.0	8.8	9.2	10.6
Robbery..............	46.3	44.3	40.4	64.3
Aggravated assault.........	64.7	50.1	107.3	80.8
Burglary..............	129.2	160.6	184.6	265.1
Larceny..............	177.0	352.3	357.1	437.2
Auto theft.............	67.9	83.1	72.4	137.9
Total.............	499.3	707.6	785.0	1,004.0

Source: *Uniform Crime Reports—1968*, p. 34.

Although a superficial evaluation might lead one to suggest that crime increases in proportion to the size of the community, many other variables dominate the actual criminal tendency. While murder and nonnegligent manslaughter in cities of more than 250,000 persons occurred at rates seven times that found in cities under 10,000 population in 1968 (14.5 to 2.0 per 100,000), rural areas reflected a 4.0 rate per 100,000 ruralities (see Table A–4). The rural aggravated assault rate (35.2), however was far less than that found in large cities possessing a population of more than 250,000 persons (83.4). Larceny arrests, on the other hand, were higher in cities of 100,000–250,000 size than in cities of over 250,000 population. Although suburban arrests continued to increase

[22] *Ibid.*, p. 34. Also see Richard Quinney, "Structural Characteristics, Population Areas, and Crime Rates in the United States," *Journal of Criminal Law, Criminology, and Police Science*, Vol. 57 (1966), pp. 45–52.

at a fast pace, much of this increase is due to the attraction which suburban wealth offers the property criminal.[23]

SEASONAL VARIATIONS

Crime is also influenced by the weather and by sociocultural factors related to seasonal changes. Murder, for example, occurs most frequently during July and December (see Appendix, Figure A-1, pp. 721-22), being stimulated by such diverse factors as summer heat and Christmas arguments. On the other hand, negligent manslaughter, affected by snow or icy roads, increases sharply in November and December. Forcible rape and aggravated assault reach their peak during the summer months when sexual stimulation (for example, due to revealing clothing or swimsuits) and group contact are most extensive. Robbery tends to increase during the early fall as days become shorter and fewer persons go out in the later evening and the sharp decline in robbery during the months of January to March is partially due to weather conditions which keep more people indoors. Burglaries and larcenies follow similar patterns, becoming more pronounced in August and December. Auto theft, on the other hand, is more common when automobiles are not in continuous use by their owners. Although seasonal and weather factors are not central determinants of the criminal act, they nevertheless influence criminal desire and opportunity. Property crimes, for example, tend to increase during the summer months when families are vacationing, fewer employees are on duty, stores are crowded, and mobility is enhanced.[24]

CRIMINAL CAREERS

Since 1963, the FBI has been engaged in a study of criminal careers on the basis of data submitted to its offices by local, state, and federal enforcement agencies. Utilizing a combination of fingerprint record keeping and computer data storage, the FBI study has found that a large volume of the continuing index crime increase is due to the recidivism of previous offenders who have simply continued their participation in crime despite attempts of the judicial system to redirect their behavior. In fact, 39 percent of those persons arrested in 1967-68, it found, had been arrested earlier for some index violation. A low of 6 percent of murder and a high of 51 percent of burglary offenders repeated violations of the same type.[25] Of the 94,467 offenders arrested and studied

---

[23] *Ibid.*, pp. 110-11.
[24] *Ibid.*, pp. 20-21.
[25] *Ibid.*, p. 36.

TABLE 3-8

Profile of offenders arrested in 1968 by type of crime

	Murder	Aggravated Assault	Rape	Robbery	Total Violent Crime	Burglary	Heroin	Marijuana	Auto Theft
Total number of subjects	688	3,640	494	4,176	8,998	6,106	1,636	2,850	6,687
Percent with prior arrest	65.6	68.5	64.6	66.8	67.3	75.1	67.1	39.6	56.9
Average age first arrest	21.2	21.3	20.5	19.7	20.5	19.5	21.4	21.0	19.9
Average criminal career years	10.7	10.4	7.6	8.3	9.3	9.5	10.4	4.6	7.1
Average number of any arrests during criminal career	7.8	8.5	6.7	7.9	8.0	9.5	9.1	4.6	7.0
Average number of violent crimes during criminal career	3.4	3.6	3.2	3.7	3.6	4.2	4.0	2.3	3.0
Frequency of arrest on specific charge (percent):									
1	86.0	59.1	78.9	61.5	63.4	42.2	61.6	78.2	55.7
2	12.6	23.6	14.8	24.7	22.8	26.0	22.5	15.8	24.0
3 or more	1.3	17.3	6.3	13.7	13.8	31.8	16.0	6.0	20.2
Leniency on specific charge (percent)	4.4	9.6	6.5	13.8	10.9	22.0	18.7	23.5	34.8
Frequency of leniency action (percent):									
0	46.5	42.6	44.5	44.0	43.7	32.7	40.2	56.6	41.8
1	29.5	31.5	31.0	29.1	30.2	33.8	28.7	31.4	32.6
2	15.6	14.9	11.7	15.2	14.9	18.1	16.3	7.1	13.0
3 or more	8.4	11.0	12.8	11.7	11.2	15.4	14.9	5.0	12.6
Mobility (percent):									
1 State	36.3	35.4	35.8	40.2	37.7	32.8	54.3	59.8	28.7
2 States	32.6	32.2	32.4	27.6	30.1	31.3	29.8	27.3	31.8
3 or more States	31.1	32.4	31.8	32.1	32.2	35.9	15.9	12.9	39.5

Source: *Uniform Crime Reports—1968*, p. 37.

in 1968, 44,272 were charged with new index offenses. Of the latter group, 47.7 percent had been charged, convicted, and imprisoned previously (see Table 3–8).

A more detailed follow-up study of 18,333 offenders who were released from the federal criminal justice system and were involved in additional arrests through 1968 showed that 63 percent had been arrested by the end of the fifth calendar year after release. Of those who were acquitted or had their cases dismissed in 1963, 91 percent were later rearrested for new offenses. Commenting on the situation, the FBI notes:

Of those released on probation 55 percent repeated, parole 61 percent, and mandatory release after serving prison time 74 percent. Offenders receiving a sentence of fine and probation in 1963 had the lowest repeating proportion with 36 percent rearrest. This type of sentence is generally found in connection with violations such as income tax fraud and embezzlement. This

FIGURE 3–4
Percent repeaters by type of crime, 1963
(persons released in 1963 and rearrested within five years)

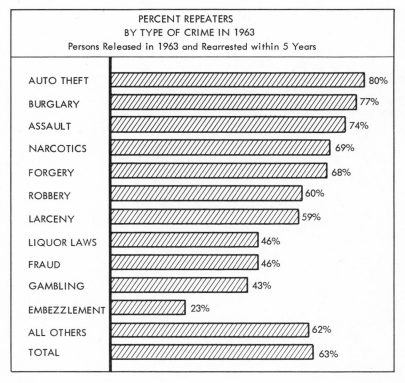

PERCENT REPEATERS
BY TYPE OF CRIME IN 1963
Persons Released in 1963 and Rearrested within 5 Years

Type of Crime	Percent
AUTO THEFT	80%
BURGLARY	77%
ASSAULT	74%
NARCOTICS	69%
FORGERY	68%
ROBBERY	60%
LARCENY	59%
LIQUOR LAWS	46%
FRAUD	46%
GAMBLING	43%
EMBEZZLEMENT	23%
ALL OTHERS	62%
TOTAL	63%

Source: *Uniform Crime Reports—1968*, p. 38.

offender has roots in a community, and as a result, detection and conviction serve as a deterrent to further unlawful activity.[26]

Rearrests, the FBI reports, range from a low of 19 percent for income tax violators to 80 percent for auto thieves (see Figure 3–4). Overall, the probability of repeating (or recidivism) is highest for youth who commit their first offense while under 20 years of age (see Table 3–9).

TABLE 3–9
Percent of offenders released in 1963—arrested on new charge
(by age group and year)

Year	Under 20	20–24	25–29	30–39	40–49	50– Over	Total all Ages
1963	21.9	25.3	24.2	21.6	18.4	11.0	21.4
1964	51.9	49.4	45.9	42.4	34.1	24.6	42.6
1965	62.3	59.0	55.8	51.9	43.0	31.6	52.0
1966	67.5	64.0	61.8	57.4	48.1	35.7	57.2
1967	70.3	67.1	64.7	60.6	51.5	37.9	60.3
1968	72.4	69.1	67.1	63.3	53.9	40.1	62.6

Sources: *Uniform Crime Reports*—p. 39.

By the end of 1968, the 11,477 persons released in 1963 and later re-arrested had committed over 28,000 new offenses, in the categories of violent crime (11 percent), crime against property (32), crimes against public morals (24), contempt of justice (16) and crimes against public order (17 percent).[27] Although the study continues, its early findings suggest greater efforts must be made to redirect youth from criminal conduct if the crime increase is to be contained.

VICTIMIZATION

The issue of victimization poses special problems inasmuch as it refers to questions related to being a criminal's victim. Just as each criminal has his victim, each victim, Stephen Schafer recognizes, has his criminal. Until recently, little attention has been given the relationship of the victim to the criminal. However, the growing body of new data point out that a large proportion of crimes in each category involve victims and offenders who are known to each other.[28] But the question is even greater than this. Many contemporary states accept no responsibility

[26] *Ibid.*, p. 37.
[27] *Ibid.*, p. 39.
[28] Stephen Schafer, *The Victim and His Criminal* (New York: Random House, Inc., 1968), pp. 3–152.

for the criminal victim, even though the offender may have committed his crime against the person while on probation or parole under the legal supervision of the state.[29] In such instances, the costs of being a victim are borne solely by the victim, his family and/or an insurance company. In place of this practice, Schafer proposes a reassessment of the state's responsibility in the total crime situation.[30]

Crime and victimization occur most frequently among the lower income classes.[31] Forcible rape, robbery, and burglary victims are especially concentrated among the lowest income groups (see Table 3–10).

TABLE 3–10
Victimization by income
(rates per 100,000 population)

	Income			
Offenses	$0 to $2,999	$3,000 to $5,999	$6,000 to $9,999	Above $10,000
Total..............	2,369	2,331	1,820	2,237
Forcible rape.............	76	49	10	17
Robbery..................	172	121	48	34
Aggravated assault.........	229	316	144	252
Burglary..................	1,319	1,020	867	790
Larceny ($50 and over).....	420	619	549	925
Motor vehicle theft.........	153	206	202	219
Number of respondents......	(5,232)	(8,238)	(10,382)	(5,946)

Source: President's Commission, *The Challenge of Crime in a Free Society*, p. 38.

Although victims of aggravated assault, larceny ($50 or over), and auto theft are most representative of the general white population, larceny victims are most likely to come from the highest income categories. Nonwhites, however, are the disproportionate victims in all crime categories with the exception of larcenies $50 and over (see Table 3–11). Women in the 20–29 age group are most frequently victimized, especially in the crimes of forcible rape and robbery. Although males in the 30–39 age category evidence the highest index crime rate, the picture is misleading, since burglaries are most often assigned to male heads of households.[32] While property crime victims are found among males of all ages, male aggravated assault and robbery victims are most often between 20 and 29 years of age (see Table 3–12).

---

[29] Richard D. Knudten, *Criminological Controversies* (New York: Appleton-Century-Crofts, 1968), pp. 307–33.
[30] Schafer, *op. cit.*, pp. 31–38.
[31] President's Commission, *op. cit.*, p. 38.
[32] *Ibid.*, p. 39.

TABLE 3–11
Victimization by race
(rates per 100,000 population)

Offenses	White	Nonwhite
Total.................	1,860	2,592
Forcible rape...............	22	82
Robbery....................	58	204
Aggravated assault..........	186	347
Burglary...................	822	1,306
Larceny ($50 and over).......	608	367
Motor vehicle theft..........	164	286
Number of respondents.......	(27,484)	(4,902)

Source: President's Commission, *The Challenge of Crime in a Free Society*, p. 39.

TABLE 3–12
Victimization by age and sex
(rates per 100,000 population)

Offense	Male						
	10–19	20–29	30–39	40–49	50–59	60 plus	All ages
Total.................	951	5,924	6,231	5,150	4,231	3,465	3,091
Robbery....................	61	257	112	210	181	98	112
Aggravated assault..........	399	824	337	263	181	146	287
Burglary...................	123	2,782	3,649	2,365	2,297	2,343	1,583
Larceny ($50 and over).......	337	1,546	1,628	1,839	967	683	841
Motor vehicle theft..........	31	515	505	473	605	195	268

Offense	Female						
	10–19	20–29	30–39	40–49	50–59	60 plus	All ages
Total.................	334	2,424	1,514	1,908	1,132	1,052	1,059
Forcible rape...............	91	238	104	48	0	0	83
Robbery....................	0	238	157	96	60	81	77
Aggravated assault..........	91	333	52	286	119	40	118
Burglary...................	30	665	574	524	298	445	314
Larceny ($50 and over).......	122	570	470	620	536	405	337
Motor vehicle theft..........	0	380	157	334	119	81	130

Source: President's Commission, *The Challenge of Crime in a Free Society*, p. 39.

CRIME COSTS

Crime is costly to all participants. Insurance, enforcement, property or health loss, court adjudication, and treatment of offender costs have increased through the decades. Although there are no known figures which accurately define the economic costs of criminal and related activ-

FIGURE 3–5
Economic impact of crimes and related expenditures
(estimated in millions of dollars)

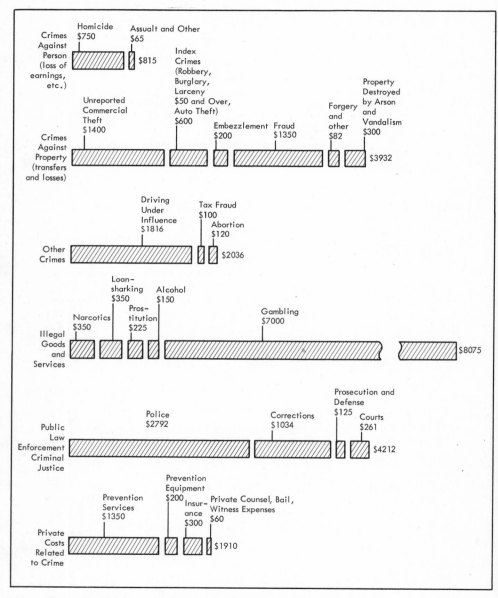

Source: President's Commission, *The Challenge of Crime in a Free Society*, p. 33.

ity, preliminary estimates stagger the imagination (see Figure 3–5). Especially disconcerting is the revelation that organized crime is estimated to yield more than *twice* the dollar volume of all other forms of traditional criminal activity from its gambling and its other operations involving legal and illegal goods and services.[33] Estimated *unreported* commercial theft losses in turn are more than double the rate evidenced for

FIGURE 3–6
Public expenditures for prevention and control of crime

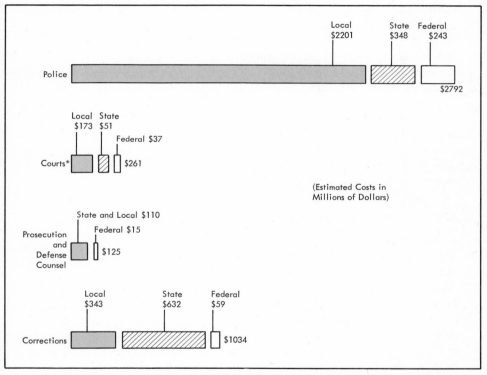

* Total court costs are estimated at $782 million—$109 federal, $155 state, and $518 local; criminal court costs were estimated at one third of the total based on studies in several jurisdictions.
Source: President's Commission, *The Challenge of Crime in a Free Society*, p. 34.

those commercial thefts reported to the police. Willful homicides, although few in number, involve the highest cost. Surprisingly, only two of the seven crimes creating the greatest economic impact (willful homicide and larceny of $50 and over) are included in the FBI's crime index.

---

[33] *Ibid.*, p. 32.

Although embezzlement, employee theft, and other forms of business deviance result in high crime costs, police data record few offenses of this type. The unclear line separating shrewd business practices from criminal fraud, too, confuses the issue. Recent cost analyses suggest, however, that robbery, burglary, larceny, and auto theft account for only one sixth of the estimated total dollar loss involved in property crimes. Even then, the largest volume of costly criminal activity may be unreported and, thereby, may be unknown to the police.[34]

Crime prevention and control costs an estimated $4 billion a year. Although enforcement and correctional costs have increased, treatment expenses have expanded at a more rapid rate. (see Figure 3–6). Some 85 to 90 percent of all enforcement costs, however, simply involve wages and salaries, leaving only a small proportion for modern equipment or evaluative research. Because of restrictions imposed by increased costs, police, courts, and correctional institutions continue to operate at substandard levels of need and efficiency. Only a fraction of the money expended for criminal justice is ever allotted to rehabilitative programs or research. Although an adult offender can be supervised within the community for as little as 38 cents per day, imprisonment in a penal institution costs about $5.24 per day in a context which offers minimal, and often superficial, rehabilitation programs.[35]

SHORTCOMINGS IN CRIME MEASUREMENT

American crime statistics, unlike their European counterparts, are dominated by a concern for traditional crime ("crime in the streets"). While valid for an agrarian or rural society dominated by local aristocrats, the reporting system minimizes that type of crime which is stimulated by rapid industrialization and urbanization. Since crime categories have been formulated with the basic assumption that criminals who refuse to uphold the values of the legitimating classes offer the greatest challenge to established society, only a limited amount of crime data, largely concerning crimes threatening personal security and property ownership, have been gathered. As a result, current crime indexes tend to measure the types of crime which are most likely to be committed by persons of limited income and sophistication. Although a wealthy person may occasionally steal, his normal economic condition generally precludes this activity. Although murder knows no class limits, the bulk of aggravated assaults are committed by persons who are prone to use force to settle an argument. Laws against the passing of bad checks

---

[34] Thorsten Sellin and Marvin Wolfgang, for example, found some years ago that more thefts were *known* to the employees of three Philadelphia department stores than were *known* to the Philadelphia police.

[35] *Ibid.*, p. 31.

("hanging paper") and misuse of stolen credit cards even now protect the commercial entrepreneur and the credit-stimulated consumer from those seeking to profit at another's expense. The harms and crimes of a modern complex society, however, transcend the minimal forms of personal and property crime. The emergence of industrial corporations, unionized labor, urban communities, and technical management has resulted in the definition of a whole new series of violations which are ultimately more costly and more serious than a large number of traditional crimes.

Although the FBI attempts to measure the changes in the national crime picture through its use of the crime index, the index is incomplete and omits those categories which involve the greatest crime volume and which may lead to other serious social consequences. The *Uniform Crime Reports* fail, for example, to measure the psychological and sociological behaviors involved in the criminal act. Since the *Reports* only record the most serious of several potential violations which may occur in the commission of a crime, the intent and behavior involved in the initiation of the act are ignored as the end result of the act is tabulated. The role and behavior of the victim, too, is unexplored in the crime data. And yet, many murders are unintended, and some action of the victim turns what would have been a less serious felony into a murder.

Laws regulating working conditions, factory procedures, wage commitments, and corporate organizations evolved as the complex society felt the need to control potentially dangerous commercial and industrial practices. The growth of large-scale American industrial organizations, however, was paralleled by the rise of a new form of administrative law which removed the control of commerce and industry from criminal law, thereby allowing management and corporate boards the flexibility necessary for a modern industrialized state. As federal agencies were created to supervise interstate commerce, aviation, communication, transportation, food and drugs, utilities, and banks and trusts, corporations were generally freed from the jurisdiction of the police, grand jury, public prosecutor, and criminal court. At the same time, they were required to respond to the less serious mechanisms of cease and desist orders, stipulations, and consent decrees, which were periodically supplemented by contempt-of-court citations for failure to comply with agency requests or directives. Private agency hearings replaced the earlier public trial of corporate violations, thereby minimizing the publicity given to the continuing violations of basic economic and legal principles. The content of laws against usury (exorbitant interest charges) even now are ignored as modern banks cooperate with other commercial businesses to extend credit at an 18 percent interest rate equivalent per year, although defining this as a "service charge." The overemphasis upon traditional crime in the meantime fosters a distorted picture of criminal deviance and focuses upon the criminal act while dismissing the deviant behavior involved. The modern inability to understand the threat of white-collar and organized crime results from this traditional stereotype of criminal activity. Crime, however, involves political manipulation, economic advantage, and individual or group oppression.

Although current crime reports recognize crime rate variables, the data, as categorized, reinforce the belief that criminality is a direct product of individual rational choice, and, thereby, only subject to control by punishment. Ignoring the social basis of criminal behavior, those who so believe offer more severe punishment as the only means of social control. Attention is shifted, as a result, from the social and systematic nature of crime to concepts of free will, constitutional defects, personal handicaps, localized poverty, and delinquent subcultures.[36] Crime, however, is part of the general and specific social system. As long as the public and the agencies of crime control are governed by traditional myths and collective emotion rather than by rational evidence gathered in an unbiased manner, law enforcement, together with its legal counterparts, will continue to lack social coherency and integration.

Since each man is both a criminal and noncriminal throughout his life, he determines and is determined by the context of his situation, which changes from day to day. If he is undetected, he remains a respected citizen. If apprehended, his future may disintegrate in a moment. For some persons, crime is a life pattern; for others, it is a momentary response. Until a clear picture of the crime problem is available, the full dimensions of the crime rate can never be fully revealed nor fully understood. Punishing a petty thief by increasing his sentence with each added conviction, while placidly minimizing the harm of the stock market manipulator or misleading advertiser, often involving hundreds of thousands of dollars, only illustrates the obvious insensitivity of current statistical measurement devices to criminal activity.

---

[36] Harry M. Shulman, "The Measurement of Crime in the United States," *Journal of Criminal Law, Criminology, and Police Science*, Vol. 57 (1966), p. 492. See also Nicholas de B. Katzenbach, "Crime Reporting," *Vital Speeches*, Vol. 32, No. 1 (1966), pp. 351–52.

Chapter
4

A CRIMINOLOGICAL
APPROACH TO
ANALYSIS OF DEVIANT
BEHAVIOR

CRIMINOLOGY AS A SCIENCE

The field of criminology cannot be classed a science, since its diverse concerns cover a variety of theoretical, normative, emotional, and substantive problems.[1] It can, however, use the scientific method to gather objective data wherever conditions permit controlled comparisons or other forms of empirical validation. Because the field is so vast, including such diverse problems as the formation of criminal law, the procedures of law enforcement, the processes of court judgment, and the punishment or treatment of the offender, total objectivity, a primary requisite of the scientific method, is not easily realized. The mere definition of crime, the failure to refrain from prohibited behavior or to complete a required act as defined by law, implies a value judgment, for example, which automatically restricts the development of a totally objective criminological approach to criminal deviance.[2]

---

[1] Gilbert Geis, "Sociology and Crime," in Joseph S. Roncek (ed.), *The Sociology of Crime* (New York: Philosophical Library, 1961), pp. 7 ff.
[2] Marvin E. Wolfgang, "Criminology and the Criminologist," *Journal of Criminal Law, Criminology, and Police Science,* Vol. 54, No. 2 (1963), pp. 156–58.

ASSUMPTIONS OF THE SCIENTIFIC METHOD

Since the scientific method assumes an objective investigative procedure, the problem of methodology is central to the scientific criminologist. Forming and operationalizing hypotheses, he gathers, records, analyzes, compares, interprets, and classifies data. Completing this task, the investigator uses his data to develop conclusions and generalizations which help him to understand the problem under study. Generalizations, however, are not end goals, since the process of verification continues into the future. The scientific researcher solves his problem by ascertaining the validity of his hypotheses or theoretical presuppositions. The continuous reexamination of known results leads to the expansion of knowledge as new variables introduce new conditions and change the relationships which were measured earlier.

Lacking a scientific approach, some attempts to deal with particular aspects of the crime problem produce results which may serve to mislead rather than lead to crime control. Nowhere is this more apparent than in the system of corrections, which has been dominated by a philosophical belief in the eventual penitence of the criminal. Permeated by philosophical-theological dichotomies of good and evil or right and wrong, the judicial system still isolates criminals from society in the false belief that all deviants have expressed a form of extreme behavior which cannot be redirected. And yet, it halfheartedly seeks the rehabilitation of a man by his own efforts through the system of parole. Social research employing scientific methodology, however, reveals that the majority of human decisions are not clear choices between right and wrong, but are more often made after taking into consideration multiple alternatives, which are, in themselves, gradations between the polar choices. The discovery that the less successful method of penal isolation costs 12 to 15 times the amount involved in probation or parole challenges the myth that rehabilitation is best accomplished in a congregate setting at the lowest cost. Inasmuch as law enforcement, the judicial process, and the penological system are not committed to the empirical process, their procedures are closely bound to experiential but nonempirical public values.[3]

Free will versus determinism

Difficulties in analysis arising out of the conflict between free will and social determinism compound the scientific approach to the study of criminal deviance. Although jurisprudence necessarily assumes that

---

[3] Travis Hirschi and Hanan C. Selvin, *Delinquency Research* (New York: Free Press, 1967), pp. 1–34. The authors have completed a valuable evaluation of methodological problems confronting the investigation of criminality. *See* also Leonard Savitz, *Dilemmas in Criminology* (New York: McGraw-Hill Book Co., 1967).

each man rationally violates a given law for good and sufficient reasons, social determinists argue that human choices depend upon sociocultural conditions. Since variables of age, sex, religion, education, occupation, and region affect the basic character of the existential personality and the individual's interpretation of culture, determinists argue that man is a product of his environment in which "free choices" are largely responses to culturally defined alternatives. Recent evidence suggests that each criminal act involves differential levels of criminal cognition (knowing) and that cognitive recognition, too, is governed by sociocultural conditions. Some violators commit criminal acts only after an agonizing struggle with their conscience; others violate normative behavioral standards with minimal guilt feelings. The normal human tendency to reduce cognitive dissonance causes the criminal to justify his deviant behavior and to modify his own self-image in the process.[4]

The scientific basis for criminology rests on the assumption that behavior is generally patterned and predictable, and if studied, will reveal causes which stimulate deviant action. Although crime has historically been attributed to such diverse factors as demons, personal sin, social disorganization, a decline in social norms, and the rise of technological society, no one answer explains the origin and continuance of criminal activity.[5] Crime remains a functional part of the social system, offering necessary, but less desirable, channels through which to achieve culturally defined goals.

METHODS OF DEVIANCE ANALYSIS

Current criminology is engaged in a quest for scientific accuracy.[6] Dominated in the past by semitheoretical and nonempirical conceptions, the modern criminological search has been for scientific verification. Using the discoveries of the classical, positivist, cartographic, socialist, technological, and sociological schools of criminology, modern criminologists have moved to a more integrated frame of reference in their attempt to understand the many dimensions of criminal deviance. They have progressed beyond the particularistic *single-factor* theoretical postulates of past generations.

The multiple-factor approach

Modern researchers attempt to comprehend the many factors involved through the *multiple-factor* approach, which presumes that each criminal

---

[4] Leon Festinger, *A Theory of Cognitive Dissonance* (Stanford, Calif.: Stanford University Press, 1957).

[5] George Vold, *Theoretical Criminology* (New York: Oxford University Press, Inc., 1958), evaluates the origins and development of criminological theory.

[6] Leon Radzinowicz, *In Search of Criminology* (Cambridge, Mass.: Harvard University Press, 1962), reveals the exact international scope of this search.

act entails different behaviors and cultural conditions. While eclectic, the approach theorizes that no one single positive factor produces crime, even though one factor may predominate in causing the specific criminal act of the particular offender.

A study of family relationships and delinquent behavior by F. Ivan Nye, for example, illustrates how a single factor (family relationship) may actually involve multiple dimensions, but such an examination, nevertheless, focuses upon the sequential characteristics of family relations and relates juvenile deviance to these patterns. Obviously only one of several potential factors available for study, the singular study of familial relationships, despite its limitations, offers a deeper qualitative insight into the influence of such patterns upon delinquency causation.[7] However, the study of the multiple factors of crime, age, and employment by Daniel Glaser and Kent Rice also includes a qualitative dimension. Examining the relationship between crime and economic conditions through the use of Uniform Crime Reports and Boston, Cincinnati, and Chicago police data, these researchers discovered that while the frequency of crimes committed by juveniles varies inversely with unemployment rates on the basis of FBI data, this finding was not as clearly supported by municipal data. Similarly, differences were found among the data concerning the frequency of crimes committed by adults in relationship to unemployment rates.[8] However, regardless of these findings, the multiple-factor approach enabled the researchers to pass beyond an analysis of single factors in their attempt to ascertain the variable relationships of several factors in the causation of crime.

The multiple-factor approach possesses many deficiencies. Its inherent relativity makes accurate scientific evaluation of common causation difficult, if not impossible. Although it emphasizes a more integrated frame of reference than found in earlier particularistic theories of crime, the multiple-factor approach fails to interpret criminal behavior as part of the functional nature of the social system. Scientific criminology has recently discovered, for example, that crime *was* or *is* found in the majority of a "normal population," shattering the earlier view that crime was solely an act of social outcasts. The greatest number of modern criminal acts are crimes prohibited by national legislation rather than universal prohibitions commonly held by all international cultures. Consequently, the study of crime cannot be divorced from the study of legal processes. Specific crimes and particular punishments are always defined within a functional social system. They serve, as a result, to give structure and substance to the existing society. Although the single-

---

[7] Examine, for example, F. Ivan Nye, Family Relationships and Delinquent Behavior (New York: John Wiley & Sons, Inc., 1958).

[8] Daniel Glaser and Kent Rice, "Crime, Age, and Employment," American Sociological Review, Vol. 24 (October, 1959), pp. 679–86.

and multiple-factor approach gives analytical insight into the specific causes of criminal activity, the tendency to separate the criminal act from its environmental setting has, at times, hindered the development of a scientific criminology.[9] The systematic configuration of crime, as a result, has been largely ignored.

The lack of detailed and accurate statistical data retards the quest for a scientific criminology. Since any adequate insight into crime causation ultimately depends upon the valid statistical correlation of many variables, the need for statistical accuracy, although not fully realized, remains ultimately critical to the scientific enterprise. Since the validity of presently available data is uncertain (see Chapter 3), current information concerning criminality is open to serious question. A variety of additional scientific methods may be used to gain meaningful data and pertinent insight into the crime problem, each of which has its basic strengths and deficiencies.

Statistical studies

Representing the most common criminological approach, these studies attempt to develop crime categories in order to establish correlations between arrests and/or convictions and other specific physical and social variables. The data reported in the *Uniform Crime Reports* illustrate this approach (see Chapter 3). The value of this method depends fully upon the accuracy of the gathered statistics. Inaccurate categories or presuppositions, for example, automatically render the gathered data useless from a scientific viewpoint.

The study of traits

The *study of traits* is a methodological approach to an understanding of criminals which attempts to compare one or more of their conditions or characteristics with those of noncriminal equivalents. Probably the most ambitious attempt to correlate delinquency with various traits has been made by Sheldon and Eleanor Glueck. In their several studies of delinquency causation, they have related juvenile delinquency in varying degrees to qualities of family life, personal characteristics, numbers and characteristics of friends, age and sex aspects, gang characteristics, and many other factors. Partly because of the inclusiveness of the studies many questions of research methodology were raised. The possible value of their findings has often been ignored in the debate over the method by which the investigators operationalized the factors studied. Because

---

[9] See Thorsten Sellin and Marvin Wolfgang, *The Measurement of Delinquency* (New York: John Wiley & Sons, Inc., 1964).

their work often overgeneralized the importance of personal familial or peer group traits, it frequently oversimplified the exact nature of exceedingly complex trait relationships.[10]

The focus may be placed upon a particular characteristic or trait or multiple-trait relationships may be explored. Since such studies center upon factors of personality, race, alcoholism, home life, and the like, they ignore the greater relationship of these traits to the criminal system, restricting, therefore, the exact picture of observed and hidden criminality. Because their method depends upon an evaluation of known offenders, their basic sample, the prisoners studied, may represent a biased and invalidating sample. The incarcerated prisoner, for example, can hardly represent his more successful counterpart who remains undetected. Since a preselection occurs even in detection and incarceration, the less serious offender being placed on probation, the prison population becomes nonrepresentative of the total criminal population.

The case study

The *case study* method overcomes several deficiencies inherent in the earlier procedures. Clifford R. Shaw, for example, utilized the case study approach in his examination of the "jack-roller," a young male named Stanley, whom he studied for six years until he reached the age of 22. Emphasizing the "integratedness" of Stanley's personality and social environment, Shaw was able to capture the total context of his problems and design a detailed but individualized treatment program. Central to Shaw's research approach was the availability of the young delinquent's own autobiography, which Shaw gathered in the form of multiple interviews during which Stanley recounted his experiences. Through this approach (methodology), Shaw was able to comprehend the point of view of the delinquent, evaluate the social and cultural situation to which the delinquent responded, and understand the sequential relationship of experiences and situations in delinquency causation.[11]

The case study approach was used successfully by Shaw to gain an evaluation in depth of a delinquent's life orientation. Studies such as this of the total configuration of the criminal act often minimize the more quantitative aspects of the criminal activity. Based upon a subjective analysis of the individual in his behavioral setting, the case study approach minimizes the use of statistics such as are employed in juvenile or presentence investigations. It falls victim to individual values and whims, public "knowledge," political pressures, and academic

---

[10] See Sheldon and Eleanor Glueck, *Unraveling Juvenile Delinquency* (New York: Commonwealth Fund, 1950).

[11] Clifford R. Shaw, *The Jack-Roller* (Chicago: University of Chicago Press, 1930), pp. 1–199.

bias. A modified case study approach using a combination of statistical and case study procedures allows for a blending of quantitative and qualitative data.

Participant observation

The method of *participant observation* is extremely difficult and filled with inherent hazards. Although the observer may face minimal risks in observing acts of a small-scale professional property offender, he becomes immediately vulnerable to physical harm if he infiltrates organized crime. Since a "syndicate" thrives on secrecy, too much knowledge is likely to be interpreted as a threat to the organization. The need of the researcher to identify with the group offers an added limitation of the investigatory process. While his involvement with the deviant group may give him insight into the specific factors of the crime problem, his data will be subject to the same difficulties inherent in the case study approach. The inability of the investigator to control the observation setting, of necessity, limits the interpretation of gathered data to a semidescriptive level.[12] The method is useful, nevertheless, since it offers sensitive insight into the more subjective aspects of criminal behavior.

The participant observation approach refers less to the number of factors studied and more to the method used to gain pertinent data. As an approach, it may lead to an evaluation of single or multiple variables, an examination of traits, or even a case study analysis of a delinquent or criminal life situation. William F. Whyte's *Street-Corner Society,* which describes the interactional relationships of young men as they struggle to achieve goals defined by the group and society that frequently lead to participation in politics and rackets, has become one of the best-known studies utilizing the participant observation method.[13]

Experimental methods

The attempt to overcome the deficiencies of other approaches has led to the development of *experimental methods,* which are continuing attempts to develop new methodology and insight. Based upon the scientific method, experimental methodology tests reasoned hypotheses in order to reach implicit conclusions concerning criminal behavior and to develop new methodological approaches to crime measurement. However, the tenuous nature of the experiment makes the results suspect.

---

[12] Refer to Ralph Schwitzgebel, *Street Corner Research* (Cambridge, Mass.: Harvard University Press, 1964).

[13] William F. Whyte, *Street-Corner Society* (Chicago: University of Chicago Press, 1955).

Since all variables cannot be adequately controlled in the experimental study, the specific research must be continuously reevaluated.

The results of applied methodology cannot be interpreted as lasting facts. Generalizations are not immutable truths; they are only directional and procedural indicators. Since the scientific approach is not bound to a single scientific methodology, the methodological process often reflects the procedures in vogue during a given historical period. Therefore, the process used depends partially upon the investigator's previous knowledge, personal judgment, basic values, and professional commitment. Although he attempts to eliminate subjective elements from his investigation, the method which he chooses is often subject to his own culture-bound bias. As a result, the quest for a scientific criminology is also a quest for an empirical methodology.

CRIMINOLOGY AND SOCIAL THEORY

At present criminology suffers from an overconcentration on *ad hoc* experimentation which tends to overemphasize single or particularistic factors. Such experimentation, however, does little to aid the development of the more inclusive middle-range theoretical explanations of crime causation. Since applied methodology is only as valuable as the perception of the problem, methodological questions cannot be divorced from the theoretical framework in which the method is operationalized. Because theories of criminal behavior lack rigor and preciseness, methodology, of necessity, reflects this ambiguity.[14]

The theoretical framework within which the investigation is conducted is the heart of social research. Criminological research is no exception to this rule. Since it is in its empirical infancy, most contemporary criminological studies offer limited value. Many are nothing more than approaches to the crime problem which are devoid of any theoretical evaluation. To date, few attempts have been made to relate criminal behavior to the functional social system. Criminologists, enforcement officials, politicians, justices, and penal administrators are slowly coming to understand that crime is part of the *general* social system and that criminals cannot be divorced from their *general* culture.[15]

The problem of criminological methodology is aggravated by the emotional context of crime. The vested interests expressed by police, enforcement, prosecution, judicial, penological, and empirical agencies

---

[14] Schlomo Shoham, "The Theoretical Boundaries of Criminology," *British Journal of Criminology* (January, 1963), pp. 230–31.

[15] F. Ferracuti and Marvin E. Wolfgang, "Clinical v. Sociological Criminology: Separation or Integration?" *Excerpta Criminologica*, Vol. 4 (1964), pp. 407–10. Donald R. Taft has consistently emphasized the importance of culture upon crime and criminal systems.

dominate many of the investigations concluded to date. The unwillingness to share information, or open files to the researcher, undoubtedly restricts the development of a science of crime. The myth that a criminal violator is a social "nonperson" colors any attempt to evaluate and reorganize contemporary social reactions to the crime problem. Dominated by the belief that man either *is* or *is not* a criminal, the public only reluctantly agrees to return a criminal to society, unconvinced that he can ever change from his criminal ways and unwilling to undertake major necessary risks to bring about behavioral change.

The lack of research funds has limited the quest for a scientific criminology. However, new stirrings suggest that this limitation will soon be overcome. As Congress makes more funds available to the U.S. Department of Justice, criminological research should uncover new dimensions of the crime-criminal process, shattering many previous myths and vested interests. However, the lack of adequate samples, the inability to control complex variables, the overemphasis upon minor problems, the gathering of doubtful data, and the use of incomplete methodology or inadequate theory compound the quest. Although continued research will continue to lead to further knowledge of crime, the delineation of the precise factors involved in crime causation and the formation of middle-range explanations of criminal behavior will only slowly merge.[16]

---

[16] See Dennis Szabo, "The Teaching of Criminology in Universities," *International Review of Criminal Policy*, No. 22 (New York: United Nations, 1964). Also refer to Radzinowicz, *op. cit.*

Part TWO

Differential criminal expressions

Chapter
5

PROPERTY CRIMES AND OFFENDERS

The growth of modern technology has been paralleled by the increase in criminal laws designed to protect property and property rights. Each chapter in the history of man has led to the enactment of new definitions of illegal and legal conduct and specific attempts to control undesired practices. Earlier Western society formulated common-law concepts which punished those who stole cattle, farm products, or furniture. The full development of criminal property law, however, did not emerge with much clarity until the 15th century. The *Carrier's* case of 1473, law professor Jerome Hall notes, set forth a new principle which has continued in expanded form to the present day. The defendant in this case, hired to carry bales to Southampton, transported the goods to another location, broke open the bales, and took their contents. Upon apprehension and after lengthly public and judicial discussion, he was charged, tried, and convicted of a felony. The decision issued in the significant judgment that property in or about the house of the master is the master's possession and that any servant utilizing this property has mere custody without personal possession or ownership.

The *Carrier's* case decided that servants or middlemen, maintaining goods on behalf of another, were not exempt from prosecution if they used these goods for their own purposes. As a result, earlier Anglo-Saxon law, restricted by minimal and immobile concepts of property, were reinterpreted to include the basic requisites for a complex technological mass society.[1] Although judicial interpretations passed beyond the exist-

---

[1] Jerome Hall, *Theft, Law and Society* (Indianapolis: Bobbs-Merrill, Co., Inc., 1952), pp. 5-9. Similar problems still exist in treating traffic offenses as criminal

ing frame of legal reference, the practical needs of the day made these reinterpretations necessary. The emergence of a mercantile society demanded new institutional interpretations which could structure and reinforce its existence. Expanding intrastate commerce and foreign trade forced the formation of new statutes of new codes. The later need to control the growing number of acts of embezzlement, fraud and larceny by trick, false pretenses in property acquisition and receiving stolen property led to the inevitable expansion of property laws. In each case, however, the new law was formed in relationship to factors of general social need, economic practice, and acceptable cultural norms.

While property codes have continued to evolve in a pragmatic manner to the present time, modern criminal property laws have failed to adequately distinguish between the nonprofessional or amateur property offender and the professional dealer in stolen goods. Property laws, as a result, tend to focus upon the minor offender and to minimize similar or expanded controls necessary to regulate the full-time professional property offender. Traditional criminal codes continue to place the eventual nonprofessional consumer in the same category with the professional receiver of criminal property.[2]

The professional property criminal

The professional criminal generally follows a particular operational method (*modus operandi*), particularly if he specializes in one crime form. As a professional thief, he must manipulate the situation. As a professional confidence man, he must develop the skills needed to manipulate his "pigeon." The human manipulator works within a contrived social situation and seeks his ends at the expense of the man he manipulates. Performing the role as an actor, he stages a drama designed to facilitate his end goal. The fledgling is trained by experienced criminal tutors and is slowly acculturated to the full dimensions of professional criminality. The recruit first becomes part of an active, professional group of thieves. He only reaches full status as a professional thief when he is accepted by other professionals. Until he proves himself, he may, for example, merely complete minor tasks requiring limited skill. As he begins to commit himself to his fellow professionals, he gradually acquires a professional identity, a subculture, and an occupational conception and a unique argot. In time, however, he divorces himself from the singular professional culture and assumes the character of his new cultural surroundings. Although he may continue to follow

---

acts, See Wolf Middendorff, "A Criminology of Traffic Offenses," *Federal Probation*, Vol. 27, No. 3 (September, 1963), pp. 36–42.

[2] *Ibid.*, p. 156.

the code of conduct based upon a concept of professional integrity, the new and broadened social setting blurs the former sharp dividing line between honest men and professional criminals.[3] As he uses the "fix" and the "fence," his professional self-image bridges the chasm between the legitimate and the illegitimate, the legal and the illegal.

PROPERTY CRIME

Burglary

Burglary, larceny, and robbery, basically property crimes (see Figure 5–1), represent three forms of theft. *Burglary*, commonly defined as the

FIGURE 5–1
Crimes against property,* 1960–68
(percent change over 1960)

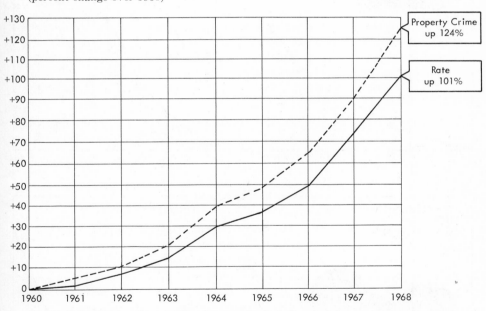

* Limited to burglary, larceny $50 and over, and auto theft.
Source: *Uniform Crime Reports—1968* (Washington, D.C.: U.S. Department of Justice, 1969), p. 3. FBI chart.

unlawful entry into a structure to commit a felony or a theft, omits the use of force or threat against the person. Definitions of burglary, which vary from state to state, may be broken down into three classifications: (1) attempted forcible entry, (2) unlawful entry without force,

---

[3] See *The Professional Thief* (Chicago: University of Chicago Press, 1937).

FIGURE 5-2

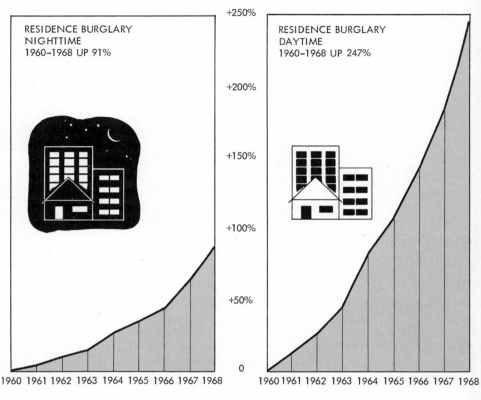

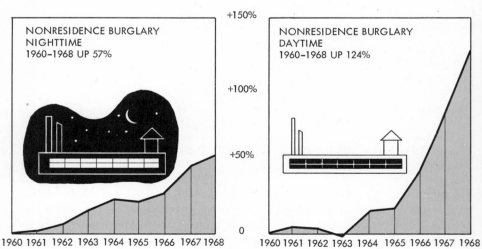

Source: *Uniform Crime Reports—1968*, p. 19.

and (3) forceful entry. Although traditionally conceived as a crime against property occurring during the evening hours, burglary may occur at any time during the day (see Figure 5–2).

The burglary rate has increased from nearly 495 per 100,000 inhabitants in 1960 to more than 915 in 1968. By comparison, 1968 rates for larceny ($50 and over) reached 636, auto theft approximated 389, and aggravated assault 141.3 per 100,000 persons. Burglary was the largest single index crime expression in 1968. Of all 1968 burglaries, 40 percent occurred in large cities of over 250,000 population. Burglary reached its peak during the last half of 1968, especially during the month of July.[4] The highest 1968 burglary rate, however, was recorded in the Western states with 1,347 per 100,000 citizens.

Since burglary is primarily a crime of opportunity and stealth, it is easily completed by amateurs and professionals. Although 7 percent of all reported 1968 burglaries were only attempts and 15 percent involved unlawful entry without force, forcible entry to the premises occurred in the remaining 77 percent. Nonresidential burglary, however, accounted for 46 percent of all 1968 burglaries. The evident increase in daytime and nighttime burglary during 1968 is due to the simplicity of this form of theft, the lack of evening police coverage, and the security offered by darkness. The FBI reports that the mean 1968 burglary resulted in an average loss of $298, although property owners suffered an estimated economic loss of nearly $545 million. Since more than four of every five burglaries during the year were not cleared by the arrest of the offender, the burglar was generally free to continue his profitable activity.

Nearly 177 persons per 100,000 population were arrested for burglary during 1968. The cities produced an offender rate of 191.8 per 100,000 inhabitants, the suburbs recorded an offender rate of 142.9, and rural areas 108.8. Persons under 25 accounted for 83 percent of all 1968 burglary arrests. Juveniles under 18 were arrested for 55 percent of the solved burglary crimes. Ninety-six males were arrested for every four females; white outnumbered black arrests by nearly two to one.[5] Although the police placed formal charges against 8 of every 10 persons arrested for burglary, 58 percent of all persons charged were juveniles who were eventually referred to the jurisdiction of the juvenile court. Fifty-six percent of those adults charged for burglary crimes, however were found guilty as charged, while 16 percent were convicted on a lesser charge and 28 percent were freed through acquittal or dismissal of charges.

---

[4] *Uniform Crime Reports—1968* (Washington, D.C.: U.S. Department of Justice, 1969), pp. 16–17.
[5] *Ibid.,* pp. 20–22.

Nearly one of every five businesses and organizations surveyed by the President's Commission on Law Enforcement and Administration of Justice in eight selected neighborhood precincts was burglarized at least once during the year of the study. Sixty-two percent of these organizations were burglarized from two to seven times. Although Chicago and Washington burglary victimization rates were highest in the precincts marked by the highest overall crime rates, Boston did not share a similar tendency. Therefore, the Commission concluded that some businesses, like some people, are more likely victims than others.[6]

Larceny

Larceny, a second form of theft, involves the unlawful taking or stealing of property and/or articles of value without the use of force, violence, or fraud. Although the *Uniform Crime Reports* include shoplifting, pickpocketing, purse snatching, thefts from autos, bicycle thefts, auto thefts, and thefts of auto parts and accessories in their tabulations, the data exclude losses of crimes involving embezzlement, confidence games, forgery, and passing checks with insufficient funds. Although auto theft, one of the seven index offenses, is evaluated as a special crime, it is properly a form of grand (major) larceny. The exclusion of thefts involving goods valued at less than $50 from the list of index offenses is based on the assumption that simple theft is less serious than thefts of $50 or more. While the point separating petty (small) larceny from grand larceny may vary from state to state, the distinction is based upon an arbitrary breaking point, whether $50, $75, or $100, as determined by each state legislature.

Burglary constitutes the largest volume of index offenses and larceny represents the second largest criminal form, representing 28 percent of the 1966 Crime Index total. Reported larcenies ($50 and over), excluding auto theft, increased from 894,600 in to 1,271,070 in 1968. The reported 1968 larceny crime rate rose to 636 offenses per 100,000 inhabitants, an increase in volume of 224,000 such offenses over 1967 (see Figure 5–3). The Standard Metropolitan Statistical Areas (SMSA) registered a 1968 larceny rate of 781.2 per 100,000 persons; the "other cities" larceny rate, on the other hand, was 480 and the rural rate reached 217.[7]

The average value of property stolen in each 1968 larceny, including

[6] President's Commission on Law Enforcement and Administration of Justice, *Commission Report: The Challenge of Crime in a Free Society* (Washington, D.C.: U.S. Government Printing Office, 1967), p. 42.

[7] *Uniform Crime Reports—1968*, pp. 22. See Donald R. Cressey, *Other People's Money* (New York: Free Press, 1953), for the dimensions of embezzlement. Note Henry Williamson, *Hustler! The Autobiography of a Thief* (New York: Doubleday & Co., Inc., 1965).

FIGURE 5–3

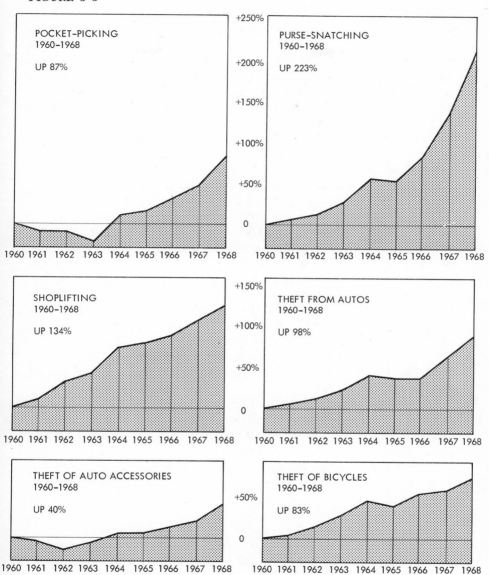

POCKET-PICKING
1960–1968

UP 87%

PURSE-SNATCHING
1960–1968

UP 223%

SHOPLIFTING
1960–1968

UP 134%

THEFT FROM AUTOS
1960–1968

UP 98%

THEFT OF AUTO ACCESSORIES
1960–1968

UP 40%

THEFT OF BICYCLES
1960–1968

UP 83%

Source: *Uniform Crime Reports—1968*, p. 25.

more than 2,172,000 thefts under $50, was $100. The total known dollar loss to victims alone exceeded $344 million. Although a portion of the stolen goods was eventually recovered and returned to victims, recovery of goods was primarily limited to the less than 20 percent of theft crimes which resulted in the arrest of an alleged offender. The value of goods stolen in miscellaneous thefts from buildings amounted to $97, from purse snatching to $53, from shoplifting to $28, and from thefts from automobiles to $142.[8] Forty-one percent of all larcenies were thefts of auto parts and accessories or other thefts from automobiles. Thefts from buildings (18 percent) and thefts of stolen bicycles (15 percent) accounted for another 33 percent of the total. The remaining larcenies occurred in varied locations and categories, being distributed among pickpocketing, purse snatching, and thefts from coin-operated machines (for example, vending machines and telephone boxes).

Only 18 percent of known 1968 larceny offenses were cleared by the police. Forty-four percent of those crimes cleared by arrest, however, resulted in the arrest of persons under 18 years of age. Suburban areas showed a juvenile clearance rate of 45 percent, while rural areas evidenced a 30 percent clearance among persons under 18 years of age. Urban clearance rates, however, were even lower than the national average, reaching only 15 percent in the suburbs and a high of 18 percent in cities with over 250,000 inhabitants. Larceny crimes resulted in 319 arrests per 100,000 inhabitants in the United States; the rate reached 382 in cities over 250,000 population, 261 in suburbs, and 112 in rural areas. The highest arrest rate (434) occurred in cities between 100,000 and 250,000 population.[9]

Forty-two percent of the total 1968 index arrests involved some form of larceny. Fifty-four percent of those arrested were persons under 18 years of age; approximately 66 percent were under 21 years of age. Surprisingly, 24 percent of all larceny theft arrests involved women. White outnumbered black arrests by more than two to one. Although nearly 83 percent of those arrested for larceny-theft were formally charged and held for prosecution, 42 percent of those processed were referred to the juvenile court. Adults were found guilty as charged in 71 percent of the cases. They were judged guilty of a lesser charge in 5 percent and either had their cases dismissed or were acquitted in the remaining 24 percent of the cases coming before the court.[10]

Larceny property crime subform: Shoplifting. Although exact data concerning shoplifting losses are not available, some estimates indicate that shoplifting accounts for 30 percent of all company inventory shrink-

---

[8] *Ibid.*, p. 24. David W. Maurer presents a lucid evaluation of pickpocket operations in his *Whiz Mob* (New Haven, Conn.: College and University Press, 1964).

[9] *Ibid.*, p. 26.

[10] *Ibid.*, pp. 26, 105.

age or loss.[11] Approximately 100,000 thefts, averaging $15 each larceny, were committed nationally each week, accounting for a minimal loss of $78 million per year.[12] In general, however, total inventory shrinkage, including shoplifting losses, range between 2 and 5 percent of sales per year. Although merchandise shrinkage may take the form of price markdowns, losses from disappearance of minor merchandise, damaged merchandise not replaced by insurance or other variations resulting in paper losses, shoplifting and employee theft account for a substantial amount of the annual loss. Businessman Norman Jaspan, for example, estimated that 70 percent of all inventory shortages in 1961 resulted from employee malpractice, twenty-five percent from honest clerical errors and five percent from shoplifting. Losses from employee dishonesty, however, varied by merchandising units (see Table 5–1). The sharp

TABLE 5–1
Losses from employee dishonesty
(in $million)

Type of Store	Total Value of Sales	Amount of Loss
Department stores..........	16,000	140
Supermarkets...............	50,000	100
Hardware stores............	9,000	90
Discount houses............	4,500	25
Variety stores..............	4,000	60
Drug retailers..............	6,000	50
Others.....................	135,000	140

Source: Mary Owen Cameron, *The Booster and the Snitch* (Glencoe, Ill.: Free Press, 1964), p. 13.

growth of self-service supermarkets and retail trade outlets has encouraged the major shoplifting increase.[13]

Of the neighborhood wholesale and retail entrepreneurs surveyed by the President's Commission, 35 percent reported no problem with shoplifting. Construction companies (30 percent); manufacturers of nondurables (33 percent); and finance, insurance, and real estate firms (25 percent), not normally expected to have shoplifting problems, reported difficulties.[14] Highest shoplifting rates were recorded in high crime rate

---

[11] Loren E. Edwards, *Shoplifting and Shrinkage Protection for Stores.* (Springfield, Ill.: Charles C. Thomas, Publisher, 1958), p. v.

[12] Based upon a 1958 estimate.

[13] Mary Owen Cameron, *The Booster and the Snitch* (Glencoe, Ill.: Free Press, 1964), p. 13.

[14] President's Commission, *op. cit.,* p. 41.

areas where the most common items stolen were food, liquor, beer, clothing, footwear, or other items worth less than $10.

Shoplifters, generally women, are classified as either commercial shoplifters or pilferers. The *commercial shoplifter*, also called "heel" or "booster," steals merchandise in order to profit by its sale. The *pilferer* or "snitch," on the other hand, steals merchandise for her own use. The commercial shoplifter steals for profit, sells her merchandise, and, in effect, operates her own illegal business. As a professional thief, the commercial shoplifter may be differentiated into a *heel* or a *booster*. While the *heel* is a professional shoplifter who rarely becomes involved in other crime forms, the *booster* is often involved in narcotic addiction, alcoholism, or prostitution.

Pilferers, stealing with a degree of regularity, form the largest group of shoplifters. Although they may include a few impulsive persons who occasionally steal merchandise for their own benefit, most pilferers intend to steal upon entrance into the store.[15] Legitimate customers, Mary Owen Cameron found in a study of Chicago shoplifters, usually enter the store *without* an intent to steal; if the thought of stealing occurs to them when in the store, they reject it immediately. Between 90 and 95 percent of intending shoplifters, on the other hand, are known to enter with prepared lists of merchandise to be shoplifted, tools (for example, razor blades) to eliminate identifying marks on the merchandise,[16] and equipment for hiding stolen merchandise.

A professional shoplifter prefers to work in a community of many small stores where the chances of being recognized are lessened. Utilizing such props as *booster boxes* (a garment or other box designed to look like a wrapped package but constructed with a hidden opening through which articles can be inserted) or *booster clothing* in the form of booster skirts, bloomers, pants, coats, or aprons (garments designed to hold stolen merchandise), the commercial shoplifter secures such items as she desires. The *skin worker* specializes in a theft of furs. The *crotch worker* shoplifts by carrying merchandise between her legs under her dress as she walks out of the store. One reported crotch worker became so efficient that she was able to jump over a 7-foot fence and outdistance two pursuing patrolmen without dropping the merchandise. Some shoplifters simply exchange cheaper price tags for higher ones. Others use ruses or stage dramas to effect their desired goals. A member of a shoplifting team, for example, may divert attention by simulating a heart attack or a fainting spell or by starting a small fire as other members of the group steal preselected merchandise.

Although most professional shoplifters work in small groups, a few

---

[15] Cameron, *op cit.*, p. 41.
[16] *Ibid.*, p. 145.

prefer to work alone. Ninety percent of all shoplifters are snitches. Even without criminal associations or connections, the amateur may shoplift 1 to 30 items in the same day, confining her snitches to smaller items that are easily concealed. Shoplifting, including pilfering, appears to be a chronic, habitual, or systematic form of human behavior. Only 5 to 10 percent of women caught shoplifting had purchased other merchandise which they had in their possession at the time of detection. Most shoplifters, Cameron concluded, are noncommercial pilferers.

A maximum of 2 percent of the female and 12 percent of the male shoplifters in Cameron's sample possessed a prior criminal record with either private or public Chicago enforcement agencies. Most pilferers were "respectable" housewives or employed persons who lived throughout the urban area. Fifty percent of the women charged in court with shoplifting were accused of stealing merchandise worth less than $14.95. The median price tag value of stolen merchandise, for example, was $6.74 for adult women and $8.30 for adult men.

The implications of an arrest did not seem to enter the shoplifter's mind. Once discovered and arrested, the pilferer often offered to purchase the stolen merchandise, not recognizing that she had committed an act of theft for which she could be charged in court.[17] As a result, recidivism was either limited or absent among pilferers who were apprehended and interrogated by store police but set free without formal charge. Since the adult pilferer had not viewed herself as a thief prior to her arrest, the arrest forced her to reject the pilferer role and to redirect her conduct.[18]

Larceny property crime subform: Auto theft. Although classified as a separate serious index offense, auto theft is a form of grand larceny. Defined as an attempted or unlawful stealing and/or driving of a motor vehicle, auto theft has increased with the teen-age population and the mass production of automobiles. An estimated 777,800 automobiles were stolen in 1968; the number was closer to 493,000 in 1965. Auto theft, a form of larceny, accounted for 17 percent of the 1968 index offenses, and it and the index larceny category comprised a total of 45 percent of all serious index crimes. Since 1960, the increase in auto theft has more than tripled the percentage increase in automobile registrations and the juvenile and young adult population between 15–24.

The sharpest automobile theft increase occurred in large cities of more than 250,000 (21 percent) and suburban areas (16 percent). However, rural areas, reporting an 8 percent rise in 1968, were not exempt from the increase. Overall, 389 auto theft offenses per 100,000 inhabitants took place during 1968; however, the highest auto theft rate, 1,060,

---

[17] *Ibid.*, pp. 147–48.
[18] *Ibid.*, p. 165.

was recorded in cities between 500,000 and 1 million inhabitants. Auto theft reached its highest average rate of 934 in large core cities; suburban and rural rates were only 237 and 67 offenses per 100,000 persons. One out of every 108 registered automobiles was stolen during 1968, a rate of 9.3 per 1,000 nationally registered automobiles. The average 1968 value of the pilfered automobile was near $991. Although 86 percent of the stolen vehicles were recovered by the police, the remaining 14 percent represented a victim and insurance loss of $100 million excluding the costs incurred in vehicle and property damage or personal inconvenience.[19]

Although the offender is usually young and white, black youth arrests for auto theft have more than doubled since 1960. More than two thirds of all auto thefts occur at night; over one half are stolen from private homes, apartments, or residential streets. Although 86 percent of all stolen vehicles during 1968 were eventually returned to their owners, only 19.6 percent of known thefts are cleared by an arrest of an alleged offender. Seventy-five percent of the stolen cars are primarily used for transportation; the remainder are taken for resale, stripped for parts, or used in some other criminal act.

Nearly 42 percent of all auto theft crimes in rural areas were solved, during 1968, but only 23 percent of suburban auto thefts and 17 percent of large city auto thefts were cleared. Where arrests did occur, juveniles under 18 were detained for 55 percent of large core city, 42 percent of suburban, and 41 percent of all rural auto thefts. Eighty-six auto theft arrests per 100,000 population were completed during 1968. Sixteen percent of all persons arrested for auto theft in 1968 were under 15 years of age, 61 percent were under 18, and 79 percent were under 21.

The largest percentage of juvenile arrests occurred in the auto theft crime category. Whites were arrested for 62 percent, blacks for 35 percent, and all other races for the remaining 3 percent of all thefts. Sixty-five percent of all persons charged for auto theft in 1968 were referred to the jurisdiction of the juvenile court. Fifty-four percent of the remaining adult auto theft offenders, however, were prosecuted and found guilty as charged. Fourteen percent were convicted or admitted guilt to a lesser charge, 32 percent were acquitted or had their cases dismissed.[20]

Larceny subform: Confidence games. The confidence game is a form of fraud. Its fundamental goal is to separate a victim from his property or money through manipulation. The basic confidence operation depends upon the ability of the operator to gain the trust of the victim and

---

[19] *Uniform Crime Reports—1968,* pp. 26–28.
[20] *Ibid.,* pp. 27. 100–101, 110.

to stimulate the victim's greed. The confidence man, therefore, preys upon his victim's latent gullibility and tendency toward larceny.

The confidence game may be divided into the two categories of *big* or *long con* and *short con*. The distinction is based upon the elaborateness of the operation and the number of props and accomplices involved in the drama. The multiple operatives in the big con activate the drama, cultivate the victim's (the "mark's") confidence, and stimulate his participation in the operation. The "steerer" or "roper" introduces the victim to the "buildup man," a second accomplice, who gains knowledge about the victim's potential susceptibility and resources, and access to his funds. While a third contact stimulates the man's greed, the fourth operator works to relieve him of his money. Once the mark has been "fleeced," the victim is either "cooled" or "shaken off," depending upon the operators' estimate of the probable action which the victim might eventually carry out. Although the con man may "cool off" the victim by helping him to adjust to an impossible situation and to maintain his self-respect, he may unceremoniously "shake off" the mark by bluntly telling him that any report to the police can only lead to his own incrimination. Short-con operations sometime take the form of elaborate off-track betting activities designed to get the victim to bet on a "sure thing." A variety of long-con operations use sales approaches offering the mark a worthless object at a high cost.

Since the *short con* is designed for smaller profit, usually the amount of money quickly available from the victim, less preparation, finesse, originality, and fewer actors and props are involved. Because the con man must move quickly to avoid detection, the short con is essentially a fast operation. Successful short-con manipulators, however, are often recruited as "insidemen" or actors in long-con operations, in which they can more readily escape detection. Most incarcerated confidence men are short-con operatives who were quickly detected and apprehended.[21] Common short-con operations include the "pigeon drop," in which the victim puts up money to show good faith in order to receive a special benefit, or the "Spanish prisoner," which promises the victim a share in buried wealth if he assists the prisoner financially in gaining release from prison. Each has multiple variations.

Julian Roebuck conducted an in-depth study of the 10 operatives taken from a sample of 400 Negro offenders at the District of Columbia Reformatory in Lorton, Virginia, during 1954–55. He found that confidence men represented a median age of 38 and came from homes that were criminalistic, conflict-oriented, demoralized, or dominated by the mother.

[21] Julian Roebuck, *Criminal Typology* (Springfield, Ill.: Charles C. Thomas, Publisher, 1966), p. 184. Robert L. Glaser discusses the victim-confidence man relationship in "The Confidence Game," *Federal Probation*, Vol. 27, No. 4 (December, 1963), p. 47 ff.

While avoiding violence patterns, the confidence operator frequently had delinquent and gang contacts before the age of 10. Having success-fully used deceit in his youth, the child continued the process through adult life. Con men, Roebuck found, showed a higher incidence of child-hood training in deceit than any other single subgroup he studied. The mother often protected the youth from truant officers or school adminis-trators, for example, in return for silence concerning her own illicit sexual activity with males in the community.[22] The effect of social change upon confidence operations is evident in one imaginative short-con operation in which the operator successfully sold Clevelanders seven tickets for the first trip to the moon before his detection and arrest.

Larceny subform: The numbers operation. Numbers operations are known as lotteries, policy, or bolita, depending upon the community in which they operate and the characteristics of the activity itself. In each, however, the player normally bets on a three-digit number (for example, 2–4–7) selected from some predetermined source such as the volume of money bet at a racetrack, the number of the last $1 bill printed at a particular U.S. mint, or some other similar possibility. Bet-ting pennies, nickels, quarters, and usually dollars, the player seeks to increase his investment 500 to 600 times. In many instances, bets may also be made on a "leader" (first digit) or "bleeder" (last two digits) number. While the normal bet is a three-digit bet (a "gig"), the player in Syracuse, New York, often receives a printed ticket for a fixed sum and views the five-digit number only after purchase. In Chicago, bolita, operated in Spanish-speaking communities, depends upon the selection of numbers from the throw of dice, the spin of a numbered wheel, or selection of numbers from a hat. In Italian and some other districts, it is referred to "policy," a term believed by some to be derived from the Italian word *polizza*, referring to a lottery ticket. Other authori-ties think that the name comes from the insurance policy, since money intended for insurance premiums often went for numbers tickets.

Operatives assume many roles in the lottery operation. The *writer* sells lottery tickets to the bettor. Frequently, he is known as a *policy writer,* a *pickup man,* a *walking writer,* or a *runner.* Normally working from a fixed location (a "spot"), he is often susceptible to police "protec-tion" at a rate near $2 per day per officer. In Harlem the policy writer has been known to take $1,000 in bets per day, keeping about 10 percent of the gross. Commonly, he receives 10 to 25 percent of the gross and 10 percent of the value of a winning ticket. *Fieldmen* or *controllers,* often organized crime "soldiers," supervise about 10 writers. Charged with organizational maintenance, they check dishonesty, pay court fines

---

[22] *Ibid.,* p. 187. See Roebuck, *op. cit.,* pp. 199–200, for bibliographic source listings on confidence operations.

and attorney fees, and act as general troubleshooters. In addition, they drop the slips and money at their superior's *substation* or *turn-in station* for further transmission to a *manager* (also known as *owner* or *banker*), frequently a syndicate lieutenant but sometimes an "independent" operator. Normally, the same routine is used in reverse for the payoff of winners.[23]

Numbers operators, Roebuck discovered in a study in depth of 16 black violators in the same sample of 400 offenders, were a comparably older, more intelligent, and more literate group of offenders (see Table 5–2). Numbers men often grew up in neighborhoods of moderate income and had close ties to other family members. Coming more frequently from patriarchal homes, they failed to reflect the typical matriarchal influence witnessed in most other offender groups. Generally unmarked by emotional conflict in the home, their childhood activities were generally well supervised. Several operators, however, admitted emotional conflict where parental supervision was lax. Evidencing a minimal amount of juvenile delinquency, alcohol or drug addiction, or a tendency to violence, the numbers men had had only a limited previous juvenile contact with the police or juvenile court. Their surreptitious beer drinking, gambling, dice or card betting, and sexual intercourse, begun at the age of 17 or 18, remained hidden from their parents and the police. Since they grew up in communities tolerant to the numbers operation, a large proportion of the numbers men became gambling addicts. Gambling was both their profession and their recreation.[24]

Many of the numbers men maintained a stable of "slick chicks," "fine broads," "foxes," and "party girls," whom they passed around among their group at three- to six-month intervals. Several of the "playmates" performed, Roebuck discovered, added clerical functions in the numbers ring. Fifteen of the sixteen numbers operatives were products of the Negro middle-class home, reared in nonslum neighborhoods by respected parents. Having rejected the view that the numbers operation was a real form of criminal behavior, they were able to view themselves as respectable middle-class persons in a stable, churchgoing, homeowner- and father-centered community.

Robbery

The crime of robbery involves the attempted or successful stealing of anything of value from a person or taking it by the use of threat or force, with or without actual physical assault. Robbery by definition,

---

[23] Donald R. Cressey, *Theft of the Nation* (New York: Harper & Row, Publishers, 1969), pp. 135–37.

[24] Roebuck, *op. cit.*, p. 140.

TABLE 5–2

Comparison of single pattern of numbers game violators with all other offenders

Selected Social and Personal Attributes	Numbers Men (N = 16) N.W.C.*	All Others (N = 384) N.W.C.	Sign of X^2
Reared in more than one home............	3	158	N.S.†
Mother figure southern migrant............	3	171	N.S.
Mother figure domestic servant...........	13	287	N.S.
Dependent family.......................	6	290	0.01
Family broken by desertion..............	2	138	N.S.
Demoralized family......................	1	195	.01
Criminality in family...................	1	170	.01
Mother figure dominant..................	2	217	.01
Inadequate supervision—father...........	3§	193	.05
Inadequate supervision—mother..........	4	278	.01
Conflict in family......................	3	231	.01
Overt hostility toward father.............	2	269	.01
Overt hostility toward mother............	1	78	N.S.
Disciplinary problem at home.............	2	117	N.S.
History of running away.................	3	182	.05
Inveterate gambler‡.....................	16	154	.01
Problem drinker........................	2	191	.05
Weak parental family structure..........	0	214	.01
No parental family ties..................	2	280	.01
Reared in urban area...................	9	325	.01
Reared in slum area....................	1	250	.01
Living in slum when arrested............	0	301	.01
History of school truancy................	2	201	.01
Disciplinary problem at school...........	3	185	.05
Street trades as juvenile.................	3	200	.05
No marital ties.........................	3	285	.01
Juvenile delinquent companions..........	5	231	.05
Member delinquent gang.................	1	141	.05
Adjudicated juvenile delinquent..........	4	173	N.S.
Committed as juvenile...................	1	145	.05
Police contact prior to age 18............	1	220	.01
Criminal companions as juvenile.........	1	162	.01
Drug addict...........................	0	69	N.S.
Positive attitude toward work............	11	142	.01

* Number with characteristic.
† Not significant.
‡ Nonprofessional gambling.
§ Based on those with fathers.
Source: Julian Roebuck, *Criminal Typology* (Springfield, Ill.: Charles C. Thomas, Publisher 1966), p. 150.

therefore, implies a wide range of behavioral-situational alternatives, including the use of weapons or the infliction of physical harm against the person. The 261,730 robberies committed during 1968 constituted nearly 6 percent of the total crime index. Robberies were most frequently committed in the period August through December. The 1968 robbery rate reached 131 victims per 100,000 population, the highest rates occurring in the largest cities. Cities over 250,000 population evidence a rate of 433; suburban communities recorded only 45 and rural areas 12 victims per 100,000 citizens.

Although 58 percent of the robberies were committed in the street, bank robbery, a small part of the total robbery volume, resulted in an average 1968 loss of more than $5,200. Gas and service station holdups reported to the police between 1960 and 1968 increased by 187 percent, chain store robberies by 210 percent, robberies of residences by nearly 100 percent, and of commercial and business establishments by 107 percent (see Figure 5–4). Sixty percent of the 1968 robbery offenses involved armed action. Nearly 40 percent resulted in muggings or other violent confrontations without extraneous weapons (see Table 5–3).[25] The aver-

TABLE 5–3
Robbery by geographic region

	Total	Northeastern	North Central	Southern	Western
Armed—any weapon..........	60.3	61.6	56.3	60.2	64.1
Strong-arm—no weapon.......	39.7	38.4	43.7	39.8	35.9

Source: *Uniform Crime Reports—1968*, p. 15.

age value of the victim's loss amounted to $269 per robbery, and the total 1968 loss neared $70 million. Twenty-seven percent of all robberies known to the police were cleared by arrests in 1968; approximately 80 percent of all robbery arrests were of adults. Twelve percent of all 1968 armed robberies and 34 percent of strong-arm robberies were cleared by the arrest of juveniles.

Forty-seven persons per 100,000 population were arrested for robbery in 1968. While cities above 250,000 inhabitants recorded an arrest rate of 113 per 100,000 persons, the suburban and rural arrest rates were substantially lower at 21 and 9. Seventy-five percent of the persons arrested for robbery during 1968 were under 25 years of age; over half (56 percent) were under 21. Thirty-three percent of the robbery arrests were completed among youth under 18. However, females accounted for only 6 of every 100 robbery arrests. Sixty-two percent of those arrested were black; the remaining 38 percent of those arrested were whites (36 percent) or members of other ethnic groups (2 percent).

Nearly 80 percent of all adults arrested for robbery in 1968 were

---

[25] *Uniform Crime Reports—1968*, pp. 13–17.

FIGURE 5–4

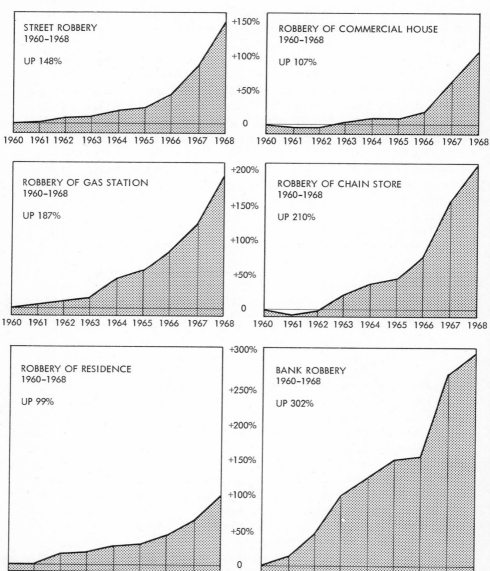

Source: *Uniform Crime Reports—1968*, p. 16.

TABLE 5–4
Comparison of single pattern of armed robbery offenders with all other offenders

Selected Social and Personal Attributes	Armed Robbers (N = 32) N.W.C.*	All Others (N = 368) N.W.C.	Sign of X²
Reared in more than one home	25	136	0.01
Mother figure southern migrant	29	145	0.1
Mother figure domestic servant	31	269	.01
Dependent family	30	266	.01
Family broken by desertion	15	125	.05
Demoralized family	27	169	.01
Criminality in family	25	146	.01
Mother figure dominant	26	193	.01
Inadequate supervision—father	19†	177†	.01
Inadequate supervision—mother	29	253	0.5
Conflict in family	19	215	N.S.†
Overt hostility toward father	18	153	.01
Overt hostility toward mother	6	73	N.S.
Disciplinary problem at home	18	101	.01
History of running away	27	158	.01
Inveterate gambler	18	152	N.S.
Problem drinker	9	184	.05
Weak parental family structure	29	185	.01
No parental family ties	25	257	N.S.
Reared in urban area	32	302	N.S.
Reared in slum area	32	219	.01
Living in slum when arrested	30	271	.05
History of school truancy	29	174	.01
Disciplinary problem at school	30	158	.01
Street trades as juvenile	28	175	.01
No marital ties	29	259	.05
Juvenile delinquent companions	31	205	.01
Member delinquent gang	31	111	.01
Adjudicated juvenile delinquent	30	147	.01
Committed as juvenile	29	117	.01
Police contact prior to age 18	32	189	.01
Criminal companions as juvenile	31	132	.01
Drug addict	1	68	.05
Positive attitude toward work	8	145	N.S.

*Number with characteristic.
†Based on those with fathers.
Source: Roebuck, *Criminal Typology*, p. 115.

formally charged by the police. Since only 61 percent of those arrested were adults, the remaining 39 percent were referred to the juvenile court for appropriate action. While 50 percent of the adults charged were convicted for robbery, 15 percent were convicted of lesser charges, and 34 percent were either acquitted or had their cases dismissed.[26]

[26] *Ibid.*, p. 17, 110. Refer to President's Commission, *op. cit.*, pp. 239–43.

Robbers, Roebuck found, are frequently single, migratory, intelligent, and more emotionally maladjusted than other offenders. Although their intelligence and criminal style, whether amateur or professional, varies with their social class and background, they frequently lack strong family attachments and possess feelings of insecurity.[27] Thirty-two armed robbers from Roebuck's sample of 400 Negro offenders differed to a significant degree in 28 social and personal characteristics from other offenders in the study (see Table 5–4). While slightly younger and more intelligent, the armed robber grew up in unfavorable slum neighborhoods to a greater extent than the rest of the sample. Their homes were more frequently marked by criminality, desertion, conflict, or inadequate parental supervision. Their fathers were often heavy drinkers, and their mothers or sisters were often prostitutes or openly entertained men in their homes. Since the mother was the dominant figure, the youths often expressed open hostility to their incomplete father figures. They were more often brought to the attention of the juvenile court for delinquency as members of juvenile gangs. Since they experienced many police contacts before the age of 18, they were periodically committed to corrective institutions.

Although armed robbers were less frequently addicted to drugs and alcohol than other offenders, they evidenced, Roebuck found, a greater tendency to use physical force, whether in the form of destruction of property, fighting with schoolmates, or a periodic mugging or purse snatching.[28] Early violence, however, progressed from petty thefts and playground fights to the eventual rolling of drunks or homosexuals and to holdups using pistols or knives. The armed robbers as a group were highly self-centered and coldly unemotional. They were, Roebuck concluded, a group of hardened, anti-social recidivists, who rejected poorly supervised and somewhat perverted homes charged with emotional conflict. Many were on the street by six years of age. Several had been amateur boxers. Most, however, had been gang leaders who participated in violence and destruction of property at an early age.[29]

---

[27] Roebuck., *op. cit.*, p. 107.

[28] *Ibid.*, p. 108. The sense of minority hopelessness is captured in Claude Brown, *Manchild in the Promised Land* (New York: Macmillan Co., 1965).

[29] *Ibid.*, p. 112.

Chapter 6

CRIMINAL VIOLATIONS AGAINST THE PERSON

Crimes against the person occur less frequently than crimes against property in the United States. Thirteen percent of all serious 1966 index crimes reported to the police were crimes against the person; the remaining 87 percent were forms of property violations. While crimes of violence increased 49 percent in volume and 37 percent in proportion to the estimated population between 1960 and 1968 (see Figure 6–1), they remain a clear minority of the crimes reported from all sources.

The crime of robbery illustrates the artificial distinction between crimes against property and crimes against the person. As an act it involves the threat or use of violence against the person. The end goal of the robbery, however, is monetary. On the other hand, alcohol and narcotic violations, not usually categorized by the FBI as crimes against the person, are crimes which a person may commit against himself. Sex offenders, too, cover a wide range of attitude, behavior, and conduct. While the forcible rapist commits an act of sexual plunder against the person, the statutory rapist may be engaging in mutually accepted courtship activity. Acts of aggravated assault or murder also involve varying behavior patterns. Many occur when the participants are drunk or are temporarily hostile to each other. The categories of crimes against property or against the person, therefore, are oversimplifications of the behavioral goals or acts involved in the criminal process. An analysis of sex crimes, alcohol or narcotic violations, and aggravated assault-homicide felonies illustrates the basic problem central to the establishment of simple crime dichotomies.

FIGURE 6–1
Crimes of violence,* 1960–68
(percent change over 1960)

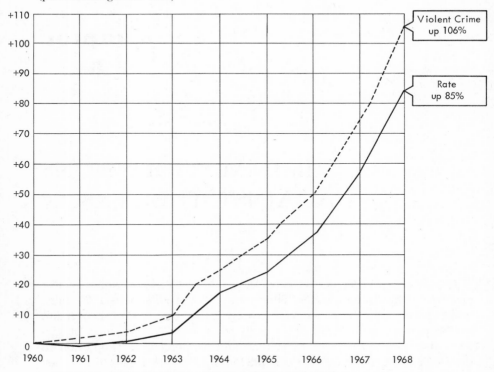

* Limited to murder, forcible rape, robbery, and aggravated assault.
   Source: *Uniform Crime Reports, 1968* (Washington, D.C.: U.S. Department of Justice, 1969), p. 3.
FBI chart.

SEX OFFENSES AND OFFENDERS

American sex laws were designed to control forced or undesired sexual relationships, unnatural or homosexual acts, statutory rape, child molestation or indecent liberties with children, and in limited degree, fornication or adultery between consenting partners. Not all acts, however, are automatically constrained by mere codification in law. Many occur in private where they are not quickly detected and are expected and ignored. The same acts occurring in public may lead to an arrest of the offender. A person, for example, who is nude as he washes in his own bathroom or at a nudist camp is unlikely to be charged with indecent exposure. On the other hand, if he invites friends to a home nudist party, he may be charged with a sex offense. While some laws, therefore, attempt to control deviant acts, others are formulated to control the setting. Sex crimes, as a result, cover a wide spectrum and involve many personality types and patterns. Since sex statutes represent moral and pragmatic legislation, they are generally inconsistent and contradictory. Each statute is a composite response to the community's sense of revulsion and concept of morality, the social harm involved in the act, the practical problem of controlling the undesired behavior, and the degree of psychopathology evidenced in the offense by the offender.[1]

Heterosexual offenses

Forcible rape, statutory rape, fornication, and incest represent four types of heterosexual relations. *Forcible rape,* comprising less than 1 percent of the 1968 Crime Index, totaled an estimated 31,000 offenses. Forcible rape offenses, as might be expected, reached a peak during the warmer months between April and September. Thirty women per every 100,000 females were forcible rape victims during 1968. Larger cities recorded a risk rate of 62 victims per 100,000 female inhabitants; suburban and rural communities had a rate of 23 and 17. Since the category of forcible rape, defined as carnal knowledge of a female forcibly and against her will, includes assaults with the attempt to rape, the FBI rape statistics are not limited to acts of genital contact. Approximately two thirds of all reported rape offenses involved actual rape by force; the remaining third were attempted rape or assaults to rape.

Although 55 percent of all forcible rapes were cleared by the arrest of an alleged offender in 1968, the arrest rate represented a 9 percent decrease from the 1967 clearance level. Fifteen percent of the arrests were made among persons under the age of 18. Of the arrests for forcible rape during the year, 64 percent were of persons under the age of 25. The total city forcible rape arrest rate was 9.2 per 100,000 persons, while the suburban and rural rates reached 6.4 and 6.5 respectively.

The largest concentration of arrests occurred among 17- to 20-year-old males. Fifty-one percent of all arrested rapists were white and 47 percent were black; the remaining 2 percent represented multiple ethnic or racial origins. Of the adults formally arrested for forcible rape by the police in 1968, 73 percent were eventually charged. Only 40 percent of the adults charged, however, were found guilty of forcible rape. An additional 16 percent of the charged adults were convicted of lesser offenses; 44 percent were either acquitted or found the charges dismissed. Of all forcible rape charges occurring during 1968, 23 percent were referred to the juvenile courts for appropriate action.[2]

---

[1] Stanton Wheeler, "Sex Offense: A Sociological Critique," *Sexual Deviance* (New York: Harper & Row, Publishers, 1967), p. 83. Ex-warden Clinton Duffy argues that sex and sex inadequacy is the cause of nearly all crime; see Clinton Duffy, *Sex and Crime* (Garden City, N.Y.: Doubleday & Co., Inc., 1965). See also *Wisconsin's First Eleven Years of Experience with Its Sex Crime Laws* (Madison: Department of Public Welfare, 1965).

[2] *Uniform Crime Reports—1968* (Washington, D.C.: U.S. Department of Justice, 1969), p. 13.

All rapes are not forcible rapes; many forcible rapes for that matter do not even involve the use of "force." *Statutory rape,* for example, usually does not involve force or violence and ultimately depends upon female cooperation. In fact, statutory rape participants may later contract an effective marriage if parental charges are not brought against the male participant. The violation of a female under 12 despite her consent, too, falls outside the simple forcible rape classification. Since she is considered legally incapable of consenting to sexual intercourse, the violation of her person normally constitutes *aggravated rape,* a crime often punished by the execution of the male offender.

Coitus of a male over 17 with an unmarried female below 17 even with consent or without previous knowledge of her age, constitutes the crime of *carnal knowledge of a juvenile* or *statutory rape.* Under American law, even though a woman suggests sexual relations, thus stimulating the rape event, the male participant may be convicted of rape, provided that the woman later refused to complete the act. *Fornication,* sexual intercourse between unmarried persons, whether controlled through statutory rape or other legislation, is prohibited in all but 10 states and calls for penalties ranging from a $10 fine in Rhode Island to a three-year prison term in Arizona.[3] Legal inconsistencies, however, allow the successful prosecution of the male who has sexual intercourse with a girl under 17, even though she may have been previously divorced, worked as a prostitute, or even been jailed for her own sex violations. The law, on the other hand, does not prohibit sexual intercourse between older women and boys under 17.

Incest, sexual relations between parents and children or between brothers and sisters, is also prohibited by law. Although more prevalent in rural areas, it also occurs in urban families marked by feeblemindedness, alcoholism, or lack of restraint. Since the prohibition against incest is one of the strongest social taboos, it is the most consistently prohibited sex practice. Incest violations account for only 2 to 6 percent of all sex offenses. Although the father-daughter relationship is most common, the brother-sister and mother-son relationships also occur in descending order of commonness.[4]

Alternate forms of sexual deviation

American society, influenced by Judeo-Christian and Puritan values, has traditionally viewed sexual contacts beyond the "normal" genital-to-genital relationship as abnormal and subject to legal control. Sexual

---

[3] Ralph Slovenko, "A Panoramic View: Sexual Behavior and the Law," *Sexual Behavior and the Law* (Springfield, Ill.: Charles C. Thomas, Publisher, 1965), p. 10.

[4] *Ibid.,* p. 37.

deviations may take many forms and are subject to a variety of criminal controls.

Sadomasochism is the derivation of sexual pleasure from inflicting or accepting pain or humiliation. Sadism and masochism are two aspects of the same underlying tendency. Sadism is subject to criminal control when it surfaces in acts of brutality and violence that come to the attention of the police. When sadomasochistic impulses are released through the willing cooperation of a lover, spouse, or prostitute, this form of sexual deviation usually escapes the attention of the public or the police.

Fetishism involves a compulsive sexual attraction to an inanimate object (for example, glove, panty) or an abnormal libidinal interest in some part of the human body other than the genital organs (feet, legs, breasts, hips). Almost always males, most fetishists are heterosexual.[5] Fetish commitment may differ in intensity and type. Modern American and European fashions cater to a mild fetishistic interest in their overemphasis upon the female bust (plunging necklines, topless bathing suits) and thighs (miniskirts), but acts which overextend "acceptable" fetishistic behavior are disallowed. Although the college panty raid does not usually result in the imposition of criminal charges, similar activity in a downtown store or private home would bring quick police response and action.

Transvestism is the practice of adopting the dress, manner, and sometimes the sexual role of the opposite sex. The male transvestite feels inwardly that nature has made a mistake and that he is really a woman, and vice versa. He may obtain specific gratification from the sensuous feel of women's clothing or from a sense of increased self-confidence or fulfillment gained by dressing in female garments. Since he resents his own masculinity, the transvestite feels more comfortable in playing the role of a female. He may even seek a change-of-sex operation to make his physical characteristics conform to his feelings. Because the male may dress as he desires, transvestism is usually not illegal as long as the deviant does not violate public decency.

Homosexuality, erotic love between two persons of the same sex, may be either male or female. It tends to be more commonly recognized among males, since social custom permits expressions of affection between females which would be suspect in men. Society ostracizes male homosexuals while it tends to ignore *female homosexuality* (*lesbianism*).

Female homosexuality, psychiatrists believe, often develops from a sense of sexual inferiority. Particular family patterns may especially encourage the development of male homosexuality. A negative father relationship accompanied by an overintimate mother relationship tends to

---

[5] Anthony Storr, *Sexual Deviation* (Baltimore, Md.: Penguin Books, Inc., 1965), pp. 35–59.

encourage the development of homosexual conduct. The mother's ability to arouse a premature but unfulfilled eroticism may lead the juvenile, some researchers think to generalize the female as a seductress who may later deprive him of his masculinity. Although many homosexuals marry, they usually continue to view the woman with fear or indifference and prefer to keep the relationship platonic. While male homosexuals frequently prefer a rugged and highly masculine-appearing companion, others prefer "pretty boys" who approach the female stereotype. Few of those engaging in homosexuality however, are "self-indulgent lechers"; the greater number of participants are simply lonely and are unable to fulfill a heterosexual desire in the traditional biological manner.[6] The tendency to find sexual satisfaction within one's own sex when heterosexual relations are unavailable, for example, explains the practice of homosexual relations in penal institutions, schools, and even religious communities. While some societies accept both homosexual and heterosexual relations as a legitimate masculine expression, contemporary American society rejects this viewpoint.

No American law prohibits homosexuality per se. Homosexuality, as a result, is minimally regulated by prosecutions under laws prohibiting sodomy, crimes against nature, and unnatural sexual acts. Although homosexuals usually do not engage in other forms of sex or property crime, their fear of discovery makes them highly susceptible to blackmail, extortion, or pressure.

Homosexual activity, especially among males, is more widespread than commonly believed. An estimated 50 percent of the white American male population have engaged in some type of homosexual activity by the age of 55.[7] While bachelors sharing the same apartment, or an excessive number of males associating together over long periods of time, are immediately suspected of homosexual activity, American society tends to accept female togetherness. The same cultural norms which encourage all males to assume heterosexual relations in order to reproduce the race make some forms of female homosexual contact a social virtue. A large amount of female homosexuality, as a result, is disguised by social customs which encourage women to share an apartment, embrace upon meeting, or hold hands in public without incurring social sanctions. While Kinsey found male homosexuality to be more wide-

---

[6] *Ibid.*, pp. 70–90. See Hendrik M. Ruitenbeck, *The Problem of Homosexuality in the Modern Society* (New York: E. P. Dutton & Co., Inc., 1963), and Slovenko, *op. cit.*, pp. 81–91. Especially note J. F. Wolfenden, *The Wolfenden Report: Report of the Committee on Homosexual Offence and Prostitution* (New York: Stein & Day Publishers, 1962).

[7] Edward H. Knight, "Overt Male Homosexuality," *Sexual Behavior and the Law*, p. 437. Refer to Daniel Cappon, *Toward an Understanding of Homosexuality* (Englewood Cliffs, N.J.: Prentice-Hall, Inc., 1965), and Edwin M. Schur, *Crimes Without Victim's* (Englewood Cliffs, N.J.: Prentice-Hall, Inc., 1965).

spread than lesbianism, Magnus Hirschfield and Havelock Ellis estimated that female homosexuals outnumber their male counterparts almost two to one.[8]

Exhibitionism, frotteurism, voyeurism, and acts of sodomy are other forms of sexual deviation. *Exhibitionism,* also known as *indecent exposure,* involves the public exposure of one's genitals. Almost always a male deviation, exhibitionism may recur in spite of the legal penalties or treatment of offenders. Of 1,985 English sexual offenders studied at the Cambridge Department of Criminal Science during the 1950's, 490 had committed some form of indecent exposure. Nineteen percent of those involved in a follow-up study of convicted exhibitionists were reconvicted for the same crime within four years. While indecent exposure often occurs as an incidental part of homosexual contact, exhibitionism is basically a heterosexual act. The exhibitionist generally attempts to prove his manliness by eliciting a female response of horror, disgust, or excitement by the exposure of his sexual organs. His ability to shock a female, in effect, allows him to overcome his inability to command her love. Since exposure is usually followed by masturbation rather than by sexual violations, exhibitionism represents a deep-seated but generally passive psychological problem. Exhibitionism often serves as a means for relieving tension and, in effect, allows the person to enter upon a sexual exploit without the need to effect any personal relationship with a member of the opposite sex.[9]

A survey of the 54 exhibitionists represented in the 132 cases studied by the Forensic Clinic of the Toronto Psychiatric Hospital revealed that exhibitionism and indecent exposure are generally products of personal impulsive-compulsive drives or recognized mental illness which leads to a general deterioration of behavior.[10] The exhibitionist's victim is usually a female child or adult. Since the exhibitionist usually reveals himself from a distance, actual physical and/or social interaction and previous victim-offender acquaintance are rare. While the victim-object is usually a single stranger, an offender occasionally exposes himself to a larger group of children. He is rarely able to define the reasons for the act or the selection of the particular victim. Although some female victims simply regard exhibitionism as a little more than a nuisance, others become seriously disturbed emotionally by the indecent exposure.

---

[8] Edmund Bergler, *Homosexuality: Disease or Way of Life* (New York: Hill & Wang, Inc., 1957), p. 261. Note William Simon and John Gagnon, "Female Homosexuality," *Sexual Deviance* (New York: Harper & Row, Publishers, 1967), pp. 247–85, and Charles W. Socarides, "Female Homosexuality," *Sexual Behavior and the Law*, pp. 462–77.

[9] Storr, *op. cit.*, pp. 94–95. See Slovenko, *op. cit.*, pp. 74–81.

[10] Johann W. Mohr, R. E. Turner, and M. B. Jerry. *Pedophilia and Exhibitionism* (Toronto: University of Toronto Press, 1964), p. 112.

Although some exhibitionists are psychologically inadequate, the completion of an exhibitionist act does not automatically indicate the presence of mental illness, mental defectiveness, or gross personal immorality. The exhibitionist is most often in his 20's. Exhibitionist activity declines rapidly among men in their 30's and is rare among persons over 40. Although the exhibitionist shows a slight tendency toward above-average intelligence, his educational achievements are often below his intellectual capacities. Overly aggressive or overly passive and often lonely, he generally leads an unhappy existence. Many exhibitionists are hard-working and conscientious in their occupation—often in one of the skilled trades.[11]

Frotteurism, the practice of rubbing one's genitals against another person, usually in a crowd, in order to achieve sexual stimulation, is another type of sexual deviance. Fetishistic interest in, and ready availability of, the buttocks makes them a primary contact point. Although the offender may sometimes be charged with indecent assault on a female or some form of minor crime, few of these violations are ever reported to the police or brought to court.

Sexual gratification without contact with the victim is possible in *voyeurism* or scopophilia. "Peeping tom" activity represents the most common form of voyeurist conduct. Girlie magazines, nudie movies, and burlesque and striptease performances satisfy the same sexual-psychological goals. Voyeurism serves as a substitute sexual act for these who are emotionally immature or are unable to find acceptable sexual alternatives.

From a biblical and medical standpoint, *sodomy* (also known as buggery) refers to the sexual relationship between the male penis and the rectum of a male or female. The term, however, is used in a legal sense to cover almost any sexual act, whether in the form of sexual stimulation by use of the mouth or tongue or actual intercourse through the anus or with an animal, bird, or dead body, which is unnatural or is defined as a crime against nature. The definitions in sodomy statutes are often vague. Penalties normally bring 5 to 30 years' imprisonment and/or a large monetary fine. In one state, sexual acts with an animal can result in a minimum penalty of five years' imprisonment, and any form of sexual variation with one's wife outside of the normal male-female relationship can bring a penalty of 60 years to life. Most statutes make no distinction between potential male or female and married or unmarried relationships.[12] Under existing laws, marriage manuals which encourage marital partners to develop mutually satisfying and special sexual techniques are, in effect, advising the couple to violate sodomy statutes.

---

[11] *Ibid.*, p. 134.
[12] Robert V. Sherwin, "Sodomy," in Slovenko, *op. cit.*, p. 427.

The crime of *pedophilia* generally refers to the seduction of female children by adult males, although male homosexuals who attempt to seduce young boys are included within its scope. The "lovers of children" often fondle children without specific genital contact, make verbal approaches to them or exhibit their genitals to juveniles. In a minority of cases, the adult attempts to persuade the child to stimulate his sexual organs or attempts to caress those of the child. Contrary to public assumption, the youthful participant often finds the association pleasant and meaningful. Since the pedophilic offender's attraction to children is compulsive and is related to his emotional development, medical and psychiatric aid is central to any treatment of the violator.[13] Sexual offenses against children rarely result in death or violence. Only a small proportion of the heterosexual offenses result in actual intercourse. Where they do, the offense generally involves a consenting victim over the age of 14. The majority (55–70 percent) of all sexual offenses against children under 14 are consistently heterosexual. Most pedophilic offenses are forms of immature gratification.[14]

The sexual offender

Forty-three percent of the inmates in a study of 300 sex offenders committed to a New Jersey diagnostic facility evidenced normal or mild neurotic tendencies. Aggressive offenders, the study revealed, were more likely to be judged normal by psychiatric diagnosis and they were less inhibited sexually. The aggressive offenders evidenced fewer severe emotional disturbances. Although their arrest history revealed few previous sexual offenses, it included multiple nonsexual violations. While the more aggressive individual attempted or completed intercourse with a person of the opposite sex beyond the age of puberty, the passive sex offender sought emotional release through exhibitionism and pedophilia.[15]

Similar patterns were discovered in a 1954 California report on sexual deviation. Over half of the 37 serious offenders studied had previous records for nonsexual offenses, although only 3 possessed previous sex arrests. Gang attacks were most frequently directed toward girls in middle

---

[13] Storr, *op. cit.*, pp. 60–180.

[14] Mohr *et al.*, *op. cit.*, p. 82. For a special but somewhat dated discussion of the sex offender problem, see "Sex Offenses," *Law and Contemporary Problems*, Vol. 25, No. 2 (Spring, 1960).

[15] *Ibid.*, p. 15. Paul H. Gebhard and associates present one of the most detailed investigations of the sex offender. See Paul H. Gebhart, *et al.*, *Sex Offenders* (New York: Harper & Row, Publishers, 1965). Their study included 1,356 white males convicted of one or more sex offenses (total sex offender group), 888 white males never convicted of sex offenses but who had been convicted of some other misdemeanor or felony (prison group), and 477 white males who had never been convicted for anything beyond traffic violations (control group). Some surveys report that up to 50 percent of their random samples can be variously defined as neurotic.

or late adolescence; acts against the extremely young female were more commonly committed by lone offenders. While Mexicans and Negroes were overrepresented in the rape category, they were underrepresented in offenses against children.[16] In many instances, the physical rape was only a form of general plundering extended to a human being.

A study of 132 pedophiles, exhibitionists, and homosexuals referred to the Forensic Clinic of the Toronto Psychiatric Hospital between April, 1956 and July, 1959 revealed that the form these offenses took varied in the extent of their occurrence. The sexual acts ranged from sexual intercourse (coitus) to immature gratification violations. Actual penetration of children in coitus was rare among sexual acts. Cases of statutory rape or carnal knowledge, involving girls of 14 and above, were somewhat more common, but they were committed by a different group of offenders. Although sadistic acts against children were relatively rare and were atypical for pedophiles, they were highly publicized and dominated the public conception of the typical sex offender.

Exhibitionism and adult homosexuality cases were the major deviation coming to the attention of the courts. Most exhibitionists exposed themselves to adults rather than children. The known cases of adult homosexuality, however, were only a fraction of the total volume. Heterosexual pedophilia, the Forensic Clinic study revealed, generally took the form of looking, showing, fondling or being fondled, acts often reflecting the physical and emotional immaturity of the offender and the sexual appeal of the victim. Pedophilic attraction represented an incomplete growth and maturity, a regression from adult life to childhood, or a general modification of sex drive in old age.[17] Pedophilic activity, the Toronto study noted, was distributed among three distinct age groups which reached the highest activity level in puberty, the mid-to-late 30's, and the mid-to-late 50's.[18] While a small minority of chronic offenders continued to engage in pedophilic activity throughout their lives, most pedophiles concentrated their activity in one of the three peak periods. Pedophilia, the Toronto study revealed, can be divided into adolescent, middle-aged, and senescent pedophilia.[19]

The greatest number of pedophilic offenses were committed by middle-aged offenders. The majority of victims had not only known the offender previously but had also frequented the place where the offender made contact. Since the victim frequently participated willingly in the sexual activity, emotional damage more often occurred as a result of ensuing adult hysteria or prosecutor interrogation than from the act

---

[16] Wheeler, *op. cit.*, p. 99.

[17] Mohr *et al.*, *op.* cit., p. 19. Refer also to the Joint State Government Commission, *The Dangerous Sex Offender* (Harrisburg: State of Pennsylvania, 1963).

[18] *Ibid.*, p. 20.

[19] *Ibid.*, pp. 20–21.

itself.[20] Pedophilic offenders, the study revealed, were not only at the level of intelligence and education of the general population but they also came from all occupational groups. The offenders were often inclined toward artistic concerns. They were more often isolated from adult social contacts than the average person. Many of their social outlets, the Toronto group found, came in youth work or church youth group activity. Two thirds of the 55 persons studied in the pedophilic group participated in religious activities.

Sexual psychopath laws

More than 13 states have legislated sexual psychopath laws, establishing administrative procedures for custody, treatment, and release of sexual offenders. On the assumptions that sex crimes were growing in the community, that treatment could best be accomplished in penal or psychiatric institutions, and that punishment would control the supposed increase, many states quickly followed Illinois in legally defining (largely inadequately) in 1939, the nature of a sexual psychopath. Although the laws were passed in the name of science, little scientific data supported their enactment. Currently viewed as legislative mistakes, they are increasingly being challenged on grounds that sex offenders are less likely to repeat their crimes than are other offenders, that few sex offenders present a grave or serious social danger, that current psychiatric techniques cannot distinguish between the potentially dangerous and nondangerous, that techniques of treating sexual offenders have not been evaluated, that definitions of the sexual psychopath are vague and unreliable, and that the laws tend to deny, if not eliminate, the due process of alleged offenders. Since the laws were often open-ended, they prescribed no maximum-sentence safeguard. Because psychiatrists could not guarantee that the offender would not repeat a sex offense, minor offenders were often incarcerated for a longer period than was either necessary or expedient. One Illinois offender, for example, served more than 10 years after having been convicted of the three separate "sex crimes" of window peeping, propositioning a prostitute, and jostling a woman in public location.

Sexual psychopath laws are under current attack because they are said to be scientifically, legally, and socially invalid. The singularistic moral philosophy upon which they are based has been challenged by the conflicting value and cultural systems which are characteristic of ethnic, religious, and social pluralism. Criteria for control of sex offenders, therefore, have shifted from a strict moral to a more pragmatic

[20] *Ibid.*, p. 37. Refer to Thomas J. Meyers, "Psychiatric Examination of the Sexual Psychopath," *Journal of Criminal Law, Criminology, and Police Science,* Vol. 56, No. 1 (March, 1965), pp. 27–31.

frame of reference. The English Wolfenden Report and the American Model Penal Code, rejecting a strict moral definition, hold that the potential social harm involved in the act should be the key determinant in the codification of sex laws. Recognizing that many laws are unenforcible, the modern pragmatic movement has emphasized a personal control of self-indulgence rather than group moral control through legislative processes. The Wolfenden Report led the British Parliament to eliminate proscriptive laws against private homosexuality by consenting adults, except those in government. The American debate over legalization of homosexuality, as well as over abortion, continues.

NARCOTIC OR DRUG OFFENSES

The attempt to control narcotic or drug offenses has centered in criminal enforcement and penal sanctions. Legally, addiction is not a crime. An addict, however, in his continual search for drugs and means by which to purchase drugs, inevitably comes in contact with the police. With few exceptions, however, the sale, purchase, or possession of drugs are state and/or federal criminal offenses. Some states prosecute those who possess needles or syringes designed for nonmedical opiate use. Others punish known or convicted addicts under vagrancy statutes designed to lessen contacts between addicts and pushers. Because the addict perpetually lives on the fringe of disclosure, he is highly susceptible to police pressures.

Current drug addiction laws are differentiated into two general types: (1) those involving the possession, purchase, sale, and transfer of narcotics in violation of state or federal narcotics laws, and (2) those prohibiting the commission of other crimes in order to gain the necessary funds for the purchase of narcotic drugs. The narcotic addict, like the drinking offender, commits criminal acts in relation to his addiction; theft by addicts, therefore, is usually a means to an end rather than an end in itself. Since he is personally unstable, the narcotic addict is rarely found among professional and organized criminals or racketeers. His actions are usually stimulated by the need to gain access to the narcotic which his body craves, and his primary effort is exerted toward the guarantee of an adequate drug or narcotic supply. Drinking offenders have been responsible for a large number of murders, rapes, assaults, and armed robberies. Narcotic addicts under the influence of the depressant drugs, on the other hand, are rarely stimulated to sex offenses or other crimes against the person. While some women become prostitutes in order to support the habit, male addicts generally do not engage in sexual violations. The police often claim that criminality develops after addiction, but the exact relationship between addiction and traditional forms of crime is unclear. The addict possesses strong feelings of personal inadequacy and general dependency. Narcotic arrests represent a mere fraction of the annual criminal volume. Narcotic law offenders, however, tend to repeat their violations.

The belief that narcotic violations could be controlled by the imposition of severe sentences led to coercive legislation following World War II. The growth in reported addiction led to the introduction of mandatory minimum sentences of 2 years for the first, 5 years for the second, and 10 years for the third and subsequent narcotic and marihuana offenses. Suspended sentences and probation were prohibited for second offenders. Even more severe sentences were legislated in 1956, when the minimum sentences for the unlawful importation or sale of drugs was raised to 5 years for the first offense and 10 years for the second and subsequent offenses. Penalties for unlawful possession remained at 2, 5, and 10 years. Suspensions of sentence, probation, and parole were prohibited for all but the first unlawful possession offense.

The use of narcotics has continued to grow in spite of the severity of the imposed punishment, a trend well documented by the increasing number of narcotic violators in the federal prison population. In 1950, only 2,017 drug law violators, 11.2 percent of all persons incarcerated in the federal prisons, were confined. All were then eligible for parole. The 3,998 drug law violators confined in the federal prisons in 1965, on the other hand, represented 17.9 percent of all incarcerated persons in the federal system. The average sentence served by the violator was 87.6 months, and more than 75 percent of these offenders were ineligible for parole.

The recent tendency to establish high and arbitrary minimum sentences has made the local judge a mere rubber stamp of the Congress or state legislature. The discretionary power of the court, an essential ingredient to a functional system of justice, has been replaced by a legislative demand to enact the legislator's inflexible will. Instead, state and federal law, the President's Commission recommends, should give enough discretionary power to the court and correctional agencies to enable them to deal flexibly with violators, giving consideration to the nature and seriousness of the offense, the prior record of the offender, and other relevant information or circumstances.[21]

The more recent Federal Drug Abuse Control amendments of 1965 limited the manufacture, distribution, and sale of designated drugs to persons or groups, whether narcotics pusher, wholesale druggist, or li-

---

[21] The President's Commission on Law Enforcement and the Administration of Justice, *Task Force Report: Narcotic and Drug Abuse* (Washington, D.C.: U.S. Government Printing Office, 1967), p. 12. For a basic discussion of the narcotic problem, see Daniel M. Wilner, *Narcotics* (New York: McGraw-Hill Book Co., 1965), Isidor Chein *et. al.*, *The Road to H* (New York: Basic Books Inc., Publishers, 1964), Reneé Buse, *The Deadly Silence* (Garden City, N.Y.: Doubleday & Co., Inc., 1965). The latter volume is a popular treatment of the issue.

censed physician. Placing restrictions on the refilling of prescriptions, the act required each drug producer, distributor, and retailer to maintain strict inventories, records, and receipts under penalty of law. While all amphetamines and barbituates were automatically included in these provisions, other sections of the law allowed the government to prohibit any depressant, stimulant or hallucinogenic drug. More than 22 drugs, including all hallucinogens and three tranquilizers, were quickly proscribed under the amendments' control provisions. Steps may be taken in the near future to lessen the penalties on the use of marihuana, however.

The Bureau of Drug Abuse and Control of the Food and Drug Administration supervises the control and distribution of all narcotics and drugs insofar as its resources allow. Although the importation or sale of heroin is prohibited in the United States, less than an estimated 10 percent of all heroin entering the country is ever seized or discovered by customs officers or narcotics agents. The Bureau of Drug Abuse is expected to have 500 agents assigned to nine fields in 1970.

Since little is known about the overall effects of illicit drug use or drug distribution procedures and organization, narcotic control efforts have been focused upon the apprehension of the addict and street supplier. Working in reverse, enforcement agencies have attempted, without much success, to use the addict as an informant in their attempt to gain convictions against the upper echelons of the narcotic distribution system.[22] Wide variations in state narcotic statutes have made their task even more difficult. Legislative, enforcement, and control procedures have been undermined by the increased numbers of middle-class users of marihuana and LSD, who have confused the narcotic and drug problem for the public. Although many police officers believe that the user of marihuana will automatically progress to heroin addiction, this assumption remains unverified. The large numbers of marihuana users who do not graduate to heroin addiction appear, in fact, to undermine this assumption.

The powerful stimulant cocaine no longer provides a major form of drug abuse. The use of marihuana, on the other hand, has reached a new high among middle-class Americans. Marihuana comes from the dried leaves and female flowers of the hemp plant (*Cannabis sativa*). It is variously known as grass, pot, tea, gage, reefers, hash, and other names. Marihuana smoke either stimulates or depresses the user, depending upon his personality. Its, sale, possession, and use are illegal. Some antimarihuana laws are essentially tax statutes designed to raise revenue.

---

[22] *Ibid.*, p. 8. See Gilbert Sandler, "The Statutory Presumption in Federal Narcotic Prosecutions," *Journal of Criminal Law, Criminology, and Police Science,* Vol. 57, No. 11 (March, 1966), pp. 7–16, and *Drug Arrests and Dispositions in California* (Sacramento: Bureau of Criminal Statistics, State Department of Justice, 1962).

Few "pot" handlers, however, have registered under the provisions of the narcotic laws to act as importers or wholesalers of the product.

Hallucinogens, particularly LSD, have been kept from general circulation, since they are powerful and dangerous drugs. Minute amounts of LSD, for example, can induce prolonged psychosis and suicidal impulses, as well as the acting out of character disorders and sexual urges. The activation of previously latent psychosis and even the reappearance of the drug effect at a later time are also possible.[23]

The 1961 Report of the Joint Committee on Narcotic Drugs of the American Bar Association and the American Medical Association noted that the major increase in drug addiction immediately following World War II largely occurred in minority areas of large metropolitan centers. Although many states and the federal government passed legislation designed to control drug usage through the infliction of severe penalties, the core problem, the committee noted, was largely bypassed. Severe punishments and coercive prison sentences, it argued, are hardly rational approaches to the narcotic problem.[24] Since narcotic addiction involves a physical and psychological drug dependence, simple coercion without due consideration of personality factors merely subverts the real issues.

Further research, the committee held, should be encouraged in order to ascertain whether the problem of addiction is best aided by open community clinics or by closed state and federal institutions. The causes of the high addict relapse rate must be investigated; solutions must be sought. The relationship between the high price of illicit drugs and crimes committed to obtain money to purchase the drug, too, must be probed more fully.[25] The reasons why addicts rarely commit violent or sex crimes and attempt to withdraw from world activity rather than to seek status or monetary reward through major criminal acts need further investigation. Ultimately, further research, the committee recommended, must be undertaken in the five major areas of out-patient treatment, causation and relapse factors, drug addiction prevention programs,

[23] *Ibid.*, p. 5. See John C. Ball, "Two Patterns of Narcotic Drug Addiction in the United States," *Journal of Criminal Law, Criminology, and Police Science,* Vol. 56, No. 2 (June, 1965), pp. 203–11.

[24] *Drug Addiction: Crime or Disease? The Interim and Final Reports Joint Committee of the American Bar Association and the American Medical Association* (Bloomington, Ind.: Indiana University Press, 1961), p. 63. Also note Emanuel Celler, "An Alternative Proposal for Dealing with Drug Addiction," *Federal Probation* (June, 1963), p. 24, Samuel C. McMorris, "The Decriminalization of Narcotic Addiction," *American Criminal Law Quarterly,* Vol. 3, No. 2 (Winter, 1965), pp. 84–88; Richard H. Kuh, "Civil Commitment for Narcotic Addicts," *Federal Probation* (June, 1963), p. 21; and Lewis Yablonsky, *The Tunnel Back: Synanon* (New York: Macmillan Co., 1965).

[25] *Ibid.*, p. 165. Alfred R. Lindeswith, *Opiate Addiction* (Bloomington, Ind.: Indiana University Press, 1947) offers a basic early discussion of the narcotic problem. For a report of Hong Kong addiction turn to Albert G. Hess, *Chasing the Dragon* (New York: Free Press, 1965).

narcotic drugs and drug addiction legislation, and narcotic law administration.[26]

The Bureau of Narcotics identified 57,199 known opiate addicts, nearly 52,000 of whom were addicted to heroin, at the end of 1965. Although the figures were undoubtedly incomplete, some estimates ranging as high as 200,000 actual addicts, fewer addicts are now believed to exist in proportion to the population than in previous American history. While more than one half of all known heroin addicts live in New York, large numbers also reside in California, Illinois, Michigan, New Jersey, Maryland, Pennsylvania, Texas, and the District of Columbia. The addict tends to be an urban male between 21 and 30, poorly educated, unskilled, and member of an ethnic minority.[27] Since the Uniform Narcotic Drug Act (Harrison Narcotic Act of 1914) prohibits the importation, possession, unauthorized sale or purchase, and manufacture of heroin, such transactions are criminal acts. Much of the heroin is imported from the Middle East. By the time it reaches the American addict, it usually has been highly diluted in order to stretch its value.

Although the rehabilitation of narcotic addicts has been attempted by the federal government at Lexington, Kentucky, and other locations, through intensive treatment, the relapse rate of addicts has reached as high as 90 percent. However, new insights into possible methods for treating and curing addiction have come from the efforts of the Black Muslims and Synanon to help narcotic and drug addicts to return to normal life. The Black Muslim effort has been largely limited to blacks and involves a high degree of personal commitment to a fundamentalist-type religious system. Working in prisons and in the community to "redeem" and reorient addicts, the Muslims claim greater success than have been evident to date in federal programs.

The Synanon approach is an outgrowth of the efforts of Charles E. Dederich, a former member of Alcoholics Anonymous, who extended small-group and community techniques to the treatment of narcotic addicts by creating a self-help cure station in Santa Monica, California. Using ex-addicts to provide understanding and support to addicted persons, the Synanon project has cut the relapse rate to as low as 20 percent. The success of this approach has led to additional efforts to expand this program into several prisons. At Nevada State Prison, for example, the program had an unexpected consequence when a group of nonaddicts also joined the effort in order to overcome personality weaknesses.[28]

---

[26] *Ibid.*, p. 161. *See* Alfred R. Lindeswith, *The Addict and the Law* (Bloomington, Ind.: Indiana University Press, 1965).

[27] President's Commission, *op. cit.*, p. 3. *Refer* to Isidor Chein, "Narcotics Use among Juveniles," in John A. O'Donnell and John C. Ball (eds.) *Narcotic Addiction* (New York: Harper & Row, Publishers, 1966), pp. 123–41, and Jeremy Larner, *The Addict in the Streets* (New York: Grove Press, Inc., 1965).

[28] Lewis Yablonsky, *Synanon: The Tunnel Back* (Baltimore, Md.: Penguin Books, Inc., 1969), pp. 334–43. Also see Rita Volkman and Donald R. Cressey, "Differential

The 50 black narcotic law violators in the sample of 400 Negro offenders studied by Julian Roebuck at the District of Columbia Reformatory
during 1954–55 revealed that drug offenders were generally younger
than other criminals and possessed average intelligence (see Table 6–1).
Coming from more favorable family, school, and community origins,
drug addicts possessed strong family ties. Although infrequently members of delinquent gangs, 86 percent of the drug addicts maintained
contact with adult criminals in their adolescence. Overprotected and
dominated by maternal concern, the addicts expressed an inability to
govern their own behavior. Although 49 had previously been married,
only 9 were currently married. The addict lived a cheap existence in
a rooming house close to drug sources in self-imposed isolation. Nearly
50 percent of the addicts performed as jazz musicians in local nightclubs.
Of the 50 offenders, 43 had never been arrested before their first narcotic
apprehension. Although the addict periodically engaged in the sale of
drugs to other persons on the street, his immediate goal was simply
to sustain his own habit rather than to engage in professional
criminality.[29]

The average daily cost of heroin for the 991 narcotic offenders arrested
in New York City in May, 1965, was $14.34,[30] a sum largely raised
through prostitution or property crime. Since the addict could only realize between one fifth to one third of the value of stolen merchandise
in resale, he had to steal property worth approximately $50 in order
to gain the average $15 needed for daily drug purchases. Only 11.1
percent of those arrested for property felonies by the New York Police
Department in 1965 were admitted drug users, however. Even fewer,
2 percent, were arrested for selected felonies against the person. Approximately 9.8 percent of New York arrests for petit larceny involved admitted drug users. Almost 40 percent, however, of the average population
of 10,000 persons under the supervision of the New York City Police
Department of Corrections in 1966 possessed a history of drug use.[31]
An average of 8 percent of all persons admitted to federal prisons or
other penal institutions during the fiscal years 1956–65 admitted drug
use.

In 1966, the Continuing Criminal Careers Program of the FBI identi-

Association and the Rehabilitation of Drug Addicts" in O'Donnell and Ball *op.
cit.*, pp. 209–33.
[29] Julian Roebuck, *Criminal Typology* (Springfield, Ill.: Charles C. Thomas, Publisher, 1966), p. 123. See Harold Firestone, "Narcotics and Criminality," *Narcotic
Addiction*, pp. 141–64.
[30] President's Commission, *op. cit.*, p. 10. A shorter version of the report is found
in the President's Commission on Law Enforcement and Administration of Justice,
Commission Report: The Challenge of Crime in a Free Society (Washington, D.C.:
U.S. Government Printing Office, 1967), pp. 211–32. A later December, 1965, sample
spent an average of $14.04 daily on narcotics.
[31] *Ibid.*, p. 11. See Edwin M. Schur, *Crimes Without Victims* (Englewood Cliffs,
N.J.: Prentice-Hall, Inc., 1965), pp. 120–68.

TABLE 6–1
Comparison of offenders with a single pattern of narcotic drug law offenses with all other offenders

Selected Social and Personal Attributes	Drug Offenders (N = 50) N.W.C.*	All Others (N = 350) N.W.C.	Sign of X²
Reared in more than one home...........	6	155	0.01
Mother figure southern migrant..........	9	165	0.01
Mother figure domestic servant..........	29	271	0.01
Dependent family.....................	33	263	N.S.†
Family broken by desertion.............	4	136	0.01
Demoralized family...................	8	188	0.01
Criminality in family.................	6	165	0.01
Mother figure dominant................	41	178	0.01
Inadequate supervision—father..........	28	168‡	0.01
Inadequate supervision—mother.........	45	237	0.01
Conflict in family.....................	10	224	0.01
Overt hostility toward father............	9	162	0.01
Overt hostility toward mother..........	7	72	N.S.
Disciplinary problem at home...........	3	116	0.01
History of running away...............	8	177	0.01
Inveterate gambler....................	7	163	0.01
Problem drinker......................	3	190	0.01
Weak parental family structure..........	16	198	0.01
No parental family ties................	18	264	0.01
Reared in urban area..................	47	287	N.S.
Reared in slum area...................	29	222	0.05
Living in slum when arrested............	34	267	N.S.
History of school truancy..............	12	191	0.01
Disciplinary problem at school..........	5	183	0.01
Street trades as juvenile...............	16	187	0.01
No marital ties.......................	41	247	N.S.
Juvenile delinquent companions..........	17	219	0.01
Member delinquent gang...............	6	136	0.01
Adjudicated juvenile delinquent..........	5	172	0.01
Committed as juvenile.................	4	142	0.01
Police contact prior to age 18...........	14	207	0.01
Criminal companions as juvenile.........	43	120	0.01
Drug addict..........................	50	19	0.01
Positive attitude toward work...........	15	138	N.S.

* Number with characteristic.
† Not significant.
‡ Based on those with fathers.
Source: Julian Roebuck *Criminal Typology* (Springfield, Ill.: Charles C. Thomas, Publisher, 1966), p. 133.

fied 4,385 persons as heroin users who averaged a 12-year criminal career marred by an average of 10 arrests. Of their average of 10 arrests, 6 were for violent crimes. Crimes against property accounted for 74 percent of the arrests. However, the nonnarcotic criminal population evidence a similar distribution of offenses. Of all heroin users, the FBI revealed

72 percent had been arrested for some other criminal act before their first narcotic arrest. Although preliminary evidence suggests a correlation between narcotic addiction and property crime, no valid data yet exists to support the hypothesis.[32]

The use of drugs is not limited to narcotic addicts. The California Bureau of Narcotic Enforcement, for example, estimated that five and one half doses of opiates for every man, woman, and child in the United States were consumed in 1963.[33] A pilot study by Blum, Brownstein, and Stone revealed that 67 percent of 200 adults interviewed indicated that they had used medical opiates. While 10 percent of those who admitted past medical use of opiates said that they used the drugs only occasionally, 5 percent admitted their regular dependence upon an opiate.[34] They concluded that although continued usage does not automatically assume the presence or absence of drug addiction, it does presume that the constant user's behavior was not aberrant enough to bring him to the attention of enforcement officers.

Richard H. Blum suggests that up to 4 percent of the metropolitan population has experimented with addictive drugs without detection or apprehension. Although between 50 and 75 percent of all adult Americans have been exposed to opiates, only 1 in 1,000 Americans has become an active illicit addict. While exposure to opiates may lead to addiction, the chances are only 1 in 500 that exposure alone will result in addiction. Addiction seems to depend upon socioeconomic and personal circumstances. Addiction risks for patients given opiates in medical treatment are much lower than for slum delinquents.[35] Medical doctors, on the other hand, are disproportionately represented among drug addicts.

ALCOHOL VIOLATIONS

Crimes involving the use of alcohol include violations of laws governing the production, storage, packaging, distribution, and sale of alcoholic

---

[32] *Loc. cit.* Earlier data concerning the narcotic problem is given in *Illicit Narcotics Traffic: Hearings before the Subcommittee on Improvements in the Federal Criminal Code* (Washington, D.C.: U.S. Government Printing Office, 1956), and *Proceedings—White House Conference on Narcotic and Drug Abuse* (Washington, D.C.: U.S. Government Printing Office, 1962).

[33] Richard H. Blum, "Mind-Altering Drugs and Dangerous Behavior: Narcotics," President's Commission, *Task Force Report: Narcotic and Drug Abuse*, p. 46.

[34] *Ibid.*, p. 47. Also note Samuel Levine, "Narcotic Addition as Viewed by a Federal Narcotic Agent," *Federal Probation* (December, 1964), p. 30; Charles T. Hurley, "Anti-Narcotic Testing: A Physician's Point of View, *Federal Probation* (June, 1963), p. 32 and Thorwald T. Brown, "Narcotics and Nalline: Six Years of Testing," *Federal Probation*, June, 1963, p. 27.

[35] *Ibid.*, p. 48. Refer to John A. O'Donnell, "The Lexington Program for Narcotic Addicts," *Federal Probation* (March, 1962), p. 55, and Alfred R. Lindesmith, "Basic Problems in the Social Psychology of Addiction and a Theory," in O'Donnell and Ball, *op. cit.*, pp. 91–109.

beverages; infractions of laws prohibiting public drunkenness; violations of regulatory laws limiting the circumstances and places where alcohol may be purchased and consumed; and other violations committed under the influence of alcohol. Although more than 35 percent of all annual arrests in the United States are for *drunkenness,* additional persons committing more serious crimes while intoxicated are included within other crime categories (for example, drunken driving, assault, or murder). Between 40 and 50 percent of all alleged offenders are drunk at the time they are jailed. The profile of the chronic drunk often indicates that he possesses low educational and job achievement. He has frequently participated in a variety of other criminal acts. Often a product of a lower-class home, he tends to become less felonious after 35 and to become increasingly dependent upon alcohol.

The use of alcohol impedes self-control and critical judgment. Marvin Wolfgang, for example, found a significant relationship between violent homicide and the presence of alcohol in the offender in his five-year study of 588 Philadelphia homicides. Sixty-four percent (374) of the 588 cases involved alcohol. While 9 percent (54) of the homicides involved a drinking victim, 11 percent (64) involved drinking offenders. In nearly 70 percent (374) of the cases, both the victim and the offender had been drinking.[36] An earlier Columbus, Ohio, study of 882 alleged offenders arrested during or immediately following the commission of a felony in the period between 1951 and 1953 revealed that 64 percent of all offenders were under the influence of alcohol at the time of their offense. Crimes involving physical violence, police chemist Lloyd Shupe discovered, were frequently associated with intoxication. Cutting and stabbing assaults by persons under the influence of alcohol were 11 times more common than similar assaults by sober persons. Although property crimes were less frequently related to drinking, the carrying of concealed weapons was eight times more common among persons influenced by alcohol. Nonfelonious assaults were 10 times as high among alcohol users, and shootings and murders by persons under the influence of alcohol were 4 times as frequent.[37]

A statistical comparison was made by Julian Roebuck of the personal and social characteristics of 40 offenders showing a double pattern of drunkenness and assault included in a sample of 400 Negro offenders

---

[36] Marvin F. Wolfgang, *Patterns in Criminal Homicide* (Philadelphia: University of Pennsylvania, 1958), pp. 136–37. For a discussion of the drinking-driver problem, see Lowell Bradford, "Drinking Driver Enforcement Problems," *Journal of Criminal Law, Criminology, and Police Science,* Vol. 57, No. 4 (December, 1966), pp. 518–20.

[37] Lloyd M. Shupe, "Alcohol and Crime," *Journal of Criminal Law, Criminology, and Police Science,* Vol. 44, (January–February, 1954), pp. 661–65. Also see Lloyd M. Shupe and K. M. Dubowski, "Ethyl Alcohol in Blood and Urine," *American Journal of Clinical Pathology,* Vol. 22, (1952), pp. 901–10.

at the District of Columbia Reformatory in Lorton, Virginia. It revealed that the *double-pattern offender,* as opposed to most other offenders, came significantly more often from patriarchal than from matriarchal homes (see Table 6–2). Although the group possessed fewer police contacts before the age of 18 and were less often brought to the attention of the juvenile court, they provoked, Roebuck discovered, significant

TABLE 6–2
Comparison of double pattern of drunkenness and assault with all other offenders

Selected Social and Personal Attributes	Drinkers and Assaulters $(N = 40)$ N.W.C.*	All Others $(N = 360)$ N.W.C.	Sign of X^2
Reared in more than one home	15	146	N.S.†
Mother figure southern migrant	30	144	0.01
Mother figure domestic servant	38	262	0.01
Dependent family	28	268	N.S.
Family broken by desertion	8	132	N.S.
Demoralized family	5	191	0.01
Criminality in family	7	164	0.01
Mother figure dominant	8	211	0.01
Inadequate supervision—father	39‡	157	0.01
Inadequate supervision—mother	31	251	N.S.
Conflict in family	33	201	0.01
Overt hostility toward father	23	148	0.01
Overt hostility toward mother	11	68	N.S.
Disciplinary problem at home	11	108	N.S.
History of running away	2	183	0.01
Inveterate gambler	28	142	0.01
Problem drinker	40	153	0.01
Weak parental family structure	13	201	0.01
No parental family ties	22	260	0.05
Reared in urban area	37	297	N.S.
Reared in slum area	13	238	0.01
Living in slum when arrested	31	270	N.S.
History of school truancy	12	191	0.01
Disciplinary problem at school	28	160	0.01
Street trades as juvenile	9	194	0.01
No marital ties	13	275	0.01
Juvenile delinquent companions	8	228	0.01
Member delinquent gang	3	139	0.01
Adjudicated juvenile delinquent	4	173	0.01
Committed as juvenile	4	142	0.01
Police contact prior to age 18	6	215	0.01
Criminal companions as juvenile	5	158	0.01
Drug addict	0	69	0.01
Positive attitude toward work	30	123	0.01

* Number with characteristic.
† Not significant.
‡ Based on those with fathers.
Source: Roebuck, *Criminal Typology,* p. 169.

scholastic disciplinary problems, including truancy and home runaway. Possessing fewer delinquent companions, they were less often members of juvenile gangs. They showed more positive work attitudes and were more often married. Yet the double-pattern offenders revealed a disproportionate tendency toward gambling and alcoholism. Of the 40 dual-pattern offenders, 35 had migrated from rural and small-town areas, becoming the first of their family to become city dwellers. They had backgrounds of a strong Baptist fundamentalism which prohibited drinking, gambling, card playing, and dancing. Family members were frequently dominated by a rigid and self-righteous father whose discipline was erratic and severe.[38] Physical violence, Roebuck hypothesized, was a personality pattern adopted in childhood as the juvenile adjusted to society.

Public drunkenness is treated unevenly in the United States. More than 2 million arrests occurred for drunkenness during 1966, accounting for one of every three American arrests. Many drunks or alcoholics, however, are never arrested or prosecuted. Since some states have no laws prohibiting drunkenness, drunks are arrested only for other offenses (for example, disorderly conduct). In other states, overlapping local ordinances and state laws are both used in the attempt to regulate alcoholic behavior. While the most common maximum sentence is 30 days in jail, some ordinances or laws provide for penalties which generally range from five days to six months. Habitual drunks may receive a two-year sentence in some states. A District of Columbia committee on prisons, probation, and parole found in 1957 that six chronic offenders had been arrested for 1,409 acts of drunkenness and had served a total of 125 years in penal institutions.[39] A second study revealed that nearly one fifth of all persons arrested for drunkenness in Los Angeles during 1964 accounted for approximately two thirds of the total drunkenness arrest volume during the year. Several were arrested as often as 18 times.

Although police practice and policies vary, many arrests are simply made to protect the drunk from predatory thieves or robbers. In several jurisdictions, the offender is quickly released once he has become sober. In others, he is released only if he posts bond and guarantees his court appearance. If taken to court, the drunk is quickly processed, often with 15 to 25 fellow drinkers. Since his arrest is taken as an indication of guilt, his case is quickly disposed of, sometimes in as little as three minutes. If not released, the alcohol offender may be sentenced to several

---

[38] Julian Roebuck, *Criminal Typology* (Springfield, Ill.: Charles C. Thomas, Publisher, 1967), p. 162.

[39] The President's Commission on Law Enforcement and the Administration of Justice, *Task Force Report: Drunkenness* (Washington, D.C.: U.S. Government Printing Office, 1967), p. 1.

days or weeks in jail. One homeless alcoholic, the President's Commission on Law Enforcement and the Administration of Justice discovered, faced arrest 31 times in a period of four months and six days, a feat only possible if he were arrested once out of every two days that he appeared on the streets of the District of Columbia.[40]

Outmoded attitudes continue to dominate the police and court approach to alcoholism. Recognition that alcoholism is a form of addiction and a disease has only slowly permeated the American enforcement and justice systems. Arrests, for drunkenness, as a result, are most often completed in order to remove an unsightly object or community nuisance from public view. Since the time spent processing drunks diverts enforcement personnel from more serious tasks, better use of police manpower can be achieved only by new legislation which would remove the crime of drunkenness from the criminal code. At present the homeless and the poor are most often arrested, while the home drinker or social inebriate are largely undetected by the police.

The President's Commission suggested that drunkenness should be prosecuted only when it involves disorderly conduct or some other criminal offense. Since drunkenness is a personal health problem, it can best be approached by the use of detoxification centers, staffed by civilian personnel, where the individual can receive adequate assistance in facing his problem. Since alcoholism, the fourth largest American health problem, reflects a serious physical and emotional condition, after-care facilities, the President's Commission suggests, should be coordinated in order to bring about the successful social reintegration of the drinking offender. The "revolving door" policy of evening arrest and morning release does little to solve the problem of an estimated 5 million American alcoholics.

The costs of present procedures dictate a change in present policy. The city of Los Angeles, for example, spent an estimated $4 million during 1958 to handle alcohol offenders.[41] Mere incarceration in a local jail at an estimated $5 per day cost the city of Baltimore nearly $750,000 for custodial care during 1964 and 1965. Two million arrests for public drunkenness at an estimated cost of $50 per arrest for police, court, and correctional services suggest the major economic and social dislocation caused by the problem of drunkenness. Current procedures in most jurisdictions, however, do little to attack the basic causes of alcoholism (see Figure 6–2).

A disproportionate number of alcoholism arrests occur among those in the lower income groups, members of ethnic minorities, and those

---

[40] *Ibid.,* p. 3.
[41] David J. Pittman, "Public Intoxication and the Alcoholic Offender in American Society," President's Commission, *Task Force Report: Drunkenness,* p. 9. A concise presentation of pertinent data on the alcoholism problem is contained in David J. Pittman, *Alcoholism* (New York: Harper & Row, Publishers, 1967).

FIGURE 6–2
Model of the deviancy reinforcement cycle for public intoxication

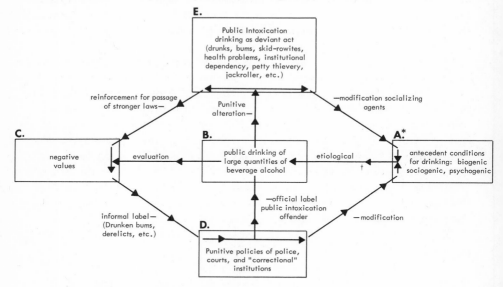

* Letters indicate theoretical sequence of events.
† Arrows indicate theoretical direction of influence.
Source: President's Commission on Law Enforcement and Administration of Justice, *Task Force Report*: *Drunkenness* (Washington, D.C.: U.S. Government Printing Office, 1967), p. 10.

dependent upon institutionalized living arrangements (for example, those living in social shelters, and members of the armed forces or merchant marine). Current jailing practices, David Pittman argues, undermine meaningful family and marital relationships, jeopardize possible employment, and generally encourage the kind of behavior which the arrest is believed to control. The jail has become little more than a public shelter where the drunk can regain his physical strength and mental faculties.[42]

A study by David Pittman and C. W. Gordon of 187 cases of men sentenced at least twice to a New York penal institution on a charge of public intoxication and incarcerated at the county jail revealed that the chronic police case drunk or inebriate offender possessed a mean age of 47.7 years. Two thirds of the Negroes and approximately one third of the whites were under 45 years of age. While black members of the sample possessed disproportionately lower-class backgrounds, coming from southern rural or small-town hometowns, white representatives were most frequently from English or Irish stock. Thirty-five per-

---

[42] *Ibid.*, p. 11. Also see David J. Pittman and C. W. Gordon, *Revolving Door: A Study of the Chronic Police Case Inebriate* (Glencoe: Free Press, 1958).

cent of the samples, for example, were Americans of Irish descent. Italians, on the other hand, only composed 2 percent of the total. Of the group under study, 42 percent were Protestant, 40 percent Roman Catholic, and 18 percent possessed no religious affiliation. Of this group, 42 percent were never married, 32 percent were separated, 19 percent were divorced, 6 percent were widowed, and 2 percent were living with their spouses before their most recent arrest. Of the sample who were married, 96 percent reported broken marriages, a markedly higher proportion than the national equivalent of 11 percent.[43] Seventy percent of the group possessed an eighth grade education or less. Of the sample, 68 percent were unskilled workers as opposed to 13 percent in the general population. The mean number of their arrests for all causes was 16.5. Of the sample, 31 percent had been previously arrested for intoxication, 32 percent on charges related to excessive use of alcohol, and 37 percent for serious violations including homicide, rape, robbery, or burglary.

AGGRAVATED ASSAULT

Aggravated assaults, similar to murder in their victim-offender relationships, most frequently occur in families or among neighbors and acquaintances. Of all 1968 serious assaults, 23 percent involved the use of firearms. Although knives or other sharp instruments were utilized in 31 percent of the assaults, other blunt objects or weapons inflicted the harm in 24 percent of the cases (see Table 6–3). Hands, fists, feet, and handy personal weapons accounted for another 21 percent of the aggravated assault volume. Of every 100 aggravated assaults known to the police, 66 resulted in a 1968 arrest. While cities of over 250,000 reported an attack rate of approximately 295 aggravated assaults per 100,000 inhabitants, the suburban (85) and rural (81) rates were substantially lower. The highest aggravated assault rate (180) was reported in the southern states. Although 30 percent of the aggravated assault arrests during 1968 were among persons under the age of 21, seven males were arrested for every one female. Blacks accounted for nearly 50 percent of all aggravated assault arrests during 1966; they were also the primary victims.[44]

An assault arrest did not automatically lead to a criminal charge

---

[43] *Ibid.,* p. 12. Marvin A. Block, "The Drinking Man's Philter," *Federal Probation* (September, 1963), pp. 25 ff., discusses the facets of the alcoholsim problem and its solution. See also George L. Maddox *et al., Drinking among Teenagers* (New Brunswick, N.J.: Rutgers Center for Alcohol Studies, 1964).

[44] *Uniform Crime Reports—1968,* p. 120. See Alex Pokorny, "Human Violence: A Comparison of Homicide, Aggravated Assault, Suicide and Attempted Suicide," *Journal of Criminal Law, Criminology, and Police Science,* Vol. 56, No. 4 (December, 1965), pp. 488–97.

TABLE 6–3

		Aggravated Assaults, Type of Weapon Used—Percent		
Region	Firearms	Knife or Other Cutting Instrument	Blunt Object or Other Dangerous Weapon	Personal Weapons
Northeastern states	15.7	34.5	30.7	19.1
North Central states	25.3	31.0	21.3	22.4
Southern states	26.5	32.0	20.9	20.7
Western states	22.5	25.6	26.1	25.8
Total	23.1	31.0	24.2	21.7

Source: *Uniform Crime Reports—1968*, p. 10.

or court conviction. Large numbers of victims, as in the past, were unwilling to cooperate with the police or to testify for the prosecution against their spouse, neighbor, or acquaintance. Nearly 4 out of 10 cases, therefore, resulted in either an acquittal or dismissal. Although 75 of every 100 persons arrested for aggravated assault were eventually charged by the police, only 49 percent of those adults charged were eventually convicted. An additional 14 percent either admitted guilt or were convicted on a lesser charge. Of all persons charged, 17 percent were referred to the juvenile court.[45]

A detailed study of assaults and assaulters in London during the decade between 1950 and 1960 revealed that nearly one half of all recorded crimes of violence involved attacks in and around public houses, cafes, and/or streets. One third of the violent attacks resulted from family and domestic disputes; another 12 percent involved attacks on police and civilians. Sexual assaults reached only 6 percent; other miscellaneous attacks accounted for only 2 percent of the total. The assault volume doubled in all categories during the decade, and violent street attacks showed an above-average increase. The victim and the offender were known to each other prior to the event in more than one half of the cases. The highest proportion of harm by strangers was inflicted in a sexual or street attack. The majority of these violent crimes were committed among working-class people in slum neighborhoods. Nearly 95 percent of all assailants were male. Two thirds were over 21. The proportion of victims and assailants under 21, however, increased significantly during the decade. Firearms were rarely used; more than one

[45] *Ibid.*, p. 11. See "Patterns of Violence," *The Annals,* Vol. 364 (March, 1966); the issue is given to a discussion of violence.

half of the assailants attacked their victims with physical force, most commonly kicking or punching. Although violent assaults, as researcher S. H. McClintock discovered, reflected indigenous violence patterns, only 3 percent of all victims were killed, disabled, disfigured, or detained in a hospital due to injuries for more than a month.[46]

Only 20 percent of the known offenders had been previously convicted of a violent crime, although nearly 50 percent had prior records for nonviolent offenses. While a major proportion of the offenders were aggressive or indicated unstable personality patterns, their aggressiveness was associated with heavy drinking patterns. A hard-core group of violent offenders, however, repeatedly used violence to escape detection in the commission of a property offense. Aggressiveness, stimulated by drinking or a social overemphasis on toughness or aggression, was part of the assaulter's way of life. Violent offenders, McClintock found, were disproportionately single, unskilled, residents of high-crime areas, and either divorced or separated if previously married.[47]

HOMICIDE

Homicide, generally divided into criminal and noncriminal homicide, varies in form from first-degree murder to justifiable homicide. Criminal homicide, chargeable upon the death of the victim within one year and one day from the time of the attack, includes *first-* and *second-degree* murder as well as *nonnegligent* (voluntary) and *negligent* (involuntary) manslaughter. First-degree murder, including both premeditation and malice aforethought, is the most serious of these homicide forms. Second-degree murder lacks the element of premeditation although it continues to possess the element of malice aforethought. Nonnegligent and negligent manslaughter, however, are primarily differentiated by the probability of a lethal outcome if the act were completed (for example, if a person is attacked with a switch blade, death may occur from a stabbing), as assumed in nonnegligent manslaughter. *Excusable homicide,* the killing in self-defense, and *justifiable homicide,* performed as a legal duty by a police officer or public executioner, are forms of noncriminal homicide.[48]

---

[46] Roebuck, *op. cit.,* p. 159.

[47] *Ibid.,* p. 160. Refer to Georges Sorel, *Reflections on Violence* (Glencoe: Free Press, 1950).

[48] Marvin E. Wolfgang, "A Sociological Analysis of Criminal Homicide," *Studies in Homicide* (New York: Harper & Row, Publishers, 1967), p. 16. See also Marvin E. Wolfgang, "A Sociological Analysis of Criminal Homicide," *Federal Probation* (March, 1961), pp. 48 ff. Under certain instances a felony which results in an accidental or unintended murder may result in a charge of murder under felony-murder provisions. See Paul A. James, "The Felony Murder Doctrine," *American Criminal Law Quarterly,* Vol. 1, No. 2 (February, 1965), pp. 33–46.

Homicide data comes from two primary sources: (1) the death statistics of the National Office of Vital Statistics and (2) the FBI's *Uniform Crime Reports*. While FBI data include all willful killings without due process as interpreted from police investigation within its categories of murder and nonnegligent manslaughter, deaths caused by negligence, attempted assaults, attempted murder, suicide, accidents, or justifiable homicide are excluded from the FBI's Crime Index. Murder and nonnegligent manslaughter constitute less than one-half of 1 percent of all index offenses; they comprise less than 2 percent of all violent crimes.

Of all murders reported in the United States, 47 percent occurred in the southern states. The north central (22 percent), northeastern (17), and western states (13) reflected noticeably lower patterns during 1968. While more homicides were committed during the summer months, October replaced December as the peak single murder month. Cities over 250,000 population reported 14.2 murder victims per 100,000 population, and the suburban and rural rates by comparison reached 3.3 and 6.3. More than six victims (6.8) per 100,000 inhabitants were reported in 1968.

TABLE 6–4

	Murder by Circumstance—Percent						
Region	Spouse Killing Spouse	Parent Killing Child	Other Family Killings	Romantic Triangle and Lovers Quarrels	Other Arguments	Known Felony Type	Suspected Felony Type
Northeastern	11.8	3.7	6.6	6.4	39.3	20.2	12.0
North Central states	13.3	3.6	10.7	6.4	39.4	20.1	6.5
Southern states	14.6	2.1	9.2	7.8	48.4	12.0	5.9
Western states	14.1	5.8	6.1	7.6	33.5	25.0	7.9
Total	13.7	3.3	8.7	7.2	42.2	17.4	7.5

Source: *Uniform Crime Reports—1968*, p. 8.

Murder victims, the 1968 *Uniform Crime Reports* noted, were predominantly male (75 percent). Of every 100 victims, 45 were white and 54 were black. The remaining 1 percent represented other ethnic or racial groups. Of the murder victims, 60 percent were between 20 and 45 years of age. Five males were arrested for murder for every one female.[49] A spouse was the victim in more than 50 percent of the intrafamily murders (see Table 6–4). In about 11 percent of the intrafamily cases parents murdered their own children. Seventeen percent of all 1968 murders were by-products of robberies, sex crimes, gangland

---

[49] *Uniform Crime Reports—1968*, pp. 6–8.

slayings, or other felonious acts. The wife was the victim of her husband in 54 percent of the cases, while the husband was murdered in 46 percent of the homicides involving a spouse. Of the husband-wife victims, 48 percent were white, 51 percent were black, and 1 percent were of other races. The female was the victim in 51 percent of those cases which involved lover's quarrels; the male, on the other hand, was the victim in 90 percent of the cases involving romantic triangles. Of the felony-type murder victims, 63 percent were white, 35 percent were black, and 2 percent represented other racial or ethnic groups or were not stated.[50]

Eighty-six percent of all known 1968 criminal homicides were cleared by an arrest. Although the majority of those arrested were above 18 years of age, juveniles under 18 accounted for 6 percent of all murder arrests. Nationally, the murder arrest rate reached 7.2 persons per 100,000 inhabitants. Cities over 250,000 population had a 14.5 arrest rate, suburban communities (3.4), and rural areas (4.0). Forty percent of all persons arrested for murder were under 25 years of age. Blacks were arrested for 60 percent of the murders and represented 54 percent of known 1968 victims. Only 64 percent of all adults arrested for murder, however, were eventually charged by the police. Although 43 percent of those charged were found guilty, 19 percent entered guilty pleas or were convicted on a lesser charge. Of those charged, 38 percent, however, were acquitted or faced dismissal of charges. The 9 percent of the murder cases which involved youth were referred to the juvenile court for action.[51]

The Philadelphia homicide study

The typical homicide offender, Marvin Wolfgang discovered in a study of 621 offenders arrested by the police for 588 cases of homicide in Philadelphia between 1948 and 1952, was a young male in his 20's who killed a man only slightly older than himself. Both participants were generally of the same race. The Negro murderer tended to use a knife in the commission of his crime. The Caucasian murderer, however, commonly beat his victim to death on the public street with his fists or feet. Nearly one half of the wives were killed in the bedroom. Wives often killed their husbands in the kitchen with a butcher knife.

Although 94 percent of the victims and offenders were of the same

[50] Ibid., p. 8. See John M. MacDonald, The Murderer and His Victim (Springfield, Ill.: Charles C. Thomas, Publisher, 1961).

[51] Ibid., p. 9. Refer to Robert C. Bensing and Oliver Schroeder, Jr., Homicide in an Urban Community (Springfield, Ill.: Charles C. Thomas, Publisher, 1960), and Alex D. Pokorny, "A Comparison of Homicide in Two Cities," Journal of Criminal Law, Criminology, and Police Science, Vol. 56, No. 4 (December, 1965), pp. 479–87.

race, they were of the same sex in only 64 percent of the cases. Of the 100 husband-wife homicides in the sample, 47 victims were husbands and 53 wives. While 41 percent of all women killed were murdered by their husbands, only 11 percent of the slain men were eliminated by their wives. Sixty-five percent of the Philadelphia offenders and 47 percent of the victims possessed a previous police arrest record.[52]

Whereas the Philadelphia mean annual victim and offender rates were 5.7 and 6.0 per 100,000 population, comparable victim rates at the time of the study ranged from a low of 2.3 in Milwaukee to 15.1 in Miami.[53]

Criminal homicide, Wolfgang discovered, was largely an unplanned act, often marked, however, by observable and predictable behavior patterns. Philadelphia Negro males, who committed an equivalent of 41.7 homicides per 100,000 inhabitants, were more likely to commit criminal homicide than Negro females. The Negro female rate (9.3), however, was greater than the white male (3.4) and white female (0.4) rate.[54] Although the female homicide rate was higher in England at that time, the British Isles reported no more criminal homicide than the city of Philadelphia in one year. Males between 20 and 24 evidenced the highest Philadelphia homicide rate (12.6 per 100,000). The highest victim rate was found in the age group between 25 and 34. Of all Philadelphia homicides, 39 percent were caused by stabbing, 33 percent by shooting, 22 percent by beatings, and 6 percent by other miscellaneous methods. Criminal homicides were more likely to occur during the weekend, especially on Saturday night between 8 P.M. and 2 A.M. However, 65 percent of the criminal homicides (380) occurred between 8 P.M. Friday night and midnight Sunday. The other 35 percent (208) filled the remaining days of the week. Sixty-five percent of the Philadelphia homicides, Wolfgang discovered, were inflicted within a 52-hour time span of a 168-hour week.[55]

Approximately one third of all Philadelphia homicide victims died within 10 minutes after the assault. Slightly less than three fifths succumbed within the first hour. Four fifths died within one day; only 5 percent lived more than 10 days after the assault. More homicides occurred in the home; otherwise, the highway, public street, alley, or field offered the most dangerous homicide locations. While 84 percent of the female offenders murdered males, 87 percent of all female victims were killed by males.[56]

The homicide offender often possessed a previous history of offenses

---

[52] Wolfgang, *Patterns*, pp. 222–37.
[53] *Ibid.*, p. 25.
[54] Wolfgang, *Studies in Homicide*, p. 18. Stuart Palmer, *A Study of Murder* (New York: Thomas Y. Crowell Co., 1960) presents a semipopular discussion of the murder problem.
[55] Wolfgang, *Patterns*, pp. 106–19.
[56] Wolfgang, *Studies in Homicide*, p. 21.

against the person. His criminal record revealed a larger proportion of arrests for aggravated assault than for all other types of property offenses combined.[57] The criminal homicide generally was caused by a domestic quarrel, altercation, act of jealousy, argument over money, or as a result of robbery. Most of the known victim-offender relationships were close, intimate, and frequent. Of all victim-offender relationships, 69 percent among males and 84 percent among females were of primary quality. In robbery-slaying cases the victim and the robber were most often strangers who were brought together by chance.[58]

Although middle- and upper-class homicidal acts may be stimulated by a sudden emotional crisis, they are more likely to betray evidence of major psychopathology or planned deliberation. The infrequency of upper- and middle-class homicide suggests that social and cultural variables are highly influential in the person's tendency or decision to commit homicide. Murder or manslaughter, for example, is more likely to occur if violence is a tolerable part of the personal and subcultural value system. The disproportionate black involvement in homicide, 4 to 10 times higher than the regional white rate, is largely a result of racial discrimination, social helplessness, and an exaggerated subcultural emphasis upon force.

International homicide data

Fewer than 7,500 murders, less than the average annual American rate, were known to the police in England and Wales between 1900 and 1949.[59] Between 1900 and 1960, the average number of murders known to the police varied from 3.6 to 4.4 per 1 million population. The most common English murder was performed by the husband on the wife, by parents on their children, or by a lover on a woman. Between 1900 and 1949, 161 persons who killed in connection with robbery and 19 who murdered police or prison officers were convicted. Two hundred twenty-four persons were convicted for killing a wife, husband, lover, or sweetheart.[60]

African homicide, Paul Bohannan found, ranged in annual rate from 0.7 to 11.6 per 100,000 inhabitants as compared to Wolfgang's identified Philadelphia male and female Negro rate of 24.0 per 100,000 during

---

[57] *Ibid.*, p. 23.

[58] Wolfgang, *Studies in Homicide*, p. 5. Harry J. Anslinger, *The Murderers: The Shocking Story of the Narcotic Gangs* (New York: Farrar, Straus, and Cuhady, 1962), presents a popularized and argumentative thesis that those who encourage addiction are also murderers.

[59] Terence Morris and Louis Blom-Cooper, "Homicide in England," *Studies in Homicide* (New York: Harper & Row, Publishers, 1967), p. 29.

[60] *Ibid.*, p. 33.

1948–52.[61] The murder of the husband by the wife rarely occurred in Africa. Women, who more frequently killed their children as a result of emotional stress or marital breakup, periodically followed the murder with an attempted or successful suicide. Comparative annual offender homicide rates per 100,000 inhabitants varied, Bohannan discovered, from 0.5 in Britain to between 1.1 and 11.6 among the Uganda tribes; from 2.3 to 15.1 among 18 American cities between 1948 and 1952, and from 2.5 to 7.4 in Ceylon.[62] Arthur L. Wood found that the Ceylonese rate had remained constant from the 1920's, while the suicide rate increased from about 5 to 7.3.[63] The largest percentage of homicides in Ceylon occurred in urban villages in the maritime area, where landlessness, unemployment, and subordinate status were frequent.

A typology of murderers

Psychiatrist Manfred Guttmacher suggests murderers and murder patterns can be grouped into 12 types. The *normal murderer* exhibits no marked psychopathology, but instead engages in murder as easily as a child plays with other children. Since normal murderers disproportionately come from deprived backgrounds, they are products of economic want and social misery. Undervaluing human life, they complete the greatest number of homicidal acts. A *sociopathic murderer,* on the other hand, wars with society; his victims tend to be persons who are nearby when he begins his war. Often a product of a cruel father and a hysterical-seductive mother, he overcompensates for his previous experiences through personal rebellion and social antagonism. The *alcoholic murderer* represents a third type of homicide offender. He commits murder when his inhibitions are released or when he attempts to defend himself against his alcohol influenced imagination. Although the *avenging murderer* acts to punish a former partner who has suddenly withdrawn from their exotic relationship, his homicide activity is primarily a personal defense mechanism. Sexual aggression in this murder type, no longer satisfied by the rejecting partner, is redirected to the former participant's death.

The *schizophrenic murderer* vents his hostility in homicide. Although schizophrenics rarely commit homicide, the act is more common among

[61] Paul Bohannan, "Patterns of Homicide among Tribal Societies in Africa," in Marvin E. Wolfgang (ed.), *Studies in Homicide* (New York: Harper & Row, Publishers, 1967), p. 217.

[62] *Ibid.*, p. 218. See also Paul Bohannan, *African Homicide and Suicide* (Princeton, N.J.: Princeton University Press, 1960).

[63] Arthur L. Wood, "Murder and Other Deviance in Ceylon," *Studies in Homicide* (New York: Harper & Row, Publishers, 1967), p. 242. Note also Stuart Palmer, "Murder and Suicide in Forty Non-Literate Societies," *Journal of Criminal Law, Criminology, and Police Science,* Vol. 56, No. 3 (September, 1965), pp. 320–24.

temporarily psychotic murderers. While their crime may suggest a psychotic act, evidence of psychosis is often undetected at the time of the psychiatric examination. These murderers, essentially lonely men, lack guilt or remorse. Not only do they alternate between fantasy and reality but their personality patterns evidence feelings of transient depression. Although they often dream of violent killings, mutilations, burnings, or other forms of destruction, temporarily psychotic murderers fear their violent thoughts and potential consequences. The *homicide-suicide,* on the other hand, engages in the act of self-murder in which he symbolically kills some hated individual or attempts to destroy that part of himself which he identifies with his victim. Therefore, the murder, which is ultimately followed by suicide, represents the symbolic suicide of the murderer before his own act of self-destruction. The *gynocidal murderer,* usually a husband or a male sexual mate who kills a woman, acts to defend himself against castration. Fearing castration, he takes the life of the person whom, he believes, is a threat to his potency. The *homosexual murderer,* on the other hand, acts to punish his homosexual partner who has deserted their single-sex relationship.

The *passive-aggressive murderer,* usually passive and favoring peace at any price, suddenly explodes and directs his pent-up emotion against his victim. The neutralization of social restraints, whether by the use of alcohol or some other agent, encourages his deviation from normal conduct and the abnormal infliction of harm. The *sadistic murderer,* however, differs in type and in psychological characteristics. While sadism is a perverted form of aggression, the offender is nearly always psychotic. Since many sadists are sexually impotent, sadistic murder is largely an extension of an attempt to force love through cruelty. Early atrocities against animals, substitute scapegoats for human beings, often reveal the hostile impulses which may lead to later acts of sadistic murder. Few murders, however, are committed by this type of offender.[64]

Murder followed by suicide

Most people believe that the criminal murder event ends with the death of the victim. Such, however, is not the case. Nearly one third of all murders in England and Wales, for example, were followed by the suicide of the murderer.[65] Many suicide participants, of course, were mentally ill, suffering from a depressive psychosis or other form of mental illness. Others, however, evidenced normal behavior or were overcommitted to normative concepts and values. Although the proportion of

---

[64] Manfred Guttmacher, *The Mind of the Murderer* (New York: Grove Press, 1962), pp. 2–100.
[65] Donald J. West, *Murder Followed by Suicide* (Cambridge, Mass.: Harvard University Press, 1966), p. 1.

suicidal murderers was somewhat smaller in New South Wales, where 767 persons were held responsible for all murders occurring in the period between 1953 and 1957, nearly 22 percent of the murder offenders (125 male and 41 female) killed themselves after their act and another 4 percent (17 male and 14 female) attempted suicide unsuccessfully.[66] A study of 545 cases of murder occurring in Denmark over a 28-year period revealed that 42.2 percent of Danish killers eventually took their own lives, while an additional 9.6 percent attempted suicide. Nearly 64 percent of the female offenders killed themselves; another 16.1 percent completed a serious suicide attempt.[67]

The offender murder-suicide frequency approximated a male to female ratio of 11 to 1 in the United States, 3 to 1 in Australia, 1.7 to 1 in England, and nearly 1 to 1 in Denmark.[68] These variations are partially explained by the data which show that English and Danish suicides are 30 to 40 times more common than homicides. Suicide in the United States, however, is only about twice the rate of homicide. The analysis of 148 murder-suicide offenses in the sample studied by D. F. West revealed that murderer-suicides constituted a less deviant group than a second study sample of ordinary murderers. While the common murderer was primarily a young, unmarried male member of the lower social classes, the murder-suicide offender was more representative of the general community, often married and living in a conventional family setting. The murder-suicide group reflected both sanity and insanity among its members.[69]

A significant number of infanticides, mercy killings, death pacts, and possible accidental killings, resulting in murder-suicide, are stimulated by feelings of despair rather than hostility. Murder-suicide offenders possess a close relationship with other members of their family whom they may murder in order to protect. While social isolates are more inclined to take their own lives, young married persons are more likely to murder without committing suicide.[70] Preliminary data, however, suggest that male murder-suicides reveal violent tendencies in previous criminal activity or in earlier domestic situations. Uncontrolled violence, for example, was especially evident among psychopathic offenders.[71] Murder-suicides, D. F. West noted, disclose a high aggression level and may turn against others or against themselves as circumstances warrant. Although murder-suicides come from all socioeconomic classes, they possess an unusual tendency to self-destruction. While younger than suicides

---

[66] *Ibid.*, p. 7.
[67] *Ibid.*, p. 7.
[68] *Ibid.*, p. 8.
[69] *Ibid.*, pp. 113–30.
[70] *Ibid.*, p. 145.
[71] *Ibid.*, p. 146.

but older than murderers, they are more often married than common murderers or suicides. An over-identification of mothers with their children at a time of depression, West believes, accounts for the large number of young married women who commit both murder and suicide. The number of murder-suicides, however, still remains a small fraction of the total homicide volume in a given year (see Table 6–5).

TABLE 6–5
Homicides, suicides, and homicide-suicides

Annual Number per 100,000 of Population	Homicide Offenders*	Homicide Offenders Who Kill Themselves	Suicides†	Suicide-‡ Murder Ratio
England and Wales......	0.27	33% = 0.09	8.5	0.97
Denmark..............	0.53	42% = 0.22	21.0	0.98
U.S.A................	4.5 approx.	4% = 0.18	10.0	0.69
Australia..............	1.7	22% = 0.36	11.0	0.87

* Figures taken from Interpol: *International Crime Statistics* for years 1959–60.
† Figures for year 1959 taken from World Health Organization *Epidemiological and Vital Statistics*, 1961.
‡ This ratio represents the number of suicides divided by the total of suicides plus murders.
Source: D. J. West, *Murder Followed by Suicide* (Cambridge, Mass.: Harvard University Press, 1966), p. 153.

Suicide rates vary throughout the world (see Table 6–6). Ordinary American suicides, however, increase during depressions and decrease in all status categories during periods of prosperity. Conversely, homicides increase during prosperity as suicides decline. Since persons of higher status are more sensitive to the frustrations of the business cycle, they are more likely to terminate their life by self-inflicted harm than are the lower status persons.[72] Andrew Henry and James Short found that a *high* psychological probability of suicide and a *low* psychological probability of *homicide* can be expected if the individual internalized harsh parental demands and discipline as a youth. On the other hand, strong external adult restraints may produce a *high* sociological probability of *homicide* consequent to frustration and a *low* sociological probability of *suicide* related to frustration.[73] Each tendency, however, is also further influenced by other socioeconomic factors. A 1969 publication by Ronald W. Maris further notes that the lower the socioeconomic

---

[72] Andrew F. Henry and James Short, *Suicide and Homicide* (New York: Free Press, 1965), p. 44. Also see Erwin Stengel, *Suicide and Attempted Suicide* (Baltimore, Md.: Penguin Books, Inc., 1966), and Herbert Hendin, *Suicide and Scandinavia: A Psychoanalytic Study of Culture and Character* (New York: Grune & Stratton, Inc., 1964).
[73] *Ibid.*, pp. 118–19.

TABLE 6–6

Suicide death rates
(per 100,000 population)

	1951	1955	1959	1961
Australia.................	9.5	10.3	11.1	11.9
Austria..................	22.7	23.4	24.8	21.9
Belgium.................	13.8	13.5	13.1	14.6
Canada..................	....	....	7.5	7.6
Ceylon..................	7.4	6.9	8.3	9.9†
Czechoslovakia...........	....	....	....	20.6
Denmark.................	23.6	23.3	21.0	16.9
Egypt...................	0.7	0.2	0.1*	....
Finland.................	15.7	19.9	20.0	20.6
France..................	15.5	15.9	16.9	15.9
Germany.................				
W. Germany............	18.2	19.2	18.7	18.7
W. Berlin.............	34.5	34.3	33.9	37.0
Democratic Republic.....	29.0	27.7	28.4*	....
Hungary.................	....	20.6	25.7	25.4
Israel..................	6.5	5.5	7.0	6.4†
Italy...................	6.8	6.6	6.2	5.6
Japan...................	18.3	25.2	22.7	19.6
Netherlands.............	6.0	6.0	7.0	6.6
New Zealand.............	9.9	9.0	8.7	8.4
Portugal................	10.2	9.2	9.2	8.7
Republic of Ireland........	2.6	2.3	2.5	3.2
S. Africa (Europeans).......	10.1	11.3	12.0	14.1†
(Africans)...............	....	....	3.1	4.3†
Spain...................	5.9	5.5	5.2	5.5†
Sweden..................	16.2	17.8	18.1	16.9
Switzerland.............	21.1	21.6	19.4	18.2
United Kingdom...........				
England and Wales.......	10.2	11.3	11.5	11.3
Scotland...............	5.4	7.7	8.5	7.9
N. Ireland.............	4.1	3.3	4.1	5.0
United States (all races)....	10.4	10.2	10.6	10.5
White..................	11.1	11.1	11.3	....
Negroes................	4.1	3.8	3.3	....

* 1958
† 1960
Source: Erwin Stengel, *Suicide and Attempted Suicide* (Baltimore, Md.: Penguin Books, Inc., 1966), p. 18.

status, the higher the suicide rate; that restraint deriving from being in a subordinate status (identified as vertical restraint) aggravates suicide; that suicide varies inversely with social integration; that mental illness seems to be disproportionately high among suicides; and that alcoholism, race, and physical factors have some effect upon the suicide rate.[74]

[74] Ronald W. Maris, *Social Forces in Urban Suicide* (Homewood, Ill.: Dorsey Press, 1969), pp. 159–66.

Chapter
7

THE CONTEXT OF
JUVENILE DELINQUENCY

Juvenile delinquency refers to antisocial conduct and legally defined delinquency by youth under a defined age limit. Although the majority of states hold that an individual is a juvenile if he is over 6 but under 18, the upper age limit in the remaining states varies from 16 to 21. A typical Massachusetts law, for example, says that a juvenile delinquent is a "child between seven and seventeen who violates any city ordinance or town by-law, or commits an offense not punishable by death."[1] The law is so inclusive that it includes every potential Massachusetts child within its definitions of delinquency. Part of the recent major increase in delinquency is due to the overinclusiveness which subjects many minor preteen and teen-age acts to juvenile court "rehabilitation." While delinquent conduct may vary from playing with firecrackers to running away from home, from drinking beer in a public park to sassing a schoolteacher, from stealing hub caps to murder of a rival gang member, the inability of some parents to maintain family respect and discipline has caused them to use delinquency statutes as a means to restrain the conduct of their own children.

While American definitions of juvenile delinquency are broad and encompassing, the English definition limits it to those acts which would be considered criminal if committed by an adult.[2] The American system

---

[1] Clyde B. Vedder, *Juvenile Offenders* (Springfield, Ill.: Charles C. Thomas, Publisher, 1963), p. 4. Also see Herbert A. Bloch, "Juvenile Delinquency: Myth or Threat," *Journal of Criminal Law, Criminology, and Police Science*, Vol. 49 (November–December, 1958), p. 305.

[2] *Ibid.*, pp. 3–4. See Herbert C. Quay, *Juvenile Delinquency: Research and Theory* (Princeton, N. J.: D. Van Nostrand Co., Inc., 1965). Also note William C. Kvara-

of juvenile delinquency and justice by comparison to the English is ambiguous and inconsistent. Although the American juvenile court system was developed to allow greater opportunity for juvenile treatment free from the stigma of criminal law, it has failed to realize its full promise. Not only has the court moved far from its original purpose, but it has failed to guarantee juveniles constitutional due process and equal justice.

Juveniles are legally exempt from the requisites and sanctions of criminal law unless they have committed major criminal violations for which the juvenile court may waive jurisdiction to the criminal court. An estimated 90 percent of all youth commit at least one delinquent act during their preadult years, and the juvenile court system protects them from the harsh recriminations of the criminal code in the attempt to correct their undesired behavior at a critical point in their lives.

Delinquent conduct has been known in some form or another to every generation, and the present generation is not unique in this respect. As the growth of the mass society has led to an even greater overdependence upon legislation and law enforcement to guarantee social conformity and cohesion, the court has extended its "protective" arm to include family problems within its jurisdiction. Ten premises, Donal E. J. MacNamara suggests, are central to an understanding of modern delinquency.

Premise One—Neither human nature nor the characteristics, drives and conduct of boys and girls have changed significantly through the centuries . . . Modern youth is no worse and no better than the youngsters of any preceding generation.

Premise Two—Our crass statistics in general are inadequate; delinquency statistics are frequently so distorted, manipulated and misinterpreted—and so fraught with "built-in error"—as to be almost useless.

Premise Three—Adjudications of delinquency in juvenile courts are quite frequently made on "evidence" which would be either inadmissable or insufficient to support a finding of guilt in the trial of an adult charged with the same offense.

Premise Four—Much so-called juvenile delinquency is in reality a healthy, normal response on the part of the juvenile to the negative circumstances which may impinge upon him.

Premise Five—Much juvenile delinquency is merely conduct imitative of adult behavior patterns, accepted as normal in our society but prohibited to those who have not as yet attained an age which differs from jurisdiction to jurisdiction.

---

ceus, "Juvenile Delinquency: A Problem for the Modern World," *Federal Probation*, Vol. 28 (September, 1964), p. 12; and Joseph F. Eaton and Kenneth Polk. *Measuring Delinquency: A Study of Probation Department Referrals* (Pittsburgh: University of Pittsburgh Press, 1961).

Premise Six—Adults frequently label delinquent juvenile conduct which is qualitatively undifferentiated from the accepted conduct patterns of the older generation at a similar age level.

Premise Seven—Youngsters from minority groups and from the socially and economically under-privileged classes are disproportionately represented in our delinquency statistics.

Premise Eight—Neither our juvenile institutions nor our extra-institutional preventive and/or rehabilitative programs—nor the more punitive and repressive campaigns favored by the Neanderthal substratum in some of our communities—can claim much success in coping with the juvenile problem.

Premise Nine—We have imposed consistently more restrictive limitations on our youngsters while at the same time exposing them to increasingly more attractive temptations inconsistent with the imposed restrictions—and we have subjected them to a longer and more terrifying experience of threatened mass annihilation than has been the lot of any previous generation.

Premise Ten—Sparing the rod does not spoil the child. If there is one thing I have learned in dealing with the more serious delinquents, it is that they have been subjected whether by their parents or those in authority who stood *in loco parentis* to far more than their share of physical abuse—and they have almost to a man been denied their needed allotment of affection, sympathy and understanding.[3]

Juvenile offenses cover a wide range of juvenile conduct. Although the specifics vary with the particular state, common juvenile "violations" in order of their frequency include:

1. Violates any law or ordinance.
2. Habitually truant.
3. (Knowingly) associates with thieves, vicious or immoral persons.
4. Incorrigible.
5. Beyond control of parents or guardian.
6. Growing up in idleness or crime.
7. So deports self as to injure or endanger self or others.
8. Absents self from home and without consent.
9. Immoral or indecent conduct.
10. (Habitually) uses vile, obscene or vulgar language.
11. (Knowingly) enters, visits house of ill repute.
12. Patronizes, visits policy shop or gaming places.
13. (Habitually) wanders about railroad yards or track.
14. Jumps train or enters car or engine without authority.
15. Patronizes saloon or dram house where intoxicating liquor is sold.

---

[3] *Ibid.*, pp. ix–xiv. Foreword by Donal E. J. MacNamara. Consult Fritz Redl and David Wineman, *Children Who Hate* (New York: Collier Books, 1962), and John M. Martin and Joseph P. Fitzpatrick, *Delinquent Behavior* (New York: Random House, Inc., 1965). For a discussion of the value of the juvenile court, see: Richard D. Knudten, *Criminological Controversies* (New York: Appleton-Century-Crofts, 1968).

16. Wanders street at night, not on lawful business.
17. Patronizes public pool room or bucket shop places.
18. Immoral conduct around school.
19. Engages in illegal occupation.
20. In occupation or situation dangerous or injurious to self or others.
21. Smokes cigarettes, or uses tobacco in any form.
22. Frequents place whose existence violates the law.
23. Is found in place for permitting which adult may be punished.
24. Addicted to drugs.
25. Disorderly.
26. Begging.
27. Uses intoxicating liquor.
28. Makes indecent proposals.
29. Loiters, sleeps in alleys, vagrant.
30. Runs away from state or charity institution.
31. Operates motor vehicle dangerously while under the influence of liquor.
32. Found on premises occupied or used for illegal purposes.
33. Attempts to marry without consent, in violation of law.
34. Given to sexual irregularities.[4]

American children under seven are not held responsible for their acts. The age of responsibility has been fixed at 9 in Israel, 10 in Great Britain, 12 in Greece, 13 in France and Poland, and 14 in Austria, Czechoslovakia, West Germany, Italy, Norway, Switzerland, and Yugoslavia. The minimum age of legal responsibility in Belgium has not been defined.[5]

TRENDS IN INTERNATIONAL DELINQUENCY

Arrests of 8- to 13-year-old juveniles in London increased 86 percent in 20 years—from 2,670 in 1938 to 4,965 in 1958. Arrests of 14- to 16-year-olds in London rose by nearly 95 percent—from 2,675 in 1938 to 5,203 in 1958.[6] Juveniles between 8 and 16, 20,413 boys and 1,333 girls, were charged in the Scottish courts during 1961. In the four years between 1954 and 1958, arrests among 18- to 21-year-old Germans rose nearly 47 percent, from 88,705 to 129,853.[7] Delinquents coming before the Italian courts more than doubled, from 10,530 to 22,796 during the

---

[4] Frederick Sussman, *The Law of Juvenile Delinquency* (New York: Oceana Publications, Inc., 1959), p. 21. Refer to Sol Rubin, "The Legal Character of Juvenile Delinquency," *The Annals*, Vol. 49 (January, 1949), pp. 1–8.

[5] T. C. N. Gibbens and R. H. Ahrenfeldt, *Cultural Factors in Delinquency* (Philadelphia: J. B. Lippincott Co., 1966), p. 27.

[6] Walter A. Lunden, *Statistics on Delinquents and Delinquency* (Springfield, Ill.: Charles C. Thomas, Publisher, 1964), p. 31.

[7] *Ibid.*, p. 35. Also note Peter P. Lejins, "American Data on Juvenile Delinquency in an International Forum," *Federal Probation*, Vol. 25 (June, 1961), p. 18.

period between 1948 to 1960. The numbers of East German juvenile and youthful offenders rose by nearly 97 percent, from 4,346 in 1951 to 8,532 in 1957. The number of juvenile offenders in the Greek courts advanced from an approximate 3,000 in 1951 to 4,203 in 1956. Juvenile convictions in Nationalist China (Taiwan) between 1952 and 1956 grew nearly 252 percent—from 1,657 to 5,874.[8] Similar increases in juvenile delinquency were recorded in Belgium, Sweden, Finland, Norway, Yugoslavia, Austria, Australia, and Japan. Denmark experienced a decline in delinquency between 1948 and 1955.[9]

Since the definition of delinquency varies from country to country, comparable data are not available for analysis. Delinquency in Cairo, Egypt, for example, includes the collection of cigarette butts from the street. Vagrancy was the second most common juvenile offense in two Indian urban areas in 1963. Defiance of the family or disrespect and disobedience of parents was the primary juvenile violation in Lagos, Nigeria. In Hong Kong, 90 percent of the 55,000 juveniles brought before the magistrate court had committed the delinquent act of hawking goods without a license.[10] Interpol international crime statistics in 1963 recorded a total of 39 juvenile offenders in the United Arab Republic. Laos reported even fewer (23) in 1950. The Federation of Malaya disclosed 508, Ghana 89, and the Philippines 6,082.[11] The limited number of international delinquents reported is largely due to the absence of public fear of delinquency, the lesser emphasis upon juvenile crime, and the greater use of informal rather than formal mechanisms to maintain social control.

THE AMERICAN SCENE

Juvenile delinquency has been rising sharply in the United States. Data concerning actual delinquency arrest and court actions, however, are incomplete. Even the statistics published by the Children's Bureau or the FBI can only indicate delinquency trends rather than reveal the context of delinquency. The total "arrests" of juveniles made by the police in a given year is generally unknown, since many cases are differentially processed without formal records or eventual court action. The wide discretionary power given the juvenile court, too, allows it to make a distinction between official and unofficial cases coming to its attention. An *official* case usually involves the filing of a formal petition and an ensuing court hearing. If the case, however, is adjusted by a referee,

---

[8] *Ibid.*, p. 56.
[9] *Ibid.*, pp. 35–54.
[10] Gibbens and Ahrenfeldt, *op. cit.*, p. 26.
[11] *Ibid.*, p. 28.

probation officer, or another court official, it may remain *unofficial*. Dade County (Miami), Florida, for example, reported 1,893 official (except traffic) and 1,312 unofficial cases (except traffic) in 1961. Cook County (Chicago), Illinois, noted 6,235 official and 6,721 unofficial cases in the same year. Philadelphia recorded 10,051 official and no unofficial cases.[12]

American arrest data reveal that nearly 39 percent of all 1968 arrests were among persons under 21. Juveniles under 18 accounted for approximately 49 percent of all index crime arrests and nearly 26 percent of the total 1968 crime arrest volume (see Table A–5 in the Appendix, pp. 732–33). More surprisingly, juveniles under 15 were arrested for nearly 23 percent of all reported 1968 index crimes including larceny (28.9 percent), burglary (26.3 percent), auto theft (16.4 percent), and robbery (11.9 percent). Fifteen and sixteen generally represented the peak years of delinquency (see Figure 7–1). Juveniles under 18 were arrested for 50 percent or more of all burglaries, larcenies, auto thefts, and acts of arson or vandalism.[13]

Although male juvenile outnumbered female juvenile arrests by nearly five-to-one in 1968, index crime arrests of males under 18 were closer to a seven-to-one ratio (see Table A–8). The number of arrests of males under 18 increased by more than 20 percent in the categories of murder and nonnegligent manslaughter (27.2 percent), robbery (21.7 percent), stolen property possession (28.7 percent), and narcotic drug violations (96.4 percent) between 1967 and 1968; female juvenile arrests increased more than 20 percent in the areas of manslaughter by negligence (36.8 percent), robbery (31.7 percent), auto theft (21.7 percent), arson (69.5 percent), embezzlement (64.0 percent), stolen property possession (26.4 percent), illegal weapons (27.7 percent), narcotic drug violations (144.9 percent), and vagrancy (31.1 percent) during the same period. While the percentage increases in many instances were rather sharp, a review of the actual number of arrests reveals a less dramatic picture. For the whole nation, male juvenile robbery arrests increased nearly 21.7 percent, from 17,480 to 21,266; female juvenile robbery arrests rose by a reported 31.7 percent, from 921 to 1,213. The major increase in narcotic drug arrests, too, is partially due to the sharp rise in juvenile marihuana use and the accompanying crackdown by the police.[14]

Of the 1,382,725 arrests among persons under 18 in 1968, white juve-

---

[12] Lunden, *op. cit.*, p. 23. See Stanley Turner, "Some Methods of Investigating Uncleared Juvenile Offenses," *Journal of Criminal Law, Criminology, and Police Science*, Vol. 56, No. 1 (March, 1965), pp. 54–58.

[13] *The Uniform Crime Reports—1968* (Washington, D.C.: U.S. Department of Justice, 1969), pp. 115–117. Consult Sol Rubin, *Crime and Juvenile Delinquency* (New York: Oceana Publications, Inc., 1961).

[14] *Ibid.*, p. 119.

nile arrests outnumbered black juvenile arrests nearly three to one. For all ages, the ratio was closer to two and one half to one (see Table A–6). Negro youth and adults were overrepresented in the arrest data in proportion to the Negro juvenile population. Approximately two thirds of all juvenile robberies were committed by Negro youth. Blacks disproportionately accounted for nearly one half of all 1968 aggravated assault, one third of all burglary, three tenths of all larceny, and one third

FIGURE 7–1
Delinquency in the life cycle
(the 10 years of 8 to 18 years constitute the zone of greatest hazards for youth. This decade is the period between early youth and young adulthood when the individual passes from the sphere of the family into the arena of the Great Society.)

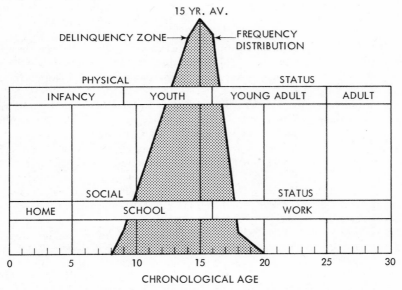

Source: Walter A. Lunden, *Statistics on Delinquents and Delinquency* (Springfield, Ill. Charles C. Thomas, Publisher, 1964), p. 61.

of all auto theft arrests. All other nonwhite racial groups accounted for less than 20,000 of the 1968 index arrests.[15]

Rural delinquency studies suggest that rural delinquency tends to be less serious than its urban counterpart. Not only are rural delinquents less sophisticated in methodology and knowledge of the types of offenses which might be committed but they are also without the support of

---

[15] *Ibid.*, pp. 119–20. See Robert D. Livingston, *Narcotic Drug Addiction Problems* (Washington, D.C.: U.S. Public Health Service, 1963).

a delinquent culture structured by professional and organized crime. Rural delinquency, John Koval and Kenneth Polk believe, is not supported by a "troublemaking" or a "parent-delinquent" culture.[16]

TYPES OF DELINQUENCY

R. D. Wirt and P. F. Briggs suggest that the delinquency can best be described in terms of a particular diagnostic type of delinquent person.

Diagnostic Category One: Delinquency is primarily due to lack of emotional integration of the family. Such families provide ineffective example setting and disciplining for developing a social conscience. The family is hence an ineffective mediator of positive social values, and the youngster is receptive to the least desirable influence emanating from associates and mass media of communication.

Diagnostic Category Two: This includes cases where the antisocial disorder is primarily the result of the child responding to an integrated home, but where the child fulfills the conscious or unconscious antisocial impulses and desires of the parents.

Diagnostic Category Three: This includes those cases where antisocial behavior is primarily the result of disorder within the child. An example would be where the sibling may be making an adequate adjustment, but the delinquent youngster suffers from a sociopathic, schizophrenic, neurologic, low intellect, or severe neurotic syndrome promoting antisocial behavior.

Diagnostic Category Four: This includes the adolescent without major home or personality disorder whose normal hyperactivity and rebelliousness cannot be constructively integrated by his present environment because of a lack of acceptable outlets.

Diagnostic Category Five: This includes those children whose delinquency is largely a result of efforts to seek or maintain status in their peer group.[17]

Peter Lejins believes that delinquency may more easily be divided into two forms of basic delinquent behavior. The *conformist delinquent* learns delinquent behavior from other members of his primary group; the *nonconformist delinquent,* on the other hand, is in rebellion against his generally law-abiding primary group. Although these forms represent

---

[16] John P. Koval and Kenneth Polk, "Problem Youth in a Small City," *Juvenile Gangs in Context* (Englewood Cliffs, N.J.; Prentice-Hall, Inc., 1967), p. 125. Also refer to Robert G. Andry, *Delinquency and Parental Pathology* (Springfield, Ill.: Charles C. Thomas, Publisher, 1961).

[17] Robert D. Wirt and Peter F. Briggs, "The Meaning of Delinquency," in Herbert C. Quay (ed.), *Juvenile Delinquency* (New York: D. Van Nostrand Co. Inc., 1965), pp. 17–18. Consult Jacob I. Hurwitz, "Three Delinquent Types: A Multivariate Analysis," *Journal of Criminal Law, Criminology, and Police Science*, Vol. 56, No. 3 (September, 1965), pp. 328–34; and Albert J. Reiss, "Social Correlates of Psychological Types of Delinquency," *American Sociological Review*, Vol. 17 (December, 1952), pp. 710–18.

polar positions, most delinquency, Lejins notes, is a combination of both dimensions.[18]

The typology of Hyman Rodman and Paul Grams recasts the psychological and social dimensions of juvenile conduct into eight basic delinquency types.

Type One. Adjusted-Occasional Gang Delinquent: The gang consists of members showing relatively good personality adjustment in the major activities of the gang or nondelinquent.

Type Two. Adjusted-Habitual-Gang Delinquent: The members of the gang show relatively good personality adjustment; their behavior is frequently or habitually delinquent.

Type Three. Adjusted-Occasional-Lone Delinquent: This type refers to the relatively adjusted adolescent who occasionally engages in delinquency on his own.

Type Four. Adjusted-Habitual-Lone Delinquent: The delinquent is relatively well adjusted and engages in delinquent behavior largely on his own.

Type Five. Maladjusted-Occasional-Gang Delinquent: This delinquent as an individual may have difficulty remaining a member within a gang of relatively well-adjusted boys. Delinquent behavior, therefore, takes place only occasionally.

Type Six. Maladjusted-Habitual-Gang Delinquent: The members of the gang show relatively poor personality adjustments; their behavior is habitually delinquent.

Type Seven. Maladjusted-Occasional-Lone Delinquent: The personality disturbance ordinarily manifests itself in non-delinquent ways and occasionally in lone delinquent acts.

Type Eight. Maladjusted-Habitual-Lone Delinquent: Personality maladjustment behaviorally or habitually manifests itself in some type of lone delinquent behavior.[19]

Theodore N. Ferdinand hypothesizes that social class factors influence the action patterns of the individual adolescent in gang delinquency (see Table 7–1).

The *Mischievous-Indulgent Pattern* is evident among upper-class cliques which develop in preparatory schools or other institutionalized settings frequented by persons of similar social class. Since these friendship groups are neither large nor fundamentally cohesive, they find a community of interests in an adolescent club or gang. As the clique

---

[18] Peter Lejins, "Pragmatic Etiology of Delinquent Behavior," *Social Forces,* Vol. 29 (March, 1951), pp. 317–20. Some of the most basic studies of delinquency were completed by Eleanor and Sheldon Glueck. See their *Juvenile Delinquency Grown Up; One Thousand Juvenile Delinquents: Their Treatment by Court and Clinic; and Crime and Correction.*

[19] Hyman Rodman and Paul Grams, "Juvenile Delinquency in the Family: A Review and Discussion," President's Commission on Law Enforcement and Administration of Justice, *Task Force Report: Juvenile Delinquency and Youth Crime* (Washington, D.C.: U.S. Government Printing Office, 1967), p. 205.

TABLE 7-1
A social typology of delinquency

Type	Social Structure	Degree of Alienation from Community	Delinquent Patterns	Class Origins of Members
Mischievous-Indulgent	Weakly organized, clique structures at best.	Somewhat alienated from conventional peers and adults.	Delinquent exploits exhibit style and taste, indulgent toward appetites.	Primarily upper-upper-class youths, upwardly mobile lower-status youths.
Aggressive-Exploitative	Well organized into clubs and gangs of adolescent society.	Delinquent activities are unknown to conventional adults, minimally alienated.	Emphasis upon proving oneself through sexual, drinking, and physical competition.	Lower upper, upper-middle-class, and upwardly mobile youths.
Criminal	Loosely organized in terms of clique structure.	Well integrated with criminal elements, not rejected by most conventional adults in immediate neighborhood.	Emphasis upon skill in criminal techniques, pursuit of criminal activities related to adult criminal practices.	Upper-lower- and upwardly mobile lower-lower-class youngsters.
Fighting	Very well organized with formal positions and strong solidarity.	Condemned and despised by immediate community, high degree of alienation.	Major emphasis upon attitudes and skills needed in physical combat.	Upper-lower- and upwardly mobile lower-lower-class youngsters.
Theft	Loosely organized in terms of friendship cliques.	Not rejected by immediate community, not seriously alienated.	Indulgence of appetites, theft for excitement, assaultive when challenged, vandalism toward schools.	Upper-lower and upwardly mobile lower-lower-class youngsters.
Disorganized Acting-Out	Very loosely organized, little structure at all.	Behavior not easily distinguished from normal adult patterns.	Indulgence of appetites, impulsive assaults, thefts and use of narcotics.	Lower-lower class.

Source: Theodore N. Ferdinand, *Typologies of Delinquency* (New York: Random House, Inc., 1966), p. 143.

neutralizes the attitudes and values of its members, its participants are immunized against their teachers or parents and increasingly evidence marginal characteristics. The clique primarily focuses upon sexual fulfillment, beer and liquor consumption, mischievous theft, and property destruction. It tends to remain nonviolent and does not develop any systematic property offense patterns.

The *Aggressive-Exploitative Pattern,* found among lower- and upper-middle-class adolescents, results in greater gang activity. Found largely among nonathletic teen-ager cliques, the aggressive-exploitative pattern is often expressed in assaults, drinking bouts, and excessive sexual delinquency. Since parents may move quickly to control these groups, cliques rarely mature into defiant delinquent gangs.

The *Criminal Pattern* is encouraged in the lower-class community by the successful criminal. The rewards of organized crime attract the limited skill adolescent of the upper-lower class who finds that successful organized criminality is compatible and consistent with the values of his class. Since the delinquent group is an integral part of the community, its activity leads to limited alienation or local conflict.

The *Fighting Pattern* is generally less common than the organized criminal gang pattern. Preoccupied with concepts of honor and revenge, the fighting gang works to rule its turf, revenge actual or believed injustice, and establish a sense of security in the face of community disorganization. As the fighting group becomes increasingly isolated from the community, it develops a siege mentality marked by estrangement from the community and a preoccupation with clique values. Possessing a clear identity and internal structure, the fighting gang, composed of upper-lower-class members, strives to compete and periodically erupts in violence.

The *Theft Pattern* is a typical upper-lower-class delinquency pattern. The antisocial activity of these delinquents may take a wide variety of forms, including sexual indulgence; minor offenses against property; illegal consumption of beer, liquor, and wine; and general intolerance of authority. Since the community considers these violations to be normal acts of lower-class youth, these activities are not interpreted as characteristic forms of delinquent behavior. Theft becomes a simple means of achieving acquisitive goals and of violating established norms of the middle and upper classes.

The *Disorganized Acting-Out Pattern* is most evident among the lower-lower-class peer group. Already estranged from the community and marked by an anomic feeling, the delinquent group acts out its disorganization in acts of petty theft, assault, robbery, and sexual indulgence. Since the clique or gang is generally apathetic and resigned to its fate, it rarely evidences aggressive-exploitative or fighting patterns. While the fighting gang may use violence to defend its honor, the disorganized acting-out clique tends to withdraw from any form of conflict. The lack of rigid internal structure and group discipline keeps the gang from becoming an organized community power or threat.[20]

THE DELINQUENT—A PROFILE

Most data suggest that the delinquent comes from areas of low socio-economic status characterized by major social change and disorganization. One of many children, he is most often 15 or 16 years old. Family wholeness and male guidance may be lacking or limited, since he disproportionately lives in a female-centered or -dominated home without a resident father. Even where a male adult serves as a nominal head of the house, his leadership may be negated by his drinking or prison incarceration and by welfare laws which prohibit payments to families which have a "man in the house."[21] Unemployed and often unemployable, the delinquent finds security in a gang or other congregate group which establishes its "turf" and controls its neighborhood.

The quest for juvenile companionship and life meaning is fulfilled by the gang which engages in delinquent acts as it attempts to reach satisfying group goals. Since an estimated 60 to 90 percent of all delinquent offenses are committed in companionship with others, many delinquent acts primarily reflect the inability of the individual or community to offset the reinforcement of deviance which the delinquent group imposes upon the individual.[22] While the modern teen-ager seeks independence from his parents, he paradoxically overdepends upon the ambivalent standards of the group as it experientially strives to reaffirm viable group values. When rebellion becomes a value in its own right, it may be operationalized rebelliously in personal taste, dress, and conduct. The President's Commission on Law Enforcement and Administration of Justice, however, discovered that gang violence against persons is less frequent, more controlled, and less violent than is commonly believed. Only 17 percent of all offenses recorded against 700 members of 21 delinquent gangs included a semblance of violence. Nearly one

---

[20] Theodore N. Ferdinand, *Typologies of Delinquency* (New York: Random House, Inc. 1966), p. 143. Review Martin Gold, *Status Forces in Delinquent Boys* (Ann Arbor: University of Michigan Press, 1963). For discussion of gang delinquency, see Thomas Gannon, "The Emergence of the 'Defensive' Gang," *Federal Probation,* Vol. 30 (December, 1966), p. 44; and *The Cost of a Juvenile Gang* (Los Angeles: Los Angeles County Probation Department, 1964).

[21] The President's Commission on Law Enforcement and Administration of Justice, *The Challenge of Crime in a Free Society* (Washington, D.C.: U.S. Government Printing Office, 1967), p. 60.

[22] *Ibid.,* p. 66. Note the *Interim Report of the Committee on the Judiciary* (Washington, D. C.: U.S. Government Printing Office, 1955), and *Hearings of the Subcommittee to Investigate Juvenile Delinquency* (Washington, D.C.: U.S. Government Printing Office, 1955).

half of all violent offenses were enacted against rival gang members who attempted to invade the gang's territory.[23]

The mean age of 918 youths in 27 known Philadelphia Negro delinquent male gangs, Gerald D. Robin discovered, was 17.6 years. Although nearly three fourths of the gang members had passed beyond juvenile status by the time the study was completed on January 7, 1962, the data suggest the dimensions of the delinquency problem (see Table 7–2). Of the 711 youths for which home police records were available,

TABLE 7–2

Disposition of gang members, by charge*

	Charge†	No. of Offenders	No. Arrested	Percent Arrested
Part I Crimes	Homicide	15	15	100.0
(Index Crimes)	Robbery	205	190	92.7
	Rape	39	36	92.3
	Burglary	301	263	87.4
	Aggravated assault	239	199	83.3
	Larceny	619	446	72.1
Part II Crimes	Sex offense	34	30	88.2
	Weapon violation	160	135	84.4
	Threats	39	25	64.1
	Assault and battery	302	161	53.3
	Other offense	94	42	44.7
	Liquor violation	116	50	43.1
	Disorderly conduct	1,117	445	39.8
	Gambling	69	20	29.0
	Trespassing	114	29	25.4
	CLV	476	113	23.7
	Total	3,939	2,199	55.8

* Within Part I and Part II offenses, the charges appear in decreasing order of the proportion arrested for each charge.

† Curfew violations were excluded from this table because it was the policy of the Juvenile Aid Division not to arrest on this charge.

Source: Malcolm W. Klein, *Juvenile Gangs in Context* (Englewood Cliffs, N.J.: Prentice-Hall, Inc., 1967), p. 22.

20 percent were charged with 10 or more offenses. Each gang member was accused of 1 to 25 offenses, and the mean number of delinquency charges was 6.2. The average number of delinquencies committed by 12-year-olds was 3.0, by juveniles under fifteen 3.8, and by those 15 or over 6.4. The average time between the first and second police contacts was 14.0 months. The time lapse between the 9th and 10th police contacts lessened to 3.6 months.

---

[23] *Ibid.*, p. 67. See Donald J. Tyrell, "Why Can't We Understand Juvenile Delinquency," *Federal Probation*, Vol. 28 (June, 1964), p. 20.

Slightly less than 14 percent of all juvenile acts in the gang study involved violence against the person. Of the other delinquent acts, 25 percent were against property, 37 percent involved general disorderly conduct, 18 percent were distinctly juvenile offenses, and 7 percent covered all other delinquent acts. Of the 711 Philadelphia gang members, 31 percent had been charged at some point in their careers with some severe physical attack against the person, whether in the form of homicide, aggravated assault, or forcible rape. Although 81 percent of those Negroes charged with index crimes were arrested, only 42 percent of the Negro males accused of less serious crimes faced arrest.[24]

Two thirds of the 291 juvenile vandals known to New York City law enforcement agencies, studied by John M. Martin, were boys between 12 and 20 years of age. While the mean age of 287 vandals was 12.94 years, the mean age of a control group of 6,776 Bronx delinquents was 14.46 years. Nearly 68 percent of all vandals were whites. Nearly 16 percent were Puerto Rican, and the remainder were nonwhite.[25]

A more detailed study of police selection of juvenile offenders for juvenile court referral and general investigation conducted in four communities identified as Steel City, Trade City, Milltown, and Manor Heights and served by the Juvenile Court of Allegheny (Pittsburgh) County, Pennsylvania, revealed that arrest rates vary widely in relationship to community characteristics (see Table 7–3). Nathan Goldman, for example, found that arrests among youths 10 to 17 years of age ranged from 12.4 to 49.7 per 1,000. The average rate, however was 32.6 per 1,000 juveniles between 10 and 17. The gross variations in arrest rates, he believed, were due largely to the tendency of several communities to complete and record minor-offense arrests with greater frequency. Few juveniles apprehended by citizens were ever brought to the attention of the police or the juvenile court. Although nearly one half of the juveniles apprehended by the police were taken to the police station, less than 36 percent of those registered by the police were reported to the juvenile court for official action. The police, Goldman discovered, differentially processed juvenile arrests in relationship to the seriousness of the offense. The more serious offenders were referred to the court with greater frequency, and Negro youths under arrest were more often brought to the attention of the court than white juveniles. Nearly 34 percent of white juvenile arrests led to juvenile court action; approximately 65 percent of Negro youth arrests followed the same route. Although Negro juvenile arrests accounted for 5.7 per-

[24] Malcolm W. Klein, *Juvenile Gangs in Context* (Englewood Cliffs, N.J.: Prentice-Hall, Inc., 1967), p. 22.

[25] John M. Martin, *Juvenile Vandalism* (Springfield, Ill.: Charles C. Thomas, Publisher, 1961), pp. 16–21.

cent of the arrest volume, they constituted 10.5 percent of all juvenile court referrals. The rate of Negro juvenile court referrals ranged from a low of 51.2 percent to a high of 84.6 percent in the three communities recording a representative Negro population, depending upon the frequency with which minor offenses were referred to the juvenile court. Although Goldman found evidence to support the belief that girls brought to the attention of the police were more likely to be referred to the court than boys, the limited number of cases in his sample restricted the formation of any conclusion.

TABLE 7–3
Social characteristics of areas studied*

	Allegheny County	Steel City	Trade City	Manor Heights	Mill Town
Population (1940 census).........	1,411,539†	55,000	29,900	20,000	12,700
Population, age 10–17............	—	8,117	3,387	2,631	2,070
Land use......................	—	Industrial	Residential and commercial	Residential	Industrial
Population density (per gross acre)...................	3.02	25.6	23.1	6.0	18.9
Percentage foreign born (white)......................	12.71	15.77	7.03	4.84	13.77
Percentage Negro..............	6.38	3.95	1.58	0.45	3.28
Nationality groups.............	Italy Br. Isles Poland	Hungary Czech. Br. Isles	Br. Isles Germany Italy	Br. Isles Germany	Italy Poland Austria Br. Isles
Median rental..................	$28.57	$28.56	$42.06	$81.88	$27.87
Occupations...................	Clerical-sales operatives	Laborers operatives clerical	Clerical craftsmen foremen	Clerical proprietor managers officials	Laborers clerical operatives
Median school grade completed...................	8.3	10.7	12.6	14.8	10.5
Percentage completed college......	5.5	3.4	10	21.5	3.5

* From *Social Facts about Pittsburgh and Allegheny County* (Pittsburgh: Federation of Social Agencies, 1945).
† Living outside Pittsburgh: 52.4 percent.
Source: Nathan Goldman, *The Differential Selection of Juvenile Offenders* (New York: National Council on Crime and Delinquency, 1965), p. 28.

The four Allegheny County communities processed juvenile cases differentially. One community evidenced a low arrest rate coupled with the high court referral rate. A second recorded a higher arrest rate marked by a major arrest rate for minor offenses and a third revealed a moderately high arrest pattern together with a moderately high court referral rate for all offenses. Race and age were especially prominent factors in the differential selection process. A fourth community evidenced a moderately high arrest rate coupled with a low court referral rate. Its referral practices varied with the seriousness of the offense, the sex and race of the offender, and the age of the youth. The differential police selection of juvenile offenders for court appearance, Goldman found, was largely determined in relationship to the policeman's attitude toward the offender and toward his own family; toward the offense completed, the juvenile court, and himself as a policeman; and community attitudes toward delinquency.[26]

The analysis of five sets of data collected during the years of 1927–33, 1934–40, 1945–51, 1954–57, and 1958–61 from the Cook (Chicago) County Juvenile Court led Henry D. McKay to conclude that delinquency rates tend to follow existing distribution patterns, remaining high where they were high in spite of social and ethnic change. Where societies remain rather rigid and unchanging, delinquency or group rebellion is largely negated. If change, on the other hand, is rapid, traditional institutions, McKay observed, may be unable to integrate the change or stabilize the threatened or threatening social groups. Most city areas, however, strive to replace disorder with order. Only in the extreme inner city areas is this tendency minimized. As adults assume new industrial or commercial roles and create new institutions, old institutions are usually modified to bring about the necessary social adjustments.[27]

THE ROOTS OF DELINQUENCY

Although it is inaccurate to claim that juvenile delinquency and adult crime are direct products of poverty and ecology, all data indicate that an overconcentration of criminal activity occurs in areas of major social disorganization. Clifford Shaw and Henry McKay, for example, found that German, Irish, Polish, and Italian delinquency patterns changed as they moved from the center of the city to better-organized and -stabilized neighborhoods. Continuing studies reveal that the delinquency and crime of a particular area are often encouraged and supported by the cultural and social conditions of the neighborhood and by the normative redefinition which legitimizes aggressive personal response. Although Negro delinquency and crime rates remain disproportionately high in these areas, Negro delinquency rates, too, have decreased as Negroes have moved from the center of the city. In fact, when blacks and whites share a comparable economic status, the extreme differentials in delinquency rates no longer continue to exist. The patterns of residential segregation which have prevented blacks from moving to better neighborhoods have subjected many persons seeking to improve their

---

[26] Nathan Goldman, *The Differential Selection of Juvenile Offenders* (New York: National Council on Crime and Delinquency, 1965), pp. 125–32. Refer to Mary Holman, *The Police Officer and the Child* (Springfield, Ill.: Charles C. Thomas, Publisher, 1962).

[27] President's Commission, *Juvenile Delinquency*, p. 115.

status to the aggressive subcultural norms of the ghetto community.[28] However, part of this decline is also due to the fact that persons in so-called "better" communities are frequently loath to notify the police of delinquent acts.

Youth, blacks, and the poor, Marvin Wolfgang believes, possess subcultural value systems which are different from, but yet subsidiary to, the larger culture. Deprived of some civil liberties and rights, they are often manipulated by the established power structure rather than given their opportunity to influence the structure. Since they are dominated by matriarchs and excessive feminine influences, male members of these groups commonly reject authority and stress masculine characteristics. Unable to emerge within the normal socioeconomic channels, they reject the whole system. All three groups, Wolfgang believes, tend to be more impulsive, nonrational, aggressive, and romantic. While they may aspire to goals similar to those of the successful, their achievement, of course, is not commensurate. Socially powerless, they seek power where competition is limited or where success without major skill or education is possible. Delinquent and criminal activity, Wolfgang hypothesized, may be a search for identity, meaning, and social justice brought about by alienation and hopelessness.[29]

Delinquency and youth crime have increased to the highest degree in those countries which have experienced the greatest economic affluence. The rise in living standards has stimulated a desire to possess goods which indicate higher status and prestige. While industrial societies distribute produced goods to members of the population more equitably, enhanced consumer good distribution itself generates greater expectations of further equality in consumption. If the availability of goods is restricted by law, the desire to possess the item may lead to conduct which is designed to gain momentary possession. Auto theft, for example, is an international juvenile attempt to overcome driver's license and car ownership restrictions.[30]

The lack of uniform quality in the American educational system poses distinct problems for marginal youth attending marginal schools. Schools with the most limited resources, least qualified personnel, and most in-

---

[28] President's Commission, *Challenge of Crime*, p. 57. Also note Clifford R. Shaw, Henry D. McKay, and James F. McDonald, *Brothers in Crime* (Chicago: University of Chicago Press, 1938); and Bernard Linder, *Towards an Understanding of Juvenile Delinquency* (New York: Columbia University Press, 1954).

[29] Marvin E. Wolfgang, "The Culture of Youth," President's Commission, *Juvenile Delinquency*, pp. 153–54. James S. Coleman discusses the problem of adolescence in *The Adolescent Society* (Glencoe: Free Press, 1961); also refer to Sheldon and Eleanor Glueck, *Unraveling Juvenile Delinquency* (Cambridge, Mass.: Harvard University Press, 1950).

[30] Jackson Toby, "Affluence and Adolescent Crime," President's Commission, *Juvenile Delinquency*, pp. 132. See Erwin Schepses, "Boys Who Steal Cars," *Federal Probation*, Vol. 25 (March, 1961), p. 56.

adequate facilities and programs are most likely to be found in slum areas. Since the school is the first step in the ultimate employment of the youth, its scholastic program in large part determines his future occupational and general social success. Because most public school systems do not evidence enough flexibility in solving individual problems, the educational system's potential for diagnosing, discouraging, or controlling delinquent behavior is minimized. The expulsion of the school troublemaker, for example, makes it possible for the larger numbers of students to learn unhindered, but it consigns the already marginal student to a life of exaggerated marginality. The lack of community alternatives automatically consigns the delinquent to a position where he cannot compete effectively in the highly competitive American socioeconomic system.

When an inadequate school system is combined with motivational difficulties, the result may be a cycle of deterioration and failure. Although the individual may advance each year as he is promoted from grade to grade, he may also be engaging in a form of *cumulative failure*. A marginal student in an inadequate school may be only one-half year behind the average youth in the fourth grade, but his achievement gap may widen to three quarters of a year by the sixth grade and one and one-half years by the eighth grade. The lack of scholastic success automatically sensitizes the youth to defense mechanisms which include the potential of delinquent action. Since students on the "C" and "D" level are seven times more likely to be delinquent than students continuing on the "A" and "B" standard, the importance of meaningful educational programs cannot be underestimated. Boys from blue-collar families who failed in school have a delinquency pattern almost seven times as frequent than those who do not fail.[31]

Although the educational dimensions of the delinquency problem cannot be immediately solved by the greater infusion of monetary or financial aid into the slum schools, such aid is a first step in the correct direction. In addition, more teachers who possess a peculiar ability to relate to difficult students must be allowed to work with delinquent students through more flexible school administrative assignments. The increased use of group techniques to encourage student involvement and peer-group control offer potential value. Early detection of delinquent tendencies at the elementary school level, if supported by necessary counseling and social services, offers some hope for delinquency prevention and control. The current tendency to segregate the delinquent

---

[31] President's Commission, *Challenge of Crime*, p. 71. A further discussion of the delinquency school problem is presented by Bruce Balow, "Delinquency and School Failure," *Federal Probation*, Vol. 25 (June, 1961), p. 15; also by Milton F. Shore and Fortune V. Mannino, "The School Dropout Situation: An Opportunity for Constructive Intervention," *Federal Probation*, Vol. 29 (September, 1965), p. 41.

within inferior or slow-learning classes and marginal programs, however, only undermines his long-range success potential. The use of meaningful curriculum materials which relate to inner city and slum problems, too, can make education more vivid and central to the youth's experience, since interest and learning are best encouraged and sustained when the educational system capitalizes on the delinquent's world of reality. While Federal Head Start and Upward Bound programs are still in the early stages, their successes have offered new insight into the educational problem. More realistic vocational training programs, designed to relate the student to current employment opportunities, can overcome the too common tendency to train marginal students for obsolete occupations.

A new emphasis upon high school counseling and job placement is necessary to bridge the gap between the school and the community. College preparatory educational programs, often unrealistic for slum youth or those of lower intelligence, must comprise only one of several future program alternatives. Since educational success depends so heavily upon youth, parent, teacher, and community interests, greater collusion must be encouraged. Farsighted communities have already begun to utilize the concept of the community school which operates during the day and evening to fulfill the basic needs of the youth, their parents, and the community.

The male youth's inability or failure to win the affection of his father is also a major factor in the formation of delinquency patterns. Delinquent activity, for example, correlates more frequently with the affection the child receives from both parents than with the consistency of discipline invoked against his person. Since a disproportionately large number of aggressive delinquents express attitudes which reveal that their parents have been either unable or unwilling to accept their feelings of dependence, juvenile delinquency tends to disclose family maladjustment rather than simple antisocial delinquent acts. Because the father's authority within the family is either strengthened or undermined by his employment or unemployment, adult male unemployment takes a major toll upon juvenile respect.

The problem of delinquency is compounded by the fact that no form of public intervention or program development can effectively deal with the daily interactional problems included in the consistency of discipline, family status in the community, husband-wife relationships, inadequate motivation, extended family pressures, and prejudicial attitudes toward law enforcement, public officials, or majority-minority members. While better housing, recreational facilities, employment opportunities, programs of family planning, and revision of welfare laws may ultimately change the structure of individual-family-government relationships, attitudinal inadequacies, developed over generations, are not quickly changed. Juvenile court philosophy, which assumes that delinquency can be controlled either by punishing a parent or by "rehabilitating" the youth through weekend sentences in a city or county jail, largely ignores the basic behavioral and social context of the delinquency problem. Public and private agencies, therefore, must take immediate steps to reduce unemployment, devise methods of providing minimum family income, reexamine or revise welfare regulations so that families may be encouraged to stay together, improve housing and recreational facilities, insure availability of family planning assistance, provide assistance in the adjustment of domestic management and child care problems, make counseling and therapy available, and develop community activities which involve the whole family. The problem of adult crime will never be controlled until intelligent solutions to the problems of juvenile delinquency are reached. Since the majority of all acts against property are committed by persons under the age of 21, the need to solve this dimension of delinquency is immediately critical.[32]

The arbitrary separation of juvenile delinquency and adult crime by statutory definition at the common age of 18 is arbitrary and behaviorally unrealistic. Youthful offenders above 18, too, may engage in conduct which is a result of frustration and personal conflict. Although many individuals under the age of 24 may be hardened and dangerous offenders, the greater bulk of offenders in this age category participate in less serious crime forms which reveal emotional and physical immaturity. Treating them as offenders only enhances the probability of their lifetime participation in crimes.[33] Few provisions have even been made for *minors* between the age of 18 and 21. Forty-four of the fifty states and the Commonwealth of Puerto Rico, for example, offer no separate procedures or protections for law-violating minors above the juvenile age limit. Many are quickly jailed or incarcerated with major offenders from whom they may learn even greater criminal knowledge and skills. The failure to differentiate the minor from the major and the younger from the older offender only encourages the growth of the delinquency-crime problem. Postjuvenile and preadult immaturity and malleability have too often been ignored by the local enforcement, justice, and corrections systems. If adult crime is ever to be controlled, the youthful offender, too,

---

[32] *Ibid.*, p. 66. See Richard S. Sterne, *Delinquent Conduct and Broken Homes* (New Haven Conn.: College and University Press, 1964), and Mark C. Roser, "On Reducing Dropouts," *Federal Probation,* Vol. 29 (December, 1965), p. 49.

[33] Milton Luger, "The Youthful Offender," *Task Force Report: Juvenile Delinquency and Youth Crime,* p. 119. Edward H. Stull discusses, "Thirty Years Work with Problem Children," *Federal Probation,* Vol. 26 (September, 1962), p. 14. Also note Albert W. Silver, "Operating a Psychiatric Clinic in a Juvenile Court," *Federal Probation,* Vol. 26 (September, 1962), p. 24; and Dorothy E. Bradbury, "The Children's Bureau and Juvenile Delinquency," *Juvenile Delinquency Facts and Facets* (Washington, D.C.: U.S. Government Printing Office, 1960).

must be allowed greater treatment alternatives than are currently available to their age category.

Delinquent groups may respond to responsible community involvement. Youthful Florida rioters, for example, became members of the black "White Hat" subenforcement group which worked with the police to "cool" the Miami ghetto riot area in 1967. Chicago police working with the Blackstone Rangers, too, were partially able to redirect the energies of an aggressive black gang into theatrical productions and community stabilization during the same year, before departmental policy turned to one of gang suppression in 1969. Similar discoveries in other communities led the President's Commission on Law Enforcement and the Administration of Justice to recommend the active employment of youth in civic activities whether as subprofessional aids or in other forms of active involvement. Coordinated community programs, including the participation of religious institutions, private social agencies, fraternal groups, other interested civic groups, and representatives of those groups which they seek to aid, offer new hope for community restabilization. Only this type of cooperation can utilize the full facilities of the Commission's proposed community residential center and the long-range promise of its recommended community Youth Service Bureau.[34]

---

[34] President's Commission, *Challenge of Crime,* p. 69. The need for emergency shelter care is presented by I. W. Fellner, "Children in Emergencies," *Federal Probation,* Vol. 25 (June, 1961), p. 12.

Chapter
8

SPECIAL FORMS OF
FEMALE CRIMINALITY

Female criminality reaches its highest volume in the crimes of drunkenness and larceny. Prostitution and commercialized vice, runaways, and disorderly conduct constitute secondary female crime categories (see Table 8–1). Girls under 18 committed nearly one half of all female theft violations during 1968 and were overrepresented in crimes of disorderly conduct, curfew and loitering law violations, and runaways. But they accounted for only 589 of the 33,007 arrests made for female prostitution. Of the 6,669 arrests for sexual offenses other than prostitution and forcible rape, over one third (2,422) were of teen-age girls.

Certain types of sex crimes, of course, are peculiar to the female. Although having an abortion is an obvious female violation, uneven abortion laws and the tendency to prosecute the abortionist rather than the one who has the abortion obscure the data concerning this form of medical crime. Since abortion violations are difficult to prove in court, many abortion offenders are eventually prosecuted for the more vague violations of vagrancy, offenses against family or children, or other statutes designed to control abortion practices. Prostitution is primarily a female criminal act. The prostitute engages in a commercial transaction in which she renders sexual services through the use of her body in exchange for a monetary payment of, say, $5 to $200 or more. A full- or part-time participant, she professionally engages in the trade in order to make a living or to supplement other income.

ABORTION VIOLATIONS

Nearly 10,000 legal abortions are performed in the United States each year. An estimated 1 million additional illegal operations are per-

TABLE 8–1

Total female arrest trends, 1967–68
(4,216 agencies; 1968 estimated population 136,780,000)

	Females					
	Total			Under 18		
Offense Charged	1967	1968	Percent Change	1967	1968	Percent Change
Total...........	629,730	681,777	+8.3	220,420	251,170	+14.0
General homicide:						
a) Murder and non-negligent manslaughter......	1,389	1,588	+14.3	78	75	−3.8
b) Manslaughter by negligence.........	294	299	+1.7	19	26	+36.8
Forcible rape.........	......	......	......	......	......	......
Robbery..............	2,969	3,793	+27.8	921	1,213	+31.7
Aggravated assault.....	13,005	12,704	−2.3	2,318	2,016	−13.0
Burglary—breaking or entering..........	9,078	10,223	+12.6	4,636	5,261	+13.5
Larceny theft..........	100,695	109,143	+8.4	48,244	50,640	+5.0
Auto theft............	4,729	5,941	+25.6	3,082	3,751	+21.7
Subtotal for above offenses.	132,159	143,691	+8.7	59,298	62,982	+6.2
Other assaults.........	22,980	26,543	+15.5	5,730	6,812	+18.9
Arson................	521	700	+34.4	210	356	+69.5
Forgery and counterfeiting........	6,289	7,182	+14.2	692	809	+16.9
Fraud...............	11,905	13,077	+9.8	423	457	+8.0
Embezzlement.........	1,125	1,012	−10.0	25	41	+64.0
Stolen property; buying, receiving, possessing..	1,982	2,709	+36.7	568	718	+26.4
Vandalism............	6,315	6,882	+9.0	4,196	4,519	+7.7
Weapons, carrying, possessing, etc.......	4,418	5,103	+15.5	452	577	+27.7
Prostitution and commercialized vice..	29,694	33,007	+11.2	565	589	+4.2
Sex offenses (except forcible rape and prostitution).........	6,669	5,467	−18.0	3,178	2,422	−23.8
Narcotic drug laws.....	13,195	23,367	+77.1	3,219	7,884	+144.9
Gambling.............	7,082	6,267	−11.5	64	41	−35.9
Offenses against family and children..	4,853	4,251	−12.4	308	128	−58.4
Driving under the influence............	16,980	18,817	+10.8	120	140	+16.7
Liquor laws...........	23,220	24,132	+3.9	9,206	10,074	+9.4
Drunkenness..........	100,435	94,895	−5.5	3,404	4,059	+19.2
Disorderly conduct.....	70,788	76,147	+7.6	14,880	17,450	+17.3
Vagrancy.............	9,093	9,740	+7.1	1,112	1,458	+31.1
All other offenses (except traffic).......	85,221	90,942	+6.7	37,964	41,808	+10.1
Suspicion (not included in totals)............	16,082	13,826	−14.0	2,575	2,769	+7.5
Curfew and loitering law violations........	15,936	17,687	+11.0	15,936	17,687	+11.0
Runaways............	58,870	70,159	+19.2	58,870	70,159	+19.2

Source: Adapted from *Uniform Crime Reports—1968* (Washington, D.C.: U.S. Department of Justice, 1969), p. 119.

formed annually.[1] Police officials rate criminal abortion as the third largest form of illegal activity in the United States, surpassed only by gambling and narcotic violations.[2] This rating, however, cannot be verified, since few abortions come to the attention of police unless they result in the hospitalization or death of the victim. Even mortality data are incomplete and inaccurate. Ransom S. Hooker, studying maternal mortality in New York City, discovered that a false diagnosis was recorded on the death certificate prior to autopsy in 25 to 30 percent of deaths due to abortion.[3]

Historical attitudes toward abortion

Attitudes toward abortion have varied throughout history. Although abortion is known to have been practiced in antiquity, ancient Hebrew, Egyptian, Greek, and Roman writings provide little concrete information concerning it. Plato and Aristotle supported abortion for eugenic or philosophical reasons. While abortion was rare during the period of the Roman consuls, it gained popularity in Imperial Rome as a means by which to maintain one's figure or to control population size.

Antiabortion proscriptions of the Christian era placed severe sanctions upon those who terminated pregnancies for their own pleasure. St. Paul, for example, articulated a theology which stressed the sinfulness of the flesh and viewed sexual intercourse as a necessary evil to maintain the race, a view which issued in the attitude that the fertilized ovum possessed the right to reach full development, birth, and eventual adulthood. Sexual asceticism, encouraged by the Christian reiteration of earlier Jewish ritualism pertaining to childbirth and celibacy, was extolled as the highest form of Christian expression. Although St. Paul argued that it was better to marry than to burn, he held that the celibacy offered the highest form of personal and religious fulfillment.

Roman Catholic theology accepted the early Aristotelian notion of the quickening of the fetus after 40 days, although it later stipulated that the fetus possessed a soul from the moment of the union of the

---

[1] Charles C. Dahlberg, "Abortion," in Ralph Slovenko (ed.), *Sexual Behavior and the Law* (Springfield, Ill.: Charles C. Thomas, Publisher, 1965), p. 379. Bertha J. Payak, "Understanding the Female Offender," *Federal Probation,* Vol. 27, No. 4 (December, 1963), pp. 7 ff., discusses the social psychological dimensions of female crime.

[2] Edwin M. Schur, *Crimes Without Victims* (Englewood Cliffs, N.J.: Prentice-Hall, Inc., 1965), p. 25. For discussion of abortion in Korea, see Pyong Choon Hahn and Byong Ji Jan, "The Criminality of Abortion in Korea," *Journal of Criminal Law, Criminology, and Police Science,* Vol. 56, No. 1 (March, 1965), pp. 18–26.

[3] Ransom S. Hooker, *Maternal Mortality in New York City* (New York: Commonwealth Fund, 1933), p. 33.

sperm and ovum. The Muslims held that life does not exist in the fetus until the start of the third trimester of pregnancy.[4]

Current abortion practices

Russia, which introduced state-supported abortion in the 1920's, reversed this policy in 1936. The state assumed its original position in 1955, however, when it gave the individual greater choice in the continuation or termination of pregnancy. Scandinavian countries have continued the practice of abortion, introduced more than 25 years ago, for a wide variety of social and medical reasons. Japan, attempting to control a rising birth rate and to allow greater family planning, legalized abortion in 1948. Although abortion receives little legal approval in the United States, many legitimate physicians periodically practice it illegally.[5]

Abortion refers to the termination of pregnancy before the fetus reaches a point of viability or capability of life outside the womb and is usually distinguished from a miscarriage, which occurs during the first three months of pregnancy. Although American legal statutes, modeled after an 1803 English law, make no attempt to control spontaneous abortion, most states prohibit the grounds for therapeutic abortions designed to interrupt or terminate a pregnancy willfully. Restrictions on abortions rose as legislative attempts to control sexual promiscuity, to guarantee social continuity, and to maintain a value system which supported the concept of the inviolability of human life. A few states permit therapeutic abortions—the interruption of pregnancy to preserve the mother's life or health or to secure the safety of the mother—but most prohibit abortions performed simply because of a desire to avoid childbirth.

Existing state abortion laws are inconsistent. State statutes generally fall into three categories. The abortion of any supposedly pregnant woman is a crime in Kentucky, Rhode Island, Indiana, Delaware, Vermont, Pennsylvania, and Wyoming. In Florida, Iowa, the District of Columbia, Connecticut, Ohio, Massachusetts, Virginia, and West Virginia, on the other hand, abortion is a criminal act if any woman merely intends to procure an abortion. However, a simple attempt by any pregnant or nonpregnant woman to secure an abortion results in a lesser charge in New York, Minnesota, Missouri, and Washington.[6] Abortion

---

[4] Jerome E. Bates and Edward Zawadski, *Criminal Abortion* (Springfield, Ill.: Charles C. Thomas, Publisher, 1964), pp. 14–21.

[5] Dahlberg, *op. cit.*, p. 381.

[6] Bates and Zawadski, *op. cit.*, p. 101. Refer to Richard D. Knudten, *Criminological Controversies* (New York: Appleton-Century-Crofts, 1968), for a further discussion of the current abortion issue.

laws, like many laws are commonly ignored. The legal criteria of abortion, therefore, range from factors of mere intent to gain an abortion to the actual completion of the act while pregnant.

Proof of an actual pregnancy and a subsequent operation are inadequate evidence of criminal violation. The state bears the additional responsibility to show that the abortion was not therapeutic and was, therefore, illegal. Although a female who gives her consent to her own abortion under criminal conditions is usually not defined as an accomplice to a crime, she can be charged with the killing of a child in attempting a miscarriage in New York State. On the other hand, she is not criminally liable in the District of Columbia and is held to be the victim under Pennsylvania law. While a woman can be convicted as a co-conspirator in the attempt to commit abortion in some states, she cannot be charged as an accomplice to abortion in Alabama if she cooperates with the abortionist in the sincere belief that her life was in danger without the therapeutic termination of pregnancy.[7]

Since most abortion laws are unenforceable, only a small fraction of these cases are ever successfully prosecuted. Because criminal liability in abortion cases cannot be determined by the mere willingness of the abortionist to perform the operation, conviction usually can be sustained only if evidence of the actual abortion is presented in court. The specific act must reasonably be in progress before intent can be established. Records, blood samples, urine specimens, and medical instruments, therefore, are necessary evidence in the successful prosecution of the female participant or the illegal abortionist.

The abortant and the abortionist

Women who desire the termination of pregnancy, Charles Dahlberg believes, can be divided into four categories. The *young unmarried woman,* who becomes pregnant at an early age, comprises the first category. The *older, previously married woman* represents a second group. Whether a widow or a divorcee, she attempts to void the pregnancy because the child is undesired and the potential stigma may threaten her immediate status in the community. *Married mothers having an accidental pregnancy,* comprising a third category, represent the largest group seeking abortions. They are motivated by medical, psychological, economic or even self-indulgent reasons. *Women with a contraindication* to pregnancy, representing the final group, often find pregnancy to be a psychological threat leading to a psychiatric illness. Some women may show evidence of mental deterioration as a result of pregnancy, and others may commit or attempt to commit suicide. The number of such

---

[7] *Ibid.,* p. 105.

cases has decreased. In recent years, however, a rise has occurred in the number of mothers who seek an abortion because they have been exposed to German measles in the first three months of pregnancy or taken Thalidomide or other potentially deforming drugs.[8]

The highest illegal abortion rate among married women occurs in the 16 to 25 and 40 to 50 age brackets.[9] Fewer than 1 percent of all abortions performed today meet the requirements of state laws, which prohibit abortion unless the operation is necessary to save the life of the woman or child. Women in the lower economic classes, least able to pay the price necessary to secure the services of a legitimate doctor, more frequently fall victim to the illegitimate abortionist. On the other hand, strong evidence suggests that respectable middle- and upper-class women more often receive understanding and sympathetic referral or surgery from their local physician. While neighbors generally refer lower-economic-class females to the local abortionist, middle- and upper-class women make contact with the abortionist through a general practitioner, druggist, former patient, or other secondary source.

The late Alfred Kinsey found that 22 percent of the married women in a study of over 5,000 white nonprison females had had one or more induced abortions by the time they were 47 years old.[10] Nearly 80 percent of the women patronizing the abortionist had previously attempted to complete the abortion themselves. While many of the illegal abortionists represented in Kinsey's study were doctors working in a clandestine manner, others had had little or no former medical training. The abortionist, however, was more skilled than Kinsey expected him to be. Although the legitimate physician practiced abortion with a threat of loss of his medical license if discovered, the nonmedical abortionist had little to lose. He easily rationalized his behavior, claiming that he was performing a necessary public service which the law, somewhat backwardly, restricted. Although reputable physicians periodically utilized his services, the abortionist received little, if any, support from the local medical association when discovered and prosecuted.

A review of 363 medical histories of abortion patients recorded during several months in 1948 by two abortion specialists in a large eastern city revealed that 102 of the 363 women were single, 180 married, and 81 previously married. Nearly one half of the formerly married group, studied by Christopher Tietze, were widows, while the remainder were divorced. Almost one half (170) of the 363 abortants were first offenders. The women in the sample ranged from 13 to 47 years, with an average age of 28.6 years. Criminal abortion, Tietze found, tended to increase

---

[8] Dahlberg, *op. cit.*, pp. 383–36.
[9] Bates and Zawadski, *op. cit.*, p. 4.
[10] Schur, *op. cit.*, p. 12.

with parity (increased births), an indication that abortion among older women was often sought to limit family size (see Table 8–2). J. H. Simons found similar evidence. Although his sample included an over-representation of Minneapolis charity hospital patients, three fourths of those treated for abortion were married women.[11]

Jerome Bates and Edward Zawadski delineate five major abortionist types. The *physician-abortionist* is a medically licensed professional who

TABLE 8–2
Women undergoing illegal abortion by marital status, age, number of children ever born and previous induced abortions

	Single	Married	Previously Married	Total
Age (years)				
10–14	3	...	..	3
15–19	22	10	2	34
20–24	29	44	15	88
25–29	21	42	28	91
30–34	18	42	20	80
35–39	6	19	10	35
40 and over	3	23	6	32
Children born				
0	100	45	25	170
1	2	39	31	72
2	...	52	16	68
3	...	27	8	35
4 and over	...	17	1	18
Previous abortions				
0	87	147	64	298
1	10	18	15	43
2	2	10	2	14
3 and over	3	5	..	8
Total	102	180	81	363

Source: Jerome Bates and Edward Zawadski, *Criminal Abortion* (Springfield, Ill.: Charles C. Thomas, Publisher, 1964), p. 45.

provides a special service for his clientele. The *abortionist with some medical training* possesses lesser qualifications and comes from the ranks of registered or licensed practical nurses, chiropractors, physiotherapists, licensed masseurs, dentists, midwives, or other quasi-medical professions. The *quack doctor* is usually an unlicensed general practitioner of medicine who possesses little or no formal medical training. The *amateur abortionist* often is recruited from the ranks of salesmen, elevator operators, prostitutes, barbers, or unskilled laborers. The *self-abortionist* in-

---

[11] Bates and Zawadski, *op. cit.*, p. 44.

cludes those persons who perform, often in desperation, the operation on themselves.[12] Thirty-one (27.9 percent) of 111 convicted abortionists studied by Bates and Zawadski were physicians who had little economic reason for engaging in the abortion traffic. Personal inadequacy or insecurity seemed to stimulate their abortionist activity.

PROSTITUTION

Prostitution is an indiscriminate commercial transaction involving the giving of one's body in sexual relationships for money.

The prostitute

American prostitutes, Frederick W. Egan suggests, fall into four basic types. The *call girl* works by telephone, contacting customers and making arrangements to meet at designated places. The *hustler* usually operates as a streetwalker or tavern pickup and services her clients in taxicabs, nearby hotels, or handy apartments. The *door-knocker* walks the halls of cheaper rooming houses or small hotels soliciting customers. The *factory girl*, working under the supervision of a madam takes on all comers.[13] Although not mentioned by Egan, the *party girl* and the *male homosexual prostitute* represent additional types who sell their sexual capacities to interested parties.

The *general prostitute* has often been described as masochistic, infantile, unable to attain mature interpersonal relationships, regressed, and emotionally dangerous to males. The call girl has been depicted as a person marked by a confused self-image, high dependency, gender-role confusion, personal aggressiveness, and incomplete internal controls. Thirty-three call girls, reported in a Los Angeles study by James H. Bryan, were between 18 and 32 years of age. Thirty-two had had contact with a person professionally involved in call-girl activities, whether a pimp or another call girl, immediately before their entrance into the trade. Nearly one half reported that their initial contact was a call girl whom they actively sought out in the attempt to enter into prostitution. Several women became call girls in order to maintain the love of the pimp, who generally arranged for the training of the girl. Twenty-four of these girls were initially trained by experienced call girls in a local apartment, usually over a two- or three-month period. Their education included an orientation to the way to obtain the fee, to consume drugs and alcohol, to converse with clients, to practice sexual and physical

---

[12] *Ibid.*, p. 35.
[13] Frederick W. Egan, *Plain Clothesman* (New York: Greenberg, 1952), pp. 100–104.

hygiene, and to solicit customers by telephone. Call girls, Bryan found, represent a low-level skill group whose economic existence centered around the pimp, or the prospect "book" through which they maintained contact with their potential clientele.[14]

The regulation of prostitution

The first serious efforts to control prostitution were made in 16th century in Europe following an epidemic of venereal disease. Prostitutes were registered in Paris as early as 1785. Napoleon Bonaparte established a system of segregated control in 1808. Brothels and solicitations for prostitution were restricted to particular city districts; houses of prostitution were licensed by the state. There were also provisions for registration and periodical medical examination of prostitutes. Similar plans introduced in various parts of the world have proved ineffective. A congress in London in 1899 sought international cooperation to stamp out the "white slave" traffic. The League of Nations set up a fact-finding body in 1919, and the United Nations took over the international attack on prostitution in 1946.

Today prostitution is still ignored in many parts of the world and is even state sponsored in some. However, prostitution was banned by law in France in 1946, in Belgium in 1948, and in Italy in 1958. Although the extension of voting right to Japanese women after World War II led to legislation to suppress commercial prostitution in Japan, cultural attitudes favoring the practice still remain.

No efforts were made by the federal government in the United States to regulate prostitution until 1910, when the Mann Act, prohibiting the interstate transportation of women for immoral purposes, was passed. Other legislation included the May Act (1941), which made it a federal offense to practice prostitution in designated military neighborhoods. Certain provisions of the federal immigration laws prohibit the introduction of alien prostitutes into the United States and the participation of prospective immigrants in prostitution for a five year period upon entrance to the country upon penalty of deportation.

American society formally finds prostitution inconsistent with traditional moral concepts. Most states have attempted to develop public educational programs designed to inform citizens about sex, prostitution, venereal disease, and organized crime. Everywhere in the United States except Arizona and Nevada keeping a house of prostitution is illegal.

---

[14] James H. Bryan, "Apprenticeships in Prostitution," *Social Problems*, Vol. 12, No. 3 (Winter, 1965), pp. 287–97. A dimension of the prostitution problem is discussed in Arthur J. Bilek and Alan S. Ganz, "The B-girl Problem," *Journal of Criminal Law, Criminology and Police Science*, Vol. 56, No. 1 (March, 1965), pp. 39–44.

In Nevada, local towns or cities may prohibit prostitution by ordinance; it is unlawful in Nevada for anyone to live off the earnings of a prostitute or to engage in procuring.

Laws against streetwalking, loitering in bars, solicitation for acts of prostitution, and being an inmate of a disorderly house have been progressively refined over the decades. Although the typical prostitution statute is designed to control female-male prostitution relationships, some communities also restrict homosexual prostitution.

Laws against the panderer or procurer are designed to control the agent who books the female into a house of prostitution and/or supervises her career. The panderer-procurer uses physical or psychological coercion to control the female in the trade. The pimp, also recognized in law, works actively for his stable of prostitutes and solicits customers for them, living parasitically from their earnings. In some states, statutes against pandering or pimping also include prohibitions and sanctions against husbands who cause or permit wives to commit prostitution and against parents who permit children to engage or remain in the "profession."

The possession or operation of a house of prostitution is a criminal offense in most political communities of the United States. The practice of mobile prostitution has led to the formulation of laws designed to control modern prostitution procedures. Penalties, therefore, can be lodged against bars or other businesses which permit known prostitutes to frequent the premises, against persons who operate employment agencies and refer women to places of ill-repute, taxi drivers who transport customers to prostitutes, or even persons who knowingly permit prostitutes to operate on premises which they own. Local ordinances often overlap state statutes. City restrictions are likely to be more detailed. Since dance halls, dance academies, Turkish baths, massage parlors, escort agencies, or other seemingly legal operations often front for prostitution activity, special ordinances and laws are periodically enacted to cover these situations. Laws designed to control the male customer, although uncommon, do exist in some jurisdictions. Although solicitation, loitering, and aiding or abetting laws may also apply to the customer, they are infrequently applied against the male participant.[15]

Additional attempts to control prostitution have involved civil actions under so-called "red-light abatement laws." Designed to overcome unwillingness of the police or prosecuting attorneys to enforce criminal statutes against prostitution, the citizen, under the provisions of these laws, possesses the right to affirm that a particular operation is a public nuisance. He may request that the court issue an abatement order which

---

[15] B. J. George, Jr., "Prostitution," in Ralph Slovenko (ed.), *op. cit.*, pp. 646–50. Refer to Harry Benjamin, *Prostitution and Morality* (New York: Julian Press, Inc. 1964).

directs the sale of furniture, fixtures, and other contents of the building in which prostitution takes place and the sealing of the premises for a one-year period under the supervision of the court. The denial or revocation of a license or permit to engage in a business activity is a form of repressive abatement designed to constrain those who resort to prostitution. The revocation of the liquor license, taxi permit, business license, or other local or state enabling license often drastically hinders the continuance of prostitution.

Common health laws offer an alternate avenue of control. Under current legislation, most health departments possess the power to seek out persons with communicable diseases and to quarantine the patient and premises until the disease has been cured.[16] This power, however, is rarely used, in spite of the threat of prostitution to community health. A large number of prostitutes, seemingly free from venereal disease, may actually spread gonorrhea and syphilis. Since a heavy dose of antibiotics taken before a vaginal smear test can result in a negative reading, periodic medical examinations are ineffective in controlling the transmission of venereal disease. A study of venereal disease among American troops in Europe after World War II, for example, revealed that licensed houses of prostitution represented the greatest single source of G.I. infection.[17]

---

[16] *Ibid.*, pp. 651–56. For a historical and cultural analysis of prostitution, refer to Fernando Enriques, *Prostitution and Society* (New York: Grove Press, Inc., 1966).

[17] *Ibid.*, p. 659. Also see Great Britain, The Committee of Homosexual Offenses and Prostitution, *The Wolfenden Report* (New York: Stein & Day, Publishers, 1962).

Chapter 9

ORGANIZED CRIME

Organized crime, diverse and encompassing, may be conceived as a crime committed by a person occupying a position in an established division of labor designed for the commission of crime.[1] Traditionally structured in the form of gambling, loan-sharking (usury, shylocking, or "juice"), narcotics, prostitution, and labor racketeering, its system now extends into legal business enterprises, including private garbage collection, jukebox operations, meat processing, nightclub enterprises, laundry services, and food sale and distribution.[2] Using terror, extortion, or other forms of fear and force to monopolize whole economic areas and to avoid income taxes, organized crime undermines the basic tax structure, causes inflated prices for legitimate and illegitimate goods and services, and encourages local corruption.[3] Commonly, the group engaging in organized crime is marked by eight characteristics, as follows:

1. Has a substantial number of members.
2. Aggressively attempts to subvert the process of government by well-organized endeavors to capture or otherwise make ineffectual the three branches of our local and federal government by various forms of bribery and corruption.
3. Its primary purpose is to dominate those categories of crime which we refer to as "organized crime." By "organized crime" is meant the

---

[1] Donald R. Cressey, *Theft of the Nation* (New York: Harper & Row, Publishers, 1969), p. 313. Also see a newly published volume by Ralph Salerno and John S. Tompkins, *The Crime Confederation* (New York: Doubleday & Co., Inc., 1969).

[2] *Chicago Daily News,* October 26, 1967, p. 64. Also recorded in *Chicago's American,* October 26, 1967, p. 54.

[3] Chicago Crime Commission, *Spotlight on Organized Crime in the Chicago Syndicate* (November, 1967), pp. 11–18.

following: commercialized prostitution, labor and management racketeering, loan-sharking, and the infiltration of the crime syndicate into
legitimate enterprises.
4. Anticipates a continuous, indefinite life-span of operation.
5. Members habitually engage in similar criminal activity as a primary
source of income.
6. Top leadership and management people primarily engage in crimes
of conspiracy and are usually divorced from operations by two or
more levels.
7. Is dedicated to commit murder and other acts of violence on any
member who informs on the group and to commit similar violence
on any outsider who seriously threatens the security of the group.
8. Does not recognize any geographical boundaries of operation and
is often associated in crime with similar groups in other cities, states,
and in some instances, in other countries.[4]

The high profits which such organized-crime operations entail provide
the means by which complete communities are controlled through a
"fix" in city hall or among enforcement officials. The economic strength
of organized crime has grown so great that it now possesses the power
to undermine stock market share prices, costs of goods purchased by
average family members and goals of industrial institutions. Writing
in his book *Theft of the Nation*, Donald R. Cressey delineates several
facts which explain the nature and operation of the Cosa Nostra, one
of several syndicates or crime organizations.

1. A nationwide alliance of at least twenty-four tightly knit "families" of
criminals exists in the United States. (Because the families are "fictive,"
in the sense that the members are not all relatives, it is necessary to
refer to them in quotation marks.)
2. The members of these "families" are all Italians and Sicilians, or of Italian
and Sicilian descent, and those on the Eastern Seaboard, especially, call
the entire system "Cosa Nostra." Each participant thinks of himself as
a "member" of a specific "family" and of Cosa Nostra (or of some equivalent term).
3. The names, criminal records, and principal criminal activities of about
5,000 of the participants have been assembled.
4. The persons occupying key positions in the skeletal structure of each "family"—consisting of positions of boss, underboss, lieutenants (also called
"captains"), counselor, and for low-ranking members called "soldiers" or
"button men"—are well-known to law-enforcement officials having access
to informants. Names of persons who permanently or temporarily occupy
other positions, such as "buffer," "money mover," "enforcer," and "executioner," are also well-known.
5. The "families" are linked to each other, and to non-Cosa Nostra syndicates,

[4] Ed Reid, *The Grim Reapers* (Chicago: Henry Regnery Co., 1969), pp. 12–13.

by understandings, agreements, and "treaties," and by mutual deference to a "Commission" made up of the leaders of the most powerful of the "families."

6. The boss of each "family" directs the activities, especially the illegal activities, of the members of his "family."

7. The members of this organization control all the tiny parts of the illegal gambling in the United States. They are the principal importers and wholesalers of narcotics. They have infiltrated certain labor unions, where they extort money from the employers and at the same time, cheat the members of the union. The members have a virtual monopoly of some legitimate enterprises, such as cigarette vending machines and juke boxes, and they own a wide variety of retail firms, restaurants and bars, hotels, trucking companies, fruit companies, linen-supply houses, garbage collection routes, and factories. Until recently, they owned several state legislators and federal congressmen and other officials in the legislative, executive, and judicial branches of government at the local, state, and federal levels. Some government officials (including judges) are considered, and consider themselves, members.

8. The information about the Commission, the "families," and the activities of members have come from detailed reports made by a wide variety of police observers, informants, wire taps, and electronic bugs.[5]

TRADITIONAL ORGANIZED CRIME

Gambling

Illegal numbers or *bolita* lotteries, off-track horse or sports betting through bookies, floating crap games, and illegal casino operations are among the forms of gambling controlled by organized crime. Although smaller communities may have their own small-time bookies, allowed to exist on the police assumption that a local product provides useful services under local, not syndicate control, gambling operators in larger cities are invariably integrated into the large-scale criminal organization. If sufficiently successful, the independent operator, moreover, is likely to be coerced to share his profits with the syndicate or to be forced into ruin as his customers are redirected to a mob member.

Large-scale gambling demands multiple-role operatives. The *operator* who takes the customer's bet on the street or in his own shop represents the bottom of the gambling hierarchy. He transfers the receipts to the *runner* or *bagman;* the bagman transmits them to the *district overseer,* who further processes the receipts according to predetermined distribution patterns. In larger cities, a *syndicate coordinator* provides additional channels for quick dispersal of profits to organization leaders.[6] One De-

[5] Cressey, *op. cit.*, pp. x–xi.
[6] The President's Commission on Law Enforcement and Administration of Justice, *The Challenge of Crime in a Free Society* (Washington, D.C.: U.S. Government Printing Office, 1967), p. 189.

troit lottery, supervised by a *section chief,* involved over 100 persons. Fifty *pickup men,* divided into five groups, reported to a substation supervisor, who in turn transmitted lottery receipts to the main office through a trusted messenger. Six workers at the main office tabulated the bets, judged the winning numbers, recorded pertinent data concerning betting activity, and processed the proceeds to the section chief, who transmitted a proportionate share to his immediate superiors. The division of labor, insulated at each level, served to maintain security and to minimize risk.[7]

Organized gambling depends upon immediate communication between the operator and his "layoff" sources in other communities. When "overbooked" on a particular number, selection, or combination, the operator may protect himself by "laying off" some of his own money on the same number or sports team at another location. Although no accurate figures are currently available, the estimated organized gambling intake is believed to vary from $7 billion to $50 billion per year. Legitimate racetrack betting reaches a yearly gross of almost $5 billion and annual illegal betting on horses, lotteries, and sports events totals an estimated $20 billion, resulting in a $6 billion to $7 billion annual illegal profit after payment of operational expenses in the form of wages, bribery, rent, and armanents.[8]

Loan-sharking or "juice"

Loan-sharking, the lending of money at exorbitant interest rates, offers the second largest source of revenue for organized crime. Gambling profits provide the initial capital for loan-sharking or "juice" operations. These operations produce large profits earned through excessive interest charges, varying from 1 to 150 percent per week, depending upon the relationship of the lender and borrower, the purpose and size of the loan, the borrower's repayment potential, and his loan security. The 20-percent-per-week loan, known in its classic form as "6-for-5," is the most common small loan. Since the lender is more concerned with continued interest payments than collection of principal, the loan shark attempts to keep the borrower perpetually in debt. Frequently, juice victims are gamblers borrowing to pay betting losses, narcotic addicts seeking loans to purchase heroin, or small businessmen borrowing in

---

[7] The President's Commission on Law Enforcement and Administration of Justice, *Task Force Report: Organized Crime* (Washington, D.C.: U.S. Government Printing Office, 1967), p. 35.

[8] *Ibid.,* p. 3. The problem of pinball gambling is discussed in Arthur J. Bilek, "The Pinball Problem: Alternate Solutions," *Journal of Criminal Law, Criminology, and Police Science,* Vol. 56, No. 4 (December, 1965), pp. 432–45, and Rufus King, "The Pinball Problem in Illinois," *Journal of Criminal Law, Criminology, and Police Science,* Vol. 57, No. 1 (March, 1966), pp. 17–26.

desperation when legitimate credit is unavailable. Lower organized crime echelons, too, are encouraged to place loans with their immediate superiors in order to keep profits within the family and to guarantee personal loyalty to the organizational hierarchy.

Because a man coming to a usurer is commonly in a vulnerable position, the loan shark immediately assumes a sense of moral superiority over the borrower. However, the victim also assists the development of this attitude by recognizing the usurer's "moral right" to collect any indebtedness by the use of force against his person. Because he has, in effect, placed his body as collateral for the loan, the infliction of harm against his body is expected if the offender fails to repay.[9]

While the Internal Revenue Service possesses little information concerning the take of the "juice" racket, it is believed to be a multibillion-dollar annual business.[10] One New York City usurer loaned a million dollars in the morning and a second million in the afternoon of the same day; a second usurer increased his net worth from $500,000 in 1960 to $7.5 million in 1964 through this method.[11]

Narcotics

For the most part, organized crime only operates in the importation and wholesale distribution of narcotics, where profits are great and risks of detection minimal. Since a $5,000 heroin investment may ultimately result in a $300,000 profit for the importer, distributor, and retailer, organized crime profitably imports and wholesales large-scale narcotic lots in order to maximize quick profits. It minimizes risks of detection by refusing to engage in small-profit street sales. Independent narcotic pushers, who receive drugs from organized-crime outlets, maintain contact with the "junk" addict. The total annual American heroin trade grosses an estimated $350 million. The syndicate importer and distributor, operating in a few urban areas affected by the "horse" problem, gross an approximate $21 million in profits annually.[12]

Multikilo narcotic importers operate at the top level of the narcotic traffic. Subdividing their imports, they transmit a kilogram of heroin to the *kilo man*, who subdivides his purchase for later delivery to a *courier*. After diluting the heroin by adding 3 kilograms of milk sugar for each kilo of heroin, the kilo men sell the product to *quarter-kilo men*. As the heroin is further diluted and broken down into smaller units, it is progressively sold to *ounce men* or *deck men* who retail the narcotic at going prices. By the time the 5-grain narcotic packets,

[9] Cressey, *op. cit.*, p. 85.
[10] President's Commission, *Challenge of Crime*, p. 189.
[11] Cressey, *op. cit.*, p. 77.
[12] *Ibid.*, pp. 189–190.

called *bags* or *packs,* are finally sold to addicts by the street peddler, the cost (or kilo profit) has increased 300 times.[13]

Prostitution and bootlegging

Changing sex attitudes and practices have undermined the prostitution traffic. Although prostitution still exists, its practice faces increased community resistance and hostility. Since prostitution is difficult to organize and maintain, discipline being challenged by the cultural and social freedom of the modern female, the control of organized crime over prostitution has diminished. While organized crime continues to facilitate the flow of prostitutes to convention areas, prostitution profits no longer dominate organized-crime assets.

Bootlegging, an original stimulus in the development of organized crime during the Prohibition era, has also been reduced to a minimal position in recent years. Discovery and destruction of stills and equipment by enforcement agencies during the initial stages of the bootleg operation have resulted in major losses and high risks which minimize profits to organized crime.

Labor racketeering

Labor racketeers, operating in an insidious manner, attempt to control labor contracts and to infiltrate labor unions. Motivated by the desire to steal union profits, to extort money from industry through threats of possible labor conflict, or to appropriate union pension and welfare funds for organized-crime business ventures, syndicate operatives maintain either direct or indirect influence over several major trade unions, especially those involving trucking, construction, and stevedore operations.[14] Labor racketeers, in effect, guarantee business continuity and labor-management peace as long as management kicks back a percentage of the profits, allows syndicate gambling on the premises, disregards loan sharks, and fails to report pillage of transported goods or company property to the police. In some instances, the syndicate grants concessions to local operators in return for a percentage of the profits. A son of a major New York City organized-crime leader, for example, was selected as broker for a number of union pension and welfare funds, although he had only recently received an insurance broker's license. Strategically placed, he divided his earned commissions with silent syndi-

---

[13] President's Commission, *Organized Crime,* p. 35.

[14] The scope of organized crime in the postwar era is discussed in John L. McClelland, *Crime Without Punishment* (New York: Duell, Sloan, and Pearce, 1962), a volume based upon the hearings of the Senate Select Committee on Improper Activities in the Labor and Management Field.

cate partners. When questioned, he claimed his early success was merely due to his listing on the telephone company's Yellow Pages.[15] In other instances, so-called legitimate contractors or administrators have hired organized-crime representatives in order to prevent union organization or to minimize the economic goals of collective bargaining.

ATTEMPTS AT BUSINESS LEGITIMACY

In recent years, organized crime has moved to infiltrate legitimate business in order to invest funds received through other illegal channels and to establish legitimate political and social influence necessary for modern operations. Although legitimate business profits are less than those gained by illegitimate means, investment in acceptable business enterprise allows a form of economic diversification which guarantees continued profits despite police pressures against illegal gambling or loan-sharking. The ownership or control of nightclubs, linen supply companies, entertainment booking agencies, parking outlets, wholesale meat enterprises, or other companies which offer substantial profits or diverse opportunities for hiding gambling profits from detection often form an interlocking economic system through which all assets are kept within the syndicate.[16]

The diversity of organized crime in legitimate business was first noted after the 1957 detection of a meeting of racket leaders at Apalachin, New York. Of the organized-crime representatives at the meeting, a controlled highly profitable coin-operated-machine routes (for example, jukebox, cigarette, candy), 16 maintained influence in the garment industry, 10 possessed substantial power in the grocery business, 17 regulated bars and restaurants, 11 held major control of olive oil and cheese businesses, and 9 were influential in construction companies. All this was in addition to other illegal activities. The remainder controlled legitimate automobile agencies, coal companies, funeral homes, entertainment outlets, horse and racetracks, linen and laundry companies, trucking or waterfront services, and local bakeries. One crime syndicate, the President's Commission found, possessed real estate interests valued at $300 million.

Although organized crime previously gained control of legitimate business through a variety of methods, whether by investing or concealing gambling or other illegal profits in silent partnerships, by outright purchase of legitimate firms, by receiving business firms as payment for the owner's gambling debts, by closing out usurious loans or by

---

[15] President's Commission, *Challenge of Crime*, p. 191.

[16] Chicago Crime Commission, *op. cit.*, pp. 3–18. See William J. Duffy, "Organized Crime Enterprises—Legal," in *Proceedings of the First National Symposium on Law Enforcement Science and Technology*, pp. 29–32, 21–27.

other forms of extortion, some syndicates have begun to use more sophisticated operational techniques. In one instance, for example, a syndicate group offered loans to legitimate business representatives in return for a guarantee that a syndicate racketeer would be appointed to the company's board of directors and that a syndicate nominee would receive first option to purchase company stock if such stock were ever placed on the open market. In another instance, the control of a brokerage firm, gained through loan-sharking, enabled syndicate operatives to make a quick profit through the sale of more than $2 million worth of fraudulent stock.

Even banking has not been able to remain free of organized-crime influence. One San Francisco bank, for example, declared bankruptcy soon after the syndicate gained control and siphoned off its assets. If the business enterprise is worthless to the syndicate, organized crime has been known to recover its usurious debt by burning the building and its contents and recovering immediate investment capital from its fire insurance coverage.[17]

THE ECONOMIC ANALYSIS OF ORGANIZED CRIME

Since syndicate operations have been largely exempt from previous governmental regulation, few attempts have been made to determine the exact economic dimensions of organized crime. Although data are few, organized crime, economist Thomas C. Schelling suggests, can be tentatively divided into several subcategories.

Black-market operations, the sale of commodities and services contrary to law, constitute a major part of organized crime activity. Traffic in narcotics, prostitution, gambling, illegal liquor, abortion, pornography, stolen goods, contraband, cigarettes, and even contraceptives are forms of black-market operations. Profitable interstate transportation of cigarettes, however, occurs only when profits can be made through avoidance of the cigarette tax in a high-tax state.

Racketeering, evidenced in extortion or criminal monopoly, is a form of unfair business operation. Extortion implies the use of threats of criminal violence and/or criminal competition to force payments of goods or money. Criminal monopoly suggests the use of criminal means to destroy competition. In both instances, organized crime minimizes or eliminates competition in order to maximize potential profits.

The *black-market monopoly,* another form of organized-crime activity, is often encouraged by laws guaranteeing the existence of an illegal monopoly which, in effect, protect the black marketeers from competitors

---

[17] Insight into syndicate operations can be gained by referring to Gus Tyler, *Organized Crime in America* (Ann Arbor: University of Michigan Press, 1962).

unwilling to pursue criminal careers. Legal prohibitions against the use of narcotics, for example, automatically create a black-market monopoly which yields excessive profits for the syndicate importers and local pusher.[18]

Cartel relationships take the form of price-fixing collusion. Working with other firms operating in the same area of enterprise, cartel representatives restrain trade in order to maximize profits. Although syndicate members may assume price-fixing leadership, they are more frequently called upon to enforce a predetermined agreement.

In *organized cheating*, mob operatives evade taxes, process adulterated foods, declare bankruptcy, or engage in unethical business practices. The use of "fronts" to distribute goods or hide illegal earnings are by-products of the cheating process.

Organized criminal services involve both legitimate and illegitimate business and service operations. The need for access to legitimate legal services, financial and tax advice, periodic credit, places to conduct business, communications facilities, and the general public causes organized crime to hire representatives of legal service and professional occupations. Where conditions demand more than consultation and services, organized crime attempts to maximize profits through the *corruption* of police, politicians, influential community leaders, and public prosecutors through bribery, intimidation or payoff.[19]

THE STRUCTURE OF ORGANIZED CRIME

La Cosa Nostra ("Our Thing") represents the inner core of organized crime (see Figure 9–1). Although it is not organically connected to the Sicilian Mafia, the Cosa Nostra presents a similar organizational form and code of conduct. Based upon a patriarchal familial relationship, the code demands that each family member remain responsive to the interests of his superior. Each participant is obligated to remain silent if detected and to refrain from seeking police protection. Loyalty, honor, respect, and obedience are central values in the exploitative authoritarian relationship of family members. Suspected or actual disloyalty may result in the immediate execution of any family member, regardless of his official position.[20] However, the trained syndicate man, Ed Reid contends, "is devoid of any moral concepts. He believes he has the right

---

[18] Thomas C. Schelling, "Economic Analysis and Organized Crime," President's Commission, *Organized Crime*, pp. 116–17.

[19] *Ibid.*, p. 117. Also refer to John A. Gardiner and David J. Olson, "Wincanton: The Politics of Corruption," President's Commission, *Organized Crime*, pp. 61–79.

[20] President's Commission, *Challenge of Crime*, p. 10. A popularized treatment of the organized crime problem is found in Hank Messic, *The Silent Syndicate* (New York: Macmillan Co., 1967).

FIGURE 9–1

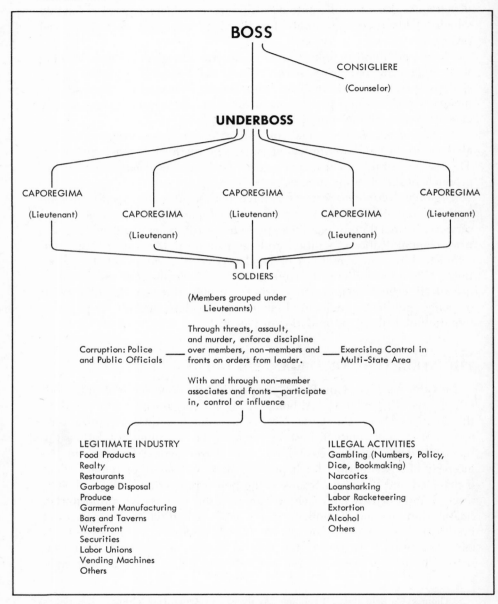

Source: The President's Commission on Law Enforcement and the Administration of Justice, *Task Force Report: Organized Crime* (Washington, D.C.: U.S. Government Printing Office, 1966), p. 9.

to steal, corrupt, even murder. His world of crime and punishment is different. In the place of shame and degradation he expects rewards: power, money, honor, glorification by a fraternity that has spread its influence around the world."[21]

Despite existing syndicate shortcomings, a national *Commissione*, composed of nine known members from the New York, Philadelphia, Buffalo, Detroit, and Chicago syndicates, serves to clarify Cosa Nostra organizational and jurisdictional disputes, set larger policy, and determine the more general organized crime tactics. Neither a representative assembly nor an elected judicial body, the *Commissione* reflects the informal authority and power patterns already recognized among its 24-constituent member syndicates. Composed of major representatives or leaders from the larger and more influential combines of Italian groups known as "families," the *Commissione* acts on behalf of its own organization and other organized crime groups in nearby communities. It is currently dominated by the five New York families. It ratifies or rejects agreements with other non-Italian criminal organizations and supervises the family selection of a new chief in order to minimize family and territorial conflict. The Baltimore, Dallas, Kansas City, Los Angeles, Pittsburgh, San Francisco, and Tampa families are not currently represented in formal *Commissione* membership.[22]

The *Boss* remains the titular head of the family, possessing both absolute authority over family structure and membership and absolute rule within his recognized territorial or geographical area of influence. The actual work of the organization is often delegated to a large number of subadministrators, charged with the task of operationalizing family or Cosa Nostra policy and ultimately responsible to the head of the family. The Boss, however, works closely with the *Consigliere* (Counselor), a crime elder statesman, and the family *Sottocapo* (Underboss) to maximize profits and maintain order.[23] Since the Counselor is often retired from the actual authority structure, his influence is largely indirect. The Underboss, on the other hand, is second in command, relaying information and transmitting instructions as a functional vice-president.

The *Caporegema* (Lieutenant) serves as the buffer between the top family member and the lowest echelon of the organization. As a go-between, he insulates the leaders of the hierarchy by channeling all command information, complaints, and money through this position. A functionary rather than a decision maker, the *Caporegema* activates the system. In some instances, his task is shared with other associates

[21] Reid, *op. cit.*, p. 2.
[22] President's Commission, *Organized Crime*, p. 34.
[23] *Ibid.*, pp. 33–34.

who work under his direction. As the manager of the organization, he operationalizes family policy decisions among the *Soldati,* the *Soldiers* or *Button men,* directly responsible to the Lieutenant. Although the Soldier holds the lowest prestige within the family, he may engage in a business partnership with one or more of his superiors. If he operates an illicit loan-sharking, dice, lottery, bookmaking, smuggling, or vending-machine operation, the Soldier usually pays a commission to the larger organization for the privilege of maintaining a business monopoly.[24] Between 3,000 to 4,000 men are members of the organized family confederations.[25]

The family ultimately depends, however, upon an even greater number of employees and agents to fulfill syndicate tasks and functions (see Figure 9–2). Neither members of the family nor necessarily of Italian descent, these workers are susceptible to discovery and apprehension by law enforcement agencies. As functionaries, they man bookie telephones, transport illicit goods, push narcotics at favored locations, or even pull wages in a legitimate business. Existing outside the semiformal family structure of organized crime, they often represent diverse ethnic groups. In one Chicago Negro neighborhood, for example, the workers were Negro, the lottery bankers were Japanese-Americans, and the lottery was licensed by an Italian family member.[26]

Organized crime depends upon a continuing system of recruitment, selection, and promotion. Local boys, attracted by the self-evident success of mob operatives in the community, offer the raw material from which the lower echelons of the syndicate operation are fashioned. Seeking to rise above their environment, they are readily subjected to syndicate promises of quick status, money, liquor, women, promotion, and security. The recruiter is protected by a lower-class distrust for the police, and therefore finds ready community response as he offers marginal services to persons who discount their marginality.

The early cooperation of the youth eventually grows into more complex forms of individual commitment to organized crime. Working originally as an accomplice rather than an originator of criminal acts, the youthful recruit soon becomes a "pure" offender in his own right. His first arrest, sentence, and potential incarceration insure his continued commitment to the organization, as he recognizes his own vulnerability to prosecution and the legal protection offered by the syndicate spokesman. As the social myths of equal justice for all social classes and of crime unprofitability are shattered, the realization that loyalty brings

---

[24] President's Commission, *Challenge of Crime,* p. 193.

[25] President's Commission, *Organized Crime,* p. 34. See Peter Maas, *The Valachi Papers* (New York: G. P. Putnam's Sons, 1968) for a special insight into the Cosa Nostra.

[26] *Ibid.,* p. 8.

Positions in a Cosa Nostra "family" organization

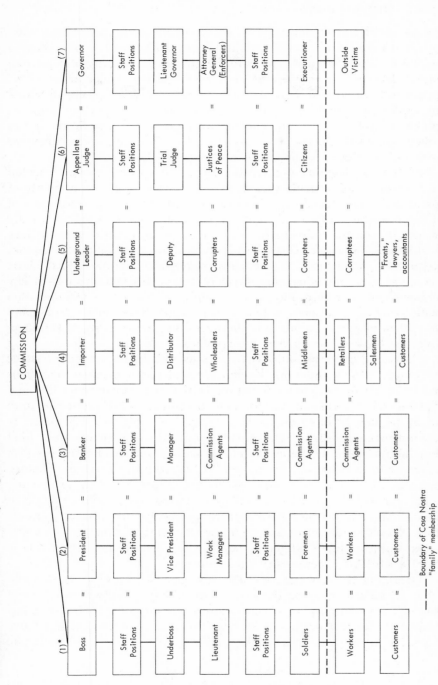

Note: (1) Authority structure; (2) production structure; (3) sales structure; (4) sales structure; (5) corruption structure; (6) judicial structure; and (7) law-enforcement structure. Most Cosa Nostra members occupy positions in structures (1) through (5), and many occupy positions in all seven structures.
Source: Donald R. Cressey, *Theft of the Nation* (New York: Harper & Row, Publishers, 1969), pp. 146–47.

quick profits and that justice can be corrupted serve to reinforce commitment to the syndicate. The youth perceives his future to be unlimited within the operation and returns to the guaranteed security of organized crime. Not only does the recruit receive a salary which often is six or seven times as high as that available in any other job commensurate to his skills but he also recognizes that political leaders, judges, attorneys, police officials, and accountants respond quickly to syndicate desires when offered significant monetary rewards.[27] The power of money, he quickly learns, exceeds the functioning power of the law.

Since every legitimate enterprise depends upon one or more essential individuals, each organization is especially susceptible to attempts of organized crime to corrupt. Because the compromise or subversion of a total institution is costly and impractical, organized crime usually works to corrupt individuals, whether in schools, businesses, unions, legislatures, executive offices, courts, political parties, or other agencies potentially antagonistic to the aims of organized crime. Most efforts to compromise individuals are directed toward the neutralization of law enforcement. But corruption is not simply limited to overt cooperation with criminals. In some instances, subversion is far more subtle and is evidenced in the failure to fulfill one's duty, the inability to act effectively, or the tendency to move precipitously.

Organized crime periodically reaches its ends by encouraging passage of tough laws in order to develop black-market monopoly conditions which eliminate marginal competitors. Even now, organized crime and the federal government vie for narcotic profits, whether in the form of illegal income or taxes. Harsh narcotic laws, which are intended to control narcotic distribution, actually punish the pusher and the addict but hardly affect the importer. The syndicate's financial resources give it power to dispense largess through legislative committees, prosecutors, witnesses, and jury members and to affect the nature of community enforcement. The position of the public prosecutor, whose judgment finally determines which cases will be prosecuted, is especially critical to successful enforcement. In one midwestern state, syndicate representatives unsuccessfully attempted to buy a county prosecutor for a $100,000–$125,000 "guaranteed annual income."

Operating as an illegal, invisible government, the Cosa Nostra and other syndicate organizations tend to nullify effective government through the neutralization of law enforcement and the system of criminal justice and/or the attempt to render local, state, and federal legislative agencies ineffective. Because the political process is so vulnerable to

---

[27] Ralph F. Salerno, "Syndicate Personnel Structure," *Proceedings of the First National Symposium on Law Enforcement Science and Technology* (London: Academic Press, 1967), p. 11.

moneyed interests, organized crime is able to corrupt actual and potential political leaders through well-placed financial contributions to their election campaigns. Organized crime depends upon corruption and by dispensing rewards undermines the objectivity and effectiveness of law enforcement. In its attempt to insulate syndicate members and leadership from police arrest and exposure to actual criminal acts, organized crime leadership utilizes 10 self-protective measures:

1. *Insulation*—Top-ranking members avoid involvement in actual crimes. They limit social contacts and eliminate all obvious links to criminal operations. The strongest insulation is Cosa Nostra's inherent philosophy that bosses must be protected. A combination of fear and traditional distaste for informing has helped preserve 30 years of silence, broken publicly by Joseph Valachi;
2. *Respect*—Deference is given to position, authority, and seniority, and is unmistakable when observed. Status is often revealed by the tone of voice, the held door, the proffered seat. "Sleepers" (high-ranking members whose importance was relatively unknown) have been revealed to police by displays of respect;
3. The *buffer*—Leaders do not mix or deal with underlings, but use a trusted aid to stand between the boss and trouble. This buffer has many functions and knows all the boss' operations;
4. The *appointment*—Infrequently, with utmost security a leader may meet an underling upon an urgent matter. Ordinarily, even the most important matters go through regular channels;
5. The *sitdown*—Meetings known as "sitdowns" are peace conferences within families or among allied families. Usually these are held at lower levels, although sometimes the heads of Cosa Nostra families must meet on vital questions. Decisions at the upper level are final;
6. *Discipline*—Whenever necessary, as it frequently is, discipline is kept within a family and is carried out by associates. Punishment ranges from warnings to sanctions on criminal enterprises to murder;
7. The *disappearance*—When murder is decreed, trusted fellow members carry out the sentence and the man vanishes without a trace—no violence, no gun play, no blood, no body, no public outcry. The case is carried by police as a disappearance; the victim is a missing person;
8. *Permission*—All illicit activities within the family require the approval of the boss. The family that gives permission will help if anything goes wrong. Family policy is the criterion; crimes which arouse the ·public are forbidden;
9. The *money mover*—One or more trusted members handle much of the cash pouring into the family from its illegal sources. The money mover has commercial connections; he puts the profits to work while hiding their sources. He invests in importing, real estate, trust funds, stock and bonds, and certain other favored enterprises. The bulk of the profits clandestinely go to the bosses; and
10. *Public relations*—The organization is always concerned with public opinion, and all strong actions which might influence the public must be

cleared with the Cosa Nostra leaders. Failure in this area reflects upon the boss. The front of respectability and propriety must be maintained.[28]

THE LOCUS OF ORGANIZED CRIME

Although organized crime is commonly viewed as a problem of large-scale organization, a President's Commission on Law Enforcement and Administration of Justice survey of 71 cities revealed that 80 percent of the police departments in cities of over 1 million inhabitants reported the existence of organized crime in their environs. An additional 20 percent of the cities with populations between 250,000 and 500,000 and over 50 percent in cities between 100,000 and 250,000 also indicated functioning syndicate operations. Several communities which denied the existence of any organized crime were known by federal intelligence agencies to possess syndicate contacts. Six of the nine other cities which failed to report or to respond to the inquiry possessed the organizational stability necessary to continue without significant disruption in spite of the death or incarceration of the local boss. Although organized crime in smaller cities has been unmeasured to date, evidence suggests that organized crime may possess a substantial foothold in cities of less than 100,000 population.[29]

The camouflage granted by corrupt local officials makes organized crime less identifiable to the public. The expansion of government regulation, however, increases the power of organized crime to circumvent the law and to gain monopolistic profits. The ability of organized crime to neutralize police officials, prosecutors, legislators, judges, regulatory agency officials, mayors, councilmen, or other leading citizens who possess either political or moral authority to block syndicate operations, as a result, has rendered the community helpless. In one California community, for example, the syndicate silenced local ministers by a simple tactic of offering a few thousand dollars to the church building fund. In another instance citizen efforts to control organized crime were neutralized by the prosecutor who held that any citizen presenting evidence of payment to public officials to secure government criminal action would also be prosecuted for unlawful conduct or participation in an illegal activity.[30] Since the public has been overly concerned for the individual violator, the criminal organization has remained largely undetected and often unidentified. Because organized crime is essentially a business enterprise, its promotional system allows for continued operation on the death or incarceration of a particular member.

---

[28] Reid, *op. cit.*, pp. 13–14.
[29] President's Commission, *Challenge of Crime*, p. 191.
[30] *Ibid.*, pp. 190–91.

ATTEMPTS TO CONTROL ORGANIZED CRIME

Investigations of organized crime instigated in the early 1900's by New Orleans and New York City police officers ended abruptly with their murder. In the 1920's, the rise of large-scale crime during the Prohibition era led to a Treasury Department investigation, eventuating in the conviction of Al Capone for income tax evasion. In New York, attempts to control organized crime in the 1930's under the leadership of Thomas E. Dewey resulted in the conviction of many syndicate leaders, including Lucky Luciano, the organizational developer of the present criminal confederation. The FBI moved to investigate and prosecute the offenders in a million-dollar movie industry extortion plot in the 1940's. The 1950's, the U.S. Attorney General convened a national conference on organized crime. While the Special Senate Committee investigations under Estes Kefauver televised the wide penetrations of organized crime to the public during the early 1950's, local law enforcement failed to utilize the leads provided by the Select Committee hearing. The Department of Justice embarked upon a major drive against the leading racket figures, but local efforts proved minimal and rather unrewarding. Using deportation proceedings, the Department successfully returned many racketeers to their country of origin. Resistance to deportation from the native country, often encouraged payoffs to foreign government officials, later limited the effectiveness of this procedure.[31]

The formation in 1954 of a Justice Department Section on Organized Crime and Racketeering resulted in only a limited coordination of investigative efforts and minimized early antiracketeering intelligence reports. Following the 1957 Apalachin meeting of organized crime representatives, the Department of Justice established a Special Group on Organized Crime, charged with the tasks of gathering intelligence, coordinating prosecution, and following up the results of grand jury proceedings. Although syndicate members attending the Apalachin meeting were later convicted of conspiracy, their successful appeal from conviction led to the eventual incorporation of the Special Group into the Organized Crime and Racketeering Section of the Justice Department.[32]

A new drive against organized crime began in the 1960's, when the FBI began to supply regular intelligence reports on 400 organized-crime leaders to appropriate enforcement agencies. The successes of the 1961–65 period, however, were slowed by the public argument over the legitimacy of federal wiretapping, as a result of a violation of a Nevada law prohibiting illegal electronic surveillance during Justice Department

---

[31] President's Commission, *Organized Crime,* pp. 10–11.
[32] *Ibid.,* p. 11.

investigations into Las Vegas casino "skimming" practices.[33] Personnel turnover and charges of enforcement overcentralization added to this general slowdown.

The 1967 creation of the "Strike Force," composed of investigators representing the Treasury Department's Alcohol and Tobacco Tax Division, Bureau of Narcotics, Bureau of Customs, Internal Revenue Service's Intelligence and Audit Divisions and the Labor Department's Racketeering Division, was designed to probe all dimensions of organized-crime operations in order to find areas for successful prosecution. Coordinated by the Justice Department's Criminal Division, the Strike Force moved to remove organized crime profits and to charge personnel essential to syndicate operations.

The recent attempt to control organized crime has been hindered by a lack of local concern.[34] A President's Commission survey of 71 cities revealed that only 12 of the 19 cities that admitted the existence of organized crime had specialized police units that were designed to gather information concerning syndicate activity. Special public prosecutors were assigned to work on organized crime cases in only six of these cities. Only 3 of 43 police departments which responded that they possessed no organized crime had developed units to restrict its development. As local police and prosecutors, however, became more aware of the threat of organized crime, new units began to emerge.[35] Prosecution attempts were still restricted by the problems of obtaining proof, limited local and state law enforcement resources, interagency suspicion, lack of enforcement coordination, basic failures to develop tactical and strategic intelligence information, problems of judicial leniency, and public and political indifference to organized crime.

TOWARD THE CONTROL OF ORGANIZED CRIME

The large-scale emergence of organized crime led the President's Commission on Law Enforcement and Administration of Justice to recommend that a minimum of one investigative grand jury be impaneled annually in each area which possesses major organized-crime activity. Under its provisions, the grand jury would possess the right to replace local prosecution and investigation teams with special counsel or investigators authorized to probe any areas designated by the grand jury.

---

[33] For a discussion of the practical problems involved, see G. Robert Blakey, "Aspects of the Evidence Gathering Process in Organized Crime Cases: A Preliminary Analysis," President's Commission, *Task Force Reports: Organized Crime*, pp. 80–113.

[34] *Chicago Sun-Times*, November 26, 1967, p. 3.

[35] President's Commission, *Organized Crime*, p. 13. Refer also to the *Hearings before the Subcommittee on Criminal Laws and Procedures of the Senate Committee on the Judiciary of the Eighty-Ninth Congress, Second Session* (Washington, D.C.: U.S. Government Printing Office, 1966).

A state and federal general statute, guaranteeing the nonprosecution of any witness testifying on behalf of the state, would encourage sufficient and adequate testimony against organized crime. Since the incidence of perjury is higher in organized-crime cases than in any other criminal form, Congress and the state, the Commission recommended, should abolish the rigid two-witness and direct-evidence rules in perjury prosecutions while retaining the requirement of proving an intentionally false statement. Congress should enact legislation which deals with wiretapping and electronic eavesdropping. Federal and state legislation should be enacted to provide extended prison terms when evidence, presentence reports, or sentence hearings show that a felony was committed as part of the continuing illegal business in which the convicted offender occupied a supervisory or management role. Residential facilities, the Commission noted, should also be provided in order to protect witnesses from the influence of organized crime during the period of litigation and prosecution.

Since eventual prosecution depends upon adequate investigatory personnel and procedures, every attorney general in states influenced by organized crime should form a unit of attorneys and investigators trained to gather specific information concerning syndicate activity. Each major urban police department, too, should form a special intelligence unit to detect and collect information concerning local mob operations. Local, state, and federal data, in turn, should be computerized and processed in order to coordinate the flight on organized crime. Although a permanent Joint Congressional Committee on Organized Crime should be created in Congress, special local and state groups, commissioned to investigate syndicate crime, should probe local crime activities.[36] Not only should businessmen's associations work to prevent and uncover organized crime and unfair business practices in the local community, but newspapers should also designate competent reporters to discover and disclose pertinent criminal activity when committed in the local community. Only a full-scale revelation of organized criminal activity, the Commission hypothesized, can lead to specific action designed to restrict syndicate power and to renew the community.[37]

THE CONTINUING PROBLEM OF ORGANIZED CRIME

The need to recognize that criminal behavior is more than a problem of individual maladjustment has led to the analysis of deviance as a

---

[36] *Gary Post-Tribune,* November 26, 1967, p. 85.

[37] President's Commission, *Challenge of Crime* pp. 200–209. See also Earl Johnson, Jr., "Organized Crime: Challenge to the American Legal System," *Journal of Criminal Law, Criminology, and Police Science,* Vol. 53 (December, 1962), pp. 399–425, and Vol. 54 (January, 1963), pp. 1–29.

functional part of the social system. Modern law enforcement is designed to control individuals, not organizations. Institutional or corporate crime forms, however, are only indirectly controlled through the apprehension of the individual violator. Few organizations are ever tried for criminal violations, although periodic trials of management officials occur, as witnessed in the price-fixing trials in the electrical industry. Organized crime, as a result, is most often attacked through the periodical prosecution of the individual criminal violator—for income tax evasion rather than for crimes of criminal conspiracy. The individualistic focus of modern law and enforcement have caused the public to ignore the even greater threat of group crime. And yet, group crime is evident in ghetto conflict, city hall inaction, inferior educational systems, higher taxes, and poor public services.

Until modern law recognizes the systematic aspects of the syndicate, La Cosa Nostra, or any other monopolistic criminal group, any legislative attempt to control deviant behavior will remain inadequate. While law enforcement continues to apprehend the narcotic pusher and user, it has done little to control the cartel dominating the narcotic traffic. Criminologist Donald Cressey notes that it is not a crime to plan, establish, and develop a criminal division of labor in order to commit a crime except where specific state conspiracy statutes are violated.[38] While legitimate corporations face political regulation designed to force responsible corporate action, few laws, if any, have been enacted to regulate illegitimate organizations, which remain free from arrest, prosecution, and imprisonment unless individuals within the organization are specifically charged with violations of a specific legal code. Until legislators itemize the limitations upon organized crime as explicitly as they have violations of theft and burglary, large-scale crime will continue to remain unpunished and uncontrolled.

Legal codifiers must recognize the techniques employed by systems analysts. A mass society yields, at least in some form, mass crime. Techniques utilized by large-scale institutions are logically transferred to large-scale deviant organizations. Organized crime evidences a division of labor similar to that of any legitimate organization, and therefore it possesses sensitive positions which may affect its overall operations. Since organized criminal deviance does not possess the force or the structure of law to maintain its structural forms, the *enforcer*, the person charged with maintenance of syndicate goals through threats and acts of intimidation, occupies a pivotal social control role.

A basic problem in the control of organized crime is the lack of

---

[38] Donald R. Cressey, "Organized Crime as a Social System," *Proceedings of the First National Symposium on Law Enforcement Science and Technology*, pp. 4–5.

legislation dealing with those types of activities in which organized crime participates. However, recent years have seen the growth of conspiracy legislation designed to severely hinder Cosa Nostra and other syndicate operations. Because organized crime is not a legal category, but rather a descriptive one, using it to describe the syndicate phenomena falls far short of securing successful prosecution for illicit activities. However, organized criminality involves two basic dimensions which are clearly outside the range of professional or white-collar criminal behavior—corruption of police and the use of force—which are potentially vulnerable to prosecution attempts.[39] Nevertheless, they are not easily divorced from other syndicate characteristics.

Participants in the Oyster Bay Conferences on Combatting Organized Crime, sponsored by Governor Rockefeller of New York, offer specific insight into those special characteristics which differentiated the most highly developed forms of organized crime from other legitimate and illegitimate enterprises. Organized crime, one participant summarized, is marked by (1) totalitarian organization; (2) immunity and protection from the law through professional advice, fear, or corruption, or all three, in order to insure continuance of their activities; (3) permanency and form; (4) activities which are highly profitable, relatively low in risk, and based upon human weakness; (5) use of fear against members of the organization, the victims, and, often, members of the public; (6) continued attempt to subvert legitimate government; (7) insularity of leadership from criminal acts; and (8) rigid discipline in a hierarchy of ranks. However, another evaluator suggested that organized crime may also be characterized in terms of the following principles:

1. Organized crime is a *business venture*.
2. The principal tool of organized crime is *muscle*.
3. Organized crime seeks out every opportunity to *corrupt* and *have influence* on anyone in government who can or may in the future be able to do favors for organized crime.
4. *Insulation* serves to separate the leaders of organized crime from the illegal activities which they direct.
5. *Discipline* is of a quasi-military character.
6. Interest in *public relations*.
7. A *way of life* in which members receive services which outsiders either do not receive or receive from legitimate sources.[40]

Organized crime, Donald Cressey suggests, is an informal criminal organization which is free of legal limitations affecting leadership, structure, monetary policy, and interstate trade. Although each syndicate

---

[39] Cressey, *Theft,* p. 310.
[40] *Ibid.,* pp. 314–315.

family, largely of Italian-Sicilian descent, evidences a multiplicity of roles and statuses, it also exhibits a complex series of interactional relationships, which compound the formal structure of the organized-crime operation.[41] Since organized crime operates in marginal areas designed to maximize profits and minimize risk, apprehension of syndicate violators becomes exceedingly difficult. A successful "fix" of a sensitively placed police officer or politician serves to insulate the syndicate from eventual prosecution. Although the syndicate largely remains a semiformal criminal organization, its major division of labor gives structure and substance to the organization. Organized crime, according to Cressey, is "any crime committed by a person occupying an established division of labor, a position designed for the commission of crime, providing that such division of labor also includes at least one position for a corruptor, one position for a corruptee, and one position for an enforcer."[42] It is possible, therefore, that the activities of organized crime may be delimited in the future by the successful prosecution of those persons who occupy the roles of corruptor, corruptee, or enforcer.

Inasmuch as organized crime depends upon the collusion of illegitimate and legitimate groups of representatives, a concentrated attack designed to shatter the corporate working arrangement, Cressey suggests, would immediately limit the profitability of organized crime. The prosecution of the *enforcer* offers an even greater probability of long-range success. Since he serves as the police officer of the illegal syndicate, the enforcer assumes functional responsibility for the integrity of the illegitimate structure. Since organized crime can rarely appeal to the legitimate court for adjudication, the role of the enforcer remains pivotal in the maintenance of organizational security. Consequently, the successful prosecution of the corruptor, corruptee, and enforcer, he reasons, would strike at the heart of the organized crime problem.[43]

Although the public has commonly demanded stricter enforcement in order to effect the control of organized crime, this approach, as witnessed in the attempt to prohibit drinking through Prohibition, has largely been ineffective. In fact, Prohibition gave birth to the large-scale criminal cartels which currently exist and threaten legitimate government. The Cosa Nostra is not so quickly put out of business. Like any corporate body, it maintains an effective bureaucracy and opportunity for leadership advancement. Therefore, the effectiveness of any attempt

---

[41] See Donald R. Cressey, "The Function and Structure of Criminal Syndicates," President's Commission, *Organized Crime*, pp. 25–60.

[42] Cressey, *Theft*, p. 319.

[43] Cressey, "Organized Crime as a Social System," p. 7. An interesting cultural analysis of organized crime is developed by Robert L. Emrich in "Cultural Anthropological Analysis of Causes and Threat of Organized Crime," *Proceedings of the First National Symposium on Law Enforcement, Science and Technology*, pp. 41–46. Also see "Combatting Organized Crime," *The Annals*, Vol. 367 (May, 1963).

to eliminate organized crime through cracking down on a syndicate's members is limited by the fact that many recruits are always waiting for leadership vacancies to occur. Then, too, successful prosecution of top-level leaders is made difficult because they rarely participate in bet taking, usury, extortion, murder, or other forms of organized crime. While undoubtedly involved in multiple conspiracies, this is difficult to prove in court. In addition, whenever crackdowns do take place, a large number of accountants hired by the syndicate quickly move to take advantage of any loopholes and syndicate lawyers seek to gain acquittals.

Some persons propose to reduce organized-crime profits by the legalization of gambling, in the belief that lessening of such profits would reduce the corruptive powers of the crime syndicate. In practice, this might not turn out to have the effect intended. Donald R. Cressey points out that such an approach is not without shortcomings and must take into consideration that the removal of certain restrictions will actually encourage many current buyers of services to become sellers. While the total volume of profit would probably increase with the legalization of gambling, state-sponsored lotteries would continue to face major syndicate challenges. Even if any of the syndicate's gambling operatives were to be displaced by changes in betting demand following legalization, they would probably only be assigned to new locations to develop new territories or enterprises. However, the possibility of total legalization is remote, due to the fact that wide variances exist in local, state, and federal laws. Because the federal government is not in the position to legalize national gambling, local operators would continue to reap the monopolistic benefits of any local option to prohibit gambling.[44]

Ultimately, the control of organized crime, if it can ever be controlled, rests in the distant future. The passage of any laws attempting to restrict syndicate activities will be met quickly with syndicate attempts to find legal loopholes. Nevertheless, while such organizations may not be effectively outlawed, they may be severely undermined in the future by the continued gathering of intelligence and the prosecution of key personnel. Organized crime, Cressey believes, may also be circumscribed informally on the state and national levels through a series of negotiations. He writes, "Once Cosa Nostra has been precisely identified as a unit, in somewhat the way the Soviet Union and Cuba are identified as units, then there can be 'tacit or explicit understandings analogous to what in the military field would be called limitation of war, the control of armament, and the development of spheres of influence.'"[45] Once the Cosa Nostra and other similar organizations have been pre-

---

[44] Cressey, *Theft*, pp. 290–95.
[45] *Ibid.*, p. 323.

cisely identified and defined, government may be able to reach a form of diplomatic accommodation with such syndicates. Although it is highly unlikely, it is not inconceivable, Cressey hypothesizes, that "the Cosa Nostra would agree to give up its political involvements and its legal operation of legitimate businesses, which in combination threaten to undermine the whole nation," it may do so if it were guaranteed profits after payment of taxes on bet-taking and other gambling forms.[46] Not only would such an action eliminate the critical roles of corruptor, corruptee, and enforcer, but it would force Cosa Nostra bosses to acknowledge their organizational existence.

We may now state the drawbacks of such a proposal. Its gravest danger rests with the assumption that organized crime would be content to maintain such a limited position in the governing hierarchy. Previous experience suggests that syndicate operations will expand into any and all spheres in which maximum profits may be realized. To legitimize the syndicate's existence does not come to grips with the problem of reinvestment of syndicate profits nor deal with the question of a society's usual tendency to define cultural ideals at a higher level than actual human practices. Would the establishment of a detente, we may ask, result in the lessening or elimination of syndicate corruption within the community or would it lead to new attempts to gain control of legitimate political and economic processes through price cutting, large-scale intimidation, stock market manipulation, and zoning board control? It is possible that such a detente would only free the syndicate for more lucrative investments of time and energy and for cooperative but coercive arrangements with large-scale corporations which already influence the course of legislation and taxation, frequently at the expense of the small businessman and the citizen-taxpayer. In short, we may conclude that the development of an accommodation does not guarantee a decline of "family" activity; in fact, it may only encourage new outreaches into unanticipated areas.

---

[46] *Ibid.*, p. 324.

Chapter 10

WHITE-COLLAR CRIME

SUTHERLAND'S VIEWS

White-collar crime, as defined by the late Edwin H. Sutherland, consists of violations of criminal law by members of the upper socioeconomic classes (as defined in terms of wealth, respectability, or general prestige), perpetrated in connection with their occupations. Although these acts are often exempted from the scope of criminal law or court judgment, they are, Sutherland insisted, as serious as any single form of recognized theft or robbery. White-collar crime, obviously, is not associated with poverty or any personal or social pathology which may accompany poverty. It is an act, often unrecognized as a formal crime, which is committed against an individual, a corporation, or even the broader society. Therefore, it may take the form of restraint of trade; misrepresentation in advertising; infringement of patents, trademarks, and copyrights; unfair labor practices; illegal rebates; financial frauds and violations of trusts; violations of war regulations; and other miscellaneous acts. While these violations are seemingly controlled through administrative boards and political procedures, they are, Sutherland argued, actually forms of unprosecuted crime.

Sutherland maintained that white-collar crime meets two tests central to the definition of crime; (1) white-collar crimes can be described legally as acts that are socially harmful, and (2) they give rise to legal provisions for punishment.[1]

Anti-infringement laws, Sutherland argued, are designed to protect

---

[1] Edwin H. Sutherland, *White-Collar Crime* (New York: Holt, Rinehart & Winston, Inc., 1961), p. 31. For detailed bibliographic sources, see Dorothy C. Tompkins, *White-Collar Crime: A Bibliography* (Berkeley; Institute of Governmental Studies, University of California, 1967).

owners of patents, copyrights, and trademarks from those who would steal or violate them. Regulations of false advertising are merely extensions of common-law fraud restrictions and laws against larceny or theft.

The concept of white-collar crime, rejected by many who argue that a crime cannot exist if no criminal code defines the act as a criminal offense, was later expanded by Sutherland and others to include violations in medical practices (including illegal abortions), illegal services to criminals necessary to the operations of organized crime, income tax fraud, illegal alcohol and narcotics sales, fee splitting, unnecessary surgical operations, unnecessary repairs, violations of the spirit of the law, bribery, and attempts to block the enactment of laws to prohibit wrong or injurious practices.

Sutherland's data

Sutherland supported his contention with an analysis of 980 decisions by the courts and administrative commissions against 70 large corporations. Of these corporations, 60 had received unfavorable decisions for restraint of trade, 53 for infringement, 44 for unfair labor practices, 43 for miscellaneous offenses, 28 for misrepresentation in advertising, and 26 for rebate practices. One hundred and fifty-eight decisions were made against 41 of the 70 large corporations by criminal courts, 298 decisions against 59 of the corporations by civil courts, and 129 decisions against 43 of the corporations by equity courts. The administrative commissions enacted 361 decisions, approximately one fourth of which were referred to and sustained by the courts.[2] Of the 70 corporations, 30 were either illegal in their origin or had begun illegal activities immediately after their incorporation. These corporations committed 27 restraint-of-trade violations and three infringements of patents. Eight additional corporations, probably illegal in origin or in their initial policy, evidenced five instances of restraint of trade, two of patent infringement, and one of fraud violation.[3]

THE WHITE-COLLAR CRIME AND OFFENDER

The line between shrewd business practices and white-collar crime is at times extremely thin. These violations are generally excluded from criminal prosecution, and they are usually processed through such ad-

---

[2] *Ibid.*, pp. 19–25.

[3] *Ibid.*, p. 18. See George B. Vold, *Theoretical Criminology* (New York: Oxford University Press, Inc., 1958), pp. 243–61, for a specific theoretical treatment of white-collar crime.

ministrative agencies as the Federal Bureau of Internal Revenue, National Labor Relations Board, Federal Trade Commission, Food and Drug Administration, Securities and Exchange Commission, or Interstate Commerce Commission. The high status of business executives, the public insensitivity to white-collar crime, and the ability of offenders to evade punishment encourages the continuance of white-collar criminality. Since the white-collar criminal operates in both legitimate and illegitimate channels without involvement in organized crime, his apprehension and prosecution are difficult. His occupational and community prestige often serves to insulate him from the stereotyping criminal court and, therefore, allows him to maintain a legitimate public image while committing acts which often lead to more serious consequences than those that have been committed by the majority of the prison population.

Early white-collar crime was encouraged by the legal principle that corporations are unable to commit crimes. The courts in the nineteenth century held that the corporation was a legislative artifact and did not possess a mind or soul; it could not, therefore, form a criminal intent or commit a criminal act. Since the corporation was held to be unable to commit unlawful acts, its agents could not be held accountable for corporate violations. When this theory proved untenable in corporate practice, however, new administrative boards or agencies and necessary legislation were created to restrain corporate abuses. The deliberate and consistent corporate tendency to commit harm against consumers, competitors, stockholders, other investors, inventors, employees and the government through restraint of trade and development of cartels, therefore, eventually led to legislation against corporate practices in the latter part of the nineteenth century. These controls, however, fell short of the severity or scope of sanctions enacted in criminal law. As a result, a businessman who participates in persistent and widespread violations customarily does not lose an equal amount of status among his business associates as does one convicted in a criminal court. Frequently, he is rewarded with a promotion and/or a salary increase for demonstrating his loyalty to the corporate institution. Many businessmen, similar to professional thieves in attitude, express, therefore, open contempt for law, government, and regulative agency personnel. Arguing that the least government is the best government, they regard legal restrictions as an infringement upon their free enterprise.

White-collar crimes are usually organized and deliberate, designed to maximize profits without regard for the public. As corporations attempt to make the best possible profit, their acts are often detrimental to the public interest. Defects in expensive products, for example, are often undisclosed, since repair would necessarily add to production costs. The 1967 investigations of the automobile industry revealed that faulty brakes, tires, or other safety items were rarely brought to the attention of the consumer, even though a malfunction could result in his death. And yet, if a noncorporate individual failed to repair his faulty car and killed another through negligence in an accident, his act could be penalized through criminal and/or civil action. Similar action by a corporation, however, is still largely exempt from any criminal charge. Industrial price-fixing, disproportionate costs of drugs, and excessive and fraudulent claims against medicare by doctors offer other illustrations of white-collar crime in a present-day society.

The quest for profits, inherent in the corporate objective, encourages the corporate executive to adopt illegal business practices in order to maximize profits in an extremely competitive economic system. Since an informal collusion exists between business corporations, local newspapers, and other opinion-making agencies, white-collar crimes are often kept from public attention. Although the conventional offender is quickly noted in the press, the white-collar offender is rarely cited in criminal law since the case is most often processed in the confidential and secure confines of an administrative or civil agency.

The white-collar criminal, who ultimately may commit more serious and expensive crimes than the small-scale professional thief, undergoes little challenge to his image and feels little public pressure to conformity. Operating in a reinforced, homogeneous atmosphere which sanctions corner-cutting and shrewd business operations, the white-collar criminal, Sutherland believed, violates the public trust through unfair competition. Since government depends upon business stability, both business and government work together to minimize serious abuses and to maintain a sound functioning economic system. White-collar crime, like organized crime, continues because the public has failed to recognize its threat. The criminal courts are lenient toward persons accused of white-collar crimes because criminal law has developed no effective method of dealing with offending corporations. Business interests have hindered legislative efforts to develop criminal controls against corporate practices, leaving the functional control of white-collar criminality to civil courts and administrative boards or commissions, whose regulations have purposefully held minimal effectiveness.

The lack of effective regulation of white-collar crime is not without its social cost. Marshall Clinard and Frank Hartung, supporting Sutherland, suggest that white-collar crime encourages feelings of mistrust, lower community morality, and general social disorganization.[4] While

---

[4] Marshall B. Clinard, *The Black Market* (New York: Rinehart & Co., 1952), pp. 35–48, and Frank E. Hartung, "White-Collar Offenses in the Wholesale Meat Industry in Detroit," *American Journal of Sociology*, Vol. 56 (July, 1950), pp. 25–34.

Clinard believes that any businessman, professional man, or politician who engages in any illegal activity in relation to his occupation is a white-collar criminal,[5] Frank Hartung limits the concept to a "violation of law regulating business, which is committed for a firm by the firm or its agents in the conduct of its business."[6] Holding a functional view of crime, Sutherland and Clinard and Hartung minimize the importance of the actual criminal court conviction as the essential element in the definition of a crime. Instead they focus upon the act and its resulting harm.

The white-collar offender, Donald Cressey believes, rationalizes his actions in relationship to the answers available in his operational subculture to explain his behavior. His rationalizations, therefore, are somewhat selective and primarily are determined by the context and the type of crime which the white-collar offender needs to justify. The existing socioeconomic structure serves as the foundation of white-collar criminal activity and influences the direction of the offender's conduct. White-collar criminals, Cressey notes, often turn to criminal activity because they have a problem which cannot be shared with any other person (for example, major debt, heavy betting losses, secret lover). Since the problem normally can only be solved by money, the individual violates his trust and at the same time rationalizes the impact of his conduct. Often, he merely imitates similar actions he sees among those around him. White-collar crime, therefore, is functionally related to the operating principles of the organization or enterprise. Marginal economic enterprise, in effect, stimulates the marginal man to marginal conduct.[7]

Walter Reckless and Simon Dinitz, on the other hand, explain white-collar criminality in terms of their insulation theory, which suggests that as persons undergo differential socialization experiences, they accept fundamental values and are increasingly insulated and reinforced in their practices. New commitments and identifications assume greater importance as the individual experiences variable family or other major reference group relationships.[8] The neutralization theory of Gresham Sykes and David Matza suggests that "good" people are released from the influence of anticriminal norms as they find rationalizations which

---

[5] Clinard, *op. cit.*, p. 35. Also see Donald R. Cressey, "The Respectable Criminal," *Transaction*, Vol. 2 (March–April, 1965), p. 12.

[6] Frank E. Hartung, "White-Collar Crime: Its Significance for Theory and Practice," *Federal Probation*, Vol. 17 (June, 1953), p. 31.

[7] Donald R. Cressey, *Other People's Money* (Glencoe: Free Press, 1953), pp. 33–37.

[8] Walter Reckless, Simon Dinitz, and Barbara Kay, "The Self Component in Potential Delinquency and Potential Nondelinquency," *American Sociological Review*, Vol. 22 (October, 1957), pp. 566–70.

permit them to preserve a favorable self-image in spite of their criminal activity.[9]

THE OPPOSITION TO THE CONCEPT

Not all criminologists agree that white-collar violations are a form of crime. Since crime by definition is a violation of a specific law which results in some form of social harm, white-collar crime, they argue, cannot be classified as a criminal act. If law is unstated, crime does not exist. In this view, although the specific conduct may be undesirable, it is not a crime. Paul Tappan, trained as a lawyer, argues that the concept of white-collar crime is inaccurate. Morality, Tappan notes, is not law unless legislated into formal legal codes. To maintain that violations of morality are automatic violations of law is unrealistic and unscientific. The specificity of law is only undermined and minimized by the attempt to include vague noncriminal categories in criminal definitions.[10]

Gilbert Geis argues that Sutherland failed to differentiate between the corporation and the management of the corporate institution. Geis, therefore, questions the wisdom of restricting white-collar crime to a corporate setting and the reality of assuming that the corporation or its officers commit crimes. The extension of guilt from an individual within the corporation to the corporation itself, Geis argues, overextends the act of the individual.[11]

Earl R. Quinney proposes that white-collar crimes be differentiated into the two categories of *occupational crimes* and *occupational deviation*. Most occupations develop practices and procedures which are either professionally unacceptable or are deviations from general occupational norms. While some occupational deviations are subject to legal sanctions or directives through regulatory or criminal law, others continue unchecked. On the other hand, occupational crimes, Quinney's term for white-collar crime, are violations of legal business controls and involve behavior similar to that expressed in unethical legal or medical activity, illegal work practices, or abnormal labor procedures. The concept of occupational crime, therefore, explains those crimes committed by individuals, by employees against the corporation, and by

---

[9] Gresham M. Sykes and David Matza, "Techniques of Neutralization: A Theory of Delinquency," *American Sociological Review*, Vol. 22 (December, 1957), pp. 666–67. Also see Richard A. Ball, "Neutralization as a Self Factor in Delinquency Risk" (Ph.D. dissertation, Ohio State University).

[10] Paul W. Tappan, "Crime and the Criminal," *Federal Probation*, Vol. 11 (July–September, 1947), pp. 41–44.

[11] Gilbert Geis, "Toward the Delineation of White-Collar Offenses," *Sociological Inquiry*, Vol. 32, No. 2 (Spring, 1962), pp. 162–65.

policy-making officials for the corporation. Since occupational crime ultimately transcends the status and class-oriented actions noted by Sutherland, the concept of occupational crime would serve, Quinney believes, to explain the acts which are committed by farmers, repairmen, or others who do not occupy white-collar positions or occupations. Occupational deviation covers those actions which are significant departures from legitimate, recognized, and shared occupational conduct.[12]

A SPECIFIC EXAMPLE: THE EMBEZZLER

Two studies of 1,001 embezzlers conducted by the U.S. Fidelity and Guarantee Company before and after World War II revealed that white-collar crime is common throughout all areas, states, and occupations in the nation. The 845 men and 156 women in the postwar study worked in a wide variety of single- or multiple-employee establishments. Two thirds of the 845 men were married, although approximately 6 percent were divorced or separated, and slightly more than 1 percent were widowers. They ranged in age from 15 to 75, and their length of service varied from less than 1 to 48 years. Although one man embezzled for 17 years, a number only embezzled once. The 845 men, together with 150 blue-collar workers, stole a record $3,544,222.89. The average male embezzler, the postwar study revealed, was 35, married, had one or two children, lived in a respectable neighborhood, and was buying his own home. In the top 40 percent of the national income distribution, he had been stealing for only eight months from the firm, which had employed him for an average of three years. He augmented his annual salary by 20 percent through theft or embezzlement (see Table 10–1).[13] The average female embezzler, on the other hand, equaled her annual salary through theft. However, her salary, at an average age of 31, primarily represented the bottom third of the national income distribution. Although she had worked for her current employer for less than two and one-half years, she had been embezzling for an average of six and one-half months. The female embezzler was or had been married.

Today's embezzler, the postwar study summarized, is younger, is less often married, earns more money, and has fewer dependents than embezzlers who worked during the Depression years. His past record revealed problems of personal character and stability which were affected

---

[12] Earl R. Quinney, "The Study of White-Collar Crime: Toward a Reorganization of Theory and Research," *Journal of Criminal Law, Criminology and Police Science,* Vol. 55, No. 2 (June, 1964), pp. 208–12. Also see Earl R. Quinney, "Occupational Structure and Criminal Behavior: Prescription Violations by Retail Pharmacists," *Social Problems,* Vol. 11 (Fall, 1963), p. 179.

[13] Norman Jaspan and Hillel Black, *The Thief in the White Collar* (Philadelphia: J. B. Lippincott Co., 1961), pp. 23–24.

by the faster and less "normal" pace of modern life.[14] The growth of embezzlement and theft was largely due to the expanded opportunity to steal, which increased with the expansion and decentralization of industry together with the lessening of management control over employee behavior. However, less than 15 percent of the nation's manufacturers, wholesalers, and retailers, the postwar study noted, bond their workers against employee theft in spite of continual losses.

TABLE 10–1
White-collar thieves: occupational distribution

Position	Number	Percentage
Men		
Executives, Managerial and professional	261	37.6
Sales	190	27.4
Clerical	142	20.4
Government	52	7.5
Labor officials	50	7.1
Total	695*	100
Women		
Executive, Managerial and professional	26	17.2
Sales	37	24.5
Clerical	73	48.3
Government	7	4.7
Labor Officials	8	5.3
Total	151†	100

* This excludes 150 blue-collar workers.
† Excluded are five blue-collar workers.
Source: Norman Jaspan, *The Thief in the White Collar* (Philadelphia: J. B. Lippincott Co., 1960), p. 24.

The difficulty of the white-collar crime concept rests in the fact that white-collar criminality exceeds the normal limits of traditional crime. And yet, the concept necessarily bridges the chasm between the defined and undefined forms of criminal behavior. A strict legal approach too often ignores the basic violations of conduct norms which in time may be legislated into the criminal code. Since undefined conduct may be equally as costly as behavior specifically defined in criminal codes, it remains a legitimate area of criminological concern.

The problem of white-collar crime is similar to that of organized crime. In both cases, antisocial behavior is far in advance of the legislative definition restricting the antisocial act. The acceptance of Tappan's

---

[14] *Ibid.*, p. 25.

criticism, therefore, would lead the criminological investigator to ignore wide areas of antinormative and generally harmful social conduct which may legitimately be included in future criminal codes. The full acceptance of Sutherland's imprecision, however, can only result in unscientific investigation. Since laws are created to regulate problems facing the social group, sociologists-criminologists must study both conduct norms and criminal statutes if they are to understand the full dimensions of delinquency and crime. The primary difference between the two is merely one of legislative codification.

White-collar crime produces at least three major social effects. The sale of harmful drugs or impure foods in violation of drug and food laws may result in physical injury or death of the consumer. Fraud, embezzlement, and the marketing of worthless, defective, or even injurious products may also lead to major financial losses. White-collar crime, however, takes its greatest toll when it undermines group values and the sense of honesty which undergird all social, economic, and political institutions.

Since the judge, legislator, commission member, and white-collar offender belong to the same social class and share similar status identification, white-collar criminals are not generally processed as common criminals. The lack of punishment, together with the inability of the consumer to secure adequate legal protection has allowed the white-collar criminal to exploit the lower-class consumer, who is denied effective appeal to the criminal courts. While the blue-collar offender who steals a television or radio from a local business is likely to be arrested, judged, and sentenced if detected, the businessman who regularly misleads the public through false advertising generally goes scot-free. Yet it is the businessman, wielding his economic and political influence, who effectively lobbies to secure special laws designed to protect the merchandise which he may eventually misrepresent to the public. At the same time, he may use similar influence and pressure to seek legislation which will exempt his own harmful actions from public control or criminal sanctions.

The confusion inherent in the concept of white-collar crime is a product of the complex society. The growth of formal organizations has not been without costs in the form of increased informal and formal crimes. Although recent revelations suggest that price-fixing and other forms of economic collusion are widespread among the major industries, white-collar criminality is most evident among marginal or declining enterprises. The failure to sustain associational-organizational business ethics has allowed many businessmen to disregard or violate the law and its intent largely without penalty or sanctions from peers or associational members. Although some acts of white-collar criminality have been due to ignorance, other forms of white-collar conduct have been encouraged by ambiguous laws which encourage the overt violation of the law and its intent. The rise of the impersonal corporation has encouraged an impersonal occupational commitment. Modern economic competition, which stimulates customer exploitation and shrewd business practices, only adds to the process. As long as the end, financial success, justifies the means, shrewd or marginal business practices and white-collar crime will continue to dominate the middle ground between normative conduct and illegal criminal behavior.

Part
THREE

Theoretical origins of
delinquent and
criminal behavior

Chapter 11

PHYSIOPSYCHOLOGICAL EXPLANATIONS OF CRIME CAUSATION

Historically, attempts to comprehend the origins of crime have centered in either demonological (spiritistic) or naturalistic explanations. The prehistoric *demonological* interpretation assumed the presence of otherworldly powers or spirits in the criminal event. Attempts to control these influences stimulated the growth of animistic religion and the use of magic. Early Judeo-Christian teaching attributed antisocial attitudes and uncommon practices to the presence of demons. In the later Middle Ages[1], the influence of naturalistic conceptions of the causes of crime began to be felt, and during the period of the Renaissance and Reformation, the social and humanistic dimensions of criminal conduct began to be understood. The idea of the impersonal and detached devil was modified by the recognition that crime is fundamentally a social product.

Although the *naturalistic* explanations of criminality had their origins in the early Phoenician and Greek worlds, such explanations did not gain wide acceptance until the 16th and 17th centuries, when the works of Hobbes, Spinoza, Descartes, and Leibnitz cast new light on human behavior. Naturalistic theory eventually took three separate directions, depending upon whether intellectual, cultural, or biological determinism was emphasized. While the *intellectual determinist* assumed that crime had its origin in the general social system and the social contract, the *cultural determinist* believed that man's behavior was merely a reflection

---

[1] George B. Vold, *Theoretical Criminology* (New York: Oxford University Press, Inc., 1958), pp. 5–6.

223

of man's sociocultural world. The *biological determinist,* on the other hand, argued that the natural laws of heredity determine the eventual actions of the basic organism. These three naturalistic schools were further differentiated in later years into other particularistic theoretical explanations which sought to relate criminality to specific causes (for example, endocrine gland malfunction, defective intelligence).

Because many other factors which could contribute to the causation of crime were closely related to these particularistic explanations, the attempt to establish direct causal relationships was marked by many difficulties. Early investigators, for example, could not fully separate economic explanations of crime from questions of native intelligence, weather conditions, or ecological characteristics. Just as physical factors could not be easily separated from cultural dimensions, psychological characteristics were not readily distinguished from social factors. Nevertheless, while each crime reveals the causative influence of many varied factors, it also discloses, later researchers found, an apparent predominant characteristic. Some types of crime primarily reveal psychological disorganization; others reflect economic goals. While many acts are stimulated by the heat of the moment, others are accomplished for political or ideological ends. While physical, mental, and social factors are involved in the commission of any crime, their proportional relationship varies in each instance.

ORIGINS OF MODERN CRIMINOLOGICAL THEORY

The Beccarian hypothesis

Modern criminological theory emerged from the argument between the Classical school of Cesare Beccaria (1738–94) and the Positivistic school of Cesare Lombroso (1836–1909). While the Classical, and later the Neoclassical, school focused upon the influence of free will, rationalism, and hedonism in crime causation, their emphasis was essentially prescientific. The Positivistic school, on the other hand, stimulated the first serious study of the criminal person as it challenged the original Beccarian emphasis upon the criminal act.

Classical theorist Cesare Bonesana, Marquis de Beccaria, at the age of 26,[2] questioned the nature of 18th-century European criminal law in his publication *On Crimes and Punishments* (*Dei Delitti E Delle Dene*). Arguing that the existing crimino-legal system was arbitrary and allowed abusive practices, Beccaria held that punishment should only be applied in proportion to the seriousness of the crime. For public

[2] Cesare Beccaria, *On Crimes and Punishments* (Indianapolis: Bobbs-Merrill Co., Inc., 1963), pp. 1–99.

officials to deprive citizens of freedom, property, and life, Beccaria argued, is beyond the scope of the state. The function of law is to bring free and independent men into an ordered society. Its task is not to coerce but to coordinate. The sum of all portions of freedom which each individual surrenders, therefore, constitutes the sovereignty of nations, which is deposited in and administered by a legitimate sovereign. Consequently, the foundation of punishment rests in the social contract which each individual possesses with society at large.[3] The right to punish does not rest automatically with the state but is founded upon the absolute need for punishment. Punishment is legitimate, Beccaria argued, only when it is used by the state or sovereign to defend the total sovereignty against the acts of any individual. Ultimately, punishment must be based upon law, which in turn is enacted by the legislator who represents the broader society. Although severe punishment, Beccaria noted, has little influence in crime prevention and is contrary to enlightened reason and justice, the type and degree of punishment inflicted upon the violator should vary in proportion to the individual's threat to society. While the more serious crimes should receive the more serious penalty, the only measure of the seriousness of crime is the amount of harm done to the particular society.

Crimes, Beccaria theorized, may be divided into three categories: crimes that threaten the existence of all members of society, crimes that injure the security or property of individuals, and crimes that disrupt public peace and tranquility. Each category represents a different degree of harm and should command varying degrees of penalty. However, the goal of punishment, Beccaria quickly added, is not to inflict pain upon current offenders. Instead, the end of punishment is the deterrence of potential future criminal offenders and the prevention of further social harm by current offenders. Punishment, therefore, must be prompt, inevitable, and equal in order to accomplish these ends. The *certainty* of punishment, Beccaria argued, is ultimately more meaningful than the fear of severe punishment. While men may be frightened from committing crimes if they are aware that apprehension is inevitable, they may be stimulated conversely to further crimes in order to escape punishment if punishment is too severe. Not only do the minds of men grow more cruel, severe, hardened, and calloused as punishment grows more cruel and severe, but severity of punishment naturally leads to tyrannical social conditions.[4] The imposition of the death penalty, Beccaria noted, is not a part of the original contract and usurps the individual's right to life. Consequently, the death penalty, an act of violence and barbarity,

---

[3] Elio Monachesi, "Cesare Beccaria," *Pioneers in Criminology* (Chicago: Quadrangle Books, Inc., 1960), pp. 36–49.
[4] Beccaria, *op. cit.*, p. 45.

is, Beccaria argued, a type of injustice which is a form of homicide in repayment for previous homicide.

The Lombrosian contribution

In contradistinction to Beccaria, Cesare Lombroso, an Italian physician-psychiatrist, maintained that the criminal represents a distinct anthropological type. The "born criminal," Lombroso held, is characterized by particular malformations of the skeleton and skull, especially evidenced in peculiar cranial or facial asymmetry. An under- or oversized brain, high cheek bones, big ears, minimal beard, projecting or receding jaw, and overdeveloped arms are potential indicators of his eventual criminality. However, sociocultural characteristics are also causative crime factors. Vanity, cruelty, idleness, the use of criminal argot, a lack of moral sense, specific nervous sensibility to pain, contempt for death and suffering, and interest in tattooing, Lombroso believed, are common indicators of criminal potential.[5] The congenital (born) criminal, a reflection of primitive human life, represents an atavistic type. Although the *born criminal,* Lombroso hypothesized, is always epileptic, epileptics are not always born criminals.

Even so, Lombroso's concept of the born criminal was only applicable to about 35 percent of the criminal population, since other offenders were merely occasional criminals or among the criminally insane. Lombroso, however, further subdivided the category of *occasional* criminals into subcategories of *pseudo criminals,* whose crimes are not intended to seriously harm society and are generally devoid of evil intent; *criminaloids,* who are products of adverse criminal environments; *criminals of passion,* who commit crimes as they respond to their emotions; and *habitual criminals* devoid of the characteristics found in the born criminal.

Although Lombroso divided the criminal population into the multiple categories of the epileptic criminal, the insane criminal, and the born criminal, he presumed a common epileptoid base. While the occasional criminals were individuals drawn into crime due to particular situations, the criminaloids were identified by innate traits which result in crime due to environmental or situational influences. Although criminaloids, Lombroso reasoned, may differ in degree, they do not differ in kind. Because the greatest number become habitual criminals, the distinction between criminaloids and born criminals is founded upon slight differences in physical characteristics. However, the habitual criminal does not possess serious anomalies or constitutional tendencies toward crime. While this individual is a victim of poor socialization, the criminal

---

[5] Hermann Mannheim, *Comparative Criminality* (Boston: Houghton Mifflin Co., 1965), p. 216.

of passion commits his crime out of anger, platonic or filial love, offended honor, or other characteristic passionate and irresistible forces. Even political criminals and suicides are passionate offenders. Although Lombroso first applied the same terminology to female criminality, in his later years he maintained that the female criminal possesses less exaggerated atavistic characteristics.[6]

Despite these variations, Lombroso theorized that criminals may be identified by multiple physical anomalies which are either atavistic or degenerative. The atavistic man represents a reversion to a primitive or subhuman mind which is evidenced physically in a variety of inferior morphological features. The degenerative violator is an offspring of pathological individuals who pass on to their children rudimentary physical and mental attributes common among primitive men. Biological "throwbacks," such men act in opposition to the rules and the expectations of modern society.[7]

Lombroso's work had an immediate influence upon Ferri, Garofalo, and other Italian scholars; such men as Lacassagne, Manouvrier, Joly, and Topinard opposed his ideas. Recognizing that Lombroso had freely established relationships between two factors, they also noted that he had failed to correlate their relationships in scientific terms. Nevertheless, his supporters and critics alike recognized that his work was instrumental in shifting the focus of criminology and penology from the previous metaphysical, legal, and juristic emphasis to a potentially scientific foundation. Lombroso's argument that the crime is secondary to the act of the criminal was not without effect. They came to accept in part or in full Lombroso's belief that the criminal and not the crime should be considered and penalized or punished. Since Lombroso had substituted ideas of individuality, social defense, and danger of the individual to society for earlier concepts of punishment, responsibility, and legal equality, their later work could not avoid the influence of Lombroso's thesis.[8]

The meaning of the Classical-Positivist argument

The Classical school represented by Beccaria focused primarily on reform within criminal law, criminal procedure, and the general system

---

[6] Cesare Lombroso, *Crime, Its Causes and Remedies* (Boston: Little, Brown & Co., 1918), p. 183.

[7] Marvin E. Wolfgang, "Cesare Lombroso," *Pioneers*, p. 183. For a discussion of glandular effects, see Max G. Schlapp, "Behavior and Gland Disease," *Journal of Heredity*, Vol. 15 (1924), p. 11; and A. W. Rowe, "A Possible Endocrine Factor in the Behavior Problems of the Young," *American Journal of Orthopsychiatry*, Vol. 1 (1931), pp. 451–75.

[8] Lombroso, *op. cit.*, pp. 365–84. Refer to Alfred Lindesmith and Yale Levin, "The Lombrosian Myth in Criminology," *American Journal of Sociology*, March, 1937.

of penalties. Opposing the arbitrary and cruel punishment apparent in the contemporary administration of criminal justice, the Classical school attempted to eliminate abuses occurring in the formation of legal codes and the existing dependence upon the use of torture, capital punishment, and transportation. Since it favored equality before the law, the Classical school encouraged trial by jury, fixed penalties, and an objective crime evaluation. The punishment applied to any crime, its followers believed, should be defined in objective terms. Although the later Positivists argued that free will and moral responsibility are incompatible with actual criminal behavior, they emphasized the legal and social responsibility of the society to the criminal. While the Classical school focused upon the relationship of crime and punishment, the Positivists viewed the crime equation as a question of the individual criminal and the treatment he receives. In essence, the Positivistic school attempted to reduce crime by the effective treatment of offender needs; the Classical school, on the other hand, worked to reduce punishment and avoid judicial arbitrariness.

Enter Ferri

Enrico Ferri (1856–1929), building upon the earlier works of Beccaria and Lombroso, theorized that crime results from anthropological or individual, physical, and social causes which are interrelated and yet may be intentionally separated for examination. Among such *anthropological* or *individual* factors, Ferri included the defendant's age, sex, occupation, civil status, social class, residence, education, organic and mental constitution, degree of training, and residence. While he held that race, climate, daily cycle, fertility, distribution of soil, meteorological characteristics, annual temperature, and the nature of the seasons are influential *physical* factors, he included the increase or decrease of population, migration, customs, religion, public opinion, family characteristics, political forms, financial practices, commercial characteristics, public administration of safety, education and welfare, penal and civil legislation, and agricultural and industrial production and distribution within his *social* causes.[9] Since physical and anthropological factors change at a relatively slow rate, radical increases in crime during one's lifetime, Ferri believed, must be due to changes in the social environment.

Criminals may be divided, Ferri hypothesized, into five basic classes—a classification which Raffaele Garofalo later criticized as inexact and unjustified. The *born* or *instinctive criminal* is unable by birth to resist criminal stimuli, and evidences a propensity to crime. The *insane criminal*, grouped with the mentally abnormal, is marked by a mental

---

[9] Thorsten Sellin, "Enrico Ferri," *Pioneers*, p. 283.

disease or a neuropsychopathic condition. The *occasional criminal,* the most common type of lawbreaker, is a product of the family and social situation more than of personal and abnormal conditions. The *passionate criminal* commits crime through inability to control his emotions. The *habitual criminal,* Ferri's fifth subtype, is an offender of habit.[10]

The Positivists, under the leadership of Enrico Ferri, rejected the concept of free will as the foundation of criminal responsibility and replaced it with a concept of the needs of society, actuated not merely by a concern for the guilt of the offender but for his potential danger to the community. Since Ferri believed that the perpetrator of every active criminal act is always criminally responsible regardless of his psychological and physical condition when he carried it out, as long as the act is an expression of his own personality, he held that defensive actions against the defendant must be determined in relation to his individual aggressive potential rather than in relation to the nature and extent of the act.[11] Man, Ferri and his fellow Positivists argued, is not responsible for crime but is made responsible for his criminal conduct by society. Consequently, the function of criminal justice is not to assess or to measure the moral guilt of an offender but to determine whether he did or did not complete the act which is defined as an offense and whether he should be restrained from committing further crimes. Because a criminal who commits a particular act violates his socially derived responsibility, the concept of "social defense," strongly utilitarian and largely unconcerned for any personal moral dimensions, suffices, Ferri theorized, to protect the society and its citizens from the threat of the offending individual.[12]

Enter Garofalo

Minimizing the atavistic theory of Lombroso, Raffaele Garofalo (1852–1932) noted that it is impossible to define a criminal without defining the nature of a crime. Consequently, he rejected the idea that crime is a violation of a law for which prescribed penalties are inflicted and held that the existing conception of the criminal is incomplete and scientifically inadequate. The "juridicial" idea, he believed, is imprecise and both includes and excludes behavior which is encompassed in "a sociologic notion of crime."[13] He argued that *natural crime* differs from conventional crime and exists in human society independent of the circumstances in a given period or the particular views of the legislator.

[10] *Ibid.,* pp. 283–84.
[11] Enrico Ferri, *Principii di Diritto Criminale* (Torino, 1928), pp. 237–38.
[12] Leon Radzinowicz, *In Search of Criminology* (Cambridge, Mass.: Harvard University Press, 1962), p. 17.
[13] Francis A. Allen, "Raffaele Garofalo," *Pioneers,* p. 257.

230 Crime in a complex society

Such crime, Garofalo insisted, consists of conduct which offends the basic sentiments of *pity* (revulsion against the voluntary infliction of sufferings on others) and *probity* (respect for property rights of others.) Since these moral attitudes are essential to individual and social co-existence, society must make its defense against the true criminal, who is either without or is deficient in pity or probity.

Natural crime, therefore, must be defined in terms of the basic altruistic sentiments of humanity. The true criminal, who lacks the proper development of altruistic attitudes and sensibilities, is more than a product of circumstance or environment. His deficiency has an organic basis. "There is no such thing," Garofalo argued, "as the casual offender—if by the use of this term we grant the possibility of a morally well-organized man committing a crime solely by the force of external circumstances."[14] The *true criminal*, he maintained, is marked by a psychic or moral "anomaly," a "psychic variation" found more frequently among members of "certain inferior races" than among members of modern civilized societies. Criminals, Garofalo held in a rather unscientific way, possess regressive characteristics which are symptomatic of lower degrees of advancement. While tradition, prejudices, bad examples, climate, and use of alcohol are the most important influences in crime causation, social and environmental factors possess secondary importance. Organic deficiency and moral sensibility may vary from one criminal to another. Persons who lack the basic altruistic sentiments of pity and probity may be classified in the simple typology of the murderer, violent criminal, thief, and lascivious criminal (sex offender). Since the true criminal reveals his inability to adapt to the social environment, society must protect itself by eliminating him from its normal confines, whether by the infliction of death, life imprisonment, overseas transportation, or other forms of segregation.

Because the true offender lacks the capacity for real remorse and repentance, punishment is unlikely to produce moral regeneration. Even the possibility of the reformation of the offender through programs of education and general rehabilitation, Garofalo maintained, are limited. Criminals have regressive characteristics; they possess primitive instincts which are expressed in predatory tendencies, a lessened concern for justice, and an absence of personal restraint.[15] All criminals, including true criminals and those who revolt against the law, fall into the four general classes of murderers, violent criminals, criminals deficient in probity, and lascivious criminals. Each of these types may evidence a corresponding form of alienation or neurosis.[16] The crimes in the first

---

[14] *Ibid.*, p. 262.
[15] Raffaele Garofalo, *Criminology* (Boston: Little, Brown & Co., 1914), p. 109.
[16] *Ibid.*, p. 131.

two categories, for example, are often expressed in homicidal mania, pyromania, epilepsy, and hysteria. Criminals deficient in probity often participate in acts of kleptomania; lascivious criminals in sadism. However, each group, Garofalo concluded, may also include youthful offenders who do not fully understand their actions or erringly imitate behavior which is common in their environment.

THE PHRENOLOGICAL EXPLANATION

Franz Joseph Gall (1758–1828) and John Gaspar Spurzheim (1776–1832), prominent phrenologists, assumed that skull conformations reveal the person's facilities or propensities to behavior. Since skull characteristics are biologically inherited, tendencies toward criminality, they believed, are transmitted from father to son. One could perceive the mental faculties of an individual by studying the size of the lobes or protuberances of the skull. According to Gall, combativeness, secretiveness and inquisitiveness, central causes of criminal behavior, are readily identifiable by this method. Since higher propensities combat lower depravity, the organs of destructiveness can stimulate violence and murder unless the other organs of piety and self-esteem are able to overcome this destructive threat.[17]

In lesser degree, J. K. Lavater (1741–1801) and Charles Caldwell (1772–1853) accepted the phrenological position that the exterior shape of the skull, unusual cranial protuberances, or other cranial or structural brain abnormalities closely correspond to criminal tendencies and that crime is directly related to one or several basic skull or brain characteristics. However, Hamilton D. Wey suggested that the "criminal class" may possess a variety of peculiar physical characteristics. Thieves' heads, Wey argued, are small; murderers', large. While the ears of criminals are often large, lengthy, and projected, crafty offenders possess a snake-like appearance.[18]

THE EXAMINATION OF PHYSICAL TYPES

The failure of the phrenological approach encouraged the growth of physical explanations of crime. Ernst Kretschmer divided basic body types into the categories of the asthenic, athletic, pyknic, and other mixed or unclassifiable types. The *asthenic,* marked by deficient vitality,

---

[17] Walter Bomberg, *Crime and Mind* (New York: Macmillan Co., 1965), p. 54. Frances MacGregor, "Some Psycho-Social Problems Associated with Facial Deformities," *American Sociological Review,* Vol. 16 (October, 1951), pp. 629–38.
[18] Vold, *op. cit.,* p. 58. Also see Ralph S. Banay, "Physical Disfigurement as a Factor in Delinquency and Crime," *Federal Probation,* Vol. 17 (January–March, 1953), pp. 20–24.

is of slender build and has weak and underdeveloped muscles. The *athletic,* identified by a strong development of skeletal muscles, shoulders, chest, and stomach, presents a graceful symmetry. The *pyknic* individual is of medium height, body rotundity, rounded shoulders pushed forward, soft hands, and rounded limbs.[19] Although Edwin Sutherland later held the work of Kretschmer to be generally useless, Kretschmer's somatotyping technique has been widely utilized in continuing research.

Goring and Hooten

Attempting to relate crime to criminal types, Charles B. Goring (1870–1919), a medical officer, engaged in detailed biometric examinations of 3,000 English convicts. Assuming that each person possessed a "criminal diathesis," which he defined as "a hypothetical character of some kind, a constitutional proclivity," Goring theorized that physical types should vary accordingly.[20] Although Goring discovered that insanity and epilepsy were more frequent among the prison than among the general population, the difference, he believed, holds little significance. Arguing that potential criminality is determined by one's heredity, Goring maintained that social injustice or environmental influences are minor stimulants to actual criminality. Even the force of circumstances, Goring argued, has little effect upon actual criminality.[21]

Charles Goring undermined the findings of Cesare Lombroso in his 1913 work entitled *The English Convict.* His own work was eventually challenged by Earnest Hooten, who argued that Goring's interpretations were preconceived attempts to disprove Lombroso's theory of criminality.[22] Hooten held that the practice of comparing the physique of the criminal with that of the noncriminal outside the context of his specific racial or nationality group is totally misleading. A measurable difference in anthropological measurements and morphological observations, Hooten concluded as a result of his studies, exists between the criminal and noncriminal population. Among other things, this difference includes a constitutional inferiority of the criminal in comparison with noncrimi-

---

[19] Ernst Kretschmer, *Physique and Character* (New York: Harcourt, Brace & World, Inc., 1925).

[20] Mannheim, *op. cit.,* p. 227.

[21] *Ibid.,* p. 228.

[22] Peter Lejins, "Hereditary Endowment, Environmental Influences and Criminality," in Herbert A. Bloch (ed.), *Crime in America* (New York: Philosophical Library, Inc., 1961), p. 320. Also see A. J. Rosanoff *et al.,* "Criminality and Delinquency in Twins," *Journal of Criminal Law and Criminology* (January–February, 1934), pp. 923–24; and Clifford Shaw, *Brothers in Crime* (Chicago: University of Chicago Press, 1938).

nals. When classified according to their offenses, they present measurable differences in physique. His detailed findings were published in his 1939 volume entitled *Crime and the Man,* and his conclusions came under immediate attack because he failed to consider other than imprisoned offenders within his definition of criminality, failed to select an adequate noncriminal sample, to formulate a clear definition of his central concept of physical inferiority, and to identify clearly the offender with the specific type of offense committed.[23] Hooten studied over 13,000 prisoners in 10 states during a 12-year period, but his primary conclusion that crime is a result of biological inferiority gained little support.[24] Nevertheless, he continued to propose his viewpoint and to recommend consequent eugenic and sterilization programs designed to control criminal behavior through the elimination of defective biological specimens.

Studies of the Jukes and Kallikak families

The belief that crime represents an atavistic throwback to primitive human existence and a degeneracy of the nervous system, furthered by the theories of French physicist Benoit Morel, who believed that misshapen heads, prognathous jaws, dental defects, abnormal ear structure and size, or other abnormalities were closely related to criminal behavior, led to further studies of criminal heredity patterns. Richard L. Dugdale, one of the earliest investigators of defective heredity, examined the members of the now-famous Jukes family after finding six members of the family in New York jails. Tracing the genealogy of the Jukes family to the early 18th century in order to discover the original biological source of existing deviance, Dugdale found that 24 of the 41 males descending from two of the five living sisters were criminals. Consequently, Dugdale concluded unscientifically that crime was more common among the elder sons when "Jukes blood" and non-Jukes blood were mixed illegitimately. The criminal's physical and mental capacity, Dugdale believed, are limited by heredity, and crime is an indication of personal vigor, pauperism, and "idiotic helplessness."[25]

A second study of the Kallikak family by Henry H. Goddard added further support to the hereditary hypothesis. Goddard discovered that 143 feebleminded and 46 normal children were among the 480 descendants of Martin Kallikak, a Revolutionary War soldier, and an allegedly feebleminded bar maid. Of the descendants, 36 were illegitimate, 33

---

[23] *Ibid.,* p. 322.

[24] Earnest A. Hooten, *Crime and the Man* (Cambridge, Mass.: Harvard University Press, 1939), p. 130. Also see Earnest A. Hooten, *The American Criminal* (Cambridge, Mass.: Harvard University Press, 1939).

[25] Richard Dugdale, *The Jukes: A Study in Crime, Pauperism and Heredity* (New York: G. P. Putnam's Sons, 1942).

sexually immoral, 24 confirmed alcoholics, and 3 epileptics. Three were criminal and eight kept houses of ill fame; another 82 died in infancy. Kallikak's legitimate marriage to a girl of a good family, on the other hand, produced 496 normal descendants who married into the best families of their state without producing feebleminded or other defective offspring.[26] However, like Dugdale, Goddard failed to control for environmental influences, a failure which rendered his study largely useless.

THE GROWTH OF EXPERIMENTAL PSYCHOLOGY

Congruent attempts to measure individual differences led to the emergence of experimental psychology. The development of the intelligence test led to early attempts to evaluate the intelligence quotient (I.Q.) of the criminal offender. Administering these tests to the newly admitted inmates at the New Jersey Training School for the Feeble-Minded, Henry H. Goddard discovered that the new inmates possessed a mental age above 13 years, a finding which led him to conclude that the community functionally defined the mental age of 12 (I.Q. 75) as the upper age limit of feeblemindedness. This premise, however, proved faulty as Goddard's later studies of criminal intelligence disclosed that 89 percent of the persons in one study were feebleminded while only 28 percent in a second institutional study possessed the same characteristics.[27]

The discovery that more than one third of the potential World War I draftees had received an I.Q. rating of feeblemindedness merely served to confirm the earlier doubts. Specific intelligence testing of prisoners by Carl Murchison and Calvin P. Stone, for example, disclosed that criminals were not inferior persons but instead were able to perform more consistently than draft Army soldiers.[28] In 1939, Simon Tulchin disclosed similar findings.[29] Lacking this evidence, Goddard continued to maintain in 1921 that the greatest single cause of delinquency and crime is "low grade mentality, much of it within the limits of feeblemindedness."[30]

---

[26] Henry H. Goddard, *The Kallikak Family* (New York: Macmillan Co., 1912), pp. 18–19. Also examine M. F. Ashley Montagu, "The Biologist Looks at Crime," *The Annals*, Vol. 217 (1914), pp. 46–58.

[27] Henry H. Goddard, *Feeble-Mindedness: Its Causes and Consequences* (New York: Macmillan, 1914), p. 569.

[28] Calvin P. Stone, "A Comparative Study of Intelligence of 3,503 Men of the United States Army," *Journal of Criminal Law and Criminology*, Vol. 12 (1921), pp. 238–57; and Carl Murchison, *Criminal Intelligence* (Worchester, Mass.: Clark University Press, 1926).

[29] Simon Tulchin, *Intelligence in Crime* (Chicago: University of Chicago Press, 1939).

[30] Henry H. Goddard, *Juvenile Delinquency* (New York: Dodd, Mead & Co., 1921), p. 22.

The investigation of mental disorders and deficiencies

Because tests confirming the relationship of crime and feeblemindedness were inconclusive, later investigations focused upon the relationship of mental deficiencies or disorders and crime. The early studies seemed to show that a large number of the criminal population are psychopathic, but the attempt to validate this conclusion revealed a less definite pattern. In the 10 years between 1910 and 1920, 99.5 percent of the Pontiac Reformatory (Illinois) inmates were classified as psychiatrically abnormal. While most were diagnosed as psychopathic offenders, this evaluation was later disputed through the development of more refined measurement and classification procedures.[31] Other early investigators found strong relationships between crime and mental disorders, which were challenged in later studies by Paul Schilder, H. Warren Dunham, and M. H. Erickson, members of the Psychiatric Clinic of the New York Court of General Sessions.[32] As a result, the term *psychopathic criminal* has come under major attack in recent years.

Several German and American researchers attempted to relate criminality to identical or fraternal twins, but their efforts achieved only limited success. Generally, these studies assumed that genetically similar twins each possessed a greater tendency to criminal behavior than their nonfraternal counterparts. Although researchers at first believed they had found a promising lead in their attempt to unravel the problem of crime causation, their hopes soon proved to be false. They were unable to answer whether the identical appearance of twins from a single fertilized ovum (identical) caused delinquency or whether it merely encouraged close companionship and familial interaction which resulted in both members facing similar environmental situations together. Consequently, the promise of identical or fraternal twin research has borne little fruit to date.

Sheldon and somatotypes

When William H. Sheldon reinvestigated the relationship of body type to total personality in stimulating criminal behavior, he reopened

---

[31] Paul W. Tappan, *Crime, Justice and Correction* (New York: McGraw-Hill Book Co., 1960), p. 117.

[32] Paul Schilder, "The Cure of Criminals and the Prevention of Crime," *Journal of Criminal Psychopathology*, Vol. 2 (October, 1940), p. 152. Also refer to H. Warren Dunham, "The Schizophrene and Criminal Behavior," *American Sociological Review*, Vol. 4 (June, 1959), pp. 352–61; and M. H. Erickson, "Criminality in a Group of Male Psychiatric Patients," *Mental Hygiene*, Vol. 22 (July, 1938), pp. 459–76.

a question which researchers had long neglected. Sheldon identified basic somatotypes (body types) which he defined as *endomorph, mesomorph,* and *ectomorph.* The endomorph was described by Sheldon in terms similar to those used by Kretschmer to explain his pyknic classification (medium height, body rotundity, soft hands). While his ectomorph was characterized by linearity, body delicacy, prominent skeletal structure, small face, sharp nose, and fine hair, the mesomorph was conceived by Sheldon as a person possessing a heavy chest and highly developed arms, limbs, and connective tissue. His central contribution appeared in his volume entitled *The Varieties of Delinquent Youth* (1949), in which he noted that all 16 delinquent youths identified among the 200 residents of the Hayden Goodwill Inn in South Boston were endowed with residual or primary criminality and happened without exception to be endomorphic mesomorphs.[33] Although Sheldons' work was quickly received and given central attention, his limited sample presented an obvious drawback.

The Gluecks

The publication of *Unraveling Juvenile Delinquency* by Sheldon and Eleanor Glueck (1950) extended the physiological investigation of criminality. Using Sheldon's somatotyping method, the Gluecks found that 60.1 percent of the delinquents revealed mesomorphic characteristics while only 30.7 percent of the nondelinquents fell into this classification.[34] Although the Gluecks reaffirmed Sheldon's presupposition of a high correlation between mesomorphy and delinquent behavior, they offered a more specific insight into the nature of the correlation. Arguing that the mesomorph is generally a man of action, the Gluecks assumed that he would act to resolve a problem situation in its context. If he acts against the law in the resolution process, he is immediately stereotyped as a delinquent. On the other hand, the ectomorph, a thinker and brooder, fails to act decisively. Rather than seek a solution to his problem, he suffers with it. By contrast, the endomorph is more apt to ignore his problem and to face life in his own particular way. Therefore, his delinquency potential is close to that of the average person his age. However, each basic morphological physique type possesses

---

[33] Peter Lejins, *op. cit.,* p. 323. Sheldon used the term *primary criminality* to refer to legal violations which are not due to mental deficiencies or psychiatric causes. Also see William H. Sheldon's other works: *The Varieties of Human Physique* (New York: Hafner Publishing Co., Inc., 1940); *The Varieties of Temperament* (New York: Harper & Row, Publishers, 1942); and *Varieties of Delinquent Youth* (New York: Harper & Bros., 1949).

[34] *Ibid.,* p. 324. See Sheldon and Eleanor Glueck, *Unraveling Juvenile Delinquency* (Cambridge, Mass.: Harvard University Press, 1951).

a difference in the incidence of certain traits which are either potentially or actually associated with delinquency. Such differences in physical and temperamental structures partially explain, the Gluecks suggested, the variable responses of each body type to environmental pressures. The fact that the reaction of each body type or subtype to its environments is so diverse helps to explain why it is so difficult to delineate the causes of delinquency.[35]

The *mesomorphs* possess a sturdy physical, nervous, and emotional structure and tend to participate in impulsive action. The *endomorphs* are more sensitive and aesthetic in their interests. Since they are more tense, inhibited, and conflict-ridden, they often express their restrained impulses in destructive-sadistic acts. The *balanced physique* type, on the other hand, does not fear defeat and failure as much as the other types. While this type possesses many of the characteristics of each of the other types, it represents a more composite physique and more balanced personality.[36]

The Gluecks had undertaken their first attempt to unravel juvenile delinquency in 1950 with a volume examining the statistically significant differences of a representative sample of true delinquents and a matched sample of true nondelinquents. In 1956, they published a book investigating the essential constitutional traits which seemed to underly delinquent conduct. Their later efforts turned to an inspection of the familial, sociocultural, and environmental influences in home and community socialization and their impact upon particular physique types. "A social factor," the Gluecks hypothesized, "acts selectively upon delinquent boys possessing certain traits."[37] Neither the trait nor the social factor, however, singly contribute to the distinction between delinquency and nondelinquency because delinquency is ultimately a product of the combined traits and factors. Consequently, the impact of a child's family environment on his ultimate involvement in delinquency is related to factors reflecting parental pathology, unfavorable aspects of the home atmosphere, abnormal family relations, and lack of parental concern. Hostility, unconventionality, a feeling of not being appreciated, a sense of parental inadequacy, defensive maternal attitudes, a tendency toward fantasy, involvement in alcoholism, culture conflict, family financial dependence, emotional conflict in the home, and a lack of family self-respect enhance the probability of delinquent activity.

Delinquency may develop in three or more ways. While some sociocultural factors stimulate the formation of traits which are significantly

---

[35] Sheldon and Eleanor Glueck, *Physique and Delinquency* (New York: Harper & Bros., 1956), p. 249.

[36] *Ibid.*, p. 251.

[37] Sheldon and Eleanor Glueck, *Family, Environment and Delinquency* (Boston: Houghton Mifflin Co., 1962).

associated with antisocial juvenile behavioral tendencies, other social characteristics impel normally neutral traits to become criminogenic. Still other sociocultural factors influence the total complex of criminogenic forces "quite apart from the influences of the various delinquency-linked physiologic, neurologic, or psychologic traits."[38] However, home environmental influences, even when oriented to the criminogenic, only selectively propel the youth toward maladjustment and delinquency in relationship to his general vulnerability to such traits. Therefore, the core process of delinquency formation, the Gluecks argue, is related to differential *contamination* rather than differential *association,* as assumed by Edwin Sutherland and Donald Cressey. The ultimate degree of contamination, however, depends "not merely on exposure but also on susceptibility as opposed to immunity."[39] The weakening of family life plays a large part in the rise of delinquency.

The rise of the psychoanalytic approach

In opposition to the Gluecks' conclusions, psychoanalytic theorists August Aichorn, Kate Friedlander and David Abrahamsen maintain that environmental and social elements are only minor factors in causation and never hold a primary role, an assumption characteristic of the Freudian-dominated psychoanalytic approach. In the Freudian scheme of explanation, all behavior, no matter how absurd or contradictory, possesses significant and meaningful personality relationships. Because it is purposive, it must be understood as a substitute or symbolic expression of repressed personality elements if it is not a direct expression of the purposes of the conscious ego. Under the Freudian model, criminal behavior is a substitute response for repressed complexes. Conflict in the unconscious mind creates feelings of guilt or anxiety, a desire to remove guilt feelings, and a wish to restore the proper balance of good against evil through punishment. As a result, the criminal commits the criminal act, the Freudians believe, in order to be caught and punished.

Sigmund Freud held that many criminal tendencies are related to neurotic symptoms. As crises develop, conflict occurs and tension increases before this situation is fully resolved. Crime, therefore, involves unanticipated elements which may lead to catastrophic ends. Two opposing sets of instincts, Freud concluded, operate within the life of the individual. The *death instinct,* manifested in a destructive or aggressive tendency, limits the organism's potential. The *libidinal instinct,* an instinct for life, serves to maintain the higher development of the person. The *destructive instinct,* a third variation, often found in the unconscious

---

[38] *Ibid.,* p. 154.
[39] *Ibid.,* p. 155. Refer to Sheldon and Eleanor Glueck, *Ventures in Criminology: Selected Recent Papers* (Cambridge, Mass.: Harvard University Press, 1964).

of neurotic patients, is not only evident in tendencies towards criminal activity but also in human expressions of cruelty, strife, and war.[40]

The followers of the psychoanalytic school of criminological theory even now believe that behavior is largely a product of biological-psychological drives or instincts which are unconscious, unrecognized, and generally not understood by the actor. They maintain that consequent functional behavior disorders, often expressed in criminality, are the results of conflicts involving these basic drives. Repressed instincts or faulty socialization may easily result in expressed criminality. Since offensive behavior is often rooted in the unconscious, the individual may only be able to control his conduct when he gains insight into the nature of his unconscious being through some form of psychoanalysis or psychoanalytic therapy.

Freud and his followers saw the human psyche as having three components: the id, the ego, and the superego. The *id*, often viewed as the person's instinctual characteristic, is centrally prominent at the time of birth. At this point in his life, the child's universe is primarily his own awareness. However, as the child becomes aware of his new environment, his *ego* begins to emerge. This ego represents a postponement or repression of instinctual drives either because of the child's inability to fulfill such instincts or the unwillingness of others to respond to his instinctual desires. The id, therefore, is partially modified in the attempt of the ego to mediate between the id and the child's world of broader reality. As a result, the id, which seeks pleasure, is modified by the ego which attempts to reduce and minimize pain.

As the child emerges into youth and manhood, the *superego,* an extension of the ego, is formed by internalization in response to advice, example, threats, warnings, and punishments by parents, teachers, and other authority figures. Because it represents a concept of morality and a development of a conscience, the superego internalizes parental value expectations and other significant infringements of authority upon the id and the ego. The superego, therefore, is composed of the social norms, values, and ideas which the child internalizes. Because the ego represents self-discipline and the internalization of value commitments, it also includes a means for punishing failure through sensitization to psychic guilt feelings or anxieties. Because the superego represents the standards of parents and normative authority, it functions to constrain the individual and to channel his actions to acceptable ends. While the id, ego, and superego work in relative harmony for most individuals, abnormal or neurotic persons may develop guilt feelings, abnormal behavior, or variations in personality patterns. If the superego has not reached its proper balance in personality development, antisocial behavior based

---

[40] Bomberg, *op. cit.,* p. 96. Also see Philip Q. Roche, "Mental Health and Criminal Behavior," *Federal Probation,* Vol. 29 (September, 1965), p. 7.

upon mere instinctual fulfillment without proper superego modifications may result.

Modifications in psychoanalytic theory

More recent psychoanalytic theorists have reconceptualized many of the assumptions of the earlier Freudians. Writing in his volume *The Psychology of Crime,* David Abrahamsen notes that the etiology of criminal behavior is related to the interplay of multiple causative factors. Although one factor may contribute more to the criminal tendency than others, no one element is ever the single cause of crime. Socioenvironmental factors influence the individual; and yet psychological and personality factors involve the person in reactions toward his environment. Consequently, each factor, which differs in quality and quantity, may combine with others in a diversity of ways. Criminal behavior, Abrahamsen suggests through the use of a pseudo-mathematical formula, can be approached through an understanding of two laws.

The first of these laws is that *criminal behavior is composed of a multiplicity of causative factors.* Because these factors vary qualitatively and quantitatively in each instance, the causes of criminal behavior are relative.[41] Heredity, Abrahamsen argues, determines what the person can do, although the environment determines what and how he does do it. Individuals, he concludes, participate in criminal activity:

1. When antisocial inclinations are exposed to criminal influences, further stimulated by the act of a precipitating event.
2. Where the offender possesses a strong unconscious desire for punishment, owing to unconscious deep-rooted guilt feelings, developed through past experience.
3. As an indirect or false expression of aggressiveness.[42] If the deficient individual is exposed to criminalistic influences, a strong emotional stress may appear in his total emotional environment. Whether one completes an antisocial or criminal act, however, depends upon the basic response of the ego and superego to instinctual impulses. Since the total situation stimulates the eventual action, criminal behavior must ultimately be understood in terms of a second law concerning the relationship of factors.

Abrahamsen's second law states that: *A criminal act (C) is the sum of a person's criminalistic tendencies (T) plus his total situation (S) divided by the amount of his resistance (R).*[43]

---

[41] David Abrahamsen, *The Psychology of Crime* (New York: Columbia University Press, 1960), p. 30.

[42] *Ibid.,* p. 33.

[43] *Ibid.,* p. 37.

Presented in formula form this law reads:

$$C = \frac{T + S}{R}$$

A criminal act, Abrahamsen reasons, only occurs if the individual's resistance is unable to offset criminalistic tendencies inherent in the situation. Since criminal behavior is an expression of many personality types, variable situations, and diverse abilities to resist, it is relative. "The external criminal situation," Abrahamsen argues, "is the total environmental situation—all the stresses and strains which contribute to mobilizing a person's criminalistic tendencies." The internal criminal situation, on the other hand, "is the person's psychological state."[44] The individual's capability of resistance is related to his emotional, intellectual, and social conditioning, which are intimately reflected in the formation of a superego and its relationship to the situation and to the person's ego. The degree of resistance which an individual offers, therefore, depends to a large extent, Abrahamsen hypothesizes, upon the individual's previous resolution of his unconscious incestuous desires, otherwise defined as his degree of emotional maturity.[45] Abrahamsen relates the incidence of criminality to the person's ability to resist or overcome his own tendencies and the enticements offered by various situations.

An English researcher, J. B. Mays, believes as a result of his Liverpool findings that delinquency represents a juvenile life episode which usually begins at 11, peaks at 13, and tapers off at 15 upon leaving school.[46] Other English researchers hold that delinquency reaches its peak in the 15th year of the individual's life. Mays finds that those who persist in delinquency above the age of 16 are those who are more inclined to criminal activity and are psychologically maladjusted or disturbed. Although the community and its youth, Mays believes, are disenchanted with the local school and feel that they derive little benefit from it, they are not openly antagonistic to it. Nevertheless, the nondelinquent Liverpool boy is a rare individual. While group but not gang delinquency is highly evident, "social delinquency" is largely confined to early and middle adolescence. As might be expected, the delinquent prefers a target (victim) that is an outgroup distinct from his family, peer, or community group.[47]

In an overextended psychological explanation of delinquency Fritz Redl and David Wineman focus upon the aggressive child whose ego

---

[44] *Ibid.*, p. 38.

[45] *Ibid.*, p. 38.

[46] J. B. Mays, *Growing Up in the City* (New York: John Wiley & Sons, Inc., 1964), pp. 76–82.

[47] David M. Downes, *The Delinquent Solution* (New York: Free Press, 1966), p. 105.

is "afflicted in many areas of functioning with a severe performance weakness."[48] The ego, that part of the personality which keeps the individual and his impulses in touch with reality, is unable to master the demands of the broader social reality. However, aggressive children, Redl and Wineman found, cannot face fear, anxiety, or insecurity without expressing some form of organized aggression. Therefore, aggression represents feelings of guilt and the inability to fulfill oneself through fun or recreational gratification. Desiring immediate gratification, aggressive children respond in a hostile manner if fulfillment is not immediately rendered. They blame destiny, some trick, or another person for their plight. While the ego is unable to control impulses for immediate gratification, it is able to defend against extreme forms of impulse satisfaction. Although the child remains unaffected by a sense of guilt, embarrassment or shame, he may nevertheless fight a battle with his own conscience, the inner enemy of impulse and license. Searching for support in his delinquency, the aggressive child seeks to identify with others of similar ego attitudes. Since the ego offers a direct defense against change, it resists identification with those elements which might control its behavior. Consequently, overly close identification with the adult enemy results in the immediate social death of the aggressive youth. Remaining "socially blind," the aggressive youth maintains a form of mechanized warfare against change by protecting the ego from attempts to identify with the aggressive youth and his problem.[49]

Because their poorly equipped egos are unable to provide the children with adequate channels for achieving satisfactions, they resort to a primitive impulse-dominated form of behavior, which stimulates punitive counterwarfare by those who find this behavior abnormal. Since the average parent or teacher is unable to understand their problem empathetically, their situation is only aggravated if therapy is suggested at a point too late in their life. Even if applied in time, therapy may possess only limited value, since ego reorientation or redefinition occurs most fully only when the ego is supported by the total environment, whether in the form of activity roles, program structures, or a coherent strategy of ego-supportive life experiences.[50] Therefore, delinquency, Redl and Wineman believe, is a product of the juvenile's inability to reach behavioral self-control. Psychiatrist Karl Menninger chooses to express a similar idea in another way. Periodic juvenile outbursts of anger often evident in impulsive homicidal attacks, Menninger writes,

---

[48] Fritz Redl, *Controls from Within* (Glencoe, Ill.: Free Press, 1952), p. 16.

[49] Fritz Redl and David Wineman, *Children Who Hate* (Glencoe, Ill.: Free Press, 1951), p. 20. Also see Sara G. Geiger, "Early Recognizable Personality Deviations," *Federal Probation*, Vol. 25 (December, 1961), p. 29.

[50] *Ibid.*, p. 37. Also see H. J. Eysenck, *Crime and Personality* (New York: Houghton Mifflin Co., 1964).

are really revelations of impulse "syscontrol," a state at which the ego is no longer able to contain the surge of emotions underlying the expression of aggression.[51]

Other interpretations

But delinquency and criminality, Franz Alexander and Hugo Staub maintain, may also be either chronic or accidental. The *chronic* criminal, whose deviancy results from his own psychic apparatus, may be differentiated into five distinct types. *Organic* or *toxic* criminals, represented among mental defectives, alcoholics, and drug addicts, are characterized by a disabled ego which allows rather weak but unconscious needs to gain expression through delinquent or criminal behavior. The crime of the *compulsive* or *symptomatic* criminal, on the other hand, is alien to his otherwise normal personality patterns. He differs from the *neurotic acting-out* criminal, who also becomes criminal due to powerful unconscious impulses, because he is momentarily overwhelmed and his ego controls are modified by the demands of the id. However, the neurotic acting-out criminal is more inclined to operationalize these unconscious needs in behavior patterns. The *normal* criminal is one whose ego and superego are committed to criminal behavior, while the *genuine* criminal primarily evidences an immaturity of the superego.

Compulsive or symptomatic criminals, the second of the major categories of Alexander and Staub, are those who emerge due to unusual environmental pressures and demands.[52] The *mistaken* criminal, a subtype, may cause damage or injury as unconscious wishes are acted out in the environmental situation. The *situational* criminal, another subtype whose crime results from an intense crisis situation, is a product of a momentary response. Consequently, while most chronic or symptomatic criminality is a product of intrapsychic personality dimensions, situational criminality is stimulated by the environmental situation.

Physician-psychiatrist Walter Bomberg does not share this outlook. Crime, Bomberg argues, must be interpreted as an act which is an expression of self-assertion springing spontaneously from the wrongdoer's impulses and inner needs. The meaning of criminal behavior, therefore, must be found in that state of "acting" which is not yet understood as a crime but which results in the assignment of punishment. Social

---

[51] Karl Menninger and M. Nayman, "Episodic Dyscontrol: A Third Order of Stress Adaptation," *Bulletin of the Menninger Clinic*, Vol. 20 (July, 1956), p. 153. For a discussion of crime and insanity, see Richard W. Nice, *Crime and Insanity* (New York: Philosophical Library, Inc., 1958).

[52] Franz Alexander and Hugo Staub, *The Criminal, The Judge, and the Public* (Glencoe: Free Press, 1956), p. 123. See Harold F. Uehling, "Crime Breeds on Smothered Feelings," *Federal Probation*, Vol. 30 (March, 1966), p. 11.

values are significant in the expression of crime only when they influence individuals and become a form of evident behavioral or symbolic expression. The entire personality of the offender, including his unconscious conflicts, defenses, personality traits, habitual responses, conscious and subliminal motivations, fantasies, wishes, conative drives, rationalizations, displacements, projections, and psychic scotomata are involved in his crime and punishment.[53]

As a result, crime from a behavioral standpoint can be viewed as a product of three natural modalities. Criminal responses, Bomberg believes, may occur in the form of aggressive drives, aggression under the cover of passivity, and psychophysiological stresses. Essentially *aggressive* crimes include murder and manslaughter, assault, forceful rape, extortion, robbery, libel, slander and professional crime (racketeering). *Passive-aggressive* violations include burglary, larceny, embezzlement, swindling, arson, bigamy, gambling, conspiracy to defraud, and carrying concealed weapons. *Psychophysiological* stress crimes include sexual crimes, which are divided into homosexuality, exhibitionism, statutory rape, pedophilia, obscene telephone calls, pornography, and indecencies in public and prostitution. In addition, there are offenses involving the possession, use, and/or sale of narcotics.[54] Crime represents a form of spontaneous self-assertion which clearly exposes the violator's impulses and inner needs to trained investigators.

---

[53] Bomberg, *op. cit.*, p. 9. Also see William Goldfarb, "Psychological Privation in Infancy and Subsequent Adjustment," *American Journal of Orthopsychiatry*, Vol. 15 (April, 1945), pp. 254–55; Edward R. Bartlett and Dale B. Harris, "Personality Factors in Delinquency," *School and Society*, Vol. 43 (1936), pp. 653–56.

[54] *Ibid.*, p. 90. Investigate Prescott Lecky, *Self-Consistency: A Theory of Personality* (New York: Island Press, 1945); and Lester E. Hewitt and Richard L. Jenkins, *Fundamental Patterns of Maladjustment: The Dynamics of Their Origin* (Springfield, Ill.: Charles C. Thomas, Publisher, 1947).

Chapter 12

SOCIOENVIRONMENTAL
AND SOCIOCULTURAL
CAUSATION THEORIES

THE OPENING DISCUSSION

Gabriel Tarde and Gustav Aschaffenberg

Gabriel Tarde, rejecting biological and physical explanations of crime causation, maintained that crime is predominately a social product. Although biological and physical factors may play some role in criminality, the influence of the social environment, he argued, is of paramount significance in the development of criminal conduct.[1] Recognizing that individual choice is evident in every criminal career, Tarde theorized that elements of chance are also central influences. The simple fact of birth places individuals in potentially criminogenic positions.

Crime is partially a product of *imitation,* which can be most clearly defined, Tarde suggested, in three basic laws: (1) Men imitate each other in proportion to their close contact (*i.e.,* imitation is greater in crowds or cities); (2) the superior is imitated by the inferior (*i.e.,* drunkenness or murder, originally crimes of royalty, have become generalized to all social levels); and (3) when two mutually exclusive patterns converge, one may be substituted for the other (*i.e.,* murder by knifing has been modified by the availability of the gun). On the basis of these

---

[1] Margaret Vine, "Gabriel Tarde," *Pioneers in Criminology,* in Herman Mannheim (ed.), (Chicago: Quadrangle Books, Inc., 1960), p. 229. See Donald R. Taft, "The Influence of the General Culture on Crime," *Federal Probation,* Vol. 30 (September, 1966), p. 16.

"laws," Tarde argued that an increased standard of living, stimulated by industrialization, enhances rather than reduces criminality.

Tarde rejected Lombroso's theory of the born criminal and the philosophical concept of free will; instead he hypothesized that individual identity and personal memory or social similarity are central ingredients in any functional concept of moral responsibility. Because each person receives some moral training and assumes social obligations, he is responsible for his acts. However, if his memory is impaired, he ought not be held responsible for his crime. Responsibility depends upon social similarity, the individual's familiarity with the society in which he lives. However, social similarity exists only if persons are aware of the nature of the society, have experienced a common education, understand prevailing customs, and have been conditioned to the basic interests and desires of the group.

Although the biological and physical capabilities of the individual may influence his moral response, they are ultimately shaped by the social context. Consequently, the function of the courts, Tarde theorized, should be confined to the rendering of a decision concerning the guilt or the innocence of the accused. Any punishment should be defined in relationship to the responsibility of the accused and should be related to the person's psychological potential for understanding. Legal uniformity should likewise be avoided because it is basically unfair to inflict the same punishment on a rural thief as on an urban thief. Rural criminals, for example, should receive more physical punishment than their urban counterparts because they commit more crimes of violence.[2] Primary focus must be placed upon the individual in the criminal event rather than upon the mere crime itself.

While Tarde emphasized the laws of imitation, *Gustav Aschaffenberg* placed greater emphasis upon society's role in crime causation. According to Aschaffenberg, society is basically responsible for the criminal because many of the causes of crime are inherent in society. Although the criminal is responsible to society because he essentially lives a life that is filled with criminal activity, society cannot escape the duty of eradicating crime causes where possible.

Despite his awareness that criminals are disproportionately marked by characteristics of mental abnormality, Aschaffenberg placed less importance upon these abnormalities than Lombroso. In opposition to the view of many of his colleagues, he maintained that alcoholism is a major crime-producing force. Arguing that penal responsibility should be determined on the basis of biological or social criteria and not according to a metaphysical or theological theory of free will, Aschaffenberg held that the use of the indeterminant sentence and probation are central

---

[2] *Ibid.*, p. 236. The student of crime should refer to Karl O. Christianson, *Scandinavian Studies in Criminology* (London: Tavistock Publications, 1965).

to any meaningful treatment program. However, the study of crime and the treatment of the offender must eventually be approached from a statistical standpoint so that qualitative evaluation and meaningful program planning can be based upon accurate and meaningful quantitative data.[3]

SOCIOENVIRONMENTAL EXPLANATIONS

Early attempts to secure quantitative and qualitative data concerning crime led to an emphasis upon geographical and ecological explanations of criminal conduct. Because questions of population, political organization, economic development, familial patterns, distribution of intelligence, characteristics of crime, and religious attitudes were believed to be related to the physical environment, human activity in the 19th century often was interpreted in terms of temperature, humidity, wind velocity, storms, precipitation, sunshine, topography, or other physical or environmental factors. The search for causal laws sometimes led to a general geographical determinism which contemporary behavioral scientists have since rejected. Although *Edwin Dexter,* writing in 1904, held that geographical factors influence the commission of particular types of crime, he also noted that such influences are mediated to some degree by social factors. Basing his conclusions upon an investigation of 20,000 cases of assault and battery in New York City and 184 cases of homicide in Denver, Dexter suggested that crimes of violence are most frequent when humidity and atmospheric pressure are low, when winds are mild, or on clear days. Fewer crimes of violence, he contended, are associated with high humidity, high pressure, rain, or cloudiness.[4]

Quetelet, Lombroso, Ferri, Aschaffenberg and other criminologists attempted to demonstrate statistically that crimes against the person are more frequent in the hot climates of France, Italy, and Germany during the summer months. Crimes against property, likewise seasonal, are more common in cold climates and in the winter.[5] These writers generally failed to consider the size of the population, variations in police procedure, and public attitudes, tending to overemphasize geographical factors. They did note variations in murder and manslaughter patterns, but their failure to consider the various types of murder apparent in the definition of homicide seriously weakened the value of their data.

Although Edwin Dexter, as noted earlier, found a relationship be-

---

[3] Gustave Aschaffenburg, *Crime and Its Repression* (Boston: Little, Brown & Co., 1913), p. 321. For a later discussion of the crime problem, see Arthur E. Fink, *Causes of Crime* (Philadelphia: University of Pennsyylvania Press, 1938).

[4] Sidney J. Kaplan, "The Geography of Crime," *The Sociology of Crime,* in Joseph S. Roucek (ed.), (New York: Philosophical Library, Inc., 1961), p. 163.

[5] Herman Mannheim, *Comparative Criminology* (Boston: Houghton Mifflin, Co., 1965), p. 203. Also see Frank A. Hankins, *Quetelet as Statistician* (New York: Longman, Green & Co., 1908).

tween weather and assault arrests, he, too, was unable to reach definitive conclusions.[6] *H. C. Brearley's* study of the relationship between seasonal variations and South Carolina homicide in 1920 and 1927 also failed to reveal a consistent correlation.[7] Nevertheless, these researchers discovered that less violence is evident during the months of heavy agricultural work. The highest homicide volume occurred during December and July, due largely to the increased social interaction taking place during these months. *Marvin E. Wolfgang* found no statistically significant differences between the hot and cold months, a finding which led him to reject the hypothesis of any relationship between monthly or seasonal changes and rates of homicide.[8] Other theorists have similarly attempted to relate criminal incidents to the existence of daylight, hours of the day or other similar factors. *Manfred Curry*, a physician, suggests that criminality may be related to the presence of "aran," an ozonelike substance, in the atmosphere.[9]

The English researcher *Cyril Burt* found that juvenile offenses in London reach their highest level in June and December and lowest level in February and August. Offenses against the person attain their climax during the summer months. Property offenses, most frequent in the winter, are, Burt believes, due to the many Christmastime temptations rather than to actual climatic conditions. The fact that malicious injury is highest in November is a consequence, Burt suggests, of the observance of Guy Fawkes Day.[10] However, most data indicate that crimes against the person tend to increase during the summer months, while crimes against property are more frequently committed during the winter.

Urban-rural factors

Although the exact influence of geographical factors on criminal conduct is unclear, preliminary evidence suggests that urban and rural crime variations are related to:

1. The population of the city or adjacent metropolitan area.
2. The composition of the population by age, sex, race, or other factors.

---

[6] Edwin Dexter, *Weather Influence* (New York: Macmillan Co., 1904); and see C. Bernaldo Quiros, *Modern Theories of Criminality*. Trans. by Alfonso de Salvio (Boston: Little, Brown & Co., 1911).

[7] H. C. Brearley, *Homicide in the United States* (Chapel Hill: University of North Carolina Press, 1932), p. 68.

[8] Marvin E. Wolfgang, *Patterns in Criminal Homicide* (Philadelphia: University of Pennsylvania Press, 1958).

[9] Manfred Curry, "The Relationship of Weather Conditions, Facial Characteristics and Crime," *Journal of Criminal Law and Criminology*, Vol. 39 (July–August, 1948), pp. 253–61.

[10] Cyril Burt, *The Young Delinquent* (London: University of London Press, 1938).

3. The economic status and activity of the population.
4. Climate conditions and variations.
5. Availability of educational, religious, or recreational facilities.
6. The number of police employees per unit of population.
7. The standards governing the appointment of the law enforcement officers.
8. The policies of prosecuting officials in the courts.
9. The problems of the public toward law-enforcement problems.
10. The degree of efficiency of the local law enforcement agency.[11]

This listing, however, is inconclusive and omits other significant factors.

An early study of 60 rural property offenders between the ages of 17 and 30 by *Marshall Clinard* uncovered that rural offenses are related to the greater mobility of the rural offender in comparison to the rural nonoffender and to his more limited participation in community affairs, less frequent personal relationships with other youth in his community, and the tendency to participate in criminal activity late in his youth. Most rural property offenders, Clinard found, engage in adventurous but unorganized activity which demand limited criminal knowledge or technique and a minimal change in their self-image.[12]

Delinquency and ecology

Clifford R. Shaw reported in his 1929 book, *Delinquency Areas,* that juvenile delinquency and adult crime are unevenly distributed throughout the city of Chicago and are concentrated in particular ecological areas. While outlying residential communities, Shaw disclosed, possess the lowest crime rates, the areas adjacent to the central business districts and large industrial centers record the highest volume. Delinquency and crime are more common in areas undergoing transition and characterized by physical deterioration, population change, and disintegration of the cultural and organizational neighborhood.[13] As business and industry move to the area, elements of community social controls cease to function effectively. The diverse cultural and ethnic groups entering the transitional area, in turn, create value conflicts and decrease social control. The disorganization caused by the influx of business and industry is subsequently supported by the added flow of foreign national groups into the new cultural and racial urban community. Since few elements within the area are able to resist this disorganization process,

---

[11] Kaplan. *op. cit.,* pp. 182–83.
[12] *Ibid.,* p. 184.
[13] Clifford R. Shaw, *Delinquency Areas* (Chicago: University of Chicago Press, 1929), p. 204. Also see Solomon Kobrin, "The Conflict of Values in Delinquency Areas," *American Sociological Review,* Vol. 16 (October, 1951).

members of the community, Shaw theorized, become highly susceptible to normally unacceptable behavior patterns. Low community resistance allows the transmission of delinquent and criminal patterns together with other cultural and social norms. Consequently, if delinquent patterns dominate the area, the attitudes and behavior of community members, are likely to be shaped by these dominant attitudes.[14]

Two years later, Clifford R. Shaw with *Henry D. McKay* investigated additional dimensions of the delinquency area and established a series of relationships between the neighborhood social system and its underlying social values. Since the more prosperous persons move from the neighborhood as soon as it is feasible, the area continues to retain those diverse elements which are culturally slow to assimilate. The intensity of antisocial norms and the lack of consistent cultural standards, Shaw and McKay suggested, actually limit the juvenile's access to conventional traditions and norms and undermine traditional agencies of social control. Even the intimate socialization of the familial group is undermined by the diversity of activities and norms of the juvenile's local play group. In such a context, family disharmony and frustration serve to reinforce the play group's social meaning and stability. The specific goals and discipline of the peer group, in effect, order a seemingly disordered home life,[15] a finding supported by subsequent studies by Shaw and McKay in Philadelphia, Boston, Cincinnati, Cleveland, Richmond, Columbus, Birmingham, Little Rock, Denver, Seattle, Portland, Vancouver, Spokane, Evansville, Peoria, Omaha, Baltimore, and Minneapolis–St. Paul.[16]

The cultural-ecological transmission theory of delinquency and crime, proposed by Shaw and McKay, suggests that criminality in urban neighborhoods is transmitted from one generation to another despite basic ethnic, ecological, and demographic changes. Much of slum delinquency, therefore, is ˋa result of the intimate relation of youth with older and more experienced criminals. As "big shots" become juvenile role models, youths emulate their behavior. If the youth serves an apprenticeship with older offenders, he acquires the values and skills which are ultimately required for full participation in the criminal culture. Since the

---

[14] *Ibid.*, p. 206. See Joseph S. Roucek, *The Sociology of Crime* (New York: Philosophical Library, Inc., 1961); and Milton L. Barron, "Juvenile Delinquency and American Values," *American Sociological Review*, Vol. 16 (April, 1951), pp. 208–14.

[15] Terence Morris, *The Criminal Area* (New York: Humanities Press, Inc., 1958), p. 79.

[16] Clifford R. Shaw and Henry D. McKay, *Juvenile Delinquency and Urban Areas: A Study of Rates of Delinquents in Relation to Differential Characteristics of Local Communities in American Cities* (Chicago: University of Chicago Press, 1942). Also see Clifford R. Shaw and Henry D. McKay, "Social Factors in Juvenile Delinquency," (Washington, D.C.: National Commission on Law Observance and Enforcement, 1931), pp. 60–108.

delinquent and adult criminal world possesses a structure of its own, members of the structural system possess opportunities for upward mobility and higher status achievement.

Other perspectives

Despite their convincing arguments, the work of Shaw and McKay was not without its opponents. Some critics questioned whether Shaw's basic theory could be applied to cities in urban areas outside the North American continent. A study by *Andrew Lind* in 1930, partially answering this question, disclosed that the spacial distribution of delinquent homes, dependency cases, organized vice arrests, and suicides in Hawaii followed ecological patterns similar to those of North American cities. However, because Hawaii was a composite ethnic state, group moral and social competition was more severe.[17] Although Hawaii was not an American state at the time, the influence of American cultural and ecological patterns undoubtedly possessed important urban influence.

Sophia Robison, also an early critic of the work of Shaw and McKay, held that the gradation of delinquency from inner to outer city was due to coincidence and to urban development rather than to the existence of precise delinquency patterns. Since Shaw and McKay's work is based upon court appearances, those who are able to avoid police contact, she argued, are not recorded in delinquency statistics. Noting that social disorganization is not characteristic of all slum areas and that delinquency often fails to correspond to particular natural boundaries, Robison maintained that Shaw should have compared the basic differences between groups sharing the same socioeconomic status and living in similar areas.

William F. Whyte's study of "street-corner society" also disclosed that the urban slum is not so much disorganized as it is unintegrated into the structure of society surrounding it. The "Cornerville" man, unable to achieve class mobility, must choose between the two worlds of business and politics or of rackets and politics, a decision which is largely determined by existing opportunities. While success in the world of business and politics immediately alienates him from the world of Cornerville, success in the *rackets and politics* gains him prompt recognition, even though he may become marginal to the larger community. The rackets and local politics, therefore, offer the Cornerville man more realistic and meaningful rewards.[18]

---

[17] A. W. Lind, "Some Ecological Patterns of Community Distribution in Honolulu," *American Journal of Sociology,* Vol. 36 (1930), pp. 206–20. Also note Marshall Clinard, *Slums and Community Development* (Illinois: Free Press, 1966).

[18] William F. Whyte, *Street Corner Society* (Chicago: University of Chicago Press, 1955), pp. 272–74.

The borough of Croydon

The study of Croydon, a county borough near metropolitan London with a 1951 population of 249,870, led *Terence Morris* to conclude that the three highest rates of delinquency occur in wards which include and surround the central business district. While his discovery seems to justify the earlier studies of Shaw and McKay, Morris questions whether the data are either relevant or completely valid. While Shaw and McKay found that the physical deterioration of the neighborhood is vitally related to delinquency and crime problems, Morris argues that the physical characteristics of Croydon have little relevance for the delinquency and crime problem except as an indirect determinant of social status in the area. Low status and low rental, generally found in urban areas of physical deterioration, naturally attract members of the core problem group. Therefore, delinquency is more closely related to the lack of planning or social organization and to the lessened emphasis within the specific area upon the individual family cultural unit.[19] The delinquent, Morris suggests, is not always maladjusted. Instead, he is more often a member of a family which possesses low social aspirations and which lives in close proximity to other families of similar type. Invariably, his partners in deviant activity are members of the same local street play group or peers at the same school. Coming from families of skilled or semiskilled manual workers, these juveniles witness more parental disharmony and have more upsetting early childhood experiences, emotional disturbances, and feelings of personal rejection.[20]

Delinquency, Morris argues, is related to factors associated with social class. Although it operates in a subtle manner, social class determines the social norms, attitudes, and responses of the individual through the mechanism of subculture. The family represents the socioeconomic matrix which is called the class system. "However reluctant," Morris writes, as he ignores the problems of middle-class delinquency and white-collar crimes, "we may be to feel that the poor are less honest or the rich more law-abiding, the facts of the matter are that crime and delinquency are almost exclusively a proletarian phenomenon."[21] While a *juvenile delinquency potential* is related to the area of delinquent residence, it is ultimately based upon a constellation of factors which can be summarized in three propositions:

1. Delinquent or criminally antisocial behavior of a "social" kind tends to be characteristic of working-class culture and to be perpetuated by it.

---

[19] Morris, *op. cit.*, pp. 129–30.
[20] *Ibid.*, p. 149. Also consult Edward Glover, *The Roots of Crime* (New York: International Universities Press, 1960).
[21] *Ibid.*, p. 165.

2. Factors engendering "psychiatric" delinquency are likely to be aggravated in working class situations by poor housing and cognate socioeconomic factors.
3. Working-class families and, therefore, working-class culture dominate on housing estates.[22]

British government housing policy, Morris concludes, is a central determinant of the concentration of delinquents in a particular ecological area.

Stepney and Poplar

A survey of all crimes known to the police in the English communities of Stepney and Poplar by *David M. Downes* in 1960 disclosed that no necessary relationship exists between high crime-rate areas and areas of criminal residence. Within certain limits, a high crime rate is related to the physical, economic, and sociocultural characteristics of the high crime-rate area.[23] Although Stepney, the slum area, evidenced a larger adult criminal population than Poplar, the characteristic offenses were crimes of violence, illegal gambling, prostitution, larceny, immoral earnings, and drug use. Adult crimes in the unintegrated slum area were highly individualistic, unprotected, unorganized, petty, and poorly paid.

Future analysis, Downes proposes, should focus upon the implications of disassociation rather than upon alienation as a normative response of the working-class male adolescent to semiskilled, unskilled, or no work. Because adolescent male delinquency was found to be related to this dimension, future research should consider the functions of work, school, and leisure in delinquency causation. Research should also be directed to the efficacy of various intervening variables which operate to keep "the delinquency-prone youth from delinquency, assuming that all working-class boys whose 'life chances' push them inexorably toward semi- and unskilled work are in a delinquency-promoting life situation."[24] The working-class boy, Downes hypothesizes, begins in a delinquency-prone situation in which various intervening variables, including broken homes, maternal-parental deprivation, family fragmentation, and individual character structure, serve to aggravate an already unsettled situation. Consequently, researchers should look for those variables, whether in the form of higher performance in school, stable but respectable working-class family background, promise or skilled performance, outlets for political activity, stable courtship relations, legitimate leisure opportuni-

---

[22] *Ibid.*, pp. 182–83.
[23] David M. Downes, *The Delinquent Solution* (Glencoe, Ill.: Free Press, 1966), p. 140.
[24] *Ibid.*, p. 259.

ties, or other similar factors, which allow the working-class boy to break free of delinquency.[25]

SOCIOCULTURAL EXPLANATIONS

The shift away from ecological explanations of delinquency and crime causation led to investigations of associations, subcultures, structures, social status, and economic life. In proposing one of the most influential theories of causation in the late 1930's in his hypothesis that crime is a product of learning and group relations, *Edwin H. Sutherland* recognized the wide diversity of criminal behavior and the multiplicity of influences in criminal conduct. Sutherland divided his differential association and learning theory into nine basic phases.

1. Criminal behavior is learned, whether in the form of habitual, professional, organized, or white-collar criminality.
2. Social interaction and communication are central to the learning process.
3. Criminal behavior is acquired through participation within personal groups, as opposed to simple contact with mass media and formal agencies or institutions.
4. The learning process involves the learning of techniques for committing crime and the formation of new attitudes, motives, drives, and forms of rationalization, evidenced in the systematic reinforcement toward criminality.
5. The specific direction of motives and drives is learned from legal definitions of favorable or unfavorable acts.
6. Delinquency occurs because definitions *favorable* to the violation of the law exceed definitions *unfavorable* to violation of the law. These definitions, however, are usually reinforced by the group commitments or the associational relationships which the individual has established.
7. Since the degree of individual participation in the group may vary, factors of intensity, priority, duration, and frequency determine the actual tendencies toward criminal behavior.
8. All the mechanisms of learning are involved in learning criminal or anticriminal behavior.
9. Criminal and noncriminal behavior are expressions of the same needs and/or values and, therefore, cannot be explained in terms of these variable needs and/or values.[26]

---

[25] *Ibid.,* p. 260.

[26] Edwin H. Sutherland, *Principles of Criminology* (Philadelphia: J. B. Lippincott Co., 1947), pp. 6–7. Also note C. R. Jeffery, "Criminal Behavior and Learning Theory," *Journal of Criminal Law, Criminology, and Police Science,* Vol. 56, No. 3 (September, 1965), pp. 294–300; and Donald R. Cressey, *Delinquency, Crime and Differential Association* (The Hague: Nijhoff, 1964).

Crime, Sutherland argued, is learned in a systematic manner as persons associate within deviant groups. While some crimes (murder and rape, for example) may involve a mental or emotional disturbance which is largely independent of group relationships, most crimes are products of group commitment or subcultural conditioning.

The pioneering differential association and learning theory has been open to many criticisms since it was proposed, including complaints that its changing frame of reference over the years has limited its real meaning, that the theory is excessively deterministic and offers a closed theoretical system, and that biological and major psychological factors are totally overlooked. Other criticisms hold that the differential association and learning theory oversimplifies the process of learning and is too general to be tested effectively.

The delinquent subculture

Albert K. Cohen's hypothesis of the delinquent subculture, more inclusive than Sutherland's differential association approach, affirms that delinquency is neither an innate nor self-acquired disposition but is rather a behavior form which children learn as they become members of groups in which delinquent conduct is already established and operative.[27] Just as every society is internally differentiated into numerous subgroups, juvenile delinquency is in its own way a subculture within the broader culture. However, the delinquent subculture, Cohen assumes, is largely nonutilitarian, malicious, and negativistic.[28] Much gang stealing, for example, has no previous motivation but is rather indiscriminate action for the sake of self-fulfillment. The norms of the delinquent subculture are taken from the larger culture and inverted to delinquent ends. Since the delinquent subculture of the delinquent gang emphasizes short-run hedonism, group autonomy, and intolerance of restraint, juvenile gang members frequently express imperious group solidarity.

Although juvenile delinquency in the delinquent subculture is overwhelmingly concentrated in the male working-class sector of the juvenile population, the data which lead to this assumption may be a result of an exaggerated bias of the police and courts. Regardless of social class, nearly all juveniles commit delinquencies in their youth. The greater number, of course, are never arrested or taken before the court. Therefore, the belief that juvenile delinquency is largely a product of working-class families and neighborhoods, Cohen contends, turns out to be nothing more than an illusion. However, in terms of actual volume

---

[27] Albert K. Cohen, *Delinquent Boys: The Culture of the Gang* (Glencoe, Ill.: Free Press, 1955), p. 11.
[28] *Ibid.,* p. 25.

and contact with police, lower-class adolescents are overrepresented in juvenile delinquency.

The delinquent subculture arises from the need to overcome tension, frustration, resentment, guilt, bitterness, anxiety, and hopelessness. All aspiring members of society do not achieve in equal degree, and the delinquent subculture provides an answer for those who find the realization of traditional norms impossible. Since the delinquent subculture, Cohen suggests, provides its members with group security and meaningful roles, it continues to exert a profound influence upon persons who find few outlets for their personality needs. Becoming part of a consensus rewarded by acceptance, recognition, and respect, the youth also participates in a valid frame of reference which justifies and validates his new conduct orientation.[29] His integration into the delinquent subculture is encouraged by the fact that the acquisition of status within the group is accompanied by a loss of status outside the delinquent subculture. As ingroup isolation occurs, ambivalence concerning delinquent subcultural goals is minimized.[30]

Family membership confers a particular status upon each person within the family. For most adolescents, the family is the early representative of the social class system.[31] Although the child lives in a particular community, his status universe, the people against whom he measures himself, extends beyond his immediate community.[32] Since he is evaluated in terms of the total society rather than in relation to his relative status among his peers, the juvenile's individual characteristics are often ignored because of his limited relationship to middle-class values. Juveniles from the most disadvantaged classes will naturally be delegated to the bottom of the status pyramid, since they are unable to compete on the same terms as youths with greater prestige and cultural training. Because middle-class norms, Cohen contends, dominate the American value system, working-class children, of necessity, must come to terms with their implication. The middle-class emphasis on ambition, individual responsibility, development of skills, tangible achievement, "worldly asceticism," rationality, courtesy, personability, physical self-control, wholesome recreation, and respect for property are often antagonistic to working-class forms of self-expression.

Middle-class socialization tends to be conscious, rational, deliberate and demanding; working-class socialization, especially in the lower-lower class, however, tends to be relatively easygoing.[33] Middle-class parents,

---

[29] *Ibid.*, p. 57. See Thorsten Sellin, *Culture Conflicts and Crime* (New York: Social Science Research Council, 1938).

[30] *Ibid.*, p. 69.

[31] *Ibid.*, p. 78. See Gordon E. Jereczek, "Gangs Need Not Be Delinquent," *Federal Probation*, Vol. 26 (March, 1962), p. 49.

[32] *Ibid.*, p. 85.

[33] *Ibid.*, pp. 98–99.

Cohen hypothesizes, are more likely to contrive the child's physical environment, social milieu, and time usage in order to enhance his socialization to the middle-class ideal than are working-class parents. Therefore, while the working-class child learns less and more slowly than the middle-class child, the middle-class juvenile or youth is provided powerful motivation to conform to parental expectations. Because the working-class child is more dependent emotionally upon his peers for satisfaction, he is more inclined to participate in group-oriented activities which offer personal gratification. Consequently, the delinquent subculture primarily provides criteria of status which children at the bottom of the status ladder are able to meet.

While Cohen explains delinquent conduct in terms of the delinquent subculture, *J. Milton Yinger* turns to the concept of contraculture to describe the patterns of gang or street-corner society which oppose the norms of the dominant conventional society. As the boys participate in peer groups, they internalize, says Yinger, the dimensions of the contraculture and act out its interactional demands in relationship to the individuals' potential.[34]

Differential opportunity

Richard A. Cloward and *Lloyd E. Ohlin* assert that delinquent subcultures are differentiated into criminal, conflict, and retreatist types in relationship to the opportunity structure which delinquent youth confront as they pursue conventional goals, and to the degree of integration which they have achieved with older persons.[35] However, many of the opportunity structures have become closed to the young and lower-class youth, and their contacts with adult support have declined. As government housing replaces slum dwellings, as families move to quarters among strangers, as impersonal government replaces known community politicians in dispensing aid, and as organized crime continues its operations in the area, the concentration of poverty-dominated lower-class members in a particular community enhances the potential for continuing deviance.

Each individual occupies positions in relation to both legitimate and illegitimate *opportunity structures*. If an illegal (criminal) structure is not readily available in a given social location, a criminal subculture is not likely to develop among adolescents. If violence offers a primary channel to higher status in a community, greater participation of juveniles in conflict (violence) will normally occur. In each community alter-

[34] J. Milton Yinger, "Contraculture and Subculture," *American Sociological Review*, Vol. 25, No. 5 (October, 1960), pp. 628–30.

[35] Richard A. Cloward and Lloyd E. Ohlin, *Delinquency and Opportunity: A Theory of Delinquent Gangs* (New York: Free Press, 1960), p. 150.

nate legitimate and illegitimate adaptations are available to adolescents who attempt to reach new status levels. The eventual delinquent's or nondelinquent's response will depend upon the degree of access available to success goals, the nature of existing legitimate structures, and the strength of illegitimate influences in defining individual opportunity.[36]

Three more or less distinctive types of delinquent subculture give rise to modern delinquency. The *criminal subculture,* Cloward and Ohlin hypothesize, leads to the development of the gang which is devoted to theft, extortion, or other means of securing profit illegally. The *conflict subculture,* on the other hand, finds expression in a gang which manipulates violence as a means for winning status. By contrast, the *retreatist subculture* is evidenced in the gang which consumes drugs or otherwise retreats from situations of social conflict.[37] Consequently, the delinquent subculture, a special category of deviant culture, is one "in which certain forms of delinquent activity are essential requirements for the performance of the dominant role supporting the subculture."[38] Delinquent activity is a product of the performance of social roles which are specifically provided and supported by the appropriate delinquent subculture. Each of the criminal, conflict, and retreatist subcultures prescribes specific responses and role alternatives for its participants.

Although the three predominant subcultures are readily identifiable in large urban centers among lower-class males, they may exist in mixed form. Members of a predominantly conflict subculture, for example, may engage in systematic theft; criminal subculture participants may periodically participate in street combat with rival gangs. While some gang members are totally socialized to the subcultural perspective, others participate selectively and maintain other viable roles in their family, school, or church. However, the adolescent's ability to successfully segregate delinquent and conforming roles over a long period of time is highly limited.

In the *criminal subculture,* prestige is offered those who achieve material power and gain through illegitimate avenues or through avenues which are defined as illegitimate by the larger society. Learning to admire and respect older criminals and to adopt the "right guy" as his role model, the adolescent, Cloward and Ohlin believe, learns to master the techniques and orientations of the criminal subculture while exhibiting hostility and distrust toward members of the society at large. Rationalizing that big businessmen avoid taxes through large expense accounts, politicians engage in graft, and suckers are his natural victims, the juvenile successfully neutralizes the controlling effect of conventional norms.

[36] *Ibid.,* p. 152. Also refer to David J. Bordua, "Some Comments on Theories of Group Delinquency," *Sociological Inquiry,* Vol. 32 (Spring, 1962), pp. 245–60.
[37] *Ibid.,* p. 1.
[38] *Ibid.,* p. 7.

In order to prove that he has no obligations to the odd group of non-criminals, he emphasizes loyalty, honesty, and trustworthiness toward his criminal associates. Cultivating meaningful "connections" within the criminal subculture, he usually serves an apprenticeship with some other older and successful offender. With maturity, he learns to utilize bondsmen, unethical lawyers, policemen on the take, grafting politicians, dishonest businessmen, and corrupt jailers in order to enhance his mobility.[39]

The *conflict subculture* role model, evident within the lower-class culture, is the "bopper" who moves with his gang, uses weapons to enforce respect from other gangs, and maintains his status by fear and threat of violence. A successful warrior, he is unpredictable and engages in destructive assaults upon persons and property, often without any apparent reason. With fearless abandon, he willingly defends his personal integrity as a member of the gang. Developing a reputation for toughness and destructive violence, he receives, Cloward and Ohlin note, adulation from his peers and admiration for physical strength and masculinity from those he subjugates. He possesses "heart"; he fights and does not "chicken out," even when confronted with clearly superior odds or force. Since he views adult role models as weak, he rejects the role models they consider appropriate and defines his own in terms of toughness and courage. He seeks to overcome the apparent indifference and insincerity of the adult world and attempts to win status by use of violence.

The *retreatist subculture* pattern is expressed in a variety of individual or group expressive, sensual, or consummatory experiences.[40] Emphasizing the pursuit of the "kick," the "cat," a drug user in a lower-class area who believes himself culturally and socially detached from the life-style and preoccupations of the conventional world, finds pleasure and meaning, in alcohol, marihuana, addictive drugs, unusual sexual experiences, hot jazz, cool jazz, or a combination of such experiences. The retreatist attempts to maximize the awareness of life and overcome the limitations of the present world. In order to maintain his kick, however, the successful cat-retreatist engages in a lucrative "hustle," which centers in the manipulation, persuasion, or conning of others to obtain the necessary "goods." He will beg, borrow, steal, or engage in confidence games; he may also peddle drugs or work as a pimp. He generally lives in idleness and concentrates on organizing, scheduling, and eventually experiencing the aesthetic pleasure of the kick. Dressing and acting as

---

[39] *Ibid.*, p. 23.

[40] *Ibid.*, p. 25. For a sharper focus upon the ideological causes of crime. refer to Leon Radzinowicz, *Ideology and Crime* (New York: Columbia University Press, 1966); and Robert M. Frumkin, "Ideological Aspects of Crime," in Roucek (ed.), *op. cit.*

a "cool cat," the retreatist attempts to present a stable self-assured but aloof image. He rejects the world of the traditional squares and seeks status and recognition within the retreatist subculture by maximizing the effect of the kick and the hustle.[41]

Although Cloward and Ohlin's theory of differential opportunity holds great promise, it faces the need of further testing. D. J. Bordua believes that the Cloward and Ohlin theory is a unidimensional analysis of gang life which lacks the thoroughness and diversity of Thrasher's classic account of gang activity.[42]

Racketville, Slumtown and Haulburg

Following the lead of Robert Merton, Richard A. Cloward, and Lloyd E. Ohlin, *Irving Spergel* studied three distinctive areas within a large eastern city; the areas were characterized by three delinquent subcultures: "Racketville" (racket subculture), "Slumtown" (conflict subculture), and "Haulburg" (theft subculture). Racketville reveals an emphasis on the *racket subculture* as a means of achieving success goals. Youths facing limited legitimate opportunities to fulfill aspirations are under direct or indirect pressure to engage in numbers and other gambling activities or in loan-shark rackets in order to achieve success. Delinquents in the racket subculture, therefore, evidence the most extreme value orientations and believe that right connections are more important than education in getting ahead.

Slumtown, the *conflict subculture*, is represented by the deteriorated slums within which many delinquent youths live.[43] A product of its social conditions often is aspiration seeking through gang fighting. The pattern of values and expectations, rules and regulations, and rewards and punishments are central ingredients of the reputation ("rep") of the successful gang fighter. On the other hand, the Haulberg *theft subculture* emerges from social conditions in which conventional and criminal opportunities to achieve success goals exist simultaneously. Theft allows the juvenile to attain desired status in an area in which an organized criminal system has not yet gained prominence. Delinquents in the theft subculture, therefore, participate in the highest incidence of joyriding, car theft, and burglary.[44]

---

[41] *Ibid.*, p. 27.

[42] Downes, *op. cit.*, p. 67. See David J. Bordua, "Delinquent Subculture: Sociological Interpretations of Gang Delinquency," *Annals,* Vol. 338 (November, 1961), pp. 119–36.

[43] See Irving Spergel, "An Exploratory Research in Delinquent Subcultures," *Social Services Review,* Vol. 35, No. 1 (March, 1961), pp. 33–47.

[44] *Ibid.*, pp. 33–47.

Although each subculture is in its own way different from the others, Spergel notes that drug using and drug addiction are adaptations which may occur in each of the three delinquent subcultural types. The use of drugs, for example, may aid the user to maintain unrealized and otherwise unrealizable wealth, prestige, or power goals despite personality limitations which may undermine these aspirations. While each subculture may simultaneously contain elements of the others in limited degree, the dominant orientation of each delinquent subculture is to the racket, conflict, or theft orientations.[45]

The subculture of violence

Focusing more specifically upon a subculture of violence, *Marvin E. Wolfgang* and *Franco Ferracuti* suggest that a subculture of violence is composed of a cluster of values that are related to the life-style, socialization process, and interpersonal relationships of individuals living under similar conditions. Because probably fewer than 5 percent of all known homicides are planned or premeditated killings, violence, Wolfgang and Ferracuti suppose, is characteristic of the offender's subcultural context. They conclude that the overt use of force or violence in impersonal relationships and/or group interaction is a general reflection of basic values that "stand apart from the dominant, the central, or the parent culture."[46] Overt and often illicit expressions of violence are part of a subcultural normative system which is reflected in the psychological traits of these subcultural participants. Consequently, the subculture of violence, Wolfgang and Ferracuti believe, can best be understood in terms of the following corollaries:

1. No subculture can be totally different from or totally in conflict with the society of which it is a part. A subculture of violence shares interlocking value elements with the dominant culture.
2. To establish the existence of a subculture of violence does not require that the actors sharing in these basic value elements should express violence in all situations. In some types of social interaction a violent and physically aggressive response is often expected or required of all members sharing in that system of values.
3. The potential resort or willingness to resort to violence in a variety of situations emphasizes the penetrating and effusive character of this culture theme. The recourse to violence serves as an index of the extent to which assimilated values are associated with violence.

---

[45] Irving Spergel, *Racketville, Slumtown, Haulburg* (Chicago: University of Chicago Press, 1964), p. xviii.
[46] Marvin E. Wolfgang and Franco Ferracuti, *The Subculture of Violence* (New York: Tavistock Publications, 1967), p. 158.

4. The subcultural ethos of violence may be shared by all ages in a sub-society, but this ethos is most prominent in a limited age group, ranging from late adolescence to middle-age.
5. The counter-norm is nonviolence. Consequently, violation of expected and required violence often results in group ostracism.
6. The development of favorable attitudes toward and the use of violence in a subculture usually involves learned behavior and a process of differential learning, association, or identification. The subcultural aspects of violence must be considered in relation to differential personality variables.
7. The use of violence in a subculture is not necessarily viewed as illicit conduct and the users, therefore, do not have to deal with feelings of guilt about their aggression. Because violence may become a part of life-style, it may become normative and expected.[47]

The process of social deviance

Upon reviewing the delinquent subculture theory of Cohen and the differential opportunity hypothesis of Cloward and Ohlin, *Leslie Wilkins* defined his own postulates of delinquent-criminal behavior which he defines in the following propositions:

1. People tend to behave with regard to respective situations and things as they perceive them to be.
2. Distinctions between what is legitimate and what is illegitimate are made culturally.
3. Legitimate and illegitimate opportunities can be distinguished, and the *balance* between the two types of opportunities presents an important variable.
4. If the balance between legitimate and illegitimate opportunities remains constant, the amount of crime will tend to vary according to the total number of opportunities. Hence it follows that disturbance of the balance will modify the crime rate if the rate is considered in relation to the opportunity structure.
5. Since perceptions influence behavior, the definitions (perceptions) of the culture have an influence upon the members of the culture itself.
6. Human decision-making skill (information-processing) is influenced not only by the nature of the information, but by the "channel" through which it is received.
7. Information which is perceived as irrelevant (orthogonal) to the dimension of action is treated as no information.
8. Systems in which information regarding the functioning of the system is fed back into the system presents different characteristics from systems where such feedback information is lacking or is minimal.
9. People do not play "expected values," thus actual odds do not explain behaviour; even perceived expected values may not provide a sufficient

---

[47] *Ibid.*, pp. 158–61.

basis for prediction of behaviour since small probabilities are not treated in terms of pay-off maximization.

10. Norms are set for the culture, but different sections of culture will experience greater or less difficulty in achieving success within the norms.[48]

More acts, Wilkins implies, will be defined as deviant when information about a particular social system increases. As society becomes more tolerant and flexible in regard to deviations by its citizens, definitions of deviance will change and the number of criminal or dysfunctional acts will tend to decrease. Consequently, social control mechanisms, Wilkins hypothesizes, will secure increased stability in such a context.

Focal concerns

Walter B. Miller's theory of focal concerns points more sharply to the nature of lower-class culture and delinquent subcultures. The lower

TABLE 12–1
Focal concerns of lower-class culture
(perceived alternatives: state, quality, conditions)

Area

1. *Trouble:* law-abiding behavior	Law-violating behavior
2. *Toughness:* physical prowess, skill; "masculinity," fearlessness, etc.	Weakness, effeminacy, timidity, ineptitude, cowardice, caution
3. *Smartness:* ability to outsmart, making money by "wits"; shrewdness, adroitness in repartee	Gullibility; making money by hard work, dull-wittedness, verbal maladroitness; slowness
4. *Excitement:* thrill, danger; risk; change, activity	Boredom; "deadness"; safeness; sameness, passivity
5. *Fate:* being "lucky," favored by "fortune"	Ill-omened, being "unlucky"
6. *Autonomy:* independence; freedom; external restraint, especially superordinate authority	Dependency, "being cared for," presence of external constraint and strong authority

Source: David M. Downes, *The Delinquent Solution* (Glencoe: Free Press, 1966), p. 69.

class, Miller suggests, is characterized by distinctive values which vary markedly from the middle-class values that undergird the legal code (see Table 12–1). Consequently, simple conformity to particular lower-class values may automatically cause violations of the law. While school personnel evaluate the future life of lower-class youth in terms of lower- or middle-class values, the future positions which they presume the lower-class youth will assume are unfeasible goals in reality. Rather, lower-class youth, Miller contends, should be trained for a law-abiding

---

[48] Leslie T. Wilkins, *Social Deviance* (Englewood Cliffs, N.J.: Prentice-Hall Inc., 1964), pp. 90–91.

lower-class way of life which may be highly different from middle-class norms. If the school could capitalize upon normal lower-class socialization to particular "focal concerns," values, or preoccupations, much of existing deviant conduct could be eliminated. The focal concern of *trouble* represents a situation or type of behavior which involves unwelcome or complicating involvement with authorities or middle-class societal agencies. The desire to avoid conduct which violates moral or legal norms, however, is more often based upon a desire to remain free of official trouble than upon a commitment to uphold these moral ideals. The concern of *toughness,* on the other hand, places a premium upon physical prowess and athletic skill. Often revealed in body tattooing, toughness is also expressed in the attitude that women are objects to be conquered or in a response of bravery in the face of physical threat. The tough man is hard, fearless, skilled in combat, and undemonstrative.

Smartness, a third focal concern, focuses on one's ability to outsmart, outwit, "con," or take advantage of others without being duped oneself. The delinquent exhibits smartness if he is able to secure valued goods or attain personal status through a minimum involvement in physical activity and a maximum use of mental ability. The focal concern of *excitement,* on the other hand, is related to the variation of normal life routine by emotional stimulation. Often taking the form of gambling, use of alcohol, or sexual adventure, the search for excitement or thrill reflects the attempt to overcome existing liabilities. The focal concern of *fate* (fortune or luck) is related to the quest for excitement. Since many lower-class members believe their lives are subject to set forces over which they can exert little control, they often presume, Miller contends, that existing conditions are strictly matters of fate which one cannot control.

The concern of *autonomy* reveals the existing tension between a belief in fate and desire for self-assertion. Although the lower-class person may argue that he is being coerced by forces beyond his control, he may likewise demand his rights to self-expression. The exaggerated statement that "no one will push me around" is an example of the expression of autonomy.[49] According to Miller, delinquency among the lower class is a product of an external clash of cultural codes. While the delinquents have internalized the distinctive codes of the lower class, the power structure of the society enforces the middle-class code, which results in an increasing definition of lower-class adolescent behavior as delinquency.

Although Miller assumes that violations may be traced to such conflicts, he does not adequately explain the major increase in middle-

---

[49] Walter B. Miller, "Lower Class Culture as a Generating Milieu of Gang Delinquency," *Journal of Social Issues,* Vol. 14, No. 3 (1958), pp. 8–13.

and upper-class juvenile delinquency which, theoretically at least, is detached from lower-class values. Miller also overlooks the relationship between the delinquent act and the sociocorporate structure of the group which tends to reinforce the specific delinquency. Although delinquent acts occur throughout the social structure, his theory does not truly account for this dimension. While Miller makes a distinction between the stable lower class, the aspiring but conflicting lower class, and the successfully aspiring lower class, his categories are marked by internal contradictions.[50]

Subcultural transmission in the United States

In a report for the National Education Association Delinquency Project *William C. Kvaraceus* and *Walter S. Miller* note that delinquency is but one dimension of the *culturally transmitted values* of the lower class. Part of a larger framework, the delinquent's frame of reference consists of elements of class, type of delinquent behavior, and youth aspiration level. While the NEA project recognized that the greater number of the youthful population is nondelinquent and possesses no significant emotional problems, it also noted that a large majority of youngsters who are involved in delinquent activities are also free of emotional difficulties. While a portion of the delinquent population does evidence some emotional disturbance, a small group of juveniles who are emotionally disturbed are also nondelinquent. "The preponderant proportion of our delinquent population," the report noted, "consists essentially of normal lower-class youngsters."[51] Nondelinquency, Kvaraceus and Miller suggest in their NEA summary, is determined by the extent to which the youth reveals a real desire for upward mobility and to which these aspirations are actually feasible in relationships to the youth's early family training and personality development. As lower-class juveniles transmit their concerns to middle-class youth, norm-violating behavior among middle-class children may become more prevalent in the future.

Delinquency areas, social structures, and conduct norms

Solomon Kobrin similarly concludes that a *duality* of *conduct norms* dominate delinquency areas. Because conventional and criminal elements exist simultaneously, delinquency areas may be differentiated according to the degree of apparent integration. In highly integrated communities,

[50] Cloward and Ohlin, *op. cit.*, pp. 72–73.
[51] William C. Kvaraceus, Walter S. Miller *et al.*, *Delinquent Behavior: Culture and the Individual* (Washington, D.C.: National Education Association, 1959), pp. 55–56.

illicit entrepreneurs support churches, political parties, fraternal societies, and other conventional community institutions, while the noncriminal population sustains illicit activities through general acceptance of the existence of such activities, delinquency, therefore, is related, Kobrin contends, to existing social structures. Although the nature of delinquency is usually restricted, existing delinquent activities offer the basic foundations for the recruitment of rackteering participants.

If the two value systems do not exist in integrated form, adult criminality is neither organized nor systematic. The conventional and criminal value systems are in constant opposition, frequently reflecting the major changes in the class, ethnic, or racial composition of the population. The ensuing transition undermines many of the social controls which were formally operative. Although adult crime remains unorganized in this type of area, the criminal value system does not integrate the group, a situation which allows the juvenile violator to escape the controls of both the conventional community and organized racketeers, assumed in the integrated community. Not only does delinquency in this community become violent, but delinquent groups become isolated conflict groups oriented to the overcoming of restraints.[52]

In a later study concentrating on the group structure and "chronological career" patterns of an adolescent Chicago street-corner group, Kobrin found that the street-corner group is a natural vehicle through which the lower-class male juvenile resolves his basic problems of adolescent development. Not only is he forced to resolve the problems brought about by early adolescent autonomy, but he must resolve the problems created by incomplete socialization. For the middle-class adolescent, on the other hand, the problem is somewhat different. He must establish autonomy among parents who are less willing to concede his authority. The Chicago adolescent street-corner group, Kobrin noted, evidences five basic characteristics: a conscious deprecation of adult authority and conventional behavior, preparation and readiness for physical combat, rejection of school discipline, tendency toward sexual aggression, and willingness to participate in delinquency.[53]

Five brothers, the family and delinquency

A study by *Henry D. McKay* and *James F. McDonald* of five brothers who assumed delinquent careers revealed that the brothers were not especially different from a large number of conventional members of

[52] Solomon Kobrin, "The Conflict of Values in Delinquency Areas," *American Sociological Review*, Vol. 16 (October, 1951), pp. 657–59.

[53] Solomon Kobrin, "The Impact of Cultural Factors on Selected Problems of Adolescent Development in the Middle and Lower Class." *American Journal of Ortho-Psychiatry*, Vol. 32, No. 3 (April, 1962), pp. 387–89.

society in intelligence, physical condition, and personality traits and that their delinquency represented a gradual and progressive participation in informal training, education, new habits, and sophisticated stealing, encouraged by a variety of influences over the years. The brothers, McKay and McDonald concluded, might have learned common occupational skills and evidenced socially approved attitudes and ideals if they had lived in a more homogeneous and conventional milieu.[54]

The delinquent careers of the five brothers originated in the delinquent practices of play groups and gangs in their immediate community. Although their initial involvement in theft was part of the "undifferentiated play life" of the street, more distinct and specialized skill was required for continued participation in stealing. Consequently, the delinquent group served not only as the stimuli for further involvement but also as the necessary socialization and encouragement center for further future delinquency. Because the community offered little resistance to local delinquency and crime, counterforces against participation in delinquency and crime were somewhat neutralized. Therefore, the stealing careers of the five brothers, McKay and McDonald held, merely reflect the general attitude of their general social world. As the area physically deteriorated, the character of institutions and social life also changed, and existing social control mechanisms were undermined. Because the controls exerted by the family, neighborhood, and church were weakened, delinquency and crime were related to the physical changes in the city which actually encouraged social disorganization.[55]

Delinquency control, McKay and McDonald concluded as a result of their study, depends upon the ability of the community to organize an effective body of conventional sentiments, attitudes, and interests as substitutes for current normative conflict and divergent practices. Therefore, programs which focus upon single individuals or small segments of the community are unlikely to have much effectiveness. Ultimately, the question remains a local question. Greater unanimity in attitudes, sentiments, and social practices, they theorized, can best occur as local residents are assisted in developing their programs which might promote the well-being of their families and the community at large.

Deviance and structural strain

Ephriam H. Mizruchi, in his *Success and Opportunity,* suggests that the concept of structural strain best explains the rise of deviance that

---

[54] Henry D. McKay and James F. McDonald, *Brothers in Crime* (Chicago: University of Chicago Press, 1966), p. 350.

[55] *Ibid.,* p. 359.

is related to questions involving cultural goals, alienation, and being a success. He noted that the minimization of social class identification is not merely a product of working-class apathy but is a specific quality of the American dream. The disparity between occupational aspirations and actual achievement, greatest in the lower class in terms of four sources of structured strain, Mizruchi explains, is inherent within the social class system and includes:

1. The external limits imposed upon the lower classes by the middle classes, which impede attainment of culturally prescribed goals.
2. The disparity between the success ideology and objective conditions of American life, which limit success and achievement to a relative few at each level of the class structure.
3. The disparity between the lower-class value system and the requirements of the attainment of success in American society.
4. The distinction between achievement and success.[56]

R. Bohlke suggests that middle-class delinquency, a diffusion of lower-class cultural patterns, is an indirect result of the economic advancement of many manual workers and of increased lower-class employment mobility. The radical shifts in income levels, Bohlke, theorizes, create a "status inconsistency," which causes a similar inconsistency in values as new middle-class families move into traditional middle-class neighborhoods. Children of these new migrants, Bohlke presumes, are likely to participate in delinquent subcultures to overcome their "marginality" when they are not accepted into the middle class. Because many of the new middle class, coming from educationally insecure homes, are unprepared to complete in conventional middle-class terms, they turn to delinquent subcultures in order to find meaning in a changing context. The children of the old middle class, on the other hand, engage in delinquency if they lack the income to maintain the consumption patterns of the new middle class.[57]

Crime and the criminogenic culture

Donald R. Taft and *Ralph W. England, Jr.,* maintain that high crime rates and volume can be attributed to a criminogenic culture, evident in the United States, which is dynamic, complex, competitive, and materialistic. Because the culture rewards those who compete successfully

---

[56] Wolfgang and Ferracuti, *op. cit.,* p. 51. Also see Ephram Mizruchi, *Success and Opportunity* (Glencoe: Free Press, 1964).

[57] R. Bohlke, "Social Mobility, Stratification Inconsistency, and Middle Class Delinquency," *Social Problems,* Vol. 8 (1960), pp. 351–63.

and ignores others who are largely unsuccessful, concepts of democracy, they assume, are subservient to racial, social class, nationality or primary-peer group criteria. Not only do schools stress competition rather than socialization of the child but communications media promote the interests of privileged minorities in opposition to the needs of the greater mass. Law, therefore, attempts to prohibit or forbid aspirations or satisfactions which are widely desired by large segments of the nonprivileged classes.[58]

The "near-group" and delinquent conduct

Taking issue with the gang subculture hypothesis, *Lewis Yablonsky* argues that the traditional belief in the structured gang must be replaced with a "near-group" construct. Although the public popularly believes that the gang engages in rumbles or conflict as a part of a planned structural response, conflict, Yablonsky theorizes, serves to generate cohesion and group identity. The near-group concept describes the middle range of group existence between less definite mobs and stable organization. The near-group achieves solidarity only under the extreme pressure which is exerted in gang warfare. Yablonsky notes that the near-group is characterized by: (1) diffuse role definitions; (2) limited cohesion; (3) impermanence; (4) minimal consensus of norms; (5) shifting membership; (6) disturbed leadership; and (7) limited definition of membership expectations.[59] The "near-group" (similar to the unstructured gang proposed by other theorists) may eventually become a structured gang, Yablonsky believes, due to mistaken police and press beliefs that the near-group is a representative structured gang rather than a small conflict gang core plus a larger group of marginal members who do not maintain a continuous gang identity.

H. W. Pfautz disagrees, arguing that Yablonsky's ideas of the "near-group" and the "true-group" unnecessarily complicate delinquent gang theory. Maintaining that the violent adolescent gang does not follow delinquent subcultural patterns, Pfautz claims that it should be interpreted as an expressive social movement which involves collective behavior. Both Yablonsky and Pfautz, however, seem to assume that any doubt concerning the universality of a structured gang automatically invalidates a subcultural theory of gang behavior.[60]

---

[58] Donald R. Taft and Ralph W. England, Jr., *Criminology* (New York: Macmillan Co., 1964), p. 277.

[59] Lewis Yablonsky, "The Delinquent Gang as a Near-Group," *Social Problems,* Vol. 7, No. 2 (Fall, 1959), pp. 108–17.

[60] Downes, *op. cit.,* pp. 16–17.

In the study of 378 white delinquent Nashville (Tennessee) boys, involving some 199 triads, *Albert J. Reiss, Jr.* and *A. Lewis Rhodes* found that the boys generally choose peers who follow similar law-abiding or delinquent patterns as their close friends. The probability that an individual will commit a specific delinquent act, Reiss and Rhodes found, depends in large measure on the action of the other members of the friendship triad.[61] Although Sheldon and Eleanor Glueck discount the meaning of companionship as a factor in delinquency causation, a study by Thomas G. Eynon of 363 white boys admitted to the Boys Industrial School in Lancaster, Ohio, revealed that among these boys who on the average began their official delinquency at the age of 13 years, companionship is always a factor regardless of the age at which the delinquency occurs.[62]

The family and criminal deviance

Kerr's study of two to three generations of hardcore deviant residents of Ship Street, mainly Irish and Roman Catholic, revealed that these persons were primarily committed to family-oriented relationships. While aware of the deficiencies of their existence, their preference for slum living at times approached the border lines of "inverted snobbery." Ship Street residents, Kerr found, assume traditional roles because the rigidity of the dominant cultural pattern restricts conduct alternatives. In a matrilocal, mother-dominated society, Ship Street residents tend to reject conventional life and local agencies designed to aid their "rehabilitation period." Because competition is minimized, community members generally remain in their place and refrain from becoming "bigheaded" and "above themselves." The emphasis upon loyalty to one's group, especially one's family, leads the individual to protect other group members.[63] On the other hand, outgroup members, Kerr noted, are held to be legitimate targets.[64] The "overindulged" boy who operates in a

---

[61] Albert J. Reiss, Jr. and A. Lewis Rhodes, "An Empirical Test of the Differential Association Theory," *The Journal of Research in Crime and Delinquency,* Vol. 1, No. 1 (January, 1964), pp. 9–13.

[62] Walter C. Reckless, *The Crime Problem* (New York: Appleton-Century-Crofts, 1967), p. 475.

[63] M. Kerr, *The People of Ship Street* (1958), as cited in Downes, *op. cit.,* p. 105. See Sheldon and Eleanor Glueck, *Family Environment and Delinquency* (Boston: Houghton Mifflin Co., 1962).

[64] *Ibid.,* p. 106. Also investigate Charles W. Coulter, "Family Disorganization as a Causal Factor in Delinquency and Crime," *Federal Probation,* Vol. 12 (September, 1948), pp. 13–17; L. L. Geismar, *Understanding the Multiproblem Family* (New York: Association Press, 1964); and Lee N. Robbins and Shirley Y. Hill, "Assessing the Contribution of Family Structure, Class and Peer Groups to Juvenile Delinquency," *Journal of Criminal Law, Criminology, and Police Science,* Vol. 57, No. 3 (September, 1966), pp. 325–34.

"mother-dominated" structure of family, Kerr found, is more frequently a delinquent type than the "affectionless" youth.

Crime and economic life

Inevitably, the quest for causative understanding led to examination of economic conditions and criminality. Those who expressed a socialist or Marxist theory of causation generally explained crime in terms of economic inequality, social class self-interest, or outright poverty. Once perfect equality in reward for one's labor is established as a functional principle and all distinctions between riches and poverty are eliminated, they hypothesized, antisocial activity and general crime will be collaterally reduced. The principal cause of crime, these theorists suggest, is capitalism; crime is nothing more than a reaction against social injustice. As long as an unequal distribution of goods condemns part of the population to poverty and deprives it of education, thereby reducing it to ignorance, crime, they declared, will continue.

Raffaele Garofalo for example maintained that society is the original offender and provokes crime by protecting economic inequality and by producing unfortunates who are unable to meet life challenges.[65] On the other hand, *William A. Bonger,* also contributing to socialist theories of criminality, theorized that the capitalist economic system encourages egoism in the form of unrestrained pursuit of self-interest. Consequently, he maintained that the social instincts of man are poorly developed and the moral force in man is unable to combat his inclination toward egoistic acts which take the form of crime. Economic interests which encourage man to ignore the plight of others likewise, Bonger wrote, encourage the decline in morality.[66]

Karl Marx and *Frederick Engels* assumed that capitalist society is composed of two classes, the exploiting capitalist and the exploited proletariat. As the capitalists grow richer and richer, the proletariat, Marx theorized, become more miserable. The inevitable results is a violent explosion taking the form of a revolution of the proletariat. Fundamental social changes, Marx and Engels concluded, can only be brought about through violent social revolution. The *class struggle* is primarily concerned with the question of private ownership of the means of production. All conflicts are class conflicts. All social changes can be explained in terms of class conflicts which are predetermined in content as well as eventual course. Because the rich will never allow the sharing of power and wealth with the proletariat, class conflict, Marx maintained

---

[65] See Raffaele Garofalo, *Criminology,* trans. Robert W. Miller (Boston: Little, Brown & Co., 1914).

[66] Note William A. Bonger, *Criminality and Economic Conditions* (Boston: Little, Brown & Co., 1916).

in focusing upon the capitalist society of his day, is historically inevitable.[67]

Ralf Dahrendorf holds that the most important characteristics of social class are authority and power. Because the social structure is fundamentally unequal, social conflict continues. Classes, Dahrendorf argues, are social conflict groups which are determined in relationship to their participation in or exclusion from the use of authority. Dahrendorf points out that private ownership of the means of production, centrally important in the class conflict theory of Marx, is only one of many forms of authority.[68]

Consequently, the Marxian hypothesis of crime causation, as Dahrendorf has observed, was undermined by the cooperative and state-managed enterprises and the general managerial revolution of the 20th century. Not only did the capitalists eventually divide into two classes of owner-managers and nonowner-managers but the working classes also underwent a wide differentiation in types. Highly skilled, semiskilled, and even unskilled workers became clearly differentiated from the poor. The rise of the middle class and of the white-collar worker, too, undermined much of the Marxian thesis.

Poverty and crime

The attempt to relate crime to poverty continues. In studying the children of Sanchez, *Oscar Lewis,* for example, suggests that the culture of poverty is a major cause of delinquency and crime. A state of economic deprivation and/or disorganization, the culture of poverty fails to provide the poor with full opportunity to rise within the occupational structure. However, it provides the poor a structure, rationale, and defense mechanism with which to confront their environment. In Mexico City, the poor are locally and provincially oriented; struggle for economic survival; are not members of labor unions or political parties; are susceptible to moneylenders; lack home privacy; resort to violence among their children, wives, and friends; engage in early sexual activity; maintain a strong authoritarianism; develop mother-oriented families; and reveal a strong sense of fatalism.[69]

Frank Riesman questions whether poverty is the basic problem in

---

[67] Consult Karl Marx and Frederick Engels, *Capital* (New York: Random House, Inc., 1906).

[68] Ralf Dahrendorf, "Toward a Theory of Social Conflict," *Journal of Conflict Resolution,* Vol. 2 (1958), pp. 170–83. Also see Bertram Spilter, "Delinquency and Middle Class Goals," *Journal of Criminal Law, Criminology, and Police Science,* Vol. 56, No. 4 (December, 1965), pp. 463–78.

[69] Oscar Lewis, *The Children of Sanchez: Autobiography of a Mexican Family* (New York: Random House, Inc., 1961), pp. xii–xxvii.

Lewis' study or whether the deviance found is merely related to the slower speed of Mexican upward mobility. Riesman's illustration, for example, that only 1 in 10 children in the 14 largest cities in the United States was deprived in 1950 and that the rate was lessened to 1 in 3 in 1960, while delinquency and crime continued to rise, suggests that the poverty dimension cannot be isolated as a cause of crime in itself.[70] The concept of poverty, he maintains, is relative. Poverty in a period of affluence is often quite different from poverty in a time of famine, disease, or unemployment. Poverty, consequently, is a subjective condition relative to the general objects which are used to determine or measure wealth.

William Healy and *Augusta F. Bronner* found it expedient to classify juvenile delinquents within five categories characterized by: (*a*) destitution; (*b*) poverty, a constant struggle to make ends meet; (*c*) normality; (*d*) comfort; and (*e*) luxury. Of the 675 juvenile delinquents in their sample, 5 percent fell into the destitute, 22 percent into the poverty, 35 percent into the normal, 34 percent into the comfort, and 4 percent into the luxury classes. Because only 27 percent of the cases came from homes of poverty, great importance, they concluded, cannot be attached to poverty per se.[71]

Writing more recently, Cyril Burt reported that 19 percent of the delinquent children in his study came from homes of the very poor in London. However, only 8 percent of the total London population came from such homes. Although 37 percent came from "moderately poor" homes, the general population included only 22 percent within this category. Consequently over one-half of the total delinquency came from among the very poor and moderately poor families. Nevertheless, poverty alone, Burt recognizes, does not produce crime. The majority of the needy do not become delinquent.[72]

Crime and the business cycle. Pursuing the poverty-crime relationship further, *Dorothy Thomas* discovered that an inverse correlation between the business cycle and offenses against property *without* violence is neither strong nor constant. Offenses committed *with* violence disclosed an inverse correlation which is both significant and constant. Offenses against the person have a slight tendency to increase during prosperity, although the correlation is neither significantly high nor con-

[70] Frank Reisman, *The Culturally-Deprived Child* (New York: Harper & Row, Publishers, 1962), pp. 1–12. Also see Albert W. Silver, "Delinquency and Socially and Economically Deprived Youth," *Federal Probation,* Vol. 27 (December, 1963), p. 3.

[71] William Healy and Augusta F. Bronner, *Delinquents and Criminals* (New York: Macmillan Co., 1926), p. 121.

[72] Cyril Burt, *The Young Delinquents* (London: University of London Press, 1938), pp. 68–69. Refer to Jackson Toby, "The Prospects for Reducing Delinquency Rates in Industrial Societies," *Federal Probation,* Vol. 27 (December, 1963), p. 23.

stant. Prosecutions for drunkenness have followed a positive correlation with the favorable business cycle, especially in the past years.[73]

Daniel Glaser and *Kent Rice* note that the rates of juvenile delinquency are inversely correlated with unemployment—that juvenile misconduct is more prominent during times of prosperity. Adult criminality among those 18 to 35 years of age on the other hand, is higher during periods of widespread unemployment, a finding which led Glaser and Rice to emphasize the demoralizing influence of unemployment in adult crime.[74]

Other theorists, too, have suggested that not only have property crimes been influenced by the expansion of insurance coverage which has lessened the onus of property offenses but thefts and burglaries have also been rationalized in such a manner that the public believes that only insurance companies suffer any specific loss. Consequently, property owners often become careless when insured, actually encouraging the commission of crime by their own action. However, even children, who possess little or no property, are unlikely to respect the property of others because respect for property is ultimately related to instruction in the value and the careful handling of property. Pilfering and vandalism, they suppose, are not only products of property disrespect but often are stimulated by crowd activity, individual frustration, and a desire to participate in group action.

A general economic depression which lessens the value of currency frequently involves a wholesale shift in criminal patterns. The devaluation of currency, for example, encourages the theft of goods which possessed greater long-range value as a commodity of exchange. For example, major economic fluctuations in Germany, *Franz Exner* discovered, exert a profound effect upon the eventual character of criminality.[75] Many theorists have assumed that crime is encouraged by unemployment, but the results have been inconclusive. Official unemployment statistics are incomplete, distinctions have frequently not been made between short-range and long-term unemployment, and local variations affecting the national or regional picture have often been ignored. While unemployment insurance and other welfare programs seem to intervene in the cause and effect relationship, the exact implications of these programs in crime control are yet unclear. In general, unemployment seems to play a diverse role which varies by particular areas and for different age groups. Although Glaser and Rice found that adult crime rates vary directly with unemployment, the exact relationship of unemployment

---

[73] See Dorothy S. Thomas, *Social Aspects of the Business Cycle* (London: Routledge Kegan Paul, Ltd., 1925).

[74] Daniel Glaser and Kent Rice, "Crime, Age and Employment," *American Sociological Review,* Vol. 24 (October, 1959), pp. 679–86.

[75] Mannheim, *Comparative Criminology,* pp. 586–87.

to delinquency is not known.[76] The relationship of the employment monotony to crime activity also remains ambiguous.

Morris Ploscowe finds that unparallelled economic and social progress, which has resulted in a better life for the ordinary worker, has also created new pressures which frequently result in criminality. Democracy has blurred caste lines, and the masses now demand greater access to those goods formerly available only to the privileged classes. Thieves, Ploscowe argues, do not steal because of poverty but because they are greedy and valued property can easily be stolen without detection.[77] Nevertheless, while economic conditions may contribute to criminality, they can hardly be held to be causative factors. The economic system, Ploscowe suggests, may contribute to the defining of structural and other social arrangements but does not in itself have any direct determining influence in crime causation.

Crime and social class

The evaluation of criminality in terms of social class factors is compounded by many variables. Studies of social class or general social stratification vary widely in their findings, due to the discrepancy in their use of such criteria as wealth, education, speech, occupation, family background, housing location, and level of aspirations for determination of strata levels. Invariably, the differential use of these factors cause the same people to be classified in different levels. Although the concept of class presumes that people live, think, and feel in a particular way in relationship to their locus in society, presumed individual participation in the characteristics assumed to be typical of their stratum may be far from reality.

A study of the relationship between delinquency and ascribed social status of 9,238 white schoolboys between the ages of 12 and 18 in Davidson County (Tennessee) in 1957 led the researchers to conclude that the greater the lower-class domination of the community, the greater the chances of delinquency of boys of any social status. However, the low-status boy has an even greater chance of becoming delinquent. "There is," Albert J. Reiss, Jr., and Lewis Rhodes suggested, "a simple relationship between ascribed social status and delinquency."[78] The rela-

---

[76] Glaser and Rice, *op. cit.*, pp. 680–86. See Herbert A. Bloch, "Economic Depression as a Factor in Rural Crime," *Journal of Criminal Law and Criminology,* Vol. 40 (November–December, 1949), pp. 458–70.

[77] Morris Ploscowe, *Some Causative Factors in Criminality,* Vol. I (Washington, D.C.: U.S. Government Printing Office, 1931), p. 176.

[78] Albert J. Reiss, Jr., and A. L. Rhodes, "The Distribution of Juvenile Delinquency in the Social Structure," *American Sociological Review,* Vol. 26, No. 5 (October, 1961), p. 720.

tive prevalence of social classes in a particular area and the extent of diffusion of each class culture affects the actual probability of participation in delinquency. While the *social status context* of Reiss and Rhodes has been a valuable addition to subcultural theory, it must be tested further among nonwhite, nonschool populations.[79]

J. P. Clark and *E. P. Wenninger,* following an approach similar to that of Reiss and Rhodes, examined the relationship of delinquency and social class in what they identify as rural farm, industrial city, lower urban, and upper urban communities. Of the 1,154 state school students representing the four community types, between 80 and 90 percent of the students, regardless of class or community, committed nuisance-value offenses. However, the 10 to 20 percent who admitted participation in serious offenses possessed significant class and community differences. The lower urban (small urban) group committed "real delinquent acts" most frequently. However, the incidence of seriousness grew with movement from the rural farm to the upper urban (large urban) to the industrial city and finally to the lower urban communities. On the whole, lower-class delinquency rates are much higher in the lower urban and industrial city than in the rural farm or upper urban communities.[80]

Ernest P. Donald, investigating a sample of 354 12-year-old white and black sixth-grade boys in Columbus, Ohio, contends that the type of neighborhood and the variable of race are relatively unimportant in determining self-concepts and that the quality and the impact of family interaction in relation to supplementary social relationships possess a greater determining effect on the youth's self-concept.[81]

Deviance and class goals, educational mobility, and deferred gratification. Class goals may be related to mobility and deferred gratification. Persons seeking to rise to middle-class status or to maintain their already existing locus, *David M. Downes* argues, may renounce impulsive action and postpone gratification or satisfaction in order to reach long-range goals. Delinquency-prone individuals, on the other hand, may be strongly motivated by the desire for immediate gratification, which causes them to seek short-range goals. The Nottingham University study of "Radby," for example, showed that delinquency-prone Dyke Street people gave their children everything the children desired as a means of compensating for their own disadvantaged childhood. The working-class members on Gladstone Road, whose children were less delinquent, re-

[79] Downes, *op. cit.,* p. 92. Refer to David J. Bordua, "Sociological Theories and Their Implications for Juvenile Delinquency," *Juvenile Delinquency Facts and Facets* (Washington, D.C.: Children's Bureau, 1960).
[80] *Ibid.,* p. 93.
[81] Reckless, *op. cit.,* p. 447.

fused to indulge their children to the same extent. They encouraged their children to defer immediate pleasures and to seek future goals.[82]

The problem of deferred gratification is becoming more acute with the advent of greater personal leisure. However, even the problem of leisure, David M. Downes believes, will be less, serious if the shortcomings of education and work are solved. While the central problem of the British socioeconomic system is one of selection for advancement through education, problems in the American system center in the development of incentives for motivation.[83]

The American *dropout* and the British *early-leaver* are both individuals who have left the educational system and who, in effect, have sought immediate gratification of some sort. The American dropout is any youth who fails to finish high school and to qualify for college entrance, while the British early-leaver is any male youth who has already been preselected for higher education in the grammar school but fails or refuses to stay in the system. Differences are related to the time at which the selection for future attainment is completed. In British, educational goals are usually delineated by the age of 11 or earlier, while American youths are technically free to select future goals until the age of 17.

While the cost of early or deferred occupational selection may be equally severe, the age at which choices are made, of course, may evoke differing responses. The early selection and rejection process within the British system, for example, encourages and strengthens disassociation, creates a fatalistic attitude toward the roles of school and work, and emphasizes self-fulfillment through leisure. On the other hand, the lateness of the decision in the case of the American boy encourages and strengthens alienation through the continuance of unrealistic ambitions into later adolescence. The working-class male adolescent's problem of leisure, Downes believes, originates in school and in work situations, which are determined in large part by socioeconomic conditions. Consequently, these apparent challenges and problems are not quickly revealed nor resolved because the adolescent is more likely to disassociate than to express outright alienation or status frustration in his early stages of reaction. As the prospects for semi- or unskilled labor deteriorate, the tendency toward disassociation is enhanced, leading to an eventual reaction against the established system and operational organization.

In essence, modern secondary education, Downes argues, serves as a massive irritant for some groups within the population. Since 25 to

---

[82] Mannheim, *Comparative Criminology*, p. 447.

[83] Downes, *op. cit.*, pp. 260–63. Also see R. H. Turner, "Modes of Ascent Through Education: 'Sponsor' and 'Contest' Mobility," in Floud, Halsey, and Anderson, (eds.), *Education, Economy and Society* (1961).

30 percent of the adolescent age group has only the prospect of a dead end to which they must eventually become resigned, they tend to dis-associate themselves from full involvement in structured activity. While automation has changed the basic ground rules of competitive occupa-tional life, the educational system has remained largely unchanged. The great demand for more qualified employees in the economic system has made the low-income child marginal and even unabsorbable within the modern labor force. However, education, Downes argues, can provide no simple panacea either. The modern occupational structure is unable to absorb even fully qualified individuals and to provide necessary mobil-ity to allow all youths to fulfill their prospects of manhood. "The streets of our urban slums," Downes says, "are slowly filling with young men who *have no prospect of finding manhood through work:* who are com-ing of age in a society who neither wants them or needs them."[84] Delin-quency, Downes believes, is related to the fact that many youths are presently humiliated by a subordinate role and have increasingly become aware that they may soon be denied any role at all.

---

[84] *Ibid.*, p. 264. Note also John M. Martin and Joseph P. Fitzpatrick, *Delinquent Behavior: A Redefinition of the Problem* (New York: Random House, Inc., 1964), and Nelson Burke and Alfred E. Simons, "Factors Which Precipitate Dropouts and Delinquency, *Federal Probation,* Vol. 29 (March, 1965), p. 28.

Chapter
13

SOCIAL-PSYCHOLOGICAL
CAUSES OF CRIME

Although the physiopsychological and socioenvironmental-sociocultural theories of causation have tended to focus upon particular segments or factors, more recently major attention has been given explanations which relate delinquency and crime to social-psychological factors in a wholistic manner. Recognizing that the potential violator is both a psychological being and a social product, such theories of causation relate criminal conduct to both elements in a more integrated manner.

THEORIES RELATED TO ANOMIE

Anomie and deviant conduct

Émile Durkheim, in discussing the relationship of psychological and sociological factors in criminal conduct, reemphasized a neglected insight when he recognized that criminality is a "normal" function of human life. Abnormality, he argued, is a social distinction established to separate undesired behavior from more acceptable conduct patterns. It is neither fully desirable nor completely possible to eliminate criminal conduct because the repression of crime only leads to social stagnation and constraints upon innovation. Since crimes are defined socially, they are society's attempt to prescribe limits of permissible behavior. Therefore, the demand for conformity, he theorized, necessarily restricts the actions of individuality; the need to control potentially insatiable human desires necessitates the creation of an external regulating force to define and to maintain the legitimate bounds of human conduct. If traditional social

279

rules no longer possess authority due to the presence of collective social disorder, the inability of man to fulfill his aspirations, Durkheim believed, may create a state of *anomie* (normlessness, nonbelonging). Rapid technological change, pervasive prosperity, and unexpected depressions mislead men to unrealizable aspirations, create a state of anomic frustration, and stimulate the same persons to suicide or other potentially deviant action. Anomie, Durkheim hypothesized, results when social norms are no longer able to constrain or control men's action. The breakdown of regulative procedures disrupts the balance between constraining and deviating pressures and allows the dominance of excessive and constant pressures for unlimited fulfillment of aspirations.

The physical and social needs of the individual are regulated in different ways. The person's physical needs are automatically governed by his organic structure, which causes him to be satisfied once his original need has been met. However, his social needs, Durkheim wrote, are "an insatiable and bottomless abyss," which may never be gratified due to man's unlimited desire for wealth, prestige, and power.[1] Consequently, the social order, which normally serves to regulate social desires and aspirations, is able to exert control only if members of society accept its dictates.

In a stable society, men normally aspire only to that which is realistically possible within the social hierarchy. Accepting the legitimacy of the criteria used for distributing social rewards, members of a stable society rarely challenge the socially defined relationship between personal worth and individual status. When restraints, however, are undermined and aspirations become unlimited, uncontrolled free expression may lead quickly to delinquency and crime. Rapid social change, economic crises, swift technological development, and ideological confusion stimulate the desire for unlimited goods and social satisfactions. The overemphasis upon infinite goals strains the societal regulatory apparatus, leaving men frustrated in their efforts to reach desired goals and unsatisfied with their position.

The problem, according to Durkheim's thesis, is especially acute in industrial societies which have failed to solve the problem of frustrated aspirations in the face of expanded economic productivity. Since the problem is fundamentally critical for persons of low economic status who possess obvious intellectual capabilities, the industrial society, Durkheim argues, must attempt to solve this problem by making success goals available to all, regardless of race, creed, or socioeconomic situation.

---

[1] Émile Durkheim, *Suicide: A Study in Sociology,* trans. J. A. Spaulding and George Simpson (Glencoe: Free Press, 1951), pp. 247–57. Although Durkheim tended to reject a straight psychological explanation of criminal deviance he has been grouped with social psychological theorists due to his emphases which contained both sociological and psychological elements.

As this is done, those with greater capabilities will be able to succeed within the established economic system and thereby realize a higher percentage of their basic aspirations. An overemphasis on success goals, however, may also lead to unhappy consequences in the form of an excessive emphasis upon status and demands for stable economic employment.

Anomie and the cultural and social structure

Expanding the insight of Durkheim, *Robert K. Merton* distinguishes two features of organized social life in the cultural structure and the social structure. The *cultural structure,* Merton suggests, consists of goals and norms, which are the approved ends to which men orient themselves and the accepted ways by which they seek to fulfill these ends. The division of citizens into social classes or strata in relationship to their wealth, power, or prestige is a consequence of the recognition that *social structure* consists of patterns of human relationships. Anomie occurs, Merton argues, because of the breakdown in the relationship between desired goals and avenues of legitimate fulfillment of these goals. Stable societies are able to provide a general balance between goals and norms, while unstable societies reflect a wider diversity of these elements. "Aberrant behavior," Merton writes, "may be regarded sociologically as a symptom of disassociation between culturally described aspirations and socially structured avenues of realizing these aspirations."[2] Anomie, he assumes, may arise as a consequence of other than economic or industrial crises or conditions. Pressures toward deviant behavior may originate with variable intensity at different locations in the social structure. Class or strata differences may allow middle-class youth greater opportunities for fulfilling their aspirations than lower-class adolescents would normally find. Therefore, variable access to differential opportunities, Merton believes, is undoubtedly a significant factor in the fulfillment or nonfulfillment of one's aspirations.

Deviant behavior is not a product of mere impulsive violations of social controls but, on the contrary, represents socially induced deviations which are jointly produced by culture and the social organizations.[3] Because cultural goals may conflict with the limitations prescribed by social structures, deviant behavior may occur. If goals and norms, how-

---

[2] Robert K. Merton, *Social Theory and Social Structure* (New York: Free Press, 1957), pp. 131–36. Also see Herbert A. Bloch, "Structured Roles and Anomie," *Proceedings of the American Sociological Society* (Berkeley, Calif.: 1953).

[3] Robert K. Merton, "The Socio-cultural Environment and Anomie," in Helen L. Witmer and Ruth Kotinsky (eds.), *New Perspectives for Research on Juvenile Delinquency,* (Washington, D.C.: U.S. Department of Health, Education, and Welfare, 1955), pp. 24–50.

ever, are in near balance, a relative stability of society is achieved. On the other hand, if inordinate stress is placed upon goals, regardless of norms, stability is challenged by disorganization.[4] Because success goals hold greater allegiance than prescribed institutionalized conduct norms, American society is anomic. The imbalance between the goals of the cultural system and the social system's provisions for reaching these goals results in social tensions and a tendency to overlook the constraints imposed by the social structure. While American society encourages the fulfillment of success goals, the opportunities to reach these goals in a prescribed social manner, Merton believes, are only differentially distributed. Although common success goals have been generalized to the mass population, the social structure has restricted or even closed the channels of access to such goal achievement. Consequently, individuals adapt their behavior to the existing imbalance between cultural and social structures through either conformity, innovation, ritualism, retreatism, or rebellion.

Anomie and opportunity structure

Extending the concept of anomie, *Richard A. Cloward* and *Lloyd E. Ohlin* reason that anomic deviant behavior depends upon the nature of the situation and the existing opportunities for participation in deviant conduct. *Differential opportunities,* they hypothesize, are as real as the differential potential for fulfilling cultural goals through institutionalized procedures, as emphasized by Durkheim and Merton. Drug use, for example, depends upon the availability of narcotics. Professional and white-collar crime also necessitate certain types of contacts between individuals or employment in positions which allow these kinds of criminal acts.

However, explaining the existence or rise of subcultural delinquency, Cloward and Ohlin argue that lower-class boys share a common commitment to American success values and goals which are commonly measured in terms of consumer goods and materials. And yet, unlike middle- and upper-class adolescents, they do not have access to the legitimate means by which to attain these success goals. Victims of the chasm between aspirations and their realization, lower-class boys face extensive pressures to engage in deviant behavior generated by this cultural and social imbalance. Consequently, these youths adapt to the apparent opportunity structures within their environment, engaging in criminalistic,

---

[4] Merton, *Social Theory,* pp. 131–36. Illustrative materials are continued in Ronald C. DeBold and Russell C. Leaf, *LSD, Man and Society* (Middletown, Conn.: Wesleyan University Press, 1967); and Henry Benjamin and R. E. L. Masters, *Prostitution and Morality* (New York: Julian Press, Inc., 1964).

conformist, or retreatist subcultures as a means of resolving the existing imbalance.[5]

THE NEUTRALIZATION HYPOTHESIS

Gresham M. Sykes and *David Matza,* rejecting the delinquent subculture idea, claim that any concept of delinquency that is based upon "competing" or "countervailing" values possesses serious defects. Since the delinquent usually feels guilt or shame at the time of detection and confinement, he obviously does not view his behavior as "morally correct."[6] The adolescent frequently recognizes both the "legitimacy of the social order and its social rightness," and his delinquency, Sykes and Matza maintain, stems from his *neutralization of conventional norms.* The situational character of accepted rules of conduct, which only appear as qualified guides for action rather than as absolute norms to be fulfilled at all times, makes it possible for the delinquent to repudiate accepted rules and to justify his own delinquent conduct. While the individual youth may view his act as devoid of intent, the same act may be defined by society and the legal system as worthy of prosecution and punishment. Since the youth involved in a particular situation may interpret the event in a manner different from persons unfamiliar with the context, he may redefine existing social rules in order to maintain or accomplish desired or necessary ends. If a rival gang, for example, invades the gang's designated neighborhood, the defending gang may justify a gang rumble, even involving murder, in order to protect its turf, despite existing laws against fighting or homicide.

Not only does the delinquent experience guilt or shame but he often accords respect and admiration to law-abiding persons who present a thorough image of honesty. Delinquents, Sykes and Matza find, draw a sharp line of distinction between potential victims and legitimate citizens, whether in relationship to kinship, ethnic, social class, age, or sex variables. Since the demands for conformity to the dominant social order cannot be totally avoided, juvenile delinquents are affected in some degree by its expectations. Rather than reject these demands, the adolescent, by establishing a delinquent subculture, neutralizes their import and participates within the delinquent learning process, a theme

---

[5] Richard A. Cloward and Lloyd E. Ohlin, *Delinquency and Opportunity: A Theory of Delinquent Gangs* (New York: Free Press, 1960), Also see Howard S. Becker, *Outsiders: Studies in the Sociology of Defiance* (Ill.: Free Press, 1963); and Alfred R. Lindesmith, *The Addict and the Law* (Bloomington: Indiana University Press, 1965). As anomie relates to juvenile delinquency may be examined in David J. Bordua "Juvenile Delinquency and 'Anomie': An Attempt at Replication," *Social Problems,* Vol. 6 (Winter, 1958), pp. 230–38.

[6] Gresham M. Sykes and David Matza, "Techniques of Neutralization: A Theory of Delinquency,"*American Sociological Review,* Vol. 22, No. 6 (December, 1957), pp. 712–19.

discussed earlier in Edwin H. Sutherland's concept of differential association. Neutralization techniques, therefore, allow the delinquent to
engage in deviant behavior without extreme psychological maladjustment.[7] Through neutralization, delinquent violations are held to be "acceptable" rather than "right." The delinquent appears, therefore, as an
"apologetic failure" in that he fails to live according to conforming norms
and values. Although dominant norms, together with the potential of
social ostracism, restrain deviant conduct, techniques of neutralization
allow the individual to engage in delinquency without seriously damaging his image by redefining his relationship to the conduct norms.[8]

Previously internalized norms, morals, and values, Sykes and Matza
continue, are neutralized either *before* or *as* one participates in delinquent conduct. Although the delinquent is committed to the dominant
normative system, he neutralized the demands of the system in order
to participate in that which is less normative. Five major techniques,
Sykes and Matza find, aid the neutralization process:

1. *Denial of responsibility.* In this instance the delinquent deflects blame
   from himself by rationalizing that he was really not responsible for
   his acts.
2. *Denial of injury.* Through rationalization the delinquent denies that
   he hurt anybody, cost anyone his property, or engaged in any major
   delinquent or criminal activity.
3. *Denial of the victim.* In this instance, the delinquent accepts the
   fact that his act may have caused harm or injury, while arguing
   that the victim deserved such injury for his previous acts committed
   against others.
4. *Condemnation of the condemners.* Focusing upon the motives and
   shortcomings of those who sit in judgment, he shifts blame from
   himself to his accusers. In exposing their shortcomings, he silences
   his own sense of guilt or qualms concerning his deviance.
5. *Appeal to higher loyalties.* Ties and commitments to companions,
   family, or primary groups supercede other loyalties and take precedence over conformity to laws and social norms.[9]

Critics of this hypothesis argue that although the neutralization theory
undoubtedly describes a basic psychological process which occurs among

[7] David M. Downes, *The Delinquent Solution* (New York: Free Press, 1966),
p. 75. The relation of the criminal and his victim are examined in Stephen Schafer,
The Victim and His Criminal (New York: Random House, Inc., 1967); and Hans
von Hentig, *The Criminal and His Victim* (New Haven, Conn.: Yale University
Press, 1948).
[8] Sykes and Matza, *op. cit.*, p. 666. See Howard T. Blane, "Drinking and Crime,"
Federal Probation, Vol. 29 (June, 1965), p. 25.
[9] *Ibid.*, pp. 666–69. Also see David Matza and Gresham M. Sykes, "Delinquency
and Subterranean Values," *American Sociological Review*, Vol. 26, No. 5 (1961)
pp. 712–19.

the delinquent gang, Sykes and Matza, they argue, fail to distinguish among delinquent norms, rules of conduct, and the structure of beliefs and values. The relationship of neutralization to the normative and moral problems of the delinquent subculture and/or the general culture, they complain, also remain unexplored. Since Sykes and Matza tend to use norm, belief, and value interchangeably, their theory, its critics contend, lacks specificity and only describes the delinquency process.

Self, awareness, and rationalization

Violations by persons in positions of financial trust, *Donald R. Cressey* theorized in a manner similar to that of Sykes and Matza, involves three self-factors of self-concept, awareness, and rationalization. In a study of 133 prisoners at state and federal institutions, Cressey found support for his view that positions of responsibility are violated when persons occupying positions of trust believe they possess a financial problem which cannot be shared, can be secretly resolved by violation of this trust, and does not strain their self-conception as trusted persons or as users of entrusted properties or funds. As the person defines the problem he faces, he violates the position of trust, Cressey assumes, by producing a *rationalization* which enables him to maintain his concept of self-esteem while violating the essence of his position. The violation of financial trust, Cressey hypothesizes, "is selected by trusted persons on the basis of the rationalizations available to them."[10] Since the person maintains an internalized honesty ideal, he rationalizes his apparent dishonesty in order to fulfill the demands of the ideal. Personal and social characteristics, therefore, are important only as they operate indirectly to permit the emergence of the components of rationalization.

On the other hand, *Edwin M. Lemert* proposes a *closure* or *isolation* theory to explain criminality. Finding check forgers naïve, Lemert believes that many, finding themselves in a crisis situation, will turn to forgery as a way out of their dilemma, especially if they had little, if any, experience in crime. As events close in upon the person, the individual, according to the Lemert thesis, attempts to resolve the problem through forgery, which offers an immediate way out.[11]

Delinquency and drift

In an extended statement on neutralization, David Matza recognizes that individuals operate on a continuum between the extremes of free-

---

[10] Donald R. Cressey, *Other People's Money: A Study on the Social Psychology of Embezzlement* (Glencoe: Free Press, 1953), p. 142.

[11] Edwin M. Lemert, "An Isolation and Closing Theory of Naïve Check Forgery," *Journal of Criminal Law,* Vol. 44, No. 3 (September–October, 1953), pp. 296–307.

dom and restraint. Although some individuals act more freely than others, they exist in relative relationships to the two extremes. *Drift,* Matza supposes, is a position midway between freedom and restraint, a condition in which the individual flirts unevenly with one or the other, thereby drifting between criminal and conventional action.[12]

While Matza is willing to partially accept the idea of a *subculture* of delinquency, he rejects the idea of a *delinquent subculture.* Although the size of the group may vary, the subculture of delinquency is "the setting," Matza writes, "in which the commission of delinquency is common knowledge among a group of juveniles."[13] Delinquent acts do not necessarily result from the mere breaking of a moral commitment to law, arising from the neutralization of legal norms. Although drift is a normal result of neutralization, which makes delinquency possible or permissible, the result is not necessarily actual delinquency. Drift, Matza believes, does not mean an irreversible commitment or compulsion to complete a particular act.

In this view, the majority of delinquents are essentially drifters. Although a small proportion may engage in deviant activity due to their neurotic impulses or their personal commitments to criminal careers, the greater number share simultaneously in the tension between freedom and restraint. While the subculture of delinquency confers status upon the delinquent as he completes particular delinquent acts, it also rewards many conventional responses. Therefore, the subculture of delinquency maintains a delicate balance between convention and crime. Neutralizing many of the prohibitions of law, the delinquent minimizes a sense of responsibility for justice or for injury to his victim. Since the subculture of delinquency encourages the individual to balance personal or social violations, he operates in opposition to the demands of law, which expect the person to retreat or escape from any aggressive actions toward others. Neutralization makes delinquent infractions possible and legitimate by removing the restraint of convention or law. However, the ordinary subcultural delinquent possesses the potential to make a decision to commit infractions or violations through the use of his will either to complete or not complete the infractions.

The will is activated either under mundane or extraordinary conditions. In the mundane context, when the delinquent comes to understand that he can commit and technically implement delinquent infractions, he may participate in delinquent conduct. If neutralization, for example, has freed the restraints of conscience and law, the completion of an infraction is accompanied by a minimum feeling of guilt. As the conscience is liberated, the potential for repetition of the act is strengthened

---

[12] David Matza, *Delinquency and Drift* (New York: John Wiley & Sons, Inc., 1964), pp. 27–28.
[13] *Ibid.,* p. 33.

especially as the sense of anxiety or guilt is either managed or neutralized.[14]

The decision to commit an infraction or to activate the will is stimulated by one of two conditions, both of which operate within the permissive context of drift. During mundane occasions, *preparation,* the first condition, gives impetus for the repetition of old infractions. *Desparation,* a second condition, completes the same function in extraordinary situations; it provides the stimulus for new and previously inexperienced violations. Both provide "the nerve," Matza suggests, "required of children for the commission of infraction."[15] As one learns (prepares) means of committing infractions, he also begins to believe that an infraction *may* be done rather than *can* be done. Having overcome the constraint of law through neutralization and having come to a point of drift, the potential delinquent simply accepts the previous infraction as acceptable behavior.

Some juveniles do not participate in delinquency or crime because they are unable to control the apprehensive component or counteraction involved in an infraction. Whether "chicken" or simply deterred from crime, they are in a sense unprepared for participation in action despite their situation of drift. However, if the level of apprehension is lessened by one's belief in one's own ability or by the imposition of minimal sanctions which also serve to lessen such tensions, the juvenile may be stimulated by a will to crime. As apprehensiveness is managed, the will to repeat a crime, Matza supposes, may consequently be activated. And yet, drift is not likely to stimulate new or previously inexperienced infractions unless the will to crime is excessively activated by a feeling of desperation.

If a mood of fatalism neutralizes legal restraints, it can encourage a sense of despair. Because fatalism by definition is the "negation of a sense of active mastery over one's environment," it is closely related to desperation. "Subculture delinquents," Matza notes, "experience desperation when caught in a mood of fatalism."[16] In such a context, the delinquent may rejoin the moral order through the commission of crime. In this way, he moves from a fatalistic to a humanistic mood with the dramatic reassurance that he is able to change human conditions. Because he is also able to activate the criminal process, he receives immediate verification of his "restored potency."

The mood of fatalism neutralizes the bind of law, "elicits the situation of company, and fosters a sense of desperation," Matza concludes, "which in turn provides the will or thrust to commit a new infraction."[17]

---

[14] *Ibid.*, pp. 181–83. Refer to H. J. Eysenck, *Crime and Personality* (New York: Houghton Mifflin Co., 1964).

[15] *Ibid.*, p. 183.

[16] *Ibid.*, p. 189.

[17] *Ibid.*, pp. 190–91.

NORM CONTAINMENT THEORY

Walter C. Reckless and Shlomo Shoham hold that individuals retain norms and values at a differential rate. The extent of retention is influenced by behavior patterns, environmental situations, peer groups, delinquent subcultures, and individual socialization. The process of norm retention or norm erosion is related to an overall theory of *norm containment*. Norms (viewed as the behavior, activity, thinking, and attitudes which others expect of an individual), are revealed in performance standards, moral codes, prescribed principles, duties, or laws. They can, however, be contained and thereby be rendered ineffective. The ability of norms to bring about desired conduct depends upon the ability of the group to transmit norms effectively and to constrain group members within established normative limits. In addition, the person must also retain and act upon these norms for them to possess efficacy. Therefore, Reckless and Shoham conclude, that if erosion of norms occurs, individuals may embrace deviant behavior patterns. In this way, norms which encourage the completion of the undesired act replace previously internalized norm expectations.

Ultimately, the ability of the group to transmit its norms and to constrain the individual is limited by urbanization, migration, dislocation, political disturbance, and culture conflict. As the adolescent and young adult move from the protected confines of their family or neighborhood into the more impersonal world, the norm-holding power of the primary group is often counteracted by the added norm alternatives which multiple groups offer. The disproportionate adolescent and young adult involvement in delinquency and crime, Reckless and Shoham thus argue, implies that the period of adolescence and young adulthood represent a period of major norm erosion.[18]

In general, Reckless' containment theory presumes that some human systems are able to resist or hold deviance to a mild level, while others are unable to resist. These differentials are, Reckless believes, to be anticipated because society and nuclear groups cannot be expected to produce total conformity, but instead produce people who can be stimulated to comply with acceptable social norms only under given circumstances. Each society, state, tribe, village, family, or other nuclear group is generally able to constrain the individual within its normative limits. However, this outer or external containment, reinforced by accepted norms and expectations, presupposes, Reckless believes, the existence

---

[18] Walter C. Reckless and Shlomo Shoham, "Norm Containment Theory as Applied to Delinquency and Crime," *Excerpta and Criminologica*, Vol. 3, No. 6 (November–December, 1963), pp. 637–43.

of deviant, illegal, unconventional, immoral, or anomic patterns of behavior.

Because individuals must be motivated to comply with these external containment goals, businesses, offices, schools, and other social groups or settings attempt to encourage the individual to respond effectively to their end goals. Although violations do occur in the process, the goal of the institution is to minimize the number of infractions or hold the number of violations to tolerable levels. A lack of meaningful roles, Reckless believes, increases the potential for violations within group or institutional settings. Although individuals who have no rules or roles to follow may respond unevenly to their life existence, they may also seek the containment security of the nuclear group or small organization which views the person as an individual and provides a base for self-understanding. As the small group or organization accepts the individual, it also sustains him by offering him a sense of belonging, a feeling of acceptance, ego support, and a meaningful concept of self.

Although outer or external containment reflects the ability of societal organizations or communities to direct the individuals to the bounds of accepted norms, regulations, laws, rules, values, and expectations, modern and pluralistic societies, marked by potential conflict and alienation, are unable, Reckless argues, to maintain an external containment force which can effectively constrain the action of the individual. In the mass society, *inner containment*, which represents the ability of the person to follow the expected norms without external constraints, assumes added importance because the diversity and impersonality of society places greater importance upon the self as an agent of social control. "The more the diversity, the more the impersonalization, and the more away from homebase," Reckless writes, "the more the self must act as the directional control."[19] However, one's ability to resist external forces depends upon the components of self which make it possible for the person to contain himself in the modern mobile world. A favorable self-image, self-concept, and self-perception allows the person to act more responsibly. One's goal orientation, Reckless assumes, allows the self to steer itself. But goals depend upon the *aspiration* and *frustration tolerance* levels of the person.

Aspirations must be synchronized with realistically obtainable goals if a person is to avoid a potential normative collapse. One's frustration tolerance, too, allows the self to achieve its inner potential. A controlled, less frustrated individual is unlikely to be diverted from his course because his ability to withstand adversity, peer or group pressure, disappointment, or failure generally helps him reach new and meaningful

---

[19] Walter C. Reckless, *The Crime Problem* (New York: Appleton-Century-Crofts, 1957), p. 475.

goals. Inner containment, however, involves the adherence and commitment to, identification with, and retention, acceptance, legitimation and defense of, values, norms, laws, codes, institutions, and customs which are common within one's environment. Self-concepts, goal orientation, frustration tolerance, and retention of norms, therefore, overlap with and reinforce each other.

If individuals in mobile, urban, industrialized, and democratic societies are part of strong *outer containment,* they are unlikely to become involved in reported delinquency or crimes. If outer containment, however, is weak and inner containment strong, the person experiences only a small chance of involvement in delinquency or crime. If, on the other hand, outer containment is relatively strong and inner containment relatively weak, the individual's potential involvement with delinquency or crime is greater than in the two previous instances. "The chances of criminal and delinquent involvement," Reckless concludes, "are maximized in modern, mobile, urban democratic society when both outer and inner containment are weak."[20]

Pressures and *pulls,* which may consist of unemployment, poverty, economic insecurity, minority group status, lack of opportunities, inequalities, group conflicts, or other similar factors, influence one's membership in groups and organizations. They may dilute or divert the buffer of external containment offered by these groups and organizations and render the individual vulnerable to their influence. Pulls may also draw the person away from an acceptable way of life. Bad companions, a delinquent or criminal subculture, mass media, propaganda, or activity of deviant groups may overcome the buffer of the group or organization and pass beyond the buffer of the self. However, additional organic and psychological pushes, represented in the forms of extreme restlessness and discontent, extreme hostility and aggressiveness, marked inner tensions, self-aggrandizement and need for immediate gratification, extreme suggestibility, strong rebellion against authority, major feeling of inferiority or inadequacy, anxieties, mental conflict, phobia, compulsions, and psychoses or other variations may also challenge, Reckless argues, the containment of the self and either make the individual susceptible to, or allow, delinquent and criminal responses.[21]

CONDUCT NORM CONFLICT AND DELINQUENCY

Conflicts in conduct norms, *Thorsten Sellin* contends, are major causes of delinquency and criminality. Because each person relates daily to

---

[20] *Ibid.,* p. 478. Reckless also discusses the containment theory in "A New Theory of Delinquency and Crime," *Federal Probation,* Vol. 5 (December, 1941), p. 42.

[21] *Ibid.,* pp. 478–80. Note also F. H. Allport, "The J-Curve Hypothesis of Conforming Behavior," *Journal of Social Psychology,* Vol. 5 (1934).

a number of social groups which possess particular behavior norms, the person is continually confronted with *conflicts in conduct norms* which are not always quickly resolved. Since the individual is a member of family, play, work, religious, political, or other groups, he acquires norms which may weaken, enhance, or even contradict norms which he earlier incorporated into his personality structure. Consequently, the greater the cultural complexity, the greater, Sellin argues, the potential normative conflict.[22] Culture conflict is related to rapid social change and its ensuing social disorganization; sudden change may come about through war, immigration, technological advances, or influence of mass communications media. Because social disorganization is representative of a disequilibrium or disintegration of the previously integrated society, it can only be resolved by the reestablishment of a normative consensus. Since each normative system exists independently as a segment of society, its ultimate value, Sellin argues, depends upon its interrelationship to other normative segments.[23] The resolution of normative conflict, however, necessitates the activation of psychological processes for conflict reduction.

FAVORABLE SELF-CONCEPT AND DELINQUENCY

One means of conflict reduction is the creation of a meaningful self-concept. A good concept of self, a product of favorable socialization, directs slum boys, *Walter C. Reckless* and *Simon Dinitz* believe, away from delinquency, while a poor self-concept, a product of unfavorable socialization, offers the slum youth no resistance to deviancy, delinquent companions, or a delinquent subculture. A good self-concept, they assume, is indicative of a *residual favorable socialization* and a strong inner self, which turns the individual from bad companions and street-corner society to middle-class values and the potential of upward mobility through the opportunity structure. The poor self-concept, on the other hand, is indicative, they hold, of a *residual unfavorable socialization* and reveals a weak inner self which is unable to redirect the boy from bad companions and street-corner society and to strengthen his resolve to accept middle-class values or participate in the established system of upward mobility.[24]

---

[22] Thorsten Sellin, *Culture Conflict in Crime* (New York: Social Science Research Council, 1938), pp. 130–31. Keep in mind, Herbert A. Block, *Disorganization: Personal and Social* (New York: Alfred A. Knopf, Inc., 1952).

[23] See Louis Wirth, "Ideological Aspects of Social Organization," *American Sociological Review*, Vol. 5 (August, 1940), p. 474.

[24] Simon Dinitz, Frank Scarpitti, and Walter C. Reckless, "Delinquency Vulnerability: A Cross Group and Longitudinal Analysis," *American Sociological Review*, Vol. 27, No. 4 (August, 1962), p. 517.

A comparative study of two groups of 12-year-old white boys in a high-rate delinquency area in Columbus, Ohio, supported the Reckless-Dinitz hypothesis. Two groups of boys, the first consisting of "good" boys and the second of "bad" were interviewed, as were also their mothers. Four years after the original interview, they were interviewed again.

At the first interview, members of the "good" group perceived themselves as remaining free of trouble and also stated that they believed their friends would remain trouble-free. They likewise predicted that they would finish school. They looked upon their families in a favorable light. The mother of each of the boys in this first group agreed with the evaluation of her son—that the son would not get into trouble, would finish school, and would remain in close relationship to his family. They agreed, too, that the son's friends would follow this same pattern. After four years, nearly all of these "good" boys, Reckless and Dinitz found, were still in school, conceived of themselves and their friends as being trouble-free, and looked upon their family as good families. Only three had a minor scrape with law enforcement agencies.

The boys in the second group, the "bad" boys, gave evidence of an unfavorable self-image at the time of the first interview. They believed, Reckless and Dinitz noted, that they would get into trouble and might be jailed. Not only had many of their friends already been involved in trouble but they also believed that trouble was likely to be a part of their friends' future. Many stated that their families were simply no good. The mothers generally agree with their sons' evaluation. Four years later, approximately 39 percent of the "bad" boys had been involved with the juvenile court on the average of three times.[25]

ALIENATION AND DELINQUENCY-CRIME

Although a negative self-image is closely related to the actual alienation of the offender, the modern concept of alienation implies a general process or condition which involves a degree of normlessness, goallessness, nonbelonging, or impersonality in the modern urban world. In modern terms, alienation is a tendency to retreat from active involvement with groups and to reject society's norms or social goals. Representing a position of retreat or apartness, alienation allows the participant to reduce his commitment to, or involvement in, institutions, norms, individuals, or groups. Through an erosion of internalized norms, personal disorganization, or even broader forms of demoralization, the moral content of infractions is often reduced to self-factors.

---

[25] Reckless, *op. cit.*, p. 445.

Although his concept of alienation was not psychological or normative, *Karl Marx* viewed it as a product of the growth of capitalism.
Because the proletariat is alienated from the means of production, it
becomes hopeless, helpless, and powerless.[26]

Melvin Seeman suggests that alienation should be understood in terms
of five components, which he describes as powerlessness, meaninglessness, normlessness, isolation, and self-estrangement. In *powerlessness,*
a person does not believe that his own behavior can determine the
eventual context or outcome of events. The individual in the phase of
meaninglessness is confused and seems unable to reach conclusions or
make choices with confidence; in the state of *normlessness,* he feels
that approved norms lack effective potential. The person in the state
of *isolation* places a low value upon the reward offered to the individual
who accepts the goals or beliefs of society and feels separated from
social institutions. In the condition of *self-estrangement,* the individual
is unable to find the rewarding activities which he needs to integrate
life.[27]

Failure or the anticipation of failure in reaching success goals by
socially sanctioned means may result in alienation. If a lower-class male
adolescent, for example, is continually faced with a competitive disad-
vantage in his use of legitimate channels to success, he may become
alienated and may repudiate these channels and procedures.[28] As an
alienated failure, he may, Seeman believes, blame either society or himself for his alienation or deviant conduct. If he holds the social system
to be unjust, he may disassociate himself from its basic norms and pursue
his success goals either by legitimate or illegitimate means. On the other
hand, if he holds himself responsible for his failure, he may seek changes
in his personality rather than in the system. If he feels pressures and
loss of self-esteem, he may likewise develop mechanisms to protect himself from feelings of inferiority and group competition.[29]

Tracing the process of alienation, *Frank Tannenbaum* suggests that
the child's participation in innocent and random play activities eventually leads him to engage in conduct which conflicts with adult values
or interests. If the child is subsequently identified as a bad youth, adult
disapproval eventually creates a form of *stigmatization* and alienation.
Even the later separation of the offender from the remaining group

---

[26] Karl Marx and Frederick Engels, *Capital* (New York: Random House, Inc.,
1906).

[27] Melvin Seeman, "On Meaning of Alienation," *American Sociological Review,*
Vol. 24, No. 6 (December, 1959), pp. 785–90.

[28] *Ibid.,* pp. 783–91. Also see Jacob Chwast, "Alienation as a Factor in Delinquency," *Federal Probation,* Vol. 28 (June, 1964), p. 25.

[29] Cloward and Ohlin, *op. cit.,* p. 112.

for specialized treatment, Tannenbaum argues, increases his alienation. Therefore, the process of creating the criminal, he suggests, involves an elaborate procedure of tagging, defining, identifying, segregating, describing, emphasizing, and stigmatizing, which makes the youth consciously and unconsciously aware of his own undesired characteristics.[30] As the child is increasingly isolated from constructive adult role models, he becomes, Tannenbaum points out, dependent upon the security offered by persons of similar interests and capabilities. The peer group subsequently supports the deviant process and reinforces the individual's alienation and deviant self-image.

KINSHIP, MASCULINE IDENTIFICATION, AND DELINQUENCY

The particular features in the American kinship system and the generally sharp segregation of kinship and occupational role, *Talcott Parsons* hypothesizes, create barriers to *masculine identification* and thereby foster delinquency. Middle-class adult male involvement in occupational roles tends to encourage the development of the female-centered kinship system. In lower-class communities, especially among Negro families, the occupational instability and family transience of adult males result in a female-centered household. Therefore, boys have trouble developing a clear masculine self-image when male role models are not readily apparent or perceived. The males gravitate toward the mother as children and may encounter conflict in adolescence when they are expected to begin to behave as men. Protesting against their earlier identification with the female, they turn to malicious and destructive acts in order to prove their masculinity. Engaging in the process of "masculine protest" or "compulsive masculinity," the youthful adolescent, Parsons assumes, attempts to overcompensate for his earlier socialization and feminine domination.[31]

Although Parsons' explanation has value, he fails to define the types of deviant behavior which arise as a result of the problems of masculine identification. However, even if the masculine identity crisis is as great as Parsons assumes, it is most difficult to explain the distribution of delinquency in terms of this hypothesis. While Parsons believes that the female-centered household is primarily confined to the middle and lower classes, the full importance of female domination in delinquency and crime causation is undetermined. Even among these classes, devi-

---

[30] Frank Tannebaum, *Crime in the Community* (New York: Columbia University Press, 1938), pp. 17–20.

[31] See Talcott Parsons, *Essays in Sociological Theory* (Glencoe: Free Press, 1954), pp. 304–5; and "Certain Primary Sources and Patterns of Aggression in the Social Structure of the Western World," *Psychiatry*, Vol. 10 (May, 1947), pp. 167–81.

ance is not uniformly evident. The continuity of delinquency with increased masculinity and the development of male-dominated households is not explained within the Parsonian hypothesis.[32]

ADOLESCENT STATUS TRANSITION

The transition of boys from adolescence to adulthood, *Herbert Bloch* and *Arthur Neiderhoffer* theorize, results in juvenile adjustment problems. Delinquency is a product of a *major change in status* which culminates in an individual life crisis. The severity of a crisis depends upon the nature and availability of processes of social adjustment which may successfully facilitate change. If the transition to adulthood is not accomplished successfully, deviant conduct, Bloch and Neiderhoffer believe, may emerge from the crisis situation.

Modern technical and occupational rules require formal training and extensive preparation which complicate an already complicated adjustment process. Since male adolescents are cut off from adult roles and are kept in a longer dependent relationship to adults, they suffer from marginality, in which they are no longer children but are not yet adults. Although barred from adult roles and deprived of money, autonomy, sexual freedom, or other privileges and rewards accorded adults, they are encouraged to aspire to adult status. Consequently, the frustrations of marginality exert constant pressures toward deviant conduct. Interacting with other adolescents who share similar problems, male adolescents assume adult behavior in a somewhat awkward and exaggerated form. By doing so, they commit many acts, Bloch and Neiderhoffer note, which are deviant for youth but are quite common among adults.[33]

As an explanation of the causes of deviance, Bloch and Niederhoffer's theory of status transition and conflict fails to clearly identify patterns of delinquent behavior and inaccurately equates adolescent with delinquent gangs. Although they suggest that delinquency is diffused widely throughout the social structure, Bloch and Niederhoffer maintain that only lower-class delinquency receives strong sanctions, support, and approval which undergirds delinquency patterns. While Bloch and Niederhoffer view the gang as an attempt to fill the chasm between childhood and adulthood, they fail to deal with the location, content, persistence, and variations in delinquent gang behavior. Even though the delinquent may stress virility, toughness, and masculinity, these traits do not necessarily indicate that he desires adult status. Rather, they may well mean that he is attempting to postpone the onset of adulthood.

---

[32] Cloward and Ohlin, *op. cit.*, p. 53.

[33] Herbert A. Bloch and Arthur Neiderhoffer, *The Gang: A Study of Adolescent Behavior* (New York: Philosophical Library, Inc., 1958), p. 17.

SOCIOETHICAL SOCIALIZATION

Delinquency and crime, *Stephen Schafer* and *Richard D. Knudten* propose, are products of the socioethical personality which is formed in relationship to innate or inherited characteristics and which emerges gradually in relationship to the surrounding cultural context of the society of which the individual is a member. The individual's socioethical personality is derived from both inherited predispositions and traditional culture, and it represents an unequal fusion of these factors. While social interaction may ultimately challenge the currently developed socioethical personality, the human will in the form of personality Schafer and Knudten suggest, influences its eventual response.

All individuals are normally socialized to the norms of culture as they emerge into manhood. However, the content of these norms will vary in relationship to such factors as social class, subcultural context, occupational and religious commitment, political preference, economic capabilities, ethnic and racial membership, geographic region, and general community characteristics. Because socioethical rules, particularly in large urban and industrial states, are continually changing, the degree of community stability varies accordingly.

Although the process of normal socialization encourages the early internalization of values, which are regarded by the society and/or the dominant political power as noncriminal and nondelinquent in nature, and the development of conforming behavior patterns consistent with these values, continuing socialization, Schafer and Knudten propose, constantly exposes the individual temptation. The actual degree of individual responsibility for any antisocial conduct, therefore, involves the interaction between the person's socioethical resistance (SER) and pressures favoring participation in crime (CP). As the pressures toward crime (CP) are exerted against the person's socioethical resistance (SER), the individual's limited socioethical responsibility factor ($LSER$) emerges, a relationship which can be symbolized in the formula:

$$\frac{SER}{CP} = LSER$$

If the resultant socioethical resistance and crime pressures are of equal strength, they may cancel each other out and leave a *criminometric average*, the reaction of an average amount of socioethical resistance to an average amount of pressure toward crime. If the criminometric average is balanced or is weighted in favor of socioethical resistance, crimes should not normally occur. If the criminometric average, however, favors crime pressures, criminality is predictable. Although shortcomings in the socialization process or some psychophysical defect may explain a common tendency to criminal or delinquent action, a temporary situation or some transitory psychophysical deficiency may cause a chronic deviance pattern. The extent or limitation of this tendency varies widely from individual to individual, time to time and even place to place.[34]

STIGMATIZATION BY SOCIETY

Deviant conduct, *Edwin M. Lemert* believes, emerges from individual, situational, and systematic sources. *Individual deviation* is a product of psychic pressures, while *situational deviation* is a consequence of the stress or pressure of a particular situation. Because situational deviance is generally independent of psychic characteristics, individuals located in the same setting of stress would normally respond in a similar deviant manner. *Systematic deviation,* on the other hand, refers to the emergence of subcultural or general deviant systems of behavior. Although systematic deviance may emerge from an individual or situational context, it becomes a form of group continuity. If society makes individual survival difficult, the individual may share in a protective social system which systematizes individual or situational deviance. A systematic deviation subculture, however, defines and makes deviant values and mores normative in order to maintain its unity.

According to Lemert, deviant behavior first begins with a flirtation with risk which may result in some social reaction. The later career experiences of the deviant youth may be more heavily influenced by the resulting social response than by his earlier involvement in undesired conduct. While deviation may be either primary or secondary, it may lead to different consequences when discovered. In effect, the individual engaging in primary deviation participates in norm-violating conduct which is alien to his concept of self. In the stage of *secondary deviation,* the participant's deviant role becomes the center of unity of his social-psychological self. While primary deviation may become secondary, it usually becomes so only when repeated acts occur when the deviant experiences societal reactions. As a result, the process of norm violation and societal reaction, Lemert argues, stimulates or fails to simulate further deviant acts. The sequence of interaction, which leads to secondary deviation, normally follows, Lemert diagnoses, an eight-step developmental path:

1. Primary deviation.
2. Social penalties.

---

[34] Stephen Schafer and Richard D. Knudten, *Juvenile Delinquency: An Introduction:* (New York: Random House, Inc., 1970). For insight into the development of criminology, see Leon Radzinowicz, *In Search of Criminology* (Cambridge, Mass.: Harvard University Press, 1962).

3. Further primary deviations.
4. Stronger penalties and rejections.
5. Further deviation, perhaps with hostility and resentments beginning to focus on those doing the penalizing.
6. Crisis reached in the tolerance quotient, expressed in formal action by the community stigmatizing the deviant.
7. Strengthening of deviant conduct as a reaction to stigmatizing and penalty imposition.
8. Ultimate acceptance of deviant social status, and efforts and adjustment on the basis of the associated role.[35]

However, *Howard S. Becker* holds that societal reaction to deviant behavior is neither automatic, fixed, nor invariable. Rather, societal response depends upon the time and place of occurrence and upon the individuals involved in deviant conduct. While some persons are secret deviants, others who conform are often falsely labeled deviant. Since criminal career patterns involve more than a single event, greater emphasis, Becker proposes, should be placed upon the processes and variables which sustain deviance over a longer period of time than upon a mere escapade. Even though a distinction must be made between master and subordinate deviant statuses, the status may dominate all other statuses which the person occupies and may cause the discrediting of the person in the eyes of the public.[36] The discrediting of the individual, therefore, may have a profound influence upon the future course of his deviant career. While the *stigmatization* of the individual is not as severe as the discrediting of the individual by pronouncing him a deviant, it nevertheless lessens the value of the person and tends to categorize him as abnormal.[37]

DEVIATION DIFFERENTIAL HYPOTHESIS

Lowell J. Carr maintains that delinquency involves three sets of factors: (1) shortcomings of personality, (2) environmental pressures against conformity, and (3) the interaction of personality and the environment. The interaction of these elements, Carr suggests, leads to the potential of *conforming or deviating pressures* which ultimately results in criminal activities or conformist conduct. What each person does in a particular situation, Carr explains, is largely determined by the relationship of the factors to each other. If factors encouraging conformity outnumber pressures encouraging deviation, the youth is likely

---

[35] Edwin M. Lemert, *Social Pathology* (New York: McGraw-Hill Book Co., 1951), p. 77. Also see Edwin M. Lemert, *Human Deviance, Social Problems and Social Control* (Englewood Cliffs, N.J.: Prentice-Hall, Inc., 1967).

[36] Howard S. Becker, *The Outsiders* (New York: Free Press, 1963), pp. 36–39.

[37] Erving Goffman, *Stigma* (Englewood Cliffs, N.J.: Prentice-Hall, Inc., 1963).

to conform to the mores evidenced within the society. Conforming factors (CF) are derived from the person (I) and the environment (E). Deviating factors (DF) are likewise both internal (I) and environmental (E). Therefore, the relationship of conforming and deviating pressures in the production or nonproduction of criminal activity can be depicted in the following equation:[38]

$$CF(I \times E) - DF(I \times E) = \begin{cases} CD \\ \text{or} \\ DD \end{cases} \begin{matrix} \to CB \\ \text{or} \\ \to DB \end{matrix}$$

The internal and environmental conforming factors minus the internal and environmental deviating factors yield, according to Carr, either a conforming differential or deviating differential, depending on the general strength of the factors involved. A dominant conforming differential (CD) leads to conforming behavior; a deviating differential (DD), on the other hand, leads to deviant conduct. Therefore, specific behavior, Carr suggests, is always the interim of the whole equation.[39] Delinquency occurs when deviation supporting factors exceed factors encouraging conformity of behavior. Areas of life in which deviation is common include deviant home life, culture conflict areas, substandard areas where physical and social structures are inefficient and deteriorating, delinquency traditions, and street trades and domestic service (*i.e.*, newspaper vender, waitress, housemaid, and particular forms of commercialized recreation).[40]

PERSONALITY STRUCTURE AND DEVIANT CONDUCT

According to *Herbert A. Bloch,* crime is a reflection of a personality structure, primarily determined by class, subcultural, or ethnic conditions which define culturally oriented needs or functions for the individual's personality structure. Because the individual internalizes these characteristics, he may express behavior which reveals his inability to conform to normative role demands in his attempt to satisfy his culturally defined needs.

As *social tropisms,* these broad personality structures determine the individual's movement toward and *from* other individuals. Serving as *tendencies to action,* the personality structures, expressed in such egoistic, aggressive, withdrawal, or isolation personality states, are expressions of the individual's self-concept or *generic status.* Because the self-concept (generic status) reflects the person's personality structure, existing cultural conditions will either repudiate or enforce this self-concept. There-

---

[38] Lowell J. Carr, *Delinquency Control* (New York, Harper & Bros., 1950).
[39] *Ibid.*, p. 161.
[40] *Ibid.*, pp. 167–77.

fore, criminality, Bloch assumes, occurs if the individual is continually exposed to a series of primary relationships which are oriented to criminal or illegal behavior or if the individual is placed in situations which do not reinforce generic status but do create areas of tension and conflict. If primary relationships reinforce the components of generic status, the individual may reveal criminal patterns. However, if the person is confronted with tension and conflict, he may engage in criminal activity in order to resolve the tension between his self-concept and the actual social situation.[41] Although Bloch's theory has not been adequately tested, it presumes that crime is a product of a functional relationship between the personality and the social structure and is, therefore, an inherent element of the social situation.

PROSOCIAL, ANTISOCIAL, AND ASOCIAL DELINQUENCY

A study of 36 boys at the State of Washington Diagnostic Center led John W. Kinch to classify delinquent youth in three social-psychological categories: prosocial, antisocial, and asocial.

The *prosocial delinquents*, he found, are largely situational delinquents who participate in serious delinquency on a single occasion. Well adjusted in peer relationships, they have stable family situations and satisfactory school records. Consequently, they view themselves as friendly, loyal, warmhearted, relaxed, patient, courteous, not lazy, not quarrelsome, not selfish, not crabby, not timid, not confused, not nervous, and not disorderly.

The *antisocial delinquents*, primarily gang delinquents from urban areas, report multiple contacts with law enforcement agencies. Beginning delinquency at an early age, they come from lower-class families which reveal lax discipline and previous sibling delinquency patterns. Marked by truancy and poor achievement, the antisocial delinquents evidence poor school adjustments. While they perceive themselves as smart, excitable, dependable, stubborn, patient, and not warmhearted, their self-perceptions are less favorable than those of the prosocial delinquents.

The *asocial delinquents*, "the unsocialized aggressors," on the other hand, face early and severe parental rejection. While many are born out of wedlock, most come from broken homes and maintain poor peer relationships. The asocial delinquents, Kinch found, are generally loners in their delinquent activities. They view themselves as nervous, confused, daring, timid, not dependable, not smart, not excitable, and disorderly.[42]

---

[41] Herbert A. Bloch and Gilbert Geis, *Man, Crime and Society* (New York: Random House, Inc., 1962), pp. 125–28.

[42] John W. Kinch, "Self-Conceptions of Types of Delinquents," *Sociological Inquiry*, Vol. 32 (Spring, 1962), pp. 228–33. Refer to Theodore N. Ferdinand, *Typologies of Delinquency* (New York: Random House, Inc., 1966).

GANG DELINQUENCY IN ENGLAND

P. Scott, a clinical psychologist who attempted the first English systematic investigation of gang delinquency in England, recognizes three types of offender groups, which he identifies as adolescent street groups, structured gangs, and loosely structured (diffuse) groups, the latter subdivided into "fleeting casual groups," "groups of customary friends and siblings," and "loose antisocial groups."[43] Members of *adolescent street groups*, Scott suggests, are not oriented to delinquency but participate in delinquent acts individually or collectively as the occasion arises. *Structured gangs* possess a definite membership and leadership core, persist in time, and operate from some set location. They initiate members into the group and define their criminal objectives.

Turning to the *loosely structured* groups, the *fleeting* or *casual delinquent association*, emerges largely by chance, if predispositions toward delinquency are present among boys between 10 and 13. While *groups of friends and siblings*, offer the framework for the greatest number of group offenses, their usual activities, Scott noted, are not delinquent. However, members of the *loose antisocial group*, are more delinquency-prone and reveal signs of unhappy or disturbed adolescence. Leadership roles, which shift from follower to follower, are more catalytic than directive. Most delinquent groups, Scott believes, are unstructured, although in several instances the gang is an atypical form which arises from existing social pressures.[44] Although preliminary evidence suggests that delinquent group structures in England are somewhat different from American metropolitan delinquency structures, no real evidence yet exists to support this thesis. Ecological and demographic factors and lack of ethnic ghettos have helped to minimize gang development in England.

Slumtown in England

As a result of his investigation of the subculture of an English city slum, *John Mays* concluded that crime and delinquency are related to the situation and the personality of the individual. The cultural milieu of Liverpool, Mays noted, passively accepts certain forms of neighborhood shoplifting, malicious damage, and petty larceny. Consequently, delinquency in large city areas, Mays theorizes, is related to the psychological and environmental pressures placed upon the individual. Making a basic distinction between the temporary social pressures of the gang which lead to delinquent acts and the activity of criminals which persist

[43] P. Scott, "Gangs and Delinquents in London," *British Journal of Delinquency*, Vol. 7 (July, 1956), pp. 8–21.

[44] Downes, *op. cit.*, p. 118.

because of psychological disturbances that continue adolescent behavior into early adulthood, Mays makes a basic distinction between two ideal offender types which may merge imperceptively into one continuous delinquent-criminal orientation. Many delinquents, Mays argues, experience a degree of emotional maladjustment, while serious and persistent offenders are victims of a criminogenic social background. Therefore, delinquency and crime, Mays maintains, may be best understood in terms of two equations:

$$\text{Personal} + \text{Environmental factors} = \text{Crime}$$
$$\text{Environmental} + \text{Personal factors} = \text{Delinquency}[45]$$

Mays found that in slum town delinquency was a form of subculturally prescribed behavior in which nearly every boy in the community participated and which could bring most boys to the attention of the police at some time in early life. While the greater majority of those surveyed, Mays found, completed a delinquent act of some type in early life, most seemed to have outgrown their delinquency in the course of their lives and avoided arrest. Minor legal infringements, Mays concluded, are to be expected of young boys to whom such infringements represent normative conduct standards. These delinquents often fail to grow out of the deviant phase due to permanent social and psychological adjustment problems. While early juvenile delinquency, Mays believes, is a product of the juvenile culture, later criminal acts are characteristic of psychological rather than sociological disturbances.[46]

IDENTITY AND THE REFERENCE GROUP

Although *Theodore M. Newcomb* accepts the role of cultural factors in delinquent conduct, he tends to place greater emphasis upon the relationship of self-identity and the reference group in deviance causation. Arguing that individuals have multiple opportunities to relate to particular *associational reference groups,* Newcomb suggests that they often become dissatisfied with a group as other alternatives become evident. Reference group strength in influencing a particular person, therefore, is decreased in relationship to the degree of reduction in satisfaction which the group affords the individual.

The search for self-identity, Newcomb suggests, involves four different types of relationships which may exist between two specific kinds of groups. When membership groups serve as reference groups, the individual learns the norms accepted by group members. If the individual,

---

[45] Terence Morris, *The Criminal Area* (New York: Humanities Press, Inc., 1958), p. 79.
[46] *Ibid.,* pp. 103–4.

however, relates to multiple membership or reference groups, past membership may continue to influence his present activities which are not reinforced by current membership norms and values. On the other hand, a person may aspire to join another group of which he is not currently a member in order to reinforce the values and norms to which it is already committed. If an individual aspires to group membership, he is generally indoctrinated to the values and norms of the membership group, utilizing his new commitment as a reference group for other conduct expressions. Consequently, reference groups, either singly or simultaneously, may provide both positive and negative frames of reference.[47]

DIFFERENTIAL IDENTIFICATION AND DIFFERENTIAL ANTICIPATION

Daniel Glaser, modifying Edwin H. Sutherland's theory of differential association, suggests a concept of *differential identification,* closely related to reference-group theory, to explain the causation behind delinquency and crime. Each person, Glaser argues, assumes criminal behavior patterns to the extent that he identifies with real or imaginary persons who appear acceptable and worthy of emulation. Glaser's theory places a collateral emphasis upon social interaction. He believes that the individual rationalizes his conduct through his interaction with other persons. Although he identifies with both criminals and noncriminals through roles presented in fiction, movies, television, or other news media during his lifetime, he may also experience delinquency within a broader group context. Individuals can identify indirectly with behavior on the basis of what they have heard, seen, or read. Therefore, imitation, Glaser argues, may be a product of indirect (secondary) reference. Mass media may portray many alternative "generalized others" to the potential delinquent-criminal, who in turn may identify with the person who pursues criminal conduct and may legitimate the deviant model's choices as his own.[48]

Using a form of reference theory, Glaser assumes that individuals become criminal both through actual involvement with others who are criminal and through reference to their criminal existence. Because individuals are frequently operating in a social dynamic which encourages flexible social relationships and associational membership, their reference groups change frequently. Since modern mobility affects one's participa-

[47] Theodore M. Newcomb, *Social Psychology* (New York: Dryden Press, 1950), pp. 226–27. Also investigate Bruce Biddle and Edwin J. Thomas, *Role Theory: Concepts and Research* (New York: John Wiley & Sons, Inc., 1966).

[48] Daniel Glaser, "Criminality Theories in Behavioral Images," *American Journal of Sociology,* Vol. 61, No. 5 (1956), p. 440.

tion within associations, criminal conduct is influenced by differential identifications and not merely differential associations. Although Glaser admits that his concept of differential identification is unable to account for accidental or "loner" type crimes, he assumes that individuals identify with particular models on the basis of hidden individual factors.[49]

More recently, Glaser has expanded this idea in his theory of *differential anticipation* as a result of his recognition that the bulk of felony activity begins and terminates during adolescence, that the felonies committed after adolescence are a "fixation" in or a "regression" to adolescent behavior patterns, and that over 90 percent of the men released from prison initially look for legitimate employment as a means to self-sufficiency. Glaser hypothesizes:

Whenever there is the possibility of performing either a criminal or a noncriminal act as alternative means for achieving certain ends, or where the only possibilities are to employ a criminal means or to forsake the ends that crime might serve, people take that course of action from which they anticipate the most favorable conception of themselves.[50]

The offender's anticipations are affected by his moral beliefs and feelings through his conception of self. However, each individual possesses potentially differing criteria of morality which he applies to criminal actions. According to Glaser, the person's self-conception "in his pursuit of either criminal or noncriminal alternative actions is determined by both his prior experiences and his present circumstances."[51] While most human beings experiment with criminal shortcuts in passing from childhood dependence to adult independence, only a few are detoured for a major length of time through imprisonment. Nevertheless, the decision to commit a crime, according to Glaser, is a "dynamic emergent" of an offender's interaction with himself and with other real or imaginary persons (his reference group) in particular social and economic situations.[52] Those who continue careers as offenders consequently oscillate between criminal and noncriminal goals in relationship to the anticipated gratifications which they believe such ends offer.

---

[49] *Ibid.*, p. 440.
[50] Daniel Glaser, *The Effectiveness of a Prison and Parole System* (Indianapolis: Bobbs-Merrill Co., Inc., 1964), p. 490.
[51] *Ibid.*, p. 491.
[52] *Ibid.*, pp. 494–95.

Chapter
14

AN INTEGRATED
THEORY OF
DELINQUENCY-CRIME
CAUSATION

CONTEMPORARY THEORY OF CRIME CAUSATION

Theories of causation, like social theories generally, consider single or multiple variables and assume many forms. Some are automatically categorized as *ad hoc* theories because they relate delinquency and criminality to a single factor and offer a limited insight into the exact nature of criminal causation. The Sunday newspaper supplement stories which relate delinquency to broken homes, or crime to low intelligence, are examples of such hypothesizing. However, some theories, at the opposite pole, are *generic* attempts to relate a multitude of factors to the rise in delinquency and crime. In many instances, their very effort to be inclusive may make the broad generic approach rather meaningless. Few attempts have been made to develop generic criminological theory because of the criminologist's inability to explain the many diverse factors which enter into criminal deviance. Inasmuch as generic theorizing is an attempt to explain universal human behavior, it must eventually explain the causes of the diverse expressions of individual conduct, the varieties of legal definitions of crime, the effects of social change upon criminal behavior, and other assorted factors. Consequently, a generic theory of crime causation must be as broad, as inclusive, and as universally applicable to the field of criminology as, for example, Einstein's theory of relativity is to the natural sciences. The limited knowledge of complex human behavior, however, clearly restricts such development at this point in history.

Although social theory at the turn of the century was often more generic than *ad hoc*, the application of the scientific method to criminal behavior resulted in the publication of many studies which provided *ad hoc* explanations for the increase in criminal deviance. However, just as generic theories were unable to account adequately for criminal conduct, *ad hoc* explanations have similarly failed. While the former were often too inclusive, the latter frequently failed to consider important data which might challenge or force the broadening of *ad hoc* explanations.

Because of these limitations, Robert Merton has more recently stressed the development of theories of the *middle range*, which avoid the specificity of the *ad hoc* approach and yet do not suffer from the ambiguities of generic theorizing. As intermediate sociological theories of human behavior, middle-range formulations permit theorists of causation to pass beyond simplistic explanations without suffering the pitfalls of overgeneralization. Sutherland's differential association and learning theory, for example, successfully related learning theory to sociological discoveries concerning group behavior. And yet the promise of the middle range is even greater than Sutherland's contribution. An even larger number of variables may be considered in the continued development of a theory of crime causation which combines and recasts man's theorizing concerning juvenile and adult deviant behavior.

Because theories of causation must be able to explain crime in all its forms and in all regions of the world, attempts to explain crime in theoretical terms are far from the generic level. The value of the middle-range theory rests with its attempt to integrate data, knowledge, and hypotheses concerning human normative and deviant behavior into a coherent whole, an effort which may lead in time to the articulation of a near-generic theoretical explanation of human conduct. The mere acknowledgment that vast numbers of the population engage in delinquency as part of their "normal" adolescent socialization suggests that much of what we call deviance may in some way be rather common youthful experiences, especially among young males emerging into manhood. However, this simple recognition has received little consideration to date in most theories of causation.

Middle-range theory is not easily formulated. It must integrate many divergent facts into a coherent explanation of causation. Consequently, the emergence of sound middle-range theory depends upon a recognition of the rules of theory building which include, according to George Homans, the following principles:[1]

---

[1] George C. Homans, *The Human Group* (New York: Harcourt, Brace & World, Inc., 1950), pp. 16–17.

1. Look first at the obvious, the familiar, the common.
2. State the obvious in its full generality.
3. Talk about one thing at a time.
4. Cut down as far as you dare the number of things you are talking about.
5. Once you have started to talk, do not stop until you are finished.
6. Recognize that your analysis must be abstract because it deals with only a few elements of the concrete situation.

The relation of theory and research

Although such rules are easy to identify, the integration of social facts into a coherent theoretical model is much harder to achieve. First, social facts have to be discovered and tested. Only then can they add to the scientific quality of the theorizing taking place. In short, the development of sound theory, whether *ad hoc,* middle range, or generic, must take place in a dynamic relationship with empirical research. However, this process must include more than a passive testing and verification of hypotheses and/or theory. Social research and theory are intertwined. Empirical research must assist in the molding of theory through initiating, reformulating, deflecting, and clarifying hypotheses. Therefore, in some instances research findings may stimulate the development of social theory; at others, they may merely serve as a symbolic statement of human behavior. Moreover, empirical research tends to press for the extension of theory through its presentation of new facts which may not fully coincide with established theoretical postulates.

As new research procedures develop and as they shift the focus of interest to the frontier of new investigations, they potentially possess a major theoretical impact. As this occurs, the empirical researcher is forced to formulate and clarify his concepts in order to gather meaningful data possessing long-term consequence. Explicitly formulated theory does not invariably precede empirical inquiry; the sequence is often reversed, and theory and research, Robert Merton maintains, possess reciprocal roles which hold important consequences for the eventual articulation of middle-range or even generic theory.[2]

TOWARD AN INTEGRATED THEORY OF DELINQUENCY–CRIME CAUSATION

The findings resulting from the interaction of theory and research, presented in Chapters 11, 12, and 13, necessitate further delinquency-

---

[2] Robert K. Merton, *Social Theory and Social Structure* (Glencoe: Free Press, 1957), pp. 103–17.

crime theoretical reformulations. The many insights offered by these theorists reveal that present hypotheses are incomplete and tend to be *ad hoc* rather than middle-range conceptions of delinquent-criminal conduct. However, any attempt to integrate these findings into a more coherent theoretical system must consider the contributions of a variety of contemporary social theorists before any further recasting of theory is attempted. Although several ideas of Robert K. Merton have already found specific application in several theories, his ideas of structural-functionalism and manifest (intended) and latent (unintended) functions warrant further development. Similarly, George Homans' insights into the character of the small group and "elementary" social interaction and Talcott Parsons' conception of the social system deserve further attention. Even the processes involved in making and in consolidating a decision, examined by Leon Festinger, must be added to those ingredients which may eventually form a coherent middle-range theory of delinquent-criminal behavior. While each offers a distinct perspective, each still remains a fundamental insight into generalized aspects of human endeavor.

Elements of an integrated theory: structural-functionalism

The contributions of Merton to theories of delinquency and crime causation are many. He has observed that some proponents of functional analysis believe that standardized social activities or cultural items are functional for the entire social or cultural system, that all such social and cultural items fulfill sociological functions, and that these items are consequently indispensable. But Merton has clearly shown that the assumption of the complete functional unity of society is not always valid. In fact, it is often the case that some social sentiments or usages may be functional for some groups and dysfunctional for others in the same society. Such variations disprove the assumed unity of the society. The assumption that some practices are indispensable various functional alternatives, functional equivalents, or functional substitutes may replace existing functions.

Moreover, *manifest* (intended or recognized) functions, those objective consequences contributing to the adjustment or adaptation of the system, may yield *latent* (unintended and unrecognized) functions which may undermine or challenge the functional nature of the existing social system.[3] A change in one dimension, Merton recognizes in his differentiation of manifest and latent functions, may issue in unanticipated modifications in another phase of the system. For example, data from past decades indicate that the hardening of narcotic laws, designed

---

[3] *Ibid.*, pp. 25–51.

to lessen the narcotic traffic, latently resulted in an increase in costs of narcotic fixes, or increase in the percentage of narcotics offenders incarcerated in federal prisons and a negative public reaction to the harshness of antimarijuana laws. Therefore, as Merton writes, "to seek social change without due recognition of the manifest and latent functions performed by the social organization undergoing change is to indulge in social ritual rather than social engineering."[4] To ignore the manifest and latent functions (or their equivalents) of a system in the enactment of social change only heightens the risk of failure at the time such change in inaugurated. The social functions of an organization, Merton argues, help to determine the structure, including the recruitment of personnel involved in the structure, "just as the structure helps determine the effectiveness with which the functions are fulfilled."[5] Although the business group and the criminal group are distant from each other in terms of status, they often share similar functional organizational forms. "Structure," Merton says, "affects function and function affects structure."[6]

In many instances, social structures exert definite pressures upon some persons to participate in nonconforming rather than conforming conduct. Although every culture defines goals, purposes, and interests which are recommended as legitimate objectives for all or for differentially located members of society and which regulate and control the acceptable modes for reaching such goals, these phases of the social structure remain in a form of effective equilibrium as long as the individuals conforming to such cultural constraints receive satisfactions from these achievement goals and from the institutionally available means by which to achieve them. If persons do not derive satisfactions, they will tend to work for a change in the rules for gaining these ends. As a result, much deviating behavior may be interpreted sociologically, according to Merton, as a symptom of *dissociation* between (1) culturally prescribed aspirations and (2) socially structured avenues for realizing these aspirations. If the culturally acceptable avenue for reaching satisfactions is unavailable to particular group members, the most effective procedure for reaching these ends, whether legitimate or illegitimate, may replace institutionally preferred and prescribed conduct. At such periods, society may become unstable and individuals become anomic or normless, leading to personal demoralization or social deinstitutionalization. Individual adaptation within such a social context, therefore, may take the form of conformity, innovation, ritualism, retreatism, or rebellion. The social structure, whatever the form of response made by the individual, is highly instrumental in producing a strain toward anomie (normlessness)

---

[4] *Ibid.*, p. 81.
[5] *Ibid.*, p. 81.
[6] *Ibid.*, p. 82.

and deviant behavior. Consequently, the imperfect coordination of the goals-end-means phases of the social structure leads to anomie.[7]

In these and many other similar instances, men may define situations, whether real or not, as real, thereby having them become real in their consequences.[8] This theorem of W. I. Thomas, Merton believes, offers a continuing reminder that men respond both to the objective features of the situation and also to the meaning that such an event possesses for them. Once they have assigned some meaning to a particular situation, their consequent behavior and some of the consequences of that behavior are partially determined by the ascribed meaning of the event.[9] As a result, this recognition is a form of self-fulfilling prophecy which permits either a false or a correct definition of a situation to emerge as a true conception upon which future conduct is based. For example, if a legislature defines all sex offenders as a social threat, each sex offender, regardless of his apparent social threat, will be treated as a major criminal. Therefore, operation of self-fulfilling prophecy causes many citizens to maintain the validity of questionable laws, demand punishment in situations where punishment has little deterrent effect, find more crime where criminal deviance may have always existed, and call any meaningful move toward rehabilitation a form of coddling criminals. Merton says, "Only when the original assumption is questioned and a new definition of the situation is introduced does the consequent flow of events give the lie to the assumption. Only then does the belief no longer father reality."[10] Self-fulfilling prophecy, an example of fears being translated into reality, operates, Merton observes, "only in the absence of deliberate institutional controls."[11]

Elements of an integrated theory: Social interactionism

Small groups, George Homans contends, are the only elements which give sociohistorical continuity during periods of social disintegration, whether in the form of disruption or of elimination of trades, guilds, classes, religions, nations, empires, cultures, or civilizations. The group is a dynamic social equilibrium which possesses true uniformities in activity, interaction, sentiment, and norms. While *activity* refers to what group members do, *interaction* relates to the relation of one member to another. The idea of *sentiment* suggests the sum of interior feelings in norms or in codes of behavior which groups adopt. Because the forces which affect behavior are in a constant state of mutual dependence, in-

---

[7] *Ibid.*, pp. 132–59.
[8] *Ibid.*, p. 421.
[9] *Ibid.*, p. 422.
[10] *Ibid.*, p. 424.
[11] *Ibid.*, p. 436.

dividual actions, Homans contends, will be influenced by feelings within the group which have no direct bearing on a group's relation to the environment. The stability of society is founded to a great extent upon the vigor and durability of small groups.

Each group participates in an *external* system (involving relations between a group and its environment) which effects its behavior in an *internal* system (referring to those group sentiments toward another which have implications for behavior). Consequently, the small group is in effect a social system whose parts are mutually interdependent and which reacts with its environment as a self-adjusting organization of response. What acts and what reacts, Homans believes, is not a single part or function or a combination of parts or functions of the social system but rather the system as a whole, which is a system of mutual interdependence.

According to Homans, the activities, interactions, and sentiments of group members and the mutual relations of these elements while the group is active compose the social system that exists in some form of environment,[12] whether the physical, the technical, or the social. Although all are interrelated, one aspect of environment may be more important than others for a particular group. While the environment places limits upon behavior, the actual form that interaction takes depends to a large degree upon the activity, interaction, sentiment, and norms of members of participant groups. The *external system,* therefore, is that state and interrelationship of sentiment, activity, and interaction which provide solutions to particular problems. The external system, the relation between group and environment, is a circular relationship of action and reaction.[13]

The *internal system,* not directly conditioned by the environment, simultaneously emerges from within the external system and reacts upon it. Consequently, while the external system permits groups to survive in its environment, the internal system, a product of life together, is an expression of members' toward one another. Like the external system, the internal system is also a system because it is also expressed in the three forms of activity, sentiment, and interaction. The more frequently men interact with one another, the more likely, Homans believes, they are to hold similar norms, share similar sentiments, and participate in similar activities. Although they may share a sense of variation among persons or subgroups, group members are nevertheless "more nearly alike in the norms they hold than in their overall behavior."[14] Because norms are a product of ongoing activities, participants in activities tend

---

[12] Homans, *op. cit.,* p. 17.
[13] *Ibid.,* p. 90.
[14] *Ibid.,* pp. 109–26.

to converge upon such norms. The more frequently persons interact with each other, the stronger, Homans suggests, will be their sentiments of friendship for the other. Those persons who feel the sentiments of liking one another will also express those sentiments and activities "over and above the activities of the external system."[15]

Elements of an integrated theory: The social system

The social system, Talcott Parsons perceives, is only one of three ways in which social action is structured. Although personality systems and cultural systems also possess major importance, the *social system*, represented as a distinct sociological form deserves, according to Parsons, major attention.[16] While society is fundamentally a system of interaction, the relationship between actors within society represent the structure of the system. Each actor is located in society in relationship to status and role. Status locates the individual relative to other participant actors; roles define the various tasks he is to perform. Because the social system is antecedent to the individual actor, central emphasis must be placed upon the collectivity as a composite whole rather than upon the actor as a composite unit. Therefore, the stability and the orderly development of a social system depend upon the meeting of the minimum needs of the majority of actors, the maintenance of a minimum control over potentially disruptive behavior, and the continued internalization of a level of personality adequate for participation within a social system.[17]

Individuals who act out status-roles also share normatively ordered ideas and beliefs. However, value orientations may take many pattern alternatives in relation to the multiple types of institutionalization available within a social system. Although the actor in any given action strives to attain maximum gratification, an action system can only be organized or integrated if its actors renounce some of their gratification goals. The actor cannot realistically want everything. He must be neutral about some items. However, his basic interest will be determined in large degree in relationship to whether he is pursuing his own private interest or an interest that he shares with others.

Overall, five paired value orientation pattern alternatives, Parsons finds, define patterns of relational role expectation. *Affectivity versus affective neutrality* refers to the norms which permit or prohibit immediate expression of the emotions or needs of particular social actors. *Self-orientation versus collectivity orientation* suggests the problem of pursuing private interests or sharing common goals with others. *Universalism versus particularism* describes the problem of whether the

---

[15] *Ibid.*, p. 134.
[16] Talcott Parsons, *The Social System* (Glencoe: Free Press, 1951), pp. 7–19.
[17] *Ibid.*, pp. 26–27.

primacy of cognitive values may imply a universalistic standard of role expectation or whether the primacy of appreciative value suggests a particularistic standard in which action is determined either through ideas or through feelings. *Achievement versus ascription,* on the other hand, questions whether one values the other party within the social action because of what he is (ascription) or what he does (achievement). The problem of *specificity versus diffuseness,* which refers to the scope of the ego's interest in the object, opens to each actor the opportunity for defining his role in specific or in diffuse terms. Because these five pattern variables may be grouped in many combinations, role expectation patterns on the relational level may take some 32 different forms and result in a variety of social actions within the social system.[18]

Elements of an integrated theory: Cognitive dissonance

Despite these many alternatives, individuals within any action or social system are faced with real or seeming inconsistencies which are frequently invisible to the actor but visible to the objective observer. Because *dissonance* (inconsistency) is psychologically uncomfortable, it will motivate the person, Leon Festinger hypothesizes, to try to reduce the dissonance and to achieve consonance (consistency). If dissonance is present, the individual will actively avoid situations and information which would likely increase the dissonance.[19] Consequently, the existence of nonfitting relations among cognitions motivates individuals to reduce dissonance and to seek consonance. Because cognition refers to any knowledge, opinion, or belief about the environment, one's self, or one's behavior, cognitive dissonance covers a wide range of behavior and refers to an antecedent condition which stimulates an activity toward reduction of such dissonance. Through such a process, persons, Festinger maintains, often do things that seem irrational or hold opinions that are seemingly inconsistent with their normal attitudes.

Dissonance tends to occur when new events or new information create a momentary inconsistency in existing knowledge, opinion, or cognition concerning behavior or when similar contradictions inherent in social situations, despite the absence of new and unforseen events or information, disturb existing patterns of consonance. In some instances, the need to establish consonance may motivate a person simply to change his cognition about his behavior (*i.e.,* justify his shoplifting on the grounds that everybody else is also doing it). He emphasizes the basic value of the event to his person and lessens the emphasis upon the risk

---

[18] *Ibid.,* pp. 60–66.

[19] Leon Festinger, *A Theory of Cognitive Dissonance* (Stanford, Calif.: Stanford University Press, 1957), p. 3. Festinger is not without his critics which include Osgood, Rosenberg, Newcomb, and others. Consult psychological literature for a detailed analysis and criticisms.

or the penalty which may result if he continues the same behavior. Because one's sense of reality impinges upon his person, it will exert pressures, Festinger believes, to bring the appropriate cognitive elements into line with their reality.

Although cognitions are not fully relative to others, where relative cognitions and relationships do exist, the problems of dissonance and consonance resolution remain. Elements are dissonant if they do not fit together for one reason or another. They are consonant, on the other hand, when they uphold the consistency of each other. However, dissonance is determined to a large degree by motivations and desired consequences and may be irrelevant if such motivations and consequences are not desired. Dissonance, Festinger believes, can emerge from logical inconsistencies, differences in cultural mores, an emphasis upon one specific opinion, the inclusion of one specific opinion by definition within a more general opinion, or one's past experience.[20] Because not all dissonant relations are of equal magnitude, when two elements are dissonant the magnitude of the dissonance will be a function of the importance of the elements. If two cognitive elements are either dissonant or consonant and yet the magnitude of the dissonance or consonance increases as the importance of the value of the elements increases, the total amount of dissonance which exists between two clusters of cognitive elements is a function of the weighted proportions of all relevant relations between the two clusters that are dissonant.[21]

While the existence of dissonance encourages the rise of pressures to reduce or eliminate dissonance, the strength of these pressures is related to the magnitude of the dissonance itself. As a result, the greater the dissonance, the greater the intensity of action to reduce dissonance and to avoid situations which will increase dissonance.[22] Where dissonance does exist, it is most easily eliminated by changing one of the elements causing dissonance. It may be possible in some instances to change environmental cognitions by modifying the situation in which that element exists. However, it is easier, Festinger contends, to change the social rather than the physical environment in order to reduce dissonance. At other times, it may become important to change some cognitive element by adding new cognitive developments which may reduce existing dissonances. However, the individual may resist attempts to reduce dissonance because the change may be painful or involve a loss, because present behavior may be generally satisfying, or because change may be simply impossible.[23] Consequently, the theory of cognitive dissonance, Festinger states, recognizes that:

[20] *Ibid.*, pp. 3–14.
[21] *Ibid.*, pp. 16–18.
[22] *Ibid.*, p. 18.
[23] *Ibid.*, pp. 25–26.

1. Dissonant or "nonfitting" relations among noncognitive elements may exist.
2. The existence of dissonance gives rise to pressures to reduce the dissonance and to avoid increases in dissonance.
3. Manifestations of the operation of these pressures include behavior changes, changes of cognition, and circumspect exposure to new information and new opinions.[24]

Although dissonance is an "inevitable consequence" of a decision, the magnitude of the postdecision dissonance, Festinger believes, depends upon the importance of the decision, the relative attractiveness of the unchosen alternative to the chosen decision, and the degree of overlap of cognitive elements corresponding to the alternative. The pressure to reduce dissonance following a decision will stimulate an increase in the relative attractiveness of the chosen alternative, a decrease of the relative attractiveness of the unchosen alternative, an establishment of cognitive overlap, or possibly a psychological revocation of the decision. Consequently, following a decision, the decision maker actively seeks out information which produces a consonant cognition with the action assumed. At the same time, one's confidence in the decision or sense of discrepancy in the attractiveness of alternatives involved in the choice tend to increase. The successful reduction of postdecision dissonance, therefore, makes it exceedingly difficult to reverse this decision once made.[25] Eventually, dissonance may be reduced by a subsequent change of private opinion or by the magnification of reward or punishment in order to develop increased consonance with one's overt conduct. Throughout one's life, however, dissonance-reducing cognition is sought while dissonance-increasing cognition is avoided.[26]

AN INTEGRATED MIDDLE-RANGE THEORY OF DELINQUENT AND CRIMINAL BEHAVIOR: A THEORY OF RELATIVITY[27]

The definition, character, and incidence of delinquency and crime are relative to the cultural, social, small-group and personality factors and forces which shape and produce them.

---

[24] *Ibid.*, p. 31.
[25] *Ibid.*, pp. 47–83.
[26] *Ibid.*, pp. 260–66.
[27] This theory is proposed by Richard D. Knudten. He acknowledges the contributions of Vernon Fox of Florida State University, Daniel Glaser of the University of Southern California, George Homans of Harvard, and Stephen Schafer of Northwestern University; of his Valparaiso colleagues William Cross, LeRoy Martinson, and Nancy Sederberg; and his undergraduate and graduate students from the fall, 1969, in the reformulation of this theory.

I. Relativity and culture

1. *The definition, character, and incidence of delinquency and crime, while often similar in a number of other cultures, are relative.* Whatever their context, they are interactional products of environmental, cultural, societal, associational, small-group, and personality factors. Societal reaction to delinquent or criminal behavior depends upon the definition of criminal deviance; the time, place, and situation of its occurrence; and the person(s) involved. Although norms are delimited by culture, different segments of society will modify many norms to make them more relevant and realistic for their members.

2. *Because delinquency and crime are by definition violations of some normative legal code, they are relative to normative social definitions.* Normative content, however, varies in relationship to such factors as:

   a) Social class.
   b) Subcultural, occupational, and religious commitments.
   c) Political preferences.
   d) Familial characteristics.
   e) Economic capabilities.
   f) Ethnic and racial membership.
   g) Geographic region.
   h) Community characteristics.
   i) Educational achievements.

3. *The distinction between serious and less serious defenses is relative.* So-called serious crimes may be products of accidents and so-called less serious offenses may produce fatal results. How they will be processed will depend upon the victim-offender relationship, the degree of seriousness attached to the act, the value of the target imagined and evaluated by legislators, the philosophy of law enforcement in the area, and the like.

4. *Although crimes of young adults are specific violations of the criminal code, offenses of juvenile delinquents, while also specified in law, are generally more extensive and cover behavior often permitted adults.* Juveniles in the United States, for example, may be detained for running away from home or entering a bar. Such "offenses" may be defined and be processed in a completely different manner in other cultural or national areas.

5. *The number of delinquent and criminal offenses known to the police are only a fraction of the total volume of such violations.* More violations occur than are ever detected by law enforcement

personnel. Consequently, those apprehended, judged, and sentenced represent only a sample of the total volume of continuing offenders.

6. *Every cultural system is composed of multiple normative and deviant subsystems.* What system(s) the individual participates in will be determined in large degree by opportunity and status factors over which the person has little control during his childhood. His delinquency is closely related to a lack of social planning and social organization and a lessened emphasis upon the family sociocultural unit. However, the family in many instances may be supportive of delinquency and crime.

7. *For some persons within a social or cultural system, crime is a functional act for attaining major social and cultural goals.* What is functional to one person or group is often dysfunctional to another.

8. *Delinquency is often a product of social roles provided and supported within a subculture of delinquency.* However, the placement and maintenance of youth in asymetrical roles and subordinate statuses may also result in juvenile humiliation and attempts to express manhood.

9. *Subcultures of deviance may be of different types.* Subcultures of *delinquency* (sometimes called contracultures) may be partially described in terms of the following ideal types which are defined in relationship to existing opportunity structures:

    a) Criminal subcultures (*i.e.*, gangs oriented to theft, extortion).
    b) Retreatist subcultures (*i.e.*, drug).
    c) Conflict subcultures (*i.e.*, manipulative violence).

    Among the clearly *adult* subcultures of criminality are the (*a*) *confederational* or *organized* and (*b*) *professional* in addition to the adult variations of the three juvenile subcultures mentioned above.

    On another level, a subculture of *violence,* composed of a cluster of values related to life styles, to the socialization process, and to interpersonal relations, also exists in some regions or among some group(s).

10. *Where delinquent and criminal conduct are more a product of cultural rather than personality factors, decreased functioning of normative social controls, increased value conflicts, and greater social disorganization are likely to exist.* Some slum dwellers rationalize their situation in a form of "inverted snobbery" and express a preference for slum living despite existing deficiencies in social control, value conflicts, and social disorganization. However, delinquency and crime may also exist and grow in areas where these problems do not exist in the

same degree. The lower volume of *reported* suburban delinquency is most likely due to lessened reporting of deviance in such areas as compared with those of high social disorganization or blight.

11. *Some delinquent behavior is an anticipated outcome of "normal" adolescent socialization.* Inasmuch as the process of socialization includes cognition and the application of skills as well as learning through trial and error, delinquent conduct, especially among males, may be expected as juveniles mature. Much of this potential delinquency goes undetected and unreported, leaving the major unanswered questions: By what process do delinquents overcome their deviance and assume normative patterns? Are current procedures for identifying, processing, and treating delinquency hindrances or aids to the overcoming of juvenile deviance?

12. *Because the totality of culture is always greater than the individual or group's ability to comprehend and command that culture, delinquent and criminal groups will reveal distinct cultural patterns which are not found to the same degree among the more norm-maintaining elements of society.* Because those elements which compose the deviant system are also available to each member of the larger social group, persons largely unintegrated into deviant systems may utilize them in delinquency or crime. What norms are accepted will be largely determined by the factor of social class.

13. *Social factors act selectively upon delinquents who possess or are excessively exposed to certain personal traits and/or who belong to certain stigmatized ascriptive categories.* These include the traits and categories of:

   a) Hostility.
   b) Unconventionality.
   c) Feeling of being unappreciated.
   d) Sense of parental inadequacy.
   e) Defensive maternal attitudes.
   f) Family financial dependence.
   g) Unstable home life.
   h) Lack of familial and personal self-respect.
   i) Physical impairment.

   Delinquent conduct is related to differential exposure to ascribed environmental factors as well as to the differential association of youth with delinquency-prone groups.

14. *Male juveniles often engage in "conspicuous masculinity," proving their manhood by malicious and destructive acts.* Lower-class focal concern for trouble, toughness, smartness, excitement,

autonomy, and fate underlies a disproportionate part of its deviant conduct. These focal concerns, however, may or may not encourage deviant conduct. If such concerns (or values) are channeled effectively into normative ends, normative conduct may be expected. In addition, the same focal concerns may be expressed in many different ways by members of the various social classes.

15. *As the distance between social classes narrows forms of class delinquency and crime will become less well defined.* As lower-class juveniles, for example, transmit their concerns to middle-class youth, norm-violating behavior in a form common to lower-class youth may become more prevalent among these youth and vice versa. Lower-class mobility has created status inconsistency and blurred the boundaries of class delinquency.

16. *The volume of delinquency and crime will tend to increase in direct relationship to such factors as:*
   a) The number of adolescents and young adults in the population.
   b) The volume of new legislation relating to delinquency and crime.
   c) The ease with which such deviance may be committed.
   d) The supply of produced consumer goods.
   e) The number and efficiency of law enforcement personnel and the philosophy of enforcement.
   f) The character and efficiency of justice in the courts.
   g) The public's concern for delinquency and crime.
   h) The structured strain between ideals and institutional means for reaching these goals.
   i) The methods used to record these offenses.
   j) Pressures in favor of deviance within one's peer groups.
   k) The nature of parent-child relationships.
Each of these factors is relative to a particular cultural system.

II. Relativity and social organization

17. *While the social functions of a deviant organization help to determine the structure of that organization, the structure helps to determine the eventual effectiveness of the deviant functions of that organization.* Each function and organization is influenced or shaped in relation to the other and is, in effect, an interaction product.

18. *Some delinquency and crime functions are manifest (intended) and others are latent (unintended) consequences of a completed action.* Each planned action may possess both expected and un-

expected consequences. Inasmuch as all functions are performed in a social equilibrium at the time of enactment, a change in one element of a functional normative or deviant system will result in the modification of other facets of the same system. Similar changes will also occur if the existing social equilibrium is composed of a dysfunctional normative or deviant system.

19. *Social structures frequently exert pressures upon some persons, especially the poorly socialized, to participate in nonconforming rather than conforming actions.* Because delinquent or criminal social groups are fundamentally systems of interaction, the relationship between the actors within that group represent the structure of the social system.

20. *Deviant and normative social structures are composed of role relationships which include role transactions and sequences of role bargains.* The latter refer to interacting individuals who strive to resolve the common strains of overdemanding roles within the group setting. Because the individual's total role obligations are highly idealized and overdemanding, they are frequently ambivalent, contradictory, inconsistent, or conflicting and involve him in participation in deviant and normative social structures which are composed of interindividual transactions and accommodations which result in relative stabilities of expectations and behavior patterns.

21. *Each actor is located within the delinquent-criminal group in terms of status roles.* While *status* locates the individual in the group or in a society in relation to other participant actors, *roles* define the various tasks he is to perform. If the delinquent or criminal offender's status is low, he may complete legal or illegal acts to achieve status goals. If his status is high, he may respond to peer pressures or other forces. The greater the lower-class domination of the community, the greater the chances of a delinquent life for boys of any social status. Delinquency and crime, however, cannot be correlated with a condition of poverty.

22. *The stability and the orderly development of the delinquent-criminal social system depend upon the meeting of a minimum number of needs for a majority of actors, the maintenance of a minimum of control over potentially disruptive behavior, and the continued internalization of a personality level adequate for one's participation within that system.* The amount of functional or actual crime will tend to vary according to the total number of opportunities available for normative or delinquent-criminal conduct and the tendency of a social system to support such conduct.

23. *Delinquency and crime are potential status equalizers in a competitive society.* The skilled and unskilled, the intelligent and the less intelligent, and the rich and the poor, for example, are able to compete actively in achieving status goals. In the United States, both delinquency and crime tend to be consistent with a cultural emphasis upon competition and achievement. Culture prescribes rewards for those who compete successfully and frequently penalizes those who do not or who attempt to circumvent institutionalized norms for attaining status goals.

24. *As individuals, delinquents and criminals reveal a tendency to seek immediate gratification and an inability or unwillingness to defer their desires for fulfillment.* Although most actors in any given situation strive to attain maximum gratification, an action system can only be organized or integrated if its actors renounce some of their gratification goals. Gangs, confederational or organized-crime groups, and professional offenders seem to be the most successful in motivating individuals to defer their desires for immediate gratification.

25. *The basic delinquent-criminal interests of the juvenile or adult offender are determined in large degree by whether he is pursuing his own private interest or one which he shares with others.* However, an inconsistency in institutions may also encourage the nature and the direction of the youth's interests. For example, the early selection of students for future work training in England leads to greater dissociation, fatalism, and self-fulfillment through leisure. Later selection in the United States may encourage alienation through the continuation of unrealistic ambitions. Consequently, the educational system, which has not changed to any great extent with the advent of automation, has become a major irritant to a large proportion of youth. Delinquency is frequently more serious among those in school than peers who have dropped out.

III. Relativity and the small group

26. *Socialization to delinquency and crime generally occurs in small groups which share a dynamic social equilibrium and possess true uniformities in activity (what group members do), interaction (relation of one member to another), and sentiment (sum of interior feelings or codes of behavior which groups adopt).*

27. *Each delinquent or criminal group participates within an external system (relationship between group and environment) and an internal system (group sentiments to another which have implications for behavior).* Each system, external or internal,

consists of activity, interaction, and sentiment. While the environment affecting the deviating group's *external system* may be primarily physical, technical, social, or a combination thereof, the *internal system* of the deviating group emerges from within the external system and reacts upon it. What acts and reacts is not a single part or function or a combination of parts or functions but the mutually interdependent system as a whole.

28. *When men interact within a delinquent or criminal group or system, they are more likely to hold similar norms, believe themselves to be distinct from other persons or subgroups, and participate in similar activities.* Peer discipline serves to establish order in disorder, although the new order may be radically opposed to legal codes and middle-class values. While the degree of individual participation within such a group or system varies in intensity, priority, duration, and frequency, individual actions will be frequently influenced by feelings within the group which have no *direct* bearing on the group's relation to its environment.

29. *The size and nature of the delinquent or criminal group are variable and relative.* The possibility that a few youth will complete a delinquent act depends upon the characteristics of the other members of the friendship dyad or triad. In other instances, the scope of delinquency will depend upon the character of the larger social unit. Although many play groups or gangs do not participate in delinquency, others encourage its development through undifferentiated play life. However, the larger delinquent social units reveal more specific characteristics and associational patterns. The gangs (also known as "near-groups") that engage in conflict or "rumbles" do so in order to demonstrate manhood and they generate cohesion and personal and group identity. Such groups are generally characterized by diffuse role definitions, limited cohesion, impermanence, minimal consensus of norms, shifting membership, disturbed leadership, and limited membership expectations. All gangs are a social device which allows youth to find the power necessary for manhood through interaction with peers. Street-corner groups tend to deprecate adult authority and conventional conduct, emphasize readiness for physical combat, reject school discipline, accept sexual aggression, and participate willingly in delinquency.

30. *Although inherited physical characteristics are the raw material from which personality is formed through a process of socialization in mutliple social groups, most crimes are products of all the processes involved in learning.* Deviant actions are partially

a product of personal attitudes, imitation processes, reference group commitments and associational relationships. New attitudes, motives, drives, and rationalizations are created through learning, usually in relationship to definitions of legitimate and illegitimate conduct. On the other hand, some delinquency and crimes, as in the case of the mental defective or senile adult, are a consequence of incomplete or inadequate socialization; and still other a result of passion and emotion which lessens rational-normative personality controls.

IV. Relativity and the individual

31. *Some delinquency or crime may be a substitute or symbolic expression of a repressed personality structure and may be a product of guilt or anxiety resulting from a conflict in the unconscious mind.* Other forms, however, are a result of faulty socialization or the failure to develop a meaningful sense of socioethical responsibility. Consequently, delinquency and crime causes are relative in relation to physical, psychological, social psychological, and sociological factors.

32. *The processes of stigmatization and alienation play an important part in the development of delinquent or criminal personalities.* Once stigmatization of a youth as "bad" or an adult as "criminal" occurs, the person may become fully alienated and increasingly isolated, and may become dependent upon the security offered by persons with similar problems and interests. In order to overcome the alienation components of powerlessness, meaninglessness (confusion), normlessness (inadequacy of approved norms), isolation (feeling of separation from society), and self-estrangement (inadequate rewarding activities for the integration of life), the violator may seek a new normative security with deviant persons or deviant groups.

33. *Deviating behavior in the form of delinquency and crime may also be a product of dissociation between culturally prescribed aspirations, and socially structured avenues for realizing these aspirations.* When cultural constraints produce satisfactions for the individual, they will tend to be upheld. When achievement goals and the institutionalized means by which to achieve them no longer coincide, new rules may be devised by persons or groups for reaching these ends. In such instances youths and adults will seek out both illegitimate and legitimate means to reach such goals.

34. *Because delinquents and criminals are unable to accept continued tension and/or conflict throughout their lives, they will*

make every effort to reduce dissonance (inconsistency). This may be done through the neutralization of conventional norms or through the development of new deviant commitments which are reinforced by new norms. If neutralization occurs, it may take the form of offender denial of responsibility, denial of injury, denial of the victim, condemning of the condemnors, or an appeal to higher loyalties.

Dissonance is created when new events or new information create a momentary inconsistency with existing knowledge, opinions, or cognitions. Human decision making is influenced not only by the nature of the events or information but the channel through which they are received. Irrelevant information is usually treated as no information at all.

35. *The move to lessen dissonance (inconsistency) and achieve consonance (consistency) will include attempts of the delinquent or criminal to avoid situations or information which produce or increase dissonance and to unify one's cognition about one's self, one's behavior, and one's environment.* However, the desire to reduce dissonance will often produce attitudes and actions which are frequently irrational and inconsistent with the person's previous behavior patterns. Adolescents and adults may specifically associate with gangs or groups of criminals in order to reduce dissonance and to reinforce consonance. However, many will merely drift in commitments, making the condition of drift a commitment in itself. Drift also makes infractions possible by removing restraints and permitting a minimum feeling of guilt. Norms may similarly be contained and rendered ineffective.

36. *Because the delinquent or criminal's sense of reality will bring pressures to bear upon his person to bring appropriate cognitive elements into line, the situations which are real in their consequences will be those which persons define as real.* Following a decision favorable to committing an offense, the decision maker actively seeks out information which produces a consonant cognition with the action decided upon. As a result, the questioning of the original decision to violate tends to decrease, making it more difficult to reverse the decision once it has been made. Dissonance-reducing cognition is sought while dissonance-increasing cognition is avoided.

37. *Delinquents or criminals who become personally demoralized or socially deinstitutionalized may adapt to their social context through:*
   a) Innovation.
   b) Ritualism (often called overconformity).

c) Retreatism or withdrawal.

d) Isolation.

e) Rebellion or aggression.

Whatever the response, it is influential in relieving a condition of anomie (non-belonging, rootlessness, normlessness).

38. *Although the greater number of juveniles overcome delinquent tendencies, many continue into adult crime.* Once entrance is made into a system of juvenile or adult justice, the institutional system tends to retain many offenders within its limits through the ensuing stigmatization of the offender and institutional maintenance processes. Those coming to the attention of, and remaining within, the system of justice represent only a sample of the total volume of criminal deviance.

39. *The violator's success or failure in overcoming delinquency and crime depends in large degree upon his ability to bargain and upon his assets in the interactional negotiated exchange process.* All persons do not share equal skills, status, and prestige and are, therefore, not subject to the processes of justice to the same degree. As a result, those most likely to continue in criminal conduct are those individuals who are most dissimilar from the model projected in criminal law and who have limited negotiating reserviors.

V. Conclusion

Delinquency and crime are relative and depend upon the situation in which criminal norms and action are located as defined by the cultural environment, the person's tendency to ignore or to neutralize limits placed upon his actions by his social status and class, his ability to resist pressures which call for violation placed upon him by his group roles, and his tendency toward action as determined by his individual personality.

Part FOUR

Formal systems of social control

Chapter 15

THE SYSTEM OF LAW
ENFORCEMENT

Although what may have been one of the first "police" organizations emerged around 1340 B.C. when Hur Moheb created a rigorous security unit to guarantee safety against piracy on the Nile, the development of the modern police agency has been relatively recent.[1] An early version of a police force arose in the British Isles during the early Middle Ages within the Anglo-Saxon form of community organization. Security around 800 A.D. was maintained through a system of tens, tithings, and hundreds. Ten families constituted a *tithing*, which chose its security representative; ten tithings formed a hundred, which in turn elected a reeve as its head. Several hundreds likewise composed a county or shire with the shire reeve (sheriff) responsible for security in the larger community. Despite the fact that the Norman invasion under William the Conqueror in 1066 stimulated many social changes, this basic system of tens, tithings and hundreds was continued. However, all able-bodied men, in addition, were enjoined to pursue criminal suspects in the "hue and cry," and to contain disturbances, detain suspicious persons, and interrogate strangers after dark in "watch and ward" duty.

The subsequent growth of metropolitan society introduced new changes in these police procedures. The night watch and special police patrols to protect business places, wharves, and other potentially dangerous areas became commonplace by the 19th century. The "Bow Street Runners," created in 1749 by the novelist and magistrate Henry Fielding to serve papers for the court, arose as the early model for the develop-

---

[1] James Cramer, *The World's Police* (London: Cassell & Co., Ltd., 1964), p. 5.

ment of the London metropolitan police in 1829.[2] While the more than 300 members of the "Runners" received a small salary, it was augmented by a system of spoils and rewards which the arresting aide received for apprehending felons or recovering stolen property.

THE EVOLUTION OF THE LONDON POLICE FORCE

A more professional police force was organized by Sir Robert Peel in London during 1829. His action, however, was not without its critics, who feared that the London Metropolitan Police Force would become a coercive control agency modeled upon the lines of the pre-Revolutionary French security force.[3] Although many, like the Whigs, were anti-police, Peel's supporters urged the creation of a police force in order to maintain public order. Arguing that statistics indicated major increases in crime in London and Middlesex during the period of the early Industrial Revolution, this trend, Peel's supporters held, could only be checked by the creation of a constraining enforcement program. Although others, like F. W. Maitland, held that British liberty did not depend, and never had depended, upon a particular form of police organization but rather upon the supremacy of Parliament and the rule of law, their arguments were generally lost to the alleged need to maintain social order.

As the English system of enforcement developed, it was diffused to other countries, especially to the English Colonies, where the "watch and ward" system became widespread. During the 19th century, Boston, for example, established a professional force, initially of six men. Later, New York similarly followed with an 800-man police force designed to maintain order. As the need for enforcement grew more apparent, additional cities and towns also formed police forces to augment their special needs.

About 1,000 police officers, stationed in six divisions, had been enrolled during the first year after the passage of the (British) Metropolitan Police Act, and the development of the force resulted in many growing pains. Because the office of the prosecutor had not yet been created, any policeman making an arrest had to undertake the prosecution in court himself. If he failed in his prosecution and was unable to pay the legal costs, he could legally be imprisoned for debt.[4] Because he lacked wide legal powers, he occupied an especially vulnerable position. Nevertheless, the Metropolitan Police, after formation, evolved into an efficient enforcement system.

---

[2] *Ibid.*, p. 18.
[3] Charles Reith, *The Police Idea: Its History and Evolution in the Eighteenth Century and After* (London: Oxford University Press, 1938), p. 188.
[4] Cramer, *op. cit.*, p. 19.

The London Metropolitan Police District currently encompasses an area of 742 square miles, which includes docks, industrial and farming areas, suburbs, palaces, and very dense residential communities. Divided into four subdistricts, each operates under a commander and includes five or six divisions which are in turn administered by a chief superintendent. While the Secretary of State for Home Affairs serves as the police authority for the Metropolitan Police District, the Commissioner of Police of the Metropolis is appointed by the Queen upon the recommendation of the Home Secretary. Ultimately, the Commissioner is responsible to Parliament for promotion, discipline, and legislative matters. In 1964, the uniformed branch of the district numbered 18,326, the CID 1,700, and the Women police 581.[5] The officers of the London Metropolitan Police District only represented a portion of the total number of enforcement officers in the British Isles. Two years earlier, for example, approximately 158 police forces served a population of 53 million in Great Britain. Thirteen of these agencies, twelve in Scotland, employed fewer than 100 officers. While 49 had between 100 and 199 persons on their force, 35 had between 500 and 599, and 15 over 1,000 employees.[6]

Each of the 51 constabularies throughout England and Wales currently remain under the jurisdiction of a chief constable who is ultimately responsible for discipline and promotion within his agency. However, he is similarly supervised by a Standing Joint Committee which consists of an equal number of justices of the peace and counselors, usually appointed by the city council. The 72 city or borough police forces are likewise commanded by a chief constable, empowered to impose punishments in the form of suspension, dismissal, fine, or reduction in rank on policemen within its area of jurisdiction, if confirmed by the Watch Committee. Ultimately, the British Home office supervises the local police through its inspectors of constabulary, who report findings concerning police efficiency to the central government. If the force meets local standards, the government supplies half the cost for its maintenance. According to existing law, national police subsidies may be terminated if any local police agency fails to fulfill its intended function.[7]

Although charged with the normal responsibilities of enforcement, the British police forces possess additional responsibility for maintenance of internal security, evacuation of the civilian population, reconnaissance

---

[5] *Ibid.*, pp. 24–25.

[6] Michael P. Banton, *The Policeman in the Community* (New York: Basic Books, Inc., Publishers, 1964), p. 89.

[7] Sidney H. Asch, *Police Authority and the Rights of the Individual* (New York: Arco Publishing Co., Inc. 1968), p. 20. Also consult J. P. Clark, "Isolation of the Police: A Comparison of British and American Situations," *Journal of Criminal Law, Criminology, and Police Science*, Vol. 56 (September, 1965), p. 307.

of roads after a nuclear attack, assistance in the control of the homeless, and the maintenance of order among the public in and near fallout areas in times of nuclear war.[8] Because the British population is generally law-abiding and both criminals and police generally believe it is to their advantage to refrain from the use of lethal force, policemen in the British Isles rarely carry guns.

Recruited candidates for the various police forces in the British Isles must normally be between 19 and 30 years of age, stand between 5 feet 8 inches and 6 feet, and have completed a standard education. Upon enrollment as a constable, the recruit is sent to a Police Training Centre in one of the eight police districts in England and Wales, or to the Metropolitan Police Force's Recruit Training School. During the 13-week period, he receives instruction in routine police duties, in the prevention and detection of crime, elementary law, physical training, lifesaving and first aid, and other pertinent aids to police work. Upon completion of the course, the recruit receives further instruction in local laws and district police practices and is given practical instruction in report writing, patrolling, and other essential enforcement responsibilities.

On probation for two years, the probationary constable returns for a two weeks' intermediate and final course during that period. Upon completion of five years service, and upon passing a qualifying examination, he becomes eligible for promotion to sergeant. Those with special capabilities are likewise eligible for promotion to detective sergeant, inspector, chief inspector, or other administrative positions.[9] A 1962 Report of the Royal Commission on the Police, appointed to evaluate the nature of the believed tension between the English police and the public, made the following suggestions:

1. Constables should be subject to more effective supervision.
2. A national police service might prove to be a more efficient instrument for fighting crime.
3. Efficient policing of an area should be transferred from police authorities to the Secretaries of State.
4. Shared costs of enforcement should be equally borne as at present between the local and national government.
5. Police authorities should be made liable for the wrongful acts of police officers.
6. Overseeing councils should be reorganized.
7. Police forces should likewise be reorganized in order to gain maximum enforcement strength.

---

[8] Cramer, *op. cit.*, p. 33. Refer to Leonard F. Field, *Police Administration: A Critical study of Police Organizations in U.S. and Abroad* (New York: G. P. Putnam's Sons, 1909).

[9] *Ibid.*, p. 37.

8. Better-educated trainees should be recruited for the police service.
9. Formal and informal relations and contacts between police and the local community should be developed as far as possible.[10]

OTHER NATIONAL POLICE SYSTEMS

The forms of enforcement organization vary throughout the world. Most European police systems are centralized under the control of the national government. Even in areas in which local government is overlapped by a national police district, the national enforcement system takes precedence. In the United States and Canada, however, enforcement is highly decentralized. Nearly all levels of government maintain independent police systems, resulting in substantial overlapping and periodic confusion in enforcement. Although agencies cooperate where possible, the lack of overall coordination in the exchange of information concerning criminal violations lessens the overall effectiveness of the American enforcement system.

The French police

In France, the *Sûreté Nationale* coordinates the national enforcement system, while the quasi-military *gendarmerie* maintains law and order in smaller towns and rural areas. The *Prefecture of Police,* including the Seine department (Paris and 80 neighboring communes) which employs some 23,000 officers and men (*agents de police*), fulfills a slightly different role. The *National Gendarmerie,* which covers all the departments of France, comprises nearly 63,000 officers and men. The Sûreté Nationale, a national police force, enrolls nearly 53,000 men and officers.[11] Each of these forces, however, remains under the administration of the French Minister of the Interior, who is ultimately responsible for order and security.

In general, the Prefecture of Police maintains order in the capital and the neighboring suburbs, the National Gendarmerie in the country districts and among the military, and the Sûreté Nationale in towns and specialized branches. While candidates with ordinary educational backgrounds may enter the Prefecture of Police as *gardiens de la paix,* holders of a university degree may apply for positions as acting *officiers de police.* More highly educated individuals, too, may apply to enter the ranks of *commissaires de police* on a "direct entry" basis. In the National Gendarmerie, the men in the lower ranks are recruited from among members of the French armed forces. All enlisted members mini-

---

[10] *Ibid.,* pp. 102–4.
[11] *Ibid.,* pp. 291–92.

mally hold a noncommissioned rank. Sûreté Nationale recruits participate in a six-month study course at a police school before being posted to one of the Republican Security Guard Companies, where they serve for several years before transfer to one of the city police forces.

The West German police

The police function in the Federal Republic of Germany (West Germany) centers around the State and Communal Police Force, the Emergency Police, the Water Police, and the Criminal Police. The State and Communal Police Forces, charged with the maintenance of security and order, also direct and supervise street traffic and prevent and detect punishable offenses. While the Emergency Police deal with disasters, riots, or other emergencies, they also function as a police recruit training agency. The Water Police, working in navigable rivers, canals, harbors, and coastal waters, enforce regulations concerning ship safety, prevent crime, and control the issuance of ship certificates or other documents. The Criminal Police, an equivalent of the British CID, are largely responsible for detective and investigative efforts. Although limited to the boundaries of the area which they serve, they are neither financed nor controlled by the Federal Republic of Germany. On the federal level, the Frontier Police Force, the largest police force in the Republic, patrols the international borders of the nation. The Federal Railway Police, responsible to the Federal Transport Minister, protects the railways, stations, and other railway establishments.[12]

The Soviet police system

The Soviet police system was established during the reign of Peter the Great (1672–1725). In 1825, Czar Nicholas I accelerated the process of police control. During the period of the czars, the Russian police collected statistics, "enforced sanitary regulations, made searches and seizures in private houses, kept thousands of 'suspects' under constant watch, read all their correspondence, took charge of dead bodies and admonished all those who neglected their religious duties."[13] By the early part of the twentieth century, the regular police had achieved control over local officials. Empowered to supervise the local community, they often worked with house porters to gain information about citizens in the houses which they served. Police control reached its height with the creation of the coercive Political or State Police which Nicholas I formed to protect his person and the security of the state.

---

[12] *Ibid.*, pp. 305–6.
[13] *Ibid.*, p. 400.

Following the Russian Revolution in 1917, an All-Russian Extraordinary Commission, known as the CHEKA, emerged to combat counterrevolution, sabotage, and public speculation. Working in close contact with the People's Commissariat of Internal Affairs (NKVD) and the People's Commissariat of Justice after 1918, the local CHEKAs operated throughout the country. In addition, the militia, attached to the local Soviets of Worker's and Peasant's Deputies, worked in concert with CHEKA forces as necessary. When the CHEKA was replaced by the State Political Administration (GPU) in 1921, its functions were supervised by the NKVD. The relationships of these organizations were later modified during the periods of political trials and purges, and their functions were assumed after 1946 by the Ministries of Internal Affairs (MVD) and State Security (MGB). When the MGB was absorbed into the MVB after the death of Stalin in 1953, many of the MVB tasks were reassigned to other government ministries. Forced labor camps, for example, were transferred to the Ministry of Justice; state highways to a new Ministry of Highways and Transportation; and eastern mines to the Ministry of Metallurgy. All state security organizations were also quickly transferred to the Committee on State Security under the Council of Ministers of the U.S.S.R. (known as KGB). Currently, the KGB maintains a counterintelligence network within the Soviet armed forces, an organization of foreign and Soviet agents, and an investigatory program directed toward infringements of state security.

Even the militia was reorganized in 1956 as a department of the Executive Committee of each Soviet. While the rights, duties, and responsibilities of the militia have since been defined in statute by the Council of Ministers, each organization is ultimately supervised by its own specific Soviet. Consequently, the militiamen are charged with diverse responsibilities, including the maintenance of public order; detention of persons apprehended in the commission of a crime; issuance of passports, visas, and permits; and investigation of accidents and reported crimes for eventual prosecution by the Procurator's Office. A People's Voluntary Militia serves as needed to augment the regular militia.[14]

The police in the Soviet Union operate within a conception of law which holds that law is an instrument for education and control rather than for guaranteeing individual freedom. Used to structure correct relationships between parents, teachers, priests, and other individuals in the state, the law is held subservient to political ideology. As a result, court procedure is informal and speedy; the judge protects the offender against the results of his ignorance and redefines the new path which he is to follow. Consequently, the rule "let the punishment fit the crime,"

---

[14] *Ibid.*, pp. 404–5.

Harold J. Berman writes, is supplemented by an added dictate, "Let the punishment fit the man."[15]

THE DEVELOPMENT OF THE INTERNATIONAL POLICE ORGANIZATION (INTERPOL)

The need for international police cooperation has led to the development of what has now become known as INTERPOL. Created from the International Criminal Police Commission, which was formed at a 1923 meeting of 138 delegates from 20 sovereign countries or territories who agreed to promote mutual assistance between cooperating criminal police authorities and to establish and develop institutions necessary or likely to contribute to efficient suppression of ordinary crime, Interpol has become an international enforcement clearinghouse. Although the I.C.P.C. achieved but limited success during the period prior to World War II, it reached new prominence in 1956 with a membership of 55 countries.

Under its revised 1956 constitution, all political, military, religious, or racial activities were placed outside the bounds of INTERPOL inquiries. Each member country operates through a national bureau organized to suppress ordinary crimes. It is usually located in the central headquarters of a particular police agency. As a cooperating police system, each bureau is responsible for forwarding all information of international interest to the secretariat; undertaking all inquiries, searches, and arrests requested by other countries within its own country; and implementing all resolutions noted by the assembly. Primarily a clearinghouse operation, INTERPOL now aids all participating nations in the centralization and exchange of information. However, if INTERPOL information aids in the discovery of a fleeing offender in a foreign country, any attempted extradition is negotiated between the native and foreign country involved.[16]

SYSTEMS OF LAW ENFORCEMENT IN THE UNITED STATES

Law enforcement in the United States had its inception in the "rattle watch," established by the leaders of Nieu Amsterdam under Peter Stuyvesant in 1658 as a means of securing the community from 9 P.M. until dawn, and in the diffusion of the "watch and ward," established in the British Isles, to the Colonies. Boston established its night watch

---

[15] Harold J. Berman, *Justice in the U.S.S.R.* (New York: Random House, Inc., 1963), p. 336.

[16] Cramer, *op. cit.*, p. 443.

system as early as 1636; New York City, in 1844, founded a police force of full-time officers who covered all of the hours of the day.[17] Since that time law enforcement has grown in organizational and procedural complexity, and now encompasses five major types of police agency, including:

1. Federal agencies, especially those attached to the Treasury, Justice, and Post Office Departments.
2. Nearly 15,000 village, borough, and incorporated town enforcement agencies.[18]
3. Some 1,000 city and over 20,000 township or New England town police forces.
4. Sheriffs and deputy sheriffs in over 3,000 counties.
5. State police forces and criminal investigation agencies in 50 states.

Other minor enforcement organizations, which must also be added to this total, include those of the District of Columbia, bridge and tunnel authorities, and park and parkways agencies. Each possesses its particular purpose and specific legal jurisdiction, and is served by clearly defined personnel (see Table 15–1).

Federal enforcement agencies

Nine basic federal enforcement agencies are currently authorized by the Congress (see Table 15–2). Others of lesser consequence also serve other governmental agencies. Such agencies as the Federal Bureau of Investigation (FBI) and the Border Patrol of the Justice Department; the Bureau of the Chief Postal Inspector in the Post Office Department; and the U.S. Secret Service, Internal Revenue Service Alcohol Tax Unit, Bureau of Customs, Bureau of Narcotics and the U.S. Coast Guard in the Treasury Department serve to investigate and/or to enforce existing federal statutes. Additional federal agencies, possessing a limited enforcement responsibility, function within the Department of State (passport and extradition laws). The enforcement and investigative powers of the National Park Service (forest preservation), the Public Health Service (control of epidemic diseases), and the Department of Agriculture (animal and plant quarantine), are not as extensive as those

---

[17] Paul W. Tappan, *Crime, Justice and Correction* (New York: McGraw-Hill Book Co., 1960), p. 274. See Bruce Smith, *Police Systems in the United States* (New York: Harper & Bros., 1960).

[18] Cramer, *op. cit.*, p. 407. Refer to V. W. Peterson, "Local and State Law Enforcement Today," *Current History*, Vol. 53 (July, 1967), pp. 8–14; and J. P. Kenny and John B. Williams, *Police Operations* (Springfield, Ill.: Charles C. Thomas, Publisher, 1968).

TABLE 15-1

Distribution of law enforcement agencies; classified according to the type of government served, and extent of police authority with which they are generally entrusted

Type of Government Served (1)	Police with General Authority (2)	Police Units with Restricted Authority or of Limited Use (Maintained in Certain Jurisdictions Only) (3)
Village	Village Marshal, Constable or Police Department	
Township, County District or Magisterial District	(a) Township or District Constables AND/OR (b) Township or District Police Department	Fish and Game Wardens
City	City Police Department	City Park and Parkway Police — Other City Law Enforcement Units
Special District	Special District Police	Boulevard and Park District Police
County	(a) Sheriff and Deputies AND/OR (b) County Police	County Parkway Police — Fish and Game Wardens — Prosecutor's Detectives and Raiding Squads
State	State Police	State Highway Patrol AND/OR Motor Vehicle Inspection — Fish and Game Wardens — Alcoholic Beverage Control — State Bureau of Investigation AND/OR Identification — Attorney General's Investigators — State Fire Marshal (Investigations) — Other State Law Enforcement Units
Federal	Federal Bureau of Investigation (Justice)	Immigration Border Patrol (Justice) — Customs Border Patrol (Treasury) — Enforcement Division; Alcohol Tax Unit (Treasury) — Secret Service Division (Treasury) — Bureau of Narcotics (Treasury) — Post Office Inspectors — Other Federal Law Enforcement Units

Source: Bruce Smith, *Police Systems in the United States* (New York: Harper & Bros., 1960), p. 302.

TABLE 15–2
Federal law enforcement agencies

Agency	*Responsibility*
Treasury department	
1. Intelligence Unit of the Bureau of Internal Revenue	Major violation of internal revenue laws including evasion of income tax laws.
2. Enforcement division of the alcohol tax units of the Bureau of Internal Revenue	Violation of laws levying taxes upon intoxicants.
3. Division of Investigation and Patrol of the Bureau of Customs	Smuggling and illegal exportation.
4. Secret Service Division	Counterfeiting, forgery, and protection of President, his family, and President-elect.
5. The Bureau of Narcotics	Violation of federal narcotic laws.
Justice Department	
1. Immigration Border Patrol	Illegal entry of aliens and allied crimes
2. The Federal Bureau of Investigation	All crimes not the immediate and special concern of other federal police agencies.
Post Office Department	
1. Chief Inspector office of the Chief Inspector	Mail losses, wrongful use of the mails, and other postal violations.

Source: Robert G. Caldwell, *Criminology* (New York: Ronald Press, Co., 1965), p. 304.

possessed by agencies of the Departments of Justice, Treasury and Postmaster General.[19]

The constable, town marshal, village policeman, and the county sheriff

The constable, an officer of a township or a town who is elected by popular vote or selected by local appointment, represents the least sophisticated form of enforcement. Usually poorly trained, he is generally compensated by local governmental bodies. Often a part-time officer who engages in police functions, he may also participate in the collection of taxes and the issuance of local election notices. The town marshal and village policeman, equivalent counterparts of the constable in larger jurisdiction, too, are usually limited to the legal boundaries of their community or employment. Subjected to partisan politics, they are commonly employed on a part-time basis.

Although the town constable, local marshal, or village policeman have been slowly losing their importance and power as the United States has become more urbanized, the authority of the sheriff within the

---

[19] Asch, *op. cit.*, p. 21. Also see Fred J. Cook, *The FBI Nobody Knows* (New York: Macmillan, 1964); F. Egan, *Plainclothesman* (New York: Arco Publishing Co., Inc., 1952); and Don Whitehead, *The FBI Story* (New York: Random House, 1956).

county political unit remains strong. Because the occupant of the county sheriff's office is decided through an electoral process, local law enforcement is inevitably bound in varying degrees to partisan politics. Inasmuch as few qualifications for office beyond limitations upon age, residence, and citizenship exist, the county sheriff who responds to the desires of the dominant political party faces few threats to his security. The county sheriff is responsible for the management of the county jail in most areas of the country, and he also assumes responsibility for tax collection in some parts of the South and Southeast. The city police force maintains jurisdiction within the recognized municipal boundary; the county sheriff possesses jurisdiction in those areas of the county where provision has not been made for town or city enforcement systems.

Although this practice has been declining in recent years, in many counties and states the sheriff is compensated in direct relationship to the fees collected as the result of his enforcement activity. As a result, total compensation, a 1949 study revealed, may range from a minimum of $1,200 a year in small rural areas to $100,000 per year in a large metropolitan center.[20] Efforts to overcome the limitations of the county sheriff system and to establish efficient county sheriff operations have led to the introduction of the merit system of employment, an approach which is allowed by 1969 Indiana law, for example, only in counties with a population of more than 80,000 persons.

The municipal police

Although an estimated 40,000 separate police agencies employ some 420,000 people and spend more than $4.5 billion a year,[21] 55 of the police departments in cities of more than 250,000 population employ nearly one third of all police personnel. Policing a city of more than 1 million in 1967 cost approximately $27.31 per resident per year as compared to a city of less than 50,000, which cost less than $8.74 per resident per year. Although the ratios of policemen per 1,000 residents in cities of over 500,000 population range from 1.07 (San Diego) to 4.04 (Boston), these cities report no gross differences in the incidence of reported crime.[22]

A widespread belief in municipal police ineffectiveness undoubtedly

---

[20] Robert G. Caldwell, *Criminology* (New York: Ronald Press Co., 1965), p. 288.

[21] The President's Commission on Law Enforcement and the Administration of Justice, *Commission Report: The Challenge of Crime in a Free Society* (Washington, D.C.: U.S. Government Printing Office, 1967), p. 91. Also examine C. D. Delorch, "Relationship of Criminal Sentences to Law Enforcement," *Federal Rules Decision,* Vol. 30 (September, 1962), p. 478.

[22] *Ibid.,* p. 106. Refer to Edward L. Barrett, *Police Practices and the Law* (Washington, D.C.: U.S. Government Printing Office, 1962).

contributes to a continually high urban crime rate. Property crimes are often undetected or, if detected, unsolved, unless some clue to the identification of the criminal or some witness to the event comes forward to aid the police investigation. Of 1,095 crimes reported in Los Angeles during January, 1966, for example, 310 of the 349 cases in which the police were furnished with a suspect's name were resolved either by an arrest or by some other acceptable enforcement procedure. However, only 181 of the remaining 1,375 crimes in which no suspect was identified were cleared by an arrest. Nine tenths of the arrests were completed by patrolmen, although 25 percent of the patrolmen's arrests were products of leads provided by detectives. The average response time in cases in which arrests were completed was 4.1 minutes, while it reached 6.3 minutes in cases in which arrests were made within one half hour of the commission of the crime. More than 48 percent were completed within two hours.[23]

The city police are usually supervised by municipal councils, a local police board or commission, a state-appointed administrator or board, a commissioner of public safety, or a mayor or city manager. While supervision by the first two groups retains local control of police, it also subjects a department to community political pressures. However, when a state-appointed board or administrator regulates police activity, state political pressures replace local political interests. While supervision by the commissioner of public safety possesses some merit, his varied responsibilities in police, fire, health, and welfare forces the administrator to divert his attention to these matters. The administrative control of the police force by the mayor or city manager has similar shortcomings. If the chief of police in a smaller community, for example, is an elected official responsible to the chief executive, he may become a victim of existing political rivalries to the detriment of the police force. Consequently, most larger cities maintain both a civilian and a professional head of the police department. The civilian representative is frequently designated as commissioner, the professional administrator as chief of police. Such a dual arrangement usually, but not always, allows the insulation of the police chief and his administration from the pressures of immediate politics.

The state police

The development of state police can be traced to the inadequacy of the local constable and sheriff systems over which the state had no control. The need to regulate vice, control labor disturbances, supervise highways, and enforce the law in rural areas also aided the growth

---

[23] *Ibid.*, p. 97.

process. In recent years, the state police have developed increased facilities for criminal identification and crime laboratory, crime data gathering, police training, and communications services to aid local police forces in detecting and apprehending the more mobile modern offender.

The Texas Rangers, created in 1835 by the provisional government of Texas, were the forerunners of the modern state police. Originally conceived as a border patrol, its powers were soon expanded to include those now generally assumed in most state police systems. Nearly every state today has some form of state police. However, fewer than one third provide state police units with general law enforcement powers. State highway troopers in Pennsylvania, Massachusetts, New York, and New Jersey, among others, possess the authority to enforce all state laws in addition to their normal highway patrol responsibilities. Although the trooper is often prohibited from enforcing the laws in municipalities unless requested by local authorities, he does possess the right of "hot pursuit," which allows the policeman to go anywhere in the state to complete an arrest when pursuing a criminal fleeing from his jurisdiction. Because of their mobility and communication advantages, the state police have largely replaced the sheriff and constable system in many of the rural areas of the United States.

Organization and structure of the police

The size of police forces varies from the one-man enforcement agency in many rural areas to the 30,000 or more officers in New York City. The one-man police force, found most frequently in rural towns and townships, smaller villages, boroughs or other incorporated areas, and usually supervised by the mayor or the village or town board, is responsible for the entire scope of police work. The officer engages in uniformed patrol and traffic regulation, criminal investigation, local administration, and other functions pertinent to the police task. Since his job demands more than he is able to accomplish alone in a 24-hour period, he remains essentially on active duty during the normal duty period and on call during the rest of the day. In larger communities, the functions and responsibilities of the police officer are divided and assigned to the greater number of specialized officers available for diverse enforcement tasks. Urban police organization varies in relationship to the size of the community, the nature of criminal violations, and the need for particular types of enforcement. The division of labor reaches its highest point in the large urban police department, which allows the greatest specialization of police function (see Table 15–3). Because the priority given to each of the related major police activities varies according to enforcement policy, community need, and personnel capability, the structural organization of the police force varies with the size and politi-

TABLE 15–3

Classification of major police activities*

Major Grouping	Related Activities within Each Group
1. Patrol force	All protective patrols—foot, mounted, or motorized Recording and checking patrol-box calls Patrol wagon service Booking prisoners at district stations Custody of prisoners at district station lockups Operation of patrol and district station records
2. Traffic regulation	All traffic regulation posts and patrols—fixed post, mounted, or motorized Traffic engineering and planning Accident prevention squads and records Accident records and reports Junior traffic patrols
3. Criminal investigation	All organized crime detection activities conducted by agencies other than the patrol force: street and general duty details, specialized squads, pawnshop squad Criminal correspondence Crime laboratory Photography of crimes and criminals
4. Communication and records control	Files of crime and investigation reports Arrest records Identification files† Central Complaint Room (communication and crime reports center)†
5. Property management	Accounting and payrolls Purchasing Maintenance of police buildings and equipment (including electrical signal systems; telephone, telegraph, teletype, radio, traffic and recall lights, patrol boxes, police vehicles, etc.)
6. Personnel management	Examination and investigation of recruits Qualification and efficiency records Promotion standards Training Disciplinary trials Police surgeons
7. Crime prevention	Protective work with women and juveniles Supervision of delinquent boys' activities Juvenile aid programs
8. Morals regulation	Headquarters squads for controlling prostitution, narcotics, intoxications, and gambling

* In some jurisdictions prisoners serving sentences in the city prison or on the prison farm, as well as those awaiting trial, are placed in custody of the local police force. In that event, an additional major activity is created, which proves difficult to adjust to regular police work. The custody of such prisoners involves questions of institutional management and of penology, which are foreign to police administration.

† May be operated as a criminal investigation adjunct if necessary or more convenient.

Source: Smith, *Police Systems in the United States*, pp. 219–220.

cal posture of the local urban community. A police organization, organized and quasi-military, is marked by strict subordination by rank, a formal and rigid chain of command, and an insulation of enforcement roles. Nevertheless, each system modifies these basic characteristics in relationship to its personnel and its perceived functions. The power of the chief to command and control large police departments, for example, is proscribed by a complex system of due process which protects officer subordinates. Because the police job is politically sensitive, the policeman, as Albert J. Reiss, Jr. and David J. Bordua note, is buttressed by selection, promotion, and discharge procedures which make his position more secure.[24]

Because police departments are organized to carry out a *reactive* strategy when an offense has occurred, their *proactive* program suffers by contrast. Rather than depending upon undercover or anticipatory police work, most police departments depend upon citizen complaints for enforcement direction. The very character of enforcement, therefore, is influenced by citizen pressures and the sympathy which the victim receives as a complainant. Because the public believes the policeman is paid to maintain social order and to protect the public from personal or property harms, most individuals have little interest in doing anything themselves to aid the enforcement process. While the citizen expresses minimal concern for anticipatory police work, he reacts emotionally when a serious crime has been committed. Rather ambiguously, the public nevertheless expects the policeman not only to deter crime but also to anticipate its completion.

Although the police organization functions to protect life and property, preserve peace, prevent crime, detect and arrest law violators, enforce laws and ordinances, and safeguard individual rights, these duties are fulfilled in large urban police departments by elements within the bureaucratic organization. As with any institution, these goals are often submerged to the need of the hierarchy, the demands for specialization, the effects of competitive examinations, procedural red tape, the seniority system, the formulation of rules and regulations, the maintenance of channels of communication, and the demand for obedience to hierarchial authority. Consequently, the police ideal often becomes nothing more than the maintenance of the dominant political, social, and economic interests of the community.[25]

---

[24] Albert Reiss, Jr., and David J. Bordua, "Environment and Organization: Perspective on the Police," in David J. Bordua (ed.), *The Police* (New York: John Wiley & Sons, Inc., 1967), p. 35. See H. Goldstein, "Police Policy Formulation: A Proposal for Improving Police Performance," *Michigan Law Review*, Vol. 65 (April, 1965), p. 1123.

[25] Arthur Niederhoffer, *Behind the Shield* (Garden City: Doubleday & Co., Inc., 1967), p. 12. For an expanded discussion of several other aspects, refer to Frank J. Remington, "The Role of Police in Democratic Society," *Journal of Criminal*

Modern police functions, diverse and encompassing, include patrol, traffic, detective, vice, juvenile, records, communications, laboratory, jail operation, maintenance, planning, inspection, ledgers and accounts, personnel, public relations, and intelligence functions.[26] It may include foot, motorcycle, automobile, or other vehicle control and/or detective activities. Although the actual internal organization of the police agency may take many varied forms (see Figure 15–1), large departments generally

FIGURE 15–1
Typical organization of a small force, with subdivision by time of day

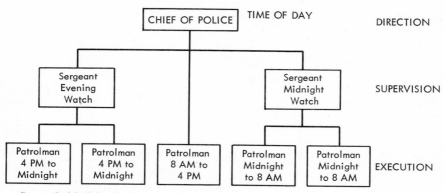

Source: Smith, *Police Systems in the United States*, p. 210.

tend to provide for three administrative branches called staff services, line operations, and inspections. Staff services refer to the personnel, records and identification, communication, property management, and public relation functions.[27] Line activities include patrol and investigation and traffic or other regulation.

The policeman

Recruits to the police force came largely from the lower economic classes until the time of the Depression. Many were poorly prepared

---

Law, Vol. 56 (September, 1965), p. 361; W. H. Parker, "Police Service—A Key to Community Quality," *Journal of Criminal Law, Criminology, and Police Science,* Vol. 55 (June, 1964), p. 273; and Richard L. Holcomb, *The Police and the Public* (Springfield, Ill.: Charles C. Thomas, Publisher, 1966).

[26] Tappan, *op. cit.,* p. 281; note William H. Hewett, *A Bibliography of Police Administration* (Springfield, Ill.: Charles C Thomas, Publisher, 1967).

[27] Caldwell, *op. cit.,* p. 292–93. Also examine Charles E. Clark and Harry Shulman, *Law Administration in Connecticut* (New Haven, Conn.: Yale University Press, 1937); and Jerome H. Skolnick and J. Richard Woodworth, "Bureaucracy, Information and Social Control: A Study of a Morals Detail," in Bordua (ed.), *op. cit.,* pp. 99–136.

for such service. A 1916 test of 30 police force candidates in San Jose, California, by Lewis Terman and Arthur Otis, for example, revealed that 21 of the sample were mentally inferior and only 3 had I.Q.'s of 100 or better.[28] A later study by Louis Thurstone revealed that the

FIGURE 15–2
Further development of the organization of a small police force, with subdivision by time of day

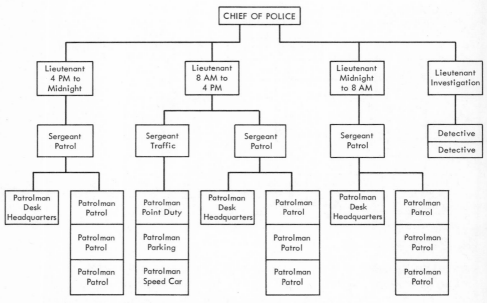

Source: Smith, *Police Systems in the United States*, p. 213.

superior officers of the Detroit police force scored on a lower level than the patrolmen serving under them. The most intelligent policemen, Thurstone hypothesized, left the department for better positions without waiting for promotion.[29] However, the economic insecurity of the 1930's stimulated many middle-class males to seek employment in the relatively stable police departments which offered relatively improved salaries and security. The entrance of better-educated middle-class officers into the law enforcement system immediately produced a tendency toward increased professionalization and greater dependence upon the use of technical and scientific skills. Serving as the nucleus of the future police

---

[28] Lewis Terman and Arthur Otis *et. al.*, "The Trial of Mental and Pedagogical Tests in a Civil Service Examination for Policemen and Firemen," *Journal of Applied Psychology*, Vol. 11 (1917), p. 21.
[29] Louis L. Thurstone, "The Intelligence of Policemen," *Journal of Personnel Research*, Vol. 1 (1922), pp. 64–74.

elite, the middle-class college graduate encouraged a new approach to the enforcement function.

In the 1950's and 1960's, when the recruitment pattern reverted back to the earlier pattern, much of this initiative was lost. During a 15-year period in the 1950's and 1960's, for example, the majority of the candidates for the New York City police force came from the upper-lower class. Although a few members of the lower-middle class did join the police force, nearly 95 percent of the total group, Arthur Niederhoffer discovered, possessed no college training. More than 85 percent of the recruits came from working-class families (see Table 15–4). While the

TABLE 15–4
Occupations of fathers of recruits
($N = 1,214$)

Type of Occupation	Number of Fathers	Percent of Total
Professional	28	2.3
Semiprofessional	7	.6
Proprietors	49	4.2
Managers and supervisors	72	6.0
Clerical	76	6.3
Sales	30	2.5
Protective service	132	11.0
Skilled workers	311	25.6
Semiskilled workers	237	19.0
Unskilled workers	96	8.0
Service (not protective)	160	13.2
Farm and kindred workers	16	1.3
Totals	1,214	100

Source: Arthur Niederhoffer, *Behind the Shield* (Garden City, N.Y.: Doubleday & Co., Inc., 1967), p. 37.

working-class youth tended to become a more dependable policeman than the middle-class college student who had not been tested in gang or street-corner society, an overdependence upon recruits of limited education, average intelligence, or cautious personality tended to accentuate, Niederhoffer believes, the medium and mediocre at the expense of the "independent and exceptional." The overwhelming majority of the recruits who joined the New York Police force did so, he found, for the security it offered.[30] Despite the low ebb of the police image, most viewed a police career as an upward step on the social scale.

Currently, each candidate for the police force must generally meet detailed physical standards, possess good moral character, and maintain

---

[30] Niederhoffer, *op. cit.*, p. 36. Include H. Lynn Edwards, "Law Enforcement Training in the United States," *American Criminal Law Quarterly*, Vol. 3, No. 2 (Winter, 1965), pp. 89–96.

prior residence in the community for a designated period. Typical physical requirements include a weight range of 150 to 250 pounds, height minimum of 5 feet 8 inches, at least 20–40 vision, and an age between 21 and 35. Although some departments give psychological tests, only about one quarter of the local departments attempt to screen the emotional fitness of each candidate. More than 70 percent of the existing departments require a high school diploma; fewer than two dozen of the 40,000 police agencies require college credits for continued employment. Despite the growing need for more police officers, national success rates on entry examinations between 1956 and 1961 decreased from 30 to 22 percent. The Los Angeles police department accepted less than 3 percent of its applicants during 1965.[31]

Police salary scales are generally low. The medium annual salary in small cities for patrolmen, as reported in 1968, is $4,600; his counterpart in the larger community receives $5,300. While the maximum salary for most urban policemen is typically less than $1,000 above the starting salary, the special agent of the FBI begins at $8,421 a year and can reach a level of $16,905 without promotion to a supervisory position. Future salaries of the proposed police agents, the President's Commission proposes, should be comparable to the FBI scale. While a police officer's salary might be $1,000 a year less, the community service officer should receive a minimum of $5,000 a year.[32]

Access to the channels for upward mobility and economic advancement have not been equally available to all. The U.S. Civil Rights Commission study of 1962, for example, revealed that 1 in every 26 Negroes is a sergeant, although the white ratio is 1 in 12. Out of every 114 Negroes, only 1 is a lieutenant; the white ratio is 1 in 26. While 1 in every 235 Negroes is a captain or above, the white ratio is 1 in 53.[33]

The dilemmas of enforcement

Modern law enforcement is faced with many fundamental dilemmas. At the outset, the policeman is asked to combine characteristics of the psychologist, sociologist, social worker, attorney, traffic expeditor, and family counselor in his person. And yet, his actual function and ultimate success depend upon the formulated rules and statutes which restrict the scope of enforcement and the conduct of the officer. Possessing

---

[31] President's Commission, *op. cit.*, p. 109. Refer to James H. McNamara, "Uncertainties in Police Work: The Relevance of Police Recruits' Backgrounds and Training," in Bordua (ed.), *op. cit.*, pp. 163–252.

[32] President's Commission, *op. cit.*, p. 111.

[33] *Report of the National Advisory Commission on Civil Disorders* (New York: Bantam Books, Inc., 1968), p. 311.

discretionary authority,[34] he is asked to use his power apart from his own basic prejudices and social commitments without training as to how this is to be accomplished. But an even greater dilemma is related to the growth of large-scale crime, which has necessitated a greater coordination of police effort and challenged the basic concept of local control of the police. The realization that some 420,000 enforcement personnel are employed in an approximated 40,000 police forces suggests that the average police force is far too small to contain the existing crime increase. Even the attempt to overcome this shortcoming by the use of volunteers or part-time personnel creates both latent and manifest social problems. Usually untrained and unprepared for law enforcement discipline, they likewise also fail to use the authority delegated them. Consequently, their action in critical social situations may do little to bring about its control or solution.

Of far greater consequence, however, is the question of whether the police system will operate on a system of meritious employment or be subjected continually to political patronage. The merit system is generally superior to the system of patronage and spoils, which causes almost automatic changes in police administration when power shifts from one political party to another. While the merit system may lead to the development of an ineffective bureaucratic organization, the spoils and patronage system may consign the local police unit to a form of generalized mediocrity. As long as the merit system is not combined with civil service tenure procedures, the police agency may correct inherent personnel and organizational weaknesses in a manner similar to that allowed under the spoils system. However, a greater dependence upon the merit system may likewise encourage the development of police unions designed to maintain officer security, lobby for salary increases, and secure more favorable fringe working benefits.

The policeman has gained greater power and influence over the community and his working conditions in recent years and tends to be much more militant than his predecessors. And yet, he is especially susceptible, Arthur S. Niederhoffer finds, to anomie and cynicism. He shows signs of anomie, for example, when the old values of the social system are supplanted by the new code of the police organization. As the move toward professionalization undermines old norms and loyalties within the police department, the policeman in the lower ranks feels uncertain

---

[34] Investigate J. M. Malone, "Problems in Law Enforcement," *New York County Lawyers Association Bar Bulletin*, Vol. 24 (1966–67), p. 77; E. F. Roberts, "Paradoxes in Law Enforcement," *Journal of Criminal Law, Criminology, and Police Science*, Vol. 52 (June–August, 1961), p. 224; Neal Osborough, "Police Discretion Note to Prosecute Students," *Journal of Criminal Law, Criminology, and Police Science*, Vol. 56, No. 2 (June 1965), pp. 241–45; and "Equal Protection as a Defense to Selective Law Enforcement by Police Officials," *Journal of Public Law*, Vol. 14 (1965), p. 223.

of his future. As professionalization becomes more important, both disappointment and failure and pride and advancement become more pronounced. Consequently, Niederhoffer believes, when this threat is added to the frustration encouraged by the public's refusal to provide the status supports which the policeman needs, the officer may well become a victim of apathy, confusion, frustration, alienation, and despair.

Anomie is often buttressed by cynicism. In one form, police cynicism is directed against life, the world, and the general public and in another form, against the police system.[35] Cynicism may become a disguise for individual failure and may include a cynical attitude toward those who seek to compete and win the professionalization sweepstakes. If the cynic tends to deprecate the entire police social system, it becomes increasingly easier, Niederhoffer finds, to reduce his personal commitment to the system and its effective values.[36] Cynicism often follows a general occupational career, beginning among recruits at the training school in the form of pseudo cynicism, which is still dominated by idealism and commitment to the police system. During the first five years of a police career, a form of romantic cynicism, a type of disillusionment, begins to emerge among the more idealistic members of the force. The growth of aggressive cynicism, on the other hand, takes the form of *ressentiment* (resentment and hostility) around the 10-year mark. Only in the last years of the policemen's career does a resigned form of cynicism replace more blatant cynicism as it comes to grips with the flaws of the existing police system.[37]

But anomie and cynicism are not the only elements complicating the police task. The combination of *danger* and *authority* assumed in the police function, Jerome Skolnick found, undermined procedural regularity in the fictitious city of Westville, California. The concern for danger inevitably provoked an attitude of self-defense, together with a corresponding sense of fear and anxiety. Authority, he discovered is often expressed in an extraordinary response to perceived threats. Consequently, as long as the policeman feels in control of the social situation, he is often prone, he argues, to use his authority in order to reduce his perceived danger.[38]

The greatest amount of police enforcement time is not devoted to criminal situations but basically to events involving social tension or

[35] Niederhoffer, *op. cit.*, p. 95.

[36] *Ibid.*, pp. 94–96. Refer to C. Ray Jeffery, "The Sociology of the Police," in Joseph S. Roucek (ed.), *The Sociology of Crime* (New York: Philosophical Library, Inc., 1961).

[37] *Ibid.*, pp. 98–99.

[38] Jerome H. Skolnick, *Justice Without Trial: Law Enforcement in Democratic Society* (New York: John Wiley & Sons, Inc., 1966), p. 90. Also note Claude R. Sowle, *Police Power and Individual Freedom: The Quest for Balance* (Chicago: Aldine Publishing Co., 1962).

conflict within families or among members of the community.[39] Because the police function involves control of barking dogs, the return of runaway children, the control of narcotics or prostitution, and even the apprehension of a murderer, it is diverse and subject to few common classifications. Inasmuch as the policeman initiates the first action against a believed offender, his decision at the outset affects the outcome of any given case. His concept of enforcement, therefore, determines the nature of justice and the quality of evidence presented to the prosecuting attorney and to the court at the very outset. Since the modern policeman too often seeks vindication through a judgment of guilt upon the arrested offender, he has been known at times to work in a biased manner in order to validate his own arrest decisions. Consequently, any court decision to dismiss charges becomes a threat to his "knowledge" about the event, which he believes is more important than the rules of evidence maintained by the court. Because "today's probationers," Albert J. Reiss, Jr. and David J. Bordua say, "are not infrequently tomorrow's work,"[40] police officers are quickly disenchanted with courts and judges that dismiss or release offenders or by rehabilitation workers who limit the scope of "justice." Where court action does not coincide with the desires of the policeman, he may well dispense justice on the spot rather than face repudiation through later court dismissal of the case.[41]

Because each element may potentially justify the action of the other, close relationships among police officers, public prosecutors, and the courts have frequently led to subversion of the goals of law enforcement. Concerned for statistical success in apprehension and conviction of offenders, the police, Reiss and Bordua find, have been known to present to the courts only those cases which have the highest probability of conviction. Consequently, the disparity between the number of crimes reported to the police and the low number of actual arrests of criminal offenders creates a further dilemma in police administration. Since only about one in four offenses known to the police is ever cleared by an arrest, the police, Reiss and Bordua believe, cannot simply justify their activity as a representation of the moral or legal order. Forced to maintain a public image of success while facing a deteriorating ratio of known crimes to arrests, the police administrator often justifies his existence by calling attention to the large number of misdemeanors which have

---

[39] See Charles Rogers, "Police Control of Obscene Literature," *Journal of Criminal Law, Criminology, and Police Science,* Vol. 57, No. 4 (December, 1966), pp. 430–82.

[40] Reiss and Bordua, *op. cit.,* pp. 25–55.

[41] Refer to "Police Procedure and the Accusatorial Principle," *Criminal Law Bulletin,* Vol. 3 (October, 1967), p. 521; H. B. Rothblatt and R. M. Pitler, "Police Interrogation: Warning and Waivers—Where Do We Go From Here?" *Notre Dame Lawyer,* Vol. 42 (April, 1967), p. 479; Fred E. Inbau and John E. Reid, *Criminal Interrogation and Confessions* (Baltimore: Williams & Wilkins Co., 1962).

been successfully prosecuted and by ignoring the wider disparity or lack of success in arresting more serious property offenders. Depending upon the accused's self-confession of guilt for court validation of their own success, law enforcement officers and administrators are quickly angered by alleged offenders who prove knowledgeable in the nuances of criminal law.[42]

Police discretionary power

The attempt to eliminate the conflict between successful arrests and court acquittals has been partially controlled by the bargaining process, which allows the prosecutor to gain convictions on a lesser charge with the consent of the defendant's attorney. Through such action, the policeman, the prosecutor, and even the defense attorney are vindicated as they serve both the state and the alleged offender. Consequently, once police concern becomes production oriented, the policeman is likely to arrest those who are quickly arrested and convicted.[43]

While both the magnitude of an offense and the previous contacts of the juvenile with the police have a clear effect upon the disposition of any case, the category of previous contacts with police possess greater impact on the final case disposition. The configuration of previous offenses or contacts is especially critical in juvenile cases in which the judgment of the juvenile offender is generally untested by legal counsel representing the offender. If his attitude is unfavorable and disrespectful, the juvenile is especially vulnerable to arrest, detention, and incarceration. Defiance, Nathan Goldman found, is likely to lead the male juvenile to the juvenile court more quickly than any other basic factor.[44]

In the United States, an arrest may be made by a policeman with or without a warrant. However, an arrest warrant is usually issued by a magistrate upon the showing of probable cause that the suspect is guilty of a crime. In most states, the warrant, Frank J. Remington recognizes, may be issued on the basis of information and belief by the courts; in others, by the prosecuting attorney.[45] The police, however, generally act and arrest without warrants and then present the case to the prosecutor, inasmuch as the enforcement officer is usually empowered to arrest

[42] Reiss and Bordua, op. cit., p. 35.

[43] Note "Good Communications Can Cut Crime Response Time," American City, Vol. 82 (August, 1967), pp. 100–101.

[44] Nathan Goldman, The Differential Selection of Juvenile Offenders for Court Appearances (New York: National Council on Crime and Delinquency, 1963), p. 106. Examine E. L. Barrett, "Police Practices and the Law from Arrest to Release or Charge," California Law Review, Vol. 50 (March, 1962), p. 11; and D. J. Bordua, "Recent Trends: Deviant Behavior and Social Control," The Annals. Vol. 369 (January, 1967), pp. 149–63.

[45] Frank J. Remington, "The Law Relating to 'On the Street' Detention, Questioning and Frisking of Suspected Persons," in Claude R. Sowle (ed.), Police Power and Individual Freedom, (Chicago: Aldine Publishing Co., 1962), p. 13.

a *felony* offender whenever he has reasonable grounds to believe that a felony has been committed and that the person he plans to arrest has committed the offense. In cases involving less serious *misdemeanor* offenses, an arrest may generally be made without a warrant only when the misdemeanor, involving a breach of peace, is committed in the presence of the arresting officer. While some jurisdictions expand this right to include any misdemeanor committed in the presence of an officer, other states allow the officer to arrest for a misdemeanor which he has reasonable grounds to believe has been committed.[46]

The so-called Uniform Arrest Act of 1942, which authorized the policeman to "stop any person abroad whom he has reasonable grounds to suspect is committing, has committed, or is about to commit a crime and demand of him his name, address, business abroad and whither he is going," suggests that the stopping of any person would not constitute an "arrest" but a detention, which could be continued for a two-hour period to permit further investigation. Although the growing crime rate would seem to indicate that greater police intervention is ultimately necessary, the act itself implies the potential loss of civil liberties. The critical word in this definition is the word "reasonable," a definition which may differ in accordance with one's view of the purpose of the law and the police.[47] Although the police in most states possess the privilege to stop and interrogate at the present time, current statutes do not place the burden of proof of innocence upon the interrogated person. Whether one is arrested or merely detained, his mobility as a suspected offender is functionally lessened. If a suspected offender resists lawful arrest, the police officer is generally allowed the use of such force as is *reasonably* necessary to secure his apprehension unless the believed violator is charged with a felony dangerous to life,[48] at which time the *general* use of lethal force is permissible.

ARREST POWERS IN OTHER COUNTRIES

France

Variations in arrest procedures occur in France where, according to the Code of Penal Procedure of 1959, a person may be taken into custody

---

[46] *Ibid.*, p. 14. See J. B. Waite, "Whose Rules? The Problem of Improper Police Methods," *American Bar Association Journal*, Vol. 48 (November, 1962), p. 1057.

[47] Caleb Foote, "The Fourth Amendment: Obstacle or Necessity in the Law of Arrest," Sowle (ed.), *op. cit.*, p. 29. Also refer to Richard H. Kuh, "Reflections on New York's 'Stop and Frisk' Law and Its Claimed Unconstitutionality," *Journal of Criminal Law, Criminology, and Police Science*, Vol. 56, No. 1 (March, 1965), pp. 32–38.

[48] Roy C. Hall, Jr., *The Law of Arrest* (New York: University of Atlanta Press, 1961), p. 93; Yale Kamisar, "Criminals, Cops and the Constitution," *Nation*, Vol. 199 (November 9, 1964), pp. 322–26; "Justified Use of Deadly Force," *Criminal Law Bulletin*, Vol. 4 (January–February, 1968), p. 3; and "Civil Liberties and Police Power," *Commonweal*, Vol. 80 (April 3, 1964), p. 29.

only if the examining magistrate delivers a warrant of arrest against him. However, no warrant of justice is necessary in cases in which the crime is being or has just been committed, a person is in possession of objects or presents signs leading to the suspicion he participated in a crime, or is prosecuted due to public outcry. While French police possess the right to maintain a surveillance, to check one's identity, or to search a suspect, these privileges are not used indiscriminately.[49]

Japan

Under the revised Japanese Code of Criminal Procedure (1948), a warrant issued by a judge is necessary to complete an arrest. However, two exceptions to this law allow any person to arrest without warrant any offender who is committing or has just committed a crime in his presence and permit an investigating official to arrest a suspect without warrant if he has committed or has reason to believe that he may have committed any of the predescribed serious crimes for which he may remain unapprehended if a warrant is procured. In such cases of urgent arrest, however, a warrant must be secured soon after the completion of the arrest.[50] The Police Duty Law of 1948, as amended in 1954, additionally permits the police officer to stop and question any person whom the officer has sufficient ground for suspecting to have committed or about to commit a crime. Such questioning may take place on the street or upon request at the local police station or police box.

Canada

Both the Canadian peace officer and the ordinary citizen are empowered to arrest without warrant in particular circumstances under provisions defined in the provincial enactments and the Criminal Code of Canada. Since crimes are simply designated as indictable offenses and offenses which are less serious crimes, the common American distinction between misdemeanors and felonies does not apply. The flexibility of the Canadian code is especially apparent in Section 435, which indicates that a peace officer may arrest without a warrant a person who has committed or who on reasonable and probable grounds he believes has committed or is about to commit an *indictable* offense, or a person whom he discovers committing a *criminal* offense.[51] Although the suspected Canadian offender cannot be forced to answer questions put

---

[49] Robert Vouin, "Police Detention and Arrest Privileges under Foreign Law—France," Sowle (ed.), *op. cit.*, p. 48.

[50] Harno Abe, "Police Detention and Arrest Privileges under Foreign Law—Japan," Sowle (ed.), *op. cit.*, p. 61.

[51] G. Arthur Martin, "Police Detention and Arrest Privileges under Foreign Law—Canada," Sowle (ed.), *op. cit.*, p. 37.

to him by a constable, the officer possesses the right to detain a suspect for questioning for up to three or four days under certain circumstances. Although this practice may be illegal, it is continued under the guise that the suspected offender voluntarily participates in his detention by responding to the request of the confronting officer.

THE POLICE IN A DEMOCRATIC SOCIETY

The issues posed at the time of the creation of the London Metropolitan police force are no less valid today. Historically, the American police force has been largely free to act as it desires under local political control. In too many instances, however, this freedom has resulted in a politically dominated police force which merely is the agent of the established community power structure. Consequently, an increasing number of voices have been questioning whether greater controls should not be enacted over the police. The primary issue, Jerome H. Skolnick notes, is whether the police should be held responsible for the constraints to due process as well as the more tenuous requirements of decency, courtesy, and civility.[52] The police in democratic society, Skolnick argues, "are required to maintain order and to do so under the rule of law."[53] And yet, because they are functionaries charged with maintaining order and are part of a bureaucracy, they often only express bureaucratic initiative and are dominated by a disciplined adherence to rules and regulations.

Because the rule of law emphasizes the rights of individual citizens and places constraints upon the initiative of legal officials, an operational tension between the ideas of order and efficiency and those of initiative and legality underlies the basic problem of the police in a democratic legal organization. If the police, Skolnick maintains, could guarantee order without regard for legality, their "short-run difficulties" would be considerably diminished. However, the essence of the criminal code is legality and specificity. Criminal law, he points out, is essentially a set of rules for the maintenance of social order which are precisely defined and substantively maintained. Because questions of legitimate search, legal arrest, and the nature of admissible evidence are involved in the enforcement and judicial processes, the procedures of criminal law operate to protect both the rights of the individual and the system of social order. Consequently, the concept of law and order attempts

---

[52] Skolnick, *op. cit.*, p. 4.

[53] *Ibid.*, p. 6. See Albert Deutsch, *The Trouble With Cops* (New York: Crown Publishers, 1954); A. B. Caldwell, "Police Efficiency in Law Enforcement as a Foundation of American Life," *American Bar Association Journal*, Vol. 48, (February, 1962), p. 130; and R. F. Kennedy, "Respect for Law," *American Bar Association Journal*, Vol. 48 (January, 1962), p. 31.

to minimize the substantial tensions between the idea of law and the maintenance of order. Since the police are organized along the lines of a military model, their concepts of law and order tend to be martial. Their emphasis upon police hierarchy, chain of command, direct obedience to superiors, and continuous responsibility encourage a strong sense of social uniformity and routine. Personal initiative may be both a hindrance and an aid to the police function, since it may either disrupt the chain of command or enhance its operation.

Nowhere is the tension between law and order more evident than in the adjudication process. Because police effectiveness, Skolnick presumes, is often determined by the number of arrested criminals which are convicted, the trial process has too often become nothing more than a reinforcement of the police image. The use of the guilty plea, which requires no trial, to achieve conviction often serves to validate the police function at the expense of the arrested defendant. Eighty-six percent of the cases coming to the federal courts between 1960 and 1963, Skolnick notes, were settled by guilty pleas, while state courts settled 75 percent of its cases in the same manner during the same period.[54] Guilty pleas have not only been used by enforcement and judicial personnel as a means of quickly processing defendants through limited court facilities but they have served to rationalize the police tension between the volume of reported crime and their ability to arrest suspected offenders. Consequently, the guilty plea, Skolnick concludes, may shield the police from criticism concerning illegal search and seizure, eavesdropping, illegitimate procedures for gaining confessions, or other situations which cover up the actual interaction between the defendant and the policeman during and after the period of arrest.

The enforcement function is compounded by the fact that an illegal arrest is both a violation of law and of the person's civil rights, although the failure to complete an arrest may ultimately lead to the infliction of harm against some property or persons. The policeman, in fact, has the responsibility of having to make immediate judgments which affect the actual future relationships of all persons in the ensuing drama. Because any arrest involves a series of complicated legal issues, the policeman must have probable cause to suspect that the person arrested has committed a specific crime. However, many arrests clearly occur without any reasonable probability that a crime has been committed.[55]

In its simplest form, an arrest is the taking of a person into custody so that he can eventually answer for the commission of any offense of which he is convicted. An arrest, Sidney Asch notes, depends upon

---

[54] *Ibid.*, p. 13.
[55] Asch, *op. cit.*, p. 48. Consult also W. R. Poage, "Enforcement of the Law," *Vital Speeches*, Vol. 34 (March, 1968), pp. 341–43; Martin Friedland, *Detention before Trial* (Toronto: University of Toronto Press, 1965); and "U.S. Crime and Law Enforcement: Symposium," *Current History*, Vol. 53 (July, 1967), pp. 1–42.

the policeman's intent to arrest under "a real or pretended authority, accompanied by a seizure or detention of the person which is so understood by the person arrested."[56] Under these provisions, an arrest may constitute nothing more than the mere consent of the person to appear in court at a designated time or it may represent a more formal action, involving the physical detention of the suspected offender, fingerprinting, booking, and arraigning. Despite the fact that arrests may occur upon the issuance of an authorized warrant by a judge or an appropriate peace officer, the warrant is legal only if the court possesses the legal power to issue the warrant and if the warrant itself is free of defects which might make it useless.

Although the private person at one time possessed the right to make arrests without warrant, most states no longer allow the free use of this privilege. In a few states, the private citizen may arrest a misdemeanor offender without a warrant if the act is committed in his presence. In recent years, state legislatures have increasingly moved to increase the power of the policeman in the arrest process.

While previously the police function centered largely in the maintenance of law and order, its responsibility in recent years has become one of maintaining neutrality in the face of challenges over civil rights. In essence, the police function in modern society has changed drastically, as the police have been asked to neutralize their emotions and opinions and to remain impartial arbiters of interpersonal and intercultural conflict. The very flow of upward and downward individual mobility, which reveals the major changes occurring within society, have effectually caused changes in the basic character of the police function. Invariably, such social displacement has encouraged an increase in criminality, which the community attempts to control by the passage of a greater number of sanctions and laws designed to maintain order and to secure social peace. At the same time, however, it renders the policeman's task even more difficult, giving him an even greater number of duties without expanding the police force to the levels necessary to guarantee law enforcement.

The enforcement problem has now passed far beyond the capacity of the individual policeman or even the total police force to fulfill effectively the expectations of the law, and police morale has suffered accordingly. Ultimately, police effectiveness depends upon the policeman's concept of the enforcement function and the public's willingness to observe established laws. If the policeman merely exists to enforce the law, his acts will tend to support a coercive enforcement pattern. However, if he sees his job as one of keeping peace in the community, he may serve as an arbiter of conflict. Since less than 15 percent of his time is used in effective police investigatory work, the greater function of

---

[56] *Ibid.*, p. 49.

the police involves the collection of information, the use of his good offices, and his continued presence in the particular community to encourage potential violators to refrain from criminal activity.

Although the law does not allow the policeman unlimited discretion in the arrest of a violator, the enforcement, justice, and correctional systems cannot exist without wide discretionary police power. Accepted by the public, police discretion may depend upon factors of social class, personal morality, racial characteristics, or even public attitudes towards law enforcement. Because the number of violators and laws defining violations always outnumber the number of policemen who can arrest or enforce, enforcement forces have been overwhelmed by the volume of criminal activity. Where racial conflict has added another variable, the enforcement function has been further compromised by the emotional commitment of the local policeman. Standards of police morality and conduct fluctuate, and therefore, the intent of the law is not always realized. Nevertheless, the public has come to expect more of the local officer, exposing his shortcomings in the process.

Alienation and the police

The police problem of modern America, James Q. Wilson believes, is largely a morale problem. Because the policeman is charged with serving incompatible ends, the officer is often unable to find a consistent and satisfactory self-concept. The problem of morale or self-respect, however, is also related to the very nature of the police role, which involves his facing his opponent as a clear-cut antagonist. Because the police officer's work involves the issuing of summonses, the making of arrests, the conducting of inquiries, the carrying out of periodic searches of homes, the halting of cars, the testifying in court and the maintaining of a jail, the police officer confronts many citizens at their time of major anxiety and hostility.

Because police officers (ambivalently) desire both symbolic and coercive enforcement, they often tolerate violations of the law. While the lower classes, Wilson contends, have become more middle class and lessened the demand for commercialized vice and manipulative municipal politics, the civil rights movement and the greater restrictions by the courts (for example, decisions concerning the admission of evidence and the procedures of police interrogation) have affected the policeman's morale. The policeman's sense of alienation from society, Wilson believes, consequently causes the emergence of a distinctive subculture or code which allows the policeman to maintain his self-respect without an overdependence upon civilian attitudes.[57]

---

[57] James Q. Wilson, "Police Morale, Reform and Citizen Respect: The Chicago Case," in Bordua (ed.), op. cit., pp. 137–62.

The tendency to evaluate the effectiveness of modern law enforcement in relationship to the FBI *Uniform Crime Reports* statistics concerning crimes known to the police and crimes cleared by arrest, often highly or totally misleading, adds to the anxiety. If police effectiveness were instead evaluated in terms of evident professionalization, quality of personnel selection, general nature of enforcement policies, apparent value of its patrol system, and its organization for crime deterrence and control,[58] much of the morale problem could be quickly lessened. Because the most effective policing is that enforcement which relates to the needs of the area, law enforcement, in effect, should be evaluated in terms of its appropriateness of service rather than of mere statistical reports.

The individual policeman is production oriented and arrests represent his successes, and court acquittals become his failures, a situation which is especially frustrating because the arresting officer has little control over the outcome of the criminal trial. If the accused is released, the policeman may well reveal a sense of moral outrage which becomes evident in his belief that he is the only element resisting the disintegration of society. Like any other functionary, the policeman desires recognition, often reached through a fulfilled sense of moral completion. Therefore, justice is often intermixed with a sense of self-fulfillment. In these instances, the specificity of the law is often submerged to the moral viewpoint of the police enforcer.

As competing complex structures of probation, parole, and treatment modify traditional procedures for handling criminal offenders, the policeman may come to view the correctional or welfare official as his opponent. Because the police role assumes the position of the interrogator rather than the interrogated, the reversal of roles, when placed on the witness stand, quickly challenges the officer's authority. Ensuing anxieties, as a result, are often reinforced by the status differentials apparent between the officer and the judge. Inasmuch as the policeman often shares a status similar to that of the charged defendant, his exact role in the courtroom drama may actually serve to undermine his believed self-image by bringing it into a more realistic context. Recent Supreme Court decisions challenging informal and oftentimes highly illegal police practices, therefore, have served to further undermine the policeman's self-concept.[59] The very characteristics of the enforcement and judicial processes create the tension which inevitably results in status anxieties among members of the local police force.

---

[58] V. A. Leonard, *Police Organization and Management* (Brooklyn: Foundation Press, Inc., 1951), pp. 404–38.

[59] Refer to J. O. Newman, "Cops, Courts and Congress: Effects of Supreme Court Decisions," *New Republic*, Vol. 156 (March, 1967), pp. 16–20; and R. C. Hoy, "Authority of Federal Law Enforcement Officers—A Need for Uniformity," *Federal Bar Journal*, Vol. 21 (Spring, 1961), p. 245.

Public antagonism further complicates the modern enforcement function. Questions concerning the effectiveness of the police force; the general public apathy which allows corrupt political machines to dominate
police departments, the emphasis upon achievement which allows unethical individuals to gain high prestige in American society; the public's
ignorance of the complexity of the modern apprehension and enforcement system; police overlapping which results in excessive duplication
of services; legal technicalities which render legal sanctions impotent
in deterring recidivism; limited and ineffective training, salary, and
equipment for adequate police work; and changing laws and court decisions on arrest and admissions of evidence encourage uncertainty among
enforcement officers.[60]

The police and minorities

Although the question of police brutality brings varied reactions from
the white and black communities, belief in its existence cannot be denied. Since the scope of "brutality" may range from the level of mere
discourtesy to actual physical beating or infliction of lethal harm, its
occurrence can take many forms. Forty-three percent of those questioned
in a 1964 study by *The New York Times* expressed belief in the existence
of police brutality. A nationwide Gallup poll also revealed that 35 percent of the black and 7 percent of the white male population say that
police brutality exists in their areas. Other studies in Watts (California)
and Detroit (Michigan) have similarly disclosed that between 70 and
83 percent of the blacks queried maintain that police use insulting language while making arrests or engage in some form of police brutality.[61]

The Report of the National Advisory Commission on Civil Disorders
further suggests that ghetto residents believe that law enforcement administrators and officers follow a double standard in their community.
Believing that the police act in one way in the white community and
another way in the black, they believe that "an assault on a white victim
produces one reaction and an assault on a Negro quite another."[62] Data
from Cleveland, Ohio, tend to support this picture of the views of the
black population. Police, the U.S. Commission on Civil Rights discovered, took nearly four times as long to respond to calls concerning robbery originating within a Negro district as compared to the district
in which the response was next slowest. The response to other kinds
of crime was at least twice as long. The challenge of the policeman

---

[60] Caldwell, *op. cit.*, p. 286.
[61] *Report of the National Advisory Commission on Civil Disorders, op. cit.*, p. 302.
Also see Shalom Endelmann, *Violence in the Streets* (Chicago: Quadrangle Books,
Inc., 1968).
[62] *Ibid.*, p. 309.

in the ghetto is most clearly depicted in a statement included within the U.S. Riot Commission Report:

The policeman in the ghetto is a symbol, finally, of a society from which many ghetto Negroes are increasingly alienated.

At the same time, police responsibilities in the ghetto have grown as other institutions of social control have lost much of their authority: the schools, because so many are segregated, old and inferior; religion, which has become irrelevant to those who lost faith as they lost hope; career aspirations, which for many young Negroes are totally lacking; the family, because its bonds are so often snapped. It is the policeman who must fill this institutional vacuum, and then is resented for the presence this effort demands.[63]

Public distrust of the police was readily revealed in a 1967 study by the National Opinion Research Center which indicated that while 23 percent of all white persons believe that the police are doing an "excellent" job of enforcing the law, only 15 percent of the nonwhites accept this viewpoint. Additionally, 7 percent of the whites held that the police were doing a "poor" job as contrasted with 16 percent among nonwhites. While 63 percent of whites and 30 percent of nonwhites, NORC reported, expressed the belief that the police are "almost all honest," 1 percent of whites and 10 percent of nonwhites suggested that the police are "almost all corrupt."[64]

Policemen, gangs, and minority group members

Police and gang or minority relations remain highly tenuous. Because the policeman views the youth who wears boots, long hair, and a club jacket as the cause of some citizen complaint or a potential threat to his own survival, the gang or minority member comes under immediate suspicion. However, the situation is especially acute when the gang member is black. As a result, the frequently interrogated Negro gang member, Carl Werthman and Irving Piliavin find, responds to his police interrogators with jibes or taunts which challenge police authority. While part of this mutual antagonism is due to the wide diversity in local customs and legal codes, which is most clearly evident in the ghetto, and to common investigation and interrogation procedures, which receive minimal acceptance in the ghetto, it cannot be explained by this fact alone. Since gang members use the street-corner hangout as a form of public "home" or "private place," they often engage publicly in wine drinking, poker games, arguments, lovemaking, or other forms of be-

---

[63] *Ibid.*, p. 300.

[64] President's Commission, *op. cit.*, p. 99; Michael J. Murphy, "Improving the Law Enforcement Image," *Journal of Criminal Law, Criminology and Police Science,* Vol. 56, No. 1 (March, 1965), pp. 105–108.

havior which are often accomplished in some private location by middle-class juveniles.[65] For the Negro gang member, the corner hangout is a place where he can feel at ease, a fact often misunderstood by the "policing" policeman. However, as the youth moves a few blocks from his home location, he often feels like a foreigner in the new environment. His uneasiness in his public role consequently leads the youth to participate with his immediate peers in frequently bitter gang conflicts over territorial and jurisdictional matters. At the same time, the policeman tends to view these happenings as a threat to social stability and to reveal his own anxieties over his own public role in a "foreign" area.

Highly active police investigation and enforcement, Werthman and Piliavin discovered, results in a disproportionate police effort to detect suspicious persons in order to uncover the criminal actor in the criminal situation. While the officer will first begin his investigation by contacting the complainant, he soon progresses to the interrogation of individual youths whom he believes are capable of committing a particular criminal act. Having categorized previous offenders on file cards or in his mind, the officer moves quickly to match wits with those identified in his written or mental juvenile lineup. The officer interrogates both the innocent and guilty and justifies his action as necessary for the apprehension of the violator. The youth often perceive this conduct, since all juveniles are not similarly contacted, as another example of police unfairness.

A study of the Watts (Los Angeles) riot by Walter J. Paine disclosed that over 90 percent of the blacks queried believed that police mistreatment, whether in the form of use of insulting language, of officer disrespect, of search of a car, home, or person for no good reason, of use of unnecessary force in making arrests, or of beating of people in custody, actually did occur. Although 53 percent declared that they had

[65] Carl Werthman and Irving Piliavin, "Gang Members and the Police," The Police, p. 58; James L. Brennan and Donald W. Olmstead, Police Work with Delinquents (East Lansing: Michigan State University Press, 1965), pp. iii–115; Alfred J. Kahn, Police and Children (New York: Citizen's Committee on Children of New York City, 1951); Juvenile Law Enforcement: Delinquency Prevention and Control (Madison: State Department of Public Welfare, 1962); Police Services for Juveniles (Washington, D.C.: U.S. Department of Health, Education, and Welfare, 1954); John Kenny and Dan G. Pursuit, Police Work with Juveniles (Springfield, Ill.: Charles C Thomas, Publisher, 1967); Richard Myren and Lynn D. Swanson, Police Work with Children: Perspectives and Problems (Washington, D.C.: U.S. Government Printing Office, 1962); Kenneth Shimota, "A Study of Police Services to Children in a Rural Wisconsin County," Journal of Criminal Law, Criminology, and Police Science, Vol. 56, No. 2 (June, 1965), pp. 257–59; M. M. Childs, "Law Enforcement and the Youthful Offender: Juvenile Procedures," Family Law Quarterly, Vol. 1, No. 4 (December, 1967), pp. 135–36; K. Lipez, "Law of Demonstrations: The Demonstrators, the Police and the Courts," Denver Law Journal, Vol. 44 (Fall, 1967), pp. 499–547; and Lynn D. Swanson, "Role of Police in the Protection of Children from Neglect and Abuse," Federal Probation, Vol. 25 (March, 1961), p. 43.

been personally subjected to insulting language, only 10 percent testified to being beaten up while in custody, 44 percent to being searched without reason, and 22 percent to being victims of unnecessary force while undergoing arrest. Whether realistic or not, such beliefs, Paine concluded, have a profound effect upon police-community interaction patterns.[66]

Occasionally, police-community tensions overflow into riots, as has happened with increased frequency in recent years. Once this has happened, the police must restore community stability. Successful police activity during riot conditions, Howard R. Leary contends, involve the application of four basic objectives:

1. Prompt evaluation and determination if the initial incident is of riotous proportions or may escalate into a riot.
2. Rapid mobilization and assembly of sufficient manpower and equipment to suppress the riot.
3. Utilization of riot control techniques to contain the riot, disperse the mob, and clear and secure the area of the riot.
4. Establishment of security plans to provide sufficient patrol coverage of the riot area, to suppress the riot and maintain law and order.[67]

The failure to follow such steps, Leary presupposes, can only increase the probability of citizen-police confrontation which riots frequently represent.

The Philadelphia riot in August, 1964, is a prime example of police failure to comprehend the magnitude of the event both during and following the riot control period. Plans for the containment and the control of the riot were largely ineffective. From this example, Leary concluded that the wise handling of either peaceful or riotous civil demonstrations must ultimately be summarized in the words *confidence, neutrality, judgment,* and *support.* Only when all elements of the police system possess confidence in their fellow officers and departmental capabilities can the police presence reach its maximum effectiveness. Only when the policeman is clearly neutral, observing his sworn commitment to uphold the law, can he serve impartially and objectively in the cause of effective law and order. Consequently, neutrality, Leary writes, "should be protected by the exercise of sound judgment."[68] Incor-

---

[66] Walter J. Paine, "Los Angeles Riot Study: The Perception of Police Brutality in South Central Los Angeles following the Revolt of August, 1965" (Dissertation, University of California at Los Angeles); and J. Edgar Hoover, "Law Enforcement States Its Views," *Villanova Law Review,* Vol. 12 (Spring, 1967), p. 457.

[67] Howard R. Leary, "The Police and Riotous Demonstrations," *Violence in the Streets,* (Chicago: Quadrangle Books, Inc., 1968), p. 374.

[68] *Ibid.,* p. 375.

rect or poorly diagnosed decisions can only inflame a situation further. In addition, the police must ultimately receive mass media and community support, since their effectiveness is only as good as the public commitment.[69]

Law enforcement and the use of force

At times, members of the police force are called upon to use force to seek observance of laws or to apprehend violators. Occasionally, this power has been used against rioters, whether justifiably or unjustifiably. Because the use of lethal force is the ultimate police sanction in controlling criminal conduct, many police homicides during any year period are enumerated in the common-law noncriminal or innocent homicide categories of justifiable or excusable homicide. *Justifiable homicide* refers to an intentional killing either commanded or authorized by the law. It may include the killing of an enemy during wartime, the execution of the legal death sentence, the unavoidable killing of a felon during the commission of an arrest or attempted blockage of an escape, or killings necessitated by lawful self-defense in which the slayer faces peril of death or threatened bodily harm. *Excusable homicide,* on the other hand, refers to an unintentional killing completed without intent to harm and without criminal negligence, and/or to homicide committed in self-defense upon a sudden event threatening danger or major bodily harm. Because the category of justifiable homicide includes those persons killed by the police in the commission of their duties, it offers an insight into the policeman's dependence upon lethal force in their commission or completion of law enforcement tasks.

A comparative study of 318 justifiable police homicides during a 10-year period in 10 cities by Gerald D. Robin revealed that one half of the 159 cases for which data concerning the age of the decedents was recorded were under 28 years of age; 32 percent of the men were between 20 to 50 years of age. While approximately 5 of the 159 victims were juveniles, 8.8 percent were above 45 years of age. Of the 269 cases in which the race of the decedent was recorded, 61.7 percent were Negroes. Chicago accounted for 54.6 percent of the 350 police slayings between 1950 and 1960 in nine of the cities. While Boston possessed the lowest volume of slayings, with less than one victim per million population, Miami led all 10 cities in the study with a yearly rate of 7.06. Akron (Ohio) policemen, the study indicated, were 45 times as likely to kill a criminal as a Boston policeman. In any given year, the policeman, the researchers found, is nearly "six times more

---

[69] H. S. Ruth and L. T. Ohlin, "Combatting Crime: Symposium," *The Annals,* Vol. 374 (Nov. 1967), pp. 1–184.

likely to kill than be killed in the course of his duty, although the probability of either occurring is extremely low."[70]

Of the 32 cases of police killings between 1950 and 1960 in Philadelphia, 30 of the 32 cases were disposed of by the medical examiner who exonerated the officers on the grounds of justifiable homicide at the inquest. Although two cases were remanded to the Grand Jury and were processed for eventual trial, the involved officers were found not guilty. In this 10-year period, 42 police officers shot and killed 32 male criminals. One officer alone, Gerald D. Robin uncovered, was responsible for the justifiable homicide in twenty-three cases. Eleven officers received injury during their attempt to apprehend the felons. Although only 22 percent of the city population during the period was Negro, 87.5 percent (28) of the 32 decedents were black.[71] A tendency to use fatal force, the study revealed, was most evident in the late evening and early morning hours, a period which generally was marked by the greatest police activity.[72] Nearly 72 percent of the shootings took place between 9 P.M. and 9 A.M. Of the 32 instant crimes, 24 were among the more serious crime index offenses. Twenty-five of the total killed evidenced various degrees of resistance; seven actually fled from the police. Six of the 25 either pulled, pushed or jerked away from the officer, 2 assaulted the policeman, and 17 committed aggravated assault and battery on the enforcement official. In each case the use of fatal force, Robin found, was authorized by law and represented a last resort.[73]

Although the number of attacks against the police has resulted in a growing demand for greater opportunities for the policeman to defend himself, the police officer faces less risk, despite his occupational demands, than many persons in so-called "less risk" occupations. One comparison of homicides of police with other occupational categories, for example, disclosed that law enforcement occupational risks are smaller than those of many larger industrial occupations, including mining, (a fatality rate 93.58 per 100,000 employees), agriculture (54.97), contract construction (75.81), and transportation (44.08). Law enforcement occupational fatalities, a 1955 study revealed, numbered a comparative 32.76 fatalities per 100,000 employees.[74]

Nevertheless, the hazards faced by the police lead some members Tamm believes, should be freed of the current atmosphere of indecision of law enforcement to seek greater police initiative. The police, Quinn

---

[70] Gerald D. Robin, "Justifiable Homicide by Police Officers," in Endelman (ed.), *op. cit.*, p. 399. Also note F. Knebel, "Police in Crisis: White Cop and Black Rebel," *Look*, Vol. 32 (February 6, 1968), pp. 14–21.

[71] Robin, *op. cit.*, p. 437.

[72] Orlando W. Wilson, "Distribution of Police Patrol Force," *Public Administration Service*, Vol. 74 (1941), p. 11.

[73] *Ibid.*, p. 439.

[74] *Ibid.*, p. 445.

which arises from court decisions that challenge the method and procedure of the arresting officer. While the courts may be expected to demonstrate dignity and sanctity, the work of the police, he argues, does not
permit the slow deliberation available to the judge. The policeman is
often forced to make immediate judgments for the protection of law
and order with little time for reflection.

Because criminal law has been enacted in a patchwork manner, it
contains many holes through which the criminal can escape. In these
instances, Tamm argues, the policeman and his work are hindered by
the lack of consistency in criminal law. Crime, which continues to soar
in number and viciousness, cannot be attributed to a decrease in police
effectiveness because the modern policeman is better equipped and
trained than at any time in previous history. Therefore, much of the
crime problem, he maintains, must be laid at the door of the judicial
process because the deterrent effect of swift, sure, and just punishment
has too often been modified by court inefficiency and an imbalance
between personal rights and the rights of modern society. When criminals are allowed to beat the rap, fellow criminals, Tamm suggests, become more bold. Consequently, the courts or the Congress must define
the exact limits and responsibilities of the policeman's role so that the
police may maintain and fulfill their function in the ordering of the
modern society.[75]

The resolution of community conflicts

While many enforcement reformers suggest the need for the professionalization of the police, mere professionalization is inadequate. The
problem involves more than the use of force. The need to improve
police–minority group relations is paramount if the problem of ghetto
crime is to be overcome. Human relations training of recruits and officers,
the enlargement of police-community relations units within police departments, precinct and citywide advisory committees, and police programs of public education have grown in importance. The attempt to
recruit members of minority groups, too, has grown in intensity. However, the effective integration of these officers into the police force
depends upon the elimination of discrimination within the police department and the integration of police patrols. However, these actions do
little to guarantee changes in community attitudes. A poll for the National Crime Commission in Washington, D.C. found 49 percent of the

---

[75] Quinn Tamm, "Police Must Be More Free," in Endelman (ed.), *op. cit.*,
p. 399; "Congress and the National Crime Problem," *Congressional Digest*, Vol.
46 (August, 1967), pp. 193–224.

Negro men responding that at least half of the police force would ultimately have to be replaced if a really good police department were
to be realized. Approximately 59 percent indicated their belief that many
police enjoy giving the Negro a hard time; and 62 percent accepted
the notion that the police discriminated against minorities.[76]

The attempt to redress the shortcomings of law enforcement has led
the President's Commission on Law Enforcement and Administration
of Justice (1967) to recommend that state legislatures enact statutory
provisions which will allow law enforcement officers to stop persons
for brief questioning, to participate formally in community planning
in all cities, to maintain community-relations programs in all larger communities, to encourage minority-group advisory committees or effective
liaison with police agencies in their neighborhoods, to recruit and deploy
minority-group officers fairly, and to provide adequate grievance procedures for citizens in the community. Police departments, the Commission
suggested, should develop and enunciate policies for police personnel
concerning matters of movement and activity of citizens, processing of
minor disputes, safeguarding of rights of free speech and assembly, and
decision to arrest or not arrest in specific situations. But police administrators should make certain that such acts are completed with a sense
of justice.

Because of the excessive cost of modern enforcement, police personnel
should be utilized efficiently. In order to provide for the service and
investigative functions necessary in the medium- and large-sized urban
departments, the police task, the Commission proposed, should be divided into three officer categories, tentatively defined in terms of the
community service officer, the police officer, and the police agent (see
Figure 15–3).

The *community service officer,* commonly a man between 17 and
29, would replace the present police cadet as an apprentice policeman
and would work in close cooperation with, and under the supervision
of, the police officer and police agent. A uniformed member of the
working police, he would nevertheless be limited to particular law enforcement tasks and not carry arms. Empowered to maintain close contact with juveniles in his community, he would represent community
members as needed before municipal agencies.

The *police officer,* charged with enforcing laws and investigating
crimes readily solved by immediate investigations, would respond to

---

[76] Albert D. Biderman, Louise A. Johnson, Jennie McIntyre, and Adrianne W.
Weir, *Report on a Pilot Study in the District of Columbia on Victimization and
Attitudes toward Law Enforcement* (Washington, D.C.: U.S. Government Printing
Office, 1967), pp. 137, 144. Also see Allan Silver, "The Demand for Order in
Civil Society," Bordua (ed.), *op. cit.,* pp. 1–24.

FIGURE 15-3
Career development and educational standards

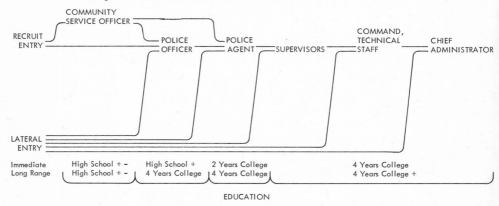

Source: The President's Commission *Commission Report: The Challenge of Crime in a Free Society* (Washington, D.C.: U.S. Government Printing Office, 1967), p. 108.

selected called-for services, perform routine patrol, enforce traffic regulations, provide emergency services, and investigate traffic accidents.

The *police agent,* chosen from those applicants who have completed at least two years of college and preferably possess a liberal arts or social science baccalaureate degree, would assume responsibility for imaginative and responsible police work. He would complete basic police jobs which are complicated, sensitive, and demanding, whether as a juvenile or community relations officer, uniformed patrolman, or career specialist in narcotics, robbery, or homicide investigation. As the most knowledgeable and responsible member of the police team, he would guide and advise the community service and police officers.

Because the enforcement function demands specialized training and problem-solving capability, police departments, the President's Commission proposed, should recruit actively from college campuses and inner city neighborhoods. Personality and intelligence testing should be continued and expanded. Police departments and civil service commissions, it concluded, should reexamine existing physical limitations placed upon employment and place primary emphasis upon the person's education, background, character, and personality. Not only must salaries be raised but promotion eligibility requirements should stress ability above seniority. Limitations upon police mobility should be eliminated so that the most capable officers may be employed. Because of the demanding character of police work, entering officers should serve probationary periods of between one year and 18 months; every continued general enforcement officer should participate in a week of intensive in-service training each year. In order to maintain police integrity, each department should provide for a well-manned internal investigation unit responsibile only to the chief administrator of the department.[77]

New directions in law enforcement

The attempt to develop more effective urban law enforcement has led to interagency cooperation and forms of contract law enforcement. In Suffolk County (New York) and Dade County (Florida), county investigators assist incorporated municipalities in crime solving. Some 29 different agencies of the county, city, and state level cooperate in the Kansas City (Missouri) Metropolitan squad, organized to handle major cases. The Metropol Operation in Atlanta (Georgia) likewise serves 38 different departments in six counties in fugitive apprehension. However, a form of jurisdictional consolidation, involving a merger of city and suburbs in a form of metropolitan government in Nashville–Davidson County (Tennessee), the only merger of its type, serves to increase law enforcement performance within Nashville and the surrounding territory. Contract law enforcement to other political jurisdictions for a fee, another approach to more effective enforcement, has had some success in Los Angeles County where the sheriff's office provides complete police service to 29 of the 77 municipalities in that California area.

Under a further variation of enforcement coverage, towns, villages, and boroughs cede law enforcement functions to the county, and citizens within the area pay a special tax for the maintenance of a high quality of law enforcement normally unavailable to the smaller community. While retaining independence of local government, such subordinate police service districts provide a contiguous policing jurisdiction. Although this service has had its most notable success in Nassau and Suffolk Counties (New York), attempts to create similar agencies in other states have run afoul of state constitutional limitations which retain the county sheriff as a constitutional state and not municipal officer. Efforts to change these provisions have usually ended in defeat because of the citizens' fear of large-scale police organizations.[78]

The meaning of the crime and enforcement problem

Crime is not a creation of our own times but has existed in one form or another in all past and contemporary societies. However, problems confronting the police are of recent origin because police forces

---

[77] President's Commission, *op. cit.*, pp. 91–123; S. Dash, "Crime, Law Enforcement and Justice: The Prospects for Reform," *Federal Bar Journal,* Vol. 26 (Summer, 1966), p. 224.

[78] *Ibid.,* pp. 122–23.

were only organized in the middle 1700's. And yet, despite the presence and the increased efficiency of law enforcement, participation in crime has continued to rise due to many factors, as discussed in earlier chapters. In the United States, the increase has been especially evident because interethnic and interracial conflicts have not been fully resolved within the urban metropolis. The current demand by citizens that political systems solve the crime problem reveals a simplistic understanding of the nature of crime and of the function of law enforcement. Fear has led much of the public to demand a form of police totalitarianism in the quest for community security. And yet, such a goal is incompatible with the philosophy of a democratic state. While all modern nations are policed societies, some totalitarian nations have become police states.[79]

The creation of the London police system in 1829 opened the way for the bueaucratic professionalization of law enforcement. Charged with the regular patrol of police beats; the adherence to strict rules, which still allowed for an element of police discretion; maintenance of order; and control of the "dangerous classes," the police provided the physical sanction of a formal organization which was charged with maintaining social control within the societal structure. In effect, they became the paramilitary force created by the peaceful and propertied classes to maintain internal peace without a full-scale commitment to military action. This enabled the otherwise-engaged respectable citizenry to refrain from participating in enforcement duties as had formerly been the custom.

Replacing the militia, posse, yeoman corps of other watch and ward committees, the beat patrolman became a social reflection of the change toward urban life.[80] The emerging police system, as a result, was designed to penetrate civil society in order to prevent crime and violence and to detect and apprehend criminals. And yet, the evolving police system in reality represented a continued presence of centralized political authority in the community, which was slowly breaking free of small-community social control mechanisms. The police system, serving as a unifying agency in the midst of change, has come to represent a core of values which are legally given precedence over values of conflicting ethnic, minority, or other social groups.

The nineteenth century police officer had to rely upon the moral assent of the general population for successful completion of his responsibilities. Without the moral cooperation of his subjects, he could be little more than an agent of coercion, an unacceptable police response in a democratic society. Consequently, a careful balance was maintained

---

[79] Silver, *op. cit.,* p. 6.
[80] *Ibid.,* p. 9.

between the seriousness of the criminal act and the use of force. In recent years, however, moral consensus of the public has been under attack. Yippies, hippies, student groups, minority protestors, union members, revolutionists, proponents of the status quo, and even the police have violated the moral consensus and staged a drama of police-protestor confrontation. The clash between police and a wide variety of protestors during the 1968 Democratic National Convention in Chicago reflects the need to create a new community-police consensus.[81]

Ironically, this happens at a time when police efficiency and capability is reaching an all-time high. However, the breakdown of spacial barriers between "the daily round of urban property classes and the criminal and unruly poor," Daniel Bell suggests, "has made the former more aware of violence in daily life."[82] The urban property classes, as a result, have tended to use the police, he believes, as a means for controlling or eliminating social problems. Reasoning that public bureaucracies have eliminated the plague, developed sound urban sanitation systems, and maintained food quality control, the urban propertied classes, Bell argues, likewise have come to expect crime and violence control through the application of power by the police bureaucracy. The extension of civil rights, municipal housing programs, mass media reporting, and objectification of informal and somewhat questionable police practices, however, have made such attempts impossible. Therefore, the inability of the police to maintain order in the large cities has led small communities which feel threatened to demand coercive police action in order to overcome violence, criminality, and riotous behavior. In this mental mood, the police, Bell contends, are given the role of a "garrison force" against an internal enemy.[83]

---

[81] See *The Walker Report*, (New York: Bantam Books, Inc., 1969).

[82] Daniel Bell, *The End of Ideology* (New York: Collier Books, 1960), pp. 151–74.

[83] Silver, *op. cit.*, p. 21. Also consult, for an added dimension: R. K. Woetzel, "Organized Crime in America and Law Enforcement," *Criminal Law Bulletin*, Vol. 1963 (Summer, 1963), p. 611; and Gus Tyler, "An Interdisciplinary Attack on Organized Crime," *The Annals*, Vol. 347 (May, 1963), pp. 104–12.

Chapter 16

OFFICERS OF THE COURT: PROSECUTION AND DEFENSE ATTORNEYS

In its attempt to remain objective the system of criminal justice theoretically guarantees that all persons receive equal justice before the law regardless of race, creed, social class, wealth or other consideration. Under the provisions of the criminal code in the United States, a man is presumed innocent until otherwise proved guilty through due process of law in a manner compatible with the democratic principles of American society. In effect, American jurisprudence is founded upon the idea that no legal guilt can exist without a prior definition of the law defining a particular act as illegal and that the prosecution must prove beyond a reasonable doubt that the act committed was intended by the conscious violator. The concept of due process to which both the prosecution and the defense are theoretically bound also include the following characteristics:

1. Definiteness of penal statutes and codes. The criminal code establishes a definite and unambiguous normative standard for conduct.
2. Accusation must give notice. The accusation of crime can be a grand jury indictment, any information, or a complaint which informs the accused person of the precise charge for which he may prepare a defense.
3. Arraignment with all possible speed. Originally not included in the

due process requirement, this principle assumes that the accused must be taken before a magistrate or other judicial functionary to determine the propriety of the charges made by a law enforcement official.

4. The privilege against self-incrimination either by personal confession, or through manipulation and psychological harassment, extensive interrogations, or other violations of the physical person.
5. Prohibition against unreasonable searches and seizures based upon the implicit assumption that the accused is innocent until proven guilty or reasonably believed to have violated a criminal statute.
6. The right to assistance of counsel.
7. Trial by jury, a principle based on the Constitution and the Sixth Amendment.
8. The right to call witnesses and confront adverse witnesses through cross-examination.
9. Right to an impartial judge.
10. Right to an impartial prosecutor who serves the accused as well as the state.
11. A presumption of innocence until the accused is proved guilty beyond "a reasonable doubt."
12. Prohibitions against cruel and unusual punishments.
13. Right to reasonable bail.[1]

However, all these provisions have not always been realized in the American system of justice.

The origin of the prosecutor's office

When barbaric justice was replaced by the controlled dispensation of justice in England in the 13th century, the public inquiry of witnesses replaced trial by ordeal and by combat. Later, when bodies of official witnesses to facts became the judges of evidence, criminal trials ceased to be a public inquiry into the act committed and became a form of private litigation. However, as the collection, presentation, and preservation of evidence assumed paramount importance, additional persons accepted new responsibility for the examination and evaluation of evidence. Although the actual origin of the public prosecutor's office is somewhat unclear, it probably arose as a general agent or representative

---

[1] Arthur S. Blumberg, *Criminal Justice* (Chicago: Quadrangle Books, Inc., 1967), pp. 22–25. Also see James W. Hurst, *The Growth of American Law* (Boston: Little, Brown & Co., 1950), and Jerome Hall, *Studies in Jurisprudence and Criminal Theory* (New York: Oceana Publications, Inc., 1958). Of limited value, see William B. Seagle, *Law: The Science of Inefficiency* (New York: Macmillan Co., 1952).

of the King or some other power who possessed a vested interest in maintaining community peace.[2]

Although these persons were the forerunners of the modern attorney general, they were the only officers assuming the responsibilities of a prosecuting attorney equivalent in England prior to 1879. Earlier, private persons or the slowly emerging police sought indictments from a grand jury and provided a solicitor and a barrister to prosecute the offender in the name of the King. Legal prosecution was operated largely as a private system, and its cost deterred many victims from pressing for a court decision. Since the existing theory of criminal law enforcement stressed a concept of vengeance, the redress of grievances was left largely to the individual or his family. Not until a director of public prosecutions was established in England in 1879 did the English system change to any important degree. His powers, however, were largely limited to those possessed by the private person. Consequently, the director prosecuted only murders, complex crimes, or other acts which had major political significance.[3]

In early colonial America the general assemblies and legislatures constituted the sole courts of law in each colony. Although courts had appeared about 1675, the governor and his deputies assumed many of the functions of justice before this time. Not until 1775 did the courts become something other than lay courts, as trained lawyers became judges. In 1704, the first public prosecutors in colonial America appeared as local assistants to the attorney general in the Connecticut colony.[4]

The current context

Both the prosecuting and the criminal attorney are in effect officers of the court, participating in the search for truth. Because each represents a particular aspect of the adversary system, the *prosecutor* is responsible to the public, for which he acts in prosecuting the alleged offender, and the *defense attorney* is devoted to the service of his client, whom he represents in the defense. In certain instances, the advocate and counselor roles, however, require that an attorney withhold relevant and truthful information from the court in a particular case, even though his action might potentially frustrate the discovery of truth, in order to maintain a privileged relationship between the client and his attorney.

---

[2] "Prosecutor Indiscretion: A Result of Political Influence," *Indiana Law Journal,* Vol. 34 (Spring, 1959), pp. 478–79. See Bernard Botein, *The Prosecutor* (New York: Simon & Schuster, Inc. 1956); and N. J. Quisumbing, "Evolution in the Prosecution Service," *Law Journal,* Vol. 22 (March, 1957), p. 112.

[3] *Ibid.,* pp. 478–79.

[4] *Ibid.,* p. 479. For discussion of later developments, read W. Scott Van Alstyne, "District Attorney: A Historical Puzzle," *Wisconsin Law Review,* Vol. 1952 (January 1952), pp. 125–38.

Because the defendant within the adversary system is presumed innocent until proved guilty of the charge beyond a reasonable doubt by the prosecution, the defense lawyer's primary obligation may be to advise his client to withhold the truth by remaining silent. However, while the defense attorney may potentially withhold evidence by refusing to put his client on the stand, the prosecutor ethically does not possess the privilege to withhold or suppress material evidence. While it is ethical for a defense counsel to cross-examine the prosecution witness in the attempt to undermine his testimony, the prosecutor is theoretically enjoined from obtaining a conviction by making a defense witness appear to be inaccurate or untruthful when he knows that the witness is offering truthful testimony. The defense attorney, however, possesses the right to "put the government to its proof" and to "test the truth of the prosecution's case."[5]

THE PROSECUTING ATTORNEY IN THE SYSTEM OF JUSTICE

The prosecuting attorney is usually empowered to participate in three types of investigations into criminal activity. Although he may initiate investigations prior to the arrest of the accused, this function is usually performed by the local police. While he is also empowered to investigate after arrest and indictment in order to gain additional evidence necessary to the prosecution of the case, he is likewise authorized to investigate solely to determine whether the police are conscientiously performing their duties, a form of examination which obviously creates many tensions in law enforcement.[6] However, the public prosecutor or district attorney most frequently makes the formal accusation and prosecutes alleged violators in relationship to the technicalities of the law and the public legitimate concern for the security of the community.[7]

In some states, the prosecutor is required to investigate acts of arson, racial discrimination, or gambling, although he may not be explicitly

---

[5] Warren E. Burger, "Standards of Conduct for Prosecution and Defense Personnel: A Judge's Viewpoint," *American Criminal Law Quarterly*, Vol. 5, No. 11 (1966), pp. 14–15.

[6] Marvin P. Aspen, "Legal Methods for the Suppression of Organized Crime: The Investigative Function of the Prosecuting Attorney," *Journal of Criminal Law, Criminology, and Police Science*, Vol. 48 (January–February, 1958), pp. 526–27. Refer to Sam E. Hobbs, "Prosecutor's Bias, an Occupational Disease," *Alabama Law Review*, Vol. 2 (Fall, 1949), pp. 40–60; and Tom M. Hillin, "Prosecuting Attorney Who Violates An Accused's Constitutional Rights," *Houston Law Review*, Vol. 4 (Winter, 1966), pp. 551–57.

[7] Arthur L. Wood, *Crminial Lawyer* (New Haven, Conn.: College and University Press, 1967), p. 20. Note article by Monroe H. Freedman, "Professional Responsibility of the Prosecuting Attorney," *Criminal Law Bulletin*, Vol. 3 (October, 1967), p. 544; and Newman F. Baker, "The Prosecutor-Initiation of Prosecution," *Journal of Criminal Law and Criminology*, Vol. 33 (January–February, 1933), pp. 770–96.

responsible for the actual enforcement of such legislative or constitutional provisions. His actual power of investigation depends upon whether he is viewed as an officer of the executive or the judicial branch of state government. In states where the prosecutor has been classified as an officer of the court, his primary duty is to see that justice is rendered. In states in which he is viewed as an executive officer, he is expected to assume a more active role in upholding the laws of the state. Consequently, the public prosecutor nominally possesses greater power as an executive officer than as a judicial officer, although this classification has seemingly little effect on the actual result of the prosecutor's efforts.[8]

The public prosecutor: Types and powers

Prosecutors are often called assistant attorney general, circuit court attorney, circuit solicitor, commonwealth attorney, county attorney, county solicitor, criminal district attorney, district attorney general, prosecuting attorney, solicitor general or states attorney, depending upon the traditional and legal practices in the various states.[9] Whatever his title, he is usually limited to jurisdiction within one county, although in approximately one third of the states, jurisdiction transcends county lines. While most states require prosecuting attorneys to have practiced a specified number of years before assuming this office, Utah did not require its county attorneys to be lawyers until 1959.

Generally, prosecuting attorneys claiming criminal jurisdiction are elected by the public. With the exception of Tennessee and Oklahoma, the prosecutor may simultaneously engage in private practice. In South Carolina, circuit solicitors and county solicitors can both maintain a private practice and defend in criminal cases against the state when they are not duty-bound to prosecute. In most states, the prosecuting attorney handles both civil and criminal matters. Usually the prosecutor possesses discretionary power to:

1. Either prosecute or not prosecute.
2. Select the actual charge.
3. Recommend sentence.
4. Bargain for a plea of guilty.
5. Request the court to dismiss the action.
6. Obtain the assistance of a special prosecutor.[10]

---

[8] Aspen, op. cit., pp. 528–29. See J. Oliver, "Lawyer's Responsibility in Criminal Cases," Journal of Bar Association of Kansas, Vol. 36 (Summer, 1967).

[9] Duane E. Nedrud, "The Career Prosecutor," Journal of Criminal Law, Criminology, and Police Science, Vol. 51 (1960–61), p. 343. See L. E. Skeel, "Role of the County Prosecutor in Public Law Enforcement," Cleveland Bar Association Journal, Vol. 29 (December, 1957), p. 19.

[10] S. C. Williams, "Discretion Exercised by Montana County Attorneys in Criminal Prosecutions," Montana Law Review, Vol. 28 (Fall, 1966), pp. 41–78.

The public prosecutor enjoys major discretionary power, which may be used for either the public good or detriment. The power of the prosecuting attorney is usually limited only by the control of the courts, the supervision of the attorney general, or the pressures of public opinion. In Great Britain, the prosecutor at all times is a minister of justice and may be approached by the defense for assistance in finding witnesses, bringing them to court, or gathering evidence which may help the case of the defense.[11] As in the United States, he possesses unlimited funds, access to the investigative reports of the police force, contact with all news media, and entrée to the scientific skills offered in forensic laboratories.[12]

The United States attorney, an agent of the U.S. Department of Justice in a particular district of a specific state, represents the nation as a prosecutor of federal crimes and as a barrister in civil cases,[13] usually in the district court nearest to his office. Most cases coming to his attention are referred by the Federal Bureau of Investigation, the Federal Bureau of Narcotics, the Internal Revenue Service, the Secret Service, the Immigration and Naturalization Service, and the Department of Health, Education and Welfare, and may range from prosecution of small postal thefts to tax fraud or subversion cases. Because general police power is still lodged in the various states, federal prosecution is generally limited to those areas defined by federal statute.

Responsibilities and discretion of the prosecuting attorney

The prosecuting attorney, a "quasi-judicial" officer of the court, must at the outset determine and judge to his own satisfaction whether the defendant is guilty of a crime or not. Although he is not responsible for a final decision on the matter, he must satisfy himself that a crime has been committed against the people and that the defendant is ultimately involved as a guilty party in order to assert the charge against the defendant.[14] Therefore, the determination of charge normally takes place once the prosecutor is personally convinced of the guilt of the

---

[11] Christmas Humphreys, "Duties and Responsibilities of Prosecuting Counsel," *Criminal Law Review,* Vol. 1955 (December, 1955), p. 741.

[12] *Ibid.,* p. 739. *See* "Prosecutor Forensic Misconduct—'Harmless Error,' " *Utah Law Review,* Vol. 6 (Spring, 1968), p. 108.

[13] Paul Williams, "Through the Looking Glass," *Practical Lawyer,* Vol. 3 (November, 1957), p. 50. Also note John G. Heinberg, "Centralization in Federal Prosecution," *Missouri Law Review,* Vol. 15 (June, 1950), pp. 244–58, and Paul W. Williams, "Through the Looking Glass—The Office of the U.S. Attorney," *Practical Lawyer,* Vol. 3 (November, 1967), pp. 49–58.

[14] Richard Mills, "The Prosecutor: Charging and Bargaining," *University of Illinois Law Forum* (Fall, 1966), p. 514. See C. W. Luther and J. F. De Meo, "Legal Evidence or Legal Ethics: Prosecutor's Dilemma," *California State Bar Journal,* Vol. 34 (May–June, 1959), p. 273.

accused. The actual charge is normally entered as a result of prosecuting and defense attorney interaction which occurs in the plea-bargaining process. More serious offenses may be downgraded to less serious misdemeanors or/crimes, depending upon the available evidence, the potential for conviction, the level of defense, or other important variables.

During the period of prosecutor-defense attorney interaction, prosecutor discretion undergoes severe tests. Throughout such sessions, for example, decisions are made as to whether a stealing charge against the violator should be one of burglary, felonious theft, or petty theft. Such diverse factors as the nature and sufficiency of existing evidence, the quality and capability of prosecution and testifying witnesses, and the spontaneous or planned character of the actual offense have a profound effect upon the eventual charge. The following selection from the *Manual for Prosecuting Attorneys* illustrates the nature and scope of the charging and bargaining process.

The prosecutor may have perfectly legitimate reasons for striking a bargain with the defendant's attorney. His case may be weak. Corroborating testimony may be missing. Complainant may be himself an unsympathetic character and may have contributed to the crime. The penalties of the law may be too harsh for the specific crime with which the defendant is charged. Jury trial is notoriously uncertain, expensive and time-consuming. The defendant may have aided the prosecutor in another proceeding, and thus deserves some mitigation in treatment.[15]

Although the public prosecutor is duty-bound to see that the accused receives a fair trial, he must also represent the state in the trial process. However, under the American adversary system his orderly presentation of the state's case often limits the free flow of information necessary to reach a just and fair conclusion. Most courts, therefore, allow the prosecutor to present only that evidence which tends to prove guilt, while it relies upon the defense attorney to produce all guilt-denying evidence. When the prosecutor becomes aware of evidence favorable to the accused in preparation for the trial, disclosure is sometimes required in order that the defense may be complete. However, since such revelation may undermine the state's case, such evidence is often disclosed rather slowly and infrequently. Neither the scope of the prosecutor's duty to disclose nor the consequences for failure to disclose have yet been defined precisely in American criminal law.[16]

---

[15] *Ibid.*, p. 516. See 2 Ploscowe, *Manual for Prosecuting Attorneys* 319 (Practicing Law Institute, 1956).

[16] "The Duty of the Prosecutor to Disclose Exculpatory Evidence," *Columbia Law Review*, Vol. 60 (June, 1960), p. 859; "Duty of the Prosecutor to Call Witnesses Whose Testimony Will Help the Accused to Establish Innocence," *Washington University Law Quarterly*, Vol. 1966 (February 1966), pp. 68–101; and D. C. Sullivan, "Prosecuting Attorney's Duty to Disclose," *Washburn Law Journal*, Vol. 6 (Spring, 1967), p. 477.

Evidence favorable to the accused may be ignored, directed to the attention of the defense, or obscured by the prosecutor as he takes active steps to hinder the discovery of evidence by his defense adversary. In most cases, the prosecutor's action is largely determined by the reliability of the evidence, its accuracy in relationship to other evidence, and its value to the court case in question. Although the possible suppression of evidence may involve a violation of the due process clause of the Fourteenth Amendment, the tentative nature of the precise problem makes any charge against the prosecutor for failing to disclose somewhat tenuous. Courts have increasingly overturned convictions on the ground that the prosecutor failed to disclose exculpatory evidence when an examination of the trial record indicates that the defendant was prejudiced by this action.[17]

Common problems facing the prosecutor

The difference in defense and prosecutor obligations is related to the overwhelming emphasis placed upon the sanctity of individuality and personality in our society, the restrictions placed constitutionally upon political power by the Founding Fathers, and the majestic and dignified character of democratic government. Because the prosecutor possesses the legal power to exercise discretion far in excess of that power available to the defense attorney, he is burdened with special responsibility in the exercise of his discretionary power. His exercise of authority is marked by many ethical problems which cannot be quickly resolved. Six common problems, for example, emerge from the general practices of the prosecution:

1. Cases where the primary motive for the prosecution relates to matters other than commission of the particular crime for which the defendant is being prosecuted (for example, Al Capone for tax evasion). In such instances, the power of the prosecutor may abuse the rights of the individual.
2. Various plea-bargaining tactics that are, to a great extent, beyond court supervision (for example, differentiating a single offense into numerous parts or adding conspiracy counts, unfair selection of trial location).
3. Condoning and covering up police abuses, such as brutality, perjury and unlawful arrests, searches, and interrogation. The need of the prosecutor and police to work in close relationship often makes it difficult for the prosecutor to move against either a police department or one of its members.

---

[17] *Ibid.,* p. 860.

4. Suppression of evidence, the purposeful introduction of false and misleading evidence and coercion of witnesses (for example, presentation of evidence which is attributed with false characteristics; coercion of witnesses by threat of prosecution or by deferment of sentencing).
5. Attempts to preclude resolution of important issues by depriving the courts of jurisdiction.
6. Failure to advise the court regarding, and even purposely taking advantage of, ineffective assistance of defense counsel.[18]

Occasional prosecutorial duties

In many rural communities, the prosecutor may be forced to assume the responsibilities of investigation if rural sheriffs or constables are unable to carry out modern police investigative techniques. In these instances, the prosecutor acts as an effective overseer of the local sheriff and constable.[19] In the larger urban counties, on the other hand, the prosecutor usually investigates crimes to insure that the police, sheriff, and coroner's investigative staffs operate in an honest manner. Because the urban prosecuting attorney's staff is incapable of investigating and supervising the entire police community, his function essentially becomes one of surveillance of other law enforcement agencies in the attempt to minimize their potential avoidance of enforcement responsibility through the excessive division of responsibility among urban enforcement groups.[20]

Plea bargaining and the public prosecutor

American criminal justice largely depends upon the use of the guilty plea. This is especially true in state or local courts, where well over 85 percent of all cases involve a plea of guilt. Even in the federal court, pleas of *nolo contendere* (no contest) and guilt represent an average of 79 percent of the disposition of all criminal defendants for the fiscal years of 1956–62.[21] Such high rates obviously involve prosecuting and

---

[18] Monroe H. Freedman, "Professional Responsibility of the Prosecuting Attorney," *Criminal Law Bulletin,* Vol. 3 (October, 1967), p. 544. For a rebuttal of Freedman's position, consult Richard L. Braun, "Ethics in Criminal Cases: A Response," *Georgetown Law Journal,* Vol. 55 (May, 1967), pp. 1048–64).

[19] Aspen, *op. cit.,* p. 529.

[20] *Ibid.,* p. 530.

[21] Dominic R. Vetri, "Guilty Plea Bargaining: Comprises by Prosecutors to Secure Guilty Pleas," *University of Pennsylvania Law Review,* Vol. 112 (April, 1964), p. 865. Also note Audrey M. Cafes, Jr., "Can We Ignore Laws?" *Alabama Law Review,* Vol. 14 (Fall, 1961), pp. 1–10; R. Klein, "District Attorney's Discretion not to Prosecute," *Los Angeles Bar Bulletin,* Vol. 32 (September, 1967), p. 323.

defense attorney plea bargaining (also known as "copping a plea"), which most commonly takes the form of: (1) a sentence recommenda-tion, (2) a plea of guilty to a lesser included offense, and (3) the dismissal of charges in an indictment, information, or other charging paper.[22] Under the sentence recommendation approach, the prosecuting attorney suggests to the court a sentence favorable to the defendant, seeks a lesser penalty, or refrains from making any recommendations which might encourage a severe punishment. Although the courts often follow these recommendations, each defendant who pleads guilty ulti-mately assumes the risk that the judge will not accept the recommenda-tion of sentence in his particular case. The actions in the other two alternatives are self-explanatory.

While plea bargaining has been held by many to be unethical and contrary to Anglo-American ideas of criminal justice, the practice is widely used. Critics argue that the practice intrudes upon society's inter-ests either by limiting the range of punishment or by opposing society's decision that certain criminal acts be met with specified penalties. How-ever, supporters of plea bargaining believe that trials are not essential to the protection of the constitutional rights of individuals. While the trial process is sound, it is at best, they argue, "only an imprecise means of determining truth."[23] Consequently, if the prosecution can prove its case, the bargain plea, they conclude, is in the interest of both the state, which benefits from a lessened work load by not having to take the case to trial, and the defendant, who is punished while also benefiting from a chance to reorient his behavior. While agreeing that the "system of justice by negotiation, without trial, probably tends to serve better the requirements of the guilty," Abraham S. Blumberg suggests that once an individual is indicted "there is little chance of escaping conviction."[24]

Many prosecutors "bargain" young defendants into military service in place of prosecution for misdemeanor, minor, or technical felony offenses. Usually offered as an alternative to prosecution which may result in a criminal record, those so processed have usually committed no serious property damage or personal injury. Actually, such "cut bar-gains" may simply be alternatives to probation, which would have nor-mally been invoked if the 18- to 20-year-old boy had not accepted the military service alternative. In these instances, the court reveals its belief

---

[22] *Ibid.,* p. 866. Refer to Richard S. Jenks, "Statutory Discretion of the District Attorney in Wisconsin," *Wisconsin Law Review,* Vol. 1953 (January, 1953), pp. 170–76.

[23] *Ibid.,* p. 882.

[24] Blumberg, *op. cit.,* p. 30. Consult Duane R. Nedrud, "The Role of the Prose-cutor in Criminal Procedure," *University of Missouri at Kansas City Law Review,* Vol. 32 (Winter, 1964), p. 142.

that military service helps the near-criminal youth to become more mature and more disciplined, to avoid a criminal record, and to make a useful contribution to society rather than merely to serve a probationary period.[25]

Not all judges accept the validity of the plea-bargaining process. Some hold that the willingness of the defendant to plead guilty should not have any independent significance in sentencing. This group argues that it is unethical to treat guilty-pleading defendants more leniently because it causes them to forego their right to trial under the pressure of the moment. While a second school agrees that a guilty plea should have no independent significance in sentencing, they maintain that a defendant who proceeds to trial with a seemingly contrived defense should be treated more severely than one admitting his guilt. Although this group presumes that a defendant who presses his case has expressed an insincere interest in rehabilitation, this approach, nevertheless, indirectly encourages the guilty plea. A third segment holds that defendants who enter guilty pleas should be accorded even more lenient treatment because they have taken the first steps toward rehabilitation in their admission of guilt. A fourth element contends that the rehabilitation concept should be considered in relationship to the particular crime for which the defender is charged. Any consideration should then be made, they argue, in relationship to the type of violation and the situation of the defendant.[26] Because a guilty plea must be voluntary and must be made with an understanding of the charge, it may be withdrawn at any time if these conditions are not met. Generally, the prosecutor's failure to comply with his promise has been held to be a violation of due process.

When opinion is so highly divided concerning the appropriate role of the prosecutor in the bargaining process, practices may be expected to vary widely. Justice George Sutherland of the U.S. Supreme Court enunciated the content of the prosecutor's role in *Berger* v. *United States:*

> The United States Attorney is the representative not of an ordinary party to a controversy, but of a sovereignty whose obligation to cover impartially is as compelling as its obligation to govern at all; and whose interests, therefore, in a criminal prosecution is not that it shall win a case, but that justice shall be done. As such, he is in a peculiar and very definite sense the servant of the law, the twofold aim of which is that guilt shall not escape or innocence suffer. He may prosecute with earnestness and vigor—indeed, he should do so. But, while he may strike hard blows, he is not at liberty to strike foul

---

[25] Mills, *op. cit.*, p. 517. Richard Mills, "Prosecutor: Charging and 'Bargaining,'" *University of Illinois Law Forum*, Vol. 1966 (Fall, 1966), p. 511.

[26] Vetri, *op. cit.*, pp. 869–70. Note "Prosecutor's Discretion," *University of Pennsylvania Law Review*, Vol. 103 (June, 1955), pp. 1057–81.

ones. It is as much his duty to refrain from improper methods calculated to produce a wrongful conviction as it is to use every legitimate means to bring about a just one.[27]

The prosecuting attorney potentially has more control over an individual's liberty and future than any other public official or public body. Although neither the statutes of Illinois nor its codified law, for example, allow the states attorney such wide discretion, he has gained this discretion over the years through the extension of case law.[28]

The prosecutor and the trial process

A formal accusation must be made against the alleged violator before the trial may commence. Although indictment by grand jury is the traditional form or method of accusation, the use of the prosecutor's information offers an alternative. When the charge is heard by the *grand jury*, the prosecuting attorney may appear before and may advise the grand jury concerning the issues involved. The accused or other parties representing the accused cannot appear as a matter of right at that time.[29] Although the grand jury is theoretically an independent and completely autonomous body, it depends practically upon the evidence and testimony brought to its attention by the prosecuting attorney. While infrequently used as the personal "tool" of the prosecuting attorney, it is often used as a "bargaining" lever.[30] The threat to present separate indictments for every offense committed by an arrested offender before the grand jury, for example, may be sufficient stimulus to encourage the defendant to plead guilty to one or two charges.

The discretionary power of the prosecuting attorney is indeed great. The California Supreme Court, for example, indicates that the prosecutor "must determine not only whether there has been a violation of law but also whether action is justified under all the facts,"[31] and this power is often extended by the prosecutor to include the discretion *not* to prosecute, even in cases in which the prosecutor may be reasonably

---

[27] 295 U.S. 78, 88, 55, Sup. Ct. 629, 633 (1935).

[28] Mills, *op. cit.,* p. 511. Refer to J. P. Johnson, "State Attorney General and the Changing Face of Criminal Law," *Wyoming Law Journal,* Vol. 19 (Winter, 1965), p. 1; and "Role of the Prosecutor in Utah," *Utah Law Review,* Vol. 5 (Spring, 1956), p. 70.

[29] "Prosecutor's Discretion," *op. cit.,* p. 1059. Also consult L. Wright, "Lawyer's Responsibility in the Administration of Criminal Justice," *Alabama Law Review,* Vol. 16 (October, 1955), p. 391; and Richard A. Chappell, "Lawyer and the Administration of Criminal Justice," *Mercer Law Review,* Vol. 6 (Spring, 1955), pp. 240–48.

[30] Mills, *op. cit.,* p. 510.

[31] Wilson V. Sharp, 42 Cal. 2d 675, 268 p. 2d 1062, 1065 (1954).

certain that he can prove the commission of the crime and the identity of the criminal.[32] Nonprosecution, too, has often been justified by the courts because of the improbability that the action could be successfully terminated, the relative importance to the county of different prosecutions which might be initiated, the existence of a plan of action formulated in collaboration with police officers which the prosecutor believes will produce the best law enforcement, the prior confinement of the criminal to a mental institution, and the fact of restitution which lessens the impact of the original crime.[33] Twenty-five percent of the cases submitted to the Los Angeles district attorney, reported in a 1967 study, were refused prosecution by the prosecutor.

Although most cases presented to the grand jury have been heard by the magistrate in a preliminary examination of evidence, the prosecutor, if he chooses, may in most states avoid such a hearing and submit charges against individuals to the grand jury without a preliminary examination in a lower court. Even if the charge is dismissed by a magistrate's court, the prosecutor still often possesses the power to resubmit the case to a grand jury for further action. Practically, however, this is harmful to any successful prosecution.

The prosecutor's information, an alternative to the grand jury indictment, permits a faster court procedure where grand juries are infrequently impanelled. More than 25 states currently permit accusation by information for felony offenses, although many exclude an accusation by information if the felonious offense is punishable by either death or life imprisonment.[34] Where the use of the prosecutor's information exists, the prosecutor's discretion is usually limited by an expectation that the defendant be examined at a preliminary hearing before a magistrate.

Usually cases may be nol-prossed (does not intend to prosecute) at the discretion of the prosecutor, the attorney general, and/or the court, despite the previous action taken by the grand jury or other charging body. While the nol-pros (also known as *nolle prosequi*) has become an important device in the disposition of cases in the criminal court, few statutory criteria governing its general use exist. In 1954, more than 12 percent of the criminal indictments in Philadelphia, for example, were disposed of by means of nol-pros due to the withdrawal of prosecution, the death of a prosecution witness, or other miscellaneous or unidentified reasons.[35] Reasons most frequently given for nonprosecution by Montana county attorneys included (1) arguments that certain

---

[32] *Ibid.*, p. 46. See J. Kaplan, "Prosecutorial Discretion—A Comment," *New York University Law Review,* Vol. 60 (May–June, 1965), p. 1174.

[33] *Ibid.*, p. 46.

[34] *Ibid.*, p. 1061.

[35] "Prosecutor's Discretion," *op. cit.,* p. 1067.

crimes represent a greater threat to society than others, (2) some old laws are not applicable to modern conditions, (3) the interests of society require that particular laws be less strictly enforced, (4) the failure of police and sheriff's office personnel to adequately investigate violations of particular laws makes successful prosecutions unlikely, and (5) law enforcement and prosecution officials should not have to engage in the strict enforcement of certain laws.

The withdrawal of prosecution is especially common in cases involving marital or extramarital relationships. Where the charge may hinder the resumption of the existing marriage, or in-law relationships, the withdrawal of charges is often in the best interest of society. Since settlement in other instances is frequently made before the case comes to trial, the nol-pros may readily serve the end of justice more equitably than an actual court trial. Nevertheless, the use of the nol-pros, by the prosecutor gives him great power, which, while subject to public scrutiny, may allow the prosecutor to take advantage of his office. Organized crime in particular has benefited from this power in many American cities.

The prosecutor and organized crime

Since organized crime attempts to immobilize local law enforcement through either the corruption or the control of the prosecutor's office, it is especially critical to eliminate the local prosecutor who fails to perform his duty. This is usually accomplished only through the prosecution of the corrupt prosecutor, who has been returned to office by the public or whose term is still uncompleted, by the state attorney general or by a special prosecutor appointed by the court. The power of the attorney general to conduct such criminal investigations varies from state to state. While he is the sole prosecutor in two states, the attorney general of Texas, for example, possesses limited criminal jurisdiction other than the responsibility of representing the state on appeal. Even in states in which such power exists, the attorney general has infrequently exercised this authority.[36]

The attempt to overcome prosecutor corruption has led to recent suggestions to centralize the machinery of law enforcement and prosecution. Included in these provisions are the abolition of the elected office of prosecutor and the authorization for the attorney general to appoint local prosecutors. While such a move would theoretically lessen the

---

[36] Louis Sunderland, "Legal Methods for the Suppression of Organized Crime: Circumventing the Corrupt Prosecutor," *Journal of Criminal Law, Criminology, and Police Science,* Vol. 48 (January–February, 1958), pp. 532. Also see "Legislative Investigations," *Temple Law Quarterly,* Vol. 34 (Winter, 1961), p. 182.

probability of the corruption of local officials, state law enforcement officers may be corrupted just as easily as their local equivalents.

The appointment of a special prosecutor is an alternative means for overcoming the corruption of an unethical prosecutor. However, the court rarely uses this power where it does exist. It usually is only when the prosecutor is absent or when the office is vacant rather than when the prosecutor fails or refuses to perform his basic tasks that such a provision is invoked. Because the practice of intervention is obscure in itself, the method of circumvention of the corrupt prosecutor by appointment of a special prosecutor is unclear.[37]

Of 91 criminal lawyers studied by Arthur L. Wood, nearly one third believed that the prosecutor should occupy his office for a maximum of five years; 69 percent indicated that his term of office should be longer and possibly even without limitation.[38]

Prosecutors and political aspirations

Studying the relationship between political aspirations and the occupancy of the prosecutor's office, Kan Ori discovered that Indiana prosecutors enter their office at a younger age than lawyers in the Indiana General Assembly and that the greatest majority of politically successful prosecutors (i.e., persons who obtain the office of governor, U.S. senator or U.S. representative) leave the office of county prosecutor before their 40th birthday. In effect, Indiana prosecuting attorneys are less experienced in years of practice than the lawyer-legislators of the General Assembly. However, the majority of Indiana prosecutors, Ori uncovered, are politically ambitious and often come from politically oriented families. Although the politically sensitive prosecutors rate their office more favorably as a means for political advancement than the politically neutral, the prosecuting attorneyship, Ori found, has not been of excessive significance in the recruiting pattern of Indiana governors and U.S. senators. While the prosecutor's office has been the most important single office in the career pattern of Indiana congressmen in the last 60 years, its importance for vertical career mobility of U.S. representatives has been declining.[39]

---

[37] *Ibid.*, p. 538–40. Refer to J. P. Hoey, "Prosecuting Attorney and Organized Crime," *Crime and Delinquency,* Vol. 8 (October, 1962), p. 379.

[38] Wood, *op. cit.*, p. 208. See "Private Prosecution: A Remedy for District Attorney's Unwarranted Inaction" *Yale Law Journal,* Vol. 65 (December, 1955), pp. 209–34; "Appointed Attorney General's Power to Supercede an Elected District Attorney," *Temple Law Quarterly,* Vol. 33 (Fall, 1959), p. 78; and R. Dilworth, "Problems in Reorganizing the District Attorney's Office in Philadelphia," *Dickenson Law Review,* Vol. 57 (October, 1952), pp. 82–85.

[39] Kan Ori, "Politicized Nature of the County Prosecutor's Office: Fact or Fancy? The Case in Indiana," *Notre Dame Lawyer,* Vol. 40 (April, 1965), p. 303.

Police, prosecutor, and the right to counsel

The attempt to countervail the obvious power of the police and the prosecutor has more recently led to increased definitions of the right of the alleged violator to possess access to counsel. Justice George Sutherland originally argued in the *Scottsboro* decision of the U.S. Supreme Court (1932) that the right to be heard in a criminal case is of little value if it does not include the right to be heard by counsel. Without the aid of counsel, a man may be tried without a proper charge and convicted upon incompetent evidence or upon evidence which is generally inadmissible or irrelevant to the particular issue.[40] This early decision applied only to capital offenses in federal trials; a 1938 decision of the Supreme Court extended the right of counsel to all serious federal criminal cases.

The 1963 Supreme Court decision of *Brady* v. *Maryland* further held that the suppression of evidence favorable to the accused by the prosecution upon request violates due process where exculpatory evidence is material either to guilt or to punishment, "irrespective of the good faith or bad faith of the prosecution."[41] In effect, defining exculpatory evidence as being that evidence which tends either to prove the defendant's innocence or to affect the punishment for the crime, *Brady* v. *Maryland* represented an early step to provide full disclosure of evidence concerning a case to both the prosecution and defense. Although the exact limits of disclosure are still being defined, the prosecutor now faces the extra responsibility of opening his files under specifically defined circumstances to the defendant.[42] In Britain, however, the defense possesses access to every fact and document upon which the prosecution propose to base its case at the opening of the trial. The prosecutor, on the other hand, has little knowledge of the defense except that which it discovered through cross-examination before the committing magistrate or is disclosed by defending counsel.[43]

Many problems involving the exact relationship of the prosecution and defense still exist. *Massiah* v. *United States* (1964) reversed the conviction of a merchant seaman charged for violation of the federal narcotics laws. Expecting the defendant to be part of the substantial criminal organization, federal narcotics officers installed a radio trans-

---

[40] Wood, *op. cit.*, p. 185. See "Achieving Teamwork Between Courts and Law Enforcement Agencies," *American Bar Association Section on Criminal Law,* Vol. 1962 (1962), p. 9.

[41] Ann Belanger, "Criminal Law: The Prosecutor's Duty to Disclose Exculpatory Evidence," *Oklahoma Law Review,* Vol. 19 (November, 1966), p. 426.

[42] Belanger, *op. cit.*, p. 429.

[43] Humphreys, *op. cit.*, p. 745.

mitter under the seat of a car of a codefendant named Colson for the purpose of overhearing conversations between Colson and Massiah. Upon conviction and appeal, the case eventually came to the attention of the U.S. Supreme Court, where the majority, speaking through Mr. Justice Potter Stewart, held that Massiah's Sixth Amendment right to counsel was violated by the introduction of the fruits of interrogation into evidence.[44] This decision was only one of several which were destined to countervail the established power of the police and prosecutor.

The 1963 decision of *Gideon* v. *Wainwright*, which required states and localities to furnish counsel for indigent persons charged with a felony, took the first step in requiring the assignment of counsel in all capital and noncapital cases involving serious crimes, a judgment which opened a wide spectrum of later actions. As an aftermath of the *Gideon* decision, the Attorney General's Committee on Poverty and Administration of Federal Criminal Justice under the leadership of Robert F. Kennedy provided recommendations for the implementation of the *Gideon* decision. The Criminal Justice Act of 1964, likewise, authorized funds for defense attorneys and other legal services for the poor charged with a crime in federal courts and also created the Office of Criminal Justice within the Justice Department. But ensuing changes did not end at this point.

The decision of *Escobedo* v. *Illinois* (1964), which reversed a murder conviction of Danny Escobedo charged with the murder of his brother-in-law, similarly added to law enforcement and prosecutor power realignment. Originally taken into custody for interrogation shortly after the fatal shooting, Escobedo was released after a number of hours of unsuccessful interrogation by the Chicago police. Ten days later, however, he was rearrested upon the accusation of a codefendant that Escobedo had fired the fatal shots. Following his rearrest, Escobedo's request to consult a lawyer, who stood outside the interrogation room, was denied by the Chicago police. When his subsequent conviction and appeal reached the U.S. Supreme Court, the Court maintained in reversing the conviction:

> We hold, therefore, that where, as here, the investigation is no longer a general inquiry to an unsolved crime but has begun to focus on a particular suspect, the suspect has been taken into the police custody, the police carry out a process of interrogations that lends itself to eliciting incriminating statements, the suspect has requested and been denied the opportunity to consult with his lawyer, and the police have not effectively warned him of his absolute

---

[44] David Robinson, Jr., Massiah, Escobedo and Rationales for the Exclusion of Confessions," *Journal of Criminal Law, Criminology, and Police Science*, Vol. 56 (December, 1965), p. 412.

constitutional right to remain silent, the accused has been denied "the assistance of counsel" in violation of the Sixth Amendment of the Constitution "made obligatory upon the States by the Fourteenth Amendment," *Gideon* v. *Wainwright* 372 U.S., at 342, 83 U.S. Ct., at 795 and that no statement elicited by the police during the interrogation may be used against him at a criminal trial.[45]

In effect, the Supreme Court's decision states that once the process of police investigation shifts from merely an investigatory to an accusatory stage, the accused, within the scope of our existing advisory system, must be permitted to consult his attorney.

The 1966 *Miranda* v. *Arizona* decision expanded the limitations placed upon police interrogation and prescribed the necessary action which the police must take to warn the alleged offender of his rights. Although conceived by the U.S. Supreme Court as an answer to enforcement inefficiency and backwardness, and to state legislature failure to modernize the enforcement and court systems, the *Miranda* decision, in effect, demanded a common national standard for interrogation and admission of evidence in the system of criminal justice. In this decision the Court stipulated the right of the accused to remain silent in order to remain free from self-incriminating statements.[46] However, the *Miranda* decision, Evelle T. Younger believes, foreclosed any future legislative attempts to adjust the inadequacies of law enforcement interrogation, and of the admission of resulting confessions into evidence in court, through its adoption of rigid and structured rules for police-criminal interaction at the time of arrest.[47]

New problems confronting the prosecutor

The problems of the prosecutor's office have multiplied in the postwar period. The *Gideon* and *Miranda* decisions concerning the right of the indigent to counsel during the accusatory process immediately caused a major increase in the number of pending cases in most criminal jurisdictions. In the city of Baltimore, for example, the prosecutor's work load increased over 35 percent from 1,787 cases pending on January 1, 1966, to 3,882 cases on January 1, 1967. In Miami, 1,600 cases on the other hand, were pending in April, 1965; 2,088 in April, 1966; and 3,015 in April, 1967. Generally, these backlogs have seemingly been due to the expansion of the rules of discovery and case disposition, which have necessitated more prosecutor time in pretrial procedures and resultant secretarial or clerical work. At the same time, however,

---

[45] 378 U.S. 478 (1964).
[46] Blumberg, *op. cit.*, pp. 95–96.
[47] Evelle J. Younger, "Prosecution Problems," *American Bar Association Journal*, Vol. 53 (August, 1967), p. 695.

the size of the prosecutor's staff and the range of offered salaries has generally remained static.[48]

The tensions between the rights of the individual and the rights of the general public, recently evident in the strained relationships between some members of Congress and the Supreme Court, may be attributed in part to the failure of the legislative and executive branches of government to confront the difficulties arising from the decisions of the U.S. Supreme Court and lower courts.[49] While due process must be accorded the criminal, it should not, Aaron E. Koota maintains, be denied to society. Although a resurgence of interest in protecting the rights of society at large must emerge if law-abiding members of society are to be protected, the issue is far greater, he argues, than the mere creation or interpretation of law. The inexperience of elected prosecutors, for example, may neutralize the efforts of enforcement and the courts. The professionalization of the prosecuting attorney's functions is necessary if the pitfalls of inexperience are to be avoided.

Because the appellate review of criminal cases is more common than in previous years, the conduct of both the prosecutor and the defense attorney, Richard H. Kuh notes, is exposed to greater scrutiny by higher courts. As a result, previous experience in criminal prosecution and defense has become more important in order to attain the ends of justice. Knowledge of the strengths and weaknesses of the various officers and detectives aids the prosecutor in the fulfillment of his duties and enables him to assess the quality of the case which he receives from the police. Because the responsibility of the prosecution covers the gamut of investigation through the appeal, the prosecutor is daily exposed to the overall weaknesses and strengths of the judicial process.[50]

The defense attorney in the system of justice

Studying 104 civil and 101 criminal lawyers in New London (Connecticut), Brooklyn (New York), Jersey City (New Jersey), Birmingham (Alabama), and Madison (Wisconsin), Arthur L. Wood discovered that

---

[48] Seymour Gelber, "Who Cares for the Prosecutor?" *American Bar Association Journal,* Vol. 54 (July, 1968), p. 683. See G. W. Anderson, "Statistical Survey of the County Attorney Salary and Work Load," *New Hampshire Bar Journal,* Vol. 7 (July, 1965), p. 381.

[49] Aaron E. Koota, "Reflections of a Prosecutor," *Brooklyn Law Review,* Vol. 33 (Fall, 1966), p. 36. Refer to O. Busby, "County Attorney System—Should It Be Replaced?," *Oklahoma Bar Association Journal,* Vol. 32 (December, 1964), p. 2317.

[50] Richard H. Kuh, "Prosecutor Considers the Model Penal Code," *American Criminal Law Quarterly,* Vol. 1 (August, 1963), p. 10. Also note Henry H. Bull, "Career Prosecutor of Canada," *Journal of Criminal Law, Criminology, and Police Science,* Vol. 53 (March, 1962), pp. 89–96; and Richard H. Kuh, "Careers in Prosecution Offices," *Journal of Legal Education,* Vol. 14 (December, 1961), pp. 175–90.

criminal lawyers disproportionately have foreign-born fathers, who represent a relatively low occupational status, and are commonly members of a minority, frequently Jewish, religious group. Nine of the practicing criminal lawyers, Wood noted, were foreign-born as opposed to six in civil practice; six criminal lawyers were Negro or Mongoloid as opposed to one in civil practice.[51]

Criminal lawyers may be divided into several contrasting types. The first type, the least successful criminal lawyers, are generally dissatisfied, Wood said, with their practice and possess a low prestige in their profession. They defend criminals not by choice but because of their need for work. Despite their participation in municipal and minor criminal cases, they are not criminal lawyers in the broader sense and possess the lowest status in the profession. The second type of criminal lawyer, Wood pointed out, enjoys the drama of his work, the thrill of the trial, is sociable and friendly, and quickly identifies with the underdog whom he later defends.[52] A third category consists of those who possess neither an adequate practice nor a welfare attitude toward their clients. However, the number of these individuals, Wood believes, is clearly less than those found in the two preceding categories.

Criminal law, according to Wood, offers a relatively common avenue for upward social mobility. And yet, while parents of criminal lawyers desire higher status for their children, they are less likely to direct their children toward criminal law than are the parents who encourage their offspring toward positions in civil legal practice. Although the law school training of criminal attorneys is of lesser quality than that of the civil group, this deficiency, Wood believes, is largely due to the lower socioeconomic origins of the criminal lawyer. Civil lawyers tend to hold salaried or managerial positions in the semiprofessional and professional business world; criminal lawyers are more frequently employed as laborers, independent businessmen, employees in a lawyer's office, clerks of court, or policemen. Although 55 percent of the criminal lawyers and 23 percent of the civil lawyers in the study were general practitioners, the remainder in both categories, Wood observed, were either semispecialists (40 to 70 percent of their time in a field of law) or specialists (70 percent or more of their time in the field of law).

Twice as many criminal lawyers as civil lawyers in Wood's study indicated that they experienced considerable difficulty in getting started in their legal practice. While 47 percent of the criminal lawyers, Wood noted, reported that they had trouble getting clients, making contacts, or gaining sufficient income, only 28 percent of the lawyers in civil practice had a similar problem. Of course, the tendency of civil lawyers

---

[51] Wood, *op. cit.*, p. 35.

[52] *Ibid.*, p. 65. Also note Jerome E. Carlin, *Lawyers on Their Own* (New Brunswick, N.J.: Rutger's University Press, 1962).

to become associated with established firms and the tendency of criminal lawyers to engage in solo legal activities accounted for much of this difference. Although 26 percent of the criminal lawyers, Wood reported, possessed a predominantly unfavorable attitude toward the practice of criminal law, 62 percent of the civil lawyers in the study revealed a negative attitude.[53] Over one half of the sample of criminal lawyers never intended to participate in the field of criminal law.

Nearly all of the criminal lawyers queried by Arthur L. Wood indicated that they accept and try cases in which guilt is already presumed on the basis of *not* guilty pleas. While criminal lawyers, due to the nature of their clientele, tend to demand a retainer fee before proceeding with the case, they also seem to accept more charity cases than other lawyers in the profession. While the criminal lawyer, Wood observed, is certified by the State Bar, he is less likely to participate in organized professional associations.[54]

Criminal lawyers are more active in community organizations than attorneys in civil practice. And yet, they are less likely, Wood noted, to occupy a leadership position within these organizations. Criminal lawyers find more frequent satisfaction in charitable, professional, and even political activities; civil attorneys more often in religious, civic, and recreational involvements. As friends, civil lawyers prefer bankers and corporation lawyers; criminal lawyers rank these people, however, among their last choices. Neither group possesses a very high regard for social workers. Surveying their political attitudes, 64 percent of the criminal lawyers, Wood observed, favor Democratic or other liberal candidates, whereas only 45 percent of the civil attorneys lean to the same political orientation. By contrast, however, 28 percent of the criminal lawyers and 41 percent of the civil lawyers have never been active in a political party. The criminal lawyer, Wood discovered, finds a friendly relationship with the police of great value because the policeman may recommend a particular attorney to a recent arrestee, suggest a lesser charge to the district attorney, or complicate the case by an overly hostile attitude toward the defendant. Since bargaining is essential to a successful criminal defense, informal contacts within the police department, Wood concluded, are centrally important to the defense attorney. Both the criminal and civil lawyers are dependent upon the structural and informal system in which they practice.[55]

---

[53] *Ibid.*, p. 501. See J. Miller, "Criminal Lawyer," *Virginia Law Weekly*, Vol. 1 (1949), pp. 81–86; J. J. Cavanaugh, *The Lawyer in Society* (New York: Philosophical Library, Inc., 1963), pp. 40–42.

[54] *Ibid.*, p. 131. Consult Lloyd P. Stryker, *The Art of Advocacy* (New York: Simon & Schuster, Inc., 1954).

[55] *Ibid.*, p. 138. Arthur L. Wood discusses this further in "Informal Relations in the Practice of Criminal Law," *American Journal of Sociology*, Vol. 62 (July, 1956), pp. 48–55.

Fifty-eight percent of the criminal lawyers are willing to accept a plea of guilty to a lesser charge. While 13 percent of the criminal lawyers hold such plea bargaining in an unfavorable light, 27 percent of the civil lawyers, more than twice as many, do so.[56] The difference is undoubtedly related to the greater acceptance of "bargain justice" by criminal lawyers who stand to gain from the often more quickly settled negotiated guilty plea.

The defense attorney as confidence operator

Not all persons believe that the criminal lawyer engages in the defense of his client. Abraham S. Blumberg, for example, argues that the assumption that the American system of criminal justice is an adversary system is open to major debate because the defense attorney often seeks justice by negotiation and lessens the impact of due process of law in his quest for professional remuneration.[57] The defense lawyer-client relationship, Blumberg argues, is a form of confidence game enacted within the criminal court. The lawyer utilizes his connections and knowledge as a service to his client in return for a stated fee. The criminal lawyer's office furnishings, his personal contacts, and his knowledge of the law often militate against the actual fulfillment of due process of the law. In this legalized "confidence game," the lawyer arranges for the payment of his fee in advance, prepares his client for defeat, cools off the client's hostility upon the rendering of the guilty plea, and satisfies the court that he has "adequately negotiated the plea so as to preclude an embarrassing incident which might invite 'outside' scrutiny."[58] Even the enlistment of the aid of the accused's relatives, Blumberg contends, is motivated by the desire to guarantee the payment of fee and the need to secure the help of others to convince the alleged offender of the need to plead guilty.[59] The criminal lawyer, says Blumberg, works on behalf of both the court and the accused to terminate the litigation with the minimum amount of expense and damage. As a double agent, the criminal lawyer, therefore, serves "higher organizational rather than professional ends," a fact, which is concealed, Blumberg believes, by the lawyer-client "confidence game."[60]

---

[56] *Ibid.*, p. 210. Also review Walter I. Wardwell and Arthur L. Wood, "The Extra-Professional Role of the Lawyer," *American Journal of Sociology*, Vol. 61 (January, 1956), pp. 304–7.

[57] Blumberg, *op. cit.*, p. xiii. See Arthur L. Wood, "Professional Ethics Among Criminal Lawyers," *Social Problems*, Vol. 7 (Summer, 1959), pp. 70–83; and N. Levy, "Dilemma of the Criminal Lawyer," *Criminal Law Review*, Vol. 7 (1961), p. 28.

[58] *Ibid.*, p. 112.

[59] *Ibid.*, p. 113. Note Morris L. Ernst, "Lawyers are Failing the Law," *Saturday Evening Post*, Vol. 237 (March 7, 1964), pp. 237–38.

[60] *Ibid.*, p. 115.

LEGAL COUNSEL AND THE PUBLIC

Legal aid for indigent and poverty-ridden persons emerged with the need to guarantee due process with the growing complexity of the modern criminal code and the move to greater humaneness by society. The pioneering Legal Aid societies designed to serve indigent offenders originated during the latter part of the 19th century; the public defender system emerged in the second decade of the current century. As public concern has shifted from the indigent to persons of lower income, a newer lawyer reference plan came into being.

The Legal Aid Society

The *Legal Aid Society*, a philanthropic agency created to serve the legal needs of impoverished persons unable to pay a private attorney, is often established as a clinic or a department of another agency. Currently found throughout the United States, such societies are generally financed through private funds, although public funds are often earmarked for agency use. While the legal aid office may provide continuity through its staff of lawyers, its services are usually available only to those who pass a "means test" which certifies their indigent state.

By June 1, 1960, 305 Legal Aid and Defender Offices existed in the United States.[61] Of these, 132 were staffed by salaried attorneys who coordinated service in civil cases in 126 cities, having a combined population of nearly 63.5 million persons. In 77 cities, legal aid offices operated with voluntary legal staffs, serving an additional combined population of 16.5 million persons. Volunteer panels of lawyers were also available to 23 million persons in 128 other communities throughout the country. Although criminal lawyers in cities without a Legal Aid Society tend to express a similar degree of skepticism concerning its benefits as civil lawyers, once it is established little opposition has usually appeared to its continuance.

The Legal and Defender Association's objectives include the establishment of legal aid offices for civil cases in all cities over 100,000 or more population which lack such facilities, the promotion and establishment of more defender offices in counties having a population in excess of 400,000 persons, the creation of legal aid facilities in urban industrial communities of less than 100,000 but over 40,000 population, and the

---

[61] Emery A. Brownell, "A Decade of Progress: Legal Aid and Defender Services," *American Bar Association Journal*, Vol. 47 (September, 1961), p. 867. Consult William M. Beaney, *Right to Counsel in American Courts* (Ann Arbor: University of Michigan Press, 1955); and B. R. Laub, "Problem of the Unrepresented, Misrepresented and Rebellious Defendant in Criminal Court," *Duquesne University Law Review*, Vol. 2 (Summer, 1964), p. 245.

strengthening of legal aid offices that are inadequate and substandard.[62] New attempts to deal with the problem of legal aid have included such diverse programs as a statewide Defenders Committee in Massachusetts to employ defendant lawyers; an intensive Legal Services Program of the New Haven Community Progress, Inc., project; the creation of legal aid program by the Hotel Trades Council of New York City; the development of a Ford Foundation supported legal aid program in California; and other similar programs.[63] The American Bar Association suggests that the minimum standards of defender service for every state should include:

1. A provision of counsel for every indigent person facing the possibility of the deprivation of his liberty or other serious criminal sanction who is unable to employ counsel.
2. The availability of representation which is experienced, competent, and zealous.
3. The provision for investigatory and other facilities necessary for the complete defense.
4. Participation in the operation at a sufficiently early state of the proceedings so as to advise fully and to protect the defendant.
5. The assurance of undivided loyalty by the defense counsel to the client.
6. The taking of appeals in prosecuting other remedies, before or after conviction, considered by the defending counsel to be in the interest of justice.
7. The maintenance in each county in which the volume of criminal cases requiring assignment of counsels is such as to justify the employment of at least one full-time lawyer to handle the work effectively, a defender office, either as a public office or as a quasi-public or private organization.
8. The enlistment of community participation and responsibility, and encouragement of the continued cooperation of the organized bar.[64]

The public defender system

The *public defender* system was initiated in Los Angeles County in 1913 in order to aid indigents in the trial process. Although many

---

[62] Wood, *op. cit.*, p. 187.

[63] Brownell, *op. cit.*, p. 869. See *Equal Justice for the Accused* (New York: Committee of the Association of the Bar of the City of New York and the National Legal Aid and Defender Association, 1959); Junius L. Allison, "Legal Aid for the Indigent Accused of Crime," *Federal Probation*, Vol. 27 (March, 1963), pp. 46–51; and Martin V. Callagy, "Legal Aid in Criminal Cases," *Journal of Criminal Law, Criminology, and Police Science*, Vol. 42 (January–February, 1952), pp. 589–624.

[64] *Ibid.*, p. 870.

critics have since questioned the right of the state to be engaged in both the prosecution and the defense through separate state-sponsored agencies, the participation of the state in both aspects of the trial process is not automatically incompatible with the search for justice. Under the public defender approach, the defense of an indigent is no longer dependent upon charity but is assumed as a legal right in order to protect all persons from unwarranted criminal prosecution.

In effect, the public defender is an attorney who is employed, together with additional assistants or deputies, on the county level in the specialization of criminal legal defense. In California, the public defender's duties and jurisdiction are specified by the California government code. These include minor civil matters, representation of persons subject to commitment under various sections of the Welfare and Institutions Code, and juvenile and criminal court cases. Operating in such large California counties as San Francisco, Los Angeles, Alameda, San Bernardino, and Orange, the public defender and his deputies theoretically represent the rights of the accused, free from political influence or control.[65]

The public defender system generally expedites the proper administration of criminal justice. In California it initially reduced "dead time" and permitted the criminal-legal system to function more efficiently. In addition, the office of the public defender acts as a constant evaluator of the activities of the district attorney's office and the effectiveness of general law enforcement. As a public agency, the public defender's office is subject to public scrutiny, and a consequence, makes the public aware of the problems involved in representing indigent defendants. Although a system of *assigned* counsel has often been used as an alternate approach to the problem, fees paid to assigned counsel in Santa Clara County (California) are generally inadequate to cover the expenses of the attorney who accepts the responsibility of an assigned case. Only by waiving a preliminary hearing and by pleading guilty in the superior court can the assigned counsel make his case economically productive. Consequently, it is questionable whether the individual is responsibly represented when the assigned counsel is forced to make an economic sacrifice to represent his client.[66]

The public defender's office, a California study revealed, is usually more costly to maintain than the payment of funds to assigned counsel for services rendered. However the inadequate compensation of assigned counsel makes any meaningful comparison difficult. The public defender can produce economic savings by eliminating unnecessary trial, reducing

---

[65] H. Reed Searle, "Argument for the Public Defender System," *Santa Clara Law Review*, Vol. 5 (Fall, 1964), p. 51. Refer to Emery A. Brownell, "Decade of Progress: Legal Aid and Defender's Services," *American Bar Association* Journal, Vol. 47 (September, 1961), p. 867.

[66] Searle, *op. cit.*, p. 57.

jail and prison sentences, lessening welfare and related programs, and minimizing dead time.[67] Where legal aid or public defender services have been unavailable, a system of assigned counsel has often been used to provide the services of an attorney for indigent offenders. Although the assigned counsel system has periodically been justified on the ground that it is the responsibility of the bar to defend the indigent, the legal profession has generally failed to fulfill this obligation. In addition, the public-private defender organization, a variation of the legal aid and defender service program which emerged after World War II in Puerto Rico, Rochester (New York), and Buffalo,[68] is a privately administered legal aid organization.

The lawyer reference approach

The Lawyer Reference Plan, first established in Los Angeles in 1937, offers legal services to members of a neighborhood or community. Serving most frequently as a referral agency, its agents direct members of the general public to competent and reliable lawyers who consult and offer services concerning a particular legal problem at a fixed moderate fee.[69] Although the plan is in operation in over 30 of the largest American cities, 57 percent of the civil and criminal attorneys in his study, Arthur L. Wood found, were unaware of it. Because the plan is not likely to have a pronounced effect upon the employment of criminal lawyers, the criminal attorney, Wood noted, expresses less disapproval of the Lawyer Reference Plan than of the public defender system. However, nearly three fourths of his criminal and civil attorney sample accepted the court-assigned counsel approach for the indigent accused of crime.

The future roles of the lawyer

The role of the lawyer in the system of criminal justice in the future must assume several dimensions. Earl F. Morris, former president of the American Bar Association, suggests that lawyers should call public attention to the low visibility areas of the criminal process which are not likely to be scrutinized by the appellate courts or to be discussed in widely reported opinions. The implementation of the various recom-

---

[67] *Ibid.*, p. 57. See David Mars, "Public Defenders," *Journal of Criminal Law, Criminology, and Police Science*, Vol. 46 (July–August, 1955), pp. 199–210; and L. M. Getly, "Five Questions on Defender Systems," *Legal Aid Brief Case*, Vol. 24 (June, 1966), p. 269.

[68] Brownell, *op. cit.*, p. 868.

[69] Wood, *op. cit.*, p. 196. Consult E. Aller, "New Hopes for Federal Public Defender Legislation," *Legal Aid Brief Case*, Vol. 20 (October, 1961) p. 26; D. M. O'Brien, Jr., "New Projects for Defense of Indigents," *Legal Aid Brief Case*, Vol. 24 (February, 1966), p. 163.

mendations of the President's Commission on Law Enforcement and the Administration of Justice falls within this category. However, the lawyer also faces the responsibility of interpreting the actual meaning and implications of the *Miranda* decision to the public. Contrary to popular belief, the *Miranda* decision, Morris contends, seems to have had little impact upon the criminal process and is but one facet of the total delinquency-crime problem.

In addition, the lawyer must also assume responsibility for seeking a public rededication to and respect for law and order. But the concept of law and order, Morris writes, does not merely imply the control of delinquency, confirmed criminality, or riotous conduct. The lawyer, in the process of securing social stability, must also involve the businessmen who participate in illegal practices in the marketplace while believing that their conduct is different from those who rob in the streets, and the professional, who views his code of conduct and the laws pertaining to him as questionable restraints upon his own desires. Crime and justice, Morris presumes, can no longer be simply defined in traditional terms. They have now become institutionalized within businesses, communities, and often within the agencies of justice. Consequently, the legal profession through its prosecuting and defense attorneys must assume social leadership to gain stability in an era of tension and change.[70] The legal profession, Morris believes, must accept a greater responsibility for modernizing the social structures which serve as the framework for human interaction.

---

[70] Earl F. Morris, "Lawyer's Role in the War on Crime," *Los Angeles Bar Bulletin,* Vol. 43 (March, 1968), p. 205. Also see Orie L. Phillips and Philbrick McCoy, *Conduct of Judges and Lawyers* (Los Angeles: Parker & Co., 1952); Albert P. Blaustein and Charles O. Porter, *The American Lawyer* (Chicago: University of Chicago Press, 1954); and Arthur T. Vanderbilt, *The Challenge of Reform* (Princeton, N.J.: Princeton University Press, 1955).

Part FIVE

The systems of justice

Chapter
17

THE JUVENILE COURT

THE EVOLUTION OF THE JUVENILE COURT

In early English common law, children over 14 were subject to the same criminal laws as adults. On the other hand, children under seven, believed to be legally incapable of forming the necessary criminal intent, could never be judged guilty of a crime. Children between 7 and 14 could be criminally charged under specific circumstances. While the English judge often showed leniency to the younger juvenile upon a judgment of guilt, he was not permitted such flexibility in adult cases. England first recognized the need to treat juvenile offenders differentially in its Juvenile Offender Act of 1847.

In the United States, the establishment of the New York City House of Refuge (1825) and later of reform schools in Massachusetts, Pennsylvania, and other states heralded the direction of future juvenile institutional development. In 1869, Massachusetts passed an act requiring the courts to give written notice to the visiting agent of the State Board of Charities before committing children under 16. Massachusetts in 1870 also enacted a law requiring separate hearings for children in Suffolk County, a provision similarly approved in New York in 1877. Another seven years passed before Massachusetts provided for a special session for juvenile offenders and for separate record and docket procedures.[1]

---

[1] Edward Eldefonso, *Law Enforcement and the Youthful Offender* (New York: John Wiley & Sons, Inc., 1967). See F. W. Nicholas, "History, Philosophy, and Procedures of Juvenile Courts," *Journal of Family Law*, Vol. 1 (Fall, 1961), p. 151; and Gustav L. Schramm, "Philosophy of the Juvenile Court," *The Annals*, Vol. 261 (January, 1949), pp. 101–8.

Special trials for those under 16 were eventually prescribed by statute in New York (1892) and Rhode Island (1898).[2]

The first juvenile court in the United States was officially established in Chicago on July 1, 1899, but it was not until 1945 that every state created some type of juvenile court. A product of a philosophy favoring treatment rather than mere punishment of the offender, the juvenile court sought to lessen the formalism of the many existing prohibitions and guarantees of due process in an attempt to permit the judicial flexibility thought to be necessary for the adequate rehabilitation of child and adolescent offenders. A legal, and yet experimental, institution, the juvenile court was created as a civil rather than criminal court in order to protect the best interests of youth.

All states, with the exception of Maine and Wyoming, had passed juvenile court acts by 1927.[3] A state-controlled juvenile court system was first established in Utah in 1908; similar systems appeared later in Connecticut (1941), and Rhode Island (1944).[4] Most European countries began to enact juvenile court laws after 1908. By 1931, some 30 foreign countries, following the earlier lead of Great Britain, had provided for a juvenile court or other substitute.[5]

THE JURISDICTION OF THE JUVENILE COURT

The juvenile court remains a combination of common and equity law. As mentioned, children could not, under English common law, be held criminally liable if they were seven years of age or under at the time of their offense, because they were believed to be below the age of reason. However, in more recent times, an intermediate age, usually between 7 and 18, has been recognized during which juvenile responsibility is somewhat diminished from that expected of adults. Although the U.S. Children's Bureau currently recommends an upper age

---

[2] Clyde B. Vedder, *Juvenile Offenders* (Springfield, Ill.: Charles C. Thomas, Publisher, 1953), p. 114. Also refer to Monrad G. Paulsen, "Legal Framework for Child Protection," *Columbia Law Review,* Vol. 66 (April, 1966), p. 679; T. A. Welch, "Delinquency Proceedings—Fundamental Fairness for the Accused in a Quasi-Criminal Forum," *Minnesota Law Review,* Vol. 50 (March, 1966), p. 653; Francis A. Allen, *The Borderland of Criminal Justice* (Chicago: University of Chicago Press, 1964); and "Juvenile Delinquency—The History and Development of Juvenile Courts," *New York Law Forum,* Vol. 12 (Winter, 1966), pp. 644–64.

[3] Eldefonso, *op. cit.,* p. 162.

[4] Vedder, *op. cit.,* p. 145. Consult Gilbert Cosulich, *Juvenile Court Laws of the United States* (New York: National Probation Association, 1939); *Basic Legal Principles of the Juvenile Court* (Blue Ridge: Training Institute for Southern Juvenile Court Judges, 1959); and M. P. Thomas, Jr., "Delinquency and Juvenile Courts: Confession and Diversity," *Federal Probation,* Vol. 25 (December, 1961), p. 417.

[5] *Ibid.,* p. 145.

limit of 18, about one third of the states support some other age limit.[6] Nevertheless, minors over 18 are nearly always referred to the criminal court for trial in most states.

If the juvenile court determines under existing procedures that the youth is not suitable for treatment in the juvenile court, his case may be transferred to a criminal court for disposition. Such dismissal is often based upon the finding that the youth does not need public help. It is more often an admission that the juvenile cannot be rehabilitated through the use of juvenile court facilities. Usually limited to specific ages or to specific offenses, a transfer from the juvenile to the criminal court is most commonly decided by the juvenile court judge. However, in some jurisdictions the adolescent may be transferred from a criminal to a juvenile court at the discretion of the criminal judge. Under a third approach, certain designated types of offenses may automatically remove juvenile court jurisdiction over the case. In Florida, for example, capital cases are tried automatically within the criminal court. However, in Illinois the right to transfer is vested in the state's attorney, who is empowered to determine the court in which the minor is to be prosecuted.[7]

Arkansas, California, and Wyoming (for females) have set the upper age limit at 21. However, the first two states share jurisdiction of persons above 18 with the state criminal court. Wyoming has designated 19 as the upper age limit for males. In Alabama, Connecticut, Georgia, Kansas, New York, North Carolina, Oklahoma (for males), South Carolina, and Vermont, the upper age limit is 16; in Delaware (for males), Florida, Illinois (for males), Kentucky (for males), Louisiana, Maine, Massachusetts, Michigan, Missouri, Tennessee, and Texas (for males), it is set at 17. Arizona, Colorado, Delaware (for females), Indiana, Iowa, Kentucky (for females), Maryland, Minnesota, Mississippi, Montana, Nebraska, Nevada, New Hampshire, New Jersey, New Mexico, North Dakota, Ohio, Oklahoma (for females), Oregon, Pennsylvania, Rhode Island, South Carolina, South Dakota, Texas (for females), federal jurisdictions, Utah, Virginia, Washington, West Virginia, and Wisconsin provide for an age of 18.[8]

---

[6] Robert W. Winslow, *Juvenile Delinquency in a Free Society* (Belmont, Calif.: Dickenson Publishing Co., Inc., 1968), p. 120; Frederich B. Sussman, *Law of Juvenile Delinquency* (New York: Oceana Publications, Inc., 1950); L. W. Schmidt, Jr., "Juvenile Court—Salvation or Damnation for Youthful Offenders?" *Michigan State Bar Journal*, Vol. 41 (February, 1962), p. 24; and Sol Rubin, "State Juvenile Court: A New Standard," *Focus*, Vol. 30 (July, 1951), pp. 103–7.

[7] "Rights and Rehabilitation in the Juvenile Courts," *Columbia Law Review*, Vol. 67 (February, 1967), p. 313. Consult D. J. Young, "How and Why of the Juvenile Court," *PTA Magazine*, Vol. 57 (December, 1962), p. 7–9.

[8] Paul W. Tappan and Ivan Nicolle, "Juvenile Delinquents and Their Treatment," *The Annals*, Vol. 339 (June, 1962), p. 152.

The criminal court possesses original jurisdiction over juvenile cases in 21 states; it is empowered to transfer juvenile cases to or shares concurrent jurisdiction with the juvenile court in 12 states.[9] In California, for example, the juvenile court maintains original jurisdiction in handling children, possessing the power to conduct a preliminary examination pertaining to any accusatory plea charging any crime or other public violation if the accused is under 18 at the time of the alleged offense. Judges of other California courts are also empowered to certify any case coming before their court to the juvenile court if the youth involved is under 21.[10]

Nevertheless, invoking the principle of *parens patriae,* the state presumes the need to exercise guardianship over a child if the parents are unable or unwilling to fulfill their responsibility. Operating as a court of equity, the juvenile court attempts to avoid the stigmatization of the child, a goal which has not been fully realized.[11] In order to facilitate this goal, juvenile courts consequently have been organized as:

1. Independent courts with jurisdiction over children.
2. Family courts with jurisdiction over specified offenses and relations and over specified types of family conduct, including jurisdiction over children.
3. Juvenile and domestic relations courts.
4. Juvenile courts as sections or parts of courts with more general jurisdiction.[12]

Each has been designed as an alternate judicial body to the criminal court in order to place greater emphasis upon the actor than upon the action and to provide protection and treatment where needed by the juvenile within an equity court setting.[13]

---

[9] *Ibid.,* p. 152; also see Stephen Schafer and Richard D. Knudten, *Juvenile Delinquency: An Introduction* (New York: Random House, Inc., 1970).

[10] Paul B. Weston and Kenneth M. Wells, *The Administration of Justice* (Englewood Cliffs, N.J.: Prentice-Hall, Inc., 1967), p. 136.

[11] Vedder, *op. cit.,* p. 148. Also see Bertram Polow, "Juvenile Court: Effective Justice or Benevolent Despotism," *American Bar Association Journal,* Vol. 53 (January, 1967), pp. 31–36; Ola Nyquist, *Juvenile Justice* (New York: Macmillan, Co., 1961); J. P. White, "Juvenile and the Court," *North Dakota Law Review,* Vol. 44 (Winter, 1968), p. 211; Harrison A. Dobbs, "In Defense of Juvenile Courts," *Federal Probation,* Vol. 13 (September, 1949), pp. 24–29; and B. Wooton, "Juvenile Courts," *Criminal Law Review,* Vol. 1961 (October, 1961), p. 669.

[12] Louis Killian, "The Juvenile Court as an Institution," *The Annals,* Vol. 261 (1949), pp. 89–91. Investigate Alfred J. Kahn, *A Court for Children* (New York: Columbia University Press, 1951); and *Justice for Youth* (New York: Community Service Society of New York, 1955).

[13] Vedder, *op. cit.,* p. 146. See *Report on the Child Offender in the Federal System of Justice* (Washington, D.C.: National Commission of Law Observance and Enforcement, 1931).

The juvenile court is also responsible for adoption, guardianship, and mentally defective and disorderly child cases. Under certain circumstances, some adult cases may likewise be included within the court's jurisdiction, especially if an adult has been charged with contributing to the delinquency of a minor or with the failure to support his children. However, juvenile courts may occasionally possess jurisdiction in matters of marital conflict, determination of paternity, criminal neglect or abandonment, and failure to support or provide for a spouse, or the like.[14]

Generally, the juvenile court permits the juvenile and related participants the following rights:

1. To a specific statement regarding the allegations of the violation.
2. To be given adequate notice.
3. To detention only when necessary.
4. To subpoena witnesses and evidence.
5. To receive a prompt and fair hearing before an impartial judge.
6. To counsel from inception of judicial proceeding until final dispositions.
7. To admission of only competent, relevant, and probative evidence.
8. To presentation of all testimony under oath.
9. To a transcript of an adjudication hearing, especially where a denial is involved.
10. To a judicial finding of fact concerning jurisdiction before consideration of unrelated social data.
11. To examination of social records and reports considered by the judge in making the disposition.
12. To appeal from a judicial determination that the juvenile is within the court's jurisdiction.

However, all courts have not recognized, encouraged, or even made available information concerning the possible use of these rights to the parties involved in the court action, thereby negating much of their potential value and impact.[15]

According to the *Handbook for Juvenile Court Judges* prepared by the National Probation and Parole Association in cooperation with the National Council of Juvenile Court Judges, a good juvenile court should recognize and adhere to the following concepts:

1. Where the social interest of the community in delinquent behavior or in a neglect situation clashes with the fundamental rights of the parent to the companionship, custody, and control of his child, it

---

[14] *Guides for Juvenile Court Judges* (New York: National Probation and Parole Association, 1957), p. 86. For special insight, see United Nations, *The Young Adult Offender* (New York: Department of Economic and Social Affairs, 1965).

[15] Horace Bellfato, "Constitution in the Juvenile Court," *New York Law Forum*, Vol. 13 (Spring, 1967), p. 7.

is essential that a thorough preliminary investigation be made, that adequate time be allowed for diagnosis, hearing, and planning, and equally important, that competent personnel carry out the treatment processes.

2. The delinquency statutes have a dual purpose: to protect the community from the child and to protect the child from himself. Many actions labeled delinquent by statute represent a threat not to the community but to the child's own personality.

3. In the great majority of instances, these ends are not basically antithetical because the delinquent acts of most children do not pose a serious threat to the community and consequently permit careful and realistic consideration and treatment of their needs without sacrificing the well-being of others.

4. The child is referred to the court on the basis of the offense, which necessarily must be considered since it colors the thinking of the child himself, his family, his school, and his neighbors, but consideration of the offense must not preclude recognition of the postulate that the overt act may or may not be indicative of the total problem. Accordingly, the disposition should be geared to the total problem—personal, family, community, or otherwise. No child can be treated in a vacuum. His home, his family, his neighborhood, his school, his church, and all other influences on his well-being must be considered.

5. Handling the case generally entails two obligations: (1) dealing with the immediate pressures created by the child's behavior as, for example, the detention of a child who is caught up in a cycle of stealing, or the return to the classroom of the persistent truant and (2) developing a long-range plan, suited to the needs of the child as they become established, and aimed at the ultimate solution.

6. The casework function is basic in carrying out the work of the court. Casework involves investigation, diagnosis, planning, and treatment.

7. Probation is casework done in the frame of authority. Authority is one of the tools used in probation.

8. When probation is not the answer, treatment in the group situation or in an institution may be called for.

9. The court recognizes that while it has a responsibility to do everything possible for the child, there may be some children so mature that the facilities of the juvenile court may not aid them and their cases must be transferred to the criminal courts.

10. The court must not try to function in a state of self-sufficient isolation.[16]

---

[16] *Guides, op. cit.*, pp. 5–6. Also see Edward S. Porter, *Conscience of the Court* (New York: Prentice-Hall, Inc., 1962); Margaret K. Rosenheim, *Justice for the Child* (New York: Free Press, 1962); and Sydney Smith, "Delinquency and the Panacea of Punishment," *Federal Probation,* Vol. 29 (September, 1965), p. 18.

THE DIFFERING PURPOSES OF THE JUVENILE
AND THE CRIMINAL COURTS

Many factors differentiate a juvenile court from a criminal court. While juvenile courts theoretically operate on behalf of the delinquent child, the adult criminal court acts upon a charge against the accused and determines the outcome in relationship to a contest between the prosecution and the defense before the judge and the jury to determine the guilt or the innocence of the accused in order to fix punishment in proportion to the crime. While juvenile court hearings are nearly always private proceedings to which only interested parties may be admitted, criminal trials are public and represent actions of the state against the alleged offender. Theoretically, juvenile courts investigate intent in order to understand the causes of behavior and prescribe a potential treatment method which can best aid the youth; adult courts, on the other hand, view intent as a matter of guilt. Juvenile courts evaluate a specific act in relationship to the other acts of the child and the total personality and situation in which the act is committed. Criminal courts, however, examine the particular act in order to determine intent and guilt.

Although criminal courts usually do not inquire into the charge before the evidence is presented by both prosecuting and defense attorneys, except through action of the grand jury, the juvenile court proceeds with an investigation of charges through the collection and evaluation of collateral reports from assorted social agencies before the hearing even commences. Jury trials in the juvenile court are waived unless demanded; they are expected unless waived in criminal jurisdictions. Many juvenile court judges may receive specialized training and become only responsible for juvenile cases; their criminal court counterparts are generally less specialized in their judicial functions. Even though adults may be released on bail under conditions determined by the judge, juveniles do not usually fall under such provisions. Instead, they may be detained at a juvenile facility or at their own homes under the supervision of their parents. Accused adults are either jailed or placed on bail, pending the actual trial or release. While criminal courts merely sentence the offender with little concern for the treatment or institutionalization which may result, children's or juvenile courts are functionally more concerned with the treatment and rehabilitation process.[17]

---

[17] Donald R. Taft and Ralph W. England, Jr., *Criminology* (New York: Macmillan Co., 1964), pp. 369–370. *Note* J. S. Gonas, "Therapy in the Juvenile Court," *American Bar Association Journal*, Vol. 48 (April, 1962), pp. 326–28; and Joseph E. Gibbs, *Juvenile Court Forum* (Tallahasse: Florida Agricultural and Mechanical University, College of Law, 1957).

PERSONNEL AND PROCEDURE IN THE JUVENILE COURT

The juvenile judge

The operation of the juvenile court depends upon the person of judge, who must be both an executive and an administrator. Because the juvenile court judge holds a less prestigious position than other judges on the criminal court, he tends to be the "low man on the totem pole."[18] Inasmuch as he often enjoys only a short tenure in office, qualified men or women are frequently discouraged from seeking a juvenile court position. In many jurisdictions, judges are chosen from a list of elected judges and are appointed by the governor, city or county authority, mayor, state commission, juvenile committee, or some other representative group. Whatever their point of origin, most are poorly prepared to assume their new responsibilities, since few law schools prepare their graduates for juvenile court judgeships. Frequently trained in law but often insensitive to juvenile needs, the juvenile court judge may attempt to change adolescent behavior through intimidation or threats of institutionalization.

Of the 1,564 judges replying to a 1963 survey by the National Council of Juvenile Court Judges, 70 percent reported their participation in juvenile matters. Of the total responding, 71 percent had received law degrees; 49 percent, however, had not completed an undergraduate degree. The average age of the judge hearing juvenile cases was 53 years; his average salary, if fulltime, approximated $12,493. Although nearly 75 percent of the replying judges had been elected to office, one third had been previously elected to another office. Of the responding full-time judges, 72 percent disclosed that they spend a quarter or less of their time on juvenile matters. One third noted that their court did not have probation officers or social workers; 83 percent reported no regular availability of psychologists or psychiatrists.[19]

Other officers of the court

In many states, the judge is empowered to appoint *referees*, who hear cases referred to their attention. In most of these states, the referee,

---

[18] Lewis Yablonsky, "The Role of Law and Social Science in the Juvenile Court," *Journal of Criminal Law, Criminology, and Police Science,* Vol. 53 (December, 1962), p. 429; Justin W. Polier, *A View From the Bench* (New York: National Council on Crime and Delinquency, 1964); and Paul W. Alexander, "Of Juvenile Court Justice and Judges," *Yearbook of the National Probation and Parole Association,* 1947 (New York: National Probation and Parole Association, 1948).

[19] Winslow, *op. cit.,* p. 123. See William H. Sheridan, *A Social Worker Takes a Case into Court* (Washington, D.C.: U.S. Government Printing Office, 1962), pp. 1–14; and Merritt Gilman and Alice M. Law, *Training of Juvenile Probations Officers* (Washington, D.C.: U.S. Government Printing Office, 1962), pp. 1–78.

usually prescribed in law, is not authorized to designate a final order. Instead, he acts as a hearing officer, attempting to reduce testimony to facts, and makes recommendations concerning disposition. The *clerk of court* is variably responsible for filing and docketing cases, keeping a variety of case records, preparing case calendars, and recording the proceedings. The *court reporter* usually makes stenographic records, furnishes copies of the proceedings to the judge and/or others entitled to their availability, and provides transcripts for appeals. The *bailiff* or *court officer* maintains order and assists the judge as needed.

The *probation staff* works under the supervision of the juvenile court judge, generally completing a social study or an evaluation of participants in each juvenile case coming to the court's attention. As necessary, it also prescribes treatment in the community for children and adults placed under its supervision. Although probation officers desirably possess a minimum of two years of graduate training in social work, the insufficiency of personnel for probation services has caused a general lowering of requirements, currently to the level of a baccalaureate degree for professional long-term employment.[20]

Existing personnel problems have been aggravated in recent years by the continuing rise in delinquency. With one of every nine children and one of every six male adolescents being referred to the juvenile court before his 18th birthday, the personnel problem has become most acute. In the District of Columbia alone, 10,000 delinquent children were processed before the juvenile court judges during 1967. Each judge of the three-man juvenile court heard 3,500 cases, or about 14 per day. While approximately 85 percent of the adolescents waived counsel and acknowledged their involvement, their admission was partially encouraged by the excessive caseload which prohibited the intimate involvement of probation personnel with the growing number of juvenile offenders coming to their attention.

In such situations, the presence of an attorney for the youth or his family may be extremely valuable if not critical to the search for justice. However, the presence of attorneys has not always been encouraged by the court or its judge. A 1960 poll of 57 judges by the Governor's Special Study Commission on Juvenile Justice in California disclosed

---

[20] *Guides, op. cit.,* pp. 20–23. Examine Joel F. Handler and Margaret K. Rosenheim, "Privacy in Welfare: Public Assistance and Juvenile Justice," *Law and Contemporary Problems,* Vol. 31 (Spring, 1966), pp. 377–412; Roscoe Pound, "The Juvenile Court in the Service of the State," *Yearbook of the National Probation and Parole Association* (New York: National Probation and Parole Association, 1950); Holland M. Cary, "Division of Responsibility between the Juvenile Court and Welfare Agencies," *Federal Probation,* Vol. 25 (June, 1961), p. 8; George E. Gardner, "The Juvenile Court as a Child Care Institution," *Federal Probation,* Vol. 16 (June, 1952), pp. 8–12; and Frank T. Glynn, "Courts and Social Work," *Social Work Yearbook, 1954* (New York, 1954), pp. 153–54.

that 10 juvenile judges believed that attorneys are helpful to the Court, 9 maintained that counsel should be present, 25 indicated counsel are welcome in their courts, 7 presented no objection to the presence of counsel, and 6 believed that "attorneys do not accomplish much."[21] The infrequent appearance of counsel, the Commission discovered, was due to a number of factors: Many of the juvenile court cases involved children of social and economically disadvantaged homes whose parents cannot afford an attorney. Many children admitted their derelictions and no issue was in dispute. Many parents were not informed of the right to counsel or this information was not transmitted until the child was actually at the hearing and the court was ready to proceed. Many judges discouraged the presence of counsel in their courts in an effort to reduce the time devoted to the assignment. Some courts, in the belief that attorneys have no place in the juvenile court, used coercive means to discourage their presence. Probation officers would frequently counsel the parents against hiring an attorney, assuring them there would be no difference in the case's outcome, in order to lessen expenses. Attorneys found juvenile court practices confusing and disturbing because their traditional role and prerogatives were not allowed. Finally, some judges were concerned that more frequent appearance of counsel would invite more appeals, thereby upsetting traditional, local juvenile court procedures.[22]

Only a minority of juvenile court judges, the Commission discovered, routinely advised their parents of the right to representation by counsel in the juvenile court before the announcement of the Gault decision.[23] Only 21 of the reporting 57 juvenile court judges indicated that the court or its probation personnel, serving 58 percent of the California population, routinely informed parents of their right to have counsel present.[24]

The discretionary role of the police

The greatest number of juveniles who appear in juvenile court are referred by the police, although more than half of all police contacts with

---

[21] William B. McKesson, "Right to Counsel in Juvenile Proceedings," *Minnesota Law Review,* Vol. 45 (April, 1961), p. 846. See Junius L. Allison, "Counsel in the Juvenile Courts," *Federal Probation,* Vol. 30 (March, 1966), pp. 25–29; and Charles Schnitsky, *The Role of the Lawyer in Children's Court* (Washington, D.C.: U.S. Government Printing Office, 1962).

[22] As reported in *ibid.,* p. 847; also see R. C. Algase, "Right to Fair Trial in Juvenile Court," *Journal of Family Law,* Vol. 3 (Fall, 1963), p. 292.

[23] *Ibid.,* p. 849. Refer to J. C. Hall, "Judicial Ethics for the Juvenile Court Judge," *Journal of Family Law,* Vol. 3 (Fall, 1963), p. 248.

[24] *Ibid.,* pp. 849–50; and B. Wooten, "White Paper on Children in Trouble," *Criminal Law Review,* Vol. 1968 (September, 1968), p. 776.

delinquent juveniles never result in juvenile court referral.[25] While the basic police function is to enforce laws and to bring criminal charges against violating adults, the very definition of delinquency necessitates changes in police response to juveniles. In order to protect the juvenile from victimization by adults, the officer must assume preventive as well as protective responsibility for adolescent actions. Consequently, the policeman exercises a wider range of discretionary powers in dealing with adolescents. He may, for example, take action to keep the youth from drag racing, experimenting with drugs or narcotics, drinking, sexual promiscuity, or loitering with gang members. Because delinquency prohibitions are so inclusive, the policeman's decisions regarding a particular event may open up a chain of consequences which will have a long-term effect upon the adolescent and his family. Frequently, he will warn the youth to cease his actual or alleged violating conduct on the spot. At other times, depending upon his perception of the seriousness of the event, the policeman will transport the child to the police station, return him to his home, refer the situation to his parents, or even warn both the child and his parents of future consequences should the behavior continue.

The fact that fewer than one half of the juvenile-police encounters result in police station or other juvenile detention only illustrates the extensive discretionary powers the police possess. Nevertheless, whatever his action may be, the policeman's decision possesses a major importance for the youth's future behavior. An officer who responds to the juvenile's violation with hostility and threatened use of force, for example, risks a response of defiance, disrespect, and ridicule. Excessive deference may likewise undermine the policeman's authority and increase the youth's disrespect for law.[26]

Initial police contact often results from a complaint or from the officer's apprehension of the juvenile at the time of an alleged offense. In other instances, the beat patrolman may make the original contact. Whatever the procedure or context, the policeman may ultimately release the juvenile, with or without a warning, after completing a brief written report for the Field Bureau or after filing a more formal report to be referred to the Juvenile Bureau for possible action. On the other hand, he may immediately turn the youth over to the Juvenile Bureau or refer the case directly to the Juvenile Court. Whatever action he actually invokes depends in part on the attitudes of the juvenile, the number of persons facing detention in juvenile facilities, the status of the offender's family, the policeman's personal attitudes, and other similar

[25] "Juvenile Delinquents: The Police, State Courts, and Individualized Justice," *Harvard Law Review,* Vol. 79 (February, 1966), p. 776.
[26] See Irving Piliavin and Scott Briar, "Police Encounters with Juveniles," *American Journal of Sociology,* Vol. 70 (1964), pp. 206–14.

factors. Although the police will refrain from referring a case to the juvenile court if evidence is insufficient or the offense is trivial, they generally, in order to keep the referral threat from losing its force, refer automatically all cases in which the juvenile does not confess to the court. In such instances, the court, however, is likely to dismiss the proceeding, possibly after lecturing the offender on the need for future good conduct.

If the policeman chooses to detain the juvenile at the police station, juvenile facility, or local jail pending further investigation of the case, he must describe the facts of the offense necessary to sustain a petition in the juvenile court; record any previous police and court or social agency action regarding the individual; detail the attitudes of the child, his parents, and the complainant to the act; and give insight into the child's home, school, and community adjustment.[27] Although the policeman is generally limited to 24 hours of investigation time before he is obligated to release the child to his parents, detention may continue once a formal petition has been filed with the juvenile court.[28]

Many are critical of police discretionary powers. Yet the practice of police screening of juvenile offenses allows a lighter juvenile court caseload, the development of more positive police attitudes toward their role in curbing delinquency, the opportunity of juveniles to avoid court adjudication, and the potential strengthening of parental control both by a threat of possible referral to the juvenile court and by police support of parental authority.[29] Conversely, informal police action may heighten the juvenile's fear of the court and distort his view of the goals of the juvenile adjudication process.

Delinquency cases are usually referred to the juvenile court under the following conditions: if the alleged act committed by the child is of serious nature; if the overt act is not intrinsically serious, but the total circumstances surrounding the child point to the need for protective action; if the child has a record of repeated delinquency extending over a considerable period, even though his past delinquency has not resulted in a previous referral; if the child and his parents have shown themselves unable or unwilling to cooperate with agencies of a nonauthoritative character; casework with the child by a nonauthoritative or voluntary agency has failed in the past; if protective services needed by the child

---

[27] Children's Bureau, *Police Serving for Juveniles* (Washington, D.C.: U.S. Government Printing Office, 1954), pp. 7–10.

[28] Richard A. Myren and Lynn D. Swanson, *Police Work with Children* (Washington, D.C.: U.S. Government Printing Office, 1962), pp. 39–57.

[29] *Ibid.*, p. 785. See Walter Gellhorn, *Children and Families in the Courts of New York City* (New York: Vail-Ballou Press, 1954); *Standards for Specialized Courts Dealing with Children* (Washington, D.C.: U.S. Department of Health, Education, and Welfare, 1954); and Hugh P. Reed, *The Handling of the Neglected and Delinquent Child in Lincoln, Nebraska, 1955* (New York, 1955).

can be best obtained by the court through its probation department; if the child denies the offense, evidence warrants referral, and if the police believe judicial determination is required; or the child is placed in detention by police.[30]

Detention and shelter care

Although the adolescent may be *detained* in a temporary care center in a physically restricting facility pending juvenile court disposition or transfer to another jurisdiction, he may be *sheltered* in some instances in a temporary care and physically unrestricting facility awaiting his return to his own home or placement for longer-term care.[31] In general, *detention* agencies are designed to protect the community and the child by restricting the youth's mobility; *shelter care*, on the other hand, offers a temporary home or shelter for the child, generally nondelinquent, whose best interests is served by his removal from his parents, guardian, or even present institution. In small communities, sheltered care may be provided in subsidized boarding or receiving homes; in larger communities, in small open-type institutions.

As a policy, detention is usually limited to those children who are likely to run away or return to another court or place of residence during the designated period of study or disposition; whose problems are so serious and family relations so strained that they are likely to encourage later trouble and to necessitate protection from threatening community or personal situations; who have a history of serious offenses and consequently constitute a threat to community safety; who are parole violators or who are awaiting transfer to another jurisdiction, agency, or institution; and for whom secure residential care is needed to complete necessary psychological or other studies.[32] Shelter care, on the other hand, is used primarily for children who require temporary assistance due to physical or moral danger in the home or to strained relationships between child and parents which may damage the child.[33]

---

[30] *Guides, op. cit.*, p. 31. Refer to Robert M. Terry, "The Screening of Juvenile Offenders," *Journal of Criminal Law, Criminology, and Police Science*, Vol. 58, No. 2 (June, 1967), pp. 173–81; and Ray Studt, "Functions of Detention—Principles, Operation" (mimeo, unpublished).

[31] *Ibid.*, p. 42. See Norman Sherwood, *Detention Practices: Significant Developments in the Detention of Youth and Children* (New York: National Probation and Parole Association, 1960).

[32] *Ibid.*, pp. 40–47. Consult also *Standards and Guides for the Detention of Children and Youth* (New York: National Council on Crime and Delinquency, 1961), pp. 1–168.

[33] *Ibid.*, pp. 47–48. Examine William H. Sheridan, "Juvenile Court Intake," *Journal of Family Law*, Vol. 2 (Fall, 1962), pp. 139–156; and Herbert D. Foster, "Foster Homes for Juvenile Delinquents," *Federal Probation*, Vol. 13 (September, 1949), pp. 46–51.

The petition and the preliminary hearing

Juvenile court proceedings are more likely to be inquisitorial than accusatorial under the concept of *parens patriae*. In order to protect the interests of the child, the juvenile court generally follows a six-step procedural process: petition; appearance, arraignment, and adjournment; parole or remand; social investigation; hearing and adjudication; and disposition of cases coming to its attention. This process may vary by states.[34] While a complaint may be registered by any member of society concerning a juvenile's conduct, the police commonly inaugurate the petition against the youth. Generally, they are expected to provide the alleged facts which give the court jurisdiction over the child and/or adult and to identify other pertinent personal data and information about any child, codelinquent, complainant, or victim, including pertinent statements regarding injuries or damages, reasons for the request for court action, together with other data concerning previous police contacts which did not culminate in referral. They also give a brief summary of any significant factors revealed in the investigation. Frequently, court records concerning parents or other circumstances which point to the need for protective action are provided in their report.[35]

The judge or referee presiding at a juvenile court hearing must determine at the outset if the acts or conditions alleged in the petition bring the juvenile within the jurisdiction of the court, if the facts as stated support adjudication of the child as a neglected or wayward delinquent, and if the youth has committed an offense defined as delinquent which might be a crime if committed by an adult. If the juvenile and his parents deny the allegations set forward in the petition, the hearing may be adjourned so that a policeman or probation officer may secure the presence of witnesses corroborating the allegations of the petition or decide whether to continue the case within the juvenile court. If the juvenile admits his participation in the alleged violation, the hearing or juvenile officer may either release the child to his parents with a reprimand or warning, direct the child to some community social service agency, or refer the case to the juvenile court for eventual disposition.

In California, a juvenile court hearing begins with the judge or clerk reading the petition concerning the case. As he does so, he explains any term or allegation contained in the petition upon the request of any of the hearing's participants. Describing procedures and possible

[34] Tappan and Nicolle, *op. cit.*, p. 162. Also see *Procedure and Evidence in Juvenile Court* (New York: National Council on Crime and Delinquency, 1962); and Paul W. Tappan, *Delinquent Girls in Court* (New York: Columbia University Press, 1947).

[35] *Guides, op. cit.*, p. 32.

consequences, he also ascertains whether the minor or his parents, guardian, or adult relative have been informed of the right to be represented by counsel. If the minor or the minor's family is indigent, the court may appoint counsel to represent the minor at this time. However, a defense attorney must be appointed if the minor is charged with conduct which constitutes a felony if committed by an adult.[36] A preliminary juvenile court hearing is designed to determine whether the court possesses jurisdiction to hear the case; to adjudicate the issue of delinquency, neglect, or dependency; and to determine disposition. The typical hearing in the Cook County (Chicago) Family Court, a National Council on Crime and Delinquency study disclosed, averages slightly over 15 minutes, approximately one half the time the Council suggests is needed for adequate consideration of a particular case.[37]

Juvenile court procedure: The social study and case disposition

The probation department engages in a social study of the juvenile and his circumstances, usually upon the filing of a petition. Intended to provide the court with all available information concerning the child and his circumstances in order to assist its development of a maximum treatment alternative, the social study is designed to present a composite picture of the juvenile's potential for probation rehabilitation. Commonly, the social study includes a description of the offense or present problem; a discussion of previous problems or prior delinquencies; a record of family and child history; an evaluation of the juvenile's home, neighborhood, church, school, and employment relationships; insight into the youth's interests, activities, health, personality, and attitude; information concerning the adolescent's contact with other community agencies; a discussion of his individual strengths and weaknesses; and a summary and plan for resolution of the problem.[38]

After this has been received, the court must determine what action should be taken and what rights of the child or parent, if any, should be restricted through judicial decision. Once this judgment has been made, the actual supervision of the continuing care and treatment of the child is delegated to the court's administrative Probation Department which operates on its behalf. The child or youth may be treated in his own home through the legal procedures of probation or through protective supervision. The use of *probation* allows the Probation Department the opportunity to supervise the youth's activities within his

---

[36] Weston and Wells, *op. cit.,* pp. 207–8.

[37] National Council on Crime and Delinquency, *The Cook County Family Court and Arthur J. Audy Home* (New York: National Council on Crime and Delinquency, 1963), pp. 28–29.

[38] *Guides, op. cit.,* pp. 53–55.

own community, often by the person who originally completed the social study. Because probation does not involve a change in guardianship or transfer of legal custody, it aids the maintenance of family unity while yet limiting some of the powers of the youth or his parents. *Protective supervision,* on the other hand, establishes a legal status under which a neglected youth is permitted to remain at home under the supervision of the department or a court-designated agency in order to evaluate the home situation.

Although probation is frequently used to allow the youth treatment in his own community, it is periodically violated by the juvenile. Usually his violation falls into one of two categories: the commission of a new offense, or a technical violation. While the commission of a new offense refers to a violation of a delinquency statute, the technical violation refers to the general or specific conditions of probation which have been violated by the individual.[39]

If home treatment is judged inadequate or inappropriate, the child may be remanded to an appropriate institution. In any case, the court generally retains control of intake and release procedures, visitation privileges, and conditions pertinent to the youth's treatment. Deciding what is best for the child, the judge subsequently may either:

1. Place the child under the supervision (probation) of a referee or counselor in the child's own home or in a suitable custodial location under conditions reasonably decided by him.
2. Commit the child to the custody or guardianship of a public or private institution or agency authorized to care for children, place him in a family home or commit him to a training or industrial school.
3. Direct the parents, guardians, or legal custodian to pay the person or institution maintenance expenses if they encouraged, caused, or contributed to the acts or conditions which caused the child to be brought before the juvenile court.[40]

There are five basic mandates, the National Probation and Parole Association believes, for the successful disposition of delinquency cases. The child must be *individualized* so that his act is not lost in the mass of cases coming before the court. In order to effectively accomplish this end, the court must possess an awareness of how the *child views himself.* Only then can the judge *weigh the past in terms of the future.* However, he must remain flexible, keeping the specific child in mind and not be dominated by some dogmatic assertion which restricts his

---

[39] Refer to "Young Adult Offender: Current Practices and Programme in Prevention and Treatment," *United Nations Monthly Chronicle,* Vol. 3 (March, 1966), pp. 38–44; and Francis A. Allen, *The Borderline of Criminal Justice* (Chicago: University of Chicago Press, 1964).

[40] Schafer and Knudten, *op. cit.,* p. 305.

conception of his function and position. Only then can he determine the *type and quality of treatment services* necessary and available for the successful rehabilitation of the juvenile.[41]

Whatever the judgment, the juvenile court's decision, however, is not a conviction. The child or youth has not been charged with a crime and cannot be found guilty of such an act or be judged a criminal. Nevertheless, he may appeal the order of the juvenile court to a proper appellate court on matters of law and/or fact, although he may not present new evidence at the appeal hearing in most states. Only the legality or severity of the court's order is generally open to question.[42]

NEW CHALLENGES FACING THE JUVENILE COURT

Kent v. United States

The operation of the federal juvenile court was first challenged by the U.S. Supreme Court in *Kent* v. *United States* (1966), a case arising from the waiver of jurisdiction over a 16-year-old defendant by the Juvenile Court of the District of Columbia and his subsequent trial and conviction in the U.S. District Court for the District of Columbia. Morris Kent, a seriously disturbed young, black male, was arrested in 1961 for housebreaking, robbery, and rape. Although in serious need of professional care and treatment for his mentally disturbed condition, the District of Columbia Juvenile Court was unable to provide him with community treatment. Consequently, it waived its jurisdiction to the adult criminal court so that its judge could remand the youth to a mental institution until he recovered his sanity, after which he would complete his 30- to 90-year sentence.[43]

Although the original conviction was upheld by the U.S. Court of Appeals, the U.S. Supreme Court reversed the decision, maintaining the juvenile court's denial of the defendant's motion for a hearing on the question of waiver was unconstitutional. In filing its decision, the U.S. Supreme Court essentially questioned whether the lower court had not denied the juvenile due process, noting that the juvenile offender never knew the constitutional protection accorded adults nor the regenerative treatment supposedly postulated for adolescents in juvenile court

---

[41] *Guides, op. cit.,* pp. 71–77. Also consult Joachim P. Sechel, *A Study of Six California Counties with a Typical Juvenile Court Commitment Rate* (Sacramento: Calif. Youth Authority, 1960); and D. M. Scaceia, "Federal Commitment Practices and Procedures for Juvenile Offenders," *Syracuse Law Review,* Vol. 15 (Summer, 1964), p. 669.

[42] *Ibid.,* p. 78–80.

[43] David L. Bazelon, "Justice for Juveniles," *New Republic,* Vol. 156 (April 22, 1967), p. 13.

philosophy.[44] While demanding the future application of due process proceedings to juvenile hearings, the Supreme Court expressed a desire for a fairer expression of the juvenile court concept in the future.

Gault v. Arizona

The *Gault* v. *Arizona* (1967) decision deciding the first state juvenile court challenge accepted by the U.S. Supreme Court since the juvenile court's organization in 1899, was derived from the case of Gerald Francis Gault, who with a friend by the name of Ralph Lewis was taken into custody by the sheriff of Gila County (Arizona) on Monday, June 8, 1964, at 10 A.M. At the time, Gerald Gault was still subject to a six months' probation order entered in February, 1964, for having been in company with another boy who stole a wallet from a lady's purse. The police action of June 8 was stimulated by a verbal complaint of a neighbor who claimed that a caller or callers made lewd or indecent remarks to her person. As a consequence of an ensuing court hearing, the judge committed Gerald as a juvenile delinquent to a state industrial school "for a period of his minority, unless sooner discharged by due process of law."[45]

During the hearing, the probation officer acted as counsel for the child, serving concurrently as an agent of the state. The state not only failed to provide adequate notice of the hearing to the family but also failed to inform Gerald's parents of his detention until some 12 hours after it had occurred. Neither Gault nor his parents were informed by the court of his right to have assistance by counsel nor his privilege against self-incrimination. Although the decision was upheld upon appeal to the state court of appeals, Justice Abe Fortas, speaking for the majority of the U.S. Supreme Court, reversed the decision, noting that the "condition for being a boy does not justify a kangaroo court."[46]

The court was not unanimous in this decision, however. Justice Potter Steward, speaking for the minority, declared that juvenile proceedings are not criminal trials but rather civil trials in which the goal is the correction of the juvenile's condition. The act of imposing constitutional due process restrictions, already applicable to adversary criminal trials, to the thousands of juvenile courts in the United States, Steward argued, is wholly unsound as a matter of constitutional law and sadly unwise

[44] Bellfatto, *op. cit.*, p. 9; and Richard D. Knudten, *Criminological Controversies* (New York: Appleton-Century-Crofts, 1967), p. 303.

[45] "In the Matter of Gault," *Current History*, Vol. 53 (August, 1967), p. 112.

[46] Also see "Juvenile Courts: The Legacy of Gault," *PTA Magazine*, Vol. 62 (March, 1968), pp. 6–8, 12–14; "Juvenile Courts," *Vanderbilt Law Review*, Vol. 20 (October, 1967), pp. 1161–66; Noah Weinstein and Corinne Goodman, "Constructive Response for Juvenile Courts," *American Bar Association Journal*, Vol. 53.

as a matter of judicial policy.[47] Because the arguments before the Supreme Court disclosed that the parents of Gerald Gault were aware of their right to counsel, to subpoena and to cross-examination of witnesses, no issue of compulsory self-incrimination, Stewart claimed, existed in the case. He said, "I would dismiss the appeal."[48]

The importance of these decisions

The *Kent* and *Gault* decisions, the first cases dealing with the juvenile court since its creation in 1899, have opened new issues in federal and state juvenile due process. Monrad G. Paulsen believes that current interpretations of the U.S. Supreme Court have pointed to a juvenile court quite different from that proposed by the reformers. As a consequence of these decisions, the new court, Paulsen anticipates, is to be a court of last resort and "not a gateway to rehabilitation and reeducation."[49] Current Supreme Court interpretations, Paulsen contends, place legal rather than rehabilitative or regenerative solutions in the position of greatest prominence.[50]

However, Gary G. Strieker disagrees, arguing that the *Gault* decision has destroyed "the childishness which had made a constitutional delinquent of that body of social experiment and legal exceptions applying to the juvenile court."[51] The youth, Strieker observes, may now confront his accusers and demand notice of charges against his person. He is specifically entitled to counsel, the confrontation and cross-examination of witnesses, and the privilege against self-incrimination currently available to adults. Nevertheless, while these provide positive benefits, they have also caused some deficiencies. For example, the *Gault* decision, Strieker notes, has created new problems, including the basic question of whether the child is ever competent to waive his constitutional rights in either the juvenile or criminal court. Can the minor who must be protected due to his adolescent character in the juvenile court under its philosophy, Strieker asks, possess the maturity or even the right to waive his constitutional and common-law guarantees? Although the

---

[47] *Guides,* p. 113. Note T. Rubin and R. S. Shaffer, "Constitutional Protections for the Juvenile," *Denver Law Journal,* Vol. 44 (Winter, 1967), p. 66; and Curtis C. Shears, "Legal Problems Peculiar to Children's Courts," *American Bar Association Journal,* Vol. 48 (August, 1962), p. 719.

[48] *Ibid.,* p. 117.

[49] Monrad G. Paulsen, "The Role of Juvenile Court," *Current History,* Vol. 53 (August, 1967), p. 75. Also examine F. A. Allen, "Juvenile Court and the Limits of Juvenile Justice," *Wayne Law Review,* Vol. 11 (Spring, 1965), p. 676; and Walter G. Whitlack, "Juvenile Court—A Court of Law," *Case Western Reserve Law Review,* Vol. 18 (May, 1967), pp. 1239–50.

[50] *Ibid.,* pp. 1239–50.

[51] Gary G. Strieker, "Waiver of Constitutional Rights by Minors: A Question of Law or Facts?" *Hastings Law Journal,* Vol. 19 (November, 1967), p. 223.

Gault decision has opened new progressive treatment opportunities to the juvenile, it has not, Strieker contends, eliminated the right of juvenile waiver to the criminal court. Under California law a minor, Strieker points out, may waive his constitutional rights only if he places this waiver knowingly. However, waiver loss ultimately depends upon the competence of the child to make a waiver.

The continuing debate and its meaning

As a result of the Supreme Court's decision to resolve a long-standing controversy over the basic due process to which the juvenile is entitled, the juvenile court is in a transitory stage. Although the juvenile court has primarily sought the rehabilitation of the child and adolescent offender, its legalistic paternalism has necessitated a clarification of the exact procedural due process permitted "court-protected" youth. Consequently, the concept of *parens patraie* is under attack from two directions. Opponents of this principle argue that the juvenile proceedings are far from being noncriminal in nature because juvenile courts do deprive children of their liberty and mobility. On the other hand, others attack the basic assumption of the entire system, arguing that juvenile justice does not come close to performing its rehabilitative function. Therefore, if the purposes of the juvenile court are not being met, the philosophy upon which the court is founded, they conclude, has little validity.[52]

Some critics of the juvenile court argue that its emphasis upon saving a child through rehabilitation is itself rather puzzling to the youth who is being saved. Coming predominantly from lower-class homes marked by major inadequacies in income, family commitment, and future goals, young offenders are confronted by the court with an optimism which is out of character in their normal environment. Still others contend that the court actually degrades the teen-ager as a youth when he has matured well beyond the concept of the child assumed in the origins of the juvenile court. Consequently, teen-agers, these critics explain, are bored, contemptuous, and impatient with the juvenile court. Its attempts to help are a source of its basic weakness. While its principal services are made disproportionately available to the poor, the operation of the court, critics note, is not designed for the convenience of the poor. At the New York Family Court, for example, all parents, regardless of work schedule, and children are called to a morning court hearing at 9:30 A.M.; no attempt is made to space the cases throughout the day so that a full day's wage is not lost. Therefore, the poor, they

---

[52] Marlene Arnold, "Juvenile Justice in Transition," *UCLA Law Review,* Vol. 14 (May, 1967), p. 1146.

note, lose income at the same moment their time is wasted. Then, too, if cases are postponed, the financial disaster confronting a limited-income family is heightened. Therefore, the juvenile court, they argue, has been transformed into a class institution which serves delinquents who come primarily from the lower class but which does not truly serve the needs of the poor.[53]

But even these criticisms dismiss an even greater dimension of the argument. One of the most serious faults of the juvenile court is its failure, Paul W. Tappan and Ivan Nicolle believe, to face the issue of guilt. Not only does the failure to confront this question partially undermine the effective power of the court, but it permits the juvenile to avoid coming to grips with his own need for a change in self-concept. The strong emphasis of the juvenile court upon the welfare of the child places an excessive emphasis upon administrative rather than legal solutions to basic legal problems. Unfortunately, the juvenile court hearing, Tappan and Nicolle contend, allows the family, the probation officer, and even the judge to circumvent the central legal issue at point, namely the act which originally caused the youth's appearance in the Court.[54]

Reactions to the juvenile court in Great Britain and Scotland

In England, too, the juvenile court concept has come under increasing attack. Because it is both a criminal court of trial and a child's welfare board in Great Britain, the juvenile court's operations have often been antagonistic to the rehabilitative goals of juvenile court philosophy. The solution to this duality of purpose, Michael Aubrey believes, rests with the removal of British-approved schools for juveniles from the sphere of prisons and punitive establishments and the integration of such institutions into the system of general education. Additionally, the juvenile court, he concludes, must be changed into a more meaningful and different type of official body.[55]

In order to overcome many of these shortcomings, the Kilbrandon Committee on Children and Young Persons (Scotland) and the Joint Central Committee of the Police Federation have recommended the creation of Juvenile Panels which would possess jurisdiction over all children below the age of 16 or school-leaving age. Responsible for the care and the protection of children, such panels would act in the child's interest in cases in which the child violated laws pertaining to crimes and offenses. The Ingleby Committee on Children and Young

---

[53] Monrad G. Paulsen, "Juvenile Courts, Family Courts, and the Poor Man," *California Law Review*, Vol. 54 (May, 1966), p. 697.

[54] Tappan and Nicolle, *op. cit.*, p. 164.

[55] Michael Aubrey, "The Future of Juvenile Courts," *Criminal Law Review*, Vol. 1965 (November, 1965), pp. 641–42.

Persons (Great Britain) suggested modifications in existing juvenile court practices, recognizing that the child should not be separated from his own parents unless specific and defined matters have been "adequately proved."[56]

However, even these alternatives, Michael Aubrey argues, are somewhat misdirected. Instead, what is necessary, he contends, is a new body which will remove these violations from the sphere of criminal proceedings. Although it must be recognized from the outset that most juveniles commit offenses similar to those committed by those children who appear in the juvenile court, the court should not de-emphasize, if rehabilitation is truly to be accomplished, the criminal or delinquent aspects of such proceedings. Children's Advice Panels, Aubrey argues, would be established as advisory bodies possessing authority to make binding orders in carefully defined circumstances but without power to make findings of fact concerning the offense. Consisting of three persons with experience in methods of treatment of children (*i.e.*, a schoolmaster, a probation officer, and an approved school or children's officer), the panel should give advice and make positive recommendations in any case in which a child, his parents, or the local authority seeks its counsel. It should have jurisdiction by consent in cases in which children below school-leaving age but not over the age of criminal responsibility admit the facts and consent to the direction which the panel sets forth. While the decision of the panel should not be appealable to the juvenile court, parents should retain the privilege of having the case reviewed by a regional body of five members. Such panels, concerned purely with these cases and held finally accountable to the Home Office,[57] should operate where they possess jurisdiction by consent, where the local authority shows that a child below school-leaving age is in need of care and of protection and the parents are incapable of exercising these responsibilities, and where the juvenile court which has found a child or young person guilty of a criminal offense.[58]

Supporters of the present juvenile court see little reason for the development of such panels, arguing that rehabilitation does indeed take place despite the shortcomings that are currently evident in the juvenile court and its agencies at the present time. Juvenile proceedings, they argue, are an integral part of the rehabilitation process. Children and youth are allowed informal and friendly hearings in the hope that the juvenile's trust and confidence in the court will lead him to reorient his basic activity patterns. Although critics of this interpretation maintain that there is little evidence of rehabilitation at the hearing stage, sup-

---

[56] *Ibid.*, p. 643.
[57] *Ibid.*, pp. 646–47.
[58] *Ibid.*, p. 650.

porters of the court continue to find great value in an informal confrontation free of restrictive due process. There are no guarantees, they note, that the full application of due process safeguards to juvenile cases would necessarily create any better atmosphere for the rehabilitation of the child and adolescent offender.

While supporters of the juvenile court system suggest that the juvenile court protects the youth from stigmatization and criminal institutionalization, its critics argue that institutionalization in an industrial or boys' or girls' school serves the same function as imprisonment does for the adult offender. Consequently, the denial of due process to juveniles in the guise of rehabilitation actually enhances, some argue, their probable participation in crime. The denial of criminal due process to juvenile offenders, Marlene Arnold argues, is an even less viable concept than the idea that rehabilitation does occur in an institutional setting.[59]

Agencies for juvenile rehabilitation are not noticeably more effective than adult institutions. Consequently, the criteria for determining the content of juvenile due process should follow the same lines as those existing in adult cases. And yet, some legitimate differences between the needs of juvenile and adults, Arnold admits, must be recognized within the system of juvenile due process. The right to jury trial and the absolute right to release on bail, she suggests, are not as important in juvenile cases as they are in adult proceedings. However, if the real foundation of the *parens patriae* system is a concern for the best interest of the juvenile, it is impossible, she concludes, to accept the traditional arguments for depriving juveniles of due process or to argue that all elements of criminal justice must be included.[60]

Although the argument goes on the continuance of privacy at juvenile court hearings receives near-unanimous support, even from those who disagree with the juvenile court procedure. Normally, the public is still barred from juvenile court proceedings, even though the judge generally possesses the discretion to allow a few representatives or observers to watch the court in action. The absence of a jury aids in the maintenance of privacy. Nevertheless, while communication media in the past have been specifically excluded from court hearings, newspapers in recent years have been able to gain access to court data and often to the juvenile court itself.[61] This relaxation of control over publicity is a form of betrayal of the original juvenile court philosophy. While the public may demand its right to know who the future offender might be, the

---

[59] Arnold, *op. cit.*, p. 1150.

[60] *Ibid.*, p. 1158. See Robert M. Sheahen, "Constitutional Law—Due Process," *Case Western Reserve Law Review*, Vol. 19 (January, 1968), p. 394; and O. W. Ketcham, "Legal Renaissance in the Juvenile Court," *Northwestern University Law Review*, Vol. 60 (November–December, 1965), p. 585.

[61] "Rights and Rehabilitation," *op. cit.*, p. 285.

average and by far the greatest number of youths coming to the attention of the juvenile court are far from being threatening criminals.

Attempts to lessen stigmatization of the juvenile

In order to provide privacy and to facilitate the juvenile's eventual social rehabilitation and acceptance, nearly one half of the states make allowance for closing provisions, which are intended to prevent examination of records by prospective employers. However, the intent of law is not always fully achieved, inasmuch as many employers secure this information informally through direct contact with detaining enforcement agencies. In order to overcome such deficiencies, provisions have been enacted in some states to foreclose public inspection of previous delinquency actions through the sealing, vacation, or expungement of juvenile court records.[62] In California, for example, a juvenile's record may be sealed some five years *after* discharge from probation or institutionalization upon petition. If the juvenile has contacts with the police *within* the five-year period, the sealing is left to the discretion of the original juvenile judge. However, if he is free of police contacts during that same period, he may exercise his legal right to have his records sealed. Under these provisions, the youth may legitimately deny any participation as a juvenile delinquent or that he has ever possessed a juvenile record upon completion of such sealing.[63] However, most state legislatures to date make no provision for the elimination of juvenile records.

In many of these states, the juvenile court judge possesses several devices which allow him to avoid entering the results of adjudication on a juvenile court record. Frequently, he will simply dismiss the case if the court is convinced of the juvenile's potential for self-rehabilitation, the parent's ability to provide a structured environment and maintain supervision over the youth, and the youth's desire to avoid recidivism. In other instances, he will simply continue the case and provide for probation through informal supervision by a person, persons, or agency acceptable to the court for a designated period.

Both of these procedures attempt to lessen or to avoid the stigmatization of youth and to provide the best treatment opportunities to serve the youth's needs. Many cases may also be simply screened from the attention of the juvenile court by the Intake Department, which is empowered to forstall a court appearance by the juvenile, either through dismissal or through informal adjustment. An estimated one half or more of all delinquency cases are simply adjusted in the intake stage. Although

---

[62] *Ibid.*, p. 288.
[63] *Ibid.*, p. 288.

the exact procedures legally permitted the Intake Department have been variably defined from state to state, the intake staff frequently possesses full discretion to investigate, dismiss, or informally adjust juvenile violations of lesser consequence. Consequently, it is often able to lessen or eliminate the potential stigmatization of the youth, either by the reduction of the charge or by the alteration of the original petition.

Even so, less serious cases, Alex Elson and Margaret K. Rosenheim propose in accordance with a British proposal, should be transferred from a juvenile court to a Community Panel created by the court specifically to hear and dispose of such cases if the delinquency problem is to be resolved. Possessing wholly voluntary jurisdiction, the panel would remain subject to the supervision of the juvenile court judge. Such a panel, they contend, would relieve the court of a portion of its cases and would draw the process of hearing and disposing of juvenile offenses into a community forum. Sitting within urban neighborhoods or regions under the jurisdiction of the court, the panel would provide greater accessibility to the children and his parents, while also bringing the delinquency problem into perspective within its own neighborhood. Essentially community based, the lay panel would permit citizens to become involved in the problems of the juvenile court and develop community leadership in mobilizing public support for effective juvenile court administration. However, the lay panel would also allow a form of adjudication which is less damaging to the reputation of a child than currently found in the formal court process. Because panel members would be community residents, an individualized and higher standard of treatment, Elson and Rosenheim believe, would ultimately be assured the delinquent and his family.[64]

While such a proposal has merit, it is highly unlikely that it will be enacted in the near future. The predominant thrust remains upon the juvenile court. However, if the juvenile court is to discharge its responsibilities adequately, it must possess, John Ellington theorizes, many necessary characteristics. A judge chosen for his sensitivity to human rights and his mature understanding of children must man the bench, and a sufficient number of emotionally mature and professionally trained probation workers must be available to achieve its goals. Facilities for medical, psychological, and psychiatric study of children with problems and well-equipped detention home and shelter care facilities must likewise be accessible. The court should possess exclusive origi-

---

[64] Alex Elson and Margaret K. Rosenheim, "Justice for the Child at the Grass Roots," *American Bar Association Journal,* Vol. 51 (April, 1965), pp. 344–45. Also consult Jacob M. Braude, "Boy's Court: Individualized Justice for the Youthful Offender," *Federal Probation,* Vol. 12 (June, 1948), pp. 9–14; and Paul W. Alexander, "What's This about Punishing Parents?" *Federal Probation,* Vol. 12 (March, 1948), pp. 23–29.

nal jurisdiction over children up to 18 and jurisdiction over adult and children's cases. Hearings should be private, and the full protection of the civil liberties of children and parents should be provided within the court's noncriminal procedure. Additionally, the community and state should create and maintain the variety of treatment facilities necessary to meet the multiple needs of children with problems. The court should likewise possess an efficient statistical and records system, supervised by adequate clerical help. It should maintain effective cooperation with other agencies serving children and with the community, providing the public with a continuing interpretation of the court's tasks and needs.[65] Only then can the full thrust of juvenile court rehabilitative philosophy be realized.

---

[65] Yablonsky, *op. cit.*, p. 427. Refer to Walter H. Bechkham, "Helpful Practices in Juvenile Court Hearings," *Federal Probation*, Vol. 13 (June, 1949), pp. 10–14; Mary Coleman, "Courtroom with a Heart," *Judicature*, Vol. 51 (May, 1968), pp. 383–85; and G. B. Hunt, "Does Get Tough Work?," *PTA Magazine*, Vol. 59 (June, 1965), pp. 8–10.

Chapter 18

THE POSTJUVENILE
AND ADULT CRIMINAL
COURT

THE STRUCTURE OF THE STATE CRIMINAL COURTS

The modern criminal trial is a refinement of the many historic attempts to determine the innocence of the accused through the *compurgation* or the *trial by ordeal*. In the compurgation, compurgators in sufficient numbers, usually neighbors, came forward to swear to the innocence of the accused. Guilt was determined in relationship to the number of the accused's supporters, a limited number implying guilt. Under the system of trial by ordeal, common in Western Europe until the advent of the jury system, an appeal was made to divine authority through various forms of ordeal to decide the guilt or innocence of the accused. Fire or water was generally used to create the conditions of the ordeal. The accused may have been required to carry a hot iron a specified distance or survive drowning after being immersed while chained. The degree to which the accused was able to resist the effects of the ordeal was taken to indicate divine confirmation of guilt or acquittal.

Modern systems of criminal jurisprudence have moved well beyond this level. The American system of criminal justice, for example, is founded upon the constitutional separation of powers, a concept of individual independence which holds that all men are created equal, an idea that the individual is innocent until proven guilty, and a belief that the criminal courts will provide due process for all litigants.[1] De-

---

[1] Paul B. Weston and Kenneth M. Wells, *The Administration of Justice* (Englewood Cliffs, N.J.: Prentice-Hall, Inc., 1967), p. 117.

fined in the Third Article of the Constitution, the courts offer a structural system in which conflicting or antisocial decisions may be ameliorated. Although U.S. Supreme Court Justice Van Deventer in *Evans* v. *Gore* noted that the judiciary is the weakest of the three powers of government, it is, he stated, "the balance wheel of the entire system, preserving an adjustment between individual rights and governmental powers."[2] Within this balanced system are a minimum of 599 federal, 5,301 state or county, and 2,280 city courts which may or may not singly serve criminal justice.[3] The system of criminal courts is extensive and complex, encompassing 52 separate jurisdictions including the 50 states, the District of Columbia, and the federal system.

THE LEVELS OF STATE COURTS

The system of *state* courts, founded upon the constitution of each state and the legisled state criminal code, is composed of trial courts and courts of appellate review. Although the *lower trial courts* for the processing of petty offenses and the examination of offenders are usually more important in rural states, those states possessing greater urban population generally share a court system which includes lower trial criminal courts, intermediate courts of appeal and a Supreme Court. Below the lower trial courts may be a *police court,* traditionally symbolized in the role of the magistrate or the justice of the peace. Either locally elected or appointed, these judges adjudicate most of the greater volume of cases involving public intoxication, disorderly conduct, traffic offenses, petty theft, prostitution, drug possession, homosexuality, or other nuisance violations. Such lower courts or courts of inferior jurisdiction may also take the form of a recorder's, mayors', city, special sessions, quarter sessions, or municipal court. Forty-three states operate magisterial courts which are often identified as justice of the peace, magistrate, or police courts.[4] More than one half of the defendants brought before a police or magistrate's court are released, convicted, and/or sentenced within 24 hours of their arrest. Depending upon the gravity and complexity of the case, the remainder complete disposition within days, weeks, or even months.

---

[2] 253 U.S. 245 (1960). Also consult Lewis Mayers, *The American Legal System* (New York: Harper & Row, Publishers, 1964); and Frank N. Jerome, *Courts on Trial* (Princeton, N.J.: Princeton University Press, 1949).

[3] U.S. Bureau of Census, *Statistical Abstract of the United States, 1964* (Washington, D.C.: U.S. Government Printing Office, 1964), p. 158. For a specialized insight, see *Scientific Investigation in Criminal Justice* (Boston: University Law-Medicine Research Institute, 1961).

[4] Glendon Schubert, *Judicial Policy Making* (Glenview, Ill.: Scott, Foresman & Co., 1965), p. 26. Also see Harry Kalven, Jr., "The Bar, the Court and the Delay," *The Annals,* Vol. 328 (March, 1960), p. 37; and Hans Zeisel, "The Jury and Court Delay," *The Annals,* Vol. 328 (March, 1960), p. 46.

The *justice of the peace court,* the rural counterpart of the lower criminal court, operates in at least 35 states. While the compensation of the justice of the peace is fixed by a fee assessed against the parties to the trial in a majority of states, in at least three states he only receives payment if he convicts a defendant and collects his fee, a practice judged unconstitutional more than 40 years ago by the U.S. Supreme Court but simply ignored.[5] In some instances, in order to guarantee his continuing income, the justice will kick back funds to a policeman who brings a violator to his court. Indiana theoretically prevents this practice by permitting the justice of the peace to earn up to $3,000 and by requiring him to remit any monies over this amount to the state treasury. Although a number of states have moved to abolish fee-system courts, the lower courts continue to fall short of the best judicial model. Ideally, all justices, according to the President's Commission, should be salaried and all fines and fees should be remitted to the state treasury. Presiding justices should be required to have completed training in law and in their basic duties and to evidence a level of competence necessary for the position they occupy.

Inferior courts traditionally maintain jurisdiction in cases up to and including the grade of misdemeanors. *County courts* try felony cases and possess jurisdiction over capital crimes. However, fewer than 50 percent of the states possess a county court structure. Where it does exist, it is basically a substructure of a court of general jurisdiction, whether circuit, superior, or district,[6] which tries more serious felony offenses. Possessing responsibility over such serious cases as murder, kidnapping, burglary, robbery, arson, and aggravated assaults, these courts of superior jurisdiction are usually empowered to inflict capital punishment or a sentence of imprisonment in a state prison for more than one year.[7]

Although this dual level of inferior and superior jurisdiction is theoretically distinct, much judicial overlapping exists within the system of justice. The inferior courts are empowered to make decisions involving minor or petty offenses and hold preliminary hearings pertaining to serious felonies, referring the latter to courts of superior jurisdiction. The *superior, circuit,* or *district courts,* the highest courts of original jurisdiction in the state, usually conduct trials involving serious cases or charges. At the *upper state court level,* the court of appeals and the supreme court assume appellate jurisdiction, although an interme-

---

[5] The President's Commission on Law Enforcement on the Administration of Justice, *Commission Report: The Challenge of Crime in a Free Society* (Washington, D.C.: U.S. Government Printing Office, 1967), p. 129.

[6] Schubert, *op. cit.,* p. 26.

[7] Abraham S. Blumberg, *Criminal Justice* (Chicago: Quadrangle Books, Inc., 1967), p. 8.

diate appellate level in some of the larger states may review and dispose of many cases which otherwise appear in the higher courts for review.

The state *supreme court* or *court of appeals* above this dual level of original jurisdiction serve as intermediate courts which hear appeals originating in one of the two lower court systems. Usually the highest courts in the state, they unify the state court system through their powers to decide appeals. However, under proper circumstances, some of their decisions may be appealed to the *U.S. Supreme Court,* which possesses the dual responsibility of serving as the court of final decision in the federal court system and as the supervising and unifying court of diverse state supreme or appeals courts.[8]

Nearly one half of the state supreme courts are staffed by seven judges. A third have five. The remainder range from three to nine, although three states have an even number of judges, ranging between four and six. While state supreme court judicial tenure ranges from a minimum of two years in Vermont to life in Massachusetts, Rhode Island, and New Jersey, the normal term is between six to eight years in most states.[9]

A state court system: California

The California Constitution limits the lower courts to municipal and justice courts. A *justice court* maintains jurisdiction in districts of 40,000 or less; a *municipal court* hears cases in communities of more than 40,000 population. Although its judges, sitting as magistrates, may conduct preliminary hearings in felony cases, the justice court, presided over by one judge, possesses jurisdiction in minor criminal cases involving a maximum penalty of six months in jail or $1,000 fine. The municipal court judge, sitting as a magistrate to conduct preliminary hearings in felony cases, maintains jurisdiction over all misdemeanor cases involving a maximum penalty of one year in jail or a fine of $1,000. Each municipal court judge must be an attorney admitted to the practice of law in California for at least five years immediately preceding election or appointment (see Figure 18–1).

The California *superior courts,* the next highest echelon within the court system, serve as the state trial courts of general jurisdiction. Possessing original jurisdiction in all criminal cases involving a felony, and appellate jurisdiction in cases arising from the justice and municipal courts, superior court judges are empowered to issue writs of *mandamus* (an order from a higher court to an inferior court or agency to compel

---

[8] *Ibid.,* p. 9. See Daniel J. Evans, "The Courts—Key to Civilizing an Urban Society," *Judicature,* Vol. 50 (February, 1967), pp. 194–98.
[9] Schubert, *op. cit.,* p. 27.

the performance of an act by that court or agency which the law enjoins as a duty), *certiorari* (a writ of review), *prohibition* (an order from a higher to a lower court or other governmental agency which restrains or prevents the lower court or agency from acting without or in excess of its jurisdiction), and *habeus corpus* (an order directing the public official detaining a person to produce "the body" in court for determina-

FIGURE 18–1
Appellate jurisdiction

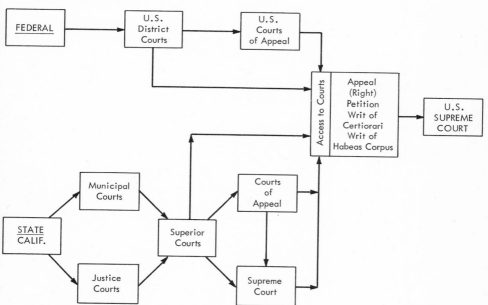

Source: Paul B. Weston and Kenneth M. Wells, *The Administration of Criminal Justice* (Englewood Cliffs, N.J.: Prentice-Hall, Inc. 1967), p. 124.

tion of the validity of imprisonment). Although each county is served by a superior court, the number of judges is fixed by the legislature in relationship to community needs. All superior court judges must be attorneys admitted to the practice of law in California for at least five years before election or appointment. Under the California constitution, the legislature may establish appellate departments within the superior courts for counties that have municipal courts.

The *District Court of Appeals of the State of California,* an interme- diate appellate court, is divided into five district courts. As in the U.S. Court of Appeals, three justices serve a district or division court, and two must concur in decisions for the completion of judgment. Also possessing the power to issue writs, the court likewise possesses appellate jurisdiction in cases on appeal from the superior court and on transfer from the supreme court. The *Supreme Court of California*, served by a chief justice and six associate justices, possesses the power to issue writs of habeus corpus, mandamus, prohibition, and certiorari. Empowered to maintain appellate jurisdiction in civil cases and in criminal cases involving the death penalty, the supreme court also exercises constitutional authority to transfer cases to and from the district courts of appeals. The supreme court is responsible for the admission of applicants to the Bar and for disciplinary action upon the recommendation of the Board of Governors of the state Bar. The court meets four times each year in San Francisco, four times in Los Angeles, and twice in Sacramento. Each week it reviews and decides applications for writs, petitions for hearings in cases decided by the district courts of appeal, and matters coming to the supreme court's attention.[10]

PARTICIPANT ROLES AND THE TRIAL PROCESS

The plaintiff, the defendant, and the community, commonly referred to as "the people," and their representatives occupy participant roles in the system of justice. Following a procedure involving many steps, the participants share in the reading of a conclusion of the trial and a decision concerning the facts of the case. At the outset of a criminal trial in the United States, a jury is selected, impanelled, and administered the oath. Following this initial step, both sides present a factual opening statement, indicating the general character of their positions in regard to the case. After the presentation of the state's case, the defense submits its arguments, an act quickly followed by the state's rebuttal and the defense's surrebuttal. Upon the conclusion of closing arguments by both sides, the jury is instructed (charged) regarding the law and is directed to retire to reach a verdict. Some time after a verdict has been reached, a judgment is pronounced and the conditions of sentence fulfilled.[11]

---

[10] Weston and Wells, *op. cit.*, p. 126. Also see Ralph N. Kleps, "Pretrial Conferences and Certificates of Readiness in California Trial Courts," *Judicature*, Vol. 50 (March, 1967), pp. 229–31.

[11] *Ibid.*, p. 185. Also see J. A. Andrews, "Criminal in the Civil Courts," *Criminal Law Review*, Vol. 1967 (August, 1967), pp. 441–54; Stuart S. Nagel, "Disparities in Criminal Procedure," *UCLA Law Review*, Vol. 14 (August, 1967), pp. 1272–1305; Donald F. Paine, "Character or Reputation of the Criminal Defendant in Tennessee," *Tennessee Law Review*, Vol. 34 (Spring, 1967), p. 482; Laura Banfield and C. P. Anderson, "Continuances in the Cook County Criminal Courts," *University of Chicago Law Review*, Vol. 35 (Winter, 1968), pp. 259–94; "Confrontation, Cross-Examination, and the Right to Prepare a Defense," *Georgetown Law Journal*, Vol. 56 (May, 1968), pp. 939–75; and "Developments in Civil Rights and Criminal Procedure," *Howard Law Journal*, Vol. 13 (Spring, 1967), pp. 358–83.

Although such a process seems cumbersome, this decision-reaching method and procedure possesses several advantages in that it:

1. Permits the application of a logical and systematic knowledge developed by reason and experience to the trial process.
2. Provides guidance through the person of the judge, who is able to relate actions in specific cases to known principles and standards as a consequence of his legal training.
3. Allows the review of judicial decisions by disinterested legally trained persons, often sitting *en banc* (as a group) to mitigate individual prejudices and misconceptions.
4. Makes the public aware of judicial actions taken.
5. Encourages the publication of the grounds for decisions by the appellate courts for the information and guidance of every interested person or agency.
6. Makes provision for trained judges who are isolated from public pressures and hysteria.[12]

However, a series of elements frequently impinge upon the organizational purpose and operation of the criminal court to redirect it from its prescribed goals and subvert these advantages. *Occupational or career commitments and drives* often generate priorities which have a greater claim upon the person than stated organizational goals. *Empire building,* too, may prevent the criminal court from meeting its responsibilities. Frequently, *attempts to maximize court production,* consistent with organizational goals, is often at odds with the concepts of due process and the rule of law. *A routine of idiosyncratic and deviant solutions* to organizational problems of production, commonly denied on an overt level, similarly may undermine organizational efforts. Even *institutional secrecy* and *relative immunity from scrutiny* together with *individual pathology* under the cloak of organizational authority and activity may delimit court effectiveness.[13]

Bail and the criminal process

Problems in the bail and bonding procedure offer a case at point. Bail, a procedure designed to allow the temporary release of a suspected or convicted offender through a written promise to appear in court as required, arose as a means to protect the health of the defendant in an age when "gaol fever" was a common malady. Utilizing a cash bail

---

[12] Roscoe Pound, *Justice According to Law* (New Haven, Conn.: Yale University Press, 1952), pp. 88–91. Of interest is Stephen M. Todd. "Pretrial Revisited," *Judicature,* Vol. 50 (January, 1967), pp. 153–57.

[13] Blumberg, *op. cit.,* p. 34.

deposit, a surety bond, or an evidence of equity in real property as collateral, the bail system works to guarantee the appearance of the offender in court at the required time to avoid loss of posted bond or collateral.

The use of bail originated in the old English practice of requiring an oath of responsible persons in order to effect the release of the accused to the custody of their person pending trial. The Statute of Westminister, enacted in 1275, formalized English bail procedures and protected the defendant from the imposition of an excessive bail. In the United States, the Judiciary Act of 1789 established a system of bail release which was incorporated into the Bill of Rights, the first Ten Amendments to the Constitution, in 1791.

Under the provisions of the Eighth Amendment, bail is permitted the charged criminal offender except in cases involving the possible invocation of the death penalty. In such instances, bail is discretionary and depends upon the nature and circumstance of the offense, the existing evidence, and the character of local legal practices. Although the amendment to the Constitution limits the requirement of excessive bail for release, actual practice varies widely. The amount of pretrial bail set ultimately depends on the facts of each individual case. Although the use of bail is designed to allow the mobility of the accused, who has not yet been proved guilty in court, high bail has often been encouraged by the state in order to keep the accused from participating effectively in his criminal defense. In such cases the basic assumption that the accused is innocent until convicted in court, a presupposition that places the primary responsibility for proof of guilt upon the office of the prosecutor, is undermined.[14]

Although bail in noncapital cases is held to be a right within the federal courts, not all states specifically define this right on a state level. However, the U.S. Supreme Court has upheld the right to bail for noncapital cases in *Stack* v. *Boyle* (1951). Unless the right to bail, it noted, is preserved on all court levels, the presumption of innocence, "secured only after centuries of struggle, would lose its meaning."[15] States differ in practice. California law supports the right to bail in noncapital cases and extends its use to the defendant convicted of a misdemeanor as a matter of right when he files an appeal to a judgment involving a fine or imprisonment. While establishing a humanitarian approach to the release of offenders on bail, California permits the court discretionary release of a prisoner who is accused of an offense punishable by death

---

[14] Weston and Wells, *op. cit.*, p. 100. See Michael Meltsner, "Pre-Trial Detention, Bail Pending Appeal, and Jail-Time Credit," *Criminal Law Bulletin,* Vol. 3 (November, 1967), pp. 618–27.

[15] 342 U.S. 1 (1951).

or who awaits action regarding an appeal from a felony judgment and sentence.[16]

Under the most common circumstances, a bail bondsman requires a fee of between 5 percent and 10 percent of the posted amount for his services. His participation in the bail process is theoretically designed to guarantee the return of the defendant to the court. Fundamentally, he serves persons with some wealth more efficiently than he does the poor. Twenty-five percent of all persons arrested, a study of the New York courts revealed, were unable to raise $25 to furnish a bond of $500; 45 percent, $70 for $1,500; and 63 percent, $125 for $2,500. During the period of their detention, persons unable to post bond were kept in some form of lockup at an expense of $3 to $10 per day to house and feed them and guard their persons. The bail system, the study disclosed, worked negatively in the majority of cases for all participants, provoking undue costs in the large volume of cases involving nondangerous offenders.[17] A 1965 report of the American bail-bond system by Ronald Goldfarb disclosed that 10 million to 12 million Americans need bail bonds each year for other than traffic cases.[18]

The Manhattan Bail Project

Attempts to overcome these shortcomings led to the development of the Manhattan Bail Project experiment, sponsored by the Vera Foundation in 1961, which disclosed the value of a system of release based upon one's recognizance. The New York Police Department, with the assistance of the Vera Institute of Justice, has processed misdemeanor and minor offenses, including simple assault, petty larceny, and malicious mischief, on a summons basis since 1964. While the individual still faces arrest, he is transported to a precinct station where he is processed and his potential for bail without bond is evaluated. If he proves to be a good risk, the precinct officer is authorized to release the alleged offender with a citation or summons, directing him to appear in court at a later date. These procedures, the department and the institute found, have saved police time and lessened detention facility overcrowding without causing excessive enforcement or court problems.[19]

The use of bail involves calculated risks. Not only may the accused fail to appear in court but he may also commit other crimes while on bail. As a result, state and federal legislatures have defined provisions

---

[16] Weston and Wells, *op. cit.*, p. 103.
[17] President's Commission, *op. cit.*, p. 131.
[18] Ronald Goldfarb, *Ransom: Critique of the American Bail System* (New York: Harper & Row, Publishers, 1965), p. 96.
[19] President's Commission, *op. cit.*, p. 132.

for the revocation of bail, the forfeiture of posted security, and the surrender of the defendant for violations of the bail process. Nevertheless, bail, although conceived of by the public as a means of constraining potential offenders, is not designed to prevent anticipated or uncompleted crimes but rather to sustain the basic presupposition that a man is innocent until proved guilty.

Offenders who commit additional crimes while on bail present special problems to the police and to the community. Law enforcement officers periodically constrain career offenders by rearresting them immediately after they have been accepted for bail in an attempt to "place them on ice" and to hinder their criminal activities. While this approach to the discretionary use of arrest and bail powers might be interpreted as in the best interests of the state and the public, it may also undermine the process of justice. The fact that release on bail usually takes place without supervision following apprehension, when emotional disturbance may be especially high, undoubtedly influences such police action. While bail may serve to protect the innocent, it may also subvert arrest and accusatory processes by making it possible for the offender to destroy evidence pertinent to his case.[20] Some data, on the other hand, suggest that the incarcerated or detained offender cannot adequately share in the preparation of his defense and is more highly susceptible to actual conviction than the individual who is able to post bond, a finding which supports the continuance of the constitutional right to bail. Although many spokesmen even now encourage the legalization of *preventive detention without bail* for charged offenders in serious cases, the very process strikes at the heart of American justice and extends the potential of the state and its agents to constrain individual and civil rights.

Such a recognition is implied in the Federal Bail Reform Act of 1966, which permits the release of defendants upon their promise to return or upon the presentation of an unsecured bond. While judges are authorized to place nonmonetary conditions upon release (*i.e.*, assign the defendant to the custody of a person or organization, restrict his travel, limit his place of residence, or place him in partial custody), the act also provides for a speedy review and appeal of bail decisions. Judges are authorized to utilize special provisions for the evaluation of bail desirability in capital cases or for convicted persons.[21]

But the debate over preventive detention continues. The fact that three separate District of Columbia homicides and one related suicide in a six-week period in early 1966 were attributed to individuals released on bail or on personal recognizance points to the seriousness of the issue. Provisions of the Federal Bail Reform Act do not provide for

---

[20] Weston and Wells, *op. cit.*, p. 101.
[21] President's Commission, *op. cit.*, p. 132.

the control of potential additional crimes by the offender before trial. If the accused is arrested for a second noncapital offense while on pretrial release, he is still permitted bail on the latter offense. Even the use of high monetary bail to detain potentially dangerous persons is lessened under the act's provisions. The President's Commission on Crime in the District of Columbia discovered that of the 2,776 persons

TABLE 18–1

Incidence of alleged felonies among persons released on bail

Method of Release	Number of Persons Released*	Persons Charged with Felonies While on Bond†		Number of Felonies Charged Against Persons Released on Bond†
		Number	Percent	
All releases..............	2,776	207	7.46	253
Trial bond..............	(**)	‡187	....	‡222
Appeal bond............	(**)	‡24	....	‡34
With surety............	§2,300	¶177	7.70	¶219
Without surety.........	571	¶35	6.13	¶40
D.C. Bail Project.......	551	26	4.72	28

* Released on bond between January 1, 1963, and October 8, 1965.

† Limited to those cases where the defendant was held for action of the grand jury as revealed by examination of U.S. District Court records from November 1, 1965, through March 4, 1966.

‡ The figures add up to more than 207 offenders and more than 253 offenses because some defendants committed an offense or offenses while on bond in two separate cases—one pending trial and one pending appeal.

** Unknown.

§ Estimate: The figure of 2,300 is somewhat larger than the difference between 2,776 total releases and 571 released without surety since some defendants were released twice, once with surety and once without.

¶ The figures add up to more than 207 offenders and more than 253 offenses because some defendants committed an offense or offenses while on bond in two separate cases—one with surety and one without surety.

Source: The President's Commission on Crime in the District of Columbia, *Report* (Washington, D.C.: U.S. Government Printing Office, 1966), p. 515.

released on bail pending disposition of felony charges between January 1, 1963, and October 8, 1965, 207 (7.5 percent) were detained for grand jury action on one or more alleged felonies committed while on bail. While 253 charged felonies were against persons released on bond, 222 were against persons released on trial bond (see Table 18–1).[22] Overall, the Commission noted that persons who allegedly commit additional offenses while on bail tend to be charged with as serious or more serious similar offenses, that a high incidence of prior arrests and convictions are recorded for those who allegedly commit crimes while on bail, and

[22] The President's Commission on Crime in the District of Columbia, *Report* (Washington, D.C.: U.S. Government Printing Office, 1966), pp. 514–15.

that there is little correlation between flight to avoid prosecution and the incidence of crime allegedly committed while on bail.[23]

The Commission concluded that the bail system must be modified sufficiently to protect the public. Because the alleged offender is presumed innocent until judged guilty under American law, moves to restrict the bail process or to use preventive detention procedures ultimately involve major constitutional questions. The Eighth Amendment provides that "excessive bail shall not be required," although it does not explicitly describe bail as a right; the Fifth Amendment also prohibits discrimination against an offender in the preparation of his defense. Proposals to provide these constitutional guarantees have included the amendment of the Bail Reform Act to consider the defendant's potential danger to the community and his likelihood of flight, additional penalties for those committing offenses on bail, expedited trials to lessen crime activity between charge and trial, and revocation of pretrial release. The majority of the Commission proposed the detention of selected accused persons who give evidence of probable future felonious conduct if released on bond or personal recognizance. However, this procedure, it recommended, should be utilized only when:

1. Conditional release under the Bail Reform Act will not provide necessary protection.
2. A hearing in which the defendant is represented by counsel sustains the government's contention that the accused falls within the purvue of the statute.
3. The accused has the right of appeal to the U.S. District Court and thereafter to the U.S. Court of Appeals for the District of Columbia.
4. Any evidence taken at a hearing shall not be admissible at the trial as impeachment or in lieu of *de novo* proof of facts alleged.
5. The trial of the detainee commences within 30 days unless extended for extraordinary cause.
6. The arrestee is permitted free access to counsel, friends, and family, and exempt from interrogation by any government officer except by his permission while detained.[24]

Even with these provisions, the use of preventive detention, the Commission held, should be limited to high risk offenders.

Judicial inquiry and contempt of court

Whatever the problem of bail release, the finding of guilt in a criminal court case is influenced by either the "fight" or the "truth" theory of

---

[23] *Ibid.,,* pp. 518–519.
[24] *Ibid,* pp. 527–528.

judicial inquiry.[25] While the "fight" theory assumes that "truth" is uncovered through the workings of the adversary system, this is generally
not certain. Many other factors may intervene. Some cases, for example,
never get to court for judgment. Statutes of limitations vary from state
to state, depending on the type of crime committed and the customs
of the area. Many states limit the prosecution of offenses for misdemeanors to one year, felonies to two or more years, and cases of fraud
by public officials or against the government without time limit. California law, for example, restricts misdemeanor prosecutions to one year
following the offense, although felonies may be prosecuted over a longer
period. Murder, embezzlement of public monies, and falsification of
public records have no limit. The limit on prosecution for the acceptance
of a bribe by a public official or public employee is six years and for
any other felony, three years.[26]

Additionally, attorney partisanship and competition frequently block
the recovery of evidence, despite High Court decisions prohibiting such
situations. Where this occurs, the Constitution and legislatures have
provided for the use of *contempt of court* proceedings to reestablish
the authority of the court or to maintain the nature of due process.
The conduct of an attorney, witness, offender, or other participant occasionally exceeds the bounds of legitimate legal inquiry, causing the court
to redress any imbalance through the imposition of contempt of court
proceedings which permit it to discipline individuals who disturb judicial
proceedings or willfully disobey the court's directives. Rarely invoked
without previous warning, inasmuch as this power effectually reinforces
the previously defined powers of the court to act as an agent of the
community, contempt of court proceedings and punishments are imposed
by a judge within the traditions of local law. While commonly processed
procedurally as a misdemeanor, criminal contempt usually includes:

1. Disorderly, contemptuous, or insolent behavior committed during the
   sitting of any court of justice, in immediate view and presence of
   the court, and directly tending to interrupt its proceedings or to im-
   pair the respect due to its authority.
2. Behavior of like character in the presence of any referee or jury
   while holding hearings authorized by law.

[25] Jerome N. Frank, *Courts on Trial: Myth and Reality in American Justice*
(Princeton, N.J.: Princeton University Press, 1949), p. 80. Also examine Harvey
Brower, "Pre-Trial Procedures in Criminal Cases," *Portia Law Journal*, Vol. 2 (Fall,
1966), pp. 1–18; "Concurrent Civil and Criminal Proceedings," *Columbia Law Re-
view*, Vol. 67 (November, 1967). pp. 1277–95; Michael Clanin, "Constitutional
Rules of Criminal Procedure and the Application of Linkletter," *Journal of Public
Law*, Vol. 16 (1967), p. 193.
[26] Weston and Wells, *op. cit.*, p. 189.

3. Any breach of the peace, noise, or other disturbance directly tending to interrupt the proceedings of any court.
4. Willful disobedience of any process or order lawfully issued by any court.
5. Resistance willfully offered by any person to the lawful order or process of any court.
6. The contumacious and unlawful refusal of any person to be sworn as a witness; or when so sworn the like refusal to answer any material question.
7. Publication of a false or grossly inaccurate report of the proceedings of any court.
8. Presenting to any court—or any member of it—with the power to order judgment after conviction, any representation of any kind in aggravation or mitigation of the punishment to be imposed, except as provided by law.[27]

However, still other procedures affect the reading of an accurate verdict while still supporting the imposition of "justice."

The negotiated guilty plea

The *negotiated guilty plea,* also known as "plea bargaining," allows the faster discharge of justice. Because all cases do not have to be tried under its provisions, the court load is lessened. Its use permits a lesser investment in staff, court time, and expended monies; it also relieves the defendant and the prosecution of the risks and uncertainties of the trial process. In many instances, the negotiated guilty plea mitigates the harshness of mandatory sentencing provisions and allows the imposition of punishments which are more closely in accord with the conditions of the particular case. Periodically utilized as a form of leverage, it is frequently invoked as a means of granting leniency in exchange for information, assistance, or testimony concerning other major cases or serious offenders.

The use of plea bargaining procedures, however, is also open to potential abuses. Dangerous offenders, for example, have been known to manipulate prosecutors and courts through plea bargaining. Then, too, the desirability of gaining testimony in return for special judicial consideration may encourage the invention of false testimony. In some instances, the threat of excessive sanctions may also induce pleas of guilty, especially if the prosecutor indicates his intent to demand a harsher sentence if the defendant does *not* plea guilty. Consequently, plea bargaining may compromise the defendant's right to trial, especially if the sentencing judge is a party to the actual negotiations.[28] Although the judge

---

[27] *California Penal Code,* Section 166.
[28] President's Commission, *op. cit.,* pp. 134–35.

must eventually become involved in the negotiated guilty plea, his judicial role demands that he determine that a factual basis for the plea exists, be certain that the defendant understands the charge and the consequences of his plea, and ascertain that the agreed-to disposition is a reasonable and appropriate sentence. His evaluation, therefore, must be grounded upon his review of the defendant's need for correctional treatment, the circumstances of the case, the defendant's cooperation, and the requirements of law enforcement.

A minimum of 5 million persons are charged yearly in court with misdemeanors other than traffic offenses. Nearly 600,000 children appear before the juvenile court in delinquency actions. Approximately 3 million persons are processed in the originating courts of superior jurisdiction in any given year on charges involving punishment by imprisonment for a year or more.[29] Guilty plea convictions constitute as high as 95 percent of all judgments recorded. An estimated 70 to 85 percent of all *felony* cases, for example, are resolved with the use of the guilty plea.

Criminal Justice in "Metropolitan Court"

Between 1950 and 1964, nearly 91 to 95 percent of all cases appearing for trial in Metropolitan Court, Arthur S. Blumberg discovered in his study of a large urban court system, were settled on the basis of a guilty plea. Of the cases processed during 1960, 92.9 percent were settled by the use of the guilty plea; only 2.85 percent faced disposition by trial.[30] Overall, the system of justice by negotiation without trial, Blumberg concludes, "probably tends to serve better the interests and requirements of the guilty than of the innocent."[31] Because jury trials involve large amounts of effort and time for relatively few convictions in comparison to negotiated guilty pleas, both the prosecution and the defense tend to avoid the trial process where possible (see Table 18–2). Consequently, once a person enters the system as an accused or indicted offender, he has little opportunity, Blumberg tentatively reasons, to escape conviction.[32] The demand for judicial efficiency, prosecutor success,

[29] Blumberg, *op. cit.*, p. 11.

[30] *Ibid.*, pp. 29–30.

[31] *Ibid.*, p. 30.

[32] *Ibid.*, p. 31. Due Process is examined in "Procedural Due Process at Judicial Sentencing for Felony," *Harvard Law Review*, Vol. 81 (February, 1968), pp. 821–46; Leonard C. Jaques, "Changed Procedures in Criminal Matters," *Detroit Lawyer*, Vol. 35 (September, 1967), pp. 127–30; Eugene A. Wright, "Courtroom Decorum and the Trial Process," *Judicature*, Vol. 51 (May, 1968), pp. 378–82; D. Taverne, "Procedure and Evidence Following the Criminal Justice Act," *Journal of the Society of Public Teachers of Law*, Vol. 9 (December, 1967), pp. 425–33; Sanford Rosen, "Contemporary Winds and Currents in Criminal Law," *Maryland Law Review*, Vol. 27 (Spring, 1967), pp. 103–30; and Lester B. Orfield, *Criminal Procedure From Arrest to Appeal* (New York: New York University Press, 1947).

TABLE 18–2
Conviction rates in cases disposed of by trial in Metropolitan Court, 1950–64

Year	Total Cases Disposed of by Trial	Convictions, Number and Percent		Acquittals	Disagreements (Hung Juries)
1950	113	92	(81.41)	21	15
1951	137	103	(75.18)	34	12
1952	127	95	(74.80)	32	22
1953	131	101	(77.09)	30	18
1954	112	88	(78.57)	24	8
1955	102	82	(80.39)	20	7
1956	114	94	(82.45)	20	11
1957	115	81	(70.43)	34	8
1958	107	90	(84.11)	17	8
1959	104	96	(92.30)	8	21
1960	116	104	(89.65)	12	6
1961	142	127	(89.43)	15	9
1962	162	142	(87.65)	20	8
1963	150	127	(84.66)	17	6
1964	145	123	(84.82)	14	8

Source: Abraham S. Blumberg, *Criminal Justice* (Chicago: Quadrangle Books, Inc., 1967), p. 32.

and defense attorney results encourages, Blumberg argues, major dependency upon plea bargaining for case settlement.

The most common defendant in Metropolitan Court was drawn from the lower socioeconomic strata and represented nearly every ethnic minority. Only 8 percent of those 3,643 persons coming to the court's probation division during 1964 were white-collar criminals. Operating with nine judges and an elaborate court staff, the justices who administer the major functions of the court constitute a Board of Judges with overall jurisdiction over record keeping and processing, probation programs, and psychiatric clinic services. A team of 15 to 18 full-time lawyers detached from any formal or direct administrative relation to the court provides a Legal Aid Defender Service which accounted in 1964 for nearly 70 percent of the Metropolitan Court caseload. Because the district attorney and his staff are also located on the same premises, the whole system of justice, Blumberg notes, represents an interactional relationship of diverse functional roles (see Figure 18–2). Consequently, these various organizations tend to serve the needs of its personnel rather than its clients.[33]

---

[33] *Ibid.*, p. 47. Also review Frank D. Day, "Administration of Criminal Justice," *Journal of Criminal Law, Criminology, and Police Science,* Vol. 56 (December, 1965), pp. 540–44; John W. Oliver, "The Citizen and the Administration of Justice," *Federal Probation,* Vol. 29 (March, 1965), p. 6; Harris B. Steinberg, "Criminal Justice in Our Time—A Review," *American Criminal Law Quarterly,* Vol. 4 (Spring, 1966), pp. 137–146; and Edward C. Gallas, "The Planning Function of the Court Administrator," *Judicature,* Vol. 50 (April, 1967), pp. 268–71.

FIGURE 18–2
Some structural relationships in the Metropolitan Court organization

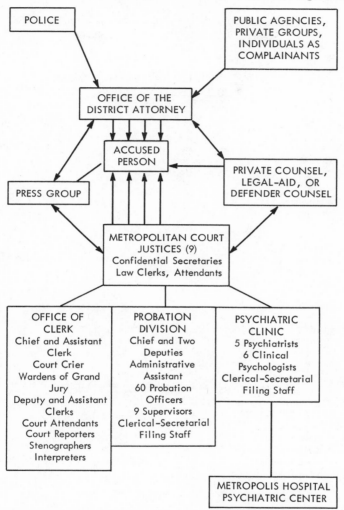

Source: Blumberg, *Criminal Justice* p. 48.

Justifying their operations, each facet of the system of justice validates its existence in terms of its production figures. However, at each stage of the process the "sieve effect" reduces the total volume of offenders at the time of *arrest* to a much smaller number at the point of sentence (see Figure 18–3). The discretionary powers within the system of justice, available to the police, prosecutor, grand jury, court of preliminary hearing, and even the presiding judge, account for much of this shrinkage

FIGURE 18–3
The sieve effect

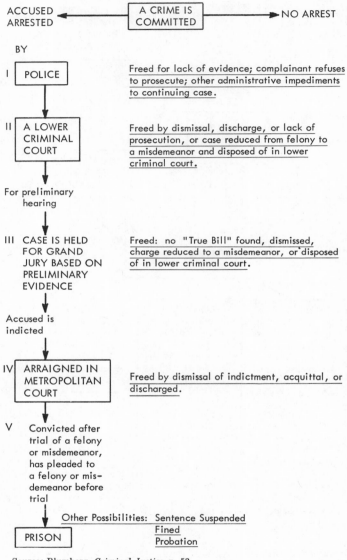

Source: Blumberg, *Criminal Justice*, p. 53.

(see Figure 18–4). Consequently, individuals sentenced to prison represent only a minority of those entering the system of criminal enforcement
and justice through an early arrest. The belief that the charged offender
is commonly a sick person, a belief which tends to reinforce the legitimacy of the criminal court, is frequently encouraged by the legal structure, Blumberg argues, because it aids the validation of many legal

FIGURE 18–4
The accused vis-à-vis his agent mediators

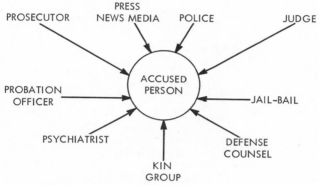

Source: Blumberg, *Criminal Justice*, p. 70.

judgments in terms of medical "science."[34] Once the offender has entered
the system of justice and has been subjected to mental and personality
examination, he is less likely to break free of the self-justifying agencies
of the judicial system.

Negotiated guilty pleas: "Cop-out" or conscious drama?

Plea bargaining, Harold Garfinkel finds, is ultimately a form of social
"cop-out," a successful degradation ceremony which reasserts ultimate
social values and strips the accused of his former status. Although the
individual, according to Garfinkel, is recast in a manner acceptable to
all participants, including potentially the accused himself, the cop-out
ceremony in which the accused publicly acknowledges his guilt and
pleads guilty to a lesser charge results in many less valuable consequences. In part, the cop-out is a charade in which the accused projects
a suitable degree of guilt, penitence, and remorse, meeting the suitable
minimum standards for such responses expected by the prosecution,

---

[34] *Ibid.,* p. 34.

defense, and court, which ultimately decides the future life of the offender.[35]

Abraham S. Blumberg disagrees, noting that the use of the guilty plea often is not a reinforcement or degradation process but rather a

TABLE 18–3
Defendant responses as to guilt or innocence after pleading (1962–1963–1964)

Nature of Response		Number of Defendants	Percent
Innocent (Manipulated)	"The lawyer or judge, police or DA 'conned me' "	86	11.9
Innocent (Pragmatic)	"Wanted to get it over with" "You can't beat the system" "They have you over a barrel when you have a record"	147	20.3
Innocent (Advice of counsel)	"Followed my lawyer's advice"	92	12.7
Innocent (Defiant)	"Framed"— Betrayed by "complainant," "police," "squealers," "lawyer," "friends," "wife," "girl friend"	33	4.6
Innocent (Adverse social data)	Blames probation officer or psychiatrist for "bad report" in cases where there was pre-pleading investigation	15	2.1
Guilty	"But I should have gotten a better deal" Blames lawyer, DA, police, judge	74	10.2
Guilty	Won't say anything further	21	2.9
Fatalistic (Doesn't press his "innocence," won't admit "guilt")	"I did it for convenience" "My lawyer told me it was the only thing I could do" "I did it because it was the best way out"	248	34.2
No response		8	1.1
Total		724	100.0

Source: Blumberg, *Criminal Justice*, p. 70.

highly structured system of exchange cloaked "in the rituals of legalism and public professions of guilt and repentance."[36] As in a modern divorce case, each participant, including the defendant, is aware of the drama which is unfolding. Consequently, the accused's self-concept of guilt

---

[35] Harold Garfinkel, "Conditions of Successful Degradation Ceremonies," *American Journal of Sociology,* Vol. 61 (March, 1956), pp. 420–24.

[36] Blumberg, *op. cit.,* p. 89; and Monrad G. Paulsen, *Equal Justice for the Poor Man* (New York: Public Affairs Commission, 1964).

is temporary and is quickly replaced in private by a sense of innocence. However, if the accused professes a sense of innocence which denies the court's expectation of offender guilt, remorse, and penitence, the violator's attempts to rationalize his actions generally are quickly subdued by the probation officer's suggestion that if he is innocent he should stand trial on the original charges rather than accept a guilty judgment.

Procedures of this type actually work to restrict the fulfillment of justice. The greatest number of defendants in Metropolitan Court between 1962 and 1964, Blumberg discovered, expressed a sense of pragmatism or fatalism in their reason for offering a plea of guilty (see Table 18–3). Less than 14 percent of the defendants admitted their guilt following the completion of the plea-bargaining ceremony; more than 50 percent immediately reasserted their "innocence" after a public plea of guilty.[37] Nevertheless, more than one third of the defendants were fatalistic, posing a near stoic attitude.

Special problems in criminal adjudications

Not all cases coming to the court's attention involve fully rational or sane participants. Consequently, special rules and procedures have been devised to protect the interests of the criminally insane and the society. *Criminal insanity,* a legal definition covering a wide variety of psychiatric states or conditions is a central ingredient in the trial process at at least four distinct points:

1. Upon arraignment, when the defense indicates that the accused is insane and incapable of making a defense.
2. During the trial process, when the defendant introduces evidence of insanity to support his plea of not guilty or postpone the trial until his sanity is regained.
3. After conviction but before judgment, when the defendant may claim insanity and the defense challenge the wisdom of sentencing an insane person.
4. After conviction, sentence, and imprisonment, when interested parties may request the transferral of the prisoner to a hospital for treatment on the presumption that he has become insane.[38]

---

[37] *Ibid.,* p. 91. For another facet, see Carolyn Jaffe, "The Press and the Oppressed," *Journal of Criminal Law, Criminology, and Police Science,* Vol. 56 (March, 1965), pp. 1–17; and Joseph Goldstein, *The Family and the Press* (Glencoe: Free Press, 1965).

[38] Robert G. Caldwell, *Criminology* (New York: Ronald Press Co., 1965). Refer to Franz Alexander and Hugo Staub, *The Criminal, The Judge, and the Public* (Glencoe: Free Press, 1956), for a volume dealing with the psychological dimensions of the process of justice.

Its applicability, however, is determined, depending upon the type of court and its precedents, in relationship to the M'Naghten and Durham Rules, which emerged from the practical need to differentiate cases involving the criminally insane from those pertaining to reasoned criminal intent.

Under the M'Naghten Rule, an 1843 English court interpretation arising from the murder of Sir Robert Peel's secretary, a violator is not criminally responsible or liable if he commits a crime while laboring "under a defect of reason," which does not permit him to recognize the nature or quality of his act or to know that his act is socially wrong. Therefore, in order to establish a defense on the ground of *insanity* within the M'Naghten provisions, the defense must clearly prove that when the accused committed the act, he was laboring under a defect of reason, from a disease of the mind, such that he did not know the nature and quality of the act he was committing, or, if he did know it, that he did not know he was doing wrong. Under this right-wrong test, which was later accepted as a standard for evaluation of criminal insanity in American courts, legal insanity could be accepted only if the accused was unable to distinguish right from wrong due to mental deficiency or disease.[39]

However, this definition has been open to continuing criticism. The arguments of noted psychologists and medical experts, who held that the preciseness of the legal concept of insanity is at odds with existing knowledge concerning mental disease, led to the adoption of the Durham Rule in the District of Columbia Court of Appeals in 1954. Under its provisions, the accused is not criminally responsible if his act is the product of mental disease or defect. Emphasizing the product rather than the knowledge of right and wrong, the Durham Rule permits the jury to consider all symptoms of mental disease or defect, the individual's knowledge of right and wrong, and the interactional setting in which the "irresistable impulse" may have resulted in a criminal offense.

But even the Durham provisions have been subject to debate. The provisions of the Model Penal Code of the American Law Institute, as a result, proposes that a person should not be held criminally responsible for his act if he lacked substantial capacity either to appreciate the criminality of his conduct or to conform his conduct to the requirements of the law due to mental disease or defect. Like the Durham Rule, the Model Penal Code's proposal is extremely broad, bringing

---

[39] Rollin M. Perkins, *Criminal Law* (Brooklyn: Foundation Press, Inc., 1957), pp. 738–55. For information on testimony procedure see Clark Sellers, "Preparing to Testify," *Journal of Criminal Law, Criminology, and Police Science,* Vol. 56 (June, 1966), pp. 235–40.

many attacks against its provisions. However, the underlying issue in this continuing debate is whether the courts, as representatives of the public, or psychiatrists, as independent medical specialists, shall in the future decide issues of criminal responsibility.[40]

The psychiatrist's role in the system of criminal justice, while important, has become highly pivotal. He may testify at a trial, offering expert testimony about the mental condition of the offender at the time of his offense. At this time, his testimony is evaluated upon the cross-examination of the defense or prosecution by the jury. The psychiatrist additionally may be called upon to examine defendants, either before or after a plea of guilty, to determine the individual's current situation from a medical rather than a legal standpoint. In this latter instance, his evaluation included in a presentence report, is not open to any rebuttal or cross-examination. And yet, his evaluation during this period largely determines the actual sentence and eventual treatment program of the accused.

Abraham S. Blumberg suggests that most criminal lawyers learn early in their career that psychiatry is imprecise, that psychiatric testimony is for sale, and that psychiatry is far from being an exact science.[41] Nevertheless, presiding judges, Blumberg believes, appreciate the manner in which psychiatric terms furnish a "scientific" framework and rationale for eventual disposition of the case. The disciplines of probation and psychiatry become "the willing handmaidens of the court organization, for individual careers," Blumberg contends, "are too often wholly dependent upon the wielders of judicial power."[42] The findings of psychiatric clinics and probation bureaus are seldom subject to review or even objective scrutiny by colleagues. Consequently, the findings of both agencies may fail to meet the standards of the profession and are often nothing more than hack pedantry. Of the 2,213 people undergoing psychiatric examination during 1964 in the Metropolitan Court, only 81 were diagnosed to be suffering from a clinically identifiable psychosis and 9 from a psychoneurosis. The remainder, Blumberg found, were

---

[40] Caldwell, op. cit., p. 364. Also see Joseph D. Tydings, "Federal Verdict of Not Guilty by Reason of Insanity and a Subsequent Commitment Procedure," Maryland Law Review, Vol. 27 (Spring, 1967), pp. 131–41; Rita M. James, "Jury's Assessment of Criminal Responsibility," Social Problems, Vol. 8 (Summer, 1959), p. 58; and Rita M. James, "Juror's Evaluation of Expert Psychiatric Testimony," Ohio State Law Journal, Vol. 21 (Spring, 1960), p. 75.

[41] Blumberg, op. cit., p. 148; and Hans Zeisel, "The New York Expert Testimony Project: Some Reflections on Legal Experiments," Stanford Law Review, Vol. 8 (1956), p. 730.

[42] Ibid., p. 149; Thomas S. Szasz, Psychiatric Justice (New York: Macmillan Co., 1965); Thomas J. Scheff, "The Societal Reaction to Deviants," Social Problems, Vol. 12 (Spring, 1964), pp. 401–13.

diagnosed as persons who show degrees of "emotional unstability," "aggressive reaction," or "aggressive and anti-social reaction."[43]

The problem of sexual psychopaths

Similar shortcomings have become increasingly evident in the administration of laws concerning sexual psychopaths. These laws were enacted in the mid-1930's out of fear that sex violations were a growing threat to the community at large. Although an offender charged in criminal proceedings could have his criminal case suspended and be committed to an institution for an indefinite period under civil procedures before 1935, the advent of a law passed after that date transferred the proceeding from civil to criminal jurisdiction. Theoretically founded upon new scientific insights, the law was and is both nonscientific and largely unnecessary. Operating under the widespread but mistaken assumption that sex crimes were becoming more common, Michigan (1935) and Illinois (1938), among others, passed such laws in an attempt to protect the female population.

While these laws presumed a major increase in the number of serious sex crimes, continuing investigation has revealed that the majority of sexual deviants are only minor offenders. Even when a vicious sex act, which in itself is usually unpredictable, is completed by such a person, he generally does not repeat this act at a later time. Although the laws originally intended the treatment rather than the punishment of the offender, the necessary services to complete this function were rarely made available. Because the concept of the psychopath has been openly questioned in psychiatry in recent years, even the functional purpose of these laws has been undermined.[44] The courts have depended heavily upon the diagnostic and treatment advice of psychiatric and psychological practitioners in defining sentences and correctional placement; psychiatric services available to sexual psychopaths have been disproportionately centered in diagnosis and not in eventual treatment for rehabilitation. Ultimately, whether the accused is judged to be criminally insane or a sexual psychopath depends upon the jury, which either affirms or rejects the charge of the prosecutor or grand jury.

[43] *Ibid.*, p. 162. Also refer to Dorothy C. Tompkins, *Insanity and the Criminal Law* (Berkeley: University of California Press, 1960); Jay Campbell, "An Accountability Approach to Criminal Responsibility," *Federal Probation*, Vol. 29 (December, 1965), p. 33; Warren E. Burger, "Psychiatrists, Lawyers, and the Courts, *Federal Probation*, Vol. 28 (June, 1964), p. 3.

[44] See Alan H. Swanson, "Sexual Psychopath Statutes: Summary and Analysis," *Journal of Criminal Law, Criminology, and Police Science*, Vol. 51 (July–August, 1960), pp. 215–35.

The rise of the jury

The modern English jury, from which the American jury is derived, probably originated in ninth-century France, which used the jury as a royal administrative device, possibly after borrowing its use from fifth-century Roman practice. When the King's rights were called into question in France, 12 neighborhood men were called to give testimony to the facts under oath. As the procedure became an implement of the powers of the King, it was diffused to England by William the Conqueror, where it became a trial procedure in competition with the practice of trial by ordeal.[45] As the jury evolved in the later centuries, it grew into a body which evaluated testimony in a manner similar to modern practice.

By the 18th century, the jury in colonial America had become highly independent of the hostile British government and was adopted in the federal and state constitutions as a freedom-guaranteeing procedure. During and after the American Revolution, juries often championed unpopular causes and served as a check on oppressive government. As trial by jury grew in America and Great Britain, the Anglo-American jury practice returned full circle to the European continent, where it similarly became a symbol of individual liberty. However, among many of the European states, especially pre-Hitler Germany, France, Scotland, and among some of the Swiss cantons, trial by jury received less enthusiasm.[46]

Currently, potential American jurors are usually selected by a commissioner of jurors within a specific county of a state. Normally, a juror must be a citizen 21 or over, a county resident for one year, in full possession of all faculties, and know the English language. While felons or convicted malfeasants are *disqualified* from jury duty, professionals such as attorneys, teachers, clergymen, physicians, dentists, and public officers are *exempt* from jury service. Previous jury duty within a year commonly disqualifies prospective jurors. *Challenges for cause* are generally unlimited if they can be substantiated by the response of the prospective juror to the questions of the prosecutor or defense counsel. Preemptory challenges (without reason), however, are generally limited. In California, for example, both sides are allowed 10 preemptory challenges in trials involving any offense other than those punishable by life imprisonment or death. In the latter instances, however, each side is permitted 20 preemptory challenges under state law.[47]

---

[45] Frank, *op. cit.*, pp. 108–9.
[46] *Ibid.*, p. 109.
[47] Weston and Wells, *op. cit.*, p. 195.

The jury in the United States

Probably the most authoritative study of the American jury system was completed by Harry Kalven, Jr., and Hans Zeisel in 1966. They used a sample of 3,576 jury cases, taken from the estimated 60,000 or more criminal jury trials in the United States per year, and 555 judges from the 1,646 who effectively cooperated with the study. The judge and jury, Kalven and Zeisel discovered, both agreed to acquittal in 13.4

FIGURE 18-5
Verdict of jury and judge
(in percent of all 3,576 trials)

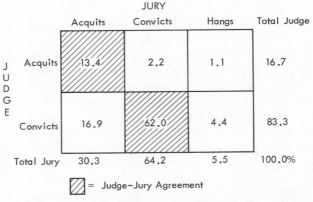

= Judge–Jury Agreement

Source: Harry Kalven, Jr., and Hans Zeisel, *The American Jury*
(Boston: Little, Brown, & Co., 1966), p. 56.

percent and to conviction in 62.0 percent of all cases, resulting in an overall agreement rate of 75.4 percent in all cases presented to both the jury and the judge (see Figure 18-5).[48] Obviously, disagreement existed in 24.6 percent of all cases. However, the judge and jury disagreed on guilt in 19.1 percent and the jury ended in a hung jury in 5.5 percent of all cases. The jury, they discovered, was less lenient than the judge in 3 percent and more lenient in 19 percent of the proceedings,[49] a net leniency of 16 percent on the part of the jury. Consequently,

[48] Harry Kalven, Jr., and Hans Zeisel, *The American Jury* (Boston: Little, Brown & Co., 1966), p. 56. Refer to Dale W. Broeder, "Previous Jury Trial Service Affecting Juror Behavior," *Insurance Law Journal* (1965).
[49] *Ibid.*, p. 59. Also see Fred L. Strodtbeck, "Social Process, The Law and Jury Functioning," *Rutgers Symposium on Law and Sociology* (Glencoe: Free Press, 1962), p. 144.

the defendant receiving a jury trial, they concluded, possessed a 16 percent more favorable response potential than persons facing a bench trial.

Overall, judge and jury disagreement in the 3,576 trials reached as high as 33.8 percent. The judge was more lenient in 5.5 percent of the cases, while the jury expressed greater latitude in 28.3 percent.[50] However, jury disagreement with the judge, Kalven and Zeisel disclosed, was not to be found exclusively in any one form of crime category as was the case in the 18th century, when the jury differed sharply with the judge over prosecutions for seditious libel, and in the early 20th century over prosecution of violators of Prohibition laws. "The jury's war with the law," Zeisel and Kalven say, is "now a polite one."[51] Net leniency, Kalven and Zeisel noted, nevertheless, varied from a high of 43 percent for game law violations to 5 percent for arson and 4 percent for miscellaneous public disorder cases. Additionally, judge and jury agreement reached a low of 53 percent for indecent exposure and a high of 92 percent for kidnapping and 88 percent for narcotics violations.[52]

Although the net leniency of the criminal jury was nearly 20 percent higher than that of the judge, such leniency, Kalven and Zeisel revealed, reaches only 6 percent in narcotics and a high of 41 percent in indecent exposure trials. In the latter cases, however, the jury tended to distinguish between indecent exposure to children and to adults. If it perceived that the complaining adult female was marked by a *de minimus* (minimizing) aspect, this tended to lessen the seriousness of the charge. While the jury tended to consider such factors, the judge conversely tended to disregard such information, inasmuch as formal law makes no allowance or references to such variations. Therefore, differences in evaluation of the trial, Kalven and Zeisel hypothesized, seemed to result from evidence factors, facts only the judge knew, disparity in counsel ability, and jury sentiments about the individual defendant and the law.[53] The jury, for example, periodically evaluated specific items of evidence somewhat differently from the judge, especially in close cases, since many important facts were available only to the judge and not to the

---

[50] *Ibid.*, p. 62. Consult Dale W. Broeder, "The Functions of the Jury: Fact or Fiction?" *University of Chicago Law Review*, Vol. 21 (1954), p. 386; Strodtbeck and Richard D. Mann, "Sex Differentiations in Jury Deliberations," *Sociometry*, Vol. 19 (March, 1956), p. 715; Fred L. Strodtbeck, Rita M. James, and Charles Hawkins, "Social Status in Jury Deliberations," *American Sociological Review*, Vol. 22 (December, 1957), p. 713; and Fred L. Strodtbeck and Hook, "The Social Dimensions of a Twelve Man Jury Table," *Sociometry*, Vol. 25 (January, 1962).

[51] *Ibid.*, p. 76. See Rita M. James, "Status and Competence in Jury Deliberations," *American Journal of Sociology*, Vol. 64 (May, 1959), p. 563; and Dale W. Broeder, "Plaintiffs Family Status as Affecting Juror Behavior: Some Tentative Insights," *Journal of Public Law*, Vol. 14, (1965), p. 131.

[52] *Ibid.*, p. 76.

[53] *Ibid.*, pp. 86–106.

jury under existing administrative procedure and rules for admission of evidence which have evolved over the centuries.

In some instances, the superiority of either the prosecution or the defense, they hypothesized, influenced the jury's disagreement with the judge; in others the basic characteristics of the individual on trial provoked a higher sense of alienation or sympathy from the jury than from the judge. In many instances, the jury, Kalven and Zeisel found, will adapt the law to specific cases if it believes its provisions are currently inappropriate or that the crime has been aided by the contributory

TABLE 18–4
Summary explanation of disagreement

	Normal Disagreements on			Crossovers on			Total Disagreements %
	Guilt %	Charge %	Hung %	Guilt %	Charge %	Hung %	
Sentiments on the law.....	53	59	32	49	72	26	50
Sentimets on the defendant...............	23	27	17	28	20	3	22
Evidence factors..........	78	62	84	93	100	100	79
Facts only the judge knew..	7	3	3	4	4	. . .	5
Disparity of counsel.......	9	6	9	5	4	. . .	8
Average number of reasons per case*...............	1.7	1.6	1.5	1.8	2.0	1.3	1.6
Number of cases.....	*559*	*142*	*127*	*75*	*25*	*34*	*962*

* Percentages add to more than 100 because, as indicated in the Average line, some cases have more than one reason, e.g., column one adds to 170 percent or 1.7 reasons per case.
Source: Kalven, Jr., and Zeisel, *The American Jury*, p. 111.

negligence of the victim. The concept of contributory fault of the victim, Kalven and Zeisel discovered, tended to emerge as a form of defense which lessened the impact of a particular crime. It created a disagreement between judge and jury in part or in whole which resulted in evidence problems in some four out of every five cases (79 percent).[54] In 50 percent of the disagreements, the reason was related to jury differences in attitude or in sentiments concerning the law (see Table 18–4). While the jury agreed with the judge about three quarters of the time, two thirds of its disagreements were founded upon some jury response to values which the law often did not take into account. The jury, in

---

[54] *Ibid.*, pp. 108–12. Alvin L. Short, "Effective Jury Management," *Judicature*, Vol. 50 (April, 1967), pp. 265–67; and Joshua N. Koplovitz, "Jury or Non-Jury: The Defense Counsel's Dilemma," *Criminal Law Bulletin*, Vol. 2 (November, 1966), pp. 3–9.

effect, resolved doubts about issues of fact in relationship to its central values, an act which often occurred unconsciously.

Practically, the American jury is neither nonrule-minded nor fundamentally defendant-prone. Concerned for existing equities, the jury responds to the given state of law and public opinion. Because jury members usually share in the widespread consensus of values assumed in the law, the randomly drawn jury does not tend to reflect dissenting viewpoints.[55] And yet, no two juries and no two judges are alike. The jury verdict to a high degree is influenced by the direction of the votes taken at the start of the deliberation process and not, as generally believed, by rational persuasion. Deliberation, Kalven and Zeisel believe, is the route by which the initial majority produces consensus from the considering group.

The role of the jury in Great Britain

The British Criminal Justice Act of 1967 has greatly modified the early practice of criminal justice in Great Britain. Under its provisions, the court may accept a jury verdict of 10 to 2 after the jury has deliberated for at least two hours, a procedure which its supporters believe effects only 1 of every 3,000 or so yearly committal proceedings. Even more important is the allowance granted the court in using written statements in place of oral testimony by witnesses, a practice which permits the sharing of testimony with the defense immediately upon the recording of such information.[56] Under the latter provision, the accused may be committed for trial on evidence disclosed in written statements of witnesses rather than in oral testimony, a procedure designed to save time for police officers and to lessen case continuances. Although these statements must be presented or served on the accused before the hearing, his lawyer may still call witnesses to give oral evidence if the accused desires to contest their contents. The accused is likewise expected to present evidence supporting his alibi to the prosecution before he is tried upon an indictment.[57]

The role of the trial judge in England differs sharply from that in the United States. Under English procedure, the judge participates

---

[55] *Ibid.*, pp. 494–96. Also see Harry Kalven, Jr., "A Report on the Jury Project," *Insurance Counsel Journal*, Vol. 24 (October, 1957), p. 368. For a more specialized discussion of juries in relation to civil damage awards, see Harry Kalven, Jr., "The Jury, the Law and the Personal Injury Damage Award," *Ohio State Law Journal*, Vol. 19 (1958), p. 158; and Harry Kalven, Jr., "The Jury and the Principles of the Law of Damages" (Dedicatory paper given at the University of Chicago Law School, 1960).

[56] Mark Carlyle, "The Criminal Justice Act of 1967—Its Procedure and Practice," *Criminal Law Review*, Vol. 1967 (1967), p. 613.

[57] *Ibid.*, p. 619.

vigorously in the trial process, especially as he summarizes evidence concerning a case and gives the jury general instruction concerning aspects of the law pertinent to the trial. As he does this, he invariably gives the jury some insight into his feelings concerning the case. However, the American judge generally does little more than instruct the jury on the ingredients of the law pertinent to the case. Twenty states, for example, permit neither comment nor summary; 17 allow only a summary; and 11 states plus the federal courts, which formerly included Hawaii and Alaska, make provision for both summary and comment on the evidence.[58]

The judge and the system of criminal justice

The American judge occupies a pivotal role in the system of criminal justice. He not only tries cases but he supervises and reviews negotiated guilty pleas and the ultimate treatment of the offender.[59] An effective system of justice consequently depends upon the selection of qualified judges. Inconsistency of judicial approach or capability may have a profound effect upon court decision-making results. The addition of one judge to a California superior court, for example, caused an increase from 26 to 53 percent of convicted offenders sentenced to prison and a decrease from 51 to 21 percent of those granted probation. His absence during the following year resulted in a decline in the percentage of those imprisoned from 53 to 31 percent and an increase on probation from 21 to 48 percent.[60] Studies in other courts revealed further disconcerting information. One 10-year study of New Jersey court procedures disclosed that the decision to imprison a convicted offender depended solely upon the judge's personality in at least 23 percent of the cases. Similarly, of those defendants accused before a Cleveland judge who suspended sentence in 31 percent of his cases, 80 percent pleaded guilty; before a second Cleveland judge who suspended sentences in 6 percent of his cases, only 30 percent pleaded guilty.[61]

The selection of judges

The method of selection varies from jurisdiction to jurisdiction and state to state. Judges in 11 states are appointed by either the governor

[58] Kalven and Zeisel, op. cit., p. 420.
[59] See Susan M. Chalker, "Judicial Myopia, Differential Sentencing and the Guilty Plea," American Criminal Law Quarterly, Vol. 6 (Summer, 1968), pp. 187–99.
[60] Sandor Frankel, "Sentencing Morass and Suggestion for Reform," Criminal Law Bulletin, Vol. 3 (July–August, 1967), p. 365; and D. A. Thomas "Sentencing— the Basic Principles," Criminal Law Review, Vol. 1967 (August–September, 1967), pp. 455–65, 503–25.
[61] Ibid., p. 369. Note Albert Wahl, "If I were a Judge," Federal Probation, Vol. 26 (June, 1962), pp. 41–47.

or the legislature. In some states, they are first appointed and then must run for election on their records. They are elected in 15 states without party labels; their election is a partisan decision in 19 states.[62] Where selection of judicial candidates has been completed under a partisan system, party considerations or other factors unrelated to the candidate's qualifications hold major influence. The partisan election of judges has not always been fully successful because it frequently minimizes the basic qualifications of the candidates for such office.

Judges in the constitutional courts of the federal system generally enjoy lifetime tenure. The terms of state court judges vary in length, depending upon the method of selection and continued tenure. Most frequently, judges of lower courts serve 6-year and justices of higher courts 12-year terms. Federal justices may be removed by impeachment for high crimes, an infrequently used method which demands conviction by a simple majority of the House of Representatives and by a two thirds vote of a quorum of senators.[63]

For the most part, judges are either appointed or elected. In recent years, several attempts have been made to modify the appointive system in order to develop a truly bipartisan, nonpartisan, or politically independent judiciary. Many states select judges through a process of bipartisan nomination and of effective screening by a special Bar association advisory committee. Because bipartisan nomination, however, has often led to deals between political leaders resulting in unapposed candidacies for judges of both parties at the time of election, and the local Bar association has periodically failed to secure the most capable judicial nominees, the Missouri plan, a compromise between these two alternatives, was created in 1940 as an acceptable substitute for the direct election of judges. It has operated successfully in Missouri for more than 25 years and is currently used in various forms in some 10 states. Under its provisions a special commission screens available candidates, evaluating their qualifications.

In Missouri, the screening is conducted by a committee composed of the chief justice of the supreme court, serving as chairman; three attorneys elected by the state Bar; and three citizens appointed by the governor who are not members of the Bar. In order to minimize the politics of the selection process, commissioner terms are staggered over a six-year period.[64] Selecting three candidates for every vacant judgeship within their area of operation, they refer these names to the governor for consideration and appointment. He in turn chooses one, appointing

---

[62] President's Commission, *Challenge of Crime*, p. 146; and Edward J. Devitt, "Ten Commandments for the New Judge," *Federal Probation*, Vol. 26 (December, 1962) pp. 15–18.

[63] *Ibid.*, p. 135.

[64] *Ibid.*, pp. 131–32.

his nominee to a vacant judgeship for a one-year term. During this one-year probationary period, the competence and character of the new appointee is evaluated by persons in the area. Upon completion of the probationary period, the appointee is automatically nominated and must have his name placed upon the ballot for the next general election as a candidate for a full judicial term, which consists of 6 years in circuit court and 12 years in appellate court.[65]

Recommendations for the future selection of judges

Although the President's Commission on Law Enforcement and Administration of Justice favors an appointive over an elective approach to the selection of judges, it can be effective only if productive screening procedures emphasize the personal and professional qualifications of the individual for office. The screening function, the Commission holds, should be established in law and be performed by a group directly responsible to the appointing authority. Representative of the community, such an authority should review the qualifications of potential judges and make appropriate recommendations. Similarly, the American Bar Association and the American Judicature Society generally support the merit selection of judges as incorporated in the Missouri plan. The value of this approach, they believe, resides in the nomination of a panel of judicial candidates by a nonpartisan commission composed of conscientious, qualified laymen and lawyers; the requirement that the executive appoint judges from the panel submitted by the Commission; the review of the appointment by the voters after a probationary term of service in which the only question is whether the judge's record warrants his retention in office; and a periodic review of the appointment by the voters at the end of each term of public service to determine whether the judge's record warrants his continued retention in office.[66]

The frequent election of judges, every four years in many states, may undermine the independence of the judiciary. Consequently, the attempt to insulate federal and many state judges from political influences has encouraged the development of a judicial term of 10 to 14 years, depending upon the state, or lifetime tenure until a fixed retirement age. While high judicial standards have generally been continued under these long-term tenure approaches, their success finally depends upon the continued competence of the presiding judge. Consequently, administrative procedures for dealing with incompetence or misbehavior possess vital importance to the operation of all judicial systems. Most states only provide for impeachment or recall, which do not really deal

---

[65] *Ibid.*, p. 132.
[66] *Ibid.*, p. 132.

with the problem of excusing physically or mentally incapacited judges from their duties without public humiliation. While some states, most noticeably California and Texas, have created state Justice Department Commissions empowered to examine judicial conduct and to take necessary action, the number following this approach are still few. Using an approach of informal conferences or discussion designed to appeal to the individual judge's sense of status and self-motivation, these commissions have attempted to preserve the dignity of the office and the man while effecting change in the interest of the community.

The selection and maintenance of California judges

In the selection of supreme court and appeals courts justices, California follows a process similar to the Missouri plan. However, it has taken the leadership in reviewing the continuing competence of the judiciary. In 1960, California created a nine-member Commission on Judicial Qualifications to review judicial performance and to administer necessary discipline upon judges who failed effectively to fulfill their judicial obligations. Composed of five judges appointed by the supreme court, two lawyers appointed by the California Bar, and two public members appointed by the governor, the Commission receives complaints and evaluates the conduct of state court judges. Possessing the power to hold hearings and to recommend whether a judge should be removed or retired from office to the supreme court, the Commission in its early years had notable successes in eliminating unfit judges from the bench. During the first four years of its operation, the Commission, for example, was able to secure the removal of 26 judges and to stimulate the retirement or resignation of others. Only one judge protested the recommendation for his removal to the state supreme court.[67]

California judges, as all elected California officials, may also be recalled by the approval of a majority of voters on a recall petition. Judges charged with a crime involving moral turpitude in any California court may be suspended by the state supreme court, pending final conviction, upon its own motion or upon a petition filed by any person.

Variations in judicial styles

Any attempt to evaluate judicial competence and effectiveness immediately involves the recognition of variation in judicial training, styles, and roles. Judges commonly disclose a minimum of three different levels of origin and practice. The model of the judge of the *lower level*, says Abraham S. Blumberg, is the most common and most susceptible to pa-

---

[67] *Ibid.*, p. 147.

tronage and to "clubhouse" politics. Often a marginal member of his profession, this judge trades upon his ethnicity or his contacts in benevolent, fraternal, or religious organizations. Since strong political contacts are necessary for reelection and promotion, the lower-level judge maintains strong party commitments. The going rate for such judgeships in New York City is equivalent, Wallace Sayre and Herbert Kaufman discovered, to a two-year salary contribution to the aspirant's political party.[68]

Judges in the *middle-level* career pattern generally occupy the intermediate appellate courts. Commonly chosen by the state governor upon the approval of the legislature or some other appropriate body, this judge is often a graduate of a nonelite but above "factory" level law school. More literate than his lower-level counterparts, he too is sensitive to party politics. On the other hand, judges of the *upper level* are commonly products of elite families and "national" law schools which possess outstanding reputations. Extremely well-trained, the upper-level judge frequently occupies an important political office before elevation to the higher bench. While some of these men may be true legal scholars, the greater number are "politically well-connected." Despite the prohibition against participation in partisan politics defined in Canon 28 of the Canons of Judicial Ethics of the American Bar Association, upper-level judges, like those in each of the other two levels, usually possess some form of politically visible contact with a partisan organization. Somewhat removed from the original conditions and testimony of the case, judges on the middle and upper level are usually far detached from the interpersonal dynamics which stimulates the initiation of the court actions.[69]

The characteristics of Metropolitan Court judges

In Metropolitan Court, the mean age of the judges was 51 years. Only one of the judges was a graduate of a national law school; eight others completed part-time proprietary, or factory law schools.[70] Although three of the nine justices had earned a baccalaureate degree before commencing law school training, nearly all were totally unprepared for a judicial career. Consequently, newly appointed judges were intially socialized to the operational court organization by court clerks or other civil service functionaries. Of the nine metropolitan judges, three had prior experience in courts of inferior criminal jurisdiction. All had exten-

---

[68] Wallace S. Sayre and Herbert Kaufman, *Governing New York City* (New York: Russell Sage, 1960).

[69] Blumberg, *op. cit.*, pp. 119–23.

[70] See Lowell S. Nicholson, *The Law Schools of the United States* (Baltimore, Md.: Lord Baltimore Press, Inc., 1958).

sive political connections and four served as assistant district attorney for brief periods. Each justice was a son of professional, proprietor, medium-sized mercantile or managerial father; in religion, four were Catholics, two were Protestants and three were Jews.[71]

The judges of Metropolitan Court disclosed six major judicial role patterns. The *intellectual-scholars* and the *routinier-hacks* served as the workhorses of the court. One judge, Abraham S. Blumberg disclosed, possessed intellectual or scholarly characteristics but yet continuously participated in courtroom wheeling and dealing. On the other hand, a second judge, identified as a routinier-hack, was more traditional and maintained a routine case production. The political *adventurer-careerist*, a third model, used the bench as a stepping-stone to other political offices and possessed no great interest in law or the administration of criminal justice. The *judicial pensioner* came to the bench as a late reward in his political life. The *hatchet man* served as a legitimate enforcer for the political clubhouse by processing difficult cases which possessed major political importance. The *tyrant-showboat–benevolent-despot* model, commonly the same judge on different occasions, usually represented a hostile, frustrated, and defeated judge who had come to a dead end in his political career. Rejected by his colleagues, his actions were frequently inconsistent and incomprehensible.[72]

PROBLEMATIC TENSIONS IN THE SYSTEM OF JUSTICE

Despite the seeming success of the present systems of negotiated-guilty plea, jury, and judicial appointment in processing cases coming before the system of criminal justice, all is not well with the system. A diversity of questions and tensions, including the tension over the distribution of state and federal power, plague the modern scene. While Article Six of the Constitution indicates that the Constitution and the laws of the federal government shall effectively serve as the supreme law of the land, each of the sovereign states, which formed the federal government, historically exercises near-autonomous judicial power in its courts. Therefore, as the federal government created a system of supreme and inferior courts, establishing an independent judiciary designed to balance the power of government, it immediately developed an over-arching court system which was theoretically separate from, but practically in periodic conflict with, the system in each autonomous state. While the Fourth Article of the Constitution sought to guarantee the validity of state court decisions in each sister state, the divergencies in the practice of law has made the resolution of existing and future

---

[71] Blumberg, *op. cit.*, pp. 125–26.
[72] *Ibid.*, pp. 139–41.

judicial conflicts somewhat difficult. Consequently, since the founding of the Republic, the U.S. Supreme Court has been extending the more demanding procedural requirements of the federal courts to the states. While the U.S. Supreme Court has not yet decided that the Fourth Amendment's due process clause makes *all* provisions of the first eight amendments to the Constitution directly applicable to the states, case law reveals a definite trend in this direction. The Fourth Amendment's protection of privacy, for example, was applied to the states in *Mapp* v. *Ohio* (1961); the Fifth Amendment's protection against self-incrimination in *Malloy* v. *Hogan* (1964); and the Sixth Amendment's right to assistance of counsel in *Gideon* v. *Wainwright* (1963).[73]

In many states and in the federal system, *search warrants* may be used in order to seize contraband or the fruits and instrumentalities of a crime but not to gain access to a man's house, his office, or papers merely to search randomly for incriminating evidence. In its decisions the courts have made definite distinctions between evidence gained as a result of reasonable knowledge that possession violates the law and that secured as a result of an intrusion into an individual's home or property without a reasonable expectation that such items would be found.[74] Consequently, illegally seized evidence is not admissible in American courts. Later applications of the exclusionary rules have increasingly clarified and restricted the scope of evidence which may be presented to a court during a trial.

While many commentators have criticized them, these tendencies have emerged because the practices of many police officials, prosecuting attorneys, and grand juries offer little real protection to an accused person. Their standards of evidence required to move the case to the next step of the screening and adjudication process are often superficial. Since the police operate upon the principle of "probable cause," believing that fact or error will be uncovered in the trial process,[75] and the prosecution acts upon a belief that those brought to the attention of its office

---

[73] Consult Dolores Knapp, "Waiver of Constitutional Rights by Counsel in a Criminal Proceeding, *John Marshall Journal of Practical Proceedings,* Vol. 1 (Spring, 1967), pp. 93–110; Luther E. Jones, Jr., "Translating Recent Supreme Court Decisions into Courtroom Reality," *Baylor Law Review,* Vol. 19 (Summer, 1967), pp. 371–408; and L. B. Schwartz and P. M. Bator, "Criminal Justice in the Mid-Sixties," *Federal Rules Decisions,* Vol. 42 (November, 1967), pp. 463–78.

[74] The problem of evidence is considered in Phillip A. Trautman. "Motions Testing the Sufficiency of Evidence," *Washburne Law Review,* Vol. 42 (April, 1967), pp. 787–816; E. L. Cady, Jr., "Objections to Demonstrative Evidence," *Missouri Law Review,* Vol. 32 (Summer, 1967), pp. 333–53; Hugh W. Morgan, "Criminal Discovery Implications of the False Evidence and Suppression of Evidence Cases," *Tennessee Law Review,* Vol. 34 (Summer, 1967), pp. 654–70; and "Evolving Methods of Scientific Proof," *New York Law Forum,* Vol. 13 (Winter, 1967), pp. 679–775.

[75] See Ronald G. Schecter, "Police Procedures and the Accusatorial Principle," *Criminal Law Bulletin,* Vol. 3 (October, 1967), pp. 521–43.

are generally guilty, each agency in the apprehension and accusatory systems finds an element of realization in the other.

The relative power of the police

When a police officer, carrying out his duty honestly and conscientiously under Scottish procedure, *ought* to know that the man he is questioning is under serious consideration as the perpetuator of the crime under investigation, he is a suspect, and all interrogation must cease.[76] However, the question is put somewhat differently in the United States, where the issue is not only at what point interrogation must cease but also at what point must counsel be made legally available to the suspect in order to guarantee due process to his person. In Scotland, after an officer arrests a person, he must inform the prisoner of the charge against him and immediately caution him that anything he may say in *answer to the charge* will be taken down in writing and may be used as evidence. After this caution is given any statement not in answer to the charge by the accused is inadmissible in evidence at the trial. However, in the United States, once the warning has been given, under the recent Miranda provisions, *any statement* gathered by the policeman *may be introduced* as evidence at a trial. While these variances seem irrational, they are due largely to the differences in legal procedure in the two countries and reflect differences in originating principles. In the United States, which developed its Constitution to protect the person from the abuses posed by the state, the accusatorial presupposition demands that the state prove the guilt of the accused. In Scotland, which was closely allied with those powers the Colonists sought to flee, the inquisitional system of criminal procedure placed a greater burden upon the person to prove his innocence.[77]

Nevertheless, in the United States many persons become victims of the bureaucratic division of labor which allows the avoidance of actual responsibility for human rights in the guise of completion of particular enforcement-prosecution functions.[78] Although the grand jury was originally designed to protect the innocent from unwarranted prosecution, it too, Jerome Skolnick argues, has lost much of its effectiveness as an agency for protection of the innocent. Therefore, as criminal justice

---

[76] Harvey Brower, "Pre-Trial Procedures in Criminal Cases: A Comparative Review," *Portia Law Journal,* Vol. 2 (Fall, 1966), p. 5.

[77] *Ibid.,* pp. 5–6.

[78] Blumberg, *op. cit.,* p. 27. See also D'Army Bailey, "Enjoining State Criminal Prosecutions which Abridge First Amendment Freedoms," *Harvard Civil Rights Law Review,* Vol. 3 (Fall, 1967), pp. 67–124.

is administered in mass, Skolnick notes:

Presumptions necessarily run to regularity and administrative efficiency. The negation of the presumption of innocence permeates the entire system of justice without trial. All involved in the system, defense attorneys and judges, as well as the prosecutors and policemen, operate according to a working presumption of the guilt of persons accused of crime. As accused after accused is processed through the system, participants are prone to develop a routinized callousness, akin to the absence of emotional involvement characterizing the physician's attitude toward illness and disease. That the accused is entitled to counsel is an accepted part of the system, but this guarantee implies no specific affirmation of "adversariness" in an interactional sense. Indeed, the most respected attorneys, prosecuting and defense alike, are those who can "reasonably" see eye to eye in a system where most defendants are guilty of some crime.[79]

Examining a series of interrelated criminal courts which processed cases ranging from minor infractions to major felonies, Abraham S. Blumberg finds similar tendencies. The institutionalized system of criminal justice is more inquisitorial than theoretically believed possible. Plea bargaining or "justice by negotiation," therefore, falls short of the standards of due process. Both judges and criminal lawyers, Blumberg believes, are hardly as objective in their roles as popular myth would have the public assume. Due process is nothing more than a form of bureaucratic due process which pays homage to constitutional principles while often ignoring their substance.[80] Although traditional due process assumes values and concerns guaranteeing individual rights, bureaucratic due process, Blumberg says, tends to exalt the goal and requirements of the agencies of criminal justice. Therefore, the institution of justice has come to overshadow the requirement of traditional due process. The enforcement-judicial demand for guilty pleas has produced an assembly-line approach to criminal justice which is incompatible, he argues, with traditional due process procedures. The full and open hearing in court is only the culmination of secret negotiations of parties or agents represented in any specific case. The interchangeable use of the concepts of "due process" and "the rule of law" have become ideological rituals rather than constitutional protections. Even the presumption

[79] Jerome H. Skolnick, *Justice Without Trial* (New York: John Wiley & Sons, Inc., 1966), p. 241.

[80] Blumberg, *op. cit.*, p. 4. See T. E. Johnston, "The Judge's Rule and Police Interrogation in England Today," *Journal of Criminal Law, Criminology and Police Science*, Vol. 57 (March, 1966), pp. 85–92; Maurice Fallipoli, "Federal Habeus Corpus, the Threat and the Challenge," *American Criminal Law Quarterly*, Vol. 4 (Summer, 1966), pp. 211–29; and J. De Weese Carter, "The Use of Federal Habeus Corpus by State Prisoners," *American Criminal Law Quarterly*, Vol. 4 (Fall, 1965), pp. 20–35.

of innocence, widely assumed by the public to be an operating principle in the system of justice, is supplanted, Blumberg finds, by a nonadversary and accusatory system which tends to favor a presumption of guilt.[81]

The case for an ombudsman

An office or person in the model of the Swedish ombudsman, Abraham S. Blumberg suggests, would be invaluable in the quest for objective justice. Operating independently of the criminal court, his task would be to supervise scrupulously each guilty plea along the following lines of inquiry to determine whether minimum standards of justice have been fulfilled.

1. Ascertain whether the indictment was read and the charges were clearly explained to the defendant.
2. Ascertain, if the defendant indicates a desire to plead guilty, what his reasons are for doing so.
3. Explain to him the right of a jury trial.
4. Ask the prosecution to summarize in detail the evidence *other than any confession* that has been obtained against the defendant.
5. Examine carefully the precise circumstances of the defendant's arrest and all police practices and activities that preceded and followed the arrest.
6. Scrutinize each lesser-plea transaction to determine whether any secret arrangements have been made under the threat or promise of some benefit that would not accrue to the accused should he agree or fail to comply.
7. Assess the health, age, education, race, and other factors, such as intelligence, which might affect a defendant's tractability and capacity to resist manipulation.
8. Evaluate the effects of any period of confinement prior to pleading, its duration, and the living conditions during such detention.[82]

While such an office still tends to be unique, interest in its development has been strengthened by the recognition that the power of the modern state far exceeds the power of the person. Simple questioning may quickly turn to the accusatory interrogation of witnesses, leaving honest citizens at the mercy of those who possess institutional power.

---

[81] *Ibid.*, p. 6.
[82] *Ibid.*, pp. 182–83.

Problems in the administration of justice

The goal of speedy justice must always be balanced with judicial fairness. Justice must proceed with deliberate speed and yet with deliberate consideration. However, the time lapse between preliminary hearing and grand jury action, normally three months, does not always allow the deliberate speed which the community may desire. Frequently, persons charged with serious crimes may await trial for more than a year. Because the individual is still innocent until proved guilty, incarceration even in preventive detention without recourse to bail undermines the constitutional guarantees to due process and the concept of innocence until judged guilty, affirmed as a working principle in the American system of justice. However, much of the problem of delay and continuance is related to the judge's failure to supervise the court's operations. In most jurisdictions, the judge manages the court's calendar. Although he may be assisted by some other officers of the court, the thrust of detail quickly becomes too great for any single judge to supervise.

In order to facilitate the trial process, the President's Commission on Law Enforcement and the Administration of Justice has suggested a model timetable for felony cases (see Figure 18–6). Under its assumptions, the preliminary hearing would occur within three days of the initial appearance for jailed defendants and within seven days for released defendants; the period from arrest to trial of felony cases would not take more than four months, and the period from trial to appellate review would occur within five months. The entire process of adjudication under this model would be completed within nine months as in Great Britain at the present time.[83]

However, the mere development of a revised timetable for the faster processing of cases is not an adequate response to the problem of adjudications. Substantive changes must also be made in the criminal code. The Modern Penal Code of the American Law Institute suggests that all crimes be redefined within three grades of felonies and two grades of misdemeanors. While each grade would be limited by a maximum penalty, most would be shorter than those currently prevalent in most states. However, if the offender is especially dangerous or the offense is rather heinous, the maximum may be extended by the judge. Under the code's provisions, the judge would possess the discretion to grant probation except in capital cases. The judge would be empowered to set minimum terms of imprisonment which could be limited to three years for all but the most serious felonies, and correctional authorities would possess discretionary authority to grant paroles. Although the

---

[83] President's Commission, *Challenge of Crime*, pp. 155–56.

FIGURE 18–6
Model timetable for felony cases

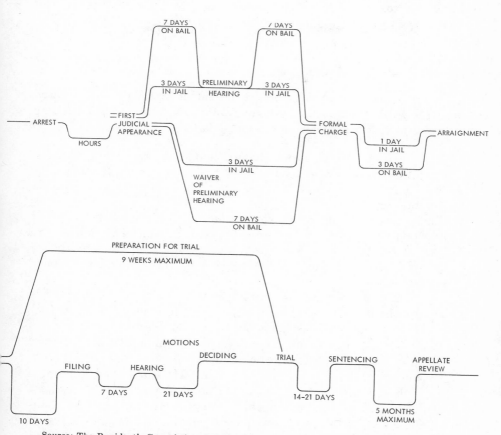

Source: The President's Commission, *The Challenge of Crime in a Free Society* (Washington, D.C.: U.S. Government Printing Office, 1967), pp. 154–55.

Notes: Arrest to First Judicial Appearance. *Many states and the federal courts require appearance "without unnecessary delay." Depending on the circumstances, a few hours—or less—may be regarded as "unnecessary delay." Compliance with this standard may require extension of court operating hours and the continual availability of a magistrate.*

First Judicial Appearance to Arraignment. *Standards here are complicated because: (a) a shorter period is appropriate for defendants in jail than for those released; (b) preliminary hearings are waived in many cases and the formality and usefulness of the hearing varies; (c) formal charge in some cases is by grand jury indictment, while in others by prosecutor's information—usually the right to indictment can be waived by the defendant; and (d) in many jurisdictions proceedings through preliminary hearing in felony cases are in one court while grand jury charge and subsequent proceedings are in another. While in all cases these steps should take no more than 17 days, in most cases it should be possible to accomplish them in substantially less time.*

Arraignment to Trial. *Many of the increasing number of motions require the judge to hear and decide factual issues. Discovery orders may require time for the assembling and screening of documents. The recommended standard would allow slightly more than five weeks for these steps and would allow a total of nine weeks between arraignment and trial. Where complicated motions are not involved, the period before trial should be shortened.*

Trial to Sentence. *During this period a presentence investigation should be completed.*

Sentence to Appellate Review. *This standard is based on the time periods of the proposed Uniform Rules of Federal Appellate Procedure. Many jurisdictions would have to change existing practices concerning printing and preparation of records to meet this standard.*

minimum sentence for any felony would be at least one year, judges would possess the authority to impose individualized sentences and parole boards to review cases after the correctional process had commenced.[84]

Proposals for criminal justice reform

In 1967, the shortcomings of the system of criminal courts caused the President's Commission on Law Enforcement and Administration of Justice to make the following recommendations:

1. That felony and misdemeanor courts and their supporting agencies, including prosecutors, defenders, and probation services be unified.
2. That judicial manpower of such courts be increased and physical facilities be improved.
3. That prosecutors, probation officers, and defense counsel be provided in courts where such officers are not present in sufficient numbers.
4. That states and the federal government enact legislation to abolish or overhaul the justice of the peace and the U.S. Commissioner systems.
5. That bail projects be undertaken at the state, county, and local levels to furnish judical officers with sufficient information about the accused's financial condition necessary to pretrial release.
6. That each state enact comprehensive bail reform legislation patterned after the Federal Bail Reform Act of 1966.
7. That every community establish procedures to enable and to encourage police departments to release in appropriate types of cases, as many arrested persons as possible promptly after arrest, upon issuance of a citation or summons requiring subsequent appearance.
8. That prosecutors discriminate in charge decisions, insuring that offenders who merit criminal sanctions are not released and that other offenders are either released or diverted to noncriminal methods of treatment and control.[85]

---

[84] Examine James M. Carter and Fred Kunzel, "Forms of Adjudication for Use in Sentencing," *Federal Rules Decisions*, Vol. 44 (June, 1968), pp. 197–224; Frank A. DeCosta, Jr., "Disparity and Inequality of Criminal Sentences," *Harvard Law Journal*, Vol. 14 (Winter, 1968), pp. 29–59; and Lyle H. Truax, "Structuring the Sentence," *Judicature*, Vol. 52 (August–September, 1968), pp. 65–70.

[85] President's Commission, *Challenge of Crime*, pp. 129–34. Refer to Robert J. Kennedy, "Crime in the Cities: Improving the Administration of Criminal Justice," *Journal of Criminal Law, Criminology, and Police Science*, Vol. 56 (June, 1967), pp. 142–54; and Joseph D. Tydings, "Modernizing the Administration of Justice," *Judicature*, Vol. 50 (April, 1967), pp. 258–61.

In addition, the President's Commission suggested that if a negotiated agreement to plea guilty is reached, prosecutor[86] and defense counsel should state explicitly all its terms, and upon the plea of guilty in open court, terms of the agreement should be stated fully on the record and in writing, especially in serious or complicated cases. In appropriate cases, prosecutors and defense counsel should share information which they secured independently if such action will aid early case disposition. Defender agencies should also adopt programs enabling the early development of basic biographical information, diagnostic evaluations, and correctional planning for offenders.[87]

Police, prosecutors, bar associations, and courts, the Commission additionally recommended, should issue regulations and standards concerning the information that can be properly released to news media without jeopardizing the trial. All states should provide adequate postconviction remedies[88] which allow a single, simple remedy for all claims of deprivation of constitutional right. Petitions should be decided upon their merits rather than upon procedural technicalities. Similarly, Congress and the states should enact statutes giving the prosecution the right to appeal from the grant of all pretrial motions to suppress evidence or confessions.[89] In order to aid the conviction process, a general witness immunity statute should be passed at the federal and state levels providing for the immunity necessary to gain a compulsion of testimony. Congress and the states should abolish the rigid two-witness and direct evidence rules in perjury prosecutions, while also maintaining the requirement of proving an intentional false statement. Sentencing provisions of state penal codes should be reviewed with the goal of simplifying the grading of offenses, removing mandatory minimum prison terms, eliminating long maximum prison terms, and removing restrictions upon parole and pro-

---

[86] See Evelle J. Younger, "Prosecution Problems," *American Bar Association Journal*, Vol. 53 (August, 1967), pp. 695–702; and Monroe H. Freedman, "Professional Responsibility of the Prosecuting Attorney," *Criminal Law Bulletin*, Vol. 3 (October, 1967), p. 544.

[87] *Ibid.*, pp. 136–37.

[88] Gerald F. Uelman, "Post-Conviction Relief for Federal Prisoners," *West Virginia Law Review*, Vol. 69 (April, 1967), pp. 277–91.

[89] For information concerning discovery, see William J. McLafferty, "Disclosure and Discovery in Criminal Cases: Where Are We Headed?" *Duquesne Law Review*, Vol. 6 (Fall, 1967), pp. 41–59; Michael Moore, "Criminal Discovery," *Hastings Law Journal*, Vol. 19 (March, 1968), pp. 865–917; Peter Langrock, "Vermont's Experiment in Criminal Discovery," *American Bar Association Journal*, Vol. 53 (August, 1967), pp. 732–34; Martin L. Skumukler, "Fresh Look at the Suppressed Evidence Rule," *Brooklyn Law Review*, Vol. 34 (Winter, 1968), pp. 269–75; Marion F. Ratnoff, "New Criminal Disposition Statute in Ohio," *Case Western Reserve Law Review*, Vol. 19 (January, 1968), pp. 279–91; and Ephraim Margolin, "Toward Effective Criminal Discovery in California—A Practitioner's View," *California Law Review*, Vol. 56 (August, 1968), pp. 1040–59.

bation eligibility.[90] Judges should possess the clear authority to impose extended prison terms upon persistent habitual offenders or dangerous criminals. Sentencing codes should include criteria designed to help judges exercise their discretion in relationship to clearly stated standards.[91]

While making no recommendation concerning the continuance or elimination of capital punishment, its use, the Commission suggested, should be strictly limited to specific types of offenses and be invoked in an even-handed and non-discriminatory manner. All felony and misdemeanor courts should have probation services based upon a standard of proficiency, common to modern probation services. Under most circumstances the defendant and his counsel should be permitted to examine the complete presentence report.[92] In order to bring the administration of justice into close relationship with and awareness of correctional programs and facilities, every state should organize and finance regular judicial institutes or conferences for judges and correctional authorities. Jury sentence in noncapital cases should be abolished; inadequate, excessive, disparate sentences should be avoided or corrected.[93]

Judicial tenure in major trial courts, the President's Commission recommended, should be set for a term of 10 or more years, although

---

[90] R. C. Thompsen, "Sentencing the Dangerous Offender," *Federal Probation,* Vol. 32 (March, 1968), pp. 3–4.

[91] *Ibid.,* pp. 137–43. Also note Richard F. Doyle, "A Sentencing Council in Operation," *Federal Probation,* Vol. 25 (September, 1961), pp. 27–30; James V. Bennett, "Countdown for Judicial Sentencing," *Federal Probation,* Vol. 25 (September, 1961), p. 22; Roszel C. Thomsen, "Sentencing in Income Tax Cases," *Federal Probation,* Vol. 26 (March, 1962), pp. 10–13; Frank J. Remington and Donald J. Newman, "The Highland Park Institute on Sentence Disparity," *Federal Probation,* Vol. 26 (March, 1962), pp. 3–9; William F. Smith, "Sentencing Alternatives Available to the Courts," *Federal Probation,* Vol. 26 (June, 1962), pp. 3–5; A. E. Gottshall, "Sentencing the Youth and Young Adult Offender," *Federal Probation,* Vol. 26 (June, 1962), pp. 17–22; Eugene N. Varkin, "Sentencing the Adult Offender," *Federal Probation,* Vol. 26 (June, 1962), pp. 11–16; B. J. George, Jr., "Sentencing Methods and Techniques in the U.S.," *Federal Probation,* Vol. 26 (June, 1962), pp. 33–40; Irving R. Kaufman, "Enlightened Sentences Through Improved Technique," *Federal Probation,* Vol. 26 (September, 1962), pp. 3–10; and Richard E. Robinson, "The Defendant Needs to Know," *Federal Probation,* Vol. 26 (December, 1961), pp. 3–6.

[92] Refer to John B. Wilson, "A New Arena Is Emerging to Test the Confidentiality of Presentence Reports," *Federal Probation,* Vol. 25 (December, 1961), pp. 6–11; Jacob B. Barnett and David H. Gronewald, "Confidentiality of the Presentence Report," *Federal Probation,* Vol. 26 (March, 1962), pp. 26–30; Paul W. Keve, "The Message of Mr. Piyo's Dream," *Federal Probation,* Vol. 25 (December, 1961), pp. 11–15.

[93] Refer to John S. Palmore, "Sentencing and Correction: The Black Sheep of Criminal Law," *Federal Probation,* Vol. 26 (December, 1962), pp. 6–15; Rosser M. Smith, "A Probation Officer Looks at Disparities in Sentence," *Federal Probation,* Vol. 26 (December, 1962), pp. 19–23; William M. Byrne, Jr., "Federal Sentencing Procedures: Need for Reform," *Los Angeles Bar Bulletin.* Vol. 42 (October, 1967), pp. 563–67; and "Institute for Sentencing," *Federal Rules Decisions,* Vol. 42 (August, 1967), pp. 175–232.

the retirement of judges at a predetermined age should also be facilitated. Community salary structures should be upgraded in order to allow district attorneys and assistants to devote full-time to their office without having to engage in outside practice. Efforts to raise the quality of the office so that highly talented lawyers will seek the position should be undertaken. Pertinent professional and governmental organizations should develop curriculum and programs for the preservice and inservice training of prosecutors. The power and authority of the state attorney general or other appropriate statewide officers should be strengthened in order to coordinate local prosecution.

Likewise, counsel should be provided every criminal defendant who faces a significant penalty if he is unable to afford counsel himself. Provided early in the proceedings and no later than the first judicial appearance, such counsel should aid the defendant in both misdemeanor and felony cases. Legal assistance should also be provided, the Commission indicated, in parole and probation revocation proceedings, juvenile delinquency proceedings if there is a possibility of coercive disposition, and all legal processes which threaten the respondent with a substantial loss of liberty. A coordinated assigned-counsel system or defender system, financed on a regular and statewide basis, should replace counsel assigned by judges. The courts and their systems should also establish standards for the completion of the various stages of criminal cases in order to insure the expeditious disposition of cases.

States should also provide for clear administrative responsibility within the courts and make professional court administrators available to assist the judges in court management. The physical facilities and compensation for witnesses and jurors should be improved. Unnecessary appearances and waiting should be minimized through the expanded use of the scheduling and witness call systems. Sworn statements, except in cases involving an immediate hearing on the arrest or charge, should be accepted as a substitute for the appearance of the arresting officer at the initial court appearance. Overall, states should reexamine their court structure and organization with the view of creating a single, unified system of courts, subject to central administrative management within the judiciary. Central administration should possess the authority to make rules and shift manpower to meet changing requirements of the court system.[94] Only then can the criminal court realize true justice and efficiency.

---

[94] President's Commission, *Challenge of Crime*, pp. 145–57. Particular aspects of the system of justice are discussed in John S. Hastings, "The Criminal Justice Act of 1964," *Journal of Criminal Law, Criminology, and Police Science*, Vol. 57 (September, 1966), pp. 426–29; A. Kingston, "Probability and Legal Proceedings," *Journal of Criminal Law, Criminology, and Police Science*, Vol. 57 (June, 1966), pp. 93–98; and Carl Martin, "Electronic Courtroom Recording," *Judicature*, Vol. 50 (April, 1967), pp. 262–64.

Chapter 19

THE SYSTEM OF
MILITARY JUSTICE

The earliest documented form of military justice appeared during the Greek and Roman civilizations.[1] The Crusaders developed the first known formal military code. The American Articles of War originated in 1775 from contributions received from the Code of Gustavus Adolphus of 1621[2] and the British Articles of War, in effect during the American Revolution.[3] Under the provision of the British Articles, the King, as chief executive and commander in chief of the armies, possessed the power, independent of any statutory authority, over the armed forces. By virtue of his position, he both commanded and legislated for the army, prescribing the Articles of War, offenses and penalties, substantive and procedural law, and courts-martial jurisdiction and procedure. The court-martial, then an agency of command rather than a judicial body, operated as his agent to accomplish defined military goals.

THE EVOLUTION OF AMERICAN MILITARY JUSTICE

The Continental Congress, adopting the Massachusetts Articles and portions of the British Military Code in its own Articles of War of

---

[1] Hikmet Sener, "A Comparison of the Turkish and American Military Systems of Nonjudical Punishment," *Military Law Review*, Vol. 27 (January, 1965), p. 111; and Primitivo Chingcuangco, "Human Rights in the Administration of Phillipine Military Justice," *Military Law Review*, Vol. 37 (July, 1967). pp. 127–54.

[2] Robert D. Byers, "Court-Martial as a Sentencing Agency: Milestone or Millstone," *Military Law Review*, Vol. 41 (July, 1968), p. 83.

[3] Donald W. Hansen, "Judicial Functions for the Commander?" *Military Law Review*, Vol. 41 (July, 1968), p. 7.

1775, accepted similar assumptions.[4] Adopted on June 30, 1775, these Articles served as the first national code of military justice, even though they were revised within the year. While the Articles made no provision for a commander to convene a court-martial, his power to do so was generally accepted in practice. At the same time, however, the Continental Congress did allow the commander the power of appellate review. By 1786, the Continental commander had been empowered by the Congress to utilize his authority without its approval in all cases, except those involving death, dismissal of a commissioned officer in peacetime, and in all sentences involving general officers.[5]

Under the 1806 revision of the Articles of War, the function of judicial review was transferred from the Congress and the commander to the President. At the same time, any general officer commanding an army, or colonels responsible for separate departments, were similarly granted power to convene a general court-martial as necessary, a decision which made the court-martial potentially subject to local pressures and to the whims of commanders. Possessing the right to select a legal adviser as a trial judge advocate, such officers were restricted only by the right of the accused to challenge court members for cause. If the commander was accuser or prosecutor, he was likewise prohibited, under the Articles of 1806, from appointing the members of the court, although this restriction was generally limited to the trial of officers and not to cases before inferior tribunals.[6]

The problems created during the Civil War, however, necessitated further changes and produced the Articles of War of 1874. Under its provisions the commander was empowered in time of war to execute certain death sentences upon confirmation of the department commander or the commanding general in the field. Usually this action was limited to special cases involving the conviction of spies, mutineers, deserters, or murderers.[7] The accused had to be brought to trial within eight days after his arrest, or as soon as a court-martial could be convened; officers had to be tried within 40 days of the original arrest or the arrest was terminated. Under the stipulations of the Articles, a judge advocate was excluded from attendance at the closed sessions of the court-martial, even though his legal assistance could be requested in open court in the presence of the accused. While the defendant was not granted a defense attorney as a matter of right, his own testimony was now accepted as a competent witness, and his failure to take the stand could not be legally presumed to be an admission of guilt.

---

[4] *Ibid.,* p. 10.
[5] *Ibid.,* p. 11. Also note Conrad D. Philos, *Handbook of Court-Martial Law* (Chicago: Callaghan & Co., 1951).
[6] *Ibid.,* p. 13.
[7] *Ibid.,* p. 13.

The Articles of War of 1916, largely proposed by Major General Enoch H. Crowder, the then current Judge Advocate General, failed to grant the right of preemptory challenge, demanded prompt court-martial of the accused, and referred to the President as the supreme court of trials by courts-martial.[8] Recognizing the President as commander in chief and chief legislator for the Army, the revised code authorized the President to provide rules of procedure and modes of proof in court-martial trials. The previous limitation that division and brigade commanders could not convene courts-martial in other than wartime, due to the changes in the approach and procedures of war, was eliminated.

A major turning point in the development of American military justice was recorded in the Articles of War of 1920. While the earlier codes had served to support the commander's authority, these Articles more effectively related the commander's power to civilian jurisprudence. The convening authority, therefore, was required to share his decision-making authority with noncommanders, to forward the file of an accused to the staff judge advocate prior to trial, and to consult with his staff judge advocate for an opinion concerning the legality of the proceedings before taking any posttrial action. While the commander still retained broad discretionary authority to appoint members of the court, his appointments were limited to officers with over two years' service who were "best qualified for the duty by reason of age, training, experience, and judicial temperament."[9] He was likewise enjoined from requesting or demanding a reconsideration of an acquittal or an increase in punishment by a court-martial.

The commander was further required in the revised Articles of War of 1948 to determine if the charges were "legally sufficient" and if conviction was supported by proof "beyond a reasonable doubt." A separate Judge Advocate General's Corps was created to insure independent legal action and advice. Enlisted men were empowered under the 1948 Articles to sit as members of the court-martial when requested by the accused, a procedure that replaced the earlier "court of honor" theory which assumed that only officers possess the requisite knowledge of discipline to make judgments in military cases. Most strikingly, court members were empowered to use their independent judgment free of commander influence and without fear of censure in later court-martials.[10]

---

[8] *Ibid.*, p. 15. For an interesting insight to the period, see Maurer Maurer, "Court Martialing of Camp Followers, World War I," *American Journal of Legal History*, Vol. 9 (July, 1965), pp. 205–15.

[9] *Ibid.*, p. 41. See Wayne E. Alley, "Overseas Commander's Power to Regulate the Private Life," *Military Law Review*, Vol. 37 (July, 1967), pp. 57–120.

[10] *Ibid.*, p. 19.

THE UNIFORM CODE OF MILITARY JUSTICE

Adopted in 1950 and made effective on May 31, 1951, the Uniform Code of Military Justice, incorporating the previously separate Army and Navy codes in Sections 801 through 940 of Title 10 of the United States Code, further defined the evolving relationship of court-martial participants. It provided for three classes of court-martial: summary, special, and general. Each was to be formed by appointment of personnel by the commander. While the Uniform Code placed no limit upon the type of offenses which could be tried by the courts-martial, it did restrict the types of sentences it could prescribe.

Charges and specifications, signed by an appropriate person before a commissioned officer of the Armed Forces, may allege military violations by the offender and may take the form of charges of conspiracy; solicitation; fraudulent and unlawful enlistment, appointment, or separation; desertion; absence without leave; contempt or disrespect toward officials or superior commissioned officers; insubordinate conduct toward warrant, noncommissioned, or petty officers; cruelty and maltreatment; mutiny or sedition; resistance, breach of arrest, or escape; misbehavior before the enemy; spying; or improper use of countersign (see the accompanying listing of selected articles from the Uniform Code). Chargeable are improper hazarding of vessel; drunk on duty; dueling; malingering; provoking speeches or gestures; conduct unbecoming an officer and a gentleman; and the general crimes of murder, rape, burglary, and the like.[11]

The *summary court-martial,* which makes no provision for defense counsel or prosecutor, is conducted by a single officer. However, all branches of the armed services have permitted or provided such counsel in recent years upon request. The least important military court, the summary court-martial is generally limited to forfeitures of two thirds of a month's pay, limited reductions in grade, and one month's confinement. A court primarily for enlisted men, it is not empowered to try commissioned or warrant officers. The court is designed to limit the formation of a negative record, and any recording of action, except in cases requiring eventual review, is limited to docket-type entries. Such review is usually completed by the staff judge advocate of the officer exercising general court-martial jurisdiction unless higher evaluation is demanded.[12] In general, the summary court-martial is the effective

---

[11] Department of the Army, *Pocket Part of the Manual for Courts Martial—United States, 1956* (Washington, D.C.: U.S. Government Printing Office, 1956), pp. 351–52.

[12] Myron L. Birnbaum, "The Effect of Recent Supreme Court Decisions on Military Law," *Fordham Law Review,* Vol. 36 (December, 1967), p. 155.

police court of the Armed Forces and is comparable to the justice of the peace or city courts.[13]

SELECTED ARTICLES FROM THE
UNIFORM CODE OF MILITARY JUSTICE*

Article 89   Disrespect Toward Superior Commissioned Officer

Any person subject to this chapter who behaves with disrespect toward his superior commissioned officer shall be punished as a court-martial may direct.

Article 90   Assaulting or Willfully Disobeying Superior Commissioned Officer

Any person subject to this chapter who—

(1) strikes his superior commissioned officer or draws or lifts up any weapon or offers any violence against him while he is in the execution of his office; or

(2) willfully disobeys a lawful command of his superior commissioned officer;

shall be punished, if the offense is committed in time of war, by death or such other punishment as a court-martial may direct and if the offense is committed at any other time, by such punishment, other than death, as a court-martial may direct.

. . . .

Article 91   Insubordinate Conduct Toward Warrant Officer, Noncommissioned Officer, or Petty Officer

Any warrant officer or enlisted member who—

(1) strikes or assaults a warrant officer, noncommissioned officer, or petty officer, while that officer is in the execution of his office;

(2) willfully disobeys the lawful order of a warrant officer, noncommissioned officer, or petty officer; or

(3) treats with contempt or is disrespectful in language or deportment toward a warrant officer, noncommissioned officer, or petty officer while that officer is in the execution of his office shall be punished as a court-martial may direct.

. . . .

Article 92   Failure to Obey Order or Regulation

Any person subject to this chapter who—

(1) violates or fails to obey any lawful general order or regulation;

(2) having knowledge of any other lawful order issued by a member of the armed forces, which it is his duty to obey, fails to obey the order; or

(3) is derelict in the performance of his duties; shall be punished as a court-martial may direct.

. . . .

---

* From: *Military Law Journal,* Vol. 31 (January, 1966), pp. 130–133.

[13] James A. Black, Jr., "The Uniform Code of Military Justice and the Right to Counsel," *University of Cincinnati Law Review,* Vol. 36 (Summer, 1967), pp. 472–86.

Article 93   Cruelty and Maltreatment

Any person subject to this chapter who is guilty of cruelty toward, or oppression or maltreatment of, any person subject to his orders shall be punished as a court-martial may direct.

Article 104   Aiding the Enemy

Any person who—

(1) aids, or attempts to aid, the enemy with arms, ammunition, supplies, money, or other things; or

(2) without proper authority, knowingly harbors, protects or gives intelligence to, or communicates or corresponds with or holds any intercourse with the enemy, either directly or indirectly; shall suffer death or such other punishment as a court-martial commission may direct.

Article 105   Misconduct as Prisoner

Any person subject to this chapter who, while in the hands of the enemy in time of war—

(1) for the purpose of securing favorable treatment by his captors acts without proper authority in a manner contrary to law, custom, or regulation, to the detriment of others of whatever nationality held by the enemy as civilian or military prisoners; or

(2) while in a position of authority over such persons maltreats them without justifiable cause;
shall be punished as a court-martial may direct.

Article 133   Conduct Unbecoming an Officer and a Gentleman

Any commissioned officer, cadet, or midshipman who is convicted of conduct unbecoming an officer and a gentleman shall be punished as a court-martial may direct.

Article 134   General Article

Though not specifically mentioned in this chapter, all disorders and neglects to the prejudice of good order and discipline in the armed forces, all conduct of a nature to bring discredit upon the armed forces, and crimes and offenses not capital, of which persons subject to this chapter may be guilty, shall be taken cognizance of by a general, special, or summary court-martial, according to the nature and degree of the offense, and shall be punished at the discretion of that court.

CODE OF CONDUCT*

I

I am an American fighting man. I serve in the forces which guard my country and our way of life. I am prepared to give my life in their defense.

---

* From: *Military Law Journal,* Vol. 31 (January, 1966), pp. 130–133.

II

I will never surrender of my own free will. If in command, I will never surrender my men while they still have the means to resist.

III

If I am captured I will continue to resist by all means available. I will make every effort to escape and aid others to escape. I will accept neither parole nor special favors from the enemy.

IV

If I become a prisoner of war, I will keep faith with my fellow prisoners. I will give no information nor take part in any action which might be harmful to my comrades. If I am senior, I will take command. If not, I will obey the lawful orders of those appointed over me and will back them up in every way.

V

When questioned, should I become a prisoner of war, I am bound to give only name, rank, service number, and date of birth. I will evade answering further questions to the utmost of my ability. I will make no oral or written statements disloyal to my country and its allies or harmful to their cause.

VI

I will never forget that I am an American fighting man, responsible for my actions, and dedicated to the principles which made my country free. I will trust in my God and in the United States of America.

The *special courts-martial*, consisting of three or more members who may be commissioned or warrant officers, requires both trial and defense counsel. If the accused is an enlisted man, a minimum of one third of the members of the courts-martial, if he requests their participation, must be enlisted personnel. While members may be lawyers, defense counsel must share similar qualifications if his trial counsel is a lawyer. Although sentences are limited to the provisions of the Table of Maximum Punishments prescribed in the Manual for Courts-Martial by the President, they may not exceed forfeiture of two thirds of pay for six months and reduction in grade, confinement at hard labor for six months, or a bad-conduct discharge. In such cases, complete records are kept in either summarized form, if sentence does not include a bad-conduct discharge, or in verbatim form, if such a discharge is included.[14] While

---

[14] Birnbaum, *op. cit.*, p. 156.

cases which do not involve a bad-conduct discharge are finally reviewed at the general court-martial level, those which do are referred to a board of review.

A *general court-martial*, consisting of five or more members designated in a manner similar to a special court-martial, usually includes the services of a law officer who occupies a position similar to that of a civilian judge with the exception that he does not rule on challenges or motions for findings of not guilty, does not determine sentences, and is not empowered to fulfill particular collateral responsibilities and powers that a civilian judge might fulfill. Assigned to a "convenient" duty station within a judicial circuit, he serves the needs within that circuit. Because his work is not supervised by the convening authority or the staff judge advocate, he is essentially free to follow the dictates of his profession and the case.[15]

Trial and defense counsel and the law officer must be lawyers. Under the provisions of the Uniform Code, the court may impose any punishment or combination of punishments within the limitations set by the President. Due to the seriousness of these cases, verbatim records are maintained and forwarded to the respective Judge Advocate General who examines less serious general court-martial trials for error. Those cases which involve an approved sentence which "affects a general or a flag officer or extends to death, dismissal of a commissioned officer, cadet, or midshipman, dishonorable or bad-conduct discharge, or confinement for one year or more" are forwarded to a Board of Review for further consideration.[16]

OPERATIONAL ASSUMPTIONS OF THE SYSTEM OF MILITARY JUSTICE

Civilian criminal justice and military justice serve different purposes. While the civilian criminal code seeks to prevent antisocial acts, the military code enforces the military demand that the soldier perform disagreeable and often dangerous responsibilities rarely asked of civilians (see accompanying Executive Order 10631).[17] In contrast to the criminal code, which is enacted through legislative action, military command regulations may assume the force of law despite the fact that they are arbitrarily promulgated by the local commander. The need for military

[15] Byers, *op. cit.*, p. 91. A civilian problem is involved in H. Thomas Howell, "Does Judge Advocate Service Qualify for Admission on Motion?" *American Bar Association Journal*, Vol. 53 (October, 1967), pp. 915–19.

[16] Birnbaum, *op. cit.*, p. 157. Also note David E. Zajicek, "General Court-Martial Authority: Air Force Prisoners in United States Disciplinary Barracks," *Air Force Judge Advocate General Law Review*, Vol. 10 (May–June, 1968). pp. 24–36.

[17] Hansen, *op. cit.*, p. 41.

security and for maintenance of order make the system of military justice fundamentally different from the context of the civilian and criminal code. And yet, at the same time, the protection afforded citizens by the systems of civilian and military justice cannot be in gross opposition with established judicial principles. The wide latitude allowed the local commander is generally modified by the interactional acceptance or non-acceptance of his dictates by the men under his command.

A complaint forwarded to the commanding officer of the accused serves as the basis for the origin of a court-martial in the system of military justice. Upon receipt of the complaint, the commanding officer is empowered to determine whether an offense has been committed,

EXECUTIVE ORDER 10631 CODE OF CONDUCT
FOR MEMBERS OF THE
ARMED FORCES OF THE UNITED STATES*

By virtue of the Authority vested in me as President of the United States, and as Commander in Chief of the Armed Forces of the United States, I hereby prescribe the Code of Conduct for the Armed Forces of the United States which are attached to this order and hereby made a part thereof.

Every member of the Armed Forces of the United States is expected to measure up to the standards embodied in this Code of Conduct while he is in combat or in captivity. To ensure achievement of these standards, each member of the Armed Forces liable to capture shall be provided with specific training and instruction designed to better equip him to counter and withstand all enemy efforts against him, and shall be fully instructed as to the behavior and obligations expected of him during combat or captivity.

The Secretary of Defense (and the Secretary of the Treasury with respect to the Coast Guard except when it is serving as part of the Navy) shall take such action as is deemed necessary to implement this order and to disseminate and make the said Code known to all members of the Armed Forces of the United States.

THE WHITE HOUSE

August 17, 1955

/s/ Dwight D. Eisenhower

whether a court-martial is warranted, and whether nonjudicial punishment might prove to be more appropriate. If the commanding officer concludes that a court-martial is in order, he proceeds to draw up charges and specifications, to define his recommendations for the disposition of the case, and to forward both to the convenient authority. At the same time, he is held responsible for notifying the accused of the charges against him. If the accused is facing a general court-martial,

---

* From: *Military Law Journal*, Vol. 31 (January, 1966), pp. 130–33.

the charges are referred to a disinterested officer, who conducts a thorough investigation and recommends final disposition of charges. However, consideration and advice must be sought from the staff judge advocate or legal adviser before the convening authority can direct a trial by general court-martial.[18] The law officer, not a member of the general court-martial, is responsible for the maintenance of fair and orderly conduct at such a trial. While he does not vote upon questions before the court, his rulings on questions of law and procedure are final.[19]

During the first phase of the actual trial, the court-martial seeks judgment concerning the guilt or innocence of the accused. If he is found guilty, a second hearing is held to consider extenuating or mitigating circumstances and to determine appropriate sentence. Any decision, however, is potentially subject to several levels of review based upon the nature of the case and the type of court-martial which was held.[20] Nonjudicial punishments imposed under Article 15 of the Uniform Code of Military Justice may take nine basic forms: admonition and reprimand, restriction, arrest in quarters, correctional custody, confinement on bread and water or diminished rations, extra duties, reduction in grade, forfeiture of pay, and detention of pay.[21] While court members in the early Army court-martial system sentenced the accused after his trial, a practice which continues even today, they originally did so because they generally represented the only legally trained personnel available in the court at that time.[22]

During 1965 and 1966, 3,029 individuals were tried in Army general courts-martial. Although 1,634 (80.01 percent) of the pleas were "entered pursuant to a pre-trial agreement,"[23] 2,024 (67.4 percent) were tried on pleas of guilty. While the all courts-martial tried 69,174 cases in a jurisdiction of some 3 million persons during the calendar year 1966, the majority involved either summary or special and general courts-martial "in which the sentence did not include a punitive discharge."[24] However, nearly 4,000 of these cases were eventually reconsidered by appropriate Boards of Review inasmuch as the sentence involved a punitive discharge or a confinement at hard labor for a year or more.

A study by Robert D. Byers of attitudes toward sentencing of 143 staff judge advocates, law officers, and senior judge advocates throughout the world revealed that 82 of the 111 officers (74 percent) replying to a questionnaire agreed that sentencing authority should be vested

---

[18] Black, *op. cit.*, pp. 474–75.
[19] *Ibid.*, p. 473.
[20] *Ibid.*, p. 475.
[21] Sener, *op. cit.*, p. 130.
[22] Byers, *op. cit.*, p. 84.
[23] *Ibid.*, p. 89.
[24] Birnbaum, *op. cit.* p. 153.

in the law officer. Only 29 urged the retention of the present sentencing system.[25] Those favoring the law officer sentencing approach suggested that this system would best permit use of comprehensive presentence inquiry; free the court members of time-consuming sentencing procedures; provide a greater freedom from command influence; secure more uniform sentences; gain the greater use of suspended sentences; reduce appellate corrective action for inappropriate or illegal sentences; and avoid instructional complications. On the other hand, proponents of the existing court-martial sentencing method argue that the present process of convening courts-martial assures fairness under the present system; discipline is the function of commander; the collective judgment of court members is more desirable than a decision by one man; law officers may be unaware of command problems; any present weakness may be corrected through the mere modification of the present structure; the sentencing burden would be too great for the law officer; modifications would be objectionable to senior commanders; law officer sentencing should be used only in trials involving guilty pleas; the system would be a violation of military tradition; and a penological approach to sentencing does not apply to military justice.[26]

THE BOARD OF REVIEW

Each military service maintains a Board of Review which serves as an intermediate appellate tribunal to review matters of fact and of law and to affirm only that part of the approved sentence which seems appropriate. While the accused is represented in cases before the Board in the United States by a judge advocate from the office of the respective Judge Advocate General, he has also been allowed the right of representation by individual counsel in recent years.[27] (The Air Force, for example, maintains Boards of Review which are comparable to the appellate courts of the federal system.) A product of a War Department general order in January, 1918, the Board was originally created in the office of the Judge Advocate General of the Army and its branches. The originating principle was later reaffirmed in the 1920 code, the 1940 revision of the code, and the 1951 Uniform Code of Military Justice.[28]

In their current composition, the Boards of Review possess the authority to weigh evidence, judge the credibility of witnesses, and determine controversial questions of fact. Under the Uniform Code, not less than three officers or civilians compose the Board of Review, although only the Navy and the Coast Guard commonly use civilian attorneys

---

[25] Byers, op. cit., p. 105.

[26] Ibid., p. 106.

[27] Birnbaum, op. cit., p. 157.

[28] Morris F. Bittle, "A Brief Look at the Air Force Boards of Review," Air Force JAG Law Review, Vol. 8 (May–June, 1966), p. 12.

on such Boards.[29] Under the 1961 revision of the Board procedures, an accused is entitled to representation by his own civilian counsel or by assigned appellate counsel. If civilian counsel is employed, he must be a member of the federal Bar or court or of the highest court of the U.S. possession or state. Generally, all arguments presented before the Board of Review must relate to areas or arguments set out in the original brief, which serve as the foundation for the evaluation of the case.

The Uniform Code of Military Justice also established a Supreme Court of the Military composed entirely of civilians,[30] which rules on all basic matters as it sees fit. Under the law establishing its operations, no more than two of the judges may be members of the same political party, and members of the court must be appointed from the membership of the Bar of the federal court or the highest state court. The Court of Military Appeals receives cases from the Boards of Review either as a matter of course, if a general or flag officer or unaffirmed death sentence is involved, or on petition of the accused or on certification of the particular judge advocate general.[31] More than 98 percent of the 19,749 cases reviewed by the Court of Military Appeals through June 1966 were received on petition.[32]

THE CONTINUING EVOLUTION OF MILITARY JUSTICE

The evolution of military justice can be seen in the concept of mistrial, which was earlier denied as an acceptable procedure in the military court. During the early 1950's, the law officer was constrained from terminating a trial prior to a finding of judgment due to the decisions of the existing service Boards of Review. However, in 1954, two of the three members of the Court of Military Appeals finally reversed this interpretation and affirmed the law officer's right to make mistrial judgments. While this change actually reflected the shift of authority from the military commander to the judicial representative of the system of military justice, the exact definition of requirements for the determination of a mistrial are still being determined. Paul E. Wilson suggests that the following code serve as a guide for the evaluation of mistrials in court martials:

1. The law officer shall terminate a trial any time before findings when he determines:

---

[29] *Ibid.,* p. 13.

[30] Frederick R. Hanlon, *Ten-Year Chronology of the U.S. Military Court of Appeals* (Washington, D.C.: U.S. Court of Military Appeals, 1961), p. 2.

[31] *Ibid.,* p. 8. Also see Delmar Karlen, "Civilian and Military Justice at the Appellate Level," *Wisconsin Law Review,* Vol. 1968, No. 3 (1968), pp. 786–805.

[32] Birnbaum, *op. cit.,* pp. 157–58.

a) It is physically impossible to proceed with the trial in conformity with the law; or

b) There is a legal defect in the proceedings which would make any judgment rendered upon the findings reversible as a matter of law; or

c) Prejudicial conduct, in or outside the courtroom, makes it impossible to proceed with the trial without injustice to either the accused or the government; or

d) A substantial question exists as to the objectivity of the court or its willingness to be bound by the law officer's instructions.

2. The convening authority may direct the termination of a trial by court-martial prior to findings when required by urgent and unforeseen military necessity.

3. A subsequent prosecution, based on the same conduct for violation of the same provision of the code, is not barred when the trial is terminated after arraignment and before findings when:

a) The termination is for any reason mentioned in 1 and 2 above;

b) The accused consents to the termination or waives, by motion or otherwise, his right to object to the termination.[33]

Because court-martial jurisdiction is derived from the First Article of the Constitution, which empowers Congress[34] to "make rules for the Government and for regulation of land and naval forces," decisions of the U.S. Supreme Court have been applied to military courts either indirectly or through analogy as Congress or the system of military justice have deemed feasible. However, while the early decisions of the Supreme Court generally limited the jurisdiction of civil tribunals to questions of whether the military court had jurisdiction over a person and subject matter or whether it exceeded its powers in sentencing,[35] the decision of *Burns* v. *Wilson* (1953) has lately extended this inquiry to the determination of whether the accused received due process.[36] In modern times, the military appellate system, therefore, has emerged as an official institution to supervise the use of court-martial authority and procedure.

Burns v. *Wilson* has effectively determined that military courts possess the same responsibility to protect the members of the military from

---

[33] Paul E. Wilson, "Mistrials in Court-Martial: A Study of the Evolution of the Judicial Character of the Military Judge," *William and Mary Law Review,* Vol. 9 (Winter, 1967), p. 348; and E. P. Wasinger, "Doctrine of Waiver," *Military Law Review,* Vol. 39 (January, 1968), pp. 85–119.

[34] Article I, U.S. Constitution. Also see Walter F. Brown, "Criminal Jurisdiction over Visiting Naval Forces under International Law," *Washington and Lee Law Review,* Vol. 24 (Spring, 1967), pp. 9–48; and Elizabeth R. Smith, "Code of Conduct in Relation to International Law," *Military Law Review,* Vol. 31 (1966), pp. 85–136.

[35] 206 U.S. 333 (1907). See Frederick B. Weiner, "Are the General Military Articles Unconstitutionally Vague?" *American Bar Association Journal,* Vol. 54 (April, 1968), pp. 357–64.

[36] 346 U.S. 137, 142 (1953).

violations of their constitutional rights as federal courts, a judgment which characteristically extends the provisions of the Bill of Rights to servicemen. However, the exact extent to which this principle will be applied remains an open question. The right of free speech, for example, is still modified by the requirements of the situation. The demand for security may make picketing by an off-duty uniformed Army lieutenant unacceptable.[37] However, even the more recent *U.S. v. Howe* decision has held that even here the issue is not one of restriction of political dissent but the contemptuous manner in which this dissent is expressed. The military, the Court of Military Appeals ruled, may impose restrictions upon free speech when the constraints are necessary to protect national security, maintain internal discipline, and promote military morale.

Even these interpretations are under attack due to the continuance of the military draft, which has forced the democratization of the Armed Forces and has undermined the previous assumption that the court-martial is a court of honor for soldiers or other Armed Forces personnel who voluntarily assume the responsibility implied in the military code.[38] Because of large numbers of young men who do not voluntarily assume the obligations of the military code, new problems in law and in military discipline have arisen.[39] One of the areas of tension has included the question of the serviceman's right to counsel. While the Uniform Code

---

[37] Robert J. Finan and Joseph E. Vorbach, "Court of Military Appeals and the Bill of Rights: A New Look," *George Washington Law Review*, Vol. 36 (1967), p. 437; and Jerome X. Lewis, "Freedom of Speech—An Examination of the Civilian Test of Constitutionality and Its Application to the Military," *Military Law Review*, Vol. 41 (July, 1968), pp. 55–80.

[38] See Frederick C. Moss, "Effect of the First Amendment on Federal Control of Draft Protests," *Villanova Law Review*, Vol. 13 (Winter, 1968), p. 347; D. M. Cohen and R. Greenspan, "Conscientious Objection, Democratic Theory, and the Constitution,". *University of Pittsburgh Law Review*, Vol. 29 (March, 1968), p. 389; Thomas G. Kienbaum, "Administrative Law," *Wayne Law Review*, Vol. 13 (Fall, 1967), pp. 722–28; John Ritter, "New Draft Law: Its Failures and Future," *Case Western Reserve Law Review*, Vol. 19 (January, 1968), pp. 292–326; J. L. Bernstein, "Conscription and the Constitution," *American Bar Association Journal*, Vol. 53 (August, 1967), pp. 708–12; Ann F. Ginger, "Minimum Due Process Standards in Selective Service Cases," *Hastings Law Journal*, Vol. 19 (May, 1968), pp. 1313–48; Ralph Reisner, "Conscientious Objector Exemption; Administrative Procedures and Judicial Review," *University of Chicago Law Review*, Vol. 35 (Summer, 1968), pp. 686–720; James W. Scouten, "States, the Federal Constitution and the War Protesters," *Cornell Law Review*, Vol. 53 (February, 1968), pp. 528–42; Alfred C. Jones III, "Draft Reclassification for Political Demonstrations," *Cornell Law Review*, Vol. 53 (May, 1968), pp. 916–34; "Selective Service and the 1967 Statute," *Military Law Review*, Vol. 39 (April, 1968), p. 33; Lawrence R. Velvel, "Freedom of Speech and the Draft Card Burning Cases," *University of Kansas*, Vol. 16 (January, 1968), pp. 149–79; and "Administrative Law," *Harvard Law Review*, Vol. 81 (January, 1968), pp. 685–90.

[39] Hansen, *op. cit.*, p. 2. Refer additionally to James A. Black, Jr., "Uniform Code of Military Justice and the Right to Council," *University of Cincinnati Law Review*, Vol. 36 (Summer, 1967), pp. 472–86; James F. Falco, "*United States*

of Military Justice (1951) permitted the appointment of defense counsel for special and general courts-martial, it usually occurred only when charges were referred to trial. Even following the Supreme Court decision in *Escobedo* v. *Illinois* (1966), the Court of Military Appeals held that the accused "is not denied the assistance of counsel unless he requests and is refused the right to consult counsel during the interrogation, or is misinformed as to his right to counsel."[40] As a consequence of the *Miranda* v. *Arizona* decision some four months later, however, the military departments instructed their law enforcement personnel to comply with the *Miranda* rules where applicable despite the fact that some confusion existed in each of the services concerning the exact application of the *Miranda* ruling. While the Fifth Amendment privilege against self-incrimination had been incorporated into the 1951 formulation of the Uniform Code of Military Justice, the *Miranda* decision, which requires the arresting officer to remind the accused of his right to remain silent, has given it greater meaning.

The case of Airman Third Class Michael Tempia is a case at point. The Court of Military Appeals reversed Tempia's conviction for indecent liberties with three young girls in a base library rest room on the ground that the *Miranda* decision pertaining to the need to inform the accused of his right to remain silent applies directly to military courts.[41] In effect, the Court of Military Appeals rejected the previous assumption that the Supreme Court does not exercise supervisory authority over courts-martial and moved toward a more clearly defined foundation of military justice. Holding that Tempia had undergone "custodial interrogation," the court maintained that the contention that the accused had knowingly and intelligently waived his right to counsel was not supported by the evidence.

Still there are other tensions. Historically, the Court of Military Ap-

---

v. *Tempia*," *Villanova Law Review*, Vol. 13 (Fall, 1967), p. 170; Gilbert A. Bartlett, "Partial Protection from Self-Incrimination in Military Justice," *William and Mary Law Review*, Vol. 9 (Spring, 1968), p. 844; M. L. Zurier, "Blankenship Revisited—Undue Questioning by Court Members," *Air Force Judge Advocate General Law Review*, Vol. 9 (July–August, 1967), pp. 18–23; Dean A. Zimmerman, "Gideon in the Military," *South Dakota Law Review*, Vol. 13 (Spring, 1968), pp. 410–15; and Edward F. Sherman, "Right to Competent Counsel in Special Courts-Martial," *American Bar Association Antitrust Law Journal*, Vol. 54 (September, 1968), pp. 866–71.

[40] Birnbaum, *op. cit.*, p. 160. For another facet see Raymond S. E. Pushkar, "Criminal Libel and Slander in the Military," *Air Force Judge Advocate General Journal*, Vol. 9 (November–December, 1967), pp. 40–44.

[41] Gaylord L. Finch, "Military Law and the Miranda Requirements," *Cleveland-Marshall Law Review*, Vol. 17 (September, 1968), p. 537. Robert D. Hamel, "Military Search and Seizure—Probable Cause Requirement," *Military Law Review*, Vol. 39 (January, 1968), pp. 41–84; and D. B. Nichols, "Compatibility of Military and Civil Legal Values: *Mens Rea*—A Case in Point," *Military Law Review*, Vol. 28 (April, 1965), pp. 169–92.

peals has denied the military prisoner the right to bail.[42] Even the Bail Reform Act of 1966 excluded the use of bail within the system of military justice, assuming theoretically that military courts protect the servicemen through an early determination of whether pretrial restraint is justified and whether his commanding officer abused his discretionary power.[43]

The continuing problem

The serviceman is not like his civilian peers. He is unable to quit his job and go home or to convince others to strike against working conditions. He does not enjoy the right to trial by jury or even the right to bail guaranteed under the Eighth Amendment, since he is continually under the control of his superiors. Because he lives publicly in a barracks with other men, the Fourth Amendment guarantee against unreasonable search and seizure offers only limited value.[44] Practically, the serviceman exists within a welfare state committed to order and to discipline in order to accomplish a defense function. And yet, this state is the most undemocratic of all institutions.

The idealism of the Code of Conduct and the discretionary nature of the Uniform Code of Military Justice have received many criticisms during the Vietnam War years. The *Pueblo* incident once again points out the vast cleavage between the demands of military necessity stated in the Code of Conduct and the physical and psychological ability of Armed Forces personnel to endure suffering. The earlier "brainwashing" of military personnel during the Korean War which gave birth to the Code similarly testifies to the problem. Since the capture of the intelligence ship *Pueblo,* several other incidents have pointed to the shortcomings of the Uniform Code of Military Justice, or at least to its usage. The "mutiny" of prisoners (a sit-down strike) at the Presidio stockade and the alleged murder of a Vietnamese employee by Green Beret personnel for suspected betrayal of American forces have both come under the jurisdiction of the Uniform Code. While those engaged in the "mutiny" have been charged, tried, and sentenced with rapidity, the eight Green Berets have been freed of charges because of alleged CIA refusal, according to the Secretary of the Army, to testify at an appropriate court-martial, a refusal which would receive little acceptance in civilian criminal cases.

The proposed Military Justice Act of 1967, embodied in Senate bill 2009, was designed to modernize the system of military justice and to

---

[42] 17 U.S.C.M.A., 135, 137 MR 399 (1967) in *Levy* v. *Resor. See* Alonzo Shields, "Supplement to the Survey of Military Justice," *Military Law Review,* Vol. 41 (July, 1968), pp. 109–50.

[43] Finan and Vorbach, *op. cit.,* p. 446.

[44] *Ibid.,* pp. 542–43.

overcome many of the criticisms of command control, lack of legal training of counsel, variations in Air Force, Army, and Navy justice, and violations of due process. An omnibus bill divided into five parts, the 1967 act would have designated procedures for administrative discharge boards, allowed the formation of a separate corps for Navy judge advocates, suggested multiple changes in the Uniform Code of Military Justice, transformed boards of review into the Court of Military Review, and consolidated presented service boards into a single Board for the Correction of Military Records under the Department of Defense.[45] The act would have provided that no member, whether enlisted, warrant, or commissioned would receive a discharge under other than honorable conditions, except where allegations of misconduct, unfitness, or threat to security are sustained either by admission of guilt or after a just hearing. While this act was not enacted, it suggests the direction likely to be taken by future changes in the Uniform Code of Military Justice. Even so, the tensions between civilian and military justice will not be easily resolved.

---

[45] Barrett S. Haight, "Proposed Military Justice Act of 1967: First Class Legislation for the 'Second Class' Citizens," *Dickinson Law Review*, Vol. 72 (Fall, 1967), p. 96.

Chapter
20

THE FEDERAL COURTS
SYSTEM

The federal court system is divided into constitutional and legislative courts. While the constitutional court was created under the provisions of Article Three of the Constitution, the legislative court, created by act of Congress, was authorized in the document's First Article. Originally empowered to act administratively and in a quasi-legislative manner within its range of authority, several legislative courts, including the Court of Claims, Customs Court, and Court of Customs and Patent Appeals (see Figure 20–1), have since been assimilated by action of Congress between 1953 and 1958 into the constitutional court system. Under the Constitution, Congress may additionally establish territorial courts, keeping with its responsibility of governing the property or territory of the United States.

The Judiciary Act of 1789 made provision for six Supreme Court Justices, including the Chief Justice, and a system of circuit and district courts. The *circuit courts*, different from the present circuit courts of appeal, were primarily trial courts which also exercised appellate responsibilities relating to the limited appeals allowed at that time from the district courts. The circuit courts under the provisions of the act were the chief trial courts and were presided over by a Supreme Court Justice. However, it was only in 1842 that they acquired concurrent jurisdiction over noncapital crimes. The *district court*, on the other hand, was generally a minor criminal court in the late 1700's, although they also accepted some responsibility for civil cases.[1] When the circuit courts

---

[1] Floyd R. Gibson, "Some Observations on Our United States Court of Appeals,"

FIGURE 20–1
The judicial system

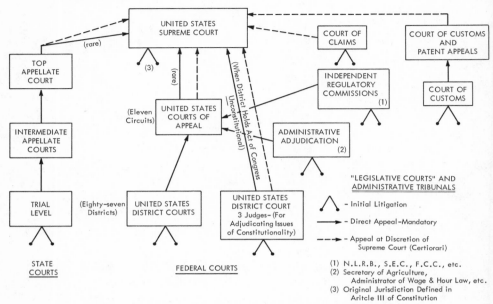

Source: John P. Roche, *Courts and Rights* (New York: Random House, Inc., 1961), p. 29.

were abolished in 1911, leaving the district courts with general trial jurisdiction and the circuit courts of appeals with appellate jurisdiction, the Supreme Court was designated as the final appellate arbitrator of all appeals.

THE U.S. DISTRICT COURTS AND THE COURTS OF APPEALS

Currently, the federal court system consists of three constitutional courts known as the U.S. district courts, the U.S. circuit courts of appeals, and the U.S. Supreme Court. The district courts essentially serve as the primary trial courts of the federal system. Maintained by a U.S. commissioner, who acts as a magistrate in each of the 87 U.S. federal districts, they serve a geographical area, its judiciary varying in size with the caseload of a particular district. U.S. district courts possess original jurisdiction in the trial of offenses against federal laws, cases

University of Missouri at Kansas City Law Review, Vol. 35 (Summer, 1967), p. 263. Also note Charles W. Bunn, *Jurisdiction and Practice of the Courts of the U.S.* (St. Paul, Minn.: West Publishing Co., 1949); and John P. Roche, *Courts and Rights: The American Judiciary in Action* (New York: Random House, Inc., 1961).

involving a "federal question" or violation of federal legislation, or in litigation relating to citizenship questions or involving the U.S. Internal Revenue Department or a national bank.[2]

Although periodic attempts have been made to reform the office of the U.S. commissioner, a position equivalent to the justice of the peace within the state judicial system, commissioners still possess the authority to issue arrest and search warrants, arraign defendants on complaints, fix bail, hold preliminary hearings on felony cases, and try petty offenses at certain military reservations. Approximately 700 commissioners, barely 1 percent of whom are full-time officers, serve in the federal system. although one third are not attorneys, the federal government does not maintain a training program for such officials. Most commissioners are compensated on a fee basis.[3]

The U.S. circuit courts of appeals possess appellate jurisdiction (see Table 20–1). Covering a circuit of several states, each of the 11 appellate courts, depending on the work load, is served by three to nine judges. Appeals are usually heard by three or more judges, although two judges constitute a necessary quorum. Cases are accepted for review from federal lower courts, regulatory commissions, and other assorted governmental agencies. The chief judge of each court of appeals names the senior judges of the court.

Most federal litigation ends in the U.S. courts of appeals. Fewer than 3 percent of the cases coming before this court are later considered by the Supreme Court.[4] While the filing of cases in U.S. district courts has increased by 16 percent in the past seven years, similar actions in U.S. courts of appeals have increased nearly 100 percent. The Supreme Court reviews approximately 100 cases from the federal courts of appeals each year, approximately 1 out of every 45 cases either heard or submitted to its jurisdiction.[5]

The U.S. circuit court of appeals is the federal tribunal of last resort. Although the Supreme Court may be asked by writ of certiorari to review the decisions of the circuit courts of appeals, litigants have no further appeal as a matter of right from its decisions.[6] The circuit court of appeals possesses jurisdiction over appeals from all final decisions

---

[2] Paul B. Weston and Kenneth W. Wells, *The Administration of Justice* (Englewood Cliffs, N.J.: Prentice-Hall, Inc., 1967), p. 124.

[3] The President's Commission, *The Challenge of Crime in a Free Society* (Washington, D.C.: U.S. Government Printing Office, 1967), p. 130.

[4] J. Edward Lumbard, "Current Problems of the Federal Courts of Appeals," *New York County Bar Bulletin*, Vol. 25 (1967–69), pp. 210–11.

[5] *Ibid.*, p. 211. See Frank Jerome, *Courts on Trial* (Princeton, N.J.: Princeton University Press, 1949); and *Field Study of the Operations of the U.S. Courts* (Washington, D.C.: U.S. Government Printing Office, 1959).

[6] T. P. Coleman, "Appellate Proceedings in the United States Court of Appeals," *Mississippi Law Journal*, Vol. 38 (October, 1967), pp. 554–55.

TABLE 20–1

United States courts of appeals: Nature of suit or offense or appeals from the United States district courts filed in the United States courts of appeals during the fiscal year ended June 30, 1966

Nature of Suit or Offense	Total	Circuit										
		D.C.	First	Second	Third	Fourth	Fifth	Sixth	Seventh	Eighth	Ninth	Tenth
TOTAL CRIMINAL CASES	1,458	252	39	170	82	88	214	131	113	88	191	90
General Offenses	1,219	245	32	144	67	54	142	96	112	70	175	82
Homicide, Total	35	27	……	……	2	2	……	……	……	2	……	2
Murder—first degree	12	8	……	……	2	……	……	……	……	1	……	1
Other homicide	23	19	……	……	……	2	……	……	……	1	……	1
Robbery, Total	176	84	3	6	6	4	8	15	16	5	20	9
Bank	94	5	3	6	6	4	8	12	16	5	20	9
Other robbery	82	79	……	……	……	……	……	3	……	……	……	……
Assault	37	21	1	5	2	1	……	2	3	1	2	1
Burglary	50	35	……	1	……	……	4	……	……	5	……	3
Larceny and Theft, Total	78	8	3	18	6	4	7	6	8	4	11	3
Interstate shipment	34	……	2	13	2	3	1	6	5	4	4	3
Transportation, etc., of stolen property	9	……	1	3	1	……	2	1	2	……	……	……
Other	35	8	……	2	3	1	4	……	1	……	7	……
Embezzlement	16	……	4	……	2	……	1	1	4	2	1	1
Fraud, Total	177	3	7	30	13	6	31	20	20	14	20	13
Income tax	41	……	1	11	……	3	10	3	5	2	5	1
Postal and interstate wire, radio, etc.	53	3	……	3	5	1	11	2	10	6	8	7
Other	83	3	6	16	8	2	10	15	5	6	7	5
Auto theft	122	11	……	3	4	20	28	6	5	11	15	19
Transportation of forged securities	39	……	……	2	6	2	8	7	3	3	4	4
Forgery	43	3	……	5	3	4	9	6	3	2	3	5
Counterfeiting	39	……	3	7	6	2	3	5	3	3	5	2

Offense	Total											
Sex Offenses, Total	34	16	...	...	...	...	5	4	...	1	6	2
Rape	19	16	...	...	...	...	1	...	...	...	1	1
White slave traffic	15	...	...	...	...	...	4	4	...	1	5	1
Other sex offenses	...	...	...	...	...	...	...	...	...	...	...	...
Narcotics, Total	246	22	6	56	1	2	23	12	30	8	78	8
Marihuana Tax Act	48	1	1	3	...	...	6	1	1	2	30	3
Other	198	21	5	53	1	2	17	11	29	6	48	5
Miscellaneous General Offenses, Total	127	15	5	11	16	7	15	12	17	9	10	10
Bribery	8	...	1	7	...	...	...	...	...	...	...	...
Extortion, racketeering, and threats	15	...	...	...	1	1	1	...	5	1	2	4
Gambling, lottery	46	4	3	2	13	5	3	5	...	5	3	3
Kidnapping	5	...	...	...	1	...	1	1	1	...	1	...
Perjury	11	...	1	1	...	1	3	3	...	...	2	1
Other	42	11	...	1	1	...	7	3	11	3	2	2
Special Offenses	239	7	7	26	15	34	72	35	1	18	16	8
Immigration Laws	2	...	...	...	...	...	...	...	...	...	2	...
Liquor, Internal Revenue	74	...	4	1	2	21	22	19	1	...	...	4
Federal Statutes, Total	163	7	3	25	13	13	50	16	1	17	14	4
National defense laws	36	2	...	10	1	4	5	1	...	1	10	2
Other	127	5	3	15	12	9	45	15	1	16	4	2

Source: Will Shafroth, "Survey of the U.S. Courts of Appeals," *Federal Rules Decision*, Vol. 42 (September, 1967), pp. 300–301.

of the district courts of the United States, except in cases where direct review is assigned to the Supreme Court. Each of the 11 U.S. courts of appeals, including that of the District of Columbia, allows its member judges to use their discretion, as may be proper, to grant writs of habeas corpus, stays, injunctions, or other writs. Responsible also for the review of the issuance of preliminary injunctions, the court of appeals also supervises orders of the National Labor Relations Board and of other federal agencies as defined by Congress. Because a special three-judge federal court possesses jurisdiction only to pass on the constitutionality of the acts of Congress or legislatures of various states, the circuit court of appeals is not empowered to review the decisions of the U.S. district courts. Appeal in these cases is directed to the U.S. Supreme Court.[7]

The Fifth Circuit Court of Appeals

The jurisdiction of the Fifth Circuit Court of Appeals includes Texas, Louisiana, Mississippi, Alabama, Georgia, and Florida. Although the court is generally housed in New Orleans, it also sits in Fort Worth, Houston, Jackson, Montgomery, Atlanta, and Jacksonville. Composed of 12 active and 3 retired judges, the court may sit *en banc* (as a whole) or more commonly as a three-man panel. Each judge sits for one week per month for nine months of each year, during which time he hears four cases a day for five days. Usually, 30 minutes is allotted to each side for each of the four arguments heard during the day. The other three weeks, after the appropriate disposition of the case is decided, are spent in preparation of opinions. Upon completion of an opinion, a copy is forwarded to each judge by the opinion writer for either his assent or dissent, after which the writing judge files the opinion with the court clerk, who thereupon publishes and distributes the opinion.[8]

The call for reform

The move for procedural reform in the circuit court of appeals has been stimulated by the population explosion and the increased number of cases coming to the attention of the court. The volume coming before the U.S. courts of appeals increased by one fiftieth between 1941 to 1960 (from 3,213 to 3,899 cases). During the next six years, from 1960 to 1966, the total increased by two thirds (from 3,899 to 6,548 cases).

---

[7] *Ibid.*, p. 556. Robert L. Stern, "Changes in the Federal Appellate Rules," *Federal Rules Decisions*, Vol. 41 (March, 1967), pp. 297–309; E. Barrett Prettyman, "Uniform Appellate Rules," *American Bar Association Journal*, Vol. 52 (February, 1966), pp. 123–26; "Appealability in the Federal Courts," *Harvard Law Review*, Vol. 75 (December, 1961), pp. 351–82.

[8] *Ibid.*, pp. 556–57.

FIGURE 20–2
Petitions filed by prisoners*
(fiscal years 1960–66)

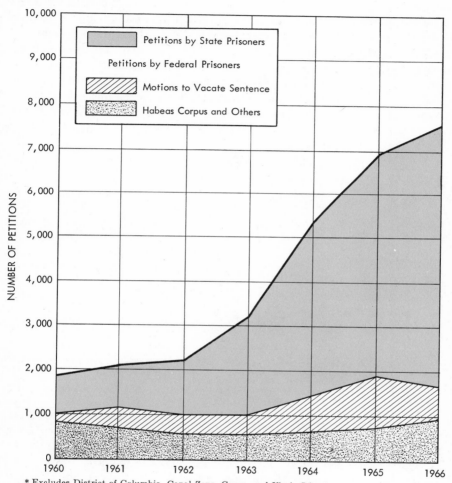

* Excludes District of Columbia, Canal Zone, Guam, and Virgin Islands.
    Source: Will Shafroth, "Survey of the U.S. Courts of Appeals," *Federal Rules Decision*, Vol. 42
(September, 1967), p. 277.

However, the addition of 10 judges in the 11 circuit courts of appeals
in both 1961 and 1966 helped to keep the court caseload within acceptable limits.[9] Caseloads between 1954 and 1960 ranged from 54 to

---

[9] Will Shafroth, "Survey of the U.S. Court of Appeals," *Federal Rules Decision*,
Vol. 42 (September, 1967), p. 250. See David Peck, *Court Organization and Procedures to Meet the Needs of Modern Society* (W. Nelson Cromwell Foundation,
1958).

57 per judge; by 1966, despite the expansion of 10 additional judges during the year, the caseload rose to 84 per justice.

During fiscal 1962, 1,523 petitions for habeas corpus and motions to vacate sentences came to the circuit courts; approximately 5,786, however, came to its attention during fiscal 1965. Much of this increase was due to the large number of prisoner appeals from denials of habeas corpus petitions and motions to vacate sentences by district judges, requests which increased from 290 in 1960 to 1,106 in 1966.[10] In addition to these prisoner petitions, an additional 2,005 proceedings, which were processed without coming to the court's attention, were reported in the

TABLE 20-2
U.S. courts of appeals: Types of cases filed, fiscal years 1950 to 1966

Fiscal Year	Total Appeals	Appeals from District Courts					Administrative Appeals	Other
		Total	Criminal	U.S. Civil	Private Civil	Bankruptcy		
1950	2,830	2,252	308	708	1,114	122	485	93
1955	3,695	3,004	677	811	1,363	153	576	115
1960	3,899	3,077	623	788	1,534	132	737	85
1961	4,204	3,251	616	903	1,617	115	846	107
1962	4,587	3,490	731	1,016	1,612	131	968	129
1963	5,039	3,915	891	985	1,902	137	1,029	95
1964	5,412	4,433	959	1,188	2,069	217	827	152
1965	6,221	5,103	1,103	1,305	2,491	204	968	150
1966	6,548	5,324	1,322	1,262	2,582	158	1,084	140

Note: Beginning in 1962, the number of appeals on each line is reduced by the number disposed of by consolidation in that year. Consolidated cases were eliminated from the filings prior to 1962.
Source: Shafroth, "Survey of the U.S. Courts of Appeals" p. 294.

various records of the U.S. courts of appeals during 1966 (see Figure 20-2). Although the greater number of these petitions involve complaints of prison maltreatment or similar charges and the majority possess not legal merit, they enable the prisoner, Charles A. Wright observes, to maintain hope.[11] The need to screen the many petitions coming to the court have led several of the circuits to assign staff law clerks to petition screening before submitting them to any judicial panel for consideration. Nevertheless, the greatest number of cases filed for action by the U.S. courts of appeals involve either private or federal civil actions (see Tables 20-2 and 20-3).

---

[10] *Ibid.*, p. 254. Examine J. Gillis Wetter, *The Styles of Appellate Judicial Decisions* (Leyden, Holland: A. W. Sythoff, 1960).

[11] Charles A. Wright, "The Federal Courts—A Century after Appomattox," *American Bar Association Journal*, Vol. 52 (August, 1966), pp. 742–47.

TABLE 20–3

U.S. courts of appeals: Trials in the district courts and civil and criminal appeals of the court of appeals, fiscal years 1961 through 1966

Fiscal Year	Number of Judgeships Circuit	Number of Judgeships District	Total Trials	Total Civil and Criminal Appeals Filed	Civil Trials	Civil Appeals	Criminal Trials	Criminal Appeals
1961.........	68	245	9,594	3,136	6,156	2,520	3,438	616
1962.........	78	307	10,048	3,359	6,260	2,628	3,788	731
1963.........	78	307	10,960	3,778	7,095	2,887	3,865	891
1964.........	78	307	11,079	4,216	7,155	3,257	3,924	959
1965.........	78	306	11,485	4,899	7,613	3,796	3,872	1,103
1966.........	78	306	12,193	5,166	7,783	3,844	4,410	1,322
Percent increases from 1961 thru 1966..	15	25	27	65	26	53	28	155

Note: Beginning with 1962, the number of appeals in each year under each category have been reduced by the number disposed of by consolidation.

Source: Shafroth, "Survey of the U.S. Courts of Appeals," p. 297.

THE UNITED STATES SUPREME COURT

The *U.S. Supreme Court*, served by nine justices, posses both orginal and appellate jurisdiction. While six judges constitute a quorum, no fewer than four must concur for a valid decision. As a body of original jurisdiction, it decides cases between the United States and one or more American states; between the United States and certain foreign ambassadors, ministers, counsels, and their servants; and between an American state and persons who are not citizens of that state and/or a foreign country. In addition, the Supreme Court maintains appellate jurisdiction over cases tried or reviewed in all other constitutional, territorial, and a majority of legislative courts, and cases referred from the highest state courts, if they involve a "substantial federal question."[12] If appeal to the Court is not a matter of defined right, the Court may move to accept a litigant's petition for a writ of certiorari (review), the application being evaluated by the entire court membership. However, a writ of application, allowing the review of the case by the court, is granted only if four or more justices approve the petition.[13]

The Supreme Court derives much of its power from its discretionary

---

[12] Wendell Mitchell, *Relations between the Federal and State Courts* (New York: Columbia University Press, 1949).

[13] Weston and Wells, *op. cit.*, p. 124; Borris M. Komer, "On the Reform of Appellate Procedures of the U.S. Supreme Court," *Chicago Kent Law Review*, Vol. 44 (Spring, 1967), pp. 28–38; and "Discretionary Powers of the Supreme Court to Dismiss Appeals from State Courts," *Columbia Law Review*, Vol. 63 (April, 1963), pp. 688–707.

authority to grant or to deny certiorari. However, because the Court is also an interpreter of the Constitution, a highly flexible document which can be widely interpreted in relationship to social needs and issues, it often finds itself in an unpopular position.[14] Because the Supreme Court popularly is granted the tradition of the "doctrine of finality," a belief that holds that its decisions are the law of the land, it functionally exercises veto power over the President and the Congress. Nevertheless, authority of the Supreme Court ultimately depends upon the power generated by the solution of a particular problem, since much of the Court's power is illusory. Because the Court does not possess any enforcement powers of its own, it depends upon the powers of other state and federal agencies for the enactment of its decisions. Operationally, the money for Supreme Court personnel, salaries, and facilities are provided by Congress.[15]

Traditionally, the Supreme Court convenes the first Monday in October and adjourns in mid-June. Although terms may vary, the Court usually hears cases four days a week for two weeks before recessing for two weeks of decision writing and research. Following the one-month midterm recess, the Court continues the same procedure into the second or third week of June. During this period, public and private group sessions begin at 10 A.M. and adjourn at noon, reconvening at 12:30 and finally concluding at 2:30 P.M. Actual court activity, however, represents only small portion of the Court's total volume of business. The continuing process of deciding whether to hear or not hear a case consumes a large portion of the Court's time. Although the Supreme Court has historically released its decisions on Monday, it has periodically since 1965 released its opinions on other days of the week, especially near the end of the court term.

The process of decision making in the Supreme Court

The heart of the Supreme Court is its decision-making process, largely based on rationality, logic, and precedents. Actually, the Court will normally write more than 100 opinions during a term, although it will decide 50 or more additional cases without written opinions. Together, these 150–175 cases, approximately 5 to 6 percent of the more than 3,000 cases presented to the Court on any given year for review, form the raw material of Supreme Court judgments. During the normal Friday

---

[14] David L. Grey, "Supreme Court as a Communicator," *Houston Law Review,* Vol. 5 (January, 1968), p. 406.

[15] Consider H. J. Hogan, "Supreme Court and Natural Law," *American Bar Association Journal,* Vol. 54 (June, 1968), p. 570.

conferences of the Justices, tentative sides are drawn, opinion writers are selected, and the necessary steps are taken to draft opinions.[16] If the Chief Justice votes with the majority, he assigns the opinion writing to a member of the majority. If he sides with the minority, the senior Justice of the majority, usually on the following Monday, assigns the opinion to an appropriate Justice. However, the process of reaching decision in the Supreme Court continues until the Justices are able to create an opinion which represent both majority and in some cases minority opinion. While the Court periodically suffers from the handicap that it is never able to prove the law conclusively, since much of legal jurisprudence is a matter of degree and negotiated interpretation, factors of judicial personality, ideology, and experiences, or necessity, are essential ingredients of the interactional decision-making process.[17]

The Supreme Court's function of judicial review sometimes implies the creation of judicial legislation. Its willingness or unwillingness to accept and to interpret particular laws referred to its attention, for example, may infer that the Court is engaging in judicial legislation in the guise of judicial review without recognizing its involvement. Traditionally, the judicial function has popularly been conceived in terms of a concept of limit judicial power which allows the Court merely to review or to interpret an earlier decision,[18] assuming that "law was rules and that law was stable."[19] Progressive theory, on the other hand, suggests that social change necessitates the reinterpretation of law in relation to the dynamics of the day. Although progressive theorists argue that general legal principles are not comprised in this process, their resultant interpretation of the relationship of law and society have often been highly diverse.

Although the Supreme Court reversed and remanded some 175 cases to state tribunals between 1941 and 1951, some 46 of these cases faced further litigation. Nearly one half, when retried, resulted in the reimposition of the original decision.[20] Nevertheless, the decisions of the U.S. Supreme Court, Leslie L. Anderson argues, often have the practical effect of increasing uniformity in the state and federal judicial systems. As a consequence of its decisions, the Court has increasingly been defining the nature of admissible evidence, the relationship between population and legislative districts, the procedure of local public school operation, acceptable local police methods, relationships between unwilling

---

[16] *Ibid.,* p. 415.

[17] *Ibid.,* p. 415. See Bernard Schwartz, *The Supreme Court* (New York: Ronald Press, Co., 1957).

[18] Fred V. Cahill, *Judicial Legislation: Study of American Legal Theory* (New York: Ronald Press Co., 1952), p. 7.

[19] *Ibid.,* p. 152.

[20] Grey, *op. cit.,* p. 407.

political leaders and government-sponsored programs, concepts of public morality, relationships of restaurant operation and interstate travel, and the right of the public to birth control information and supplies.[21]

Because these changes have been extensive and based upon knowledge which has only been acquired recently, many members of the system of justice have not been prepared either to understand or to act upon this information. In order to overcome some of this liability, Chief Justice Earl Warren proposed the establishment of a Federal Judicial Center in order to acquaint federal judges, in an organized scientific manner, with the diverse problems coming before the judicial system. Proposed as a means by which the courts could begin a "kind of self-analysis, research and planning necessary for a more effective judicial system," the Federal Judicial Center, in the eyes of the Chief Justice, could provide the stimulant for federal court modernization and experimentation.[22]

Public tensions resulting from recent U.S. Supreme Court decisions

At the heart of the tension existing between the general public and the Supreme Court is a constitutional dilemma in litigation which requires the Supreme Court, Archibald Cox believes, to be more judicial than other government bodies while at the same time being more conscious of political and policy considerations than other courts.[23] The development of the mass society, he notes, has forced a centralization of many public and community services and has caused the Supreme Court to serve as a check upon congressional regulative authority and power on behalf of the local community and the individual state.[24] Charged with the dual task of protecting the individual against the encroachment of government and maintaining the unity of the group without giving way to the libertarian demands of individual extremists, the Supreme Court, almost by default, is placed in the position of having to challenge many of the diverse statutes enacted by state legislatures in order to find a degree of national conformity. While the Supreme Court was originally preoccupied with the protection of the individual against a hostile government, it has increasingly assumed a greater con-

---

[21] Leslie L. Anderson, "Problems of the Federal Court—and How the State Courts Might Help," *American Bar Association Journal*, Vol. 54 (April, 1968), p. 354.

[22] Earl Warren, "Supreme Court—1967," *New York State Bar Journal*, Vol. 39 (October, 1967), p. 394.

[23] Archibald Cox, "Role of the Supreme Court in American Society," *Marquette Law Review*, Vol. 50 (June, 1967), p. 578.

[24] *Ibid.*, p. 580. Also note Carl B. Swisher, *The Supreme Court in Modern Role* (New York: New York University Press, 1958).

cern, Cox recognizes, for the "affirmative obligations of the government to its citizens."[25]

The Supreme Court gains its greatest power from psychological conditioning which leads the public to respect the Court's decisions and to reverence law, and its members, despite its many controversial decisions, generally receive major public honor and respect. However, the Court's mystique is periodically in serious tension with the mechanical and often contradictory operations and decisions of the lower and public courts. Operating in secrecy to guarantee the integrity of the decision-making process, the Supreme Court rather successfully remains aloof of those external pressures which often affect the operation of the government.

While the Supreme Court refrains from the manipulation of public opinion and traditionally refuses to defend its decisions publicly, it is indirectly able to manipulate public opinion through its control of news. The Court stipulates, David L. Grey notes, what it wants to stipulate without press conferences or any exegesis of its decisions. It speaks with an authority which is reserved for self-restraint. In an area in which public relations are most important, it reveals, Grey believes, a near-total disregard for modern public relations techniques.[26]

The Supreme Court, civil rights, and criminal processes

In recent years, the Supreme Court has expressed growing concern for the development of a more meaningful definition of the rules of due process in order to balance the relationship between the accused and the state. Recognizing that the powers of government far exceed the resources of the individual, the Court has sought to establish an essence of equality in strength and in resources. However, the Court's concern, Abraham S. Blumberg writes,

with better and more extensive rules has served as a façade of moral philosophy to divert our gaze from the more significant development of the emergence of "bureaucratic due process," a non-adversary system of justice by negotiation. It consists of secret bargaining sessions, employing subtle, bureaucratically ordained modes of coercion and influence to dispose of onerously large case loads in an efficacious and "rational" manner. Except for isolated cases, the bargaining or "cop-out" procedures on which our entire system of criminal law administration would appear to depend, have never been subjected to

---

[25] *Ibid.*, p. 584. Refer to Paul A. Freund, *On Understanding the Supreme Court* (Boston: Little, Brown & Co., 1949).

[26] Grey, *op. cit.*, p. 412. See J. B. Deutsch, "Neutrality, Legitimacy, and the Supreme Court," *Stanford Law Review,* Vol. 20 (January, 1968), p. 169; and Alexander M. Bickel, "Supreme Court and Political Democracy," *Federal Rules Decisions,* Vol. 44 (May, 1968), pp. 158–69.

extensive judicial scrutiny to determine their constitutionality or propriety in terms of due process.[27]

The failure of Congress and state government to implement due process legislation had led the Supreme Court to legislate changes in the criminal court system through its decisions. Although it has usually acted pragmatically, sometimes reversing its own rulings in order to systematize state criminal law and practice, it has moved to coordinate and to elevate the state system of justice to the higher standards revealed in the federal criminal justice system. Consequently, the Court has focused its attention upon the meaning of the Fourth, Fifth, Sixth, and Eighth Amendments to the Constitution, dealing with illegal searches and seizures, self-incrimination, indictment by grand jury, trial by jury, double jeopardy, excessive bail, and cruel and unusual punishments. In this action, bureaucratic due process, as conceived by Blumberg, is being challenged by the general but idealistic requirements of due process reflected somewhat optimistically in the Bill of Rights. In systematically extending individual rights guaranteed in federal courts to the state justice system through the Fourteenth Amendment, the Supreme Court has taken a controversial initiative to establish a new equilibrium of power and responsibility.

The quest for explicit definitions of due process continues in the American judicial system. Justice Felix Frankfurter, representing the majority position, has maintained that due process may mean involvement more as well as less than that prescribed in the Bill of Rights. On the other hand, Justice Black has defined due process as nothing less than a "short-hand transcript" for the Bill of Rights.[28] In both instances, the concept of federal jurisdiction, which permits and depends upon local and state court authority, confuses the exact implications of due process procedure. Although state laws may vary considerably from federal standards, they remain unchallenged by the higher courts so long as they do not violate fundamental principles of liberty and justice. But the major mobility of the modern population has increased the expectation that common criminal code standards will apply equally to all persons regardless of race, creed, or color, creating demands for greater uniformity in state criminal and civil codes.

Of the 2,903 dispositions from the 3,356 cases on the U.S. Supreme Court docket at the beginning of October, 1966, 147 cases were argued orally and were decided by written opinion, 131 cases were summarily affirmed or reversed without argument, 124 appeals were dismissed, and

---

[27] Abraham S. Blumberg, *Criminal Justice* (Chicago: Quadrangle Books, Inc., 1967), p. 213; and Ray Forrester, "Changing Role of the Supreme Court," *New York State Bar Journal,* Vol. 39 (August, 1967), pp. 277–84.

[28] *Ibid.,* p. 15.

the remaining 2,500 dispositions were processed through denial of petition for certiorari.[29] Of the 110 written opinions which decided the 147 cases, 40 dealt with criminal matters. All but four dealt with constitutional questions. Of the 53 opinions deciding constitutional issues during the 1966 Supreme Court term, 36 concerned problems of criminal law.[30]

Although the Supreme Court has attempted to protect the rights of the defendant in a criminal case is extending its various decisions, it has largely ignored, Blumberg suggests, a least three crucial areas in the judicial process which immediately undermine its judgments. Not only does the Court's informal structure encourage the seeking of goals which exceed those envisioned in the formal and traditional due process concept, but the real nature of the relationship between lawyers and other professionals within the system of court interaction is not taken into consideration. The actual lawyer-client relationship, contrary to modern television, press, or mass media propaganda, is far less client-centered, Blumberg contends, than is commonly believed. Despite continuing Supreme Court redefinitions, this situation, he believes, is unlikely to change to any significant degree.[31] Nevertheless, decisions of the United States Supreme Court have a profound effect upon the nature and the function of law. And yet, little is known about the process by which these decisions are reached or the actual impact which they possess upon and within the social system. Because few scholars raise central questions pertaining to the Supreme Court's decision-making and decision-implementing processes, investigations, Arthur S. Miller and Allan W. Scheflin contend, must be made into the following areas in the future:

1. The data relevant to the decisional process.
2. The impact of court decisions.
3. Factors influencing the court.
4. The preferred means of getting information to the court.
5. Potential aids for the court decision making.
6. The nature of the "social realities" which the court does and should consider.
7. Those goals which the court does and should seek.
8. The existing or anticipated relationship of the Court to other units of government.
9. What contributions psychology, sociology, and the other behavioral sciences may bring to the thought processes of Supreme Court Justices.

---

[29] Byron R. White, "The United States Supreme Court—1966–1967, " *Natural Resources Lawyer,* Vol. 1 (January, 1968), pp. 24–25.

[30] *Ibid.,* p. 25. *Also* see Archibald Cox, "Supreme Court and the Federal System," *California Law Review,* Vol. 50 (December, 1962), pp. 800–820.

[31] Blumberg, *op. cit.,* pp. 183–84.

10. What criteria or principles should serve as the foundation for judicial decision making and/or evaluation of the Court's work.[32]

Although these many questions yet remain unanswered, the impact of the Supreme Court's work cannot be questioned. Evaluating the work of the Supreme Court from his position as Solicitor General of the United States, Archibald Cox notes:

Only history will know whether the present court has avoided both horns of the dilemma that lie at the bottom of its work. Today the question is open to debate. For myself, I am confident that historians will write that the trend of the Supreme Court decisions during the 1950's and 1960's was in keeping with the main-stream of American history—a bit progressive but also moderate, a bit humane but not sentimental, a bit idealistic but seldom doctrinaire and in the long run essentially pragmatic—in short, in keeping with the true genius of our institutions.

But perhaps I am prejudiced. One who has sat in the Supreme Court almost daily awaiting oral argument or the delivery of opinions acquires both admiration and affection for the court and for all the justices. The problems with which they deal are so difficult, the number and variety of cases are so overwhelming, the implications are so far-reaching, that one sits humbled by the demands upon him. That the institution of constitutional adjudication works so well on the whole is testimony not only to the genius of the institution but to the wisdom and courage of the individual judges.[33]

---

[32] Arthur S. Miller and Allan W. Scheflin, "The Power of the Supreme Court in the Age of the Positive State: A Preliminary Excursus," *Duke Law Journal,* Vol. 1967 (April–June, 1967), p. 296.

[33] Cox, *op. cit.,* p. 593. Refer to Paul Bartholomew, "Supreme Court of the United States, 1956–1966," *American Bar Association Journal,* Vol. 53 (August, 1967), pp. 729–31; and Robert G. McCloskey, *The American Supreme Court* (Chicago: University of Chicago Press, 1960).

Part SIX

The disposition
of offenders

Chapter 21

THE SYSTEMS OF SENTENCING AND PROBATION

Human societies have historically responded to criminal conduct by the infliction of penalties in the form of banishment, reparations and fines, imprisonment, capital punishment, or other punishments of varying degrees of severity. Banishment often meant death, inasmuch as it deprived the offender of tribal protection. In modern times, banishment takes the form of deportation, hardly as serious or threatening, and infliction of a banishment of sorts for vagrancy. Under existing vagrancy statutes, presumed idle or undesirable persons are taken from the street and banished to unseen locations. Designed as catch-all laws, vagrancy statutes restrict the entrance of undesirables into a city or community, provide grounds for police control of suspicious individuals, and offer the necessary legal foundation for conviction and subsequent fining or sentencing of public nuisances.[1]

Fines and the offering of reparations, alternatives to jail or prison sentences, originally served a punishment sanction and permitted the person or his family to gain restitution for the harm inflicted. As political power shifted from the family and tribe to the lord and king, restitution to the victim declined as the state preempted these funds for its own expenses. Under current practices, however, the payment of a fine permits the offender to pay a monetary penalty without any restriction upon his personal mobility through detention or imprisonment, although

[1] Caleb Foote, "Vagrancy-Type Law and Its Administration," *University of Pennsylvania Law Review*, Vol. 104 (March, 1956), pp. 603–50.

he may be jailed if he is unable to pay. In such instances, he may "work off" the amount at a stated dollar value per day of incarceration, a common response of many persons economically deprived or temporarily out of funds who have been convicted of drunkenness, disorderly conduct, and vagrancy.

The civil prisoner and criminal sanctions

Under certain circumstances some offenders who have not committed a criminal act may receive fines or short-term detention sentences. Pauline Morris found, for example, that two completely different types of civil prisoners in England and Wales are occasionally included among those receiving criminal sanctions. Although those who are unable *to pay* their debts differ from those who *default on maintenance* payments to wives and/or children, they both may receive fines or incarceration. Civil debtors, Morris indicated, commonly lack social competence and reveal a degree of intellectual inadequacy. More than one half in her sample were unemployed at the time of committal and even when employed tended to accept employment for only a short time at low wages. Two thirds had previously been imprisoned either as civil prisoners or as convicted criminals, generally for petty thievery or vagrancy. On the other hand, maintenance defaulters were reluctant to pay their wives and accepted imprisonment while claiming that their wives were living with other men, a fact, they believed, that exempted them from further support responsibilities. Maintenance defaulters worked to evade arrest and imprisonment by periodically changing jobs, moving throughout the country, or avoiding work in order to evade attachment of earnings. Since British defaulters may be imprisoned only once in any 12-month period for maintenance failure, imprisonment for the majority, Morris noted, is an annual "experience."[2]

Part of the problem of the civil prisoner may be due to large family size—over 40 percent having four or more children and 26 percent having five or more. Approximately 88 percent of the civil debtors, Morris noted, live with their legal wives. Because the imprisonment of the civil debtor is rather short, it has little effect upon the material or psychological aspects of the family. For such persons debt seems to be a way of life. The offender seems to care little about his imprisonment. Because his basic problem is related to social training rather than to prison custody, imprisonment, Morris concluded, does little to aid the offender or to stop his debtor tendencies.[3]

---

[2] Pauline Morris, *Prisoners and Their Families* (New York: Hart Publishing Co., Inc., 1965), p. 298.
[3] *Ibid.*, p. 299.

TRENDS AND PROBLEMS IN SENTENCING

Although imprisonment has been commonly utilized as a means for securing individual conformity, many new trends have emerged in the process of criminal sentencing. The concept of punishment has received less weight as greater attention has been given to the use of indeterminate sentences which enable the release of the convicted offender upon demonstration of good behavior and his apparent desire to lead a normative life.[4] Additionally, several major efforts have been made to reduce the disparity in sentences evident in many jurisdictions for the same offense. Nevertheless, present data suggest that the imposition of sentences still varies considerably in relationship to such factors as the nature of the community, the type of court, the personality of the judge, the status of the defendant, and other important criteria. Consequently, several jurisdictions have attempted to overcome many of the inadequacies of the earlier system of justice by giving the judge greater insight into the character and problems of the convicted offender by more extensive use of probation department presentence reports (see Figure 21–1). If more detailed studies and data are required, the defendant may undergo a limited commitment under expert observation before actual court sentencing. Utilized for expert testing and analysis in cases involving mentally disturbed, sex, narcotic, or other types of juvenile or adult offenders, this approach permits the judge without proper facilities, training, or personnel to receive the important information necessary for the full consideration of an appropriate penalty.

Until recent years, many judges, especially in the federal system, were simply allowed the choice of either ordering imprisonment for a fixed period or granting probation when permitted under the statute in question. Recently, however, under the Federal Juvenile Delinquency

---

[4] Reed K. Clegg, *Probation and Parole* (Springfield, Ill.: Charles C. Thomas, Publisher, 1964), p. 23. For a second insight, see "Increased Sentence Upon Retrial," *Washington and Lee Law Review*, Vol. 25 (Spring, 1968), p. 60; and S. A. Weigel, "Appellate Revision of Sentences," *Stanford Law Review*, Vol. 20 (Fall, 1968), p. 405. Michigan passed the first indeterminate sentence law, which was later declared unconstitutional. The Elmira Reformatory in New York originally used the indeterminate sentence in the United States. Even this approach, however, was not fully an indeterminate procedure, since it provided for a potential minimum and maximum sentence. Also refer to E. Taylor, "Criminal Justice Act, 1967," *Law Societies Gazette*, Vol. 61 (October, 1967), p. 541; R. M. Carter and Leslie T. Wilkins, "Some Factors in Sentencing Policy," *Journal of Criminal Law, Criminology, and Police Science*, Vol. 50 (December, 1967), p. 503; Lord Parker of Waddington, "Judicial Function and Penal Reform," *Criminal Law Quarterly*, Vol. 9 (July, 1967), p. 400; J. E. Ross, "Punishments and the Punitive Articles," *Judge Advocate General Journal*, Vol. 23 (September–November, 1968), p. 43; and J. Andenaes, "Does Punishment Deter Crime?" *Criminal Law Quarterly*, Vol. 11 (November, 1968), p. 76.

FIGURE 21–1
The sentencing function

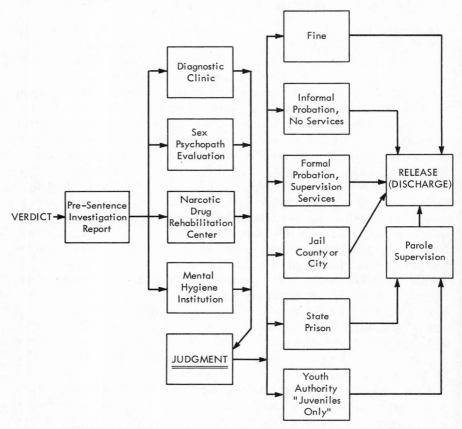

Source: Paul B. Weston and Kenneth M. Wells, *The Administration of Justice* (Englewood Cliffs, N.J.: Prentice-Hall, Inc., 1967), p. 228.

and the Federal Youth Corrections Acts, the system of federal justice has allowed greater variations, including the application of split sentences (part confinement, part probation), a choice of probation conditions, and other alternatives in sentencing. The greater use of probation with supervision is part of the continuing trend.[5]

The passage of sentence by a court is theoretically designed to deter

---

[5] George H. Boldt, "Recent Trends in Criminal Sentencing," *American Criminal Law Quarterly*, Vol. 1 (August, 1963), pp. 4–9. Also see W. H. Fox, "Sentencing the Juvenile Offender," *Western Ontario Law Review*, Vol. 5 (1966), p. 109; D. Lasok, "Treatment of the Young Offender," *New Law Journal*, Vol. 116 (December, 1965), p. 209; and "Interstate Placement of Juveniles," *Columbia Journal of Law and Social Problems*, Vol. 3 (June, 1967), p. 171.

future crimes by other potential criminals, to protect the community from the threat posed by the convicted offender, and to begin the process of rehabilitation of the violator. In varying degree, each of these three goals is evident in the sentencing and penological process. However, each offender is essentially an individual who has committed a particular crime at a particular place at a particular time. Although his sentence should be designed ideally in relationship to his basic needs and the most advanced conception of treatment methods, his actual sentence and treatment program is always limited by the realities of the court and prison systems. Because the prediction process still lacks scientific reliability, the judge attempts to apply what he believes to be the best penalty and treatment program for the offender and for the community in his sentence of the offender. Inasmuch as state and federal sentencing codes have generally reflected the attitudes and needs of the public at the moment, they often lack complete consistency and are frequently out of touch with scientific discoveries concerning human behavior.

Sentencing, therefore, may include many discretionary and often legally irrelevant factors which all the participants in the judical process take into account in varying degrees. This is partially due to the fact that many laws, theoretically designed as a punishment to fit the crime, inconsistently prescribe offenses and penalties. For example, in Pennsylvania the stealing of a carton of cigarettes from a store through burglary may result in the imposition of the same 20-year sentence to imprisonment also designated for an act of willful homicide, a form of second-degree murder. Sexual intercourse with a willing female under 16 (statutory rape) entails a risk of imprisonment for five times as long a term (15 years) as a physical assault with a deadly weapon (aggravated assault and battery) upon the same female.[6]

Many state criminal laws are noticeably inconsistent. In Colorado, for example, a person convicted of first-degree murder must serve 10 years before becoming eligible for parole; a person convicted of a lesser degree of homicide, on the other hand, must serve 15 years or more before reaching the same point of eligibility. Although killing a dog in Colorado is punishable by a maximum sentence of six months, stealing a dog carries a potential penalty of 10 years' imprisonment.[7] Moreover,

---

[6] Edward Green, *Judicial Attitudes in Sentencing* (New York: St. Martin's Press, Inc., 1962), p. 4. Also see Robert F. Kennedy, "Justice Is Found in the Hearts and Minds of Free Men," *Federal Probation*, Vol. 25 (December, 1961), pp. 3–5; W. J. Raggio, "American System of Criminal Justice," *Oklahoma Bar Association Journal*, Vol. 39 (February, 1968), p. 335; and J. C. Craven, "Sentencing," *University of Illinois Law Forum*, Vol. 1966 (Fall, 1966), pp. 523–39.

[7] The President's Commission on Law Enforcement and the Administration of Justice, *The Challenge of Crime in a Free Society* (Washington, D.C.: U.S. Government Printing Office, 1967), p. 142. Refer to Talbot Smith, "The Sentencing Council and the Problem of Disproportionate Sentences," *Federal Probation*, Vol. 27 (March, 1963), pp. 3–6.

such unevenness in punishment is not limited to state codes. Armed bank robbery under federal law is punishable by fine, probation, or a prison term of up to 25 years. However, in cases of armed robbery of a post office, the judge is limited to either granting probation or imposing a 25-year prison sentence.[8] As a result, most judges tend to choose probation rather than to invoke a long prison term. Because the Congress in its passage of federal criminal provisions places the judge in the position of having to decide between the two extremes of a minimum or maximum sentence, neither choice may truly serve the ends of justice.

Even under carefully defined circumstances, a single criminal action can result in two broad categories of multiple punishment. *Unit-of-offense* problems involve decisions as to whether to charge an alleged offender with one or more violations induced within the single interaction violation pattern. For example, when two officers are harmed in one shotgun blast, a judgment must be made concerning whether one or two punishments should be inflicted for one specific interactional offense. Problems in regard to *overlapping statutes,* on the other hand, relate to the existence of both state and federal laws which prohibit the action taken. In such instances, some decision must be made concerning the court in which the charge should be processed. Although gambling violations, for example, may be either state or federal offenses under certain circumstances, they are commonly prosecuted on the state rather than the federal level.[9]

Under the Canadian system of sentencing, the court possesses absolute discretion in fixing a *definite* term (a minimum period of detention before parole eligibility) and an *indefinite* term (a maximum period of detention) and in deciding to whom the sentence applies.[10] In the

---

[8] *Ibid.*, pp. 3–6. Consult John Wallace, "Aids in Sentencing," *Federal Rules Decisions,* Vol. 40 (October, 1966), pp. 433–39; and Myrl E. Alexander, "A Hopeful View of the Sentencing Process," *American Criminal Law Quarterly,* Vol. 3 (Summer, 1965), pp. 189–97; "Process of Juvenile Detention," *Osgoode Hall Law Journal,* Vol. 3 (April, 1965), p. 343; Conrad P. Printzlien, "Deferred Prosecution for Juvenile Offenders," *Federal Probation,* Vol. 12 (March, 1948), pp. 17–22; William H. Sheridan, "Juveniles Who Commit Noncriminal Acts," *Federal Probation,* Vol. 31 (March, 1967), pp. 26–30; and William W. Crain, "Indeterminate and Determinate Time in the Treatment of the Adolescent Delinquent," *Federal Probation,* Vol. 26 (September, 1962), pp. 28–32.

[9] Mordecai Merker, "Multiple Punishment in the Federal Courts: Consecutive Sentences Based on Overlapping Statutes Covering a Single Criminal Transaction," *American Criminal Law Quarterly,* Vol. 4 (Summer, 1966), p. 206; and D. P. Lay, "Problems of Federal Habeas Corpus Involving State Prisoners," *Federal Rules Decisions,* Vol. 45; and A. Samuels, "Sentencing Drug Offenders," *Criminal Law Review,* Vol. 1968 (August, 1968), p. 434.

[10] F. P. Miller, "Parole," in William T. McGrath (ed.), *Crime and Its Treatment in Canada.* (New York: St. Martin's Press, Inc., 1965), p. 366. Also see L. H. Truax, "Structuring the Sentence," *Judicature,* Vol. 52 (August–September, 1968), p. 65.

United States, judges are granted wide discretionary authority, rarely allowed in other countries, to impose sentences ranging from probation to prison terms of up to 25 years.[11] Although American juries fix the sentences of the convicted offender in 10 states, this practice has many shortcomings. Possessing neither the expertise nor experience for a rational assessment of the correctional needs of offenders, juries are frequently less able than judges to prescribe desired treatment alternatives. An Atlanta Crime Commission study of jury sentencing revealed that many Atlanta first offenders received more severe sentences than hardened recidivists.[12]

In many situations, the power of the judge (and jury) in sentencing is clearly prescribed. Habitual-offender laws, for example, necessitate increased penalties for offenders convicted of one or more previous felonies. While such laws have existed since the birth of the nation, their use has become more common since the passage of the New York Baumer Act (1926), which made life imprisonment mandatory for all persons convicted of a fourth felony. Designed to protect the community against criminal recidivism by increasing the penalty for each ensuing crime and by depriving judges and parole boards of discretionary power, habitual-offender laws were quickly enacted in almost all states. However, they have failed to achieve their purpose. Prosecutors have used threats to invoke the habitual-offender law as a means of coercing the defendant to plead guilty to a lesser charge in order to save trial costs and the time of the prosecutor and the court. In other instances, the habitual-offender law has had the result of encouraging plea bargaining. Consequently, the intent of the law, the increased social and physical isolation of the continuing offender, has not truly been achieved.

The effect of this type of law in actually encouraging a greater number of killings of policemen by making offenders desperate has never been fully measured.[13] The very persons for whom these laws were designed, including organized criminals and professional offenders, have been able to largely circumvent their existence.[14] In order to overcome much of the arbitrariness of the habitual-offender laws, the American

---

[11] President's Commission, *op. cit.*, p. 142. Examine also E. D. Fay, " 'Bargained for' Plea Guilty," *Criminal Law Bulletin*, Vol. 4 (June, 1968), p. 265.

[12] *Ibid.*, p. 145. Also see G. A. Martin, "Closing Argument to the Jury for the Defense in Criminal Cases," *Criminal Law Quarterly*, Vol. 10 (November, 1967), p. 34; and G. L. Murray, "Prosecution of a Criminal Jury Trial," *Criminal Law Quarterly*, Vol. 10 (November, 1967), p. 68.

[13] Robert G. Caldwell, *Criminology* (New York: Ronald Press, Co., 1965), p. 359. Also see Paul W. Tappan, "Habitual Offender Laws and Sentencing Practices in Relation to Organized Crime," *Organized Crime and Law Enforcement* (New York: Grosbry Press, 1952), Vol. 1, pp. 113–76.

[14] See Sol Rubin, Henry Weihofen, George Edwards, and Simon Rosenzweig, *The Law of Criminal Correction* (St. Paul, Minn.: West Publishing Co., 1963), pp. 391–408.

Law Institute in its Modern Penal Code suggests that the court be allowed greater flexibility in considering the particular needs of the individual through the use of indeterminant prison sentences which would be graded in relationship to the seriousness of the crime and more individualized in response to the particular situation.

However, such a proposal overlooks the fact that sentencing inconsistency is partially due to the wide latitude offered the sentencing authority in the selection of sanctions, the lack of established sentencing standards necessary to measure the appropriateness of its disposition judgment, and the delegation of sentencing authority to one person.[15] Disparity in sentencing, for example, is especially evident in a 1965 study which reveals that the average federal district court sentence for violation of marihuana laws ran from a minimum of 24 to 118 months; for narcotics violations from 21 to 165 months; for forgery from 12 to 52 months; for unlawful immigration from 3 to 23 months; and for liquor violations from 4 to 36 months. Averages for individual circuit courts for marihuana offenses, the study showed, ranged over the span of 30, 26, 24, 36, 54, 24, and 83 months; for narcotics, 12, 36, 25, 136, 51, 60, 48, 49, 75, and 123 months; for forgery 15, 14, 24, 39, 52, 19, 26, 38, and 36 months; for immigration 20, 17, 21, and 26 months; and for liquor 25, 20, 18, and 19 months.[16]

Other shortcomings in sentencing procedures are also evident in the mandatory infliction of severe minimum sentences, limitations in granting probation and parole, and the infliction of extremely high maximum sentences. Even when severe mandatory minimum sentences, especially in cases of armed robbery and narcotic sales, are demanded by law, judges have been known to dismiss cases and juries to acquit defendants. Then, too, the discretionary power of the judge to apply penalties ranging from the granting of probation to a 25-year prison term encourages the imposition of inconsistent penalties for the same offense in most states. An excessive use of high maximum sentences places an extreme strain upon the correctional system and encourages prisoner disinterest in self-rehabilitation. The failure of the penal code to adequately distinguish between an occasional and repeating offender likewise aggravates the situation. It is questionable whether justice and treatment goals are served when the man who kills his wife in the heat of emotion

---

[15] Richard F. Doyle, "A Sentencing Council in Operation," *Federal Probation*, Vol. 25 (September, 1961), p. 27. Examine "Legal Aid in Criminal Proceedings," *New Law Journal*, Vol. 118 (September, 1968), pp. 833, 857, 881; Reed Cozart, "Civil Rights and the Criminal Offender," *Federal Probation*, Vol. 30 (March, 1966), p. 3; A. M. Kirkpatrick, "Corporal Punishment," *Criminal Law Quarterly*, Vol. 10 (May, 1968), p. 320; and J. A. Andrews, "Joint Trials," *Modern Law Review*, Vol. 30 (November, 1967), p. 645.

[16] Sandor Frankel, "Sentencing Morass and a Suuggestion for Reform," *Criminal Law Bulletin*, Vol. 3 (July–August, 1967), pp. 367–68.

and the person who premeditates the murder of a family of five both receive the same sentence.

Sentencing and prejudice

Sentencing is not always objective. For example, Thorsten Sellin reported in 1935 that a study of prison sentence length for 10 different offenses by native-born whites, foreign-born whites and Negroes disclosed that Negroes received longer average sentences than whites in 3 out of 10 categories in states employing definite sentences. However, in states authorizing indeterminate sentences, they received longer minimums for all offenses except homicide and longer maximums for all offenses except assaults and burglary.[17] The majority of determinate sentences imposed in the South, Sellin projected, reflected the paternalistic attitude toward the Negro found in the region. However, even in the North the Negro was similarly subjected to the longer indeterminate sentences, due to the fact, Sellin concluded, that he was both a competitor in industry and an outsider to the community.[18]

Roscoe Martin found that Texas courts in 1930 tended to favor native Americans over Negroes, Mexicans, and European-born whites, and favored defendants native to the county of trial over Texans not native to the county of trial, American-born non-Texans, and foreign-born persons in that order. Defendants engaged in trade, he noted, were favored over those in lower-grade occupational categories, property owners over propertyless defendants, taxpayers over tax delinquents, married men over single men, widowed over divorced, defendants with children over the childless, and poll-tax payers over nonpoll-tax payers. Variables of sex, age, education, and the presence and absence of parents had little effect upon the severity of sentence. Because Martin failed to differentiate the rates of involvement of various groups in particular crime categories, his findings are open to question. However, other studies by Matthew F. McGuire and Alexander Holtzoff, Morris Ploscowe, Sam B. Warner and Henry B. Cabot, Harold E. Lane, Frederick J. Gaudet, Daniel T. O'Regan and Frank J. Schlosser, Jerome Hall, and Emil Frankel similarly reveal variant sentencing patterns.[19]

Edward Green made a pioneering study of judicial attitudes and sentencing in relation to 1,437 convictions recorded in a volume of the docket of a nonjury prison court of the Philadelphia Court of Quarter Sessions tried over a 17-month period during 1956–57. The study revealed that the nature of the offense was the primary factor influencing the

---

[17] Thorsten Sellin, "Race Prejudice in The Administration of Justice," *American Journal of Sociology*, Vol. 41 (September, 1935), pp. 212–17.

[18] *Ibid.*, p. 217.

[19] Green, *op. cit.*, pp. 9–10.

variation and severity of sentences. Sentencing was affected by the degree of specificity of the act to the victim, the degree of direct contact between the offender and the victim, and the extent to which the criminal act involved the element of bodily injury.[20] The higher the degree of violation of the person, the heavier the average penalty applied against the offender. However, the heaviness of the penalty was also influenced by the number of separate criminal acts of which the defendant had been convicted. Even the number of prior felony convictions, the number of misdemeanors disposed of through penitentiary sentences, and the number of misdemeanors resulting in short terms of imprisonment or in nonprison sentences had some, but generally less, influence. The recency of the last prior felony conviction might also have been a factor. However, the number of arrests failing to result in conviction, Green perceived, had no affect on the severity of sentence. Similarly, the enormity of a prior criminal record had no significant relationship to the length of penitentiary sentences posed by the judge.

Overall, preference in sentencing, Green concluded, is given to females over males, youthful offenders over mature offenders, and whites over Negroes. Women are convicted for less serious crimes than men, younger offenders commit more serious crimes than older males, and Negro defendents, on the average older than whites, possess more lengthy prior records of criminality. However, as offenders of both races grow older, the percentage distribution of their offenses become more alike. Consequently, the differences in sentencing in the Philadelphia court between white and Negro would tend to smooth out in time.[21] Although the recency of the last prior felony conviction, Green noted, holds a moderate "though not statistically significant relationship with variation in sentences, the more recent the conviction, the higher the sentence."[22] Disparity of sentencing among the 21 judges in the Philadelphia court was insignificant in lesser cases, although it was most pronounced in cases at an "intermediate level of gravity." Even in the most serious cases, only 1 of the 21 judges varied significantly from his colleagues. Prosecutors had no significant effect upon the severity of sentences imposed by the judge.

The Philadelphia study revealed that the judges did not favor defendants who pleaded guilty over those who did not, except in cases of minor crimes against personal property in which a judge evidenced tolerance if the offender offered restitution when he pleaded guilty.

---

[20] *Ibid.*, p. 97. Also see L. G. Schultz, "Victim-Offender Relationship," *Crime and Delinquency*, Vol. 14 (April, 1968), p. 135; and W. R. Newsome, "Vacation of Suspension," *Judge Advocate General Journal*, Vol. 20, (September–November, 1965), p. 35.

[21] *Ibid.*, p. 99.

[22] *Ibid.*, p. 98.

However, sentencing flexibility was somewhat more common in plea bargaining in which the offender pleaded guilty to a lesser charge. At this point, the normative inconsistency of the penal code, Green hypothesized, is projected into the court's judgment of the relative gravity of the offense. In effect, the judge mentally reevaluates and scales the crimes and their penalties into a coherent pattern.[23] Nevertheless, the judges, he found, differed in degree in their scales of penal values and in their impressions of case seriousness in relationship to their social background, personality, and penal philosophy.[24] Consequently, the deliberations of the sentencing judge, Green concluded, "are not at the mercy of his passions or prejudices but comply with the mandate of the law."[25]

Although the move toward allowing the sentencing judge wider discretionary power in sentencing in the United States has permitted greater flexibility in administration of justice and encouraged the development of penal rehabilitative rather than mere punishment goals, it has nevertheless done so at the "expense of precision and certainty in the law."[26] Consequently, new debates have arisen concerning the objectives of punishment, criteria for sentencing, and inconsistency in the invocation of penalties. While existing penal codes perpetuate the influence of Beccaria, who maintained the need for a set quantum of punishment as a deterrence for that quantum of pleasure received from the criminal act, the rise of the Lombrosian concern for the needs of the offender have received greater attention. While Lombroso's positivistic supporters have sought greater flexibility in the sentencing process, it is this discretionary power used in the name of prisoner rehabilitation which has

---

[23] *Ibid.*, p. 100. Consult "Guides to the Judge in Sentencing in Racketeering Cases," *Crime and Delinquency*, Vol. 14 (April, 1968), p. 97; Richard A. Chappel, "Due Process of Law as It Relates to Corrections," *Federal Probation*, Vol. 29 (September, 1965), pp. 3–6; B. R. Lamb, "Man on the Bench," *Pennsylvania Bar Association Quarterly*, Vol. 40 (October, 1968), p. 129; and T. L. Shaffer, "Judges, Repulsive Evidence and the Ability to Respond," *Notre Dame Lawyer*, Vol. 43 (April, 1968), p. 503.

[24] *Ibid.*, p. 101. Also examine "Retrial of the Successful Criminal Appellant: Harsher Punishment and Denial of Credit for Time Served: *Patton* v. *North Carolina*," 381 F. 2d 636, *Maryland Law Review*, Vol. 28 (Winter, 1968), p. 64; and T. P. O'Rourke and R. G. Salem, "Comparative Analysis of Pretrial Release Procedures," *Crime and Delinquency*, Vol. 14 (October, 1968), p. 367.

[25] *Ibid.*, p. 367. Refer to L. Setwin, "Waiver of Objections to Former Testimony," *UCLA Law Review*, Vol. 15 (November, 1967), p. 118; H. Goldstein, "Trial Judges and the Police," *Crime and Delinquency*, Vol. 14 (January, 1968), p. 14; and "To Take the Stand or Not to Take the Stand: The Dilemma of the Defendant with a Criminal Record," *Columbia Journal of Law and Social Problems*, Vol. 4 (July, 1968), p. 215.

[26] *Ibid.*, p. 1. See S. A. Weigel, "Appellate Revision of Sentences: To Make the Punishment Fit the Crime," *Stanford Law Review*, Vol. 20 (February, 1968), p. 405; and "Critical Appraisal of the Application of the Best Evidence Rule," *Rutgers Law Review*, Vol. 21 (Spring, 1967), p. 526.

come under increased attack. Many critics question whether the judge possesses the necessary formal training to impose an effective and just sentence and whether his proper role might not simply be limited to the refereeing of the judicial process. Inasmuch as crime is not a singular activity and involves multiple gradations of intent and harm, the sentencing function, they conclude, might be handled more adequately by a panel of experts trained in the sciences of human behavior.[27]

The federal government has moved for greater flexibility in youth sentencing procedures. The passage of the Federal Youth Correction Act, applicable to those under the age of 22, provides for an indeterminant sentence with release on parole not later than two years before the expiration of the sentence. The standard maximum is limited to six years, and the court may impose on a youth a term up to that maximum if the crime carries a higher maximum for adult offenders. If a youth on parole responds successfully, the Board of Parole is empowered to release him for supervision and set aside his conviction. In addition, the same act allows the federal prison system to develop special youth centers, foster homes, or other residential facilities in order to promote the rehabilitation of the youthful offender. It also extended the 1958 Youth Act to cover selected defendant types up to the age of 25. Under the latter's provision, the courts were authorized to commit any offender to the attorney general for examination and recommendation and to impose sentences which made the defendant eligible for parole as soon as such determination was made by the parole board, at a date fixed by the court, or upon completion of one third of the maximum sentence. The judge was also given the power to impose a combination sentence of both jail and probation in one-count convictions.[28]

Although these provisions permit greater flexibility in federal juvenile and young adult dispositions, they do not solve the total problem. Inequitable sentences continue to have a negative effect upon the offender and often reinforce his antagonism toward society. Creating a feeling of mistreatment and injustice, inequitable sentences cause the offender and his family to lose confidence in the law and severely undermine the effective administration of justice.[29] In an attempt to develop uniform and consistent sentencing policies within a particular jurisdiction, the appellate courts have been accorded the power of review of sentence in 12 states and for the military courts. While several other states have interpreted existing laws to grant similar authority, this power is vested solely in the trial judge in the federal system and in 31 states. However,

---

[27] *Ibid.*, p. 3.

[28] Myrl E. Alexander, "A Hopeful View of the Sentencing Process," *American Criminal Law Quarterly*, Vol. 3 (Summer, 1965), pp. 192–93.

[29] Talbott Smith, "The Sentencing Council and the Problem of Disproportionate Sentences," *Federal Probation*, Vol. 28 (June, 1963), p. 5.

if sentencing inconsistencies are to be overcome, the appellate court should be given greater powers to maintain a constant sentencing practice.

In some states the sentencing council, a panel of three judges, chosen to consider the applicability of a specific sentence to a particular case in relation to the facts and to the previous imposition of sentence in other convictions, decides the actual sentence. Because each judge has the presentence investigation report from the probation department and a study sheet prepared for all offenders at hand for consideration, he and his two colleagues are more fully able to recommend final sentences in a coherent manner. Under this procedure, each judge mentally identifies several central or important determinants of sentencing and offers his opinion, which is combined with those of his colleagues for transmission to the judge of the original jurisdiction for implementation. Serving multiple purposes, the sentencing council aids the search for justice by encouraging standardized and equal sentences, by stimulating dialogue among sentencing judges, and by expanding judicial knowledge of many often ignored areas of the criminal justice system. Such a procedure also permits the sentencing and assisting judges to evaluate the successes and failures of their previous sentencing practices.[30] In California, the determination of the length of felony sentences currently resides with the Adult Authority, although the trial judge may actually sentence the offender to the maximum sentence allowed by law.

California and New York prescribe lengthy mandatory sentences for continued felony violations. Other states often require either a mandatory sentence or a mandatory extension of the primary sentence if the crime involves narcotics, deadly weapons, violence, or sexual misbehavior.[31] California provides for the civil commitment of a drug addict upon conviction but before sentence if the defendant is addicted to habit-forming drugs. Committed to a rehabilitation center for drug habit arrest, the offender may be returned to the court's jurisdiction and sentenced as a convicted offender without a drug habit if he proves he can live in social community without drug use.

Although mandatory sentences may be prescribed in law, they are coming under increasing attack on the grounds that they undermine the basic sentencing function of the judge and limit the best use of correctional resources for individualized treatment on the basis of diagnostic and presentence investigation reports. Some laws concerning defective delinquents, the mentally disordered, sex offenders, and sexual psychopaths permit the near-automatic removal of the offender from

---

[30] *Ibid.*, pp. 8–9.

[31] Paul B. Weston and Kenneth M. Wells, *The Administration of Justice* (Englewood Cliffs, N.J.: Prentice-Hall, Inc., 1967), p. 228.

society until cured or until no longer a menace to general safety. At a later time they, too, may be returned to the court for the infliction of an appropriate sentence.

The Model Penal Code of the American Law Institute attempts to overcome many of the shortcomings of existing sentencing procedures by proposing the reduction of all crimes to three grades of felony and two of misdemeanor. While each grade carries a maximum penalty, most sentences are shorter than those currently prevalent in most states. Not only would the judge be empowered to grant probation except in capital cases but he would also be authorized to extend the maximum if the offender were especially dangerous and the offense excessively atrocious. While the code makes one year the minimum term of imprisonment for any felony, the minimum for the most serious felonies is three years. Beyond this, the judge is given the power to impose a flexible sentence pertinent to the case situation. The 1967 President's Commission on Law Enforcement and Administration of Justice proposed the reexamination of sentencing provisions of penal codes with the goal of simplifying the grading of offenses, of eliminating mandatory minimum and long maximum terms, and of removing current restrictions upon probation and parole.[32]

But even these modifications are only partial solutions. Current procedures and sentences often discriminate against the poor. The use of fines, Max Grünhut believes, would be of greater value among the poor if fines were assessed according to the offender's ability to pay rather than in relationship to the gravity of the offense, and if the poor could pay on an installment plan basis.[33] Only then would the economic impact of the fine be equivalent for all parties. Charles H. Miller points out that the use of fines is more likely to serve as a deterrent for criminal acts oriented toward the acquisition of property. Fines, Miller believes, should be determined in relationship to the number of prior offenses and the current economic situation of the offender.[34]

The presentence investigation

Although not all states require its completion, the presentence investigation and report, which examines the circumstances of the offense, the attitude of the complainant or victim, the offender's delinquent or

---

[32] President's Commission, op. cit., p. 143. Refer to Annulment of a Conviction of Crime (New York: National Council on Crime and Delinquency, 1962); and W. D. Milligan, "Certificate of Rehabilitation and Application for Pardon in California," California State Bar Journal, Vol. 43 (January–February, 1968), p. 112.

[33] Max Grünhut, Penal Reform (Oxford: Clarendon Press, 1948), p. 6.

[34] Charles H. Miller, "The Fine: Price Tag or Rehabilitative Force?" National Probation and Parole Association Journal, Vol. 2 (October, 1956), p. 379.

criminal record and social history, and other factors, has become more common in recent years in both juvenile and adult cases.

California requires the completion of such a report in all felony cases in which the defendant is eligible for probation and in discretionary misdemeanor cases. Commonly divided into six to eight sections (see Table 21–1), the presentence investigation report permits thorough re-

TABLE 21–1
Ingredients of the presentence investigation report

1. *Legal History of the Offender*
    a) Court and institutional record;
    b) Statement describing present offense;
    c) Complainant's statement;
    d) Offender's statement describing offense;
    e) Mitigating (or aggravating) circumstances:
        (1) *Offender*
        (2) *Crime*
        (3) *Codefendants*
2. *Social History of Offender*
    a) Early life and education;
    b) Employment and socio-economic condition;
    c) Character, habits, associates, leisure-time activities;
    d) Social condition and history;
    e) Religious training and observance; and
    f) Mental and physical condition.
3. *Family History of Offender*
    a) Wife and children;
    b) Parents; and
    c) Previous marriages.
4. *Home and Neighborhood Background*
5. *Community Attitudes*
6. *Other Information*
7. *Disposition Recommended*
8. *Summary*

Source: Paul B. Weston and Kenneth M. Wells, *The Administration of Justice* (Englewood Cliffs, N.J.: Prentice-Hall, Inc., 1967), p. 230.

view of the offender's history and potential for rehabilitation before the actual sentencing occurs.

Offenders may undergo presentence investigations in many different facilities, depending upon the offender's violation and needs. Many states have developed juvenile and adult diagnostic facilities to carry out this function. During a 90-day period, the offender is examined by center personnel, and data are gathered for the final report, including findings and recommendations, to the court. While a state department of correction may provide such services, larger cities, such as New York City, may furnish these services at the municipal or metropolitan court level.[35]

[35] Weston and Wells, *op. cit.*, p. 231. Also see Franco Ferracuti, Mario Fontanesi, and Marvin E. Wolfgang, "The Diagnostic and Classification Center at Rebibbia, Rome," *Federal Probation*, Vol. 27 (September, 1963), pp. 31–35.

Available to the court, the prosecutor, and defense counsel, the report becomes part of the case record and is forwarded to the officer in charge of prison assignment if probation is denied. Generally, all copies are later sealed and are made available only to case participants. While some critics claim that the presentence report merely plays to the bias of the judge, such a charge has not been effectively documented.

The federal presentence investigation report aids the court in determining the appropriate sentence, assists the Bureau of Prisons and its institutions in their classification and treatment programs and in release planning, furnishes the parole board with information relating to parole consideration, assists the probation officer in his rehabilitative efforts during probation and parole supervision, and offers a source of pertinent information for systematic research.[36]

THE SYSTEM OF PROBATION

If the offender is not sentenced to imprisonment on the basis of the presentence report, he may be placed on probation. In the English sense, probation, Max Grünhut acknowledges, is a nonpunitive sanction against a criminal offense committed with a guilty mind and, therefore, is a form of criminal sentence. It can be modified only in the case of a breach of probation, "if the probationer has committed an act, or is guilty of omission, in defiance of the requirements imposed on him that is, by an act of his own choice."[37] As conceived in the United States, probation, however, is a form of disposition under which a court, Charles L. Newman notes, "suspends either the sentence or execution of the judgment of sentence on selected offenders, releasing them conditionally on good behavior, under prescribed terms of rules and subject to the control, guidance, and assistance of the court as exercised through offi-

---

[36] *The Pre-Sentence Investigation Report* (Washington, D.C.: U.S. Government Printing Office, 1965), p. 1. Refer to James B. Parsons, "The Presentence Investigation Report Must be Preserved as a Confidential Document," *Federal Probation,* Vol. 27 (March, 1964), pp. 3–17; Roszel C. Thomsen, "Confidentiality of the Pre-sentence Report: A Middle Position," *Federal Probation,* Vol. 28 (March, 1961), pp. 8–10; *An Evaluation of Probation Success: A Study in Post-Discharge Recidivism* (Albany, N.Y.: Department of Correction, 1960); Stuart Adams, "The Value of Research in Probation," *Federal Probation,* Vol. 29 (September, 1965), pp. 35–40; Albert Wahl and Daniel Glaser, "Pilot Time Study of the Federal Probation Officer's Job," *Federal Probation,* Vol. 27 (September, 1963), pp. 20–25; and John Edgar Hoover, "Primacy in Parole and Probation," *University of Kansas Law Review,* Vol. 13 (March, 1965), pp. 343–50.

[37] Grünhut, *op. cit.,* p. 50. Consult "Judicial Review of Probation Conditions," *Columbia Law Review,* Vol. 67 (January, 1967), p. 181; "Appealability of an Order Revoking Probation," *St. John's Law Review,* Vol. 42 (January, 1968), p. 393; Frederick Benjamin, "Due Process and Revocation of Conditional Liberty," *Wayne Law Review,* Vol. 12 (Spring, 1966), pp. 638–56; and Eugene C. Di Cerbo, "When Should Probation be Revoked?," *Federal Probation,* Vol. 30 (June, 1966), pp. 11–17.

cers appointed to supervise them."[38] The fundamental characteristic of the American system of probation is the conditional suspension of sentence *plus* supervision of all activities of the offender during the period of his suspension.

As a system, probation operates in conjunction with theories of punishment which imply that behavior and conduct may be changed by the threatened use of legal force. However, probation assumes by contrast that changes in individual behavior depend upon confronting the offender with meaningful conduct alternatives, aiding him in solving the problems which have stimulated his current problem, and informing him of the probable consequences of alternate patterns of action which he may undertake.[39] Minimizing the emphasis upon deterrent punishment, the probation approach assumes that human behavior may be redirected through the mutual interaction of the probation officer and his probationers which may affect personal and environmental adjustments and may assist the juvenile or adult and his family or friends in meeting normative goals. Commonly, probation attempts to apply social casework methods in order to individualize treatment, leaving the child or adult to his normal home environment and community while rehabilitation continues.[40] As a concept, probation is personality

[38] Charles L. Newman, *Sourcebook on Probation, Paroles and Pardons* (Springfield, Ill.: Charles C. Thomas, Publisher, 1964), pp. 28–30. See Arthur P. Miles, "The Reality of The Probation Officer's Dilemma," *Federal Probation*, Vol. 28 (March, 1965), pp. 18–23; Andre Cailliet, "Treatment of a Juvenile Delinquent: A Probation Officer's View," *Federal Probation*, Vol. 28 (September, 1964), pp. 47–51; Eleanor Muhlmeyer, "A Probation Officer Looks at His Job," *Federal Probation*, Vol. 30, (March, 1966), pp. 5–10; Philip Stein, "A Probation Officer—Hmm— What Do You Do?" *Federal Probation*, Vol. 20 (September, 1966), pp. 27–30; Jane K. Ives, "The Essential Task of the Probation—Parole Officer," *Federal Probation*, Vol. 25 (March, 1962), pp. 38–43; Harvey Treger, "The Alcoholic and the Probation Officer: A New Relationship," *Federal Probation*, Vol. 26 (December, 1962), pp. 23–25; and Robert M. Carter, "It is Respectfully Recommended. . . ," *Federal Probation*, Vol. 20 (June, 1966), pp. 38–42.

[39] Robert W. Winslow, *Juvenile Delinquency in a Free Society* (Belmont, Calif.: Dickenson Publishing Co., Inc., 1968), pp. 181–82. Also see Leon J. Sims, "Supervision: An Opportunity for Rehabilitation," *Federal Probation*, Vol. 26 (September, 1962), pp. 37–40; Edward W. Garrett, "Improvement of Officer Performance Through Supervision," *Federal Probation*, Vol. 27 (September, 1963), pp. 43–47; Charles L. Newman, "Let's 'Sell' Corrections: A Straight Talk to Probation Officers," *Federal Probation*, Vol. 29 (June, 1965), pp. 21–24; and David H. Gronewald, "Supervision Practices in the Federal Probation System," *Federal Probation*, Vol. 28 (September, 1964), pp. 19–25.

[40] Clyde B. Vedder, *Juvenile Offenders* (Springfield, Ill.: Charles C. Thomas, Publisher, 1963), p. 173. Refer to Charles H. Shireman, "Casework in Probation and Parole: Some Considerations in Diagnosis and Treatment," *Federal Probation*, Vol. 27 (June, 1963), pp. 51–57; Seymour Aller, "Effecting Change in Youthful Offenders: Three Case Illustrations," *Federal Probation*, Vol. 26 (March, 1962), pp. 31–38; Charles L. Newman, "Concepts of Treatment in Probation and Parole Supervision," *Federal Probation*, Vol. 25 (March, 1961), pp. 11–18; Herbert Vogt, "Group Counseling in Probation," *Federal Probation*, Vol. 25 (September, 1961), pp. 49–54; and Walter Evans, "The Probationer's Job: An Essential Factor in His Rehabilitation," *Federal Probation*, Vol. 25 (June, 1961), pp. 30–33.

oriented. It presumes that the interests of society and the individual in rehabilitation are best fulfilled by allowing the judged or convicted offender the opportunity to remain outside a juvenile training school or the adult prison while undergoing restricted supervision in the community. Probation, therefore, encourages the individualized sentencing of offenders, using their self-motivating potential to gain conformity and commitment to established law.

Although its origin are obscure, the probation system probably grew out of the reprieves allowed offenders who claimed "benefit of clergy" in 13th-century Europe.[41] In the 19th century, the practice of sentencing youthful English criminals to a one-day term of imprisonment followed by a conditional release under the supervision of parents or master developed at the Warwickshire Court of Quarter Sessions. Magistrate Matthew Davenport Hill, keeping records of those placed on probation during the following 1841, found only 78, or 16 percent, of the 484 probationers were returned to the court for later sentencing.[42] Recorder Cox of Portsmouth, following a similar practice as Hill, listed only two failures over a 12-year period.

As the practice spread to Middlesex, Birmingham, and London, probation officers were eventually supplied by the local police force and even later by volunteer and philanthropic organizations. In order to act as sureties for young and first offenders, the Church of England Temperance Society, for example, established a category of court missionaries. In 1890, 36 were engaged in this work; in 1907, 143 served in this capacity. Their success led to the creation of a state allowance program for the appointment of salaried probation officers. As the number of probationers increased, public probation departments gradually evolved. However, the availability of probation services to English courts was not made mandatory until 1925.[43]

In the United States, probation was pioneered by John Augustus, a 19th-century Boston bootmaker, who established the earliest form of probation some 38 years prior to the 1878 enactment of the Massachusetts probation statute.[44] A self-appointed probation officer, Augustus attempted to mitigate some of the harshness of the judicial system.[45] Believing drunkards to be redeemable, Augustus provided them with

[41] David Dressler, *Practice and Theory of Probation and Parole* (New York, 1959), p. 7.

[42] William T. McGrath, *Crime and Its Treatment in Canada* (New York: St. Martin's Press, Inc., 1965), p. 223.

[43] Winslow, *op. cit.*, p. 175. Consult Herschel A. Prins, "Training for Probation Work in England and Wales," *Federal Probation*, Vol. 28 (December, 1964), pp. 12–18.

[44] Newman, *op. cit.*, pp. 72–74.

[45] Jerry L. Donnelly, "Conflict Between Probation and the Right to Appeal in Kansas," *Kansas Law Review*, Vol. 15 (May, 1967), p. 570.

bail, employment, and limited funds to assist their readjustment to society.[46] In his first 10 years of activity, he pledged bail in the amount
of $99,464 for 1,102 persons (674 males and 428 females). By the time
of his death in 1858, he had provided bail for more than 1,946 persons.[47]

Massachusetts developed the first juvenile probation service in the
United States in 1869, when an agent of the state board of charities
was authorized to appear at criminal trials on behalf of juveniles, to
find suitable homes, and to visit children periodically. Only six states
had operationalized a similar probation concept by the turn of the century. Massachusetts followed its earlier provision with an 1890 law which
made probation a mandatory feature of the state court system.[48]

Probation was first conceived as a form of release upon approval.
It was later broadened and reconceived in the United States as a form
of suspension of sentence which freed the offender for a period of time
depending on the continuance of good behavior.[49] Such a conception
was essentially stimulated by a 1916 Supreme Court decision which
held that neither federal not state courts possess authority from common
law to suspend sentences indefinitely and that the suspension of imposition or execution of sentence is a nonconstitutional usurpation of power
by the judiciary unless the suspension of sentence is specifically authorized by statute.[50]

Consequently, most federal and state probation laws provide the trial
court with discretionary power to grant or to withhold probation, although the majority of legislatures have made certain classes of convicted
offenders ineligible for probation. In Illinois, for example, probation
is left to the discretion of the trial court except in cases of capital offense,
sale of narcotics, and rape, for which probation is excluded. In 1965,
23 percent of the cases from Cook County (Chicago) which were terminated by conviction resulted in probation; 42 percent of those cases
from the downstate rural areas, by contrast, received the same
disposition.[51]

In Canada, probation is held to be the right of the offender. Generally,
its use is restricted to first offenders or to persons free of criminal conviction for five years. Canada at present does not provide a national system
of probation or legal provisions for transfer of responsibility if the probationer moves to another province. Under existing probation procedures, a defendant, found guilty of a crime upon verdict or plea, can

---

[46] Clegg, *op. cit.*, p. 9.
[47] McGrath, *op. cit.*, p. 223.
[48] Winslow, *op. cit.*, p. 176.
[49] Vedder, *op. cit.*, pp. 171–72.
[50] Donnelly, *op. cit.*, p. 570.
[51] James C. Craven, "Sentencing," *University of Illinois Law Forum*, Vol. 1966
(Fall, 1966), p. 527.

be released by the court without imprisonment, subject to conditions imposed by the court and to the supervision of the court or province probation service.[52] The Federal Juvenile Act governs the provision of juvenile probation in Canada.[53]

In the United States, through the use of *summary* or *bench probation,* a court may grant an offender probation without preliminary or presentence investigation and without ability to provide probation supervision. Since the usual benefits of probation are unavailable, this form of probation merely permits the individual to remain free in the community by avoiding incarceration. It is generally used only in low-risk cases.[54] Usually, however, probation is granted only after a thorough review of a case and when supervision is available. Among the factors which normally must be considered before granting probation are:

1. The nature of the crime committed.
    a) Type of crime.
    b) Circumstances of its commission.
    c) Defendant's motivation.
    d) Defendant's degree of culpability.
    e) Was the crime an isolated offense or a part of an organized criminal enterprise or racket?
    f) Did the crime involve the use of violence or dangerous weapons, bodily harm or threat of bodily harm or other acts disclosing a high degree of criminality or callousness?
    g) The extent of the direct impact of the crime on the public.
2. The need for deterrence of others.
3. The need for publicly vindicating the public policy embodied in statute violated by the defendant.
4. Defendant's age.
5. Defendant's criminal experience.
6. Defendant's mental and emotional makeup.
7. Significant personal traits pertinent to defendant's present predicament and the outlook for his future conduct.
8. Defendant's attitudes and feelings about himself.
9. Defendant's attitudes toward society and probation.
10. Defendant's attitude and feeling about the crime.
11. Defendant's family and domestic history and relationships, including dependents.
12. His educational background.
13. His social background, associates, interests, and hobbies.

---

[52] *Standard Probation and Parole Act, 1955 of the National Council on Crime and Delinquency.*
[53] McGrath, *op. cit.,* p. 230.
[54] Clegg, *op. cit.,* p. 19.

14. His religious training, interests, and observances.
15. His employment history.
16. Vocational capabilities, experiences, and aptitude of defendant; his outlook for gainful employment.
17. His financial condition.
18. Whether defendant pleaded guilty.
19. Whether defendant was convicted after trial and whether he took the stand and gave testimony that was patently false.
20. Whether the defendant was convicted after trial and whether he was responsible for putting on the stand witnesses whose testimony was patently suborned.
21. Whether defendant was responsible for any threats to any prosecution witnesses or for the disappearance or unavailability of any prosecution witnesses.
22. Whether the defendant pleaded guilty and took the stand as a government witness, giving truthful testimony.
23. Whether the defendant pleaded guilty and has cooperated or is cooperating with the government by furnishing information about criminal activities concerning which he has knowledge.
24. The likelihood of the defendant's repeating this type of crime or any other crime.
25. The defendant's military record, if any, and his adjustment to it.
26. The potentially injurious effects of institutionalization.[55]

Similar but somewhat modified criteria are also used in evaluating the juvenile's probation potential.

The provisions of the Model Penal Code suggest that the offender's eligibility for probation should be determined in the future in relationship to his probable dangerousness, his need for treatment, and the seriousness of his offense. Factors of continuing importance in any decision to grant probation include the general mildness of the offense, the character of the offender, the hardship imposed by imprisonment upon the offender or his dependents, and other similar elements. Only

[55] William B. Herlando, "When and How Should a Sentencing Judge Use Probation," *Federal Rules Decision*, Vol. 35 (October, 1964), pp. 495–96. Examine Henry L. Hartman, "Interviewing Techniques in Probation and Parole—Building the Relationship," *Federal Probation*, Vol. 27 (March, 1963), pp. 14–19; Henry L. Hartman, "Interviewing Techniques in Probation and Parole—The Art of Listening," *Federal Probation*, Vol. 27 (June, 1963), pp. 15–21; Henry L. Hartman, "Interviewing Techniques in Probation and Parole—The Initial Interview (Part I)," *Federal Probation*, Vol. 27 (September, 1963), pp. 8–14; Henry L. Hartman, "Interviewing Techniques in Probation and Parole—The Initial Interview (Part II)," *Federal Probation*, Vol. 27 (December, 1963), pp. 17–22; Chester H. Bartoo, "Interviewing Candidates for Probation," *Federal Probation*, Vol. 25 (March, 1961), pp. 19–23; and Seymour L. Halleck, "The Interview With the Offender," *Federal Probation*, Vol. 25 (March, 1961), pp. 23–27.

through consideration of these factors can the persistent, habitual, or hardened criminal be differentiated from his less committed counterparts.[56] However, mere division of criminal types is not enough to affect an adequate probation program. Probation standards should properly include full authority to place juvenile and adult offenders on probation, complete presentence investigation, careful selection of cases, qualified personnel, restriction of caseloads to 50 or under, and intensive supervision according to sound casework.[57]

Juvenile probation services

Although juvenile probation services are usually organized in either a centralized statewide system, a centralized county or city system reinforced by state services, or a combination of the two, every American state provides some juvenile probation services. Thirty-one states, encompassing 74 percent of all counties in the United States, maintain probation services in each of its counties. Four states including 165 counties, provide no probation services. Courts administer juvenile probation in 32 states, state correctional agencies in 5 states, state public welfare departments in 7 states, some other state agencies in 4 states, and various other agencies in 3 states. Approximately 47 percent of the court-administered departments are under merit or civil service systems.[58]

Whatever the organizational form of the probation services, the eligibility of the juvenile for probation is usually determined through the court's intake department, which screens juveniles coming to its attention. Under the leadership of a probation officer or the juvenile judge who function as *parens patrae,* the intake procedure permits the officer of the court, the juvenile, and his parents to reach collectively some decision necessary to the satisfactory adjustment of the case. Commonly, the probation officer presides at the intake session, leaving the judge to participate in informal hearings, which generally culminate in informal dispositions. Intake options may lead to the outright dismissal of the case, referral of the case to another community agency or service, informal supervision of the offender by the probation staff, detention, or filing of a petition for formal juvenile court action.[59]

---

[56] President's Commission, *op. cit.,* p. 142.

[57] Helen D. Pigeon, *Probation and Parole—A Study Manual* (New York: National Probation and Parole Association, 1942), p. 90.

[58] Winslow, *op. cit.,* p. 184. Refer to Hyman S. Lippman, "The Role of the Probation Officer in the Treatment of Delinquency in Children," *Federal Probation,* Vol. 12 (June, 1948), pp. 36–39; Ben S. Meeker, "Training of Juvenile Court Probation Officers and Related Workers Who Cannot Attend Graduate School," *Training Personnel for Work with Juvenile Delinquents* (Washington, D.C.: U.S. Department of Health, Education, and Welfare, 1954), pp. 23–43.

[59] *Ibid.,* p. 145. Also see "Juvenile Probation," *Crime and Delinquency,* Vol. 13 (January, 1967), p. 41.

Formal probation procedures permit the youth to remain in the community under probation officer supervision and guidance. A legal status within the juvenile court, probation usually depends upon a finding that the behavior of the child is legally subject to juvenile court jurisdiction and to the imposition of conditions which modify his freedom of action and that his best interests are served through supervision in the community. Consequently, the specific goals of probation services include the prevention of repetition of a child's delinquent conduct and of long-term deviant or criminal careers, and the assistance of the child through feasible probation measures designed to enhance his potential as a productive citizen.

The modern probation department, therefore, participates in a series of functions, including detention intake and screening, social study and diagnosis, and supervision and treatment, which are designed to aid the juvenile's adjustment within modern society. While the functions of intake and screening and/or social study and diagnosis are primarily provided for the juvenile court and the family, the process of supervision and treatment, which includes surveillance, service, and counseling, are fundamentally services to the youth. In surveillance, the probation officer maintains contact with the child, his parents, school personnel, and other persons important to his adjustment. At the same time, he continues to make the youth aware of his responsibilities to the society, which depends upon the mutual cooperation of its members. Representing a confrontation with reality, the probation officer provides the juvenile with the assurance that the society is interested in his person and in his normative response to the structural expectations of his social group. Through service the officer also mobilizes community agencies to assist the child or his family. In fulfilling his counseling responsibility, he uses his professional ability to aid the youth, his family, or other participants in understanding their basic problems and the potential means for their solution.[60]

Most probation officers use a variety of skills and services in their attempt to reorient the behavior of the delinquent. The utilization of foster family care and group homes frequently provides opportunities for adjustment which are unavailable to the child in his own home. Although the group home, for example, may supply the juvenile with the necessary external controls without the emotional costs which are common in foster home placements, comparatively few are available. Nearly 42 percent of the 243 agencies surveyed in the sample reported to the President's Commission on Law Enforcement and the Administration of Justice used foster homes for juvenile probation cases. Because

---

[60] *Ibid.*, pp. 179–80. Examine O. T. Irwin, "Group Reporting in Juvenile Probation," *Crime and Delinquency*, Vol. 11 (October, 1965), p. 341.

more than one half of the 4,967 probationers under foster home care at the time of the reports were placed by probation departments in three California counties, this figure may be misleading. Only 10 of the agencies, serving a total of 332 children, operated group homes.[61]

Whatever the setting, probation furnishes juveniles and first offenders a basic rehabilitation opportunity. Although potentially applicable to second offenders, its use is generally limited to the former, since their prospects for successful probation are greater than those for recidivists. In these instances, probation is a suspension of any imprisonment and a conditional release upon conviction pending good behavior for a designated period of time. It depends upon the availability of probation officer supervision and guidance, and it has its greatest value when the violator trusts the probation officer.

Probation eligibility often depends upon particular criteria designated by the state. The individual's criminal history, including conviction of a serious crime, the use of drugs or dangerous weapons as a minor or adult, and the use of torture or the infliction of bodily injury, may automatically exclude the defendant from probation consideration. In some states, a public official who has been convicted of bribery, embezzlement, or extortion is ineligible for probation. In California, a defendant can normally assume probation upon his first conviction unless specific factors militate against its use.[62]

Probation in a mobile society

An ever increasing problem in probation is the high mobility of modern society. Mobility creates a problem of supervision of offenders outside the state in which they are on probation. Originally probation (and parole) usually had to be completed in the area of court jurisdiction. However, since 1934, when Congress first authorized a compact among the states for the prevention of crime, many flexible provisions in corrections have been adopted. Under the provisions of the Interstate Compact on Parolees and Probationers, for example, members of either group may be transferred to a receptive environment where their chances of rehabilitation are greater, or they may be returned and reincarcerated if they commit further violations.[63] Additionally, the parolee or probationer may travel to a receiving state if he is a resident or has a family

---

[61] *Ibid.*, p. 195.

[62] Weston and Wells, *op. cit.*, p. 233. Also see Alexander Rheiner, "The Period of Probation," *Federal Probation*, Vol. 26 (September, 1962), pp. 33–36; and F. Lovell Bixby, "Probation is Not Freedom," *Federal Probation*, Vol. 26 (June 1962) pp. 47–51.

[63] Newman, *op. cit.*, p. 210; and M. E. Switzer, "Treatment in the Community," *Trial*, Vol. 4 (April–May, 1968), p. 11.

residing within that state, can obtain employment at that location, and is accepted for entrance by that state. Upon transfer to the new jurisdiction, he becomes subject to the probation or parole supervision terms of that jurisdiction. If for some reason he flees that jurisdiction or violates the conditions of his release, he may be apprehended and extradicted to the place of original jurisdiction for further action.

Since the initiation of the Compact, thousands of cases have been processed. Currently more than 12,000 cases are handled annually under its terms; 25 percent of the cases represent new additions which replace cases terminating each year.[64] While the Compact has filled a void, it nevertheless possesses some shortcomings. Wide variations in parole and parole systems, for example, continue to exist among the states; some jurisdictions fail to provide adequate supervision, necessary treatment facilities, and necessary personnel to discharge their responsibilities effectively; and all states still do not agree on the grounds for returning a parolee to prison.[65]

Probation in Canada

Canadian probation services are generally operated by provincial authorities. In British Columbia, where the probation service is located in the correction branch of the Attorney General's Department, the chief probation officer is also the director of correction. Probation officers under his jurisdiction furnish supervision and presentence service for both juveniles and adults, handle presupervision and prerelease planning for the British Columbia parole board, and under certain circumstances provide direct parole supervision.[66] During 1963–64, some 2,257 persons were under the supervision of the provincial Probation Service, 414 were released under parole supervision, and 365 were supervised voluntarily without a court order beyond the end of their formal probation period. In addition, British Columbia probation officers also prepared 2,467 presentence reports which led to other dispositions of offenders in that year. Of 880 cases in British Columbia under study, 88 percent successfully completed probation. Only 18 percent were resentenced to a British Columbia institution within a six-year follow-up period. Sixty-four probation officers within the Canadian provinces served an average caseload of 59 persons.

While most provinces place adult probation services within their Attorney General's Department, four now associate this function within the welfare department and a few others place it in the department

---

[64] *Ibid.*, pp. 210–11.
[65] *Ibid.*, pp. 211–12.
[66] McGrath, *op. cit.*, p. 231.

of social welfare and rehabilitation. Each, however, provides presentence service for its appropriate courts.[67]

Improvement of Canadian probation services depends upon the introduction of new procedures. Uniformity of legislation and standards must be secured. Provisions must be made for the legal transfer of cases between provinces under court supervision. Not only must probation officers be better trained and standards of supervision elevated but public relations and community involvement must also improve as well. In addition, the federal government must provide more research funds for the evaluation of penal effectiveness and the advancement of experimentation in the field. Caseloads for probation officers must be reduced and controlled and an imaginative approach to probation encouraged.[68]

Probation and the mentally ill

Probation always involves some degree of risk. In cases of apparent mental illness, the risk may be accentuated. In a follow-up study of probation of those having undergone mental treatment, Max Grünhut discovered that 255 of 369 probationers for whom full medical information was available were discharged either in a substantially or partially improved condition. Two thirds of the probationers receiving medical treatment completed their period of probation satisfactorily. An additional 42 of the 98 probationers who received an unfavorable medical prognosis also terminated their period of probation satisfactorily.[69] Within one year after the termination of probation, 32 percent of the men and 15 percent of the women were reconvicted. Nearly 50 percent of the young males between 17 and 21 recidivated. While low reconviction rates were common among persons convicted of offenses against the person, high reconviction rates were especially evident among those involved in acquisitive crimes. Psychopaths had high reconviction rates; patients suffering from anxiety, depression, or a physiologically based mental disorder had a lower reconviction rate. Nevertheless, 57 of the 128 probationers who were discharged from medical treatment with an unfavorable prognosis recorded no further convictions during the year period under study. Summarizing his findings, Max Grünhut reported:

Out of 100 offenders who received mental treatment in accordance with the requirement of a probation order, 70 are discharged with favourable prognosis. Out of the 70, 56 are not reconvicted within a period of one

---

[67] *Ibid.*, pp. 232–39.
[68] *Ibid.*, pp. 242–43.
[69] Max Grünhut, *Probation and Mental Treatment* (London: Tavistock Publications, 1963), p. 44.

year after the termination of their probation order. A further 13 out of the 30 who did not have a favourable medical prognosis also remain free from reconviction.[70]

In essence, Grünhut discovered in his study of 636 cases in 1953 that the chances of successful medical treatment are not especially impaired by the conviction of the offender followed by a subsequent court decision of probation on the condition that appropriate treatment be sought for his mental condition. The chances of keeping probationers not visibly benefiting from medical treatment within the law even ran, Grünhut found, as high as 50 percent. Such a high degree of success, he noted, is partially due to the fact that some probationers respond well to the personality of the doctor while others find greater compatibility with their probation officer. Because probation furnished a highly flexible treatment opportunity, its officers are more fully able to respond to individual needs than are institutional staff representatives. However, it is also true, he noted, that the probationer may well find other persons within the community with whom he may identify. He found that the chances for successful treatment tend to be higher if the medical practitioner who served as an expert witness regarding the advisability of his undergoing mental treatment is the same person who provides the treatment of the probationer.[71]

The value of community-based corrections

Because two thirds of the total corrections caseload on any given day is supervised through probation and parole, the development of strong community-based corrections is of utmost importance.[72] The value of these community programs is especially apparent when one compares the 1965 cost of penal institutionalization (approximately $3,600 a year) and community supervision through probation or parole (approximately $330 per year). Then, too, 15 different studies of probation show that between 60 and 90 percent of the probationers within the study samples completed their term without revocation. A California study of 11,638 adults some seven years after they were granted probation during 1956–58, for example, revealed that 72 percent completed probation without revocation.

While interest in the use of probation as a treatment method has increased in felony cases, it has received less attention on the misdemeanor level. The recommended minimum probation caseload is 50 su-

---

[70] *Ibid.*, p. 45.
[71] *Ibid.*, p. 47.
[72] President's Commission, *op. cit.*, p. 165.

pervision cases per month per officer. One third of the 250 counties evaluated in the national corrections survey provided no probation services and depended upon the use of the suspended sentence without supervision, fines, or institutionalization as a misdemeanant treatment method. Of the 212 local jails sampled, 131 (62 percent) reported an absence of misdemeanant parole procedures. Among the 81 which did not, only 8 percent released inmates on parole. Generally, the use of advanced correctional methods for less serious and more receptive misdemeanant offenders, the study concluded, is rare to minimal.[73]

The probation officer

Effective probation programs depend in large measure upon capable probation officers. They must possess maturity, integrity, and ability to form and to sustain wholesome impersonal relationships. They must also have the capacity to accept responsibility, work with aggressive individuals as well as established agencies, and motivate probationers to higher performance levels.[74] And yet, while possessing these characteristics, they must also be able to facilitate the disposition of cases, manage the controls provided by the judicial setting, aid in creating environmental changes, and assist in counseling the released offender.[75] Overall, their responsibilities are many and their rewards often slight.

If the probation officer is involved in new investigations and diagnostic studies, five supervision cases per month should be removed from his minimum load for each new investigation diagnostic study. However, even then a recommended 50-unit load only permits an average of three hours per month of supervision for each case. When this is further qualified by the time spent in court attendance, travel, supervisory services, dictation, and general housekeeping chores, the total time available for child–probation officer discourse is closer to one hour per month, a period not likely to have major impact upon the youth's deficient attitudes and behavior. Because all cases do not share the same sense of urgency, many receive even less time than the projected minimum. The fact that the median supervision load of most probation officers falls between 71 and 80 cases, not including the additional responsibilities necessitated in investigatory and diagnostic work, only further illustrates the obvious

---

[73] Ibid., p. 166. Refer to Gloria Cunningham, "Supervision of the Female Offender," Federal Probation, Vol. 27 (December, 1963), pp. 12–16.

[74] Newman, op. cit., pp. 77–80. Also see R. Dimants, M. Taber and D. E. Van-Laningham, "How Adult Probation Officers View Their Job Responsibilities," Crime and Delinquency, Vol. 12 (April, 1966), p. 97.

[75] Jane K. Ives, "The Essential Task of the Probation-Parole Officer," Federal Probation, Vol. 25 (March, 1962), p. 338.

shortcomings of the juvenile probation system. Because one half of the probation officer's time is normally spent on investigations and social studies, his supervision of probationers generally tends to suffer.[76]

Probation officers with 0 to 50 cases are responsible for nearly 12 percent of all juvenile cases, less than 1 percent of all misdemeanant cases, and slightly more than 3 percent of all felony cases in 1965. At the other extreme, officers with over 100 cases are responsible for nearly 11 percent of all juvenile, more than 76 percent of all misdemeanant, and slightly more than 67 percent of all felony cases.[77] When compared with recommended maximum caseload of 50 offenders per officer, the inadequacy of current probation and parole services becomes quickly apparent. Consequently, probation officers commonly tend to emphasize the mechanics of juvenile probation rather than the interactional potential of the probation system. Typically, probation and parole supervision consists of a 10- or 15-minute interview once or twice a month during which the officer questions and charges his advisee, refers him to an appropriate agency for employment or health care, and takes notes for a report.[78]

One study of juvenile probation services during 1966 revealed that 223,800 children were undergoing probation supervision for periods ranging from 3 to 36 months at an estimated cost of $75,916,000 per year. Although nearly 11 percent of all children on probation during the period of the survey were covered in caseloads of over 100, only two tenths of 2 percent participated in caseloads of fewer than 20 supervised cases. More than half of the probation officer's time was commonly consumed in the completion of case studies for use by the juvenile court judge.[79]

In 1965, only 1,944 officers of the needed 15,000 for a 50 to 1 coverage were employed in misdemeanant probation. By 1975, the demand is expected to be closer to 22,000. On the juvenile and felony level the situation is somewhat better but still below recommended ratios. While 7,706 probation and parole officers were employed in 1965, the estimated need approximated 13,800. The number of probation personnel necessary to complete the community treatment of juveniles adequately is estimated to be 23,000 by 1975. While one third the needed number of probation and parole officers serving adult felons were employed in 1965, an estimated 23,000 will also be needed by 1975. However, the lack of funds and trained personnel restrict the arrival at this goal.

---

[76] The President's Commission on Law Enforcement and Administration of Justice, *Task Force Report: Corrections* (Washington, D.C.: U.S. Government Printing Office, 1967), pp. 130–41.

[77] President's Commission, *The Challenge,* pp. 168–69.

[78] *Ibid.,* pp. 164–67.

[79] Winslow, *op. cit.,* p. 124.

Volunteers in probation work

In some countries, the shortage of probation officers has been over-come through the use of volunteers. The Danish Welfare Society, for example, provides 800 select volunteers for probation and parole services throughout that nation. While the majority of volunteers carry from 1 to 5 cases, a few individuals carry from between 20 to 30 cases each. Although approximately three fourths of the cases are assigned to volunteers, regular professional workers supervise the more difficult ones. Volunteers in this program are required to provide professional staff members with regular case progress reports and are paid a fee of about $3 per month for each case supervised.

The use of volunteers in probation and parole services has also been officially recognized in Sweden. Although staff members complete the presentence investigation for the court, a volunteer may assume super-vision of the case if the defendant is placed on probation. Given a nominal amount to cover annual expenses, the sympathetic volunteers tend to work most effectively in small towns and rural areas where the impersonality and diversity of the large city do not defeat the interest in, or effectiveness of, their services.[80]

The Child Welfare Department of Western Australia in Perth similarly employs volunteers to assist in the supervision of delinquents on probation. Systematically recruited, screened, and trained, the probation volunteers must have completed a high school education; preferably be married, although unmarried persons over 28 are accepted; be in good health; show employment stability; have a hobby interest; and not be involved in too many activities. Attending training sessions twice a week during a six-month period, the volunteers also visit training schools and assist staff members in handling groups of boys or girls on Saturday afternoons. Carrying a maximum of three cases, the 60 or more volunteers remain under the supervision of a staff member who allocates, reviews, and discusses cases with his volunteer assistants. For their services each volunteer receives approximately $45 annually to cover out-of-pocket expenses.

In Japan, approximately 47,000 volunteers participate in adult probation work under the formal sponsorship of the regional probation–parole supervision officers, who originally screen volunteers for this work. Formally appointed by the Minister of Justice for a two-year term upon a positive evaluation of their financial stability, motivation, and reputation in the community, these volunteers receive no salary but are com-

---

[80] Paul W. Keve, *Imaginative Programming in Probation and Parole* (Minneapolis: University of Minnesota Press, 1967), pp. 270–71.

pensated for any accident occurring in the discharge of their duties and receive reimbursement for expenses. Operating on the principle that probation is a treatment method designed to rehabilitate an offender in his community, the Japanese believe that the use of volunteers enhances the understanding and the cooperation of the community in the treatment process.[81] Japanese volunteer services for juveniles are coordinated through the 730 Women's Rehabilitation Aid Associations, which supplement state services by operating shelters, by supplying medical care, money or clothing, or by arranging employment for individual youths.[82]

Volunteer services are also utilized in the United States. One of the more interesting programs has been operationalized within the Royal Oak Municipal Court (Michigan) which places one probationer with each of nearly 75 persons who participate in its probation assistance program. Operating as friends rather than as authoritarian probation officers, the volunteers represent acceptance, understanding, affection, and concern. Meeting monthly with a counselor who represents the court, each volunteer provides his contact with a brief written report regarding his relations with the probationer. In most instances, volunteers do not assume responsibility for persons over 21 years of age, those who appear emotionally disturbed, or those who are alcoholics or sex offenders. An initial evaluation of the Royal Oaks Volunteer Program suggests that volunteer services may be adequate as a temporary expedient but are inadequate as a permanent arrangement. Although the volunteer may open up the potential of a state-funded municipal court probation service, the failure to attract some leadership early in the program's development may undermine its potential.[83]

In California, local businessmen are often used to aid probationers in finding employment. Serving as interviewers who represent the community, they offer the probationer a sense of belonging and a feeling that someone cares for them as persons.[84] Other attempts to engage parolees and probationers in interaction with professionals within the community have also shown a degree of success at Toronto and at Camp Pugsley in Michigan.[85] The Connecticut Prison Association even now maintains a statewide volunteer program which provides sponsors within the adult correctional system. Serving as a friend of the client, the sponsor, assigned to the inmate six months or more before his release on parole, is expected to visit his parolee once or twice a month. Working

[81] *Ibid.*, pp. 268–70.
[82] *The Present State of Juvenile Delinquency and Counter-Measures in Japan* (Tokyo: Ministry of Justice, 1965), pp. 25–26.
[83] Keve, *op. cit.*, pp. 260–64.
[84] David P. Macpherson, "Community Action for Employment of Probationers," *Crime and Delinquency*, Vol. 10 (January, 1964), p. 41.
[85] Keve, *op. cit.*, pp. 256–59.

under the supervision of a social worker, the sponsor attempts to lessen the inmate's sense of captivity in prison and isolation upon his return to the community.[86]

Recommendations for probation system modification

In 1967, in order to overcome limitations within the probation system, the President's Commission on Law Enforcement and Administration of Justice made the following suggestions: that parole and probation services be made available to all juveniles, adult misdemeanants, and felons able to benefit from their existence regardless of jurisdiction; that every state provide released offenders not formally paroled with adequate supervision until it is deemed unnecessary; that all jurisdictions examine their need for probation and parole officers, and provide an average ratio of 35 rather than 50 offenders per officer; that probation and parole services integrate the work of volunteers and some professional aids in demonstration projects into regular programs; that officials develop new methods and skills to assist in integrating offenders into community institutions; that substantial service-purchase funds be made available to probation and parole agencies for use in meeting important needs of individual offenders which can not otherwise be met; and that caseloads be varied in relationship to the type and intensity of treatment necessary for the offender.[87]

Because probation services depend upon adequate staffing, the Commission also recommended increases in the salary structure in order to maintain current and recruit added personnel. Common salaries of the chief probation officer at the time of the Commission report ranged from less than $2,400 to more than $18,000 with the median of $8,100 to $9,000; staff supervisor from less than $3,000 to approximately $11,000 with a median of $7,000 to $8,000; and probation officer from under $1,500 to $11,000 with a median of $5,100 to $6,000. Such a salary structure, the Commission maintained, makes it largely impossible for probation departments to compete for the services of persons with minimum let alone preferred qualifications.[88]

---

[86] *Ibid.*, pp. 266–67.

[87] President's Commission, *The Challenge*, pp. 167–71. Examine Luther Youngdahl, "Reports on Developments in the Federal Probation System," *Federal Rules Decisions*, Vol. 28 (December, 1964), p. 79; Committee on the Administration of the Federal Probation System, "Chief Justice Appoints Committee on Federal Probation System," *Federal Probation*, Vol. 27 (June, 1963), pp. 3–5; Olney Warren III, "The Federal Probation System in 1963; Where We Stand," *Federal Probation*, Vol. 27 (September, 1963), pp. 3–8; and Luther W. Youngdahl, "Developments in the Federal Probation System," *Federal Probation*, Vol. 28 (September, 1964), pp. 3–9.

[88] Winslow, *op. cit.*, p. 193.

Recommended minimum standards for probation officers, not yet fully realized, include a bachelor's degree in the social sciences, and one year of graduate study in social work or a related science, or one year of paid, fulltime experience under professional supervision in a recognized agency. In addition, on-the-job training in the essentials of probation, diagnosis, and treatment is normally assumed. However, the recommended qualifications are far from realization. While 74 percent of the departments responding to a survey of probation officers indicated that the minimum standard of a bachelor's degree is assumed, 22 percent reported staff qualifications below the recommended minimum educational standard, although 4 percent require a master's degree in social work or one of the allied social sciences. Most data suggest that probation officers and chief probation officers generally lack professional training in diagnosis and treatment, a finding which suggests the need for in-service training or other staff developmental programs. However, only 48 percent of the departments surveyed made provision for such training.[89]

The probation officer as an institutional representative

Regardless of the training he receives, the probation officer eventually becomes an operative of the juvenile or criminal court system. The 60 probation officers and additional psychiatrists and clinical psychologists operating in Metropolitan Court (New York), Abraham S. Blumberg found, eventually had to accept the reality that their work was highly routinized and represented a lesser professional opportunity than they had anticipated at the time of employment. Rationalizing on the basis of their "emotional maturity and adult responsibility," they had to compromise their professional capabilities with organizational demands.[90] Sixteen probation officers (25 percent) had graduated from schools of social work, and the rest had completed graduate work in sociology, psychology, law, business administration, education, and nursing. Most were agency transients, drifting from one low-paying private agency job to another before settling in Metropolitan Court. Attracted by the money and security which the court system offered, the greater number of graduate social workers, Blumberg found, had already become disenchanted with the professional and intellectual aspects of the social work. Because they quickly learned that the status of the worker within the probation organization was related to his willingness to accept organization goals, they willingly rationalized their ideals.

---

[89] *Ibid.*, p. 189.

[90] Abraham S. Blumberg, *Criminal Justice* (Chicago: Quadrangle Books, Inc., 1967), p. 154.

Probation personnel turnover in Metropolitan Court, however, remained low, probably due to the favorable salary structure and the lack of promotional possibilities in probation work. Although once dominated by Irish-Catholics and Jews, the probation staff, Blumberg found, now includes Negroes and Puerto Ricans, who come from the lower ranks of civil service mobility. Negroes and Puerto Ricans, Blumberg reported, accounted for one fourth of the probation staff of Metropolitan Court; the remaining staff was evenly apportioned among the Jews and Irish and Italian Catholics. Most probation recruits came from the lower and lower-middle classes and viewed their employment as an upward step on the status ladder. While serving as a "professional," the probation worker evidenced a limited "service ideal," which took the form of a primary allegiance to the organization rather than to the client.

Impossible caseload conditions often made probation and supervision services of Metropolitan Court commonplace and of dubious quality. Since the emphasis of the court was upon the negative aspects of the delinquent's or offender's career, positive values and virtues, Blumberg found, were rarely emphasized. As a consequence, probation personnel often projected their own hostilities and values into the presentence reports which were eventually used to determine the actual case disposition. As "occupational voyeurists," probation practitioners, Blumberg argued on the basis of his findings, intrude upon the lives of others and vicariously experience offender life-styles which they are unable to imitate in their pedestrian civil servant lives.[91] Ultimately, the tendency of the probation department to serve as the agent of the court rather than the client undermines the true nature of the adversary system in criminal justice. Therefore, any extension of psychiatric or probation services, Blumberg concluded, will only reinforce the already organizationally controlled system and make a real adversary system of justice even more improbable.[92] The independence and impartiality of the probation department is finally compromised by the organization motives and purposes of the court which supervises its activities and operations.

In order to overcome many of these difficulties, the National Council on Crime and Delinquency recommends the operationalizing of the following principles:

1. Probation officers should be free from improper control, political or otherwise.
2. Enough officers should be provided to carry the load with not more than 50 cases per officer in order to insure adequate guidance and supervision.

---

[91] *Ibid.*, p. 155.
[92] *Ibid.*, p. 167.

3. Adequate salaries should be paid to attract and keep properly trained probation officers.
4. Officers should be developed and trained through continuing education.
5. Judges should be encouraged to use probation where it is indicated.
6. Specialized services, whether medical, psychological, psychiatric, or through foster homes, should be made available.
7. Administrative policies should encourage full utilization of other community services.
8. Statutory provisions should permit full use of probation without arbitrary limitation as to eligibility and length of probation.
9. Comprehensive diagnostic presentence investigation, including clinical findings when necessary, should be made a fundamental part of the sentencing process regardless of anticipated disposition.
10. A favorable judicial and public climate should be created which encourages the highest potential of helpful service.[93]

Only under such conditions, the Council noted, can the potential value of probation be fully realized.

EXECUTIVE CLEMENCY AND CIVIL RIGHTS

Although probation permits the court to avoid sentencing the offender to prison or other institution, other provisions are included within the system of sentencing for correcting abuses of court powers and guaranteeing the correct disposition of offenders once imprisoned. Methods available include the use of the full pardon, a commutation of sentence to imprisonment for life or a term of years, or a reprieve or stay of execution. Each is an aspect of "executive clemency."

In England, the power to pardon offenders rested historically with the Crown; however, in the United States this authority is vested with the people, who delegate it in turn to the executive branch of the government, usually to the person of the President or the governors of the various states. A *full pardon* is rarely granted and usually only if the convicted person is truly innocent. Pardons excuse the offender of his conviction and restore his formal civil rights. When pardon is applied to a group of persons, it is termed *amnesty. Commutation,* the substitution of a lighter sentence for a heavier, lessens the length of punishment and permits earlier parole consideration. Commutations are often granted

---

[93] Mark S. Richmond, *Prison Profiles* (New York: Oceana Publications, Inc., 1965), p. 136. Consult Edward M. Taylor and Alexander M. McEachern, "Needs and Direction in Probation Training," *Federal Probation,* Vol. 30 (March, 1966), pp. 18–24; Eugene H. Czajkoski, "The Need for Philosophical Direction in Probation and Parole," *Federal Probation,* Vol. 27 (June, 1967), pp. 10–15.

in order to fulfill prosecutor promises of lighter punishment or of personal immunity in return for turning states' evidence or becoming a state witness. The *reprieve* or *stay of execution* may be used to postpone the execution of a death sentence; it does not cause the prisoner's release from custody but merely postpones the actual execution sentence. However, the reprieve or stay does permit the convicted offender more time in which to gather additional information necessary to substantiate his appeal for commutation or full pardon.[94]

In many instances, the use of clemency procedures is encouraged by the nature and content of the law. For example, until the enactment of the Narcotics Control Act in 1956, the federal courts were free to pass sentences of fines, probation, or institutional commitment upon narcotic offenders as the case required. Nearly all committed prisoners until that date were automatically eligible for parole after having served one third of the sentences.[95] However, the passage of the act, an example of a harshly punitive law, prohibited probation or parole for most individuals convicted of narcotics or marihuana violations and provided mandatory minimum penalties for such crimes. Under its provisions, relatively minor offenders may receive terms of 40, 50, 60, or 80 years. In one instance, a 19-year-old feebleminded youth, an epileptic addicted after an extended period of drug administration during hospitalization, was sentenced to life.[96] In order to overcome the excessive harshness of this Narcotics Control Act, the Kennedy and Johnson administrations eventually applied their clemency powers in a more creative manner.

One reason for the continuing interest in executive clemency is the fact that the civil rights of prisoners are commonly restricted upon conviction through civil-death statutes, other laws establishing the suspension or permanent elimination of specific rights, or the decisions of commissions or boards legally empowered to withdraw certain rights. Seventeen states permit the civil death of offenders upon sentence to life imprisonment or death. Under these statutes, such persons automatically lose their right to vote, hold office, testify, or act as jurors. In nine states and in one other not covered by civil-death procedures, many civil rights may also be suspended for an offense short of life imprisonment or death. Thirty-five states, for example, provide for the permanent deprivation of the right to vote. The majority of states do not allow the convicted felon to run for public office or to occupy positions of trust. A few states also disqualify him from jury duty.

Sentence to life imprisonment may automatically terminate a civil marriage, and conviction of felony together with imprisonment is

---

[94] Newman, *op. cit.*, pp. 43–49. Also see "Legal Services for Prison Inmates," *Wayne State Law Review*, Vol. 1967 (Spring, 1967), p. 514.

[95] *Ibid.*, p. 192.

[96] Alexander, *op. cit.*, p. 191.

grounds in 36 states for divorce. Forty-four states allow the offender's spouse to divorce her husband on the grounds of felony or imprisonment.[97] In a few jurisdictions, the felon's children can be placed for adoption without his consent. Additionally, individuals making their livelihood as accountants, barbers, civil engineers, detectives, automobile operators, embalmers, hairdressers, junk dealers, real estate brokers, liquor store owners, pawnbrokers, pharmacists, midwives, naturopaths, nurses, veterinarians, chiropodists, chiropractors, dentists, physicians, surgeons, or lawyers may be deprived of their occupations upon conviction of certain infamous crimes by a commission or board which certifies or licenses such occupations. Although the released offender may appeal any exclusionary decision, the judgment is essentially a specialized administrative consideration.[98] Under certain circumstances some of these rights may be regained, depending upon the requirements of the legal jurisdiction which removed them in the first place, upon discharge from imprisonment, upon completion of parole, upon issuance of an executive pardon, or upon the fulfillment of some special action concerning certification provided in law.

The increased use of clemency procedures in recent years provides new incentive goals for convicted offenders.[99] However, Charles L. Newman suggests that pardons may only be proper in the following situations:

1. Political appeasement in emergencies wherein pardon may be necessary to pacify a revolution-torn country or to unite a country for war;
2. Calm second judgment after a period of war hysteria, during which persons were given very severe sentences for political offenses later realized to have been very minor or upon evidence later felt to be insufficient;
3. Similarly, changed public opinion after a period of severe penalties against certain conduct which is later looked upon as much less criminal or as no crime all. Prohibition is a recent example. The present severity against kidnappers may give rise to cases which future judgment may recommend for clemencies;
4. Cases "where punishment would do more harm than good," to quote Bentham, as in certain cases of sedition, conspiracy, or acts of public disorder;
5. Technical violations leading to hard results. We can mention at least one example—where the legal "principal" in a crime may be only a comparatively innocent hireling, while the brains of the plot is legally guilty only as an accessory;
6. Cases where pardon is necessary to uphold the good faith of the state as where a criminal has been promised immunity for turning states' evidence;

---

[97] Morris Ploscowe, *The Truth About Divorce* (New York: Hawthorne Books, Inc. 1955), pp. 268–93.

[98] Newman, *op. cit.,* pp. 28–30.

[99] Weston and Wells, *op. cit.,* p. 228.

7. Cases of later proved innocence or of mitigating circumstances. Although we have recommended liberalizing judicial procedures so that most of these cases could be handled by proceedings to reverse the conviction, probably some restrictions will necessarily be retained upon the right to such judicial review, and cases may still arise in which such review is impossible, though innocence is clearly probable; and

8. Applications for reprieve or commutation, especially in death sentences. Here, too, liberalization of judicial procedure should permit reprieves to be granted by the courts. But for while there is somewhat less logical reason for retaining this power in the executive than can be found from most of the examples listed above, this last recourse, to the Governor in these cases is a benevolent power, which we shall probably want to retain and it will no doubt continue to be a major part of the pardoning power.[100]

---

[100] Newman, *op. cit.*, pp. 53–54.

Chapter 22

SYSTEMS OF INSTITUTIONALIZATION OF JUVENILES

The system of juvenile corrections, as distinguished from the system for adults, normally includes the juvenile court, juvenile probation services, and after-care services for those released from a training facility. Children coming before the American juvenile court usually (a) are those who have been neglected or are in need of parental protection, or (b) are juveniles who have participated in some form of unacceptable behavior peculiar to children or have committed offenses which would be punished by fine or imprisonment if committed by an adult.[1] In practical terms, the conduct of juveniles coming before the juvenile court, according to William H. Sheridan, may be classified into two basic categories: (1) those who have committed acts which would be crimes if committed by adults; and (2) those who have not committed such offenses. Approximately 26 percent of all cases coming before the juvenile court in the United States involve children who have broken no law but who are simply designated as "beyond control," "ungovernable," "incorrigible," "runaway," "minors in need of supervision," or "persons in need of supervision."[2] Others have been detained for violations

---

[1] Donald Sinclair, "Training-Schools in Canada," in William T. McGrath (ed.), *Crime and Its Treatment in Canada* (New York: St. Martin's Press, Inc., 1965), p. 245; and W. J. Chambliss and J. T. Lell, "Legal Process in the Community Setting," *Crime and Delinquency*, Vol. 12 (October, 1966), p. 310.

[2] William H. Sheridan, "Juveniles Who Commit Non-Criminal Acts: Why Treat Them in the Correctional System?" *Federal Probation*, Vol. 31 (March, 1967), p. 27. Also see Sydney Smith, "Delinquency and the Panacea of Punishment," *Federal Probation*, Vol. 29 (September, 1965), pp. 18–23; W. M. Headwell, "Lawyer

of specific ordinances applicable only to children, such as breaking the curfew, truancy, and use of alcohol or tobacco.

Nearly 686,000 cases of delinquency, 150,000 of dependency and neglect, and 42,000 traffic cases were referred to the juvenile courts in the United States in 1964.[3] At a time when 20,377 persons were housed in federal prisons, 201,220 in state prisons, and 141,303 in local jails and workhouses, an additional 62,773 juveniles were institutionalized in 1965 in public training schools (43,636), local juvenile institutions (6,024), and detention homes (13,113).[4] An examination of 10 studies of state and local detention programs by the Children's Bureau disclosed that 48 percent of the 9,500 children in these samples had not committed adult criminal acts. Of the 1,300 children in the study group in jail pending hearings, approximately 40 percent could be classified within the noncriminal group; 50 percent of the children in the detention homes also fell into this category.[5]

Such data, necessarily raise the question whether juveniles who commit noncriminal acts should be treated in a correctional system. The answer, William H. Sheridan suggests, is to be found in the application of new remedies, including (1) the development of a greater number of intervening services between the complainant and the court in order to reduce the need for court intervention, (2) a better intake system overseen by a responsible individual in a smaller court (or a separate unit in a larger court), and (3) greater restrictions upon the placements available to the juvenile judge in order to discourage his requests for transfer of juveniles to state institutions. Juveniles who do not commit criminal acts should be not treated in correctional institutions; minor

---

in Juvenile Court Dispositional Proceedings," *Juvenile Court Judges Journal,* Vol. 16 (Fall, 1965), p. 109.

[3] Children's Bureau, *Juvenile Court Statistics—1964* (Washington, D.C.: U.S. Department of Health, Education, and Welfare, 1965), p. 106. Note R. B. Eaton, "Detention Facilities in Non-Metropolitan Counties," *Juvenile Court Judges Journal,* Vol. 17 (Spring, 1966), p. 9; "Juvenile Detention," *Crime and Delinquency,* Vol. 13 (January, 1967), p. 11; and Hugh D. Reed, *The Detention of Children in Illinois* (New York: National Probation and Parole Association, 1952).

[4] The President's Commission, on Law Enforcement and the Administration of Justice, *The Challenge of Crime in a Free Society* (Washington, D.C.: U.S. Government Printing Office, 1967), p. 172. Also refer to George M. Lott, "The Juvenile Detention Home," *Federal Probation,* Vol. 6 (January–March, 1942), pp. 35–39; Joe W. Hart, "The Use of the 'Gossip Group' in a Juvenile Home Setting," *Federal Probation,* Vol. 28 (December, 1964), pp. 57–59; William P. Dorney, "The Educational Program as a Part of a Detention Service," *Federal Probation,* Vol. 28 (December, 1964), pp. 55–57; Ralph C. Norris, "The School in the Detention Home Should Be a Part of the Public School System," *Federal Probation,* Vol. 29 (June, 1965), pp. 17–21; and Kenneth A. Griffiths, "Program Is the Essence of Juvenile Detention," *Federal Probation,* Vol. 28 (June, 1964), pp. 31–34.

[5] Sheridan, *op. cit.,* p. 27. Also see American Law Institute, *The Problem of Sentencing* (Philadelphia: American Law Institute, 1962); *Model Sentencing Act* (New York: National Council on Crime and Delinquency, 1963); and Clyde B. Vedder, *Juvenile Offenders* (Springfield, Ill.: Charles C. Thomas, Publisher, 1963).

violators, Sheridan argues, should not be punished by a "rehabilitation" disposition to a juvenile institution.[6] Not only is such an approach injurious to treatment but the projected increase in the number of juveniles undergoing future correction makes such a solution impractical (see Figure 22–1).

FIGURE 22–1
Average daily population in corrections

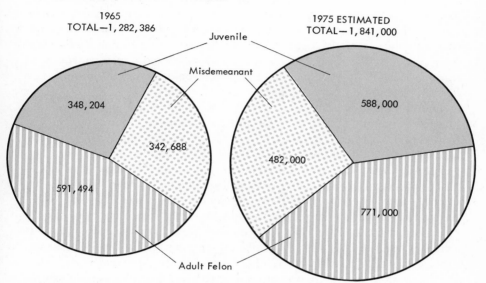

Source: The President's Commission on Law Enforcement and the Administration of Justice, *Task Force Report: Corrections* (Washington, D.C.: U.S. Government Printing Office, 1967), p. 7.

TREATMENT OF THE JUVENILE OFFENDER

The modern training school had its forerunner in the Lyman School for Boys, opened in 1846 at Westboro, Massachusetts. It was followed by the New York State Agricultural and Industrial School in 1849 and the Maine Boys Training Center in 1853. Each sought to prepare the juvenile for his eventual return to community living. Indiana, Maryland, Nevada, New Hampshire, New Jersey, Ohio, and Vermont later developed training schools, and by 1900, similar institutions had been created in 36 states. Alaska, the 50th state, only completed its facility in 1960.

Since their creation, most institutions for juveniles have sought to

---

[6] *Ibid.*, pp. 28–30. Consult Sherwood Norman, *Shelter Care of Children for Court and Community* (New York: National Council on Crime and Delinquency, 1963); and Richard Allaman, "Managing Misbehavior at the Detention Home," *Federal Probation*, Vol. 17 (March, 1953), pp. 27–32.

teach the skills necessary for future usefulness and to provide the juvenile with a normative system which enables him to "follow the right." In recent years, these goals have been expanded through the recognition that nearly one half of those undergoing treatment in the juvenile training facility will be reincarcerated and that treatment can produce lasting change only if the personal reasons behind the delinquent act are understood. Recognizing somewhat belatedly that what may be deviant to the larger society may be thoroughly normative for the juvenile at the moment of his delinquency, treatment personnel have attempted to pass beyond the mere "instillation" of values within delinquents and to respond to the emotional need of the youth. Assuming that juvenile conduct can only be changed if the juvenile himself seeks change, the new training school approaches emphasize personal reevaluation and behavior reorientation.[7]

Despite the emphasis upon personality change, training schools for juveniles, like their adult counterparts, often emphasize custody rather than actual treatment of the individual. Nevertheless, the training school maintains the multiple responsibilities of caring for troublesome or dangerous children, educating the youth in its custody, developing rehabilitation programs, resocializing youths for effective return to the community, and creating recreational or social programs designed to fill the voids of institutionalization. Frequently, the goals of custody, education, recreation, and treatment are incompatible.[8] However, the training school is supposed to offer the child under treatment a specialized program designed to ameliorate his hardened or unstable condition. While the institution strives to prepare the youth for his eventual return to the community, its ultimate success depends upon the quality and character of the aftercare services provided upon his return.

David Street, Robert D. Vinter, and Charles Perrow find that juvenile correctional institutions are "people-changing" organizations. While they actively seek the resocialization of the offender, they do so within the conditions of custody. Inevitably, therefore, they must seek the rehabilitation of the offender within a time-limited and an internally oriented setting. Staffed by trained professionals and traditional functionaries,

---

[7] Robert W. Winslow, *Juvenile Delinquency in a Free Society* (Belmont, Calif.: Dickenson Publishing Company, Inc., 1968), p. 199. See "Juvenile Institutions," *Crime and Delinquency*, Vol. 13 (January, 1967), p. 73; M. A. Zald and David Street, "Custody and Treatment in Juvenile Institutions," *Crime and Delinquency*, Vol. 10 (July, 1964), p. 249; and A. G. Novick, "Institutional Organization for Treatment," *Crime and Delinquency*, Vol. 10 (July, 1964), p. 257.

[8] Theodore N. Ferdinand, "Some Inherent Limitations in Rehabilitating Juvenile Delinquents in Training Schools," *Federal Probation*, Vol. 31 (December, 1967), pp. 30–34. Consult John B. Costello, "Institutions for Juvenile Delinquents," *Annals*, Vol. 261 (January, 1949), pp. 166–78; Bertram M. Beck, *Youth Within Walls* (New York: Community Service Society, 1950).

penal institutions for juveniles frequently strive to reach the multiple goals of confinement (custody) and of change (rehabilitation) in rather ambiguous fashion.[9]

Generalizing from their study of six juvenile correctional organizations, Street, Vinter, and Perrow identify three major organizational models within the custody-treatment continuum:

1. *Obedience/conformity.* Habits, respect for authority, and training are emphasized. The technique is *conditioning.* Obedience/conformity maintains undifferentiated views of its inmates, emphasizes immediate accommodations to external controls, and utilizes high levels of staff domination with negative sanctions. It is the most custodial type of juvenile institution presently found in the United States, for humanitarian pressures have eliminated the incarceration-deprivation institution as a viable empirical type.
2. *Reeducation/development.* Inmates are to be *changed through training.* Changes in attitudes and values, acquisition of skills, the development of personal resources, and new social behavior are sought. Compared to the obedience/conformity type, this type provides more gratifications and maintains closer staff-inmate relations.
3. *Treatment.* The treatment institution focuses on the psychological reconstitution of the individual. It seeks more thoroughgoing personality change than the other types. To this end it emphasizes gratifications and varied activities, with punishments relatively few and seldom severe. In the individual treatment-variant considerable stress is placed on self-insight and two-person psychotherapeutic practices. In the milieu treatment-variant attention is paid to both individual and social controls, the aim being not only to help the inmate resolve his personal problems within the institution but also to prepare him for community living.[10]

The study of two institutions in each of these three categories led the researchers to conclude that the implementation of the treatment goal "remains elusive."[11]

---

[9] David Street, Robert D. Vinter, and Charles Perrow, *Organization For Treatment* (New York: Free Press, 1966), pp. 1–15. Examine David Fogel, "Institutional Strategies in Dealing with Youthful Offenders," *Federal Probation,* Vol. 31 (July, 1967), pp. 41–47; Herschel Alt, "The Training School and Residential Treatment," *Federal Probation,* Vol. 16 (March, 1952), pp. 32–35; and Leighton W. Dudley, "New Horizons for the Institutional Treatment of Youth Offenders," *Federal Probation,* Vol. 30 (June, 1966), pp. 50–53.

[10] *Ibid.,* p. 21. Refer to Frank R. Scarpitti and Richard M. Stephanson, "The Use of the Small Group in the Rehabilitation of Delinquents," *Federal Probation,* Vol. 30 (September, 1966), pp. 45–50.

[11] *Ibid.,* p. 279. See Esther P. Rothman, "Teaching for a Positive Concept of Authority in a School for Emotionally Disturbed Girls," *Federal Probation,* Vol. 28 (March, 1964), pp. 36–39; Carle F. O'Neil and David Gregory, "The Metamorphosis of a Training School," *Federal Probation,* Vol. 28 (June, 1964), pp. 34–40; and A. G. Novick, "Institutional Diversification and Continuity of Service for Committed Juveniles," *Federal Probation,* Vol. 28 (March, 1964), pp. 40–47.

Three institutions failed to implement treatment to any degree; two, on the other hand, were overwhelmingly treatment oriented. If treatment is to become a reality, staff members and units, Street, Vinter, and Perrow concluded, must be given sufficient power over organizational operations. However, those implementing the treatment ideal must also recognize that special external efforts must be exerted to neutralize community hostility and to gain support from organizations of parents or other agencies. Because treatment programs require a high degree of organizational flexibility, disruption in routine, ambiguities in criteria for staff performance, and staff, inmate, and personnel conflicts must be approached with tolerance. Although meaningful change depends upon capable executive leadership, leadership success in fulfilling treatment goals is still subject to the limits imposed by the institution.[12] While the obedience/conformity institutions produce negative results, the re-education/development institutions, more conventional and open in their program, reveal mixed but generally more positive successes. "The consequences for the inmates of the treatment institutions," Street, Vinter, and Perrow conclude, "appear to be even more positive with greater development of personal and social controls and the acquisition of some skills in problem-solving and self-understanding."[13] Whether these skills will continue without reinforcement after release, however, is another question.

Most states have a limited program of juvenile institutional diversity. While 8 states have one facility and 14 states have two serving juveniles, six of the larger jurisdictions have nine or more juvenile institutions. The growing use of small camps and reception centers has changed the former pattern of the dual state boys' and girls' schools which dominated juvenile corrections for many decades. The growth of camp programs has partially been hastened by the lower cost of these operations and the fact that the setting which small camps offer is more conducive to treatment.[14] On the other hand, the overcrowding of juvenile treatment institutions has encouraged the parallel development of diagnostic parole programs in which all juvenile court commitments are referred either directly or after a short period of institutional treatment to a reception center for screening for parole eligibility. Designed to redirect

---

[12] *Ibid.*, pp. 280–81. See Anthony Catalina, "Resolving 'Built-In' Staff Conflicts in a Training School for Boys," *Federal Probation*, Vol. 30 (June, 1966), p. 60; and John B. Leibrock, "The Houseparent and the Delinquent Boy," *Federal Probation*, Vol. 28 (September, 1964), pp. 59–60.

[13] *Ibid.*, p. 282. Also see Eugene J. Mantone, "Walton Village," *Federal Probation*, Vol. 31 (June, 1967), pp. 27–32; and M. E. Switzer, "Treatment in the Community," *Trial*, Vol. 4 (April–May, 1968), p. 11.

[14] Winslow, *op. cit.*, p. 203. Refer to Kenneth S. Carpenter and George H. Weber, "Intake and Orientation Procedures in Institutions for Delinquent Youth," *Federal Probation*, Vol. 30 (March, 1966), p. 37.

juvenile treatment attempts from training schools to short, intensive treatment programs followed by parole in the community, reception center parole and short-term treatment programs have grown immensely in recent years.

Such screening in New York City's Youth House is carried out by special aftercare staff while juveniles await entrance into the state school system. Those selected return to the community and participate in an extensive casework program. In Washington, D.C., juveniles are screened in a central reception center for juvenile offenders, many being assigned immediately to foster homes, halfway houses, or other community based programs.[15] California makes the greatest use of reception center release. Approximately 20 percent of the boys and 35 percent of the girls processed by the California Youth Authority upon a normal 30-day reception center testing period are released to foster home placement or to regular parole.

Youths referred to reception centers commonly stay in these locations between 28 and 45 days. Children are frequently committed to state training institutions for 4 to 24 months; their median stay is for 9 months.[16] Three fourths of the total state institutional systems, housing nine tenths of the institutional population, commonly have an average length of stay between six months and one year.[17] Nearly 42 percent of the 233 probation departments examined in the National Survey of Corrections reported that they commonly use *foster home* placement as an alternative to institutionalization because these homes provide the youth with closer identification with respectable community members, carry less stigma than juvenile institutions, maintain the youth within or near his own community, and are far less costly. Inasmuch as the foster home implies the severing of family ties for a temporary or permanent period, it must be used with discretion.

Many states have developed *group homes* as a middle offering be-

---

[15] *Ibid.,* p. 230. Refer to Arthur W. Witherspoon, "Foster Home Placements for Delinquent Juveniles," *Federal Probation,* Vol. 30 (December, 1966), pp. 48–52; Ruth Gilpin, "Foster Home Care for Delinquent Children," *Annals,* Vol. 261 (January, 1948), pp. 120–27; Helen R. Hagan, "Foster Care for Children," *Social Work Year Book-1954* (New York: National Association of Social Workers, 1954), pp. 225–32; and F. McNeil, "Halfway-House Program for Delinquents," *Crime and Delinquency,* Vol. 13 (October, 1967), p. 107.

[16] *Ibid.,* p. 204. See R. H. Levy, "Reception and Diagnostic Center of the Illinois Youth Commission, *Juvenile Court Judges Journal,* Vol. 18 (Spring, 1967), p. 12; Martin Gula, "Study and Treatment Homes for Troubled Children," *The Child,* Vol. 12 (November, 1947), pp. 66–70; and Juvenile Division, *Philadelphia's Youth Study Center Annual Report* (Philadelphia: Youth Study Center, 1964).

[17] *Ibid.,* p. 204. For another facet, see "Transfer of Juveniles to Adult Correctional Institutions," *Wisconsin Law Review,* Vol. 1966 (Summer, 1966), p. 866; and "Facts and Law of the Inter-Institutional Transfer of Juveniles," *Maine Law Review,* Vol. 20 (1968), p. 93; and R. Mills, "Delinquent Disabled Boys," *Crime and Delinquency,* Vol. 13 (October, 1967), p. 545.

tween the foster home and the juvenile institution. The Minnesota Youth Commission, for example, pays a nominal retaining fee for each licensed bed in seven group homes serving its programs; when a youth is placed in the home operated by independent parties, the amount paid per bed is increased. Similarly, the Wisconsin Division of Corrections utilizes 33 homes for boys or girls. Placing four to eight adolescents in each location, these homes serve the equivalent number of juveniles in one institution at 25 to 33 percent less cost. While this approach is promising, the fact that it allows county probation departments to avoid responsibility for a community-based juvenile treatment program remains a drawback.[18]

Approaches to treatment

Whatever the location of the correctional attempt, a number of approaches to juvenile treatment may be used in juvenile institutional or other treatment programs. The *psychological* and *ego-alien* approaches, for example, emphasize individual treatment within a social environment. The environment is evaluated in terms of its influence upon delinquency rather than its relationship to group membership. Therefore, the focus of treatment is placed upon the restructuring of the individual's personality through the delineation of required roles, the observance of discipline, and a regimentation of the daily institutional program. Largely rejecting the possibility that delinquency may be due to a feeling of self-satisfaction rather than dissatisfaction, the supporters of the psychological treatment approach seek signs that the juvenile has internalized stable response patterns through daily interaction.

The ego-alien approach varies slightly. Franz Alexander and Lewis B. Shapiro, for example, relate delinquency to ego-alien impulses which are frequently represented in aggressive antisocial nature behavior.[19] Delinquency, they presume, is a behavioral disturbance stimulated by unconscious motivational forces which are eventually expressed in the distorted substitute of the delinquent act. Possessing a weak superego, the child is unable to repress and to control his unconscious drives and therefore expresses them in overt delinquency. The youth may be

---

[18] *Ibid.*, pp. 226–27.

[19] Franz Alexander and Lewis B. Shapiro, "Neurosis, Behavior Disorder and Perversions," in Franz Alexander and Helen Ross (eds.), *Dynamic Psychiatry* (Chicago: University of Chicago Press, 1952), p. 132. Refer to F. L. Faust, "Group Counseling with Juveniles," *Crime and Delinquency*, Vol. 11 (October, 1965), p. 349; Marvin Hersko, "Community Therapy in an Institution for Delinquent Girls," *Federal Probation*, Vol. 28 (June, 1964), pp. 41–46; R. C. Sarri and R. D. Vinter, "Group Treatment Strategies in Juvenile Correctional Program," *Crime and Delinquency*, Vol. 11 (October, 1965), p. 326.

successfully treated only if he learns to understand his conscious and unconscious actions.

The *guided group interaction* approach, a form of group counseling, attempts to involve a number of juvenile offenders in frequent but intensive discussions pertaining to motivation and behavior. Emphasizing the evaluation of current experiences and problems, the guided group interaction method strives to develop a treatment-oriented group "culture" in which participants may follow members in the solution of their problems. Presuming the principle that peer recommendations are more likely to be accepted by fellow offenders, the guided group interaction approach permits the common sharing of anxieties and hopes necessary for the eventual resolution of these personal problems. This method emphasizes the individual's participation in seeking a constructive solution to the problems at hand.[20]

Experiments in guided group interaction.   An early experiment in guided group interactions was inaugurated for 20 boys between 16 and 17 at Highfields, New Jersey, in 1950. All participants were assigned directly by the juvenile court as a condition of probation. Juveniles who were mentally retarded or deeply disturbed, or who had been previously committed to a correctional school, were screened from consideration. Working on the assumption that the major impact of juvenile corrections occurs within the first three months of contact, the program provided for group members to work at nearby psychiatric institutions during the day and to participate in group counseling sessions in the evening. On weekends each boy cleaned his residence, received visitors, participated in religious services, and shared free time. Encouraged to confront the problems of his peers and his own person, each youth was given as much responsibility as the staff believed he could manage at the time. Release depended upon his peers' evaluation of his readiness for release, itself a major change in the normal expectation that the juvenile may be released only upon the fulfillment of standards set by his incarcerators.

An examination of the effectiveness of the Highfields experiment for youthful offenders by H. Ashley Weeks indicates that the approach was effective with a large number of the boys sent to the project. In comparison to 47 of every 100 boys from the New Jersey State Reformatory for Males of Annandale, 63 of every 100 Highfields boys were able to stay free of other violations which might lead to reinstitutionalization

---

[20] Stephen Schafer and Richard D. Knudten, *The Problem of Juvenile Delinquency* (New York: Random House, Inc., 1970). Consult W. J. Granier, "Rehabilitation: Theory and Practice," *Juvenile Court Judges Journal*, Vol. 18 (Spring, 1967), p. 16; J. E. Cowden, "Predicting Institutional Adjustment and Recidivism in Delinquent Boys," *Journal of Criminal Law, Criminology, and Police Science*, Vol. 57 (March, 1966), p. 39.

upon the completion of their treatment. This difference,[21] however, was largely due to the higher success rate for Negroes in the Highfields program. Officially on probation at the time that they were included in the Highfields experiment, approximately one fifth of the boys were unable to maintain effective residence. Some ran away, viewed the program as threatening, or worked to disrupt the progress of the stable group. Despite these limitations, the Highfields program, Weeks found, rehabilitated 28 more boys per 100 than the traditional male youth rehabilitation approach. At Highfields, 8 out of every 10 white boys and 7 out of every 10 Negroes were successful.

Although Highfields white boys become more favorable toward obeying the law and less favorable in attitudes toward law enforcement, Annandale white boys showed greater favorableness toward general authority and less toward law enforcement. Highfields Negro boys, on the other hand, revealed a more unfavorable attitude toward parental authority and showed the greatest tendency for change, scoring favorably on five scales and unfavorably in attitudes toward parental authority. While the experience at Highfields and Annandale did not substantially change the primary goals or basic drives of either group, the Annandale group did not seem to recognize and to accept their basic drives or to clarify their primary goals. Among the Highfields males, on the other hand, primary goals were more clearly defined and basic drives more fully accepted. Overall, the Highfields program rehabilitated youth at a high rate of success at less cost over a shorter period of time than at Annandale.[22]

The success of the Highfields project encouraged the development of other similar programs in Essexfields (New Jersey), Pinehills and Provo (Utah), and others in San Francisco and Los Angeles and in Kentucky and New York. The Provo, Essexfields, and San Francisco variations permit each boy to live at home and participate in meaningful community employment, daily group meetings, and rigorous programs. The Provo experiment in its early years provided for the employment of every boy by the city at 50 cents per hour during the summer. After he had completed his assigned task, he participated in guided group interaction sessions until released at 7 P.M. to return home. Assuming that change must be shared by others if it is to be meaningful, the youths defined and sought solutions to problems under the guidance of group members and project staff.[23] Although both staff and offenders

---

[21] H. Ashley Weeks, *Youthful Offenders at Highfields* (Ann Arbor: University of Michigan Press, 1963), pp. 118–19.

[22] *Ibid.*, p. 122. Also see Howard W. Polsky, *Cottage Six: The Social System of Delinquent Boys in Residential Treatment* (New York: Russell Foundation, 1962).

[23] President's Commission, *op. cit.*, p. 171. Also examine James A. Lucas, "Therapeutic Use of Limits in Dealing With Institutionalized Delinquent Boys," *Federal*

were responsible for defining how much responsibility the violator shall assume for his own life, he was forced to solve these problems in the Essexfields and Pinehills programs within his own community in relationship to his family, friends, teachers, and employers. Both projects avoided the artificial characteristics of the normal training school and encouraged juveniles to live at home.[24]

The Parkland project in Louisville (Kentucky), the Girl's Unite for Intensive Daytime Education program, commonly called GUIDE, in Richmond (California), and a second girl's program in San Mateo (California) have posed variations of the guided group interaction approach. In each instance youths involved in these projects meet jointly at a designated center and participate in crafts, educational training, center beautification and development, and individual and group counseling. At Parkland, participants share in morning classes, afternoon work about the Louisville Zoo, and evening dinner and group counseling sessions.[25] Underlying this approach is the belief that work skills can overcome the limitations imposed by deviant tendencies and can assist in the development of self-reliance and institutional efficiency.[26]

The youth authority and treatment of juveniles

California, Texas, Illinois, Massachusetts, and Delaware maintain statewide juvenile correctional authorities. A number of other states have established committees, boards, or commissions to deal with the problems of juvenile offenders. The majority of the states have been reticent to utilize this approach due to the feeling of many judges that the transference of sentencing authority to these boards is a threat to their own sentencing power. Moreover, administrators and personnel in established institutions have been unwilling to modify existing procedures. In addition, many legislators, believing the authority approach to be an experiment, have refused to enact an authority measure without more conclusive information concerning its benefits.

Under the authority approach, juveniles are placed under the supervision of youth authorities through the action of juvenile and superior

---

Probation, Vol. 28 (June, 1964), pp. 46–50; William Crain, "The Chronic 'Mess-Up' and His Changing Character," *Federal Probation*, Vol. 28 (June, 1964), pp. 50–56; and David L. Haarer, "Gifted Delinquents," *Federal Probation*, Vol. 30 (March, 1966), pp. 43–46.

[24] Winslow, *op. cit.*, p. 224.

[25] *Ibid.*, p. 225.

[26] Schafer and Knudten, *op. cit.* See Norman G. Tolman, "Approaching the Institutionalized Female Delinquent Through Group Therapy," *Federal Probation*, Vol. 25 (June, 1961), pp. 34–40; M. M. Crites, "Group Counseling for Probationers and Staff," *Crime and Delinquency*, Vol. 11 (October, 1965), p. 355; and S. Silverstein, "Work Therapy Program for Delinquent Boys," *Crime and Delinquency*, Vol. 11 (July, 1965), p. 256.

courts. Offenders are usually sent first to reception and diagnostic centers where their particular needs are evaluated and treatment programs anticipated. The California Youth Authority program, created in 1941 and closely modeled after the Borstal system in England, permits the authority to accept a limited number of cases, assume responsibility for delinquency prevention, and maintain jurisdiction over juvenile and youthful offenders to the age of 23. In 1961, the California Youth Authority was incorporated into a new adult and youth corrections agency. The Youth Authority Board was subsequently expanded from three to six, each member being appointed by the governor and approved by the state senate. Organized into administrative, field, treatment, and research services, the California Youth Authority strives to provide the best possible training and environment for the juvenile or youth undergoing correctional treatment.[27]

One of its more interesting experiments has been the Community Treatment Project for juveniles in Sacramento and San Joaquin counties, which is designed for the gathering of hardcore data concerning the effectiveness of treatment programs. After screening in a reception center, boys and girls free of mental abnormality, serious offenses, or community objection to their participation are randomly assigned to the community project or are sent to a juvenile institution, eventually to be paroled. Members of the experimental group thereupon undergo individual and group counseling, group and family therapy, school training, and other group activities in a highly developed and yet individualized treatment plan. Working with a ratio of 1 staff to 12 youths at a program center which houses the staff and provides a recreation area, classrooms, and a music room, the staff attempts to correct the youths' problems. The control group, on the other hand, follows the normal routine within the traditional California juvenile institution.

The early success of the program was apparent when a check of parolees at the end of 15 months' parole exposure revealed that 28 percent of the experimental group as opposed to 52 percent of the control group had their paroles revoked. When the program was extended to the Watts area in Los Angeles and to Oakland in 1964, similar apparent successes were also revealed. At the end of 15 months of parole exposure, 39 percent of the predominantly Negro youths of the Watts and Oakland experiments underwent parole revocation in comparison to a statewide revocation rate of 48 percent for juveniles of the same age categories. While the $150-per-month cost per boy in the Los Angeles and Oakland programs was three to four times as much as the cost of regular parole,

[27] Reed K. Clegg, *Probation and Parole* (Springfield, Ill.: Charles C. Thomas, Publisher, 1964), pp. 154–57; and John R. Ellingston, "The Youth Authority Program," in Paul W. Tappan, (ed.), *Contemporary Correction* (New York: McGraw-Hill, 1951), pp. 126–27.

it was less than one half the average monthly cost of institutionalizing the offender.[28]

In another experiment of the California Youth Authority, the Marshall program was created to ease the pressure of juvenile institutions. It consisted of a three months' intensive treatment program at the Norwalk reception center and was founded on a therapeutic community concept. Youths selected for the program participate in a half day of work in institutional operation and maintenance, a few specialized education classes, and daily group counseling. Rewards for active juvenile participation include progressively longer and more frequent home furloughs and parent-youth participation in group activities. Early data reveal that 44 percent of the Marshall youths as opposed to 47 percent of a matched group undergo parole revocation within 15 months of parole exposure. The revocation rate is based upon a three-month treatment program at Marshall and an average eight- to nine-month training program at the state school. Although the apparent results of both institutions were similar, the Marshall program represented a significant saving to the public.[29]

Variations in programs for treatment of juveniles

Many other delinquency treatment programs have also been created by other state or private agencies. The Institute for Behavioral Research at Silver Spring, Maryland, for example, has created the Case Project, a development on a predetermined scale. Each youth receives one penny for each point to a maximum of $40 per week. From this amount, he pays for his private room, food, recreation, books, toiletries, schooling, and decorations. The philosophy undergirding the program implies the belief of the counselors that "a well-designed environment can, by offering select and well-designed choices, help direct the behavior of the students to those academic and social goals which are necessary for successful participation in our democratic society."[30] Under these provisions, participating students may be employed by the Project according to their educational backgrounds and level of competence. The student in the Case program is encouraged to compete actively in order to develop the skills necessary to compete effectively on the open market.

Another treatment variation was initiated in early 1968 as the National Training School for Boys at Morgantown, West Virginia. Located on a 340-acre campus, the school is designed to house a maximum population of 354 boys. It closely resembles a prep school. Included are seven

---

[28] Winslow, op. cit., p. 229.

[29] Ibid., pp. 230–31.

[30] Robert C. Byrd, "Turning a Corner in Juvenile Corrections," Federal Probation, Vol. 30 (December, 1966), p. 17.

separate housing units, a junior high school, a senior high school, a chapel, a clinical center, and outdoor recreational facilities.[31] Among the facilities are a library, hobbyshop, gymnasium, central dining hall, warehouse, commissary, and barbershop grouped about a community square. Emphasizing the education of the youth, the School is designed to facilitate his educational advancement upon diagnosis of his core problem. The school's staff seeks to channel the juvenile's interests into particular vocational and technical training programs.

The scope of institutions for juveniles

Overall, juvenile institutions are many and varied and serve a diverse constituency (see Figure 22–2). For example, the 1965 survey by the Children's Bureau of 220 state-operated juvenile institutions in 50 states, Puerto Rico, and the District of Columbia disclosed that an average daily population of 42,389 youths participated in juvenile training programs in these institutions. These institutions represent 86 percent of the juvenile training school capacity in the United States. The average daily population in 17 jurisdictions, the study uncovered, was more than 10 percent below, and in 11 was 10 percent or more above, capacity.[32] Thirty-one states reported the periodic or sustained use of private facilities for the placement of delinquents. Although existing facilities in 1965 were highly strained, anticipated new construction by 1975 in all but eight states would increase the present capacity by over 42 percent. However, a capacity of 20 or less percent is planned in only 55 percent of present construction, 63 percent of authorized construction, and 45 percent of projected construction.

The American Psychiatric Association recommends that juvenile institutions be limited to 150 children in order to maximize the value of the treatment program. The greater majority of juvenile population, however, is currently institutionalized in facilities for far larger numbers. The association recommends maximum capacity standards for living units of 20 for homogeneous and 12 to 16 for heterogeneous groupings. It also encourages the construction of private rooms for girls. Of all 1,344 living units in 220 juvenile institutions in the various states, however, only 24 percent maintain a capacity of 20 or less.[33] Many of the

---

[31] *Ibid.*, p. 14.

[32] Winslow, *op. cit.*, pp. 202–3. See American Psychiatric Association, *Guide to Planning for Training Schools for Delinquent Children* (Washington, D.C.: American Psychiatric Association, 1952).

[33] *Ibid.*, p. 209. Consult Joseph H. Kane, "An Institutional Program for the Seriously Disturbed Delinquent Boy," *Federal Probation*, Vol. 30 (September, 1966), pp. 37–44; H. M. Gary, "Help For the Retarded Delinquent," *Juvenile Court Judges Journal*, Vol. 19 (Spring, 1968), p. 20; R. B. Miller and E. Kennedy, "Adolescent

FIGURE 22–2
Juveniles under correctional supervision in the United States
(population projected to 1975)

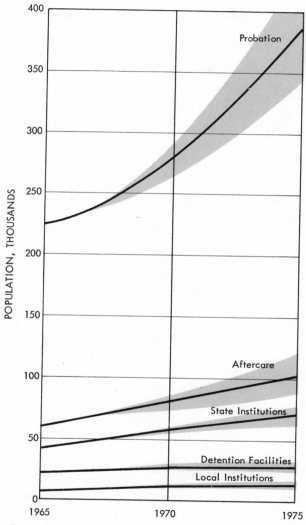

Source: President's Commission, *Task Force Report: Corrections*, p. 8.

new juvenile institutions are reception centers and boys' camps. While
the reception center, found in 10 states, provides greater opportunities
for evaluation of juvenile needs before referral to one of the many state

juvenile institutions or agencies, the growth of youth camps for 40–50 boys have been stimulated by the lower cost of operation and their generally higher success rate.

Of the 21,247 staff members employed in state juvenile institutions who served an average 1965 daily population of 42,389 trainees, only 1,154 were psychiatrists, psychologists, or social workers classified as treatment personnel. Although 282 psychiatrists were required to meet the minimum standard of 1 psychiatrist per 150 children within the average daily population of the 220 state-operated institutions recorded in the survey, only a reported equivalent of 46 psychiatrists served juvenile interests. No more than four states provided the minimum standard of psychiatric service. Of the 282 psychologists similarly required to reach to the same ratio, only 182 equivalent psychologists were employed by state juvenile institutions. While 12 states met the minimum ratio standard, 9 states alone accounted for 106 (60 percent) of the psychologists employed. Of the 1,413 caseworkers required to meet the minimum standard of 1 for every 30 children, a total of 926, approximately 66 percent of the number necessary, were engaged by the 220 responding institutions.[34]

The recommended teacher-pupil ratio was 1 to 15; the overall teacher-pupil ratio in the 220 institutions studied ranged from 1 to 17. With 2,495 teachers employed, the teaching standard was more closely realized than the standards in the casework, psychological, and psychiatric service areas. In addition, 158 chaplains served the 220 state institutions. However, 12 states offered no chaplaincy programs, 18 maintained less than half-time services per facility, and 32 employed one chaplain per institution.[35] Medical services were provided at 96 percent and dental services at 94 percent of the training facilities. Recreational services were available at 95 percent of the institutions, educational programs at 88 percent, casework assistance at 86 percent, counseling services at 79 percent, and psychological and psychiatric services at 75 and 71 percent respectively.

Per capita operating costs for the 52 jurisdictions in the survey amounted to $3,411 per child, or a total annual operating cost of $144,596,618, to house and care for an average daily population of 42,389 juveniles. The per capita cost varied widely, from $871 to $7,890 per

---

[34] *Ibid.*, pp. 204–6. Evaluate Clifford A. Lawson, "What Services Do We Want for Our Delinquent Children?" *Federal Probation*, Vol. 30 (March, 1966), pp. 32–36; and Povl W. Toussieng, "The Role of the Psychiatric Consultant in a State Training School" *Federal Probation*, Vol. 25 (March, 1961), pp. 39–43.

[35] Harvey L. Long, "The Church's Mission and Delinquents," *Federal Probation*, Vol. 27 (December, 1963), pp. 26–31; and Marshall E. Miller, "The Place of Religion in the Lives of Juvenile Offenders," *Federal Probation*, Vol. 29 (March, 1965), pp. 50–53.

capita, in the 42 institutions which operate training facilities without separate reception and diagnostic centers. Of the 42, 6 states reported per capita costs below $1,600 per year, 8 between $1,600 and $3,000, 13 between $3,000 and $4,500, and 13 above $4,500. In the 10 jurisdictions that operated reception and diagnostic centers, per capita costs varied from a low of $1,757 to a high of $5,723 during 1966–67. While the average per capita cost was less than $2,000 in 3 states, it ranged from $2,000 to $2,500 in 2, $3,900 to $4,500 in 3 states, and above $4,500 in 2 states.[36]

The majority of treatment educational and administrative staff in juvenile institutions, a 1964 study by the Children's Bureau revealed, do not possess the minimal educational requirements expected by the correctional profession. Educational background, the study disclosed, is especially low for cottage personnel, social workers, academic teachers, medical aides, and occupational supervisors. Not only are institutions facing major difficulty in retaining sufficiently well-qualified employees, but high staff turnover also reflected the failure of particular institutions to implement recommended personnel policies and practices.[37]

Although study recommends the 40-hour workweek for personnel working in juvenile institutions, the average workweek is more than 40 hours in 16 states and more than 50 in 7 others. The majority of state training facility staffs are protected under the merit system, and merit or civil service coverage is recommended for all training school personnel, but superintendents in 30 states are commonly outside such security guarantees. Superintendents are recommended to have completed graduate training in the behavior sciences or child development, but many do not come close to fulfilling such criteria. Ten jurisdictions, for example, make no formal educational demands and hire the best personnel available at the needed time. Twenty-eight, however, require college training, and twelve expect the superintendent to have completed a graduate degree. Juvenile staff standards suggest that employed caseworkers be graduates of accredited schools of social work; 36 jurisdictions require a college background and 11 require a graduate degree. Although no standard has been designated for cottage staff members, they have traditionally been at least high school graduates. Despite the fact that cottage staff members are important persons in training

---

[36] *Ibid.*, pp. 50–53.

[37] Children's Bureau, *Personnel and Personnel Practices in Public Institutions for Delinquent Children: A Survey* (Washington, D.C.: U.S. Government Printing Office, 1966), pp. 1–29. Also see Frank Flynn, "First Steps in Solving Training Needs of Court and Institutional Workers Who Treat Juvenile Delinquents," *Training Personnel for Work with Juvenile Delinquents* (Washington, D.C.: U.S. Department of Health, Education, and Welfare, 1954).

facility programs, low salaries have generally made it difficult to establish sound educational requirements for such positions.[38]

The disposition of delinquents in Great Britain

Delinquency sentencing alternatives and correctional methods in Great Britain vary. They include such alternatives as absolute discharge by the court, conditional discharge upon guarantees of good behavior, fines imposed upon the child or his parents, probation, committal to the care of a fit person, or detention in one of several alternative institutions. These include remand homes, approved schools, attendance centers, detention centers, and Borstal institutions.[39]

Remand homes. These homes provide offenders under the age of 17 safe custody as they await their court appearance, are remanded to custody temporarily while the case is adjourned, or seek admission to another institution. Used as a temporary detention center for a period not exceeding one month, the remand home provides a custodial facility in which the child's character, intelligence, and physical or mental condition may be observed.

Approved schools. These institutions are industrial schools created in the 19th century for destitute and delinquent children and named after the "approval" of the Secretary of State, who certifies specific schools for residential child care and protection. These schools classify children according to age and sex and offer "difficult" boys and girls a meaningful educational opportunity within a controlled environment. Emphasizing the remolding of character, the schools encourage the development of a sense of social responsibility among its participants. While the actual tenure of the boy or girl may be shorter for those under 12 years of age, most juveniles are detained in the approved school for a three-year period. After discharge they receive aftercare services until 21 years of age.[40]

Attendance centers. The centers are used as a means of disciplining young offenders or delinquents by placing restrictions upon their liberty of action. If found guilty of an offense as an adult, British youths between 18 and 24 may be required to attend the center during their spare time on Saturdays rather than serve a term of imprisonment. While they may be required to attend for up to 3 hours on any one occasion, they may not be restricted in their freedom for more than 12 hours. The attendance center program, designed to encourage the proper use

[38] Winslow, *op. cit.*, pp. 207–8.
[39] *The Treatment of Offenders in Britain* (London: H. M. Stationery Office, 1960), pp. 29–37.
[40] Schafer and Knudten, *op. cit.*, p. 354.

of leisure and to teach young offenders respect for law,[41] commonly includes such activities as instruction in handicrafts, lectures on practical topics and physical training, and hard physical work.

Detention center. If the offense is especially serious, the British youth between 16 or 17 and 20 may be sentenced under specific circumstances to detention centers, Borstal training, or a prison.[42] For example, magistrates courts may send an English boy to a detention center without requiring any fitness or other study pertinent to the treatment of the offender, inasmuch as detention centers are primarily designed to maintain the custody of the youth. Originally conceived as a means of punishment through a short, tough, and even unpleasant experience, boys in detention normally work hard, have little recreation time, and "spend quite a lot of time changing their clothes."[43] Serving the young males guilty of slightly more serious offenses, they offer a longer and more intensive residential training than found in the remand homes. Detained in such a center for a period of three to six months, the juvenile lives a disciplined life and engages in a 44-hour workweek. Boys of compulsory school age receive regular schooling; evening classes are provided for older youths. Designed to administer a "short-sharp-shock" to the juvenile offender, the detention center stimulates boys to participate in the center's high-powered operation.

Borstal institutions. The Borstals offer personal remedial and educational training for those between 16 and 21 years of age. Part of an overall system of reception centers, security Borstals and Recall institutions, the Borstal permits long-term training, usually over a four-year period, which is divided into two parts. During the first nine months to three years, the youth is treated at a Borstal for either boys or girls. The average time spent in the first phase is 20 months. In the second phase, which extends to the end of the four-year period, the offender undergoes treatment in a controlled and supervised environment. At first he may be placed in a reception center, where screening personnel select the Borstal best suited for his treatment requirements. Upon arrival at this location, he takes up residence in a homogeneous home of about 50 boys or girls under the supervision of a housemaster or housemistress and house staff. Within this setting, he is encouraged to participate in decision making, accept responsibility, and exert self-control through daily participation in physical training, work, entertainment, reading, and recreation.

---

[41] *Treatment of Offenders in Britain,* p. 32.

[42] Charlotte Banks, "Borstal Prison and Detention Centres," in Hugh Klare (ed.), *Changing Concepts of Crime and Its Treatment* (New York: Pergamon Press, Inc., 1966), p. 117.

[43] *Ibid.,* p. 122.

564   Crime in a complex society

The Borstal system was an outgrowth of an 1895 practice of segregating young offenders in a wing of Bedford prison. By 1902, older offenders serving sentences of more than 12 months were transported from throughout England to the Borstal Prison in Rochester and later to Dartmoor and Lincoln for basic training.[44] Currently, the Borstal system depends upon a system of graded classification which attempts to pair each offender with a suitable open, intermediate, or closed security institution. About one half are "closed" or maximum security institutions. Because many Borstals emphasize individual casework rather than group counseling, the decision which is invoked becomes highly important to the treatment process.[45] Borstal institutions at Aylesbury and East Sutton Park serve girls.

All inmates share in hard labor while in their assigned Borstal. Physical training is provided in gymnastics, play activities, handicrafts, and reading. Borstal youth may clear land, reclaim land from the sea, farm, or participate in industrial or shop employment. Training periods, often 12 to 18 months in duration, provide the youth with useful employment skills. Approximately 20 percent of the Borstal boys participate in vocational training at any one time. Upon release, the Borstal youth may be placed under the supervision of an aftercare association which counsels the youth and helps him to find employment and housing.[46] A "licensee," the youth is released pending good conduct and is subject to revocation of his license and to return to a Borstal facility for a period between 5 months to a year for violation.

The judge of the magistrates court may commit a male youth to sessions court for Borstal sentence if he meets the required age requirements and the court accepts the premise that Borstal training would be in his best interests. Generally, most boys can be sent to the Borstal only by a higher court.

While the Borstal sentence is indeterminate, it commonly includes a minimum of 6 months and a maximum of two years of treatment, the average sentence being between 14 and 15 months. Upon showing proper motivation, he may be gradually released from the institution so that he might be acclimated to the proper use of freedom. If he fails to comply with the conditions of his controlled freedom, he may be recalled at a later time to one of the Borstals or other rehabilitation centers.[47] Early release may occur for good behavior as in the United States, the decision resting with the authority of the Borstal Institutions. While the Home Secretary reported that 60 percent of the youths released from Borstals were not recommitted within a five-year period,

[44] Clegg, *op. cit.*, pp. 151–52.
[45] Banks, *op. cit.*, p. 123.
[46] Clegg, *op. cit.*, p. 153.
[47] Schafer and Knudten, *op. cit.*, pp. 354–55.

William Healy and Benedict S. Alper have reported success rates ranging as high as 84 percent.[48]

Today English magistrates courts may commit a boy over 17 convicted summarily of an indictable offense triable by Quarter Sessions to a higher court for sentence if they believe that it would best serve the needs of the person and the requirements of justice. In the past, they could sentence a boy directly to prison for not more than six months.[49] Boys sentenced to prison for less than three months generally served their time in separate facilities from older prisoners at a local prison. Because the very shortness of the sentence largely made any training or work program of limited value, commitment for less criminal boys between 1961 and 1963 shifted away from imprisonment and toward the use of detention centers.[50] The Criminal Justice Act of August, 1963, however, abolished medium prison sentences for boys sentenced to terms between six months and three years who had not been previously been sent to a Borstal or to a prison for six months or more. Under the new provisions, a sentence of 18 months or more could be given to such youths. All short prison sentences were also eliminated and substituted with detention orders.

Of the 2,178 boys discharged from all British Borstals in 1958, 1,156 (53 percent) were reinstitutionalized and 1,506 (69 percent) reconvicted within five years. Of the 3,438 boys discharged in 1961, 1,506 (45 percent) were reinstitutionalized and 2,122 (64 percent) reconvicted within a two-year period following release. Among senior British boys in approved schools, 56 percent released in 1958 were reconvicted within three years.[51] Of 331 boys examined by T. C. N. Gibbons, 67 percent similarly succeeded and 33 percent failed or were reconvicted within one year following release from detention. Within two years, the success group dropped to 52 percent and the failure one to 48 percent. Of 300 boys undergoing Borstal training, however, 58 percent succeeded and 42 percent failed after one year, and 44 percent succeeded and 56 percent failed after two years. Comparatively, 45 percent of the 307 youths sentenced to young prisoners centers succeeded and 55 percent failed after one year; 31 percent succeeded and 69 percent failed after two.

An examination of such findings leads Charlotte Banks to conclude simply that prison "is least effective, detention most effective, and Borstal between the two."[52] However, the differing failure rates, she also points

---

[48] William Healy and Benedict S. Alper, *Criminal Youth in the Borstal System* (New York: Commonwealth Fund, 1944).

[49] Banks, *op. cit.*, pp. 120–22.

[50] *Ibid.*, p. 135.

[51] Derek Miller, "A Model of an Institution for Treating Adolescent Delinquent Boys," *Changing Concepts of Crime and Its Treatment*, p. 97.

[52] Banks, *op. cit.*, p. 124.

out, are largely, if not entirely, "due to the types of boys sent to the three kinds of institution."[53] Fewer boys convicted of indictable violence, driving offenses, larceny, taking and driving away, or nonindictable crimes are sent to Borstal institutions. Although a larger number of "breakers and enterers" entered the Borstal in 1961, most sexual offenders, frauds, false pretense participants, nonindictable assaulters, malicious damagers, taking and driving away thieves and other "nonindictable" offenders were transported to a prison.[54]

Treatment of juveniles in Canada

Most Canadian training schools fall into one of two types of classification. Usually, they are either common-theft types which place little emphasis upon clinical therapy or they are professionalist oriented and emphasize the treatment capabilities of the psychiatrist, psychologist, caseworker, or groupworker.[55] The former emphasizes understanding and a common humane approach to juvenile treatment; the latter utilizes modern skills in the treatment process. Both have their limitations and strengths, and professional and staff relations are often strained by the conflict arising over the use of differing correctional methods.

The New Haven Borstal Institution of South Burnaby near Vancouver, British Columbia, was developed for delinquent use after World War II. Patterned after the English Borstal system, the New Haven institution provides a large house, dormitories, and workshops for use of youths between 16 and 23 who are confined within its premises for six to nine months.[56] Begun with 50 youths, the maximum enrollment has since been placed at 40 in order to maintain a sense of intimacy and of community. The 16 staff roles at New Haven include those of the director, assistant director house master, social worker, vocational instructor, Borstal officer, and clerical assistant. Emphasis at the institution is placed upon meaningful communication and a variety of activities rather than upon formal counseling or casework. Trades are used as therapy, and stress is placed upon vocational training as a means for encouragement of self-reliance, initiative, and resourcefulness. Once the boy is oriented to the institution, he works with the Borstal volunteer or association to plan for his release upon discharge. These free agents also assist

---

[53] *Ibid.*, p. 124.

[54] *Ibid.*, p. 125.

[55] Sinclair, *op. cit.*, p. 250. Also see R. P. Francis, "Training Schools Act, 1965," *Saskatchewan Bar Review*, Vol. 31 (June, 1966), p. 117; and B. Green, "Trumpets, Justice, and Federalism," *University of Toronto Law Journal*, Vol. 16 (1966), p. 407.

[56] John P. Conrad, *Crime and Its Correction* (Berkeley: University of California Press, 1967), p. 271.

in finding housing and jobs and in integrating the youth into the community. One of the greatest assets of the New Haven program has been the close cooperation engendered among the staff, detained youths, and members of the Borstal association.[57]

Although the New Haven Borstal administration is progressive, few Canadian training school administrators have been willing to break completely with past methods and traditions. A few have attempted to do so, however. Although the Boscoville school in Quebec has developed a "total staff involvement" treatment program, it has done so at a high cost and high staff-pupil ratio. Staff members must be part teacher, part social worker, part therapist, and part friend; they must be exceedingly well-trained, able to lay bare their own feelings and attitudes, and yet to absorb large amounts of hostility and aggression.[58] Few schools have enough trained staff to even consider such a program. In Ontario, boys are generally separated from girls and Catholics from non-Catholics. Girls are classified in relationship to the degree of supervision that each requires. Younger boys are segregated from older youths and are housed in one school. Mature youths with academic bents are sent to a second school; those with vocational interests to a third; and those in need of confinement to a small maximum-security institution.[59]

While Canadian training-schools have avoided many of the more notorious pitfalls of the American and British systems, they nevertheless use several basic procedures which may undermine specific phases of the school process. In some instances, one or more senior children are permitted to apply corrective measures to other child offenders. At other times, a group may be punished for the misdeeds or violations of a single member, an act which serves to solidify relationships in the juvenile community at the expense of the treatment program. Finally, the use of corporal punishment reinforces juvenile hostility against adults. In order to overcome these and other limitations and to develop a successful training school rehabilitation program for young delinquents, Donald Sinclair recommends that Canadian federal and provincial authorities adopt the following changes:

1. Place the responsibility for care and treatment of neglected, dependent and delinquent children on the child welfare departments of the provinces.
2. Commit to training schools only children who need the type of care these schools provide.
3. Develop a wider range of alternative forms of care, such as group foster homes, and extending the present use of foster care.

---

[57] *Ibid.*, pp. 271–72.
[58] Sinclair, *op. cit.*, p. 251.
[59] *Ibid.*, p. 256.

4. Provide appropriate hospitals for children who are mentally ill or seriously disturbed emotionally and adequate maternity care for pregnant girls, and seek to commit these children to training schools.
5. Reduce the size of training schools and drastically reduce the number of children for whom each house parent or supervisor is responsible.
6. Establish juvenile courts on a regional basis and provide them with adequate clinical facilities for thorough assessment and observation of a child before disposition of his case.
7. Provide an aftercare service that can effectively work with the family of a delinquent while he is receiving training.
8. Provide adequate training programs for training school staffs.
9. Intensify the drive to attract well-trained clinical workers to the schools.[60]

Even these reforms, however, may not be enough. The value of the training school still depends upon the accurate evaluation of the range of responsibility which the youth is able to accept and the degree of punishment which in his case possesses a deterrent value.

AFTERCARE OF JUVENILES

The value of institutionalization of juveniles depends in large measure upon the character and quality of aftercare services. Juvenile aftercare refers to the "duty of society" to assist the delinquent to reenter normal society and to resist future pressures toward deviance.[61] Such services may be provided by a state agency through training schools, by the juvenile court, by public or private casework agencies, by an adult parole authority, by a particular judge, or by volunteer organizations within a specific community or state.[62]

Aftercare, the last step in the juvenile treatment program, is theoretically an integral part of the correction process. Because it is that aspect of treatment which enables the juvenile to reenter effectively his own community as a valued person, it is especially important to the successful training of juveniles. In 1965, an estimated 59,000 youths, of whom

---

[60] *Ibid.*, pp. 266–78.
[61] Schafer and Knudten, *op. cit.* Also see "Juvenile Aftercare," *Crime and Delinquency*, Vol. 13 (January, 1967), p. 99; and D. Minge, "Youth Agencies Not Found in the Yellow Pages," *Juvenile Court Judges Journal*, Vol. 17 (Fall, 1966), p. 95.
[62] Charles L. Newman, *Sourcebook on Probation, Parole and Pardons* (Springfield, Ill.: Charles C. Thomas, Publishers, 1968), pp. 230–31; and "Interstate Placement of Juveniles," *Columbia Journal of Law and Social Problems*, Vol. 3 (June, 1967), p. 171.

12,000 were girls, were under aftercare supervision, in the 50 states. The number of juveniles cared for in state aftercare programs ranged from 110 to 13,000 in 1965.[63] Due to limitations of data concerning these programs, the exact scope and coverage of aftercare services is unclear. While 12 states maintain an active aftercare supervision program for an average of less than one year, 25 offer supervision of one year or more. Normally, girls are kept in aftercare supervision longer than boys.

The average per capita aftercare cost approximates $320 per year, even though costs in some states may range as high as $4,000 per year. Overall, juvenile aftercare costs are estimated to be $18 million per year as opposed to the over $144 million spent annually to house a daily population of 42,000 juvenile trainees at an average cost of nearly $3,400 per trainee per year. The lower costs of aftercare, however, are somewhat misleading inasmuch as they frequently represent the lack of concern most states have for the reentry of the juvenile into society. Aftercare caseloads may range as high as 250 adolescents to two or three counselors, who themselves are frequently working in communities far removed from the location of the juvenile's place of residence.

State departments which administer juvenile institutions also provide aftercare services for juveniles in 34 states. Although local probation departments frequently have no official relationship to the agency-administering training schools, they are often assigned aftercare responsibility in five states. Several of the remaining states place aftercare programs in local social welfare agencies.[64]

The median 1965 income of aftercare directors was $8,000 to $9,000; of district supervisors, $7,000 to $8,000; and of aftercare counselors, $5,000 to $6,000. Of the 40 states providing data concerning aftercare personnel, 23 maintained a civil service or merit system coverage for directors of juvenile aftercare services, 26 for the district supervisors, and 29 for aftercare workers. Thirty-four of forty reporting states noted that they required juvenile aftercare workers to possess a bachelor's degree in social or behavior sciences, one year of graduate study in social work or a related field, or one year of paid full-time casework in corrections. Nevertheless, such minimum standards frequently had to be waived in practice. The 40 reporting states employed 133 district supervisors, 76 district assistant supervisors and 1,033 aftercare counselors in 1965.

While it is recommended that juvenile aftercare counselors maintain active supervision of a maximum of 50 cases, the median 1965 caseload

[63] Winslow, *op. cit.*, p. 218.
[64] *Ibid.*, pp. 216.

range was 61 to 70. Because of the wide geographic distributions of many aftercare counselors and services, aftercare supervision is often crisis oriented in that the counselor contacts the child only in emergencies. More commonly, supervision is maintained through the reception of monthly reports from the juvenile by the caseworker.[65]

The problem of reentry

One of the basic problems in juvenile reentry to society is the reestablishment of the youth within the public school system. At the time of his detention, he is often already well behind the performance level of many of his peers. Because he is commonly a poor student, detention and institutionalization merely disrupt his marginal school experience and may even retard his scholastic development. Consequently, upon release and reentry into the school system, he faces problems in evaluation of school credits and in reintegration into a student group which may be somewhat younger than he is. Then, too, he may receive little help from teachers, who prefer to work with better students and know of his past troublemaking. Many of these teachers, Erven Brundage believes, are the same persons who sighed with relief when he was institutionalized.[66] Consequently, when the student reappears at a classroom for enrollment, the administrator is often placed in the difficult situation of having to respond to the youth's needs while still maintaining the support of the many teachers who are disinterested in working with him. Because they are not oriented to the rehabilitation of offenders, teachers and administrators alike, Brundage maintains, fail miserably in assisting in reentry.

A solution, Brundage suggests, can only be found in programs like that developed in the San Diego County (California) Liaison Procedure Plan which assigns a specific person to juvenile contact and reentry work in each county high school. These workers are charged with the responsibility of gaining and maintaining rapport with detained or institutionalized youth and of assisting their adjustment to the school system. Presuming that young offenders have been changed and now desire to integrate themselves more fully into society, the contact person attempts to reinforce changed attitudes of students and to aid them in shifting their allegiances to valuable scholastic goals. In order to facilitate this transition for both the youth and the school, the worker originates relationships with the youth while he is still institutionalized.[67]

---

[65] *Ibid.*, pp. 219–20.

[66] Erven Brundage, "Helping Institutionalized Students Re-enter Public Schools," *Federation Probation*, Vol. 27 (September, 1963), p. 55.

[67] *Ibid.*, p. 56. Also see Louis Berkowitz and Jacob Chwast "Community Center Program for the Prevention of School Dropouts," *Federal Probation*, Vol. 31 (Decem-

The continuing problem

While such a program undoubtedly possesses value, it only represents one facet of the juvenile delinquency problem and the quest for its solution. The President's Commission on Law Enforcement and the Administration of Justice maintains that juvenile delinquency can be overcome only if youth become more involved, with those affairs of society which affect them, and if modern institutions offer better educational programs, strengthen family life, improve opportunities for employment, and make "the activities of law enforcement and individual and social services more relevant and more accessible to those who need them the most."[68] However, even these suggestions may be too simplistic answers to the basic problem of delinquency. Charles H. Shireman questions whether the necessary backlog of knowledge concerning human personality has yet been developed and applied to juvenile correctional institutions in order to expect realistically the development of acceptable treatment methods and a high degree of positive results.[69] The frustrations of the delinquency problem, he assumes, may cause many to seek easy answers and to attempt irrational solutions in the guise of treatment.

In arguing against those who would solve the delinquency problem by a simple infliction of punishment upon the delinquent offender, Garrett Heyns contends that the solution to delinquency is far more complex than most laymen would have the public believe. In fact, punishment and treatment cannot coexist, Heyns hypothesizes, because each tends to undermine the effects of the other. What is needed, therefore, is an attack on the causes of delinquency and a recognition that modern progressive delinquency treatment programs are based upon years of tested experience. Contrary to public belief, threats and repression do not solve the delinquent's problems; they are more likely to aggravate them. And yet, the public is generally apathetic to the more successful positive prevention and treatment programs, which are finally necessary for the effective control of juvenile deviancy. Can juvenile delinquency,

---

ber, 1967), pp. 36–40; Mortimer Krenter, "A Public School in a Correctional Institution," *Federal Probation,* Vol. 29 (September, 1965), pp. 50–57; and F. Weiner, "Vocational Guidance for Delinquent Boys," *Crime and Delinquency,* Vol. 11 (October, 1965), p. 366.

[68] Winslow, *op. cit.,* p. 231.

[69] Charles H. Shireman, "How Can The Correctional School Correct?" *Crime and Delinquency,* Vol. 6 (1960), pp. 267–74. Consult W. E. Amos, "Future of Juvenile Institutions," *Federal Probation,* Vol. 32 (March, 1968), p. 41; Robert C. Byrd, "Turning the Corner in Juvenile Corrections," *Federal Probation,* Vol. 30 (December, 1966), pp. 14–17; and S. C. Averill and P. W. Toussieng, "Study of Release from a Training School for Delinquent Boys," *Crime and Delinquency,* Vol. 12 (April, 1966), p. 135.

Heyns asks, ever be solved in such a situation?[70] His answer is a resounding negative.

---

[70] Garrett Heyns, "The Treat-'em Rough Boys are Here Again," *Federal Probation*, Vol. 31 (June, 1967), pp. 7–10. Other sources of value include: Chester C. Scott, "Can You Get a 'Peep' Out of People?" *Federal Probation*, Vol. 29 (March, 1965), pp. 13–18; John R. Larkins, *A Study of the Adjustment of Negro Boys Discharged from Morrison Training School* (Raleigh, N.C.: North Carolina State Board of Public Welfare, 1947); C. Eugene Mallory, "People Are Dangerous," *Federal Probation*, Vol. 29 (December, 1965), pp. 36–40; David C. Twain, "Promising Practical Research in Delinquency," *Federal Probation*, Vol. 28 (September, 1964), pp. 30–34; Mabel A. Elliott, "Trends in Theories Regarding Juvenile Delinquency and Their Implication for Treatment Programs," *Federal Probation*, Vol. 31 (September, 1967), pp. 3–11; A. E. Reed and W. C. Hinsey, "Demonstration Project for Defective Delinquents," *Crime and Delinquency*, Vol. 11 (October, 1965), p. 375.; and E. Preston Sharp and Ellis S. Grayson, "How Delinquent Children Think and Feel," *Federal Probation*, Vol. 29 (June, 1965), pp. 12–16.

Chapter 23

THE INCARCERATION
OF ADULTS

The rise of the correctional institution is partially due to the influence of Cesare Beccaria's Classical penological theory which presumed that crime is largely a product of pleasure or profit and can be controlled by eliminating opportunities to commit crime or by replacing joy and profit from crime with personal pain. A product of penological "enlightment," the prison was developed to replace execution, flogging, and pillorying as a principal social response to criminal deviance. It was viewed as a more humane method for deterrance of criminality than these punishments or the infliction of the death penalty. Because it offered the offender an opportunity to reorient his behavior as he evaluated his own life in penal solitude, many religious groups supported the development of penal institutions. These groups approved the prison's amelioration of many of the more brutal aspects of the historical system of criminal justice.

Gaols were commonly provided in local European communities at the time John Howard, the son of a wealthy London tradesman, traveled to Lisbon in 1755 to assist the thousands made homeless by an earthquake. But Howard, captured by a privateer while in transit, was largely unconcerned for their existence until he was confined in a damp, dark, filthy dungeon in Brest with other prisoners. As a consequence of his experience, he accepted the appointment of sheriff of Bedford in 1773-after his return to England and proceeded to ameliorate existing prison abuses. Bringing the problems of prisons to the attention of the British Parliament in 1784, Howard and his supporters pressed many legislative attempts, some successful, to overcome the deplorable prison situation. In the late 18th and early 19th centuries, a member of the Society of

Friends (Quakers), the Englishwoman Elizabeth Fry, worked to secure remunerative activities for women in custody, to differentiate and segregate first offenders from long-term offenders, and "to provide adequate accomodations, food, and necessities for those in custody and those who were deported to the colonies, and to provide education and activities for children who were in custody with their mothers."[1] Although England moved early to correct the weaknesses within its existing system of incarceration, its focus remained upon custody and transportation until later decades.

THE USE OF JAILS IN THE UNITED STATES

The Walnut Street Jail in Philadelphia became the prototype of the later prison. Placed in solitary confinement, prisoners occupied cells which were large enough in many instances to permit the maintenance of some occupations while in custody. During their stay in confinement, prisoners were furnished religious literature, had the counsel of lay and clerical religious leaders, and were encouraged to renew their person through contemplation and realization of higher religious values. When removed from their cells for short periods of time, they were frequently hooded to prevent communication with other inmates. Although many suffered mental breakdowns under these conditions, the practices of the Walnut Street Jail were continued in several jurisdictions into the latter part of the 18th century.[2] Many jails were operated on the English piece system, which permitted the highest bidder to incarcerate offenders as a profit-making enterprise. This practice exists even today among the many county sheriffs who employ their wives as jail cooks and increase their profits from the per diem prisoner allowance by serving cheap meals.

In most American local and county jurisdictions, jailed prisoners are commonly persons who await investigations or preliminary hearings, trials, or transfer to a penal or other institution, serve a jail sentence, or remain in protective custody pending the opportunity to give their testimony to the court. However, because the jail provides a ready lockup facility, drug addicts, juvenile first offenders, habitual criminals, vagrants, runaways, rapists, robbers, family offenders, and other criminal

---

[1] A. M. Kirkpatrick, "After-Care and the Prisoner's Aid Societies," in William T. McGrath (ed.), *Crime and Its Treatment in Canada* (New York: St. Martin's Press, Inc., 1965), p. 406. Also see Gabriel Tarde, *Penal Philosophy*, trans. Rapelje Howell (Boston: Little, Brown & Co., 1912); Gordon Rose, *The Struggle for Penal Reform* (Chicago: Quadrangle Books, Inc., 1961); and Thorsten Sellin, "Look at Prison History," *Federal Probation*, Vol. 31 (September, 1967), pp. 18–23.

[2] Mark S. Richmond, *Prison Profiles* (New York: Oceana Publications, Inc., 1965), p. 3. Refer to Louis N. Robinson, *Jails: Care and Treatment of Misdemeanant Prisoners in the United States* (Philadelphia: Winston, 1944).

types are frequently jailed together regardless of the seriousness of their offense. This problem is especially acute for the 50,000 to 75,000 juveniles who are detained in police lockup or county jails annually.

Overall, local jails and misdemeanant institutions are the weakest link in the corrections process. "Because their inmates," the President's Commission on Law Enforcement and the Administrator of Justice concludes, "do not seem to present a clear danger to society, the response to their needs has usually been one of indifference."[3] Inasmuch as the prisoners in the jail are predominantly involved in petty crimes with short sentences, these institutions occupy a low priority status. Frequently administered by police or county sheriffs, the jails largely serve a custodial function pending the trial or hearing concerning a particular offense which involve the prisoner or detainee. They usually lack recreational and counseling programs and in some instances medical services.

A 1965 survey of corrections for the President's Commission revealed that two thirds of the 215 misdemeanant institutions possess no rehabilitation programs. Fewer than 3 percent of the jail or misdemeanant institutional staff complete rehabilitative duties in the form of diagnosis, counseling, or other treatment functions. Many of these are only part-time or employed in the larger institutions. Although 19,000 persons, the survey revealed, occupied these positions in local correctional institutions, they generally served only one third of the included institutions. Inmate work programs were largely nonexistent. Only 11 percent operated a work release, 10 percent an education, 9 percent a group counseling, and 7 percent an alcoholism treatment program. The failure of local corrections officials to provide opportunities for rehabilitation on the misdemeanant level, the President's Commission advises, permits many prisoners to graduate to more serious crimes by default.[4] Although jails are generally operated by law enforcement officials on behalf of a city and county, they are generally afterthoughts in the correctional process. Alaska, Connecticut, and Rhode Island maintain administrative supervision of jails through their adult authority, jail administration, or a department of social welfare. Most jail systems, however, are localized and subject to the whims of controlling city or county political officials.

Correctional facilities range from the local jail to the fortress-like prison. They are theoretically designed to protect society from the offender and to rehabilitate the offender. However, the primary emphasis is usually upon custody rather than treatment. Each state, the District

---

[3] The President's Commission on Law Enforcement and the Administration of Justice, *The Challenge of Crime in a Free Society* (Washington, D.C.: U.S. Government Printing Office, 1967), p. 178.

[4] "Correction in the United States," *Crime and Delinquency*, Vol. 13 (January 1967), p. 147. Consult "Social Adult Correctional Institutions and Jails," *Crime and Delinquency*, Vol. 13 (January, 1967), p. 137.

of Columbia, the commonwealth of Puerto Rico, the federal government, and the greater majority of the 3,047 counties in the United States, each acting independently of the others, support some type of correctional facility or program. Nearly 75 percent of the 3,500 or more local institutions for misdemeanants are jails; the remainder are workhouses, farms, and camps. More than two thirds of these institutions are more

FIGURE 23–1
Adults under correctional supervision in the United States
(population projected to 1975)

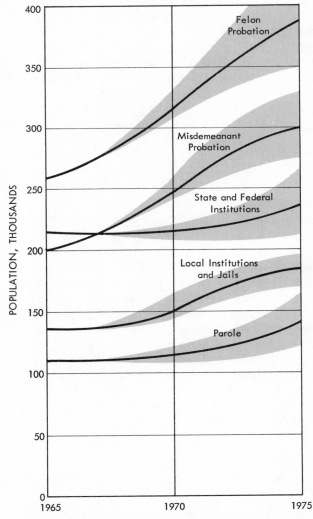

Source: The President's Commission on Law Enforcement and the Administration of Justice, *Task Force Report: Corrections* (Washington, D.C.: U.S. Government Printing Office, 1967), p. 8.

than 25 years old and fail to meet minimum standards of sanitation, housing, and offender age and category separation. Twenty-five prisons in the United States are over 100 years old.[5]

The correctional system on all levels is responsible for more than 1.3 million offenders on any given day (see Figure 23–1). It processes nearly 2.5 million admissions and spends over $1 billion annually. Designed to protect the society, rehabilitate the offender, and deter others from criminal acts, the correctional system is in fact both a success and a failure.

While a significant number of offenders end their criminal involvement once imprisoned, a large portion of the recent rising crime rate has been due to the continued recidivism of previous incarcerants. Consequently, modern corrections researchers question whether the prison truly serves the purpose for which it was intended or whether it actually hinders the treatment process. Coming rather late in the offender's career, imprisonment, they hypothesize, may have minimal influence upon the future actions of the released offender. The prison is often dominated by a concern for the custody of the convicted and minimizes the potential value of the treatment program. Yet, incarcerated offenders represent a diverse population in need of multiple treatment approaches. Alcoholics, narcotic addicts, senile males, sex deviants, professional criminals, murderers, rapists, and check forgers are only a portion of the total criminal population usually imprisoned in any one treatment facility. The majority of offenders are males between the ages of 16 and 30 who have dropped out of school and reveal unstable work records.[6]

Given this problem, the American corrections system seeks solutions on many separate levels of control and treatment. John P. Conrad finds that the American correctional apparatus includes the following elements within its system:

Jurisdictional Control	Adult	Juvenile
Local supervision	County probation	County probation
Local detention	County jail	Juvenile halls and detention homes
	County workcamps	County training schools
		County work camps
State supervision	Parole	Parole

---

[5] President's Commission, *op. cit.*, pp. 161–64. Also see *Construction and Design of Correctional Institutions* (Washington, D.C.: U.S. Bureau of Prisons, 1949); *Recent Prison Construction, 1950–1960* (Washington, D.C.: U.S. Bureau of Prisons, 1960).

[6] *Ibid.*, p. 160. Examine Arthur K. Beriner, "The Helping Process in a Hospital for Narcotic Addicts," *Federal Probation*, Vol. 26 (September, 1962), p. 57; and Lewis Yablonsky, "The Anticriminal Society: Synanon," *Federal Probation*, Vol. 26 (June, 1962), p. 50.

Jurisdictional Control	Adult	Juvenile
State detention	Prison	Training schools
Federal supervision	Integrated probation and parole services	Integrated probation and parole services
Federal detention	Local jails	Local juvenile halls
	Prisons	Training schools

The administration of criminal justice in the United States, Conrad finds, generally begins with leniency, progresses through various treatment attempts, and often ends with the preventive custodial maintenance of the offender. While American correctional practices are founded upon local autonomy, they produce a high degree of standardization regardless of the independence of jurisdictions.[7]

CORRECTIONAL SYSTEMS IN OTHER COUNTRIES

Canada

The Canadian correctional system takes both a provincial and federal form. Sentences of two years less one day are automatically served in Canadian provincial institutions regardless of the nature or type of crime or the local or federal character of the offense.[8] As a result, provincial prisons house inmates serving shorter terms, and federal institutions house the more serious longer-term offenders.[9] The federal penitentiaries are administered by the Commissioner of Penitentiaries through the Department of Justice.

Provincial institutions are often called jails, reformatories, prison farms, or correctional institutions. They serve the bulk of the offenders, frequently as high as 60 percent, who are detained for a period of only a few months. While these institutions vary widely in their facilities and structures, they show a common public neglect of the welfare of incarcerated offenders. Reflecting the influence of the Auburn system, the majority of the Canadian prisons permit the prisoner no access to outside windows, and house convicts in two- to four-tiered cellblocks.

---

[7] John P. Conrad, *Crime and Its Correction* (Berkeley: University of California Press, 1967), p. 69. Refer to Garrett Heyns, "What the Public Should Know About Adult Corrections," *Federal Probation*, Vol. 28 (March, 1964), pp. 11–15; Manuel Lopez-Rey, *Studies in Penology* (The Hague: Martinus Mijhoff, 1964); Arthur E. Fink, "Authority in the Correctional Process," *Federal Probation*, Vol. 25 (September, 1961), p. 34; Robert M. Carter, "The 'Authority Problem' Revisited," *Federal Probation*, Vol. 25 (December, 1961), p. 52; and John J. Galvin, "The Task of Corrections," *Federal Probation*, Vol. 25 (September, 1961), p. 31.

[8] Walter A. Lunden, *The Prison Warden and the Custodial Staff* (Springfield, Ill.: Charles C. Thomas, Publisher, 1965), p. 65.

[9] John V. Fornataro, "Canadian Prisons Today," in McGrath (ed.), *op. cit.*, p. 302.

However, newer architecturial designs have encouraged the development of dormitory type of housing for up to as many as 50 persons.[10]

France, England, The Netherlands

In contrast with the United States and Canada, France provides a wide variety of adult correctional facilities including the:

1. *Maison d' arrêt,* modeled along the lines of the Pennsylvania system, in which the accused awaits trial confined in complete isolation.
2. *Maison de correction* for minor offenders serving short terms.
3. *Maison centrale* for refractory prisoners undergoing sentences of hard labor and solitary confinement.
4. *Prison ordinare* for offenders considered unsuitable for programs of reeducation.
5. Minimum security farms and colonies for prisoners suitable for a program of trust and responsibility.
6. *Régime progressif* for prisoners classified for reeducation.
7. *Prison école* for special intensive training for offenders below the age of 28.
8. Special prisons for offenders suffering from mental disturbances or senility.
9. Prisons for women.
10. Preventative detention for habitual criminals accomplished in a special section of *maison d' arrêt.*[11]

Similarly, the English correctional system, directly or indirectly controlled by the government from Whitehall, maintains a high degree of institutional diversity, especially for children, youth, and young adult offenders. The Netherlands, however, presents a clear contrast. Because it only has 1,800 men and women in prison and 18,000 on probation from a population of approximately 12 million persons at any one time The Netherlands does not need large numbers of correctional institutions.[12]

Scandinavia

The organization of Scandinavian penal systems, which are undergoing a slow reshaping, is not well defined. Traditionally, Scandinavian countries have taken the Pennsylvania form based on the idea that pris-

---

[10] *Ibid.,* pp. 304–5.
[11] Conrad, *op. cit.,* p. 137.
[12] *Ibid.,* pp. 73, 113.

oners should be isolated from fellow prisoners in order to avoid further personal contamination. Metropolitan prisons in Scandinavia are used primarily for detention pending disposition or short-term sentences. These institutions emphasize a "supportive, related atmosphere which stresses the inmate's predicament as a problem to be solved rather than a guilt to be expiated."[13]

The treatment of delinquency and crime in Scandinavian countries follows a common approach, although variations in method characterize Denmark, Sweden, Norway, and Finland. Throughout the Scandinavian prison systems, the offender is met in terms of his psychological and social needs rather than on the basis of some abstract theory of punishment. Confirmed criminals may undergo preventive detention from a minimum of 1 to a maximum of 12 years. By definition, such a person is an offender who has twice previously been sentenced to prison or been judged guilty of committing an offense while in prison or within five years of release from prison. In Sweden, such offenders are administratively isolated from the remainder of the Swedish prison system within eight institutions serving 500 detainees. However, even these institutions are quite different from their modern American penal counterparts, which provide few integrated inmate treatment programs. At the Hall prison near Stockholm, for example, preventive detainees share in a therapeutic community in close contact with prison staff members. Homosexual problems are kept to a minimum through the conjugal visiting of wives every Sunday. Inmates are permitted a 72-hour furlough each quarter as a matter of right. Although more than three fourths of men released from such preventive detention return to the prison at a later date, the Hall program has had a high degree of effectiveness for high-rank offenders.

Sweden has just come through a period of penal construction eventuating in the replacement of obsolete buildings and the expansion of existing facilities. While its prisons have been undermanned in recent decades, the Swedish penal system continues to face the far greater problem of staff inadequacy due to its tendency to train correctional workers in traditional methods rather than to equip them for administration of more progressive treatment programs. Nevertheless, Swedish prisons, which are presently penological models ahead of most Western countries, are founded upon such basic presuppositions that prisoners must work, the unhealthy aspects of confinement must be minimized, modern technological advances must be incorporated within institutional design, and correction and treatment are best achieved within small-group settings. Because Sweden emphasizes a full-employment economy, its prison programs are closely related to prison industries. "First we build a factory," Conrad reports, "then we build a prison to house the

[13] Conrad, op. cit., p. 128.

men who will work in the factory.[14] Because public opinion supports such a system, prison production levels come close to those of outside industries.

Due to its low rate of property offenses, Denmark, for example, places greater emphasis upon treatment of violators who commit crimes against the person. Special institutions have been developed for psychopaths and those who have been involved in violent and in sexual offenses. The Danish *Kragskovhede* institution in north Jutland, a 400-capacity institution using California classification methods, is an example of an institution using new techniques within the Danish penal system. Through the use of a combination of vocational training, industrial employment, and remedial education techniques, together with a close staff-inmate contact, continued cooperative attempts are made to maximize the treatment of the offender. Staff members assume responsibility for aftercare services and strive to acquaint themselves with the offender's family, economic-social problems arising from confinement, and needs to facilitate his community reentry.

A smaller institution by the name of *Norre* houses up to 70 young offenders for an average stay of six months or a maximum of two years. Providing programs in agriculture and in education and emphasizing small-group relations, it encourages young prisoners to participate in a culture of mutual concern and self-respect under the guidance of a 43-man staff. The success of these programs is evident in data which reveal that recidivism rates have only reached a 35 percent level over a five-year period.[15]

Norway maintains a system of small, isolated penal institutions and has in recent years begun to adopt a new approach. Much of the contemporary interest in problems of crime and penology has been stimulated by the prison experiences of many leading citizens who were victims of the Nazi occupation during World War II. These new approaches have integrated milieu treatment and small-group programs into the Norwegian, prison system.

The Finnish labor-colony organization, developed during a period of Communist influence within the national prison system and designed for treatment of prisoners serving two years or less, is founded upon a strong belief in the therapeutic value of work. Alcoholics, for example, are assisted in overcoming their problems through short-term work on airports, roads, and within forests. Inasmuch as each inmate is paid a full wage, from which deductions are made for family care, institutional services, and restitution, each prisoner is able to leave the labor colony with some savings and a sense of social contribution.[16]

----

[14] *Ibid.*, pp. 49, 120, 250–52.
[15] *Ibid.*, pp. 120, 129, 131, 135.
[16] *Ibid.*, p. 49.

THE PRISON AND ITS INMATES

The classification of prisoners

The value of treatment in any institution depends upon the quality of prisoner classification programs and the availability of treatment facilities and staff. Classification generally refers to the distribution of offenders to different institutions and to specific functions within particular institutions. In France, classification of persons with less than two years to serve occurs in the *maison d' arrêt* and those with longer terms in a centralized location either at Fresnes (for adults) or at Toul (for youth).[17] In the United States, classification occurs at many different levels.

In most states, classification commences when the inmate is committed to a diagnostic or custodial institution. Although a few states have developed diagnostic and reception centers, the majority merely provide a series of medical, intelligence, educational achievement, and psychiatric tests and examinations once the offender has been admitted to the penal institution. In addition, the new incarcerant is usually interviewed by a classification officer, often a caseworker, and a physician, chaplain, member of the education department, identification officer, custodial supervisor, or their equivalents. Upon the completion of tests and interviews, the prisoner finally receives a program for his rehabilitation from the classification committee. Decisions regarding his work and housing will be made on the basis of this information. Corrective surgery may be prescribed and family and/or follow-up counseling designated for personality reorientation. The classification committee periodically modifies the prescribed treatment program as needed until the prisoner is eventually released from custody.[18]

Approximately 10 percent of those committed to correctional institutions are functionally illiterate and test below the fifth grade on standardized achievement tests. Prisons which possess a large number of non-white and non–English-speaking persons often have a high percentage of functional illiterates within their population. Normally, the greater number of inmates fall into the intermediate education category, which includes an equivalent of the fifth, sixth, and seventh grades. Although

---

[17] *Ibid.,* p. 137.
[18] Richmond, *op. cit.,* p. 16. Also see Frank Loveland, "Classification in the Prison System," in Paul W. Tappan (ed.), *Contemporary Correction* (New York: McGraw-Hill Book Co., 1951), pp. 92–101; Serapio R. Zalba, "A Look at Correctional Treatment," *Federal Probation,* Vol. 25 (September, 1961), p. 40; and A. M. Kirkpatrick, "Prisons Produce People," *Federal Probation,* Vol. 26 (December, 1962), p. 26.

most prison education programs have been built around the need for primary and intermediate education, a greater concern has emerged in recent years for those inmates who evidence the potential ability to complete senior high school training. Interest in general and specific enrichment and vocational programs, too, has been rising. However, critics point out common shortcomings of modern correctional programs which include the following: institutional programs of education are without apparent purpose; many are of low quality and exist primarily on paper rather than in reality; the curriculum is not really designed for prison inmates; and the program itself is poorly integrated into a program of correctional reality.[19]

Prison inmates are commonly grouped into several categories depending upon their characteristics and qualities. Some are immediately categorized as unemployable and, therefore, available only for limited work assignments. Others receive either full- or part-time assignments to general educational or vocational training schools. The vast number of inmates, however, merely engage in institutional maintenance and participate in activities and services related to the upkeep of buildings and grounds, repair machinery and equipment, alteration and new construction programs, and other general institutional needs. Still others are employed in prison industries which produce goods and services primarily for other state institutions or agencies due to legal restrictions upon the sale of prison goods on the competitive market. Inmates employed in agricultural activities work largely to supply food for state institutions. Those in conservation develop and preserve public lands while working at forestry camps or other special work projects.[20]

Phases of imprisonment

Whatever the work assignment, it is only part of the first of several phases of treatment and imprisonment which every inmate shares. In the first phase of *institutional training and treatment,* the inmate normally serves his sentence in an institution prior to parole in accordance with the defined institutional regulations. If accepted for parole, he enters the second phase, *investigation and consideration,* during which the findings of the parole service are forwarded to the parole board for evaluation and decision. The third phase *final prerelease preparation,* commences at the moment the parole is declared and continues to the point of actual release.

Special problems for both the individual and the prison exist during each of these steps. During the first phase, special efforts must be made

---

[19] *Ibid.,* pp. 30–40.
[20] *Ibid.,* p. 44.

to interpret parole and parole rules to the inmate and to others interested in his welfare, assist the inmate in planning and executing his program of training and treatment, and maintain his morale throughout the period, especially if long sentences tend to predominate. In the second phase, central problems tend to revolve around the need to assess the inmate's prospects for successful rehabilitation, the assistance needed by the offender in his release planning, the value of his plans, the level of activity of all participating officials and agencies interested in his welfare, the soon-to-be released inmate's concept of parole and the significance of his plans to parole success, and his morale in this period of adjustment. The third phase of the problem centers aroung the need to help the inmate adjust to feelings of anxiety and euphoria related to his imminent release. He must be assisted to complete final arrangements, secure clothes, arrange appointments, and write relatives; to understand his future relationship with his parole supervisor and his responsibility in the parole process; and to meet new challenges.[21] Each of these goals, however, will have to be met within the prison which is frequently hostile to their realization.

The character of the prison

The prison, according to Erving Goffman, is a total institution which circumscribes the time and interest of its members and provides a self-existing world. Each facet of human living is conducted in the same location under the same primary authority. Each person's daily activities occur in the company of a large group of other persons who are treated alike and are required to complete the same actions. Not only is the sequence of activity channeled through a system of explicit ruling by administrative officials, but each part of the program is theoretically designed as part of an overall rational plan to achieve institutional objectives. Of central importance in the full operation of the total institution is the bureaucratic organization which effectively organizes and regiments the population of the total institution.

However, not all persons who operate within the total institution are restricted to its confines. While inmates are typically restricted to contacts within the walls, staff members generally complete an eight-hour day and then integrate socially into the outside community. Conse-

---

[21] F. P. Miller, "Parole," *Crime and Its Treatment*, pp. 348–50. Consult Saleem A. Shah, "Treatment of Offenders: Some Behavioral Concepts, Principles and Approaches, *Federal Probation*, Vol. 30 (June, 1966), pp. 29–38; Charles E. Smith, "A Contemporary View of Psychiatry in Correction," *Federal Probation*, Vol. 25 (December, 1961), p. 16; Eli C. Messinger, "A Psychiatrist Views the Institutional Treatment of Young Adult Offenders," *Federal Probation*, Vol. 29 (December, 1965), pp. 40–43; and Harold F. Uehling, "Group Therapy Turns Repression into Expression for Prison Inmates," *Federal Probation*, Vol. 26 (March, 1962), p. 43.

quently, each group's definition of reality tends to be different from the other's. Staff members often view inmates as bitter, secretive, and untrustworthy, while inmates see correctional officers as condescending, high-handed, and mean. While staff officials commonly tend to feel superior and righteous, inmates, Goffman finds, tend to reflect feelings of inferiority, weakness, blameworthiness, and guilt.

Although total institutions attempt to serve the needs of both the society and the person, these aims are basically incompatible, Goffman believes, with the work-payment structure and familial commitments of one's society. Because the total institution is a social hybrid, part residential community and part formal organization, it is beset continually by tensions between conflicting goals.[22] The corruption of authority, for example, is encouraged when correctional officers overlook some conduct infractions in order to secure inmate cooperation and obedience. Through a form of negotiated exchange, inmates will create a minimum of "visible trouble," a source of difficulty for the administrator, in exchange for an officer overlooking punishable conduct. The action of the officer is partially due to the prison pressure to be a good guy; his discretionary judgment and action represents the "carrot" which he offers his prisoners in order to secure their conformity to major rules and regulations. By definition, being a good inmate is largely related to one's ability to refrain from participation in direct assaults against the administrative system within the prison.[23]

The prison, Paul de Berker notes, as did Donald R. Cressy and Erving Goffman before him, is a total institution which is often preoccupied with order and discipline. Consequently, any incarceration in a total

---

[22] Erving Goffman, "On the Characteristics of Total Institutions: The Inmate World," Donald E. Cressey (ed.), *The Prison* (New York: Holt, Rinehart & Winston, Inc., 1961), pp. 16–22. Refer to Myrl E. Alexander, "Current Concepts in Corrections," *Federal Probation*, Vol. 30 (September, 1966), pp. 33–8; Harry A. Wilmer, "Good Guys and Bad Guys," *Federal Probation*, Vol. 30 (September, 1966), pp. 8–15; Marvin E. Wolfgang, "Quantitative Analysis of Adjustment to the Prison Community," *Journal of Criminal Law, Criminology, and Police Science*, Vol. 51 (March–April, 1961), pp. 607–18; Stanton Wheeler "Socialization in Correctional Communities," *American Sociological Review*, Vol. 26 (October, 1961), pp. 699–712; Peter G. Garabedian, "Social Roles and Processes of Socialization in the Prison Community," *Social Problems*, Vol. 11 (Fall, 1963), p. 139; Walter M. Wallack, "What Price Punishment?" *Federal Probation*, Vol. 25 (March, 1961), p. 3; and Paul S. Spitzer, "Punishment vs. Treatment?," *Federal Probation*, Vol. 25 (June, 1961), p. 3.

[23] Don C. Gibbons, *Changing the Lawbreaker* (Englewood Cliffs, N.J.: Prentice-Hall, Inc., 1965), p. 204. Also see Charles Wellford, "Factors Associated with Adoption of the Inmate Code: A Study of Normative Socialization," *Journal of Criminal Law, Criminology, and Police Science*, Vol. 58 (June, 1967), pp. 197–203; L. E. Hazelrigg, "Examination of the Accuracy and Relevance of Staff Perceptions of the Inmate in the Correctional Institution," *Journal of Criminal Law, Criminology, and Police Science*, Vol. 58 (June, 1967), p. 204; and William R. Cozart, "The Man Who Waits in Between," *Federal Probation*, Vol. 25 (June, 1961), p. 27.

institution demands basic role reorientations to those role demands which support institutional expectations.[24] However, Don C. Gibbons believes that conforming behavior and the acceptance of prescribed roles is an overstatement of realistic expectations. Many of the prison riots in the 1950's, Gibbons believes, were due to the reaction of prison elites to the attempts of some administrators to reduce the power of these elites among other inmates, hardly an indication of complete role acceptance. Roles are always conditioned by the social system of the prison and the characteristics of role participants.

Whatever the roles assumed, the inmate social system, Elmer H. Johnson suggests, persists because the frustrations of confinement encourage the development of a psychology and ideology hostile to prison keepers; the inmates' inferior status continually reminds them that they have been judged untrustworthy and disreputable by society; confinement threatens inmate masculinity; the offender is unable to fulfill male economic roles or to control the events in his immediate environment; the inmate is thrown into close intimacy with persons with long records of thievery, assault, and sexual deviance; and long-term or repeatedly incarcerated offenders maintain prison traditions and pass on acquired knowledge and manipulative skills to incoming inmates.[25]

Prisonization and inmate social roles

The incarcerated inmate is influenced by the system of "prisonization," which includes, according to Donald Clemmer, the process by which the individual inmate acquires the customs, folkways, mores, institutional behavior patterns, and the general culture of the prison community. As the new inmate is socialized to the expectations of the prison, he also learns to adapt his behavior to the expectations of the prison culture. The effective prisonization of the inmate, Clemmer recognizes, is influenced by the inmate's personality, social relationships prior to his incarceration, affiliation with an informal group, assigned work placement, and own attitudes towards the prisoners' code. Prisonization, therefore,

---

[24] Paul de Berker, "The Sociology of Change in Penal Institutions," in Hugh J. Klare (ed.), *Changing Concepts of Crime and Its Treatment* (New York: Pergamon Press, Inc., 1966), p. 141. Examine Julius Leibert, *Behind the Bars: What a Chaplain Saw in Alcatraz, Folsom and San Quentin* (Garden City, N.Y.: Doubleday & Co., Inc., 1965); F. Lovell Bixby, "Treating the Prisoner: A Lesson from Europe," *Federal Probation,* Vol. 25 (March, 1961), p. 7; and Frank E. Hartung, *Theoretical Studies in Social Organization of the Prison* (New York: Social Science Research Council, 1960), pp. 130–32.

[25] Elmer H. Johnson, *Crime, Correction, and Society* (rev. ed.; Homewood, Ill.: Dorsey Press, 1968), pp. 510–11. Also see Donald R. Cressey, *The Prison: Studies in Institutional Organization and Change* (New York: Holt, Rinehart & Winston, Inc., 1961); and Derrick Sington and Giles Playfair, *Crime, Punishment, and Cure* (London: Secker & Warburg, 1965).

can best be understood as the process by which the inmate assimilates prison culture and becomes integrated into the prison world. Stripped of most of the personal identity symbols which he carries in the outside world, he begins to attach new meanings provided by the prison culture to life conditions previously taken for granted.[26] Among factors which tend to maximize prisonization, Clemmer believes are the following:

1. A sentence of many years plus a long rejection of the universal factors of prisonization.
2. A personality made unstable by an inadequacy of "socialized" relations before commitment, but possessing, nonetheless, a capacity for strong convictions and a particular kind of loyalty.
3. A dearth of personal relations with persons outside the walls.
4. A readiness and a capacity for integration into a prison primary group.
5. A blind, or almost blind, acceptance of the dogmas and mores of the primary group and the general penal population.
6. A change of placement with other persons with similar orientation.
7. A readiness to participate in gambling and abnormal sex behavior.[27]

Every prison community permits the assumption of a variety of social roles. Prisoner leadership, Clemmer found, may be differentiated into a variety of inmate roles and informal groupings. The *politicians* or *big shots,* known for their checkered criminal careers or notorious crimes, often seize power and plan strikes, sabotage, riots, or prison breaks. The *right guys,* on the other hand, strictly observe the prisoners' code and vigilantly exploit all existing opportunities for better jobs, improved living conditions, and benefits toward discharge. *Moonshiners* engage in the secret manufacture and sale of liquor to other inmates; *dope peddlers monopolize* the distribution and sale of narcotics. The *larceny boys* steal personal belongings of prisoners and sell them to other inmates. Members of the *gambling syndicate,* frequently organized into a hierarchy, extract a tax levy or toll for each game played. The *leather workers* spend their leisure time in creating artistic leather goods for sale to the public. The *religionists* share an emotional fellowship which frequently centers upon a form of religious fanaticism.

Homosexuals or *wolves* within the one-sex prison community share in homosexual promiscuity, prostitution, or temporary marriage. The *manufacturers of weapons* secretly produce knives, saws, blackjacks, whips, hatchets, or other usable weapons for use by homosexual "gal-boys" or other inmates for personal protection or by those anticipating a possible prison riot, prison break, or escape. The last group, the

[26] Donald Clemmer, "Observations on Imprisonment as a Source of Criminality," *Journal of Criminal Law, Criminology, and Police Science,* Vol. 41 (September–October, 1950), pp. 316–17.
[27] *Ibid.,* pp. 301–2.

spartans, Clemmer found, emphasize individuality and take pride in exhibiting their nude bodies to other inmates in locker rooms, showers and toilets, or other public places.[28]

The frustrations of imprisonment

Although Gresham Sykes found similar role models in his study of a captive society, he also discovered that the most painful aspects of imprisonment for male offenders are related to the deprivation of *liberty* (*i.e.,* confinement to a prison and prison isolation from family, relatives, and friends; loss of civil rights; and moral rejection by the free community), the deprivation of *goods and services,* the deprivation of *heterosexual relationships,* the deprivation of *autonomy* (*i.e.,* inability to make choices and receive information about the basis of decisions as in cases of parole denial), and the deprivation of *security* (*i.e.,* confinement in prolonged intimacy with others who have histories of violence or aggressive homosexual behavior).[29] However, despite these many frustrations, inmate attitudes, Howard S. Becker and Blanche Geer suggest, are often conceived in terms of a "latent culture" which permits the inmate to maintain a sense of self-esteem and provides boundaries for cooperation and action in a threatening environment. The general strength and influence of the latent culture in the group, they find, depend upon the characteristics of the group member (*i.e.,* whether they share the same or represent diverse cultural backgrounds).[30] John Irwin and Donald R. Cressey believe that inmate behavior is rooted in subcultural norms reflected in the outside community which restrict snitching on or exploiting one's friends, emphasize keeping cool in stress situations, and presume that only suckers cooperate with authority.[31]

George H. Grosser maintains that the prison is a service organization designed by the community for the purpose of maintaining order and safeguarding its other institutions. As a social system, it possesses both a ruling and subordinate caste which face inevitable conflicts and tensions in regard to moral obligations and achievable goals. Therefore, the prison, he contends, exists in a state of equilibrium which is slow to permit the introduction of change brought about by continued competition and technology. Exempt from competitive testing and standards

---

[28] Donald Clemmer, "Leadership Phenomena in a Prison Community," *Journal of Criminal Law and Criminology,* Vol. 28 (March–April, 1938), p. 863.

[29] Gresham Sykes, *The Society of Captives* (Princeton, N.J.: Princeton University Press, 1958), pp. 63–83.

[30] Howard S. Becker and Blanche Geer, "Latent Social Roles," *Administrative Science Quarterly,* Vol. 5 (September, 1960), pp. 306–8.

[31] John Irwin and Donald R. Cressey, "Thieves, Convicts and the Inmate Culture," *Social Problems,* Vol. 10 (Fall, 1962), p. 145.

of free society, both prison management and inmate population remain relatively free of public scrutiny. Because the administration controls most means of inmate communication with the outside world, it is able to assert its authority without too much fear of inmate response, short of riot or rebellion.[32]

Ruth S. Cavan believes that the inmate population in most prisons is commonly subdivided into five major social classes. The *upper* class, commonly interested in social power and in the control of inmate public opinion, consists of inmate politicians and others with superior status. The *middle* class, usually interested in preserving and enforcing the prisoner's code, is largely composed of the "right guys." The *lower* class, on the other hand, commonly circumscribes the uneducated, the un-skilled, the mentally retarded, and abnormal sex offenders. While the neophytes or "fish", generally young first offenders, compose the *new-comers,* stool pigeons or social outcasts who engage in intelligence and espionage activities on behalf of the prison administration usually compose the *lowest* status group.[33]

Prison culture and structure

Pentonville, an English prison.   Each penal institution is a composite of multiple and variable prisoner and staff social roles, statuses, structures, and cultures. Pentonville, a closed local English prison in an urban environment, which housed 1,250 men in 1,048 cells at the time of the 1958 study completed by Terence and Pauline Morris, is no exception. Due to institutional requirements that men be locked up singly or in groups of three, 650 men were housed in three-man lockups and the remainder in single cells. Prisoners were locked up daily from 5:30 P.M. to 6:30 A.M. and from noon until 2 P.M. The dirt and squalor of the prison, the Morrises noted, marred its physical atmosphere and under-mined inmate morale.

The typical Pentonville inmate, the Morrises found, is a recidivist who exhibits a wide range of criminal experience. Having to adjust to the social organization and routine of the prison, the inmate is forced to undergo a continuous and systematic destruction of the psyche and the adoption of new attitudes and ways of conduct which make it possi-ble for him to survive incarceration. The experience of prisonization also causes him to assume many individual behavior patterns which undermine the normal social roles in the free world. Prisonization,

---

[32] George H. Grosser, "External Setting and Internal Relations of the Prison," *Theoretical Studies in Social Organization of the Prison,* pp. 130–32.

[33] Ruth S. Cavan, *Criminology* (New York: Thomas Y. Crowell Co., 1948), p. 590.

Morris and Morris found, does not have a uniformly destructive effect upon all aspects of the prisoner's behavior or personality; its influence varies in relationship to the extent of previous exposure to prison culture (number and duration of sentences), the nature of one's relationship to the outside world, the degree to which the inmate consciously accepts the dogmas and codes of the inmate culture, and the nature of the prisoner's relationships within the prison.[34]

Overall, the inmate, the Morrises concluded, undergoes six major adjustments within the prison environment. The adjustment of *conformity* implies the inmate's recognition of the legitimacy of the custodial regime and his need to conform to its legitimate demands. Few prisoners accept this model; instead, those who represent conforming tendencies, the Morrises found, generally share only a common interest in order and stability while also accepting the common values of prison culture. Those who represent the *innovation* model, however, accept official objectives but reject the institutionalized means for their attainment. These inmates continually propose improvements for penal policy with or without erroneous assumptions.

Prisoners exemplifying a *ritualism* model reject socially approved goals and follow safe institutional norms and routines. The ritualist, the Morrises found, is the individual who has "learned to do his bird," a term similar to "doing one's own time" in the American prison cultural tradition. He simply goes along with the system as it exists, having grown wise to prison culture. While some within the ritualism model accept the system ambivalently, others accept the security offered by the prison itself. The man within the *retreatism* model, rejecting both goals and means, remains within the prison society but is not part of it. A rare individual within the institution, he represents the true alien who has escaped from the demands of prison culture. The *rebellion*-oriented prisoner works to overturn existing means and goals and to substitute alternatives; the *manipulation*-oriented prisoner adjusts to the prison situation by attempting to outwit authority rather than by creating conflict. The rebel, the Morrises found, is generally under 30, regards imprisonment as a contest of wills, and maintains a constant attitude of rebellion against authority. The manipulator recognizes his inability to change the social, physical, and psychial environment of the prison and seeks to use these factors to his own rational advantage.[35]

The California Institution for Women.   Because the majority of the female inmates of the California Institution for Women, which houses approximately one ninth of the nation's incarcerated female felons, are

---

[34] Terrence Morris and Paulene Morris, *Pentonville: A Sociological Study of an English Prison* (London: Routledge & Kegan Paul, Ltd., 1963), pp. 163–70.
[35] *Ibid.*, pp. 171–76.

parents of minor children, the problems of this institution, Serapio R. Zalba discovered, are quite different from those within male institutions. A total of 520 of the 850 female inmates, he reported, were mothers of approximately 1,200 minor children. Although the mothers had previous histories of narcotics usage, homosexuality, prostitution, or alcoholism before institutionalization, they still had managed to fulfill some semblance of a maternal responsibility. However, their children, Zalba noted, evidenced patterns of diffuse anxiety, apprehension, and uncertainty. The loss of love objects led to insecurity. Frequently, their fathers were unknown, unavailable, or disinterested in relating to their own children. Although the children needed more stable relationships, any attempts by the child to establish substitute parental contacts were undermined by the actions of the institutionalized mother. Despite the fact that many of the personal difficulties which led to her incarceration were related to the fact that she had children, the inmate-mother's rehabilitation and adjustment responses, Zalba discovered, were strongly influenced by her sense of maternal role responsibility and a personal need to maintain a continuing relationship with her children.

Although many imprisoned women make plans to reestablish contact with their children upon release, their precipitous movements often undermine the stable relationships of the child in a temporary household. At the same time, adults caring for the woman's children during her absense prefer to focus on the present and ignore the potential termination of the relationship with the child. In some situations, competition arises between the temporary parents and the mother. Rather than preparing for the day when the child may be returned to its mother, the temporary parents inevitably plan the child's program without consulting the inmate-mother. Consequently, the mother's feeling of deprivation, Zalba uncovered, actually serves to undermine potentially valuable plans for the maintenance of the mother's children in the greater number of cases.

The child who is cared for by a relative during the absence of his mother, the study revealed, maintains a greater sense of identity and belonging than does a child placed in foster care.[36] Part of the confusion arising within the parent-child relationship is due to a lack of data and information sharing between the various casework and welfare agencies assigned to assist in the maintenance of the family and in the rehabilitation of the mother. For example, the California Institution for Women receives inadequate information concerning the mother's family

---

[36] Serapio R. Zalba, *Women Prisoners and Their Families* (Los Angeles: Delmar Publishers, Inc., 1964), pp. 115–19. Refer to Annie Lorimer and Marjorie Heads, "The Significance of Morale in a Female Penal Institution," *Federal Probation*, Vol. 26 (December, 1962), p. 38.

situation and level of familial performance before institutionalization, and the public welfare department and the Women's Parole Division does not receive adequate insight into the inmate-mother's institutional performance or postrelease plans. The failure to share information creates a vicious cycle. What planning, however minimal, that does exist is rarely family oriented. Most is designed for individuals or groups of individuals rather than for family units. Prerelease plans, designed for the female inmate prior to parole consideration by the Women's Board of Trustees, are usually completed *by* rather than *with* the inmate and, therefore, are frequently unrealistic. The lack of coordination between the institution and community agencies also does little to enhance the assistance function implied in parole. While plans for the community care of the children are more realistic, the failure to plan jointly with the foster or other mother upon release often undermines the more positive aspects of an agency attempt to aid juvenile adjustment. The limited interpersonal contact of agency staff members, therefore, serves to undermine the prerelease treatment plan.

In order to correct these shortcomings, greater attention, Zalba suggests, must be given to assistance in the placement of children; aid in the development of realistic short- and long-term family plans; assistance for the mother in working out her feelings toward her children, especially in cases involving the relinquishing of children for adoption or other arrangements for long-term custody by others; and general assistance of the various community agencies in meeting the needs of family members during these periods of familial difficulty. The failure of family-oriented planning, Zalba believes, makes the need for such planning immediate.[37]

The Federal Reformatory for Women.   Rose Giallombardo discovered in her July, 1962, to July, 1963, study of the Federal Reformatory for Women at Alderson, West Virginia, that this prison is quite different from state male penal institutions. Living in 16 cottages grouped around two quadrangles located on two different levels, the women are incarcerated in a rural prison encompassed by only a cyclone fence topped with barbed wire. Because each woman is housed in a cottage for 45 to 55 inmates, there is a feeling that treatment rather than punishment is being emphasized.

The setting of the prison, Giallombardo noted, presents an immediate problem for staff recruitment. Although the inclusion of emotionally disturbed inmates within the population points to the need for a staff psychiatrist, the low salary ranges, beginning at $5,035 for a starting correctional officer, and the rural location of the institution, severely limit his employment. The 10 male correctional officers on duty primarily

---

[37] *Ibid.,* pp. 119–21.

supervise the gate, deliver medical and other items to the cottages, travel to town for mail and supplies, and assist in patrol duty as needed. Symbolically, they represent the presence of brute force to the inmates and enable women officers to deal with female inmates without recourse to force except in self-defense. The male officer represents "a negative symbol for the inmates," and he is never looked upon by them, Giallombardo observed, as a meaningful sex object.[38]

The employment of a new warden in July, 1961, led to greater attempts to encourage inmates to express themselves and to act out responsible behavior patterns. Smoking was permitted except in hazard areas, restrictions upon movement were relaxed, and custodial escort for inmates traveling to movies, church services, or other activities was eliminated. The idea of "inmates" was replaced by the concept of "resident" or "client." Homosexual behavior was punished only if participants were found in bed together, a decision which challenged the predominant views of the custodial staff.[39] The emphasis upon freedom and understanding in the new program forced correctional officers, Giallombardo found, to accept aggressive behavior, which in turn created personal tensions. Although specific attempts are made at treatment, the custodial responsibility undermines much of the treatment opportunity.

Training in good work habits constitutes the fundamental treatment program. It is supported with recreation, religious activities, medical treatment, general education, and other treatment facets. However, the problems associated with the assignment of prisoners to work tasks, and the development of individualized treatment programs, frequently restricts the value of the treatment approach. The need to maintain prisoner custody and the attempt to reach economic self-sufficiency, Rose Giallombardo noted, seriously imperils the prison's treatment function. This basic conflict of competing goals is an inherent weakness, she notes, of the prison system.[40]

Of the 653 women committed to the prison, 6 came from Mongoloid, 367 from Caucasoid, and 280 from Negroid racial backgrounds. Slightly more than 15 percent were recidivists from the Alderson prison; however, nearly half had been institutionalized for previous offenses. The incarcerated women were primarily sentenced for forgery (128 persons), narcotics violations (193), larceny (204), fraud (24), and a series of other offenses ranging from such categories as bank robbery to counterfeiting (which involved fewer than 15 persons). Of the 653 inmates, 132 were committed to the prison between the ages of 20 and 24, 129 between 25 and 29, and 114 between 30 and 34. The respective mean and median

---

[38] Rose Giallombardo, *Society of Women* (New York: John Wiley & Sons, Inc., 1966), p. 33.
[39] *Ibid.*, p. 41–44.
[40] *Ibid.*, p. 67.

ages of female prisoners was 34.4 and 30.8 years; prisoner ages at the time of the study ranged from 16 to 70. At the time of entry to Alderson prison, the female inmates were employed as waitresses or other restaurant employees (174), domestic laborers (72), factory operators (66), clerical workers (72), housewives (55), or in other jobs ranging from organists to hospital attendants. Having been earlier employed at some gainful occupation, most accommodated quickly to the prison's vocational "training program." Of the inmates, 27.1 percent were single, 31.5 percent married, 20.7 separated, 16.4 percent divorced, and approximately 4 percent widowed. More than 49 percent (325) completed only eight years or less of schooling.[41]

Even at Alderson imprisonment stripped the female offender of her individuality. A type of symbolic personal death, Giallombardo reports, occurred upon her entrance into the prison when her clothing and personal effects were itemized in her presence, packaged in brown wrapping paper, and mailed to family members or friends in civil society. Clothed in the "standard outfit original issue," she now felt depersonalized and regimented into the prison culture. The unfeminine cut of many of the clothes did little to enhance her sense of femininity and projected a clear sense of social punishment.

An estimated 5 percent of the inmate population participated in homosexual activities in the free community. The homosexual diad, Giallombardo ascertained, is viewed as a meaningful personal and social relationship by the inmates. Coercion toward prostitution, therefore, is generally lacking in the female prison. Instead, the female inmate often attempts to establish a homosexual alliance with a mutually compatible partner in order to release tension and to find solutions to the many complex problems of interpersonal prison behavior. The hardest part of living in a prison, Giallombardo discovered, "is to live with other *women*."

Female social roles at Alderson are many. The *snitcher*, the female counterpart of the male "rat," is a woman who violates the prohibitions against communications across caste lines. As a supplier of information to prison officials that may undermine inmate activities, she poses a serious threat to the inmate population. Although the snitcher who informs the prison or cottage officers of inmate activities may be regarded by them as a "good girl," she is despised by her inmate peers when discovered. The *inmate cop* or *lieutenant*, comparable to the "center man" in the male prison, is a prisoner who is in a position of authority over other inmates due to her work assignment. Fulfilling her work role, she issues orders and reports infractions of work rules.

The *square*, generally an accidental criminal, is an alien to the inmate culture and possesses "anticriminal loyalties." While the *cube square*

---

[41] *Ibid.,* pp. 78–86.

tends to support the prison administration and general social values, the *hip square* tends to sympathize with the inmate code and acts in accordance with some of its principles. The *jive bitch*, on the other hand, occupies the role of a troublemaker who often distorts facts, volunteers information, or undermines other interpersonal relationships. The role of *ramp buddies* is occupied by any two people who serve time together and develop a compatible relationship without becoming a "couple." The *homie* is an inmate from another inmate's hometown or nearby community. The female *connect*, generally occupies a good job within the prison and cooperates in the procurement of information or desired goods. In contrast with the connect, the *booster* exploits the environment through stealing from official stores and frequently maintains an illegal business enterprise. *Pinners* serve as lookouts to prevent a surprise intrusion upon unauthorized inmate activities by either staff or inmates. Occupying an important trust, she protects deviating inmates from prison punishment or loss of privilege.[42]

A series of roles are also associated with what Giallombardo calls the "homosexual cluster." The *penitentiary turnout* participates in prison homosexuality but differs from the lesbian who prefers homosexual relations in the free as well as the prison community. The *femme* or *mommy* assumes the female role in the homosexual relationship even as the *stud broad* or *daddy* assumes that of the male. The *trick*, held generally in low esteem, is one who fails to develop a sincere homosexual relationship and permits herself to be exploited. The *commissary hustler* commits herself to a single homosexual relationship with an inmate living in the same cottage, but she also establishes ties with additional tricks in other cottages for economic purposes. The *chippie* permits no stable relationship to develop and in effect plays the role of a prison prostitute. *Kick-partners* are women who participate in relatively nonpermanent physical relationships for the release of sexual tension. On the other hand, *cherries* are women who have never been initiated into homosexual practices. While they know the "score" and are not "squares," they simply have not engaged in prison homosexuality. Although she is expected to behave as a male, the *punk* assumes the passive female role. However, the *turnabout* alternately plays both male and female roles.[43]

The existence of such diverse homosexual roles is an indication of the importance for "doing easy time" of the sex relationship to these imprisoned women. The homosexual diad relationship, Giallombardo hypothesizes, serves as a kinship system which stabilizes inmate community relationships and links diverse interests, sentiments, and social and psychological needs. He writes, "Although spatially separated, the

---

[42] *Ibid.*, pp. 110–21.
[43] *Ibid.*, pp. 123–39.

cottages merge into one social unit through the interlacing of kinship ties between the inmates."[44] While the kinship network integrates inmates into the inmate social system, it also provides the foundation for the division of inmates into small family units of 2 to 15 members. The inmate kinship network is frequently composed of multiple nuclear and matricentric families, family fragments, or kinship role syndromes which in varying degrees represent the roles of husband, wife, father, mother, son, daughter, brother, and sister.[45]

Frontera Institution for Women. Imprisonment at the California Institution for Women in Frontera is especially difficult for the mother, since she not only is separated from her husband but is also unable to fulfill her maternal role of caring for her children. If pregnant at the time she enters prison, she may care for the child for a week to 10 days after its birth. However, at that point it is usually taken from her and placed, pending the mother's release, with an approved family member or in a foster home under the supervision of the state welfare department or under the authority of county agencies in which the prison is located. Of the 292 inmates responding imprisoned at Frontera, 68 percent, David A. Ward and Gene G. Kassebaum reported, are mothers, and 59 percent have minor children.[46]

At Frontera, female prisoners undergo deprivations of liberty, goods, services, heterosexual relationships, autonomy, and security. However, the disruption of familial roles of wife and mother are uniquely the most severe deprivations brought about by imprisonment for the woman. While the female institution, Ward and Kassebaum revealed, is not as harsh in appearance and function as male institutions, the absence of maternal and familial fulfillment actually makes female imprisonment equally severe.[47]

As at Alderson, female inmates at Frontera assume many social roles. However, many roles, like that of *snitch*, are further differentiated into several forms. The *dry snitch* is one who "innocently" happens to pass on information to the staff in violation of the prisoners' code. The *cold snitch* rats to staff members in the person's presence; the *plain snitch* commonly gives this information to a staff member privately, either by note or orally. Between 50 and 90 percent of the female population engage in snitching. The woman who snitches occasionally is referred to as having a *jacket* and one who does so frequently as having an overcoat.[48] Virtually absent from Frontera, however, is a role of the

---

[44] *Ibid.*, p. 159.
[45] *Ibid.*, pp. 175–76.
[46] David A. Ward and Gene G. Kassebaum, *Women's Prison* (Chicago: Aldine Publishing Co., 1965), p. 15.
[47] *Ibid.*, p. 28.
[48] *Ibid.*, pp. 32–33.

tough or *gorilla* comparable to that in male prisons, where the prisoners use physical force or violence to achieve his ends. On the other hand, equivalents of the *centerman,* who is identified with the staff, and the *square John* or prosocial prisoner type are common Frontera inmate types.

As at Alderson, a large percentage of the Frontera female population engage in homosexual relations to compensate for the loss of support and protection of parent, husband, or lover and to regain a sense of security. Homosexual love affairs, Ward and Kassebaum theorized, are forms of attempted compensation "for the mortification of the self suffered during imprisonment."[49] In effect, they lessen depersonalization by implying an inmate worth to the offender. As the older "mate" provides information, trust, and status in an institution which itself is conceived as a form of status degradation, the new inmate finds solutions to her most pressing problems in homosexual relations.

Approximately 50 percent of the Frontera inmates, Ward and Kassebaum noted, are involved homosexually "at least once during their term of imprisonment."[50] The remaining number, while not homosexual, also have to come to terms with the homosexual prison adaptation. Women rejecting homosexuality as a solution to their problems, Ward and Kassebaum found, have to learn to live in the prison inmate society dominated by homosexual ideology and behavior. For the greater number of women, the homosexual prison experience is their first such encounter. Consequently, it represents a temporary adaptation to the existing environment and implies the resumption of heterosexual relationships upon release.

Common homosexual roles at Frontera involved those of the male butch or stud broad and the female femme. Nearly one third of the 400 inmates at Frontera involved homosexually at some time, Ward and Kassebaum discovered, were butch at one time or another. Forty-five female inmate interviewees questioned as part of the Frontera study, however, estimated that the butch population included somewhere between 30 to 40 percent of the jailhouse turnouts, women introduced to homosexuality in prison for the first time. Their estimates of the proportion of butches among the true homosexual prison population, however, ranged from 60 to 90 percent.[51] Approximately two thirds of the jailhouse turnouts were femmes, a role which allowed the woman to maintain her traditional female role with only a change in the love object. Overall, "a woman turns out," Ward and Kassebaum theorized, "not as a homosexual but as a butch or a femme, and the choice she

---

[49] *Ibid.,* p. 74.
[50] *Ibid.,* p. 92.
[51] *Ibid.,* p. 104.

makes says something about her needs, her self-image, and her social and sexual relationships in the heterosexual world."[52] The main patterns of turning out in the initial phase of prison love affairs, according to Ward and Kassebaum, are summarized in the following evaluation:

Newly arrived butch inmates are rushed by femmes looking for new lovers. The butches are offered certain goods and services to heighten their interest in one girl over others. Newly arrived non-homosexuals, particularly those who are young and attractive, are wooed and often won by butches using flattery, sympathy, and advice on how to do time in and how to get out of prison.[53]

Generally, true homosexuals express little interest in converting jail-house turnouts to the gay life. Undoubtedly, this attitude is partially due to the fact that the more than one half of the Frontera female prison population who are mothers and who are reluctant to bring up children without a father are also likely to realize that the normative supports for prison homosexuality are unavailable on the outside. Homosexuality, Ward and Kassebaum hypothesize, is an expression of love in a specialized setting. Consequently, women in prison, they perceived, show the same degree of infatuation, love, jealousy, happiness, and pain as commonly found in heterosexual love experiences. Fights and emotional outbursts, property destruction, and attempted suicides are common reflections of emotional commitments.

Although female homosexuality is felt to be necessary for many doing "their own time," its practice receives little support from the staff. Many inmates believe that the negative attitude of staff members, however, is due to their faulty or inadequate understanding of the character of institutional homosexuality. Where staff hostilities are evident, most punitive action and personal ostracism tends to be focused upon the obvious butches. Inmates, Ward and Kassebaum found, feel that the staff is unable to make the important distinction between true homosexuality and the temporary-situation involvement of most inmates, and between affectional behavior (i.e., hand holding or embracing) common among women and outright homosexuality. Prisoners similarly believe that staff members are unable to differentiate between two women who are close friends and those who are lovers. Part of the problem is that female homosexuality, Ward and Kassebaum concluded, "is only a matter of official concern in the atypical world of the prison" and not outside the prison.[54]

Although the laws which apply to male homosexuality also apply to female homosexuality, greater social tolerance, Ward and Kassebaum

---

[52] *Ibid.*, p. 116.
[53] *Ibid.*, p. 155.
[54] *Ibid.*, pp. 199–204.

noted, is granted females who act in a near-homosexual manner than males. Few convictions of females have ever taken place in any of the states for homosexuality, probably because female homosexuality is not viewed as an American social problem. For example, it does not present a public health hazard through the transmission of syphilus or other venereal diseases. Because female responses are generally more expressive to begin with, they do not ordinarily arouse suspicion. And even if homosexuality among women is discovered, the public tends to believe it will cease once a virile male liaison is established.

Homosexuality and conjugal visiting

While lacking precise data to support his assumptions, Donald W. Cory hypothesizes the existence of four classes of homosexuality within the prison setting. The *exclusive heterosexuals* are unable or unwilling to engage in homosexual activities while confined. The *exclusive homosexual,* at the other extreme, finds his homosexual needs most effectively gratified within the prison setting. Frequently imprisoned for a short term, the exclusive homosexual, whose original offense may have involved solicitation in a public or semipublic place, simply continues homosexual relations with new partners. Between these two extremes, Cory believes, are those who are *primarily heterosexual but who participate* in homosexual experiences due to their new prison contacts. They differ from the fourth group of persons who are *primarily heterosexual but have maintained* occasional homosexual contacts periodically since adolescence.

Because these four types of personal responses exist simultaneously, prison officials, Cory proposes, should legalize heterosexual contacts for imprisoned inmates or make provision for periodic home visits for trustworthy prisoners. However, prison officials should also recognize that homosexual activities in the prison should not be punished as long as they represent the voluntary actions of the parties involved. Prison officials should not, he proposes, make derogatory remarks or reveal scornful attitudes toward homosexuals. And yet, they should do all they can to protect prisoners from homosexuality forced by threat, violence, or other forms of intimidation.[55]

Efforts to lessen the prison homosexual problem have largely emphasized provisions for conjugal visiting. In Mexico, conjugal visits are permitted at four prisons. Sweden similarly permits unsupervised visits of husbands and wives in a cell at open institutions. In the Philippines, the wife and family are permitted to live with the prisoner in an open

---

[55] Donald W. Cory, "Homosexuality in Prison," *Journal of Social Therapy,* Vol. 1 (April, 1955), pp. 137–40.

colony, the government paying for the transportation to the colony and for necessary support, food, and clothing.

Only one prison in the United States permits conjugal visiting. The Mississippi State Penitentiary at Parchman makes a small room available in a "red house" near each of the male camps for blacks and whites to the inmate and his wife during Sunday afternoon visiting hours. This practice, prison officials find, lessens sexual tensions, reduces homosexuality, encourages marital fidelity, and elevates inmate morale. However, many critics openly criticize the practice of conjugal visiting on the grounds that it overemphasizes physical sex, aggravates tensions for the single male prisoner, contributes to added public welfare costs through ensuing pregnancies, and encourages sexual relationship outside of marriage.[56]

The use of the weekend pass (or furlough) to permit prisoners to return home is probably most highly developed in Scandinavia, where such opportunities are defined as a matter of right even for many of the more serious criminal offenders. The Hall Institution, for example, accepts this principle as necessary to a meaningful prison treatment setting. It is a small price to pay, staff members believe, for a more therapeutically oriented community atmosphere. However, such privileges in the United States are not considered a matter of right but rather a privilege to be infrequently granted for good behavior or for preparation for eventual release. Nevertheless, weekend pass and furlough programs may receive greater future acceptance.

Although the American public has been slow to accept the idea of conjugal visitation—due to its conservative attitudes toward sex despite the seeming evidence to the contrary in the so-called sexual revolution—most nations which have adopted this practice have found it highly successful.

Imprisonment and family life

Prison places many added burdens upon marriage and family life. In a study of 177 civil prisoners, 330 "stars" (persons normally serving their first term of imprisonment), and 330 recidivists, in England and Wales, Pauline Morris discovered that married prisoners were slightly older than the prison population as a whole, 40 percent being under the age of 30 in comparison to 50 percent in the outside prison popula-

---

[56] Columbus B. Hopper, "The Conjugal Visit in Mississippi State Penitentiary," *Journal of Criminal Law, Criminology, and Police Science*, Vol. 53 (September, 1962), pp. 340–43. Also see Richard D. Knudten, *Criminological Controversies* (New York: Appleton-Century-Crofts, 1968); and Eugene Zemans and Ruth S. Cavan, "Marital Relationships of Prisoners," *Journal of Criminal Law, Criminology, and Police Science*, Vol. 49 (July–August, 1958), pp. 50–57.

tion. Nearly 37 percent were unemployed at the time they committed their offense, 31 percent were unskilled or semiskilled manual workers, and fewer than 10 percent were white-collar employees. Some form of mental or physical ill health was experienced by 21 percent, and 33 percent showed signs of psychiatric problems in regard to work. Of the unemployed, 33 percent made their living through crime.[57] Thirty-five percent of the stars, 35 percent had at least three previous convictions, while 94 percent of the recidivists had the same. Offenses involving violence were more common among recidivists, but the bulk of the prisoners had been involved in property offenses.

Although the marital stability of recidivists was clearly higher than that of the stars, nearly one third of the prisoners were involved in broken marriage. Fifty percent of the inmates had known their wives for at least two years before marriage, many wives being pregnant at the time of marriage. While 80 percent of the wives corresponded weekly with their husbands, only 54 percent visited them on every available occasion. Marital conflict for 70 percent of stars and the 80 percent of the recidivists was due to inlaw problems, unemployment, drinking, or sexual jealousy. Of the 236 star wives and 179 recidivists wives, 50 percent were under 30 and only 4 percent above 50. While less than 15 percent of the households had no dependent children, the average number of persons per household, including parents siblings, adults, children, grandchildren, wives, and dependent children, was 4.2.

The most common problems encountered during the period of separation involved the lack of money (41 percent), management of children (34 percent), loneliness and sexual frustration (32 percent), and fears of postrelease relationships (23 percent). Few wives were concerned for community hostility (5 percent) of feelings of shame (4 percent) regarding their husband's crime and imprisonment. While 30 percent of the nonseparated wives accepted part or full-time employment, 78 percent of the women received some form of national assistance, even though the assistance given was rather meager. A large number of wives expressed thoroughly negative attitudes in regard to social agencies which caused them to act as "suppliants before 'authority.'" Fifty percent of the wives suffered some degree of physical or mental illness. Interestingly, star wives most frequently expressed a feeling of injustice over the long sentences which their husbands received for a "white-collar offense," which they did not view as criminal, or for a sex violation. Although the recidivists' wives tended to regard long sentences for larceny and receiving as unfair, most wives desired their husbands back

---

[57] Pauline Morris, *Prisoners and Their Families* (New York: Hart Publishing Co., Inc., 1965), p. 290. Also see Carl S. Selsky, "Post-Commitment Family Counseling," *Federal Probation,* Vol. 26 (September, 1962), pp. 41–43.

after their release, despite their long criminal record in many instances.[58]

Twenty star and thirty-four recidivist wives were separated from their husbands at the time of the study. Their concerns were similar to those of nonseparated wives, but they had fewer children dependent upon their person, were twice as likely to be living with parents, were less likely to receive regular national assistance, received more financial aid from voluntary and statutory agencies, had fewer financial commitments, and were more adjusted to living on a small income. The reasons for their separation from their husbands were similar to the reasons for marital conflict. Of the separated wives, 54 percent continued to correspond with their husbands and 22 percent engaged in sporadic prison visits. Not only did the separated wives feel that their husbands deserve their present sentences but most claimed to be totally disinterested in their fate. In general, separated wives were much more pessimistic than nonseparated wives concerning their husbands' potential ability to give up crime as a way of life.

As a result of her study, Pauline Morris concluded that the early stage of separation is especially critical for star wives, even though each additional prison sentence tends to loosen family ties among all groups. However, the impact of any crisis ultimately depends more upon the personality of the wife than upon the quality of family adjustment. The more stable and well-adjusted wives, Morris believes, are better able to handle the separation, no matter what their relationship previously had been with their husbands. Upon his return, however, the personality of the husband assumes equal importance in determining the quality of readjustment. Usually, the pattern existing before imprisonment, Morris predicts, will tend to be the pattern reiterated upon reassuming the husband-wife relationship.[59]

Characteristics of prisoners

A study of inmates by Rodney M. Coe revealed that 22 of the 41 characteristics considered failed to differentiate significantly well-adjusted from poorly adjusted inmates. Among the many insignificant factors are citizenship, religion, education level, type of military discharge, intelligence rating, number of children in the family, sibling rank, number of times married, community or area, mobility, drinking habits, emotional stability, type of sentence, number of previous arrests, number of previous convictions, number of commitments to juvenile institutions, number of previous commitments to adult institutions, total time served,

---

[58] *Ibid.*, pp. 291–95.
[59] *Ibid.*, pp. 296–97.

number of times paroled, number of times violated parole, and number of associates on current offense.

However, 19 factors possessed significance. Well-adjusted offenders tended to be white and older at the time of prison admission. Most often laborers, they had good employment records. Although the majority of the poorly adjusted prisoners were also white, a significantly high proportion of Negroes were contained within that group. Haphazard employment and unemployment patterns were more common among the poorly adjusted prisoner grouping. Of the well-adjusted inmates, 49 percent came from homes classified as average or superior; only 29 percent of the poorly adjusted prisoners came from such homes. The remainder came from inferior homes, which were economically marginal or dependent and were frequently supervised by one parent.

Compared to 61 percent of the poorly adjusted group, only 37 percent of the well-adjusted inmates were single. Over 53 percent of the well-adjusted inmates as compared to 24 percent of the poorly adjusted group resided, Coe found, in the same community most of their lives. Somewhat surprisingly, well-adjusted inmates were more frequently involved in offenses of violence and emotion (29 percent versus 23 percent) and less frequently involved in offenses of theft and stealth (49 percent versus 69 percent) than the poorly adjusted group. Consequently, the well-adjusted offenders tended to receive the longest sentences. They were most frequently classified as improvable or questionably improvable and were commonly first or occasional offenders (57 percent). Poorly adjusted inmates were more frequently evaluated as questionably or doubtfully improvable offenders and disclosed fewer first or occasional offenders (39 percent). Not only did recidivists compose nearly one half of the poorly adjusted group in comparison to 30 percent of the well-adjusted group, but the prognosis for the self-improvement of the well-adjusted prisoner was also generally higher than for poorly adjusted inmates.[60]

More recently, Daniel Glaser has also tentatively concluded that the total prison population reveals both voluntary *isolation* and voluntary *associational* attitudes and patterns to other prisoners. Voluntary isolation, he suggests, is directly correlated with the age of prisoners, the amount of prior correctional confinement experienced, and the degree of heterogenerity of prisoners in an institution measured in terms of race, length of sentence, social class, or prior correctional confinement.

[60] Rodney M. Coe, "Characteristics of Well-Adjusted Poorly-Adjusted Inmates," in Clyde B. Vedder and Barbara Kay (eds.), *Penology* (Springfield, Ill.: Charles C. Thomas, Publisher, 1963), pp. 56–57. Examine Stanley B. Zukerman, Alfred J. Barron, and Horace B. Whittier, "A Follow-Up Study of Minnesota State Reformatory Inmates," *Journal of Criminal Law, Criminology, and Police Science,* Vol. 43 (January–February, 1953), pp. 622–36.

However, the voluntary associational patterns of prisoners can best be described as a U-shaped curve in that they are higher at the beginning of confinement, decrease near the middle, and increase near the point of release. Interinmate advice, he finds, tends to flow from older to younger inmates. Such a finding, Glaser believes, is in keeping with the predominate desire of prison inmates to fulfill the expectations of their keepers so that they might minimize trouble during confinement.[61] Most prison inmates possess strong noncriminal interests (*i.e.*, legitimate vocational aspirations). Inmates tend to get along best with other inmates at jobs which employ few inmates, maintain low contact levels with the rest of the inmate population, involve a trade-training program, offer limited access to contraband supplies or services, and screen and carefully select workers. While prisoners believe other inmates possess less commitment to staff-supported values, prisoners, Glaser suggests, in fact are highly concerned for their adjustment to the staff's value system. Isolation of inmates may impede rehabilitation if the administration encourages a "do your own time" ideology and indifference to the welfare of other inmates.[62] The development of "good-time laws" was due in part to the overcrowded conditions of prisons and the need to encourage the offender to share in his own prison rehabilitation.[63]

The problem of discipline

In some jurisdictions, prison discipline is frequently maintained through the use of solitary confinement in conjunction with dietary restrictions; prisoner cell lock-in with loss of yard privileges; loss of visitation, correspondence, canteen, or other privileges; transfer to another institution; assignment to a discipline squad for menial labor; downgrading in a grading system; forfeiture of earned "good time"; and informal corporal punishment.[64] Penalties are inflicted for such common offenses

---

[61] Daniel Glaser, *The Effectiveness of a Prison and Parole System* (Indianapolis: Bobbs-Merrill Co., Inc., 1964), pp. 98–106. Consult Clarence Schrag, "Leadership Among Prison Inmates," *American Sociology Review*, Vol. 70 (February, 1954), pp. 37–42.

[62] *Ibid.*, p. 156.

[63] Reed R. Clegg, *Probation and Parole* (Springfield, Ill.: Charles C. Thomas, Publisher, 1964), p. 23. Refer to Norman Felton, *Explorations in the Use of Group Counseling in the County Correctional Program* (Palo Alto, Calif.: Pacific Books, Publishers, 1962); Robert L. Hamblin, "Punitive and Non-Punitive Supervision," *Social Problems*, Vol. 11 (Spring, 1964), p. 345; and T. McCall, "Humaneness, Logic, and Economy," *Crime and Delinquency*, Vol. 13 (July, 1967), p. 385.

[64] Vedder and Kay, *op. cit.*, p. 116. Also see Vernon Fox, "Analysis of Prison Disciplinary Problems," *Journal of Criminal Law, Criminology, and Police Science*, Vol. 49 (November–December, 1958), pp. 321–26; and "Rules for Inmates," in Norman B. Johnson, *The Sociology of Punishment and Correction*, Leonard Savitz and Marvin E. Wolfgang (eds.), (New York: John Wiley Sons, Inc., 1962).

as gambling; fighting; homosexuality; stealing; smuggling contraband; "skating" or being in an unauthorized area without a pass; disobedience; refusal to work; manufacture of alcoholic beverages; bartering without permission; actual, attempted, and planned escapes; or other miscellaneous activities. Prison discipline is imposed to maintain institutional order and to secure inmate adherence to defined norms and staff goals.[65]

Despite the existence and use of disciplinary techniques, inmate and staff relations vary directly in relationship to the impersonal and authoritarian attitude of staff members to inmates. Where the coercive pattern is most intense, inmate pressure to avoid communication with officers is similarly most intense. As might be expected, the value of an inmate's ability to gain special access to staff or prison files and/or records varies directly with the restrictions placed upon personal communication and friendship between staff and inmates. Overall, staff influence upon inmates, Daniel Glaser says, varies directly with the same types of personal characteristics which cause a man to be liked in nonprison relationships. Staff members who are friendly and considerate possess a greater influence over inmates than those who are hostile in tone and manner. Personnel who treat inmates predictably and fairly likewise are more influential than those who do not.

Prison officers, Glaser finds, are more inclined to treat prisoners as individuals rather than as members of an inmate class or status if they deal with them in more comprehensive and nonritualized relationships. However, if the prison employee continues to relate to inmates in ritualistic and routinized duties, he is more likely to express authoritarian anti-inmate attitudes and receive a similar response from the inmate population. Therefore, the prison employee, "who has the greatest reformative influence on an offender," Glaser tentatively concludes, "is the one who is able to demonstrate sincerity and sustain concern for and confidence in the offender's rehabilitation."[66] He is able to accomplish this most effectively through "gestures of interest and acts of assistance" which exceed the minimal requirements of the employee's prison job.

Prison work and vocational training programs

In recent decades, greater emphasis has been placed upon vocational training and work opportunities as means of avoiding the drudgery of prison life. However, their effectiveness have been somewhat limited due to the restrictions placed upon such training by unions, business

---

[65] *Ibid.*, p. 120; Examine Sol Rubin, *The Law of Criminal Correction* (St. Paul, Minn.: West Publishing Co., 1963; and James V. Bennett, *Of Prisons and Justice* (Washington, D.C.: U.S. Government Printing Office, 1964).

[66] Glaser, *op. cit.*, pp. 128–62. See Lloyd W. McCorkle, "Guard-Inmate Relationships in Prisons," *Welfare Reporter,* Vol. 8 (December, 1956).

management, prison administrators, and the public. Historically, prison labor has been performed under the open-market lease, contract, piece-price, or state accounts system and the sheltered-market, state-use, or public works and ways approach. Under the *lease system* prisoners were leased to an enterpreneur for a stated amount. In turn, he accepted responsibility for their care and custody. While the entrepreneur still utilized the services of the prisoners under the *contract* approach, he paid only a daily per capita fee for their labor and the state retained control over the inmates. Under the piece-price approach the entrepreneur provided raw materials for manufacture and paid the prison a specified amount for each unit completed. In the *state account* system the state manufactured and sold its products competitively on the open market.

Due to the opposition of many businessmen and labor leaders to other approaches, the *sheltered* approach to prison industry has received greater support. The *state-use* system permits prisoners to produce goods and services for use in all types of state agencies. A compromise approach, it allows the state to provide work opportunities while it also forces each institution to sell its products to noncompetitive, nonprofit state institutions. Under the provisions of the *public works and ways* approach, prisoners assist in road construction and repair, soil-erosion control, reforestation or other similar state-sponsored tasks on behalf of the public.[67]

Although the lease and contract systems were common in the late 1800's, the later opposition of labor unions and employers' associations, which viewed prison labor as a threat to organized labor and industrial profits, caused the enactment of many laws and administrative interpretations which restricted the competitive use of prison labor. The Hawes-Cooper Act of 1929 made prison goods subject to state law and redefined their relationship to interstate commerce, and the Ashurst-Summers Act of 1935 limited the transportation of prison-made goods into states which prohibited their entry and required that all prison-made goods shipped in interstate commerce be appropriately labeled. Both laws severely undermined prison industrial work programs. Since 1940, nearly every state has prohibited the sale of prison-made goods from other states within its political boundaries and has depended upon a state-use plan,[68] suggested in 1887 and endorsed by the United States Industrial Commission in 1900, to provide the necessary work opportunities for prisoners.[69]

---

[67] *Ibid.*, p. 212; and Johnson, *op. cit.*, p. 560.
[68] President's Commission, *op. cit.*, p. 162; and Blake McKelvey, *American Prisons* (Chicago: University of Chicago Press, 1936), pp. 98–105.
[69] Frank T. Flynn, "The Federal Government and The Prison-Labor in the States, "I: Aftermath of Federal Restrictions," *Social Service Review,* Vol. 24 (March, 1950), pp. 20–21.

Although the availability of prison work opportunities is vitally important to the elimination of institutional drudgery, most of what occurs
in prison industries has only limited value for the treatment of the individual. Hardly any opportunities exist nowadays for persons trained
in license-plate making or prison farming. Even if there were such opportunities, psychiatric and social casework findings suggest that merely
teaching the incarcerated offender new skills does little to affect his
rehabilitation as long as his concept of self and social attitudes remain
unchanged. Therefore, greater emphasis must be placed upon motivating
to self-willed progress the individual who has come to understand his
own person. Implied in this assumption is the need for a personalization
of treatment based upon the semideterministic idea that an individual
does what he does because of what he has experienced. If treatment,
therefore, is to develop a greater sense of prisoner inner direction toward
more suitable ends, the impact of treatment must be realized individually.[70] And yet, those correctional treatment programs which provide
maximum reformative effects are those that enhance, Daniel Glaser
writes, "a prisoner's opportunities in legitimate economic pursuits and
those that improve his conception of himself when he identifies with
anti-criminal persons."[71]

For many younger prisoners, the regular work which they engage
in during imprisonment for even as short a time as one year is their
longest and most continuous employment experience. Unfortunately,
prisons are not able to provide work opportunities for all their inmates.
Even where work is available, incentives are often not great enough
to motivate inmates to pursue that prison job likely to be most useful
in his postrelease life. Inmate prison work performance records, therefore, are poor. Only about one fourth of the inmates working at a prison
job find later employment in those areas in which they have been trained.
Nevertheless, the prisoner's participation in the work experience may
have a direct bearing upon his postrelease success. Prison training and
work opportunities have their greatest value in acquainting inmates with
the values and rewards of employment rather than in educating the
inmate to a vocational skill. Prison educational programs, Glaser notes,
are only useful to about one fifth of the released inmates in their jobs
during their first four months after release from prison. In some instances, prison education programs may actually create unrealistic aspirations and orient inmates to goals which are not fully useful in their
postrelease life.[72]

Prisoners, according to Manuel Lopez-Rey, should participate in work
opportunities with the clear understanding that they may earn wages

[70] De Berker, *op. cit.,* pp. 145–46.
[71] Glaser, *op. cit.,* p. 512.
[72] *Ibid.,* pp. 251–83.

during their imprisonment comparable to those offered by the free community.[73] Private industry, Lopez-Rey argues, should be permitted to enter the prison to provide equipment, wage scales, and supervision necessary for effective employment of inmates. Although legal stipulations currently restrict the possibility, prison labor and industrial programs, he believes, are absolute requisites of any effective rehabilitation program. If the monotony and boredom of prison life can be overcome through the substitution of meaningful work experiences, many of the existing psychological and psychiatric services, Lopez-Rey points out, would become largely unnecessary.

In recent years, 90 to 100 percent of the prison inmates in 20 surveyed states, the District of Columbia, and the Federal Bureau of Prisons' institutions received wages.[74] In a second survey of 33 states, wages, Glaser found, range from 4 cents to $1.20 per day.[75] Six states prohibit inmate earnings, and fewer than 10 percent of the inmates earn any money in five states.

The role of the warden

The warden or superintendent of a penitentiary or prison is a figure of singular importance. He ultimately is responsible for the operation of the institution, the employment of personnel, the maintenance of security, and the enactment of any rehabilitation policy. Prison wardens rarely prepare in advance for their position. Usually they are recruited from within the ranks of the prison staff and are "field tested" in the existing prison system before assuming their new responsibilities. A study by Walter A. Lunden of 74 prison wardens in 1956 disclosed that the average age at appointment of 66 wardens in office in 1956 was 48 years. Although the wardens ranged in age at that time from 36 to 69 years, they averaged 53.9 years.[76] Only 28.8 percent were 49 or younger; 52 percent (36) had occupied the office for five or more years. However, the average length of warden tenure of office was six years and eight months. Native sons, Lunden discovered, have a greater chance of becoming wardens in their home state than outsiders.

Fifty-six percent of the wardens served in the armed forces at one point in their lives. Of the 49 wardens employed in correctional work prior to appointment, 22 (71 percent) had held earlier deputy or associate warden positions. Twenty-seven others had occupied various cor-

---

[73] Manual Lopez-Rey, "Some Considerations of the Character and Organization of Prison Labor," *Journal of Criminal Law, Criminology, and Police Science,* Vol. 49 (May–June, 1958), p. 28.

[74] Johnson, *op. cit.,* p. 568.

[75] Glaser, *op. cit.,* pp. 234–35.

[76] Lunden, *op. cit.,* p. 10.

rectional offices. The service of the 22 who had served as deputy wardens ranged from 1 to 22 years. Their promotion within the system represented a form of inbreeding which reinforced the established system of operation.

Although some critics maintain that such inbreeding is the promotion of "trained incapacity" through failure to introduce new procedures and methods into the system of corrections, this belief is not totally accepted. In past decades, John Dewey argued that such a policy could only lead to an "occupational psychosis." Others now maintain that promotion from within the ranks creates a "professional deformation" which causes the warden to fail to deal with changing conditions. Still others argue that such a system eventually develops a disciplined order which limits administrative vision, the desire to experiment, and effective leadership necessary to the development of a sound correctional program.

Part of the answer to these criticisms are discernible in Lunden's findings. Most wardens interviewed by Lunden placed major emphasis upon experience in the correctional field, administrative and business ability, education and training, honesty, integrity and fairness, well-structured personality and stable character, diplomacy, good judgment, common sense and good interpersonal relationships, initiative, willingness to try new methods, enthusiasm to achieve leadership, understanding of human nature and interest in people. They placed the greatest emphasis upon the ability of the warden to govern men under stress and to administer his office effectively.[77]

Of an additional 617 wardens completing their wardenships prior to 1956, 370 (60.5 percent) held office for four years or less. While 161 men (26.2 percent) occupied the office for 5 to 9 years, the average length of tenure was 5.3 years. The shortest average tenure was 3.4 years in Mountain states and the highest 7.0 years in the Mid-Atlantic states. In the latter, the average tenure varied from 3.6 years at Sing Sing Prison (14 wardens in 51 years) to 10.6 years at Western Pennsylvania Penitentiary (12 wardens in 129 years). However, between 1920 and 1941, a single warden occupied the position at Sing Sing prison. During the 50-year period between 1906 and 1955, approximately 17.8 percent of the prisons changed wardens in any given year. Of the 294 cases for which data were available, termination of wardenships was due to changes in state administration or political patronage (35.2 percent), resignations due to ill health or desire to enter some other field (22.7 percent), death (12.5 percent), retirement (12.5 percent), discharge or dismissal from office (6.8 percent), moved to another wardenship (5 percent), promoted to a state commissioner of correctional work within the state (3.6 percent), or killed in the line of duty (1.7 per-

---

[77] *Ibid.*, pp. 17–19.

cent).[78] Salaries of 202 wardens and superintendents, Lunden reported, ranged from a low of $4,284 to a high of $18,959.[79]

The average tenure of wardens in 6 federal penitentiaries was 5.7 years and ranged from 4.4 years at Lewisburg to 7.2 years at Alcatraz, an institution since closed. The average age of the federal wardens at the time of appointment was 48 years, although they ranged in age from 32 to 60 years when initially selected. Most common reason for turnover of federal prison wardens was transfer (44.3 percent), retirement (20.8 percent), no indication (15.8 percent), resignation (7.5 percent), reassignment to Bureau of Prisons (7.5 percent), death (2.5 percent), and reassignment to Department of Justice (1.6 percent).[80]

Prior to 1962, wardens in the Canadian federal penitentiary system were selected by the cabinet. Since 1962, however, Canadian wardens have been appointed by the Commissioner of Penitentiaries under the direction of the Minister of Justice. Commonly, most wardens have undergone military training. The 70 wardens in 7 Federal penitentiaries had an average tenure of 8.0 years, ranging from a low of 6.1 years at New Westminster to 10.3 years at Dorchester. The average age at appointment was 52 years; the lowest age of appointment was at 32 and the highest 76. The 31 wardens in the provincial correctional institutions, served an average of 8.8 years per warden. The average age at appointment was 44 years, approximately 8 years younger than the average for wardens at the federal penitentiaries.[81]

The average age for wardens in the federal prisons in the United States approximated 5.1 years between 1940 and 1962. The tenure of wardens of federal penitentiaries in Canada was 8.0 years between 1932 and 1963. Turnover in the U.S. federal institutions reached 19 per 100 wardenships as opposed to 13.5 in Canadian correctional institutions. State institutional tenure in the United States reached 5.3 years and in the Canadian provincial institutions 8.8 years during the same comparable periods. Turnover rates reached 18 per 100 wardenships in the United States and 14 in Canadian provincial institutions.[82]

TREATMENT IN A PRISON SETTING

Despite the problems and challenges of the inmates, and of the institutional and prison administration, the central issue in correction, Donald C. Gibbons maintains, is *not* one of punishment *versus* treatment

---

[78] *Ibid.*, pp. 21–36.
[79] *Ibid.*, p. 97.
[80] *Ibid.*, p. 59.
[81] *Ibid.*, pp. 67–73.
[82] *Ibid.*, p. 78.

as many have defined the problem, but rather one of treatment *and* punishment. Every violator processed through the judicial system reluctantly or unwilling participates at the outset in the application of sanctions against his previous conduct. However, as historic sanctions have been modified to include therapy, the legal machinery has been asked to change the basic personality of the individual in some significant way, a task which it is poorly equipped to perform. Because the mandate for change is often a form of punishment in itself, it further compounds the problem. Therefore, "as long as the state," Gibbons notes, "continues to define a group of individuals in society as lawbreakers and as long as the state continues to differentially exercise sanctions against such persons, punishment will continue to exist.[83] But punishment on both the juvenile and the adult level is filled with many fallacies. Sidney Smith, for example, argues that punishment of delinquents is based upon such fallacious assumptions that all children are alike and can be treated the same, that delinquents escape punishment through treatment, that the delinquent act is an isolated phenomenon, that the protective policy of the juvenile court has been tested and failed, that treatment is merely condoning delinquency, that the treatment costs too much, and that punishment cures delinquency.[84]

While the emphasis upon punishment of offenders still continues in modern times, a mid-1966 Harris survey revealed that Americans place revenge upon offenders in a low priority category. In general, the public believes that the prison should be more corrective than punitive, emphasizing rehabilitation in anticipation of the offender's reentry into society. While 12 percent of the respondents in the Harris study were uncertain, 77 percent believed prison should be primarily corrective and 11 percent felt that it should be mainly punitive.[85] Such attitudes often only reflect the attitudes of the moment, however. The 1968 Presidential election campaign bears more recent witness to an increased public interest in controlling crime and punishing offenders.

In reality, the prison is continually engaged in both treatment and punishment functions. However, many critics, as Johan Galtung notes,

---

[83] Gibbons, *op. cit.,* p. 132.

[84] Sidney Smith, "Delinquency and the Panacea of Punishment," *Federal Probation,* Vol. 29 (Summer, 1965), pp. 18–23 Consult Lyle W. Shannon, "The Problem of Competence to Help," *Federal Probation,* Vol. 31 (March, 1967), p. 32.

[85] Sanger B. Powers, "Off-Grounds Activities Present An Opportunity for Correctional Institutions," *Federal Probation,* Vol. 31 (June, 1967), p. 11. Also see Don J. Young, "Correctional Workers Must Speak Out," *Federal Probation,* Vol. 31 (December, 1967), pp. 18–21; J. Hall, Martha Williams and Louis Tomaino, "The Challenge of Correctional Change," *Journal of Criminal Law, Criminology, and Police Science,* Vol. 57 (December, 1966), pp. 493–503; and L. L. Wainwright, "Correction Rather Than Punishment: A New Concept in Florida's Prisons," *Florida Bar Journal,* Vol. 39 (March, 1965), p. 161.

argue that the following cannot be accomplished at the same time:

1. Have *punishment orientation.*

   Have *treatment orientation.*

2. Have an ideology concerning prison and prisoners such that external, exculpatory cases are only necessary cases, not sufficient causes of criminal acts by reason of the fact that individual free will and auto-causation are assumed.

   AND

   Have an ideology concerning prison and prisoners such that external exculpatory causes (social, mental, biological, and physical determinants) are seen as *both necessary and sufficient causes of crime.*

3. Portray the prison to society in negative terms, so that it functions as a collective deterrent and as a general reference for negative sanctions.

   AND

   Portray the prison to society in terms such that it stands as a neutral or positive symbol.

4. Put the inmate into the institution against his own wishes.

   AND

   Expect the inmate to adopt an attitude of willingness to undergo therapy.

5. Intentionally (and with the inmate knowing that the action is intentional) inflict evils on the inmate or deprive him of positive values during his stay in prison.

   AND

   Expect the inmate to believe what is done is done for his own good, and to cooperate in his own treatment and therapy.

6. Institutionalize secondary relations between inmates and personnel in an effort to assure equality in treatment and to prevent formation of personalities that may endanger operative efficiency in emergencies.

   AND

   Institutionalize primary relations between inmates and personnel in an effort to assure or facilitate a transfer of values to inmates.

7. Train personnel to orient themselves only to simple, consensual and highly visible variables like age, crime committed, criminal career and sentence.

   AND

   Train personnel to orient themselves to subtle, dissensual and latent characteristics of the inmates.

8. Release the inmates after time periods which are mainly a function of their behavior *before* they were institutionalized.

   AND

   Release inmates after time periods which are mainly a function of their behavior *after* they were institutionalized.[86]

---

[86] Johan Galtung, "Prison: The Organization of Dilemma," in Cressey (ed.), *op. cit.*, pp. 122–23. Refer to *Group Treatment by Correctional Personnel,* (Sacramento, California: Board of Correction, 1963); Winfred Overholser, "The Psychiatrists Role in the Treatment of the Offender," *Federal Probation,* Vol. 25 (June, 1961), p. 22; and Charles E. Smith, M.D., "Psychiatric Approaches to the Mentally Ill Federal Offender," *Federal Probation,* Vol. 30 (June, 1966), pp. 23–29.

However, Johan Galtung maintains that the fact that incompatibility exists does not necessarily mean that rehabilitation may not occur. Although persons outside the prison may believe that the punishment-treatment dichotomy is incompatible, the prisoner, Galtung holds, sees similarities between the two, since both refer to reaction, control, and efforts to change the individual.[87]

Nevertheless, institutionalization may cause major harms. Because it tends to isolate the offender from society, it often eliminates the psychological and physical supports normally offered by schools, jobs, families, and friends necessary to the gradual integration of any individual into normative life. Many prisons engage in what Austin H. McCormick calls *paregoric penology,* an approach to treatment which gives the prisoner what he wants in order to keep him quiet within the institution.[88] A few even freely dispense medication in order to maintain prisoner submissiveness. However, prisons periodically do have riots, and prisoners do attempt to escape from their custodial officers. The characteristics of those prisoners most likely to escape are described by Nelson M. Cochrane as follows:

1. Have weak or non-existent home ties.
2. Serve less than 40 percent of their prison term.
3. Have more than 18 months remaining before eligibility for parole.
4. Have more than four years remaining until attainment of maximum sentence.
5. Are habitual offenders.
6. Are less than 30 years old.
7. Have poor employment record.
8. Have detainers on file.
9. Show uncooperative attitude.
10. Show daring and aggressive personality.
11. Evidence mental instability and inferior intelligence.[89]

Challenges in treatment

Donald C. Gibbons finds obstacles to treatment in two basic areas of the juvenile and adult correctional process. "Bread and butter problems" include inadequate financial resources, low salaries, excessive caseload, or other similar limitations inherent in the social organization of correctional programs. Treatment efforts are continually undermined by

---

[87] *Ibid.,* p. 123.

[88] Austin H. McCormick, "Behind the Prison Riots," *Annals,* Vol. 293 (May 1954), pp. 18–21.

[89] Nelson M. Cochrane, "Escapes and Their Control: A Brief Study of Escape Data," *Prison World,* Vol. 10 (May–June, 1948), p. 29. Also see W. S. Loving, F. E. Stockwell, and D. A. Dobbins, "Factors Associated with Escape Behavior of Prison Inmates," *Federal Probation,* Vol. 23 (September, 1959), pp. 49–51.

the antisocial attitudes of many offenders and the conflicts which result from restrictions upon personal movement and from expectations of behavior. "Bread and butter" complaints are especially pronounced in those institutions in which correctional administation has been dependent upon the political spoils system and in which loyalty to correctional leaders rather than correctional competence is rewarded. In such contexts, the consistency and stability of correctional programs have been undermined by the easier alternative of repression rather than treatment.

When rehabilitation programs receive limited financial support, they normally assume a dominant custodial character and excessive turnover of treatment personnel occurs to the detriment of all parties. But even if these basic problems were solved, the organizational problems inherent in training school and prisons as institutions and in divergent manifest and latent responses of the staff and administration to treatment would tend to restrict the boundaries of rehabilitation programs.[90] The modern prison, Donald Gibbons argues, "must find some way of maintaining a reasonable degree of order without physical coercion and without manipulation of meaningful rewards for conformity."[91] Joseph W. Eaton however, puts the problem and its potential answer in a somewhat different framework:

Prison systems tend to have a conservative orientation. They express society's ultimate effort to enforce its laws against those whose actions or thoughts deviate from it. There is little formal opportunity for initiating changes by persons at lower echelons of its rigid caste system. Formal authority is exercised from above. Those who make policy must be responsive to the pull of conflicting values in modern societies regarding what can be expected from their prisons. For instance, the risks of living under minimum custody conditions to give inmates a chance to try out the capacity for self-control are limited by the expectation of the community that no prisoner be allowed to escape. Yet, a dynamic and a change-oriented milieu can be developed within a conservative social structure by an emphasis on humanistic, scientific and newistic values.[92]

The completion of the treatment-punishment function is made exceedingly difficult by the large number of variables involved in the basic criminal act. Leslie T. Wilkins summarizes the problem in this manner:

Persons who vary in ways that are in the main unknown (variable X_1), live in situations (X_2), and are exposed to cultural influences that vary in unknown ways (X_3). They sometimes commit deeds (X_4) which vary in many ways, except that they are classified by the laws of society as crimes, and these laws (X_5) vary both in content and interpretation. Some persons are detected by

    [90] Gibbons, op. cit., p. 189.
    [91] Gibbons, op. cit., p. 205.
    [92] Joseph W. Eaton, Stone Walls Not A Prison Make (Springfield, Ill.: Charles C. Thomas, Publisher, 1962), pp. 180–81.

systems that vary in unspecified ways (X_6); these are dealt with by persons or courts that also vary in policies (X_7) and are allocated to institutions (X_8) that also differ from each other in many unknown ways. They are committed for varying periods of time (X_9) and their interaction with the treatment (X_{10}) is expected to vary. In most cases they may be expected to interact with other persons (X_{11}) also undergoing treatment. Eventually, they are released to situations that vary both in themselves and in terms of the expected interaction with the personality of a former inmate (X_{12}). In consideration of recidivism, this process may be seen as repeated many times. Frequently in discussions of recidivism the number of times the circuit has been completed remains unspecified.[93]

Institutional or other treatment, therefore, is actually a subsystem within other subsystems, which in turn are located within a much larger system called society.

Recent advances in treatment

More recent concepts have enhanced the possibility of treatment through the development of a therapeutic community, open institutions, and a new interest in smaller correctional units. The goal of the therapeutic community approach is the creation of a treatment-oriented institution which psychologically encourages the individual to become a responsible citizen through self-evaluation and the development of inner security. Emphasizing spontaneous relationships between inmates and staff, the therapeutic community stimulates a dynamic which attempts to maximize the prisoner's participation in his own correctional program. Emphasizing the prisoner's role within the free community upon release rather than the mere adjustment of the inmate to the fact of imprisonment, this method encourages the prisoner to deal with real-life situations which he is likely to encounter upon his return to the community.[94]

The emergence of open institutions free of traditional walls, which have enacted in the past as psychological barriers to rehabilitation, represents a second treatment-enhancing development. The open institution places less emphasis upon escape barriers. It permits free movement upon the prison grounds and attempts to duplicate conditions similar

---

[93] Leslie T. Wilkins, *Evaluation of Penal Measures* (New York: Random House, 1969), p. 20.

[94] See Leonard J. Hippchen, "The Air Force's Therapeutic Community Concept," *American Journal of Correction,* Vol. 25 (January–February, 1963), p. 16; Idem, *Selection Problems in Screening Air Force Prisoners for Rehabilitation* (Amarillo Air Force Base, Texas: 3320th Retraining Group, 1963), pp. 3–4; E. H. Johnson, "A Study of Correctional Reform," *Crime and Delinquency,* Vol. 13 (October, 1967), p. 360; D. B. Hobbs and M. P. Osman, "From Prison to the Community: A Case Study," *Crime and Delinquency,* Vol. 13 (April, 1967), p. 317; and "State Correctional Institutions for Adults," *Crime and Delinquency,* Vol. 13 (January, 1968).

to those of the home community. Emphasizing self-discipline and positive social interaction, the open institution encourages prisoner correspondence, family visits, and close staff-inmate relationships. Of maximum value only for particular types of offenders, the open institution provides a greater treatment flexibility for less serious offenders than normally found within the punitive prison.

Open institutions have only recently appeared in the United States, but they have been rather commonplace in Switzerland, Denmark, and Sweden since the late 1800's. American juvenile institutions have generally followed the open pattern, and American minimum- or medium-security adult facilities in New York, (Wallkill Prison), California (Chino), New Jersey (Bordertown State), Massachusetts (Norfolk), and the federal institution near Dallas (Seagoville) possess some characteristics of open institutions.[95] The growing interest in smaller institutions, the third recent treatment development, has been stimulated by the increasing volume of data which indicate that they generally produce greater results at lesser costs than traditional large-scale situations.

Sweden, where penal policy specifies that inmates shall be treated with firmness and earnestness and yet with the consideration due them as human beings, also permits a form of preventive detention under which an offender twice previously sentenced to prison and guilty of committing an offense while imprisoned or within five years after release may be sentenced for a minimum of 1 year and a maximum of 12 years to prison confinement. Although the sentence is indeterminate, the court fixes a minimum period before parole may be granted. When permitted, parole continues for a minimum of three years under the supervision of the special board which supervises the entire preventive detention system. Provided a work opportunity and encouraged to participate in group incentives, inmates in preventive detention may earn between 70 cents to $1 per day. Detained inmates are encouraged to make as many decisions themselves as possible, including those to work, bers of the social unit. In an attempt to maintain a normal life situation, to maintain contact and communications with all members of the therapeutic community, and to build up meaningful relations with other members wives are permitted free room visits every Sunday from 9 in the morning until 6 in the evening. Each quarter, inmates are also permitted a 72-hour furlough as a matter of right. Of the 3,085 furloughs granted detainees in 1954, 442 failed to return on time, arrived drunk and disorderly, or committed other crimes while on furlough. Despite these shortcomings, prison administrators found this a reasonable price to pay for peace and respect within the prison.[96]

---

[95] Johnson, *op. cit.*, pp. 596–97.
[96] Conrad, *op. cit.*, p. 135.

In another approach to treatment, off-ground activities for the treatment of female offenders in Wisconsin were authorized in 1955. Female offenders housed at the Wisconsin Home for Women were by statute permitted to be escorted off the grounds under supervision of institutional personnel for activities associated with their rehabilitation. Trips to libraries, business establishments, church services, bowling alleys, roller rinks, athletic events, and other potentially valuable locations, helped to keep the female offender in touch with outside reality.[97] Similar opportunities were allowed men by a 1963 law authorizing their participation in this program.

No matter what the program or the availability of personnel or facilities, adequate treatment of the individual finally depends upon the existence of a valid system of classification. Because prison treatment programs are variously directed to individuals or to specified groups within minimum- to maximum-security institutions, the selection of the correct institution and program for treatment within the institution is central to any effective rehabilitation attempt. In the past, however, classification was completed without an effective coordination of treatment personnel. Diagnosis, often undertaken at a reception center or during the first few weeks after admission to a prison, was often carried out by psychologists or psychiatrists who frequently had little to do with the individual's treatment program once it was underway.

The number of diverse persons engaged in the particular dimensions of treatment fostered the continuance of this unintegrated approach. The more recent attempt to overcome divisions of staff and discipline and to bring all assets into a coherent treatment method has led to the development of the treatment-team rehabilitation approach. Under this concept, each newly incarcerated inmate comes into immediate contact with supervisory, custodial, service, or specialized institutional personnel. Covering the disciplines of clinical psychology, psychiatry, religion, recreation, scholastic and academic education, and vocational training, the treatment-team designs a correctional-rehabilitation program in keeping with the goal of prisoner change. An interdisciplinary approach, this method allows the team to view the inmate as a complete person and to share the insights of their particular disciplines in developing a unified and coherent approach to treatment. Placing greater emphasis upon inmate-treatment personnel interaction and less upon written reports, the treatment-team methodology seeks to humanize the treatment process and to overcome the many disadvantages of prisonization. However, as Gordon W. Russon recognizes, the value of treatment ultimately depends upon the readiness of the client for treatment, the com-

---

[97] Powers, *op. cit.*, p. 13.

petence of his therapists, the availability of needed time, and opportunities for creative real-life experiences in the treatment situation.[98]

Treatment and penal reform

In an attempt to alleviate the many shortcomings in corrections, the American Congress of Correction in 1960 adopted a series of principles for future penal system operations. Noting that the control of delinquency and crime are urgent challenges to the social sciences and that the forces for the prevention and control of delinquency are to be found in constructive social foundations, the Congress held that the improvement and the expansion of correctional methods should take precedence in the future. The distinction between violators of criminal law and those who are mentally sick should be maintained; a man should continue to be considered innocent until proved guilty through due process of law. Further, if a miscarriage of justice occurs, the state should offer the individual reasonable indemnification. Institutional and noninstitutional treatment, the Congress stated, should be planned and organized into an integrated system. In order to meet the variable needs of diverse offenders, a variety of treatment programs should also be enacted. Noting that repeated short sentences imposed for recurring misdemeanors or petty offenses are tentatively and correctionally ineffective, an integrated system of control, the Congress stated, should be developed through the creation of special institutional facilities and community supervision programs. Furthermore, the architecture and construction of penal and correctional institutions should functionally relate to programs carried on within their confines. These programs should be supervised by administrators who meet the higher standards of public administration and employees who serve on the basis of merit and tenure.

Because delinquent and criminal behavior is so complex, correctional personnel must possess suitable personality traits and specialized skills. Special emphasis should be placed upon a program of individualized treatment in order to maximize the potential of treatment. While a punitive sentence should remain commensurate to the seriousness of the offense and the guilt of the offender, the length of correctional treatment provided an offender for purposes of rehabilitation should depend upon the circumstances and the characteristics of the particular offender and possesses no relationship to the seriousness of the crime committed. The incarcerant, it proposed, should be accorded the generally accepted standards of decent living conditions and human relations. Because religion represents a "rich resource in the moral and spiritual regeneration of mankind," chaplains, religious instruction and counseling personnel,

---

[98] Gordon W. Russow, "Treatment," in McGrath (ed.), *op. cit.*, (New York: St. Martin's Press, Inc., 1965), p. 423.

the Congress hastened to add, should be provided within all correctional programs. Overall, the greatest emphasis should be placed upon the highest values of modern culture in the development of human character. Consequently, no law, procedure, or system of correction should deprive any offender of hope and of any possibility of his return to society as a fully responsible member.

Although the task of evaluating the individual offender should draw upon all of the available knowledge and professional skill, the correctional program should make every opportunity available to the inmate to raise his educational level, improve his vocational competence and skills, and assist his growth in knowledge. Opportunity to engage in productive work should be maintained in the prison setting without exploitation of the involuntary confinees. Diagnostic and treatment facilities for mentally abnormal offenders should be provided, developed, and maintained at appropriate stages in the correctional treatment. While the large-scale application of executive clemency provisions should be avoided, the use of executive clemency or pardon powers to restore civil rights to a rehabilitated person who has established his responsibility should be encouraged.

Work opportunities must be provided for a discharged or paroled offender if he is to regain his lost position in society. Since probation, the Congress stipulated, is a more effective and economical method of treatment for the greater number of offenders, mandatory exceptions to the use of probation for participants in specific crimes or particular types of offenders should be eliminated from the criminal code. All offenders released from correctional institutions should be freed under parole supervision at the earliest date consistent with the goal of rehabilitation and with public safety. The collection and publication of criminal statistics, and further research and scientific study into the problems of juvenile delinquency and crime, should be encouraged in order to maintain progress in corrections. The reintegration of the offender into the society as a normal citizen, the Congress recognized, depends upon popular support. Consequently, the concern for a strong foundation in corrections, adequacy of personnel, and alert and progressive administration must flow from the public as a function of its enlightened concern for the crime and delinquency problem.[99]

---

[99] Eaton, *op. cit.*, pp. 201–8; Joseph P. Evans, "A Profile of the Practitioner in a Correction Setting," *Federal Probation*, Vol. 25 (September, 1961), p. 43; Lloyd W. McCorkle, "Group Therapy and Treatment of Offenders," *Federal Probation*, Vol. 16 (December, 1952), pp. 22–27; Charles S. Prigmore, "Corrections Blueprint for National Action on Manpower and Training," *Federal Probation*, Vol. 28 (September, 1964), pp. 25–30; J. P. Conrad, "Research and the Knowledge Base of Corrections," *Crime and Delinquency*, Vol. 13 (July, 1967), p. 444; S. Rubin, "Developments in Correctional Law," *Crime and Delinquency*, Vol. 13 (April 1967), p. 356; and Rose Giallombardo, "Interviews in the Prison Community," *Journal of Criminal Law, Criminology, and Police Science*, Vol. 57, No. 3 (September, 1966), pp. 318–24.

Recommendations of the President's Commission

Presupposing many of the principles of the American Congress on Corrections, the President's Commission on Law Enforcement and Administration of Justice in 1967 further prescribed that all institutions should seek the goal of inmate rehabilitation through staff and inmate activities, educational and vocational training programs, and modern prison industrial work opportunities which may assist in the development of good work habits and a sense of personal success. Local jails and misdemeanant institutions, the Commission also concluded, should be divorced from law enforcement agencies and integrated into state correctional systems. Juveniles should be provided separate detention facilities; persons awaiting trial, if possible, should be housed separately from convicted offenders; screening and diagnostic resources should be strengthened.[100]

In the future, the penal institution should be located closer to the community from which it draws inmates, "probably in or near a city rather than in a remote location."[101] Although it may contain a few short-term high-security detention units, most difficult and dangerous inmates should be confined in more appropriate maximum-security institutions. Ideally, the desired institution would resemble a normal residential setting in which windows would have no bars, inmates would eat informally at small tables, and classrooms, recreational facilities, dayrooms and even a shop and/or library may be provided. Educational and vocational training activities should be assimilated into, and operated as much as possible within, the community. Because the penal institution should be a highly flexible institution, some of its inmates should be released soon after an initial period of detention for diagnosis and intensive treatment if their situations warrant such action. In other instances, the institution may serve as a short-term detention location designed to protect the potential offender from possible trouble. In still a third situation, the model institution might be used as a halfway house or prerelease center for those soon to be released from long-term incarceration. Conceivably, it might also serve as the foundation for a complex of separate residential area group homes created to ease the reentry problem. However, the greatest value of such a prototype, the President's Commission recognized, rests with its ability to shift the crucial treatment efforts from an idea of banishment and custody of offenders to a carefully defined system of treatment and control in which the goals of corrections might best be realized.[102]

---

[100] President's Commission, op. cit., pp. 174–78.
[101] Ibid., p. 173.
[102] K. B. Jobson, "Work Release: A Case for Intermittent Sentences," Criminal Law Quarterly, Vol. 10 (May, 1968), p. 329.

Chapter 24

DEPRIVATION OF LIFE

Taking the life of the offender has been the ultimate sanction; short of forms of death by torture, applied against the convicted violator. In primitive societies, a member of the victim's family, an avenger of blood, redressed the murder of his kin. In such an instance, capital punishment was accomplished within a family system of justice rather than through a system of state retribution. Among the Teutonic tribes, the murderer's family in later years could pay a prescribed amount to the victim's family in proportion to the rank of the individual in lieu of anticipated vengeance. English courts, by the 18th century, permitted and eventually substituted deportation to penal colonies in place of the execution of the murderer.[1] However, capital punishment was either unknown or largely restricted in Chinese, Islamic, and Slavic societies. While canon law rejected the use of capital punishment, the Roman Catholic Church nevertheless passed its condemned, especially during the period of the Inquistions, to the secular government for execution.[2]

THE SCOPE OF DEATH PENALTY CRIMES

Some 50 offenses were punishable by death in 1688, and the number rose to some 200 by the end of the 18th century. At present, crimes

---

[1] Clyde D. Vedder and Barbara Kay, *Penology: A Realistic Approach* (Springfield, Ill.: Charles C. Thomas, Publisher, 1963), p. 250. Refer to James A. Joyce, *Capital Punishment: A World View* (New York: Thomas Nelson & Sons, 1961); and Julia E. Johnson, *Capital Punishment* (New York: H. W. Wilson Co., 1939).

[2] Marc Ancel, "The Problem of the Death Penalty," in Thorsten Sellin (ed.), *Capital Punishment* (New York: Harper & Row, Publishers, 1967), p. 5. Also see Thorsten Sellin, "Capital Punishment," *Federal Probation*, Vol. 25 (September, 1961), p. 33; and John Laurence, *A History of Capital Punishment* (New York: Citadel Press, Inc., 1960).

potentially invoking the death penalty generally fall into the four categories of crimes against government, crimes against property, crimes against persons, and miscellaneous crimes. Treason and perjury are the only two offenses in the category of *crimes against government* which are subject to the death penalty. Treason, the act of levying war against the government of a particular jurisdiction or of giving aid and comfort to its enemies, is, however, punishable by death in only 20 jurisdictions of the United States, 12 demanding death upon conviction. Eleven jurisdictions, six mandatorily, punish capital perjury, the act of giving false testimony under oath which causes the conviction and execution of an innocent person, with death.[3] Capital crimes against property usually include train wrecking, arson, and burglary, although in each of these categories the act usually must result in the death, intended or accidental, of some other person. While 18 jurisdictions permit the death penalty for train wrecking, three make it mandatory. Four jurisdictions impute murder to arson if a death occurs as a result of the intended fire. Although three states make burglary a capital crime, none specify a mandatory death sentence.

The death penalty may also be invoked in *crimes against the person* which involve violence and take the form of murder, kidnapping, rape, dueling, assault by a life prisoner, robbery, willful mismanagement of explosives and bombs, attempted assault on an executive, completed assassination, lynching, or some form of aggravated assault (see Table 24–1).

Miscellaneous crimes (also known as "other offenses) usually representing an arbitrary decision by the legislature, are often capital offenses in only one jurisdiction. Examples of authorization of the death penalty in various states are the following:

1. In Arkansas for aiding in suicide, causing a boat collision resulting in death, injury or alarm causing death by night riders, or forced marriage.
2. In Delaware for showing false lights causing a boat collision and death.
3. In Georgia for castrating another while fighting or otherwise, and for possessing or controlling a poisonous snake in a manner endangering public health and safety if death ensues.
4. In Kentucky for homicide during criminal syndicalism if violence contributes to death, and for homicide from road obstruction.
5. In Nevada for assault with intent to commit murder, sodomy, may-

---

[3] Robert H. Finkel, "A Survey of Capital Offenses," in Sellin (ed.), *op. cit.*, p. 26. Examine D. H. Partington, "Incidence of the Death Penalty for Rape in Virginia," *Washington and Lee Law Review,* Vol. 22 (Spring, 1965), p. 43; and R. C. Koeninger, "Capital Punishment in Texas, 1924–1948," *Crime and Delinquency,* Vol. 15 (January, 1969), p. 132.

TABLE 24–1

Offenses punishable by death—United States, 1966

Jurisdiction	Number Offenses	Number Mandatory	Murder	Kidnapping	Rape	Dueling	Lifer-assault	Robbery	Explosives	Attempt on Executive	Lynching	Assault Intent Rape	Burglary	Arson	Train Wrecking	Perjury	Treason	Other Offenses†
Alabama	16	1	1	2	4		1*	2	1				1	2			2	
Arizona	7	3	1	1			1*	1							1	1*	1*	
Arkansas	11	1	1	1*	2	1								1			1	4
California	6	4	1	1			1*								1*	1*	1*	
Colorado	5	2	1	1			1*									1*		1
Connecticut	6	2	1	1						1*				1	1		1*	
Delaware	3		1	1										1				1
District of Columbia	3		1	1	1									1				
Federal	13		1	1				1	1	1				1			1	5
Florida	7	3	1*	1	1	1*		2						1				
Georgia	21		1	1	2	1		1	3					6	2	1	1	2
Idaho	3	1	1	1												1*		
Illinois	3		1	1													1	
Indiana	7		1	1		2								1	1		1	
Kansas	5	1	1	1										1	1	1	1*	
Kentucky	12		1	1	3			2	1		1				1			2
Louisiana	4	4	1*	1*	1*												1*	
Maryland	10		2	2	2							1		2	1			
Massachusetts	2		1				1											
Mississippi	7	1	1	1	1	2		1									1*	
Missouri	6		1	1	1			1	1						1			
Montana	4	3	1											1*	1*		1*	
Nebraska	4		1	1		1									1			
Nevada	7	1	1	1	1	1						1			1		1*	1
New Hampshire	1		1															
New Jersey	4	1	1	1							1						1*	
New Mexico	2		1	1														
New York	2						1											1
North Carolina	5	1	1		1									1	1	1*		
North Dakota	2	1					1*										1	
Ohio	8	2	1	2			1			2*					1			1
Oklahoma	5		1	1	1	1		1										
Pennsylvania	3		1				1								1			
Rhode Island	1	1					1*											
South Carolina	8		1	1	1	1						1	1					2
South Dakota	3		1	1														1
Tennessee	7		1	1	4													1
Texas	14	1	1	1	1	1		1				1		1	3	1*	1	2
Utah	4		1	1	1	1												
Vermont	3	1	1														1*	1
Virginia	13	1	1	1	1			2			1	1	1	1	2		1*	1
Washington	3	1	1	1											1		1*	
Wyoming	6		1	2		2												1

* Mandatory sentence.

† See text for enumeration.

Source: Robert H. Finkel, "A Survey of Capital Offenses," *Capital Punishment* (New York: Harper & Row, publishers; 1967), pp. 24–25.

hem, robbery, and grand larceny or for assault with extreme cruelty or great bodily injury.

6. In Ohio for the killing of a guard or officer by a convict.
7. In South Carolina for killing by poison or by stabbing.
8. In South Dakota for child molesting resulting in death.
9. In Tennessee for killing an arresting officer.

10. In Texas for abortion resulting in the death of a mother or for poisoning.
11. In Virginia for throwing stones or shooting, at a vehicle or railroad car, or other similar acts, resulting in death.
12. In Wyoming for conspiracy in kidnap for ransom.[4]

At various stages in American history, the death penalty has been inflicted for sabotage or attempted sabotage that results in a death (Alabama), anarchy and sedition that results in a death (Colorado), sabotage during preparation for war (Florida), insurrection or attempt to incite insurrection (Georgia), bombing or planting a bomb nearly anywhere with the intent to injure persons or property (Mississippi), the use of a machine gun for a crime of violence or an attempted crime of violence (Virginia), drugging a woman with intent to rape (Arkansas), attempting to kill the President of the United States or any foreign ambassador accredited to the United States (Connecticut), castration of another person (Georgia), armed assault with intent to rob (Kentucky), assault by a member of the Ku Klux Klan or similar organization where the injury results in death (West Virginia), causing death while escaping from prison (Nevada), boarding a train with the intent to commit a felony against a passenger or employee of the railroad (Wyoming), or making an assault on a jail which results in the death of a jailer (New Mexico). Even now, kidnapping without additional elements is a clear capital offense only if some other element to the crime, most commonly ransom, is present. However, Virginia considers kidnapping for ransom, kidnapping a girl with intent to defile her person, or kidnapping a girl under 16 years for the purposes of prostitution capital crimes.[5]

CAPITAL PUNISHMENT IN THE UNITED STATES AND CANADA

When the Bureau of the Census began to compile national statistics on executions in 1930, the death penalty was provided in federal law

---

[4] *Ibid.*, p. 30. See M. Carter and A. L. Smith, "Death Penalty in California," *Crime and Delinquency*, Vol. 15 (January, 1969), p. 62; G. H. Gottlieb, "Capital Punishment," *Crime and Delinquency*, Vol. 15 (January, 1969), p. 1; "Death Penalty Cases," *California Law Review*, Vol. 56 (October, 1968), p. 1270; G. E. Parker, "Corporal Punishment in Canada," *Criminal Law Quarterly*, Vol. 7 (August, 1964), p. 193.

[5] Richard Reifsnyder, "Capital Crimes in the States," *Journal of Criminal Law, Criminology, and Police Science*, Vol. 46 (March–April, 1955), pp. 690–93. See also W. J. Chambliss, "Deterrent Influence of Punishment," *Crime and Delinquency*, Vol. 12 (January, 1966), p. 70; J. Andenaes, "Does Punishment Deter Crime?" *Criminal Law Quarterly*, Vol. 6 (Spring, 1968), p. 133; and W. Bradford, "Enquiry How Far the Punishment of Death Is Necessary in Pennsylvania," *American Journal of Legal History*, Vol. 12 (April–July, 1968), pp. 122.

and in all states with the exception of Maine, Wisconsin, Minnesota, Kansas, and South Dakota. Michigan and North Dakota allowed execution for treason. North Dakota and Rhode Island permitted capital punishment for murder completed by a prisoner serving a life sentence. Kansas (1935) and South Dakota (1939) later reestablished the death penalty. Alaska, Delaware, and Hawaii rescinded their previous law in 1957; Delaware restored capital punishment in 1961. Michigan abolished the death penalty for treason in 1963. Oregon (1964) and Iowa and West Virginia (1965) totally eliminated the possibility of capital punishment in their states.

In another variation, Vermont in 1965 rescinded the penalty for murder except in cases involving a second unrelated murder or the murder of a police officer or prison official on duty. Also in 1965, New York generally abolished the death penalty while preserving its infliction in cases of murder of a policeman on duty or murder of a prison guard by a prisoner serving a life sentence for murder. Consequently, by 1966, only 37 of the 50 states generally retained the essence of capital punishment. Thirteen states, Puerto Rico, and the Virgin Islands eliminated the death penalty.[6]

Since 1961, capital murder in Canada has resulted in mandatory capital punishment, a change from an earlier period when the criminal code made no distinction between capital and noncapital murder and punished all culpable murders by death.[7]

The use of the death penalty

During the 1930's, executions in the United States averaged 167 per year. While the rate dropped to below 15 in the middle 1960's, this was largely due to changes in public attitude and in court decisions regarding deprivation of life. An average of 32 executions were completed during the years 1960 to 1965; 56 executions occurred in 1960, lessening to 7 in 1965 (see Table 24–2). Between 1930 and 1965, 33 executions of federal prisoners took place; 160 other executions were also carried out by the Army and the Air Force. All but 12 were enacted between 1942 and 1950. Of the 160, 85 were inflicted for murder, 21 for rape-murders, 53 for rape, and 1 for desertion. Interestingly, the Navy has not executed any prisoner since 1849.

Of the 3,332 executions between 1930 and 1966 for which information is available, 455 were for rape, 69 for all other crimes, and the remainder

---

[6] Thorsten Sellin, "Executions in the United States," in Sellin (ed.), *op. cit.*, pp. 31–34.

[7] Dogan D. Akman, "Homicides and Assaults in Canadian Prisons," in Sellin (ed.), *op. cit.*, p. 161.

TABLE 24-2

Executions under civil authority—United States, by state and year, 1930-65

Region and State	Total	1965	1964	1963	1962	1961	1960	1950–59	1940–49	1930–39
United States	3,856	7	15	21	47	42	56	717	1,284	1,667
Federal	33			1				9	13	10
States	3,823	7	15	20	47	42	56	708	1,271	1,657
Northeast	608			3	4	3	7	107	184	300
New Hampshire	1									1
Vermont	4							2	1	1
Massachusetts	27								9	18
Connecticut	21						1	5	10	5
New York	329			2		2	6	52	114	153
New Jersey	74			1	2			17	14	40
Pennsylvania	152				2	1		31	36	82
North Central	403	5	2	3	7	2	2	58	106	218
Ohio	172			2	2	1	2	32	51	82
Indiana	41					1		2	7	31
Illinois	90			2				9	18	61
Iowa	18				2			1	7	8
Missouri	62	1	2	1				7	15	36
South Dakota	1								1	
Nebraska	4							2	2	
Kansas	15	4			1			5	5	
South	2,305	1	12	10	22	26	32	427	832	943
Delaware	12								4	8
Maryland	68					1		6	45	16
Dist. of Columbia	40							4	16	20
Virginia	92				1	4	1	23	35	28
West Virginia	40							9	11	20
North Carolina	263					1		19	112	131
South Carolina	162				2	5	1	26	61	67
Georgia	366		2	2	1	3	6	85	130	137
Florida	170		2	1	5	2	2	49	65	44
Kentucky	103				1			16	34	52
Tennessee	93						1	8	37	47
Alabama	135	1	1		1	1	1	20	50	60
Mississippi	154		1	2	1	5	1	36	60	48
Arkansas	118		1				8	18	38	53
Louisiana	133					1		27	47	58
Oklahoma	59			1	1		3	7	13	34
Texas	297		5	4	9	3	8	74	74	120
West	507	1	1	4	14	11	15	116	149	196
Montana	6								1	5
Idaho	3							3		
Wyoming	7	1							2	4
Colorado	46		1		2	1	1	3	13	25
New Mexico	8						1	3	2	2
Arizona	38			2		1	1	8	9	17
Utah	13						1	6	4	2
Nevada	29					1	1	9	10	8
Washington	47			1			1	6	16	23
Oregon	19				1			4	12	2
California	291			1	11	8	9	74	80	108

Source: Thorsten Sellin, "Executions in the United States," *Capital Punishment* (New York: Harper and Row, 1967), pp. 32–33.

for murder. All executions for rape, except for 10 cases in Missouri, were completed in the southern states. Of the 69 miscellaneous cases, 24 executions were enacted upon conviction for armed robbery, 20 for kidnapping, 11 for burglary, and 6 for aggravated assault committed by prisoners serving life sentences. On the federal level, 8 executions involved sentences for espionage.[8] Of those executed, 49 percent were Negroes; 1,646 of these executions of blacks (80 percent) occurred in the South Atlantic, East South Central and West South Central regions of the United States. As to race, 19 American Indians, 13 Philippinos, 8 Chinese, and 2 Japanese were also included within the number executed. Ninety-two percent of all persons executed for rape were black. Of the 32 women who faced the death penalty during the period, 30 were convicted for murder. There were 12 black and 20 white. The two women federal prisoners facing execution were convicted for kidnapping and for espionage respectively.[9]

Twenty-one states and the District of Columbia in 1930 met the requirement of capital punishment with the use of electric chairs. Nevada provided for the use of lethal gas; Utah permitted the prisoner a choice between hanging or firing squad; Kentucky provided electrocution, or if the crime was rape, hanging; and 17 states and the federal system used the gallows. By 1965, 24 states were using electric chairs, 11 gas chambers, and 7 gallows. The formerly common method of hanging was retained only in New Hampshire, Kansas, Delaware, Montana, Idaho, and Washington (see Table 24–3).[10]

The death penalty in states that have abolished and later reinstated it

The states of Arizona, Colorado, Delaware, Iowa, Kansas, Maine, Missouri, Tennessee, Oregon, South Dakota, and Washington at one point in their history have abolished the death penalty only to later reinstate it. Arizona, which possessed no death penalty for murder between December, 1916, and December, 1918, had 41 murder convictions in the two years preceding, 46 during, and 45 in the two years following abolition. In Colorado, the average annual number of convictions for murder in the five years before abolition in 1897 was 15.4. The average annual number of convictions for murder reached 18 during the five years of abolition between 1897 and 1901; it averaged 19 during the five years following the reinstatement of the death penalty. The equivalent figures for manslaughter convictions during the three Colorado periods was 2.6, 4, and 1.5.

Delaware, which abolished the death penalty in April, 1958, and reinstated it in December, 1961, reported an average annual number

---

[8] Sellin, *op. cit.*, p. 34.

[9] *Ibid.*, p. 35. Also refer to James A. McCafferty, "The Death Sentence," in Hugo A. Bedau (ed.), *The Death Penalty in America* (Garden City, N.Y.: Doubleday & Co., Inc., 1964), pp. 90–116.

[10] Sellin, *op. cit.*, p. 35. Also see T. Murton, "Treatment of Condemned Prisoners," *Crime and Delinquency*, Vol. 15 (January, 1969), p. 94.

TABLE 24–3
Number of executions by states and method used, 1930–59

Electrocution		Lethal Gas		Hanging	
State	Number	State	Number	State	Number
Georgia..........	352	California.........	262	Washington.......	45
New York.......	319	No. Carolina......	262	Iowa.............	16
Texas...........	268	Mississippi........	144	Kansas...........	10
Ohio............	165	Maryland.........	67	Montana.........	6
Florida..........	158	Missouri..........	58	Idaho............	3
So. Carolina.....	154	Colorado.........	41	New Hampshire...	1
Pennsylvania	149	Arizona...........	34	Total	81
Louisiana........	131	Nevada...........	27		
Alabama.........	130	Oregon...........	18		
Arkansas........	109	New Mexico......	7		
Kentucky........	102	Wyoming.........	6		
Tennessee........	92	Total	926		
Illinois..........	88				
Virginia.........	86				
New Jersey......	71				
Oklahoma.......	54				
District of					
Columbia......	40				
Indiana..........	40				
West Virginia....	40				
Massachusetts ...	27			*Shooting or Hanging*	
Connecticut.....	20			*1930 to 1957*	
Nebraska........	4			Delaware.........	12
Vermont.........	4			Federal...........	31
So. Dakota......	1			Utah.............	12
Total	2,604			Total	55

Source: Walter A. Lunden, "The Death Penalty," in Clyde D. Vedder and Barbara Kay (eds.), *Penology: A Realistic Approach.* (Springfield, Ill.: Charles C. Thomas, Publisher, 1963), p. 254.

of murders and nonnegligent manslaughters of 22.3 during 1956–58 and 14.3 between 1959 and 1961. Iowa eliminated the death penalty between 1872 and 1878. The average annual number of convictions for murder in the seven years before abolition was 2.6, during abolition 8.8, and in the seven years following the 1878 reinstatement of the death penalty, 13.1. Iowa again abolished the death penalty in 1965. Kansas recorded no death penalty between 1907 and 1935; its annual average homicide death rate for the five years before 1935 was 6.5 and for the five years following 3.8 (see Figure 24–1). Maine first abolished capital punishment in 1876, reinstated its use in 1882, and eliminated its mandate in 1887. No meaningful data concerning the death penalty in Maine is available. Missouri, which abandoned the death penalty in 1917 only to reinstate it in 1919, recorded an average homicide death rate of 9.2 per 100,000 population between 1911 and 1916. During the years of abolition of the death penalty (1917–19), Missouri averaged 10.7, and between 1920 and 1924, 11.

Tennessee abolished capital punishment for murder in 1915, while retaining it for rape, and it reestablished the penalty in 1919. Tennessee homicide rates in 1918 were 6.9 for the whites and 29.2 for the nonwhite population; however, following the reintroduction of the death penalty, the rates of both groups rose steadily to 10.8 for whites and 52.5 for nonwhites in 1924. Oregon, which possessed no death penalty between 1915 and 1920, committed 59 "murderers" to the state penitentiary in the five years before abolition and 36 during the years of abolition. Although South Dakota abolished the death penalty in 1915, only to reintroduce its use in 1939, the state reported identical average annual homicide death rates during the five years before and the five years after restoration. Finally, Washington, which eliminated the death penalty between 1913 and 1919, reported that the average annual rate of death due to homicide was 6.8 during the period of abolition and 5.8 during the first six years after the death penalty was once again legalized.[11]

Is the death penalty a deterrent?

Most objective studies suggest that no discernible correlation exists between the actual current homicide rate and the availability of the imposition of the death penalty. In fact, William Graves, a physician, discovered in a 10-year study during the period 1946 to 1955 that more homicides occurred in Alameda, Los Angeles, and San Francisco counties (California) during Thursdays and Fridays of the week when executions were performed at San Quentin than on the other Thursdays and Fridays when no executions were completed.[12] The actual psychic contagion surrounding the event, he suggested, in its own way may actually encourage the infliction of other homicides rather than deter their occurrence. Other data further reveal that the use of the death penalty when called for is marked by inequality. Most evidence points out that it is imposed disproportionately upon the poor, the Negro, and the unpopular.[13]

---

[11] Sellin, "Abolition and Restoration of the Death Penalty in Missouri," in Sellin (ed.), op. cit., pp. 122–24. See Walter C. Reckless, "Use of the Death Penalty," Crime and Delinquency, Vol. 15 (January, 1969), p. 43; Grant S. McClellan, Capital Punishment (New York: H. W. Wilson Co., 1961); and J. F. Coakley, "Capital Punishment," American Criminal Law Quarterly, Vol. 1 (May, 1963), pp. 27–48.

[12] Vedder and Kay, op. cit., p. 143.

[13] The President's Commission on Law Enforcement and the Administration of Justice, The Challenge of Crime in a Free Society (Washington, D.C.: U.S. Government Printing Office, 1967), p. 143.

FIGURE 24–1

Homicide death rates in contiguous abolitionist and retentionist States, 1920–63
(per 100,000 population)

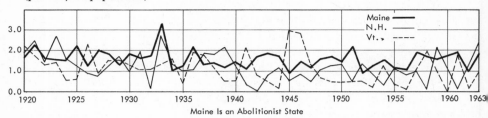

Maine Is an Abolitionist State

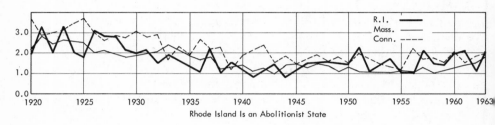

Rhode Island Is an Abolitionist State

Minnesota and Wisconsin Are Abolitionist States.

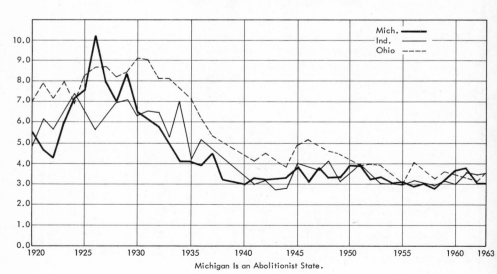

Michigan Is an Abolitionist State.

FIGURE 24-1 (*Continued*)

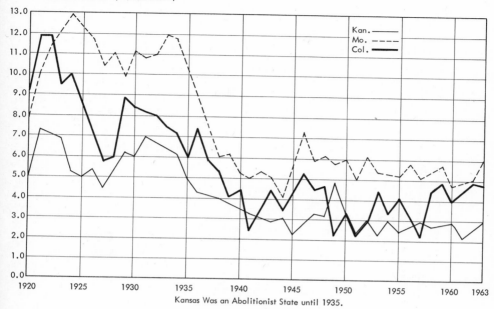

Kansas Was an Abolitionist State until 1935.

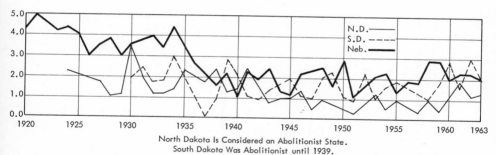

North Dakota Is Considered an Abolitionist State.
South Dakota Was Abolitionist until 1939.

Source: Thorsten Sellin, "Homicides in Retentionist and Abolitionist States," *Capital Punishment* (New York: Harper & Row, Publishers, 1967), pp. 136–37.

Although most data reveal that no significant difference exists between states which provide for capital punishment and those that do not in the safety of policemen and in the rate of assaults and murders of prison guards,[14] one of the main arguments for the retention of the capital punishment, Thorsten Sellin notes, is that only the death penalty prevents potential offenders from killing more police. Nevertheless, objective data secured from 274 schedules returned from a mailing of 593 letters pertaining to the wounding or killing of a police department member

---

[14] President's Commission, *op. cit.*, p. 143.

TABLE 24-4

Cases of police homicide, by cities grouped according to size; and rates per 100,000 population in each group of cities, by state

Abolition States	10,000–30,000				30,000–60,000				60,000–100,000			
	No. Cit.	No. Cases	Population	Rate	No. Cit.	No. Cases	Population	Rate	No. Cit.	No. Cases	Population	Rate
Maine	4		54,280	0.0	1		31,558	0.0	1		77,634	0.0
Michigan	24	8	419,904	1.9	4	1	189,609	0.5	2	3	187,912	1.6
Minnesota	14	4	259,461	1.5								
North Dakota	3	1	51,369	1.9	3	1	116,463	0.9				
Rhode Island	3		46,084	0.0	7	4	252,580	1.6	1	3	96,056	3.1
Wisconsin	13	2	207,940	0.9					4	6	361,602	1.6
Total	61	15	1,039,038	1.3	15	6	590,210	1.0				

Abolition States	100,000–350,000				500,000–650,000				All Cities			
	No. Cit.	No. Cases	Population	Rate	No. Cit.	No. Cases	Population	Rate	No. Cit.	No. Cases	Population	Rate
Maine									6		163,472	0.0
Michigan	1	1	176,515	0.6					31	13	973,940	1.3
Minnesota									14	4	259,461	1.5
North Dakota									3	1	51,369	1.9
Rhode Island					1	5	637,392	0.8	6	1	162,547	0.6
Wisconsin									22	14	1,193,968	1.2
Total	1	1	176,515	0.6	1	5	637,392	0.8	82	33	2,804,757	1.2

10,000–30,000, 30,000–60,000, 60,000–100,000

Capital Punishment States	No. Cit.	No. Cases	Population	Rate	No. Cit.	No. Cases	Population	Rate	No. Cit.	No. Cases	Population	Rate
	10,000–30,000				30,000–60,000				60,000–100,000			
Connecticut	11		190,746	0.0	5	1	212,213	0.5	1		74,293	0.0
Illinois	14	4	206,214	1.9	6	1	225,701	0.4	1	1	92,927	1.1
Indiana	10	3	170,785	1.7	4	7	171,048	4.1				
Iowa	6		85,429	0.0	2	2	64,244	3.1	1		72,296	0.0
Massachusetts	31	6	499,841	1.2	5	1	221,877	0.4	1	1	66,112	1.5
Montana	1	1	17,581	5.7								
New Hampshire	4		59,809	0.0	1	1	34,469	2.9	1		82,732	0.0
New York	24	3	426,631	0.7	7		290,304	0.0	2	4	171,546	2.3
Ohio	21	7	371,623	1.9	7	3	223,303	1.3	2	1	146,379	0.7
South Dakota	2		24,920	0.0								
Vermont	1		12,411	0.0								
Total	125	24	2,065,990	1.2	37	16	1,443,159	1.1	9	7	706,285	1.0

100,000–350,000, 500,000–650,000, All Cities

Capital Punishment States	No. Cit.	No. Cases	Population	Rate	No. Cit.	No. Cases	Population	Rate	No. Cit.	No. Cases	Population	Rate
	100,000–350,000				500,000–650,000				All Cities			
Connecticut	2	3	263,186	1.1					19	4	740,438	0.5
Illinois									21	6	524,842	1.1
Indiana	1	1	133,607	0.7					15	11	475,440	2.3
Iowa	1	6	177,965	3.3					10	8	399,934	2.0
Massachusetts	1		203,486	0.0					38	8	991,316	0.8
Montana									1	1	17,581	5.7
New Hampshire									6	1	177,010	0.5
New York	2	3	434,019	0.7	1	8	580,132	1.4	36	18	1,902,632	0.9
Ohio	3	14	635,389	2.2	1	13	503,998	2.6	34	38	1,880,692	2.2
South Dakota									2		24,920	0.0
Vermont									1		12,411	0.0
Total	10	27	1,847,652	1.5	2	21	1,084,130	1.9	183	95	7,147,216	1.3

Source: Thorsten Sellin, "The Death Penalty and Police Safety," *Capital Punishment* (New York: Harper & Row, Publishers, 1964), pp. 144–45.

through use of a lethal weapon by a criminal or a criminal suspect in the years between 1919 and 1954, completed by Thorsten Sellin's Seminar in Criminology at the University of Pennsylvania failed to support this contention. Because the data on woundings were incomplete, they were unusable. Information pertaining to the killing of policemen had greater validity.

Although the 265 usable returned schedules represented 44.8 percent of the cities queried and 55.4 percent of the abolition states, the most complete responses came from the smaller cities. Slightly more than 60 percent of the cities of under 30,000 inhabitants and 50 percent of those between 30,000 to 100,000 population in abolitionist states returned usable schedules. Approximately 42 percent of the smallest class of cities in capital punishment states also replied. While no replies were received from Detroit, Minneapolis, New York, Cleveland, or Boston, the large cities of Chicago, Milwaukee, Cincinnati, and Buffalo completed the request. Of the 138 policemen actually killed in the recorded 128 encounters in 264 cities within the 17 answering states (6 were abolition states) during 1919 and 1954, 3 policemen were killed in one event and 18 in 9 additional encounters involving the death of 2 officers. The rate of fatal attacks on police in the 6 abolition states per 100,000 population was 1.2 and in capital punishment states 1.3.[15] Of the cities between 30,000 and 60,000 population, the abolition cities evidenced a rate of 1.0 and capital punishment cities 1.1 (See Table 24-4).

When the 36-year period was divided into six six-year groupings, the 1925–36 high-hazard period could not be compared with the modern period. (See Table 24-5). However, in 62 out of 69 (89.8 percent) death penalty cities reporting, police officers testified to the added protective force of the death penalty; in 20 of 27 abolition cities (74.1 percent), fellow officers rejected this premise. Of the 168 Cook County, Illinois (Chicago), killings of police, 36 occurred when the police officer interfered with a holdup, attempted to search or arrest a person, or investigated some complaint which brought him into interaction with his suspect.

During the years 1961 to 1963, 140 policemen, an average of 47 per year, were killed in the United States by known or suspected offenders. Only 9 were killed in the abolition states; the remaining 131 occurred in death penalty states. Yet, the annual average risk for the 3-year period was 1.312 per 10,000 police in the abolition states and 1.328 in the bordering states. An additional 97 officers died in accidents during that period. Overall, the average annual rate of police officer death was 3.1 per 10,000 police in comparison to corresponding death risks of 11.0

---

[15] Sellin, "The Death Penalty and Police Safety," in Sellin (ed.), *op. cit.*, pp. 141–46.

TABLE 24–5
Trends in cases of police killings, 1919–54, as reported by 266 cities in 17 states

Years	Cases		Police Killed		Both Combined	
	Abol. States	C.P. States	Abol. States	C.P. States	Cases	Police Killed
1919–24................	8	25[c]	12	25	33	37
1925–30................	8[a]	31[e]	9	31	39	40
1931–36................	5[a]	24[a]	5	26	29	31
1937–42................	4	9	4	11	13	15
1943–48................	5[b]	5[a,d]	5	5	10	10
1949–54................	3	1	4	1	4	5
Total............	33	95	39	99	128	138

[a] Excluding a case in which the killer was insane.
[b] Excluding a case in which officer was struck by flashlight.
[c] Excluding three cases in which the killer was insane; excluding a case in which the killer used gun as club.
[d] Excluding a case in which officer was crushed by car operated by the killer.
[e] Including three cases in which the killer seized the officer's gun and killed him.
Source: Sellin, "The Death Penalty and Public Safety," p. 148.

in the mining industries, 7.7 in construction, 6.5 in agriculture, and 4.2 in transportation and public utilities. Had similar rates applied to police activities, during 1963 some 127 police officers instead of the actual 69 would have died from homicide or work injuries.[16]

In the study of homicides and assaults based upon questionnaires sent to prison administrators in all states, the District of Columbia, and those under the Federal Bureau of Prisons, some 603 persons were reported assault victims in 37 jurisdictions. Of the 603 assaulted, 61, including 8 staff members and 53 inmates, died. Nine of the inmates, each in a jurisdiction possessing the death penalty, was slain by an unidentified person or persons. In 35 events, one prisoner killed a single fellow inmate.[17] Of the 59 known assailants involved in the 52 homicides, 16 were serving sentences for murder, 19 for robbery, and 7 for theft at the time the prison homicide was committed. In all, 43 of the offenders were currently imprisoned for crimes of violence against the person at the time that they committed the prison murder. While 11 were sentenced for burglary or theft, an additional 5 were incarcerated for miscellaneous crimes. Interestingly, no fatal assault was reported in the abolitionist states of Alaska, North Dakota, Oregon, Rhode Island, West Virginia, and Wisconsin.[18]

During 1964 and 1965, 102 assaults involving 106 offenders and 107

[16] *Ibid.*, p. 153.
[17] Sellin, "Prison Homicide," in Sellin (ed.), *op. cit.*, pp. 154–57.
[18] *Ibid.*, p. 158.

victims (37 officers and 70 inmates) occurred in Canadian prisons. Six offenders were women. More than 60 percent of the assaults were completed by offenders between the ages of 20 and 29 years. Robbers accounted for over 70 percent of the inflicted harms. Over 70 percent of the casualities were among inmates convicted of theft. Of the two homicides completed during 1964 and 1965, one involved a fatal assault on a guard by an 18-year-old inmate serving a 12-year sentence for violent robbery and the second on a prison inmate by a 27-year-old prisoner serving time for armed robbery.[19] During the same two-year period, 11 officers and 13 inmates were victims of aggravated assaults. Receiving simple assaults were 25 officers and 38 inmates. Despite the actual volume of prison assaults and homicides, the argument that the commutation of death sentences increases the life occupational hazards in prison, Dogan Akman concluded, receives no empirical support.[20]

A further study of 32 wardens and prison superintendents by Paul A. Thomas similarly revealed a disproportionate rejection of the deterrent value of capital punishment. Only 3 of the 26 persons responding from the original 32 receiving questionnaires supported the contention that capital punishment is a deterrent to murder. While 24 noted that they did not believe that the offender actually considers the possible personal consequences of his criminal act at the time he committed the murder, 1 believed that he did and 2 failed to respond to the question. Of the 26 respondents, 16 (62 percent) held that the fact that innocent persons had been executed created a "fallacy" regarding the use of capital punishment; 6 (23 percent) did not, and 4 (15 percent) refrained from answering. This fact alone led 8 wardens and superintendents (31 percent) to conclude that capital punishment should be abolished or that it offered sufficient grounds for the consideration of abolition of capital punishment in the United States. Fourteen (54 percent) did not support this presupposition and four (15 percent) failed to answer the question.[21]

The movement toward abolition of the death penalty

The modern movement for abolition of the death penalty had its forerunner in the work of George Fox in the 17th century. In the latter half of the 18th century, Catherine II, Leopold II, and Joseph II of Tuscany and Austria each moved to eliminate the death penalty from the criminal codes of their nations.[22] In 1829, Sir Samuel Romilly's cam-

---

[19] Akman, op. cit., pp. 162–63.
[20] Ibid., p. 168.
[21] Paul A. Thomas, "Attitudes of Wardens Toward the Death Penalty," in Bedau (ed.), op. cit., pp. 243–44.
[22] Ancel, op. cit., p. 6.

paign for the reduction of capital crimes from the more than 200 which were then registered in England finally bore fruit in the formation of the first association for the abolition of the death penalty in London. However, the British Parliament did not fully abolish the death penalty for murder until 1965. By the 19th century, arguments and movements favoring the abolition of capital punishment intensified, leading to some effective changes in existing practices during the 20th century.

Most arguments against the death penalty followed one of six lines of reasoning. The *religious* argument suggested that the infliction of the death penalty deprives the offender of the time for repentance and of an opportunity for salvation. The *medical* and *psychological* position maintained that any person who commits murder is irrational or insane and consequently not responsible for his acts. The *legal* argument posed the view that because the death penalty is final and cannot be altered, it represents a form of dead-end penology. The *social* argument maintained that the death penalty is used so infrequently that it consequently does not truly deter others from the commission of crimes. While the *moral* viewpoint noted that capital punishment makes reformation and restitution impossible, the *cultural* argument postulated that man is not responsible for his actions because his culture essentially predetermines how he shall act.[23]

Examining the reasons in favor of the abolition of capital punishment, Donal E. J. MacNamara writes that not only is the death penalty criminologically unsound but it is morally and ethically unacceptable. The death penalty has demonstrably failed to accomplish its stated objectives, and even where it has been used, it has been applied prejudicially and inconsistently. In some instances, the innocent have been executed when a more effective alternative might have been utilized. Contrary to public opinion, police and prison officers, MacNamara notes, are somewhat safer in states that do not have the death penalty, and paroled and pardoned murderers are not a true threat to the public. Additionally, not only is the death penalty, he concluded, more costly than its alternatives, but capital punishment ultimately stands in the way of needed penal reform.[24] Thorsten Sellin tends to concur. The case for the main-

---

[23] See Walter A. Lunden, "The Death Penalty," *Police*, Vol. 5 (May–June, 1961), pp. 43–47; R. M. Carter and A. L. Smith, "Countdown for Death," *Crime and Delinquency*, Vol. 15 (January, 1969), p. 77; J. DeMent, "Plea for the Condemned," *Alabama Law Review*, Vol. 44 (Fall, 1967), p. 83; J. Greenberg and J. Himmelstein, "Varieties of Attack on the Death Penalty," *Crime and Delinquency*, Vol. 15 (January, 1969), p. 112; Sara R. Ehrmann, "For Whom the Chair Waits," *Federal Probation*, Vol. 26 (March, 1962), p. 14; and Ralph G. Murdy, "A Moderate View of Capital Punishment," *Federal Probation*, Vol. 25 (September, 1961), p. 11.

[24] Donal E. J. MacNamara, "The Case Against Capital Punishment," in Bedau (ed.), *op. cit.*, pp. 182–93. Note J. M. Stanton, "Murderers on Parole," *Crime and Delinquency*, Vol. 15 (January, 1969), p. 149.

tenance of the death penalty for the deterrence of crime is inconclusive. "The presence of the death penalty—in law or practice—does not," he categorically declares "influence homicide death rates."[25]

These and other arguments have led many religious bodies to support the abolition of capital punishment. Even now, the American Unitarian Association (1956), the Disciples of Christ (1957), the Universalist Church of America (1957), the Protestant Episcopal Church in the United States (1958), the Union of American Hebrew Congregations (1959), the United Presbyterian Church in the United States (1959), the Church of the Brethren (1957), the American Ethical Union (1960), the General Conference of the Methodist Church (1960), and the Lutheran Church in America (1966) have taken positions in favor of abolition.

In Canada, the Executive Council of the Anglican Church (1958) and the United Church of Canada (1960) have likewise stated their opposition.

The lessened dependence upon the deprivation of life

The decreasing use of capital punishment is reflected in the statistics regarding the number of prisoners on death row. During the last four decades, the number of executions has declined each year. While 200 persons were executed in 1935 for their crimes, only 1 person was deprived of his life during 1966. Persons were awaiting the completion of the sentence at the end of 1960 numbered 210; the number rose to 331 by the end of 1965. Included within the total were the 67 prisoners sentenced to death in 1965, a decrease of 31 from 1964. Sixty-two prisoners received reprieves from the death sentence during 1965.[26] Although the argument over capital punishment has continued even to more recent years, judges, juries, and political leaders seem to show an increasing reluctance to impose or authorize the death penalty in the United States.

The current trend to repeal the death sentence by disuse or to avoid its impact through elimination and substitution of life imprisonment or imprisonment for a specific length of time has been apparent for some years. Since 1930, only 7 of the 31 capital offenses commonly legislated in the United States have been used as grounds for death penalty convictions. Part of this tendency has been due to the move toward permissive rather than mandatory application of the death sentence. However, even among those who have been sentenced to death,

---

[25] Sellin, "Homicides in Retentionist and Abolitionist States," in Sellin (ed.), *op. cit.,* p. 138. Also see his "Murder and the Penalty of Death," *Annals,* Vol. 204 (November, 1951), p. 106.

[26] President's Commission, *op. cit.,* p. 143.

approximately one half escape the infliction of sentence. In 1961 alone, approximately one execution, he noted was carried out for each 115 homicides reported.[27] Much of the hesitance to use the death penalty, James A. McCafferty believes, is due to the modification of rules of evidence, requirements of counsel, and rules of court procedure, and to the extension of Federal judicial practices to the states through decisions of the U.S. Supreme Court.[28]

Capital cases are extremely costly. They take longer to litigate at the trial level, frequently tie up court time in jury selection, and demand "inordinate deliberation" because of the lack of later opportunity to correct error. Because the defense may press appeals, collateral attacks, and petitions for executive clemency following the imposition of the death sentence, a time lapse of nearly four years, if not longer, frequently occurs between the imposition and execution of sentence. Even then execution may not take place.

---

[27] See James A. McCafferty, "Major Trends in the Use of Capital Punishment," *Federal Probation*, Vol. 25 (September, 1961), pp. 15–21; W. J. Lassers, "Proof of Guilt in Capital Cases," *Journal of Criminal Law, Criminology, and Police Science*, Vol. 58 (Summer, 1967), p. 310.

[28] Sellin, "Executions," *op. cit.*, p. 35. Also consult Michael V. DiSalle, *The Power of Life and Death* (New York: Random House, Inc., 1965); Barrett Pettyman, Jr., *Death and the Supreme Court* (New York; Harcourt, Brace & World, Inc., 1961); H. A. Bedau, "The Courts, the Constitution and Capital Punishment," *Utah Law Review*, Vol. 1968 (May, 1968), p. 201; and Sol Rubin, "Supreme Court, Cruel and Unusual Punishment, and the Death Penalty," *Crime and Delinquency*, Vol. 15 (January, 1969), p. 121.

Part SEVEN

The return to the community

Chapter 25

PAROLE AND COMMUNITY REENTRY

Parole is the conditional release of a person from a penal or correctional institution under supervision within the community. It had its origins in the practices of conditional pardon (pardon for good behavior), apprenticeship by indenture (work for another for a designated period of time in return for training, room, board, and sometimes passage), the transportation (exile) of offenders to Australia and America, the Irish and English system of ticket of leave (temporary release for special reasons), and the efforts of 19th-century American prison reformers to find solutions to the growing crime problem.[1] A French derivative, the word *parole* refers to one's word of honor (*parole d' honneur*).[2] Under its terms prisoners are permitted an early release to society if they comply with certain rules designed to aid their readjustment and to prevent their recidivism or return to crime.

Because parole is a form of early release from imprisonment, it differs from probation, which permits the offender to return to the community in lieu of a prison sentence. While probation is a judicial function of the court, parole is a responsibility administered by an institutional authority on behalf of society at large. Worked in conjunction with indeterminate court sentences, which had been inaugurated as early

---

[1] Charles L. Newman, "Conditional Pardons and the Origin of Parole," in Charles L. Newman (ed.), *Sourcebook on Probation, Parole and Pardons* (Springfield, Ill.; Charles C. Thomas, Publishers, 1964), p. 4; and *Literature on Parole* (Athens, Ga.: University of Georgia, 1964).

[2] Reed R. Clegg, *Probation and Parole* (Springfield, Ill.: Charles C. Thomas, Publisher, 1964), p. 22.

as 1532 in Germany and 1832 in Spain,[3] parole seeks to capitalize upon the offender's personal efforts to rehabilitate himself.

Essentially, parole is an extension of the correctional treatment program. It is used to facilitate the rehabilitation of individuals previously confined to prisons or other institutions. Permitting release on parole or continued custody until the time at which the felon is no longer a threat to community peace and order, parole permits the inmate to live in the community while supervised at a lower cost to the public. While parole agents may help the parolee find employment and adjust to outside life in relationship to prescribed parole regulations, they are also required to act in the interest of society if the parolee violates the conditions of parole or participates in further crimes.

PAROLE IN THE UNITED STATES AND CANADA

Parole in Canada assumes the three basic elements of conditional remission of part of a sentence, a contract or agreement, and recognized supervision. First inaugurated in Canada in 1898 under the Tickets of Leave Act,[4] parolees within this system in its early years commonly reported to the local police upon their arrival. More recently, they have been reporting to the Parole Department and the office of the Dominion Parole Officer.

The enactment of the Parole Act of February 15, 1959, which established a National Parole Board for the first time, opened a new phase in Canadian parole history. Under the act's provisions, the parole board is authorized to grant parole to inmates, revoke or suspend parole, revoke or suspend any sentence of whipping, and revoke or suspend any order made under the criminal code prohibiting any person from operating a motor vehicle. Composed of five members, the board works with the assistance of the National Parole Service, which itself maintains 12 regional officers. Imprisoned offenders under the terms of the act are eligible for parole consideration when they have completed one of the following minimum requirements for parole eligibility:

1. One third of the sentence or four years, whichever is the lesser, in a sentence of a term of months or years.
2. Seven years in a life sentence imposed by the court as the maximum permitted by the Capital Criminal Code.
3. Ten years in a life sentence commuted from a sentence of death.[5]

---

[3] F. P. Miller, "Parole," in William T. McGrath (ed.), *Crime and Its Treatment in Canada.* (New York: St. Martin's Press, Inc., 1965), p. 327.

[4] *Ibid.*, p. 329.

[5] *Ibid.*, p. 340.

Although certain differences are evident in the American and Canadian systems of parole, they share many similarities. However, variations in practices among the states are quite common, especially in capital cases. In Alabama, for example, the commuted "lifer" is eligible for parole only after he has served 15 years. If conditionally released, his parole continues for life unless he receives a pardon from the Board of Pardons and Paroles. However, if he is not pardoned, a quorum of the Alabama board may revoke his parole at any time. Arkansas and Arizona follow similar practices, although the length of time to be served varies. In California, the prisoner may be paroled after he has served seven years of a life sentence commuted from a penalty of death unless the governor's commutation order contains a provision that parole shall not be granted. Although juries may recommend mercy in cases of conviction for a capital offense in Connecticut, the judge must sentence the offender to life imprisonment. As in the case of Alabama, Delaware capital offenders serving life sentences can be paroled by the parole board after they have served six months of their sentence. While the Parole Commission is empowered to release the parolee from supervision or to return him to prison for violation, only the Pardon Board, upon the recommendation of the Commission, can restore civil rights withdrawn from the individual after conviction for a felony.

In Georgia, the Board of Pardons and Paroles possesses the power to commute death penalties to life imprisonment, an action which permits parole consideration after the serving of seven years. The Idaho term served must approximate 10 years before a prisoner is eligible for parole. Parole eligibility in Illinois is determined in relation to the formula shown in Table 25–1. Although commutation of the death penalty in Kentucky is the responsibility of the governor, capital offenders are eligible for parole by the Division of Probation and Parole after serving eight years. The term before eligibility must be 15 years in Maryland. A Montana prisoner serving life may be paroled when he has served at least 25 years less the maximum possible good time of 11 years and 3 months. By contrast, North Dakota permits no commutation of death sentences to life imprisonment and allows no parole of capital offenders who commit an additional murder while serving a life sentence for homicide. An Ohio prisoner serving life for a second-degree murder is eligible for parole after having served 10 years. Those convicted of first-degree murder may become eligible for consideration only after their case has been reduced to second-degree murder through executive clemency and after they have met the requirements of second-degree murder parole eligibility.

Capital offenders serving life sentences in Oklahoma are eligible for parole after having served 15 years. They are eligible after seven years in Oregon. A South Carolina probation, parole, and pardon board, may

TABLE 25–1
Table of parole eligibility—Illinois

Minimum Sentence	Parole Eligibility
1 year	11 months
2 years	1 year, 9 months
3 years	2 years, 6 months
4 years	3 years, 2 months
5 years	3 years, 9 months
6 years	4 years, 3 months
7 years	4 years, 9 months
8 years	5 years, 3 months
9 years	5 years, 9 months
10 years	6 years, 3 months
11 years	6 years, 9 months
12 years	7 years, 3 months
13 years	7 years, 9 months
14 years	8 years, 3 months
15 years	8 years, 9 months
16 years	9 years, 3 months
17 years	9 years, 9 months
18 years	10 years, 3 months
19 years	10 years, 9 months
20 years or more	11 years, 3 months

Source: James C. Craven, "Sentencing," *University of Illinois Law Forum*, Vol. 1966 (1966), p. 536.

parole capital offenders serving life sentences following a period of 10 years of imprisonment. A governor of South Dakota may commute death sentences to life imprisonment, but capital prisoners in this category are not eligible for parole. In West Virginia, prisoners convicted or sentenced to death may have the penalty commuted by the governor and become eligible for parole after serving 10 years. However, if they have been convicted of two prior felonies, they must serve at least 15 years before eligibility. Wyoming does not permit the commutation of the death penalty to life imprisonment. Only if the jury specifies "without capital punishment" may the life sentence rather than death penalty be imposed for defined offenses. Only then can any consideration be given to parole.[6]

Criteria for parole

The American Law Institute's Model Penal Code assumes that parole will be granted except in particular circumstances which it defines thus:

---

[6] G. I. Giardini and R. G. Farrow, "The Paroling of Capital Offenders," *Capital Punishment* (New York: Harper & Row, Publishers, 1967), pp. 169–77. Also see Lloyd E. Ohlin, *Selection For Parole* (New York: Russel Sage, 1951).

1. There is a substantial risk that the prisoner will not conform to the conditions of parole;
2. His release at that time would deprecate or depreciate the seriousness of his crime or promote disrespect for law;
3. His release would have adverse effect upon prisoner discipline;
4. His capacity to lead a law-abiding life will be enhanced if his correctional treatment or vocational or other training is continued to a later time.[7]

Nevertheless, parole criteria are many. Everett M. Porter notes many of the factors considered in making parole decisions:

Probably we may assume that every parole board member has some sort of criteria that are used in arriving at a decision to vote for or against granting parole to a particular inmate. Perhaps it would be safe to conclude that in a broad sense each member of a paroling agency votes for or against granting parole after taking into consideration the following general issues:

1. The nature and gravity of the inmate's offense against society;
2. The deviant history of the person seeking parole or the absence of any misconduct in his past life;
3. The inmate's total personality as the same reflects the presence or absence of potential and capacity for harm to society;
4. The likelihood that on release the offender will return, or will not return to the life of criminal conduct and the probable injury society will suffer should the prisoner become a recidivist;
5. What efforts have been made or not been made by the prisoner since imprisonment by way of improvements in habits of social conduct-education or skills to demonstrate a honest desire to live in harmony with society and its laws; and
6. How effective or ineffective the efforts of the inmate seem to have been and will probably be when released in aiding him or her toward living a life free of crime.

On examining the foregoing general criteria, one immediately discovers that unless there is some general *a priori* agreement among us on the philosophy and nature of criminal conduct and identifiable rules for parole readiness and selection, the weight and conclusion drawn from each element of consideration are apt to be largely subjective despite a desire and perhaps a belief that one is subjective without identifiable rules. Measurements may be as varied as there are individual members of parole boards. The challenge we face, it seems, is not so much a matter of identifying what elements we will consider in arriving at our decision to vote for or against granting parole, but

---

[7] American Law Institute, *Modern Penal Code* (Report to the Thirty-Third Annual Meeting [May 23–26. 1956]). Also see *Guides for Parole Selection* (New York: National Council on Crime and Delinquency, 1963).

our great challenge is to delineate, if possible, identifiable rules by which we are guided to the decisions we make in parole selection.[8]

Parole and the community

Parole in some states is not automatic even when granted. A study completed at the Federal Reformatory in Chillicothe, Ohio, in 1958 disclosed, for example, that of the 398 men released on parole during the year, 172 were not freed on the date supposedly set for their discharge. Nearly 32 percent of the number were more than 20 days overdue at the time of final release. During that one year, the about-to-be paroled inmates spent 3,923 extra days in prison. Although the main reason for delay in parole was lack of definite employment, more than one-half of the to-be-paroled inmates were eventually released without a job. The study revealed that 87 percent of the delays in parole were due either to the lack of a suitable home plan or to lack of employment.[9]

While family attitudes toward the offender cause some offenders to spend extra days in prison, inmate parental or blood relative relationships normally tend to improve as the date of release comes closer. At the same time, prisoner hostility to persons in the free community similarly tends to diminish as he becomes more willing to accept help from anyone and especially from relatives. While 90 percent of the released men return to the communities in which they previously resided, they probably do so, despite the fact that their criminal reputation is community-wide, in order to receive assistance from kin.[10] If this aid is not forthcoming, the ex-prisoner may fail in his attempt to lead a new life. For example, discord with relatives at the releasee's place of residence, Daniel Glaser finds, is highly associated, with subsequent failure. While those expecting or already on parole tend to be most apprehensive concerning parole rules against associating with other ex-criminals, drinking, travel, and being away from home late at night, concern for rules pertaining to postrelease employment declines sharply in the first few months after release from prison.[11] Although most prisoners, Glaser believes,

[8] E. M. Porter, "Criteria for Parole Selection" (Paper delivered to Annual Meeting of the 99th Annual Congress of Corrections at Detroit, Michigan [September 9, 1958]); and note Derek Miller, *Growth to Freedom* (Bloomington: Indiana University Press, 1965).

[9] Paul W. Keve, *Imaginative Programming in Probation and Parole* (Minneapolis: University of Minnesota Press, 1967), p. 228.

[10] Daniel Glaser, *The Effectiveness of a Prison and Parole System* (Indianapolis: Bobbs-Merrill & Co., Inc., 1964), p. 400.

[11] *Ibid.*, p. 511.

hold real fears of postrelease police harrassment, only "a few percent of ex-prisoners" experience any such annoyances.[12]

Aftercare services, often offered by prisoner's aid societies, are designed in many countries and states to minimize such problems. In Canada, for example, aftercare assistance is available to parolees in every province.[13] In several provinces the Correctional Services Department of the Salvation Army, organized on a national basis and directed to give advice and general assistance to accused and released convicts, acts on behalf of the Canadian public. Using a form of spiritual therapy, the Salvation Army provides hostels, rehabilitation centers, and special institutions for alcoholic and other offenders. The John Howard Society similarly offers comparable services; it also maintains a high degree of interest in the conditions of offenders under arrest, crime prevention, and in prison reform. Other organizations such as the Catholic Rehabilitation Services, the Borstal Association, The Société de Orientation and de Réhabilitation Social, the Service de Réadaptation Social, Inc., and the Elizabeth Fry Societies operate in selected provinces.[14]

Although the Canadian provinces provide *ex gratia* grants to voluntary service groups interested in meeting the problems of prisoner reentry, the Canadian government has been slow to provide a coherent program of aftercare services. Although they work in close cooperation with the government, private social agencies are responsible primarily to their own communities through elected boards of directors. Charged with the fundamental responsibility of reintegrating the inmate to the community, most aftercare societies utilize casework services as their principal method. They employ professionally trained social workers, and an individual worker-parolee relationship is created in order to meet the many emotional needs of the discharged inmate and to build upon his personal strengths in overcoming his weaknesses.[15] Upon release, the ex-inmate, categorized for the first 30 days as a handicapped person, may use the assistance of the Canadian National Employment Service to find a suitable job. While the success rate of the National Employment Service remains high, job failures still occur due to the inability of the newly released inmate to accept direction, maintain regu-

---

[12] *Ibid.*, p. 401. Also see Bernard F. McSally "What's So Good About Parole?" *Federal Probation*, Vol. 30 (December, 1961), pp. 20–24; and Richard A. Chappell, "Federal Parole Policies and Practices," *Federal Probation*, Vol. 25 (June, 1962), pp. 27–32.

[13] A. M. Kirkpatrick, "After-care and the Prisoner's Aid Societies," in McGrath (ed.), *op. cit.*, p. 384.

[14] *Ibid.*, p. 385.

[15] *Ibid.*, p. 386; also see Harvey Treger, "Reluctance of the Social Agency to Work with the Offender," *Federal Probation*, Vol. 29 (March, 1965), pp. 23–28.

lar hours, develop good work habits, establish cooperative relationships with other employees, and to work in a steady manner.[16]

Parole sanctions

The few usable sanctions for reinforcing parole conditions are usually limited to reprimand, increased restriction, suspension of parole followed by continuation of sentence, or revocation.[17] Common parole behavior requirements include expectations that the parolee obey the law, refrain from leaving the probation jurisdiction without permission, refrain from marrying without permission, refrain from creating debts or entering into any contract without prior permission, and make contact with the parole officer at stated intervals. Other requirements in a number of jurisdictions may prohibit gambling, the use of alcoholic beverages, associations with other known offenders, or the carrying of weapons. In several jurisdictions, parolees are directed to attend church regularly; in others, his parole may be conditioned by employment requirements.[18] If the parolee violates these terms, he may be reinstitutionalized at the discretion of the supervising authority.

The following case studies[19] reveal the many dimensions of the parole revocation process. In one instance, the return to prison was caused by the isolation of the parolee's work location and the hasty action of the probation-parole officer:

"Dennis," Case V-497, left school at the age of fourteen when in the fifth grade. His I.Q. on the Revised Beta Examination, for illiterates, is 72. One factor in his school retardation may have been that he was reared in a very isolated rural area, the farm of his parents being three miles from the nearest road. From the age of seventeen on he lived with his older brother in a large city whenever he could work there, and returned to the farm whenever he could not work in the city. The farm and this city were in different states, though less than 150 miles apart. On his first arrest, when he was twenty years old, he was committed to prison under the Federal Youth Correction Act; his offense apparently was the acceptance of a ride from the city to his home area with three friends, who apparently took the initiative in their procurement of transportation by stealing an automobile.

Dennis was paroled in less than a year to live on a farm about thirty miles from his parents and to work in a coal mine. In three months the mine closed up, and after a sojourn with his parents he received permission to go to his brother's home to seek work in the city. He found a job there

---

[16] *Ibid.*, p. 393.

[17] Miller, *op. cit.*, p. 361.

[18] Clegg, *op. cit.*, p. 26. Consult Nat R. Arluke, "A Summary of Parole Rules," *National Probation and Parole Journal*, Vol. 11 (January, 1956), pp. 8–12.

[19] Case studies adapted from Glaser, *op. cit.*, pp. 75–82.

and about four months later received permission from the city U.S. Probation Officer to marry a widow, seven years his senior, whom he met on the job. A week later he was injured in an accident at his job, and he claims he received permission to return with his wife to the home of his parents. Not long afterwards he procured a farm job a few miles from the home of his parents, and he was working and living there with his wife when he was arrested as a violator.

The probation office "Referral for Consideration of Alleged Violation" requested that the U.S. Board of Parole issue a warrant in Dennis' case because of his "loss of contact, failure to submit monthly reports, and leaving district without permission." It states that reports for one month were not received and those for the next month, mailed to him by the probation office, were returned with the entry "moved—left no address." The warrant referral also mentions that the officer was told in the community of Dennis' parents home that Dennis had gone to another state.

Dennis claims to have given his report for mailing to the farmer for whom he works; there is no rural delivery in this relatively untraversable area, mail being picked up only in the village. The probation officer could not visit Dennis' parents unless he were willing to walk several miles from the road, and Dennis claims that a substitute for his regular probation officer inquired about him in the village and received some misinformation. Dennis says that his parents and employer later confirmed that he had never left the area. Regardless of the veracity of these several accounts of the violation, revocation appears to have been a much more rigid reaction than would occur in this type of circumstance in most judicial districts. In this case geographical isolation and the illiteracy of the subject added to communication difficulty.

In another, the rearrest was stimulated by the flighty character of the parolee:

"Don," Case V-458, is an illiterate youth, of rural background. When he was ten his father died. His mother did not remarry, but the home she maintained for her seven children was very impoverished. They often lived with various relatives in rural shacks, with the older males in the household frequently drunk. In Don's original offense he apparently rode with a cousin in a stolen car, for which he was given probation while his cousin went to prison. When, without permission, Don left the state in search of work, his probation was revoked and he was given a Federal Youth Correction Act sentence. He was confined for almost two years, during which great efforts were made to raise his educational level before it was concluded that he had reached his limit when he mastered third grade.

Don was supposed to be employed by a cousin on release, but the cousin did not reply to a letter about the job. When the probation officer went to check on this job, the cousin's wife told the officer to leave. This job never was available, and the officer had Don stay at a mission for homeless men rather than live in the rural community with his relatives. Nevertheless, Don repeatedly departed to visit his mother and other relatives. Several unskilled jobs were procured for him, but he was unable to keep any for long. On one occasion he visited relatives in another state without permission, to seek work there.

It is understandable that Don's probation officer became rather distraught with him, and Don also was hostile towards the officer. Don does not communicate well in any case, for which he is a frequent butt of jokes, and he has particular difficulty in expressing himself when angry. After he was seen in association with other ex-convicts among his relatives, he was returned as a violator. It was clear that Don needed an unusually protective environment for highly satisfactory adjustment, and the prison is functioning as a mental institution in his case. Efforts to facilitate and encourage his achievement of a noncriminal and self-sufficient life away from his relatives seem likely to continue to be futile, since his relatives provide his most reliable source of affection and respect, as well as economic assistance. With them, however, there also seemed to be some prospect of his joining relatives in the commission of further crime.

A third individual had his parole revoked because he traveled outside the jurisdiction to seek work:

"Tom," Case V-042, came to this country from Canada when nineteen and thereafter had a continual series of arrests in the United States, culminating in his third prison commitment in 1937, on a twenty-year federal sentence for counterfeiting. He was mandatorily released in 1949 and worked in an automobile plant for three years until a defense contract led to the discharge of all who could not prove their citizenship. After several months, during which he was able to find only temporary employment, he was assisted by a nephew in opening a small store for the sale of costume jewelry. This prospered through the Christmas season, but he had to sell out in February and was then unemployed until August. He claims that at this time he asked permission to transfer to another city to seek employment and was told that he could not do so unless he already had a job arranged there. This appears to have been a misunderstanding on his part, since the customary procedure in most federal supervision is to authorize short trips to seek work, but not to transfer a man to supervision by another district office until a satisfactory job and residence are procured in the new area. At any rate, after over five years of nonviolation, Tom absconded. Two years later, when he was approaching sixty years of age, he was returned to federal prison on a warrant for mandatory-release violation.

The cases of "Harry," "Dudley," "Ralph," and "Richard" revealed different reasons. Harry found normal life difficult and violated his parole in order to gain prison reentry:

"Harry," Case V-456, was the oldest of five children deserted by their mother when he was seven. When he was fifteen his father died, and he then ran away from three foster homes and an orphanage, until placed for a year in the Boys' Republic in Michigan. A few months after placement from there to a farm family, he was involved in a car theft for which he was sent briefly to a state industrial school. On his eighteenth birthday he joined the Army, but a year later he went AWOL and stole an automobile, for which he received his Federal Youth Correction Act sentence.

Harry was paroled after nearly three years in prison, where at first he made a poor adjustment. A job arranged for him by the probation officer proved unavailable for three weeks, during which he incurred some indebtedness, and he finally went to work for only $42 per week. However, shortly thereafter he acquired $1,300 that was left in trust for him from his father's life insurance policy. He kept his job, but proceeded to spend several hundred dollars for clothes and $740 for a used car. It proved to be a "lemon," and he spent more money to trade it for a motorcycle and another used car. Within three months these were both used as down payment for another used car, for which he also signed a note for $69 per month payments, from his salary of less than $200 per month. Within three months he had gone through his legacy, was in debt, and was involved in a complicated relationship with a woman from which he wished to withdraw. With sixty dollars left from a pay check he boarded a bus and three days later, in a remote part of the country, penniless and feverish with a cold, he turned himself in to a small-town police department.

"Dudley" yielded his parole due to his loyalty to his girlfriend:

The life of "Dudley," Case V–499, provides an extreme illustration of the habit of reacting to problems by irrational flight. As in some of the marginal-failure cases already described, frequently this flight does not involve the commission of felonies, although cars may be stolen when flight is difficult. The consequences of flight generally also increase the intensity of economic and other problems that provoke felonies.

Dudley came from a home of continuous bickering in which his parents twice were divorced and twice remarried. He was placed in a private boys' school when eleven, but was expelled when they could not control him. He was sent to a state training school when thirteen, for incorrigibility. Dudley was paroled from this school four times in the next five years, always violating parole by leaving home, and the violations always were reported to the parole officer by his mother. Dudley's federal offense was a car theft while hitchhiking far from home on his last state training school parole.

Dudley got along very well on his federal parole, working regularly a twelve-hour day at a grocery store. He had become engaged by correspondence while in prison to a girl whom he had known for many years. She lived in another judicial district, in the same state, but he obtained permission from the probation officer to visit her every other weekend. One weekday the girl called him when she was upset over a quarrel with her mother. Dudley left immediately, and joined the quarrel that evening. He says he missed the bus back to his home and he believed that his mother probably had already reported his flight, so that he would be returned to prison as a violator. He hitchhiked to the home of a friend from the training school, and after three days there they both hitchhiked across the country. Eventually they were arrested with another stolen car.

In Dudley's case the probation officer filed a report with the Parole Board recommending that no warrant be issued pending further investigation. He remarked that this was merely a repetition of Dudley's previous flight behavior, on which he generally did not commit felonies. Dudley, on the other hand, had misperceived the consequences of his initial flight to his girl's home, and in many other respects operated with an inadequate view of reality, which presumably reflected his chaotic upbringing.

Ralph had no intention of halting his criminal career and faced re-arrest and parole revocation for new crimes:

"Ralph," Case V–026, is a professional burglar and proud of it. He was thirty-three years old when mandatorily released from prison on his fifth felony conviction, and he reports that he committed a burglary that night. He committed another three days later, but that same night he was investigated by the police when he drove into a gas station and appeared drunk. He was found to have over forty dollars in coins and over three hundred cartons of cigarettes in his car, in addition to burglar tools. While free on bond following this arrest, he was caught in a gambling raid and found with identifiable stolen property. For this he served a two-year state prison term before being returned to federal prison for mandatory release violation.

Ralph told us that he concentrates on small burglaries and returns regularly to one city where he has numerous contacts for disposing of stolen goods. He also values contacts with criminal lawyers there, who can make the prosecutor's task so difficult that he can bargain for a light penalty in exchange for pleading guilty. He is a constant student of burglar alarms and continuously "cases" places for burglary possibilities, just as some insurance salesmen habitually "size up" as a potential customer every person whom they meet. He tries not to burglarize an establishment until some months elapse after he has "cased" it, so as to reduce the prospect of his presence there being recalled. When his funds permit, he spaces his burglaries a week or two apart.

Ralph is of superior intelligence and won a county spelling bee before he dropped out of school in the ninth grade. He was reared by grandparents following the divorce of his parents and illness of his mother. In prison he has served as an effective schoolteacher. It seems obvious that, had he persisted in a noncriminal occupation, by this time he would be earning as much or more than he does by burglary, and much more securely. He had a wife and three children, but she divorced him and remarried during one of his earlier imprisonments, and he no longer has any contact with them. During two interviews in prison following his quick return from mandatory release, he seemed committed to continuing his criminal career. He boasted that prior to his federal sentence he had supported himself by burglary for twenty-two months, and he hopes to have such luck again. He is careful to avoid areas where a burglary would give him a very long sentence. Whether he ever will fall into our category of "late reformation after criminal career" will long remain uncertain.

Richard was simply unable to remain free of heroin:

"Richard," Case V–254, was reared in a slum community by a paternal aunt and had little contact with his parents, who separated when he was an infant. He dropped out of school when sixteen and had very little legitimate employment thereafter. He started to use marijuana in his teens and soon graduated to heroin. He married a woman who was also an addict, and he then lived from her prostitution and from the sale of heroin, for which he received his first federal imprisonment when twenty-two years old.

Richard says that he planned not to contact his wife on release, as he feared it would lead to drug usage, and he expected to have a job at cleaning and pressing, a trade he learned in prison. On his first day out, however, he learned that the job was no longer available. That night he had some marijuana at a friend's house, and before the night was out he looked up his wife. The next day, he says, when lying in bed watching her injecting herself with heroin, he decided to try it again. He then resumed his preprison way of life, but was not caught until five months later, when he and his wife were observed making a purchase of heroin. For this he was returned to prison with a new five-year sentence.

As the foregoing cases illustrate, the reasons for parole violations vary and are sometimes valid and at other times arbitrary.

The Interstate Parole and Probation Compact and parole failure

The Interstate Parole and Probation Compact enacted by Congress in 1934, permits the states to create cooperative agreements for the supervision of probationers and parolees. Ratified by all states, the Compact permits the supervision of probationers and parolees within their areas of normal residence, often far removed from the location at which they committed their original crime. Consequently, the Interstate Compact protects the community by supervising the offender upon release rather than handing him a one-way ticket to his area of residence and increases his chances of successful reorientation in his home community with the aid and support of family, friends, and employers.

Under the detainer system which is part of the Compact, offenders who have committed additional violations in other states may be detained and transferred to the custody of the state placing the detainer. Although this practice serves the legal demands for trial of violating offenders, the detainer system may undermine the parolee's desire to prepare himself for return to society. The Compact is administered by an executive committee of the Association of Administrators and a Council of five members who delineate rules, regulations, and policies on behalf of the compacting states, subject to vote of the membership of the association.[20]

---

[20] Clegg, *op. cit.*, pp. 139–141.

Because parole is designed to supervise the prisoner's reentry into society and to assist in his rehabilitation, the failure to achieve these ends may result in the parolee's return to incarceration. Common indicators of parole failure, F. P. Miller itemizes, include:

1. Disappearance (whereabouts unknown);
2. Repeated failure to keep appointments;
3. Persistant action or inaction against the advise of the supervisor (includes the abandonment of an important phase of the parole plan without consultation);
4. Failure to meet family responsibility;
5. Persistently keeping late hours;
6. Making unauthorized journeys (should be stipulated in the early phase of the parole);
7. Keeping undesirable associations;
8. Excessive drinking (where there is no condition to abstain);
9. Breach of condition to abstain;
10. Any involvement with police including:
    a) Being checked by police,
    b) Arrest,
    c) Dismissal of charges, or
    d) Conviction. (Conviction [in Canada] for indictable offense brings automatic forfeiture).[21]

Preparation for prisoner reentry

Any program designed to prepare paroled prisoners for return to the community must take several basic factors into consideration. *Mandatory considerations* include legal and administrative aspects relating to statutory provisions for mandatory release and parole, civil rights and responsibilities of offenders, the process of release to another's custody, rules of supervision, the role of the U.S. probation officer, the determination of destination, and clearance procedures. The dimension of *planning and resources* includes employment information and counseling, financial planning, and sensitization to existing community resources, including the clergy, banking institutions, insurance companies, and alcoholic rehabilitation agencies. *Emotional elements* refer to these aspects which affect social relationships and to those attitudinal problems found among persons in process of reentering society. Tied to this dimension, although somewhat loosely, are elements related to race relations, highway safety,

---

[21] Miller, *op. cit.*, p. 353. For another dimension, consider Meyer H. Diskind and George Klonsky, "A Second look at the New York State Parole Drug Experiment," *Federal Probation*, Vol. 28 (December, 1964), pp. 34–41; George Klonsky, "Extended Supervision for Discharged Addict-Parolees," *Federal Probation*, Vol. 29 (March, 1965), pp. 39–44; and *An Experiment in the Supervision of Paroled Offenders Addicted to Narcotic Drugs* (Albany: New York State Division of Parole, 1960).

and even installment credit buying. Some individuals are never fully able to control all dimensions and eventually recidivate or live semi-successfully with such tensions.[22]

Not all reentry programs are able to respond to these dimensions. One program designed to ease many of these tensions and to assist the parolee to make the incarceration and release adjustment exists at the Patuxent Institution, a prison-type hospital for sociopathic criminal recidivists at Jessup, Maryland.[23] The program is designed primarily for individuals with a deficiency of intellect and an imbalance of emotion which required incarceration or treatment of an indeterminate length. The institution nevertheless permits the admission of a prisoner to pre-parole status (1) if he shows that he can be trusted within the community by virtue of his successful personality adjustment through psychotherapy, and (2) if the prisoner's family members or interested parties are willing to have him at their homes on leave at periodic intervals. Intended to lead to eventual parole, the preparole program permits the inmate to adjust to society and to achieve a more complete rehabilitation. Through such an opportunity, the staff establishes a new relationship with the family and with the prisoner. This approach also allows the administration to determine whether periodic leaves create financial or emotional difficulties for the family, potentially an indication of future parole failure.

When granted, these preparoles often last for five days and are usually carried out over the major holidays of Easter, Memorial Day, Fourth of July, Labor Day, Thanksgiving, and Christmas. After each visit, the leave is carefully evaluated to determine whether such opportunities should be continued in the future. If all seems well, the staff may recommend further monthly and major holiday leaves. Because inmates generally recognize that leave opportunities indicate the staff's belief in their progress, the leave tends to strengthen and reinforce the individual's confidence and personal adjustment. While such a program may possess major value, its eventual success depends on what philosophy of treatment is accepted by the family as well as by the institution.[24]

Mississippi and Michigan provide for short-time furloughs from institutions to prepare the prisoner for reentry and to stimulate his interest in personal change. Fewer than 1 percent of those chosen for participation fail to return. Similarly, various juvenile institutions permit occa-

---

[22] J. E. Baker, "Preparing Prisoners for Their Return to the Community," *Federal Probation,* Vol. 30 (June, 1966), p. 44; Louis Zeitoun, "Parole Supervision and Self-Determination," *Federal Probation,* Vol. 25 (September, 1962), pp. 44–49; and Frank T. Flynn, "Parole Supervision: A Case Analysis," *Federal Probation,* Vol. 15 (June, 1951), pp. 36–42.

[23] Nathan S. Nackman, "A Transitional Service Between Incarceration and Release," *Federal Probation,* Vol. 27 (December, 1963), pp. 43–44.

[24] *Ibid.,* p. 46.

sional short furloughs at Christmas and Thanksgiving or for weddings and funerals. Although used sparingly, these furloughs help to maintain family ties and permit the juvenile or adult to maintain meaningful contacts with free community reality.[25]

The Kingston Penitentiary in Canada operates a program of daily release prior to final release in order to lessen the problems brought about by community reentry. In 1955, prisoners were released from the women's prison at Kingston only if placed under the supervision of the Elizabeth Fry Society of that city. However, two years later, the habitual offenders were also permitted such gradual release under the supervision of the John Howard Society of Ontario at Toronto. Under the guidelines of this gradual-release program, the warden of a penitentiary is permitted to release an inmate for daily periods for whatever reason he considers advisable, with or without escort. Created to promote the inmate's reintegration into the community and to assist in his resocialization, the gradual-release program generally permits shopping trips, the opening of bank accounts, registration with the national employment service, attendance at church, visits to private homes, and recreational activities. Each aspect of the program is designed to aid the offender in reestablishing a sense of belonging to the community. While such a program has proved to be valuable, the demand for the creation of a gradual-release hostel outside penitentiary walls has also arisen in recent years in order to minimize tensions created by the reentry program among those who still must do their own time. The hostel gradual-release program provides benefits but still falls short of guaranteeing employment and of developing economic security for the inmate because most employers prefer not to employ workers, whether ex-convicts or nonconvicts, on a short-term basis.[26]

Prerelease and work furlough/work release programs

Most Canadian Prisoner's Aids provide prerelease services for prison inmates in order to assist the individual plan for his future life, adapt his personality to free society expectations, find work, and reestablish community relationships. The John Howard Society of Ontario, for example, follows up a prisoner's request for aid with the introduction of staff representative to the inmate; which develops the request; a presentation of the agency's potential services for the ex-inmate; and a more detailed discussion of agency service standards, postrelease prob-

---

[25] The President's Commission, on Law Enforcement and on Administration of Justice, *The Challenge of Crime in a Free Society* (Washington, D.C.: U.S. Government Printing Office, 1967). p. 176.

[26] Kirkpatrick, *op. cit.*, pp. 400–401; and J. P. Martin, *Offenders as Employees* (New York: St. Martin's Press, Inc., 1962).

lems, and community attitudes, if the inmate decides to use the referral service. Commonly, the discussion of postrelease problems focus on questions of:

1. Employment.
   a) An inability to use constructively the job-placing services of the community such as the national employment service.
   b) Disillusionment about the employment situation, i.e., lack of job and length of job-hunting process.
   c) The inability to find work, to sell one's self to an employer.
   d) When in employment, inability to face up to employer and barter for the best working arrangements.
   e) General feelings of insecurity in employment, such as fear of employees, someone coming in off the street and facing him, and fear of a police visit to the employer.
2. Economic insecurity over the period from release to first pay.
3. The securing of accommodations.
4. Recovery from the initial period of confusion, depression, and mental disorientation.
5. The resumption of fairly normal family and marital relationships and the difficulties that ensue.
6. The pressure to acquire material effects, particularly clothing.
7. The establishment of social relationships.
8. The constructive use of leisure.
9. The fear of finding himself back with the "rounders."
10. Handling his drive for acceptance.
11. Dealing with returning cycles of depression and lack of progress as first planned, and frustration in some cases at being unable to make any headway.
12. Hostile attitude to any authority, particularly the police.
13. Pre-conviction debts, both financial and social.
14. Problem of fantasy thinking and fabrication, such as inability to tell a straight story to employers, aftercare workers, family and friends.
15. How to use counseling effectively.
16. How to handle the overconfidence that comes with the first pay.
17. Bonding and licensing.
18. The doldrum period.[27]

The lack of income during the immediate period following release is one of the most critical of these problems. The province of Ontario permits the released offender $20 upon discharge, an inadequate amount to tide him over till his first paycheck. Consequently, many of the Prisoner's Aid Societies assist the released offender by providing money

---

[27] *Ibid.*, pp. 390–91.

for food, lodging, work clothing, and tools until he is able to get on his feet.

Many of these basic questions are also covered in the Texas prerelease program which covers 24 topics in five weeks of the prisoner's sentence at a prerelease center near Houston.[28] During his stay, the dischargee participates in an active program which begins at 5:30 A.M. with wake-up, shower, and dressing and concludes at 6 P.M. with free time. Between 7 and 11 A.M., he participates in driver training, group or individual counseling, and various sessions conducted by a guest speaker. Maintaining his assignment between 12:30 and 4:30, he prepares for an evening meal at 5 P.M. Not only do the daily discussions change but they also present the dischargee with a wide range of information necessary for his successful community readjustment (see Table 25–2).[29]

The desire to pass beyond a mere prerelease orientation program has stimulated the growth of work release programs, first permitted in Wisconsin with the passage of the 1913 Haber Law in order to provide valuable and meaningful work opportunities not available within the prison.[30] However, even before Wisonsin adopted this procedure, an unidentified New Hampshire sheriff carried out a plan which allowed prisoners to work in the community and serve nights and weekends in jail. North Carolina in 1957 inaugurated a work release program which evidenced so much early success that the state was able to close a number of prisons due to reduced recidivism among the men sharing in the program. South Carolina, Maryland, other states, and the federal system also adopted such an approach in the years following.

The enactment of the California Work Furlough Rehabilitation Law and the application of its provisions at the Elmwood Rehabilitation Center quickly stimulated California's interest in work release programs. The California work furlough approach permits the judge to sentence a prisoner to released work at his regular place of employment on the condition that he spend all his nonworking hours in jail. Such a sentence allows the offender to support his dependents, keep his job, pay part of his jailing costs, and yet satisfy the demands of sentencing.[31] During the first few years of operation of one program in Orange County, a total of 235 male offenders from municipal courts and 90 from superior

---

[28] The pioneering prerelease program was developed at the Federal Correctional Institution at Danbury, Connecticut, in 1945. See Mark S. Richmond, *Prison Profiles* (New York: Oceana Publications, Inc., 1965), p. 9.

[29] J. E. Clark, "The Texas Pre-Release Program," *Federal Probation*, Vol. 30 (December, 1966), p. 55.

[30] John D. Case, "Doing Time in the Community," *Federal Probation*, Vol. 31 (March, 1967), p. 9; and Sanger B. Powers, "Off-Ground Activities Present an Opportunity for Correctional Institutions," *Federal Probation*, Vol. 31 (June, 1967), pp. 11–15.

[31] David R. McMillan, "Work Furloughs of Jail Prisoners," *Federal Probation*, Vol. 29 (March, 1965), p. 33.

TABLE 25–2
The Texas prerelease program

Session	Topic	Guest Speaker
You and Prerelease		
1	General Orientation	Warden and staff
You and Your Job		
2	Job Opportunities	Houston Personnel Association
3	Employment Aids	Texas Employment Commission
4	Unions	Representative of AFL–CIO
5	Keeping Your Job	Businessman and Employee
6	Social Security	Social Security
You and the Law		
7	Purpose and Function of the Law	Houston Police Department
8	Motor Vehicle Operation	Department of Public Safety
9	Legal Problems	Houston Bar Association
You and Your Finances		
10	Sensible Spending and Budgeting	Businessman
11	Income Tax	Internal Revenue agent
12	Borrowing	Houston Retail Credit Association
13	Buying a Car	Houston car dealers
14	Wardrobe Tips	A retail clothier
You and Your Family		
15	The Family	Professional family counselors
16	Assisting Agencies	Community Council
You and Your Community		
17	Human Relations	Professional public relations
18	Insurance	Insurance Underwriters Association
19	Responsible Citizenship	Leaders in civic affairs
20	Personal Health	County and state departments
21	Manners and Courtesy	Representative of a service organization
22	Religious Activities	Minister
23	Personal Habits	Alcoholic and Narcotics Commission
24	Veterans Benefits	Veterans Administration

Source: J. E. Clark, "The Texas Prerelease Program," *Federal Probation*, Vol. 30 (December, 1966), p. 55.

courts were granted work furlough sentences ranging from 15 days to one year. The average sentence was 88 days. Although the procedure was used most often in cases of driving with a suspended or revoked license and drunk driving, it was also tried successfully in cases of burglary, counterfeit checks, intoxication, and assault with a deadly weapon. Of the 19 inmates returned to the court and removed for violation, 14 were arrested for using intoxicants, 3 for going to a place of residence rather than to work, 1 for failing to return to jail, and 1 for committing a new drunken driving offense. Of the $243,863 which the prisoners earned, $42,414 was paid to the county as reimbursement for expenses. Other wages went to cover personal debts, prisoner expenses, food, clothes, court fines, restitution to victims, and savings for release. Not only was the county reimbursed for part of the costs of the program, but it also received $1,393 in fines and at the same time saved an estimated $63,366 in welfare monies that did not need to be expended.[32]

Under most work released provisions, employed prisoners pay for their transportation, incidental expenses, clothing, union fees, and income taxes from their earnings made while temporarily released from prison. In some states, they must also reimburse the jurisdiction for room and board. However, surplus funds may be used for dependent support, payment of fines or debts incurred in their previous activities, and re-entry costs.

The success of work release has also led to the variation of study release which permits the juvenile or youthful offender to attend school part-time or full-time in addition to, or instead of, working. To facilitate the study opportunity, the New York State Division of Youth, for example, maintains several centers in selected apartment buildings which provide the youth with a form of institutional commitment and yet the freedom necessary to continue his education.[33] Although work release or furlough programs hold great promise, John D. Case warns that work release poses major dangers if its sole purpose is to make money for a county or other jurisdiction. In such instances, work release centers, he contends, may become little more than government-supported flop-houses. Therefore, work release programs, he concludes, must be directed toward problem solving and toward the assimilation of the offender within the society to which he was earlier alienated and must eventually return.[34] Only then can the moral and physical deterioration of prison life brought about by inmate idleness be overcome.

Problems of inmate postrelease adjustment

When prisoners are finally released from the prison under parole or outright, they immediately encounter actual reentry problems. Not only do prisoners generally come into contact with old friends soon after release but they also find their prison record is well known among

---

[32] *Ibid.*, p. 34.

[33] President's Commission, *op. cit.*, p. 177. Also see Stanley E. Grupp, "Work Release and the Misdemeanant," *Federal Probation*, Vol. 29 (June, 1965), pp. 6–12.

[34] Case, *op. cit.*, p. 9. Also consult Robert R. Hannum, "Employment Impediments for Offenders and Public Safety Regulations," *Federal Probation*, Vol. 27 (March, 1963), p. 28; and Daniel Glaser, Eugene S. Zemans and Charles W. Dean, *Money Against Crime* (Chicago: John Howard Association, 1961).

members of their postrelease social groups. Faced with a potential ostracism and the renewed influence of former friends who were originally instrumental in their criminal conduct, they may already be on the road to recidivism. Daniel Glaser finds, for example, that persistent contacts with other ex-prisoners makes the possibility of reimprisonment correspondingly higher.[35] However, most parolees tend to acquire new friends in the first few months after release who may help them make a successful adjustment.

More than 90 percent of American parolees, Daniel Glaser reports, search for legitimate careers for a month or more after leaving prison. However, when a possibility for performing a criminal or noncriminal act as an alternative means for achieving particular ends or "where the only possibilities are to employ criminal means or to forsake the ends that crime might serve," parole releasees, Glaser finds, "take that course of action from which they anticipate the most favorable conception of themselves."[36] Ultimately, the parolee's self-conception in such a situation depends upon both his prior experiences and his present circumstances. After release, most prisoners almost immediately "recapitulate" their adolescent dependence upon parent figures and their useful struggles to achieve a sense of independence in their adulthood. However, whether the individual, Glaser believes, is able to modify prior delinquent patterns when dealing with parent figures and peers depends to a great extent upon whether or not new patterns are reinforced with greater gratification in legitimate or illegitimate pursuits.

One attempt to provide a more legitimate setting for parolee decision making led to the creation of the Sioux City (Iowa) Restoration Club, which has brought parolees and townspeople into contact with each other as an expression of good will. Suggested originally by a local parole officer who had completed an eighth grade education, this approach has served to lessen the social distance between recent parolees and ordinary citizens. Paul W. Keve suggests that its success as a program is probably due to the ability of the program to overcome the parolee's apathy and hopelessness, which often undermine his attempt to accept conventional middle-class relationships.[37] At meetings held once a month with community members interested in the probationer or parolee at a local YMCA, the parolees, their sponsors and community members associate on a first-name basis. Role playing occurs during the business meeting, at which parolees have an opportunity to conduct the meeting and to fulfill some basic responsibility. As a result of these contacts, many parolees have sought advice from successful community

[35] Glaser, *op. cit.*, p. 401.
[36] *Ibid.*, p. 512.
[37] Keve, *op. cit.*, p. 254. Also see R. J. Margolin, "Postinstitutional Rehabilitation of the Penal Offender," *Federal Probation*, Vol. 31 (March, 1967), pp. 46–50.

members in the attempt to solve their problems rather than engage in later crimes.

Although this approach has been successful, other existing programs may also help to overcome postrelease problems. Daniel Glaser suggests, for example, that inmate savings programs may offer one method of meeting prostrelease expenses. Parole supervisors could assist in dispersing these funds as needed. Inmate communication with law enforcement and legitimate community members should also be facilitated through the reduction if not elimination of restrictions upon correspondence and visitation. Outside organizations, Glaser proposes, should become more involved with inmate associations whether on the level of service or hobby clubs, personal development and mutual therapy groups, religious or church organizations, or other voluntary organizations. Parole supervision staff members should likewise communicate with inmates prior to their release and should have access to loan funds for parolee assistance during the adjustment period. Parolees should be made eligible for unemployment insurance during the transitional phase. Some prison parolees and dischargees, Glaser proposes, should be employed by government agencies to reduce the general social and economic costs of recidivism and reimprisonment to the public.[38]

Easing the reentry problem

In line with many of Glaser's suggestions, the District of Columbia has included the development of work release and community furlough programs and of community treatment centers. Under the provisions of the Federal Prisoner Rehabilitation Act of 1965, 50 reformatory inmates in the Prerelease Employment Program (PREP) were first placed in District of Columbia jobs in cooperation with the Washington Labor Council in March, 1966.[39] Working at selected jobs for standard wages during the day, the prisoners returned to the institution for night lockup. A prerelease guidance center, allied with PREP, serves as a halfway house. Operating on the third floor of the Twelfth St. YMCA, the center serves 20 young men at any one time. Area boys committed for indeterminate sentences under the Federal Youth Corrections Act are eligible to live at the "Y" approximately 90 days before they are released on parole. During this period, attempts are made to solve their employment or other reentry problems. While the furlough program supplements additional efforts, it permits carefully screened inmates to leave prison on their own recognizance to attend funerals, visit relatives, complete

---

[38] Glaser, *op. cit.*, pp. 510–11.

[39] Thomas R. Sart, "Contact With a Free Community Is Basic Too if Institutional Programs Are to Succeed," *Federal Probation*, Vol. 31 (March, 1967), p. 3.

employment interviews, continue schooling, and prepare for release. Those inmates who are security risks are escorted to the city by correctional officers dressed in street clothes.[40]

The group home and the halfway house. One of the more interesting adaptations to city living and reentry is the group home provided for juveniles in an apartment home complex operated by New York City's Division of Youth. Housed in two rented contiguous apartments, remodeled to make a large living room and six bedrooms for seven boys, the group home is staffed by a husband and wife who serve as house parents and maintain 24-hour supervision five days per week. Throughout their stay at this location, juveniles share in an intimate family-style living experience. While the husband commonly works at a regular job during the day, he returns to the group home when off work for five days each week. However, both husband and wife are free to return to the privacy of their own residence on their two days off. Relief personnel spell the houseparents on a regular weekly basis. A private institution called the Children's Village also maintains three group homes for boys unable to return to their own homes after being released from an institution.[41]

Juvenile halfway houses have been used successfully in Michigan, Washington, California, and New York.[42] Youths residing in these homes must usually be provided for over a longer period of time. The Riverside Group Home in Tacoma (Washington), developed in 1962, quickly found that the expected six-month stay for each boy was insufficient and in some instances had to be extended for as long as two years. Boys were encouraged to work at neighborhood jobs after school and to pay for school expenses, dental bills, and clothes from their earnings. Ten percent of their income was deposited in a house improvement and recreational fund. Emphasizing a minimum of rules, the staff and residents attempted to maintain a family-type home.[43] An unexpected by-product of the program was the willingness of several employers to take some of the boys into their own homes on foster home placement.

The adult halfway house is somewhat more commonplace than its juvenile variation. Most houses for adult offenders are designed to provide the older releasee with some permissive supports immediately following his release from prison and during his initial phase of readjustment to the open society. However, whether the halfway house program

---

[40] *Ibid.*, p. 4.
[41] Keve, *op. cit.*, pp. 251–52.
[42] *Ibid.*, p. 226. Refer to *Children's Bureau, Halfway House Programs for Delinquents* (Washington, D.C.: U.S. Department of Health, Education, and Welfare, 1965).
[43] *Ibid.*, p. 247.

is highly structured or largely permissive depends in large part upon the basic philosophy of the supporting body. Sponsorship of halfway houses vary. The American Friends Service Committee, for example, originated the Los Angeles Crenshaw House in 1958 and operated it until its closing a few years later. The Friends also began the Austin MacCormick House in San Francisco. The Episcopal Church began and operates St. Leonard's House in Chicago.[44] One of the earliest halfway houses in the United States was organized in 1959 in St. Louis under the leadership of Father Charles Dismas Clark, who purchased an old school building with contributions from a Jewish friend. Usually staffed by a Catholic priest and many former staff residents, Dismas House serves a maximum number of 60 men. Residents not easily employable elsewhere assume much of the housekeeping and general maintenance responsibilities.[45] A second independent Catholic facility has since been provided at the Roncalli House in Minneapolis. While such houses have definite value for the rehabilitation of offenders, not all communities are willing to accept their existence. Fear of narcotic addicts led many Staten Island community members to oppose the development of Daytop Lodge, a halfway house for drug addicts.[46]

The Correctional Council of Delaware currently operates a state-owned house at 308 West Residence in Wilmington. Maintained by a prisoner's aid society, the State of Delaware and the County of Newcastle provide direct grants for its operation. In California, the Community Correctional Center at Oakland serves both as a halfway house and a headquarters for all California parole officers in that region. Established in 1965, the Center is used for recreation, counseling, group meetings, or other advantageous purposes.[47]

The Federal Bureau of Prisons maintains six halfway houses in New York City, Washington, Chicago, Detroit, Kansas City, and Los Angeles. The Bureau operates a halfway house in Michigan under a contractual agreement, serving both state and federal cases. Established under the provisions of the Prison Rehabilitation Act of 1965, the Bureau is empowered by the federal government to establish community halfway houses for selected adult offenders, permit deserving inmates to work at regular employment in nearby communities and return to the institutions during nonworking hours, and grant unescorted furloughs to inmates needing to return home for family emergencies, to seek employ-

---

[44] Ibid., p. 224.

[45] Ibid., p. 242. Examine William Krasner, "Hoodlum Priest and Respectable Convicts," Harpers, Vol. 222 (February, 1961), p. 61.

[46] Ibid., p. 230.

[47] Ibid., pp. 225–26. Also see Maurice A. Breslin and Robert G. Crosswhite, "Residential Aftercase: An Intermediate Step in the Correctional Process," Federal Probation, Vol. 27 (March, 1963), pp. 37–46.

ment, or for other important reasons thought to be consistent with the interest of the community and the prisoner.[48]

Although custodial standards vary widely, most federal halfway houses require residents to sign out and in when they leave or return to a building. During evenings or weekends, each resident must secure passes for absences. Curfews, generally 10 or 11 P.M., are common in most halfway houses. Other restrictions include prohibitions against illegal activities and liquor or women in bedrooms. Because it serves as a psychological support and helps reduce the amount of pilfering among house residents, food is readily available to all residents.[49]

Costs of halfway houses make the operation of such facilities somewhat tenuous. The operation of the Wilmington halfway house cost $37,718 in 1964. Only $1,650 of the total was covered by resident rental payments. In 1966, Dismas House charged residents between $15 and $25 per week, although a portion of this amount was returned to the resident upon discharge. However, if the resident was unemployed, not only were no charges made for his upkeep but he also was paid $5 per week for work he did within the residence. While federal prerelease centers do not charge for room and board, a number of private halfway houses depend upon room and board contributions from working residents.[50]

Group discussions play a major role within the halfway house program. Some institutions, such as the East Los Angeles halfway house hold group therapy sessions every evening in order to maximize the adjustment potential of its residents during their three-month stay. Two caseworkers plus part-time consultants in psychology, psychiatry, and group therapy assist in the Wilmington program. Each halfway house resident participates in two group meetings per week for the discussion of personal adjustment problems and maintains scheduled interviews with an assigned caseworker. Using Great Books discussions, woodworking, worship services, participant sports, and Alcoholics Anonymous meetings, the staff encourages residents to become actively involved in community life.[51]

Desiring to offer a higher quality of living experience in their halfway houses, the Black Friar Settlement in London and the Austin McCormick Halfway House have mixed a few graduate students or other mature persons with normal residents. While this move was designed to bring residents into a more normative social arrangement, the value of this procedure has not been fully established.

[48] Myrl E. Alexander, "Current Concepts in Correction," *Federal Probation*, Vol. 30 (September, 1966), p. 5.
[49] Keve, *op. cit.*, pp. 234–35.
[50] *Ibid.*, pp. 239–40.
[51] *Ibid.*, pp. 233–34.

A group meeting at the Los Angeles Crenshaw House before its demise led to the development of a halfway job to accompany the halfway house living experience. Reasoning that their reentry into society would be better accomplished if men learned to work and to understand their situation with the aid of others, Crenshaw residents attempted to create a poster-painting and display-work enterprise. However, the failure to gain state recognition or to develop a strong financial foundation ended this effort within months after its origin. At East Los Angeles, residents accept jobs and leave the halfway house only after they have received joint permission of the staff and the group.[52]

Non-residential halfway houses.   One proposal designed to overcome the high cost of facilities which has restricted the development of many useful halfway programs has been offered by Robert Meiners. Future programs, Meiners suggests, may be developed just as effectively without providing residence facilities. Instead, all apartment, rooming, or other housing arrangements for a therapeutic program may be handled by one central office. Such a procedure, Meiners argues, would move the clients more quickly into normative community living arrangements while also providing them with active reentry assistance.[53] Not only would such an approach, he believes, lessen the administrative burden of maintaining a house but it would also permit a wider variety of services and solutions for male and female clients.

Although Meiners has merely speculated upon such a possibility, the Iowa State Parole Agency and the Salvation Army have already worked out such an arrangement in Sioux City, Iowa. Any parolee needing a halfway-type placement is housed by the state parole agent in Salvation Army dormitories. Employment and other services are provided as needed by the parole agent and the Salvation Army staff. The apparent success of the program in moderate communities has led to similar approaches in other Salvation Army residence areas. Such arrangements are maintained in other living facilities for women by Dismas House in St. Louis and for all residents by Chicago's St. Leonard's House.[54]

The development of these and other counseling centers in metropolitan areas, Daniel Glaser suggests, is one of the most promising correctional developments in the last half century because they permit the prisoner to transfer to a location in the community before his release date and allow him to develop employment and postprison social relationships while still under state supervision.[55] Their full promise, however, is yet to be realized.

---

[52] *Ibid.*, pp. 236–37.
[53] Robert G. Meiners, "A Half-Way House for Parolees," *Federal Probation*, Vol. 29 (June, 1965), p. 51.
[54] Keve, *op. cit.*, p. 243.
[55] Glaser, *op. cit.*, p. 511.

Chapter 26

RECIDIVISM AND THE PROBLEM OF PREDICTION

Parole may be revoked for many different reasons (see Table 26–1).

Violations leading toward revocation potentially include the following:
1. Use of liquor (any use in 41 states).
2. Association or correspondence with persons of poor reputation (38 states).
3. Change of employment or residence (39 states).
4. Failure to report monthly (38 states).
5. Traveling out of the state without permission (2 states).
6. Marriage without permission (33 states).
7. Operation and ownership of motor vehicles without permission (30 states).
8. Use of narcotics (28 states).
9. Failure to support dependents (27 states).
10. Possession, sale, or use of weapons (12 states).
11. Travel out of the country or community without permission (25 states).
12. Failure to waive extradition (19 states).
13. Incurrence of indebtedness without permission (11 states).
14. Failure to be home at a reasonable hour (6 states).
15. Illegal assumption of lost civil rights (6 states).
16. Gambling (5 states).
17. Failure to report an arrest while on parole to one's parole officer (3 states).

TABLE 26–1
Comparison of parole regulations by states

	Alabama	Arizona	Arkansas	California	Colorado	Connecticut	Delaware	Florida	Georgia	Idaho	Illinois	Indiana	Iowa	Kansas	Kentucky	Louisiana	Maine	Maryland
1. Liquor usage	2	2	2	2	2	2	2	4	2	4	2	2	2	2	2	2	2	2
2. Association or correspondence with "undesirables"	2	2	2	2	1	2	2	2	2	2	2	2		2	2	2	2	2
3. Change of employment or residence		1		1	1	1	1	1	1		1	1	1	1	1	1	1	1
4. Filing report blanks		3	3	3		3		3	3	3		3	3	3	3	3	3	3
5. Out-of-state travel	1		1		1		1		1	1	1	1	2		1	1	1	1
6. Contracting a new marriage	1		1	1	1	1		1			1	1	1	1	1	1	1	1
7. First arrival report	3		3	3	3	3		3	3	3		3	3	3		3	3	3
8. Operation and ownership of motor vehicles		1	1	1	1		1		1	1	1	1		1			1	1
9. Narcotic usage	2		2	2			2	2	2	2	2			2	2	2	2	
10. Support dependents	3				3			3	3	3					3	3	3	3
11. Possession, sale, or use of weapons; obtaining hunting license		2	2	1	2		1	2	2		2	2	2	1	1		1	1
12. Travel out of county or community		1	1	1				1	1	1	1	1		1				
13. Agree to waive extradition	3				3			3	3	3					3		3	
14. Indebtedness					1					1								
15. Curfew					6						10:30						11:00	
16. Civil rights	1				2	2					2						2	
17. "Street time" credit if returned as P.V.																	5	5
18. Gambling	2							2				2						
19. No "street time" credit if convinced of felony					5													
20. Airplane license					1												1	
21. Report if arrested					3												3	
22. Treatment for venereal disease								3										
23. Church attendance															3			
24. Enlistment in armed forces																		

KEY—1. Allowed, but permission must first be obtained. 2. Prohibited. 3. Compulsory. 4. Allowed but not to excess. 5. May be received. 6. "Reasonable hour."
Source: Charles L. Newman, *Sourcebook on Probation, Parole and Pardons* (Springfield, Ill.: Charles C. Thomas, Publisher, 1964), pp. 204–5.

18. Failure to obtain parole officer's permission to apply for an airplane license (3 states).
19. Failure to seek treatment for venereal disease (2 states).
20. Failure to attend church regularly (2 states).
21. Enlistment in the Armed Forces without parole officer permission (1 state).[1]

Because many of these limitations are archaic, they are being increasingly challenged. But the questioning does not stop there; instead, questions concerning due process in parole revocation hearings are also being raised. Eugene T. Urbaniak maintains the traditional view that due

---

[1] Charles L. Newman, *Sourcebook on Probation, Parole and Pardons* (Springfield, Ill.: Charles C. Thomas, Publisher, 1964), pp. 206–8.

TABLE 26–1 (*Continued*)

Massachusetts	Michigan	Minnesota	Mississippi	Missouri	Montana	Nebraska	Nevada	New Hampshire	New Jersey	New Mexico	New York	North Carolina	North Dakota	Ohio	Oklahoma	Oregon	Pennsylvania	Rhode Island	South Carolina	South Dakota	Tennessee	Texas	Utah	Vermont	Virginia	Washington	West Virginia	Wisconsin	Wyoming
2	4	2	2		2	2	2	2	4	2	2	2	2	2	2	2	2	2	2	2	2	2	2	2		2		2	2
2	1	1	2	2		2	2	2/1	2		2	2	2	2	2	2	2	2	2	2	2	2	2	2		2		2	
1	1	1	1	1		1	1	1	1		1	1	1	1		1	1	1	1	1	1	1	1			1	1	1	
3	3	3	3	3	3	3	3	3		3		3	3	3	3	3		3	3	3	3		3	3	3		3	3	
1	1	1	1	1	2	1		1	1		1	1		1	1	1	1	1	1		1		1		1	1	1	1	1
1	1	1		1		1	1	1	1		1		1	1	1	1	1	1		1			1		1		1		
	3	3	3	3		3			3	3	3	3		3	3	3	3		3	3				3					
1	1	1		1		1	1	1	1		1			1	1	1	1	1	1					1		1	1	1	
2	2		2			2	2		2		2	2	2	2	2	2				1	2	2			2				
3	3		3	3		3			3		3	3	3	3		3					3	3	3	3		3			
1		1				1	1		1		2	2	1	1							2	1	2		1				
	1	1		1	1	1			1	1	1	1	1		1	1	1			1					1	1			
		3			3		3		3			3	3	3	3	3									3	3			
	1	1			1	1	1	1			1			1		1									1			1	
	6					6	6				6		6	6		2													
					2		5							5							2		5		5				
							5	5		5				5		1													
							3							3															
					3									1															

process should not be required at parole revocation hearings inasmuch as the conditional liberty granted to a parolee is an act of legislative grace and does not grant the parolee vested rights which cannot later be withdrawn at the discretion of the parole board. In effect, the conditional liberty permitted the parolee, Urbaniak argues, is a contract, and its violation is a breach of contract. Because the opportunity for conditional freedom is simply a procedure by which the parolee is allowed to serve the remainder of his sentence in the outside community, a person who has breached the conditions of his parole must inevitably accept the status of an escaped prisoner.[2]

---

[2] Eugene T. Urbaniak, "Due Process Should Not Be a Requirement at a Parole Revocation Hearing," *Federal Probation*, Vol. 27 (June, 1963), p. 50.

Sol Rubin reports that the general trend in judicial procedure is toward the amplification of due process in parole revocation hearings. Because the courts are in conflict as to whether due process evolution is derived from constitutional or statutory elements, due process procedures in parole are probably less vigorous than in probation. The trend nevertheless continues toward increased procedural requirements in parole revocation proceedings on both the state and the federal level. Although many states still have the power to revoke parole on debatable grounds more and more are requiring basic legal controls in the parole revocation process.[3]

THE PROBLEM OF RECIDIVISM

Whatever the decision concerning due process in parole revocation hearings, it is only one aspect of the total problem of recidivism. Criminal careers regardless of due process procedures, often follow, Daniel Glaser reports, a zig-zag path from noncrime to crime and back to noncrime. For some the sequence will be repeated many times; for others followed only once.[4] The rate of recidivism in countries which possess no statutory limits on the award of court probation is about 1 to 5 and for those given a form of institutional treatment 1 in every 2. While many would immediately suggest on the basis of such findings that probation is much more effective than institutional treatment, they must be careful, Leslie T. Wilkins notes, to recognize that those given probation represent better risks than those eventually institutionalized. Hence, any attempt to correlate the two is largely doomed to failure inasmuch as two dissimilar techniques cannot be evaluated in similar terms under such conditions.[5]

An early study of the recidivism of 680 Massachusetts State Penitentiary inmates by S. B. Warner in 1923 disclosed that the parole board commonly used the following criteria in deciding whether or not to parole a given inmate:

1. Whether the man had supposedly profited from his stay in the institution and had so far reformed that it was unlikely that he would commit another offense.
2. Whether his conduct in the institution was acceptable.
3. Whether suitable employment was waiting him on release.
4. Whether he had a home or other proper surrounding to go to.

---

[3] Sol Rubin, "Due Process Is Required in Parole Revocation Proceedings," *Federal Probation*, Vol. 27 (June, 1963), pp. 42–43. Also see George J. Reed, "Due Process in Parole Violation Hearings," *Federal Probation*, Vol. 27 (June, 1963), pp. 38–41.

[4] Daniel Glaser, *The Effectiveness of a Prison and Parole System* (Indianapolis: Bobbs-Merrill & Co., Inc., 1964), p. 85.

[5] Leslie T. Wilkins, *Evaluation of Penal Measures* (New York: Random House, Inc., 1969), p. 14.

5. Whether he was able to tell the exact truth when interviewed by the board.

6. Whether the seriousness of his offense and the circumstances surrounding it made parole feasible.

7. The nature of his previous record.

8. The appearance he made before the board in applying for his parole.

9. His behavior while on parole.[6]

However, most of these criteria, Warner found, were without foundation. Although the board viewed sexual offenders as major parole risks, two thirds of the paroled sex offenders were successful as opposed to a total success rate of one half. In a second study of the indeterminate sentence and the Illinois parole system in 1928, E. W. Burgess found that offenders convicted of fraud and forgery maintained a parole violation of 42.4 percent in relation to the overall institutional rate of 28.4 percent. Persons convicted of murder and manslaughter revealed only a 9 percent reconviction rate. Using his findings to produce a prediction table in which he allocated 1 negative point to each factor associated with failure and 1 positive point for each factor associated with success, Burgess found that only 1.5 percent of those men with 16 to 21 favorable points later violated while as many as 76 percent of those with only 2 to 4 favorable points did so.[7] In addition, a staff study of prison effectiveness at the Minnesota Reformatory at St. Cloud (345 men) released between July 1, 1944, and June 30, 1945, after examination of the FBI postrelease records and state parole and police records, disclosed that 21 percent of the 345 released male inmates were convicted of new felonies within the five-year follow-up period, 2 percent were returned as parole rule violators without new sentences while suspected of committing new felonies, and 15 percent were returned for other parole violations. Although a total of 38 percent were returned to prison during the follow-up period, those incarcerated ranged in age from 20 to 29 and did not represent a cross section of Minnesota prison inmates.[8]

Although the public generally believes that 65 to 70 percent of those released from prison will eventually recidivate, a more recent study by Daniel Glaser of 2,547 prisoners released from federal prisons during August and November, 1943, and January and March, 1944 disclosed that only 32.6 percent of the released federal prisoners were sentenced

---

[6] S. B. Warner, "Factors Determining Parole from the Massachusetts Reformatory," *Journal of Criminal Law and Criminology*, Vol. 14 (1923), pp. 172–207.

[7] Wilkins, *op. cit.*, pp. 64–66, Consult Louise V. Erisbie, "Treated Sex Offenders Who Revert to Sexually Deviant Behavior," *Federal Probation*, Vol. 29 (June, 1965), pp. 52–57; and Murray L. Cohen and Harry L. Kizol, "Evaluation for Parole at a Sex Offender Treatment Center," *Federal Probation*, Vol. 30 (September, 1966), pp. 50–55.

[8] Glaser, *op. cit.*, p. 18.

to new terms of imprisonment or returned to prison as parole violators within five years. This also included those who received new sentences of only one year or less, many being only a few days in the local jail. Only "about one-fourth of the men released from federal prisons in 1943 and 1944," Glaser concluded, "were returned to prison during the next five years."[9] Additionally, a two-year follow-up study of all Wisconsin inmates paroles between 1952 and 1956 further disclosed that 1.3 percent were convicted of a new offense during the parole period while an additional 22.1 percent violated some aspect of the parole or conditional release arrangement. Although 35.8 percent were eligible for imprisonment, only 31.3 percent were actually reinstitutionalized in Wisconsin prisons.[10]

Some 342 male prisoners convicted of first-degree murder were paroled in California between 1945 and 1954. By the end of June, 1956, 37 (10.8 percent) were declared parole violators. Of the group, 6 fled while on parole, 11 were returned to prison for technical violations, 11 for conviction of misdemeanors, and 9 for new felony sentences, including 2 for robbery, 2 for lewd acts with children, 1 for narcotics offenses, 1 for abortion, 1 for sex perversion, 1 for assault to murder, and 1 for second-degree murder. Of the 63 prisoners convicted of first-degree murder and eventually paroled in New York between July, 1930, and July, 1961, none committed another homicide. Fifty-six possessed no prior felony convictions before the sentence for first-degree murder; three became delinquent upon release. One committed a burglary after 18 months on parole, and two were involved in technical violations after 16 and 24 months on parole. At release their average age was 51 years. Of the 514 New York prisoners convicted of second-degree murder but paroled between January, 1945, and January, 1961, 417 (81.1 percent) possessed no previous felony convictions, 77 (15 percent) had one, and 20 (3.9 percent) had two or more. Sixty-five members of the group were returned to the prison for technical violations, thirty-three for misdemeanor convictions, and seventeen for felony convictions. Two of the new felony offenders were convicted of first-degree murder—one killed in the act of armed robbery, and the second murdered two companions while on a drinking bout.[11] One of the 273 former first-degree

[9] *Ibid.*, pp. 16–17. Also see Ralph W. England, Jr., "A Study of Post-Probation Recidivism Among 500 Federal Offenders," *Federal Probation,* Vol. 19 (September, 1955), pp. 10–16.

[10] Wisconsin State Department of Public Welfare, *Failure Rates of Prisoners Paroled From Wisconsin Adult Correctional Institutions* (Madison: Bureau of Research Statistics, 1958). Examine a second publication for this bureau entitled, A *Study of the Relationship between Time Served and Later Parole Violation Experience* (Madison: Bureau of Research Statistics, 1965).

[11] Thorsten Sellin, "Comments," in Thorsten Sellin (ed.), *Capital Punishment* (New York: Harper & Row, Publishers, 1967), p. 185.

murderers paroled in Ohio between 1945 and 1965, 143 of the 154 receiving final releases received them in 1965. During that period, 15 (5.5 percent) first-degree murderers violated parole.[12]

A separate follow-up study of California parolees released between 1946 and 1949 through January 1, 1953 disclosed that 20.2 percent of those on parole supervision were imprisoned on a new felony, 23.3 percent were returned to prison for parole violations without felony convictions, and 5.5 percent were declared parole violators but not returned to prison.[13] Of 924 Canadian parolees released during 1950 less than 4 percent were recommitted during the parole periods. Nearly 74 percent of the group (681 persons) had not violated parole nor been sentenced to a prison on a new offense at the end of a five-year period. Persons surveyed included those serving sentences as short as six months and as long as life imprisonment.[14]

A 1960 random study of 1,015 cases of adult male prisoners released from prisons in 1956 further disclosed that 26.6 percent were reimprisoned on new felony sentences, 1.7 percent on parole or conditional release violations when suspected of new felonies, and 2.8 percent for violations of parole with no felonies alleged. In addition, 3.9 percent received nonprison sentences for felony-like offenses, such as petty larceny and concealed weapons. The 65 percent classified as successful included the 52.2 percent who possessed no further criminal record and the 2.4 percent who had one or more felony arrests with no convictions, the 4.8 percent who recorded one or more arrests on felony charges with no convictions, the 4.5 percent who shared in one or more misdemeanor convictions without any arrests on felony charges, and 1.1 percent who had one or more misdemeanor convictions and one or more arrests on felony charges with no felony convictions.[15]

A study of court sentencing in England and Wales revealed that first offenders ranging between the ages of 8 and 16 years have a 65 percent probability of being convicted of another offense; those between 17 and 29, 55 percent probability; and those 30 and above a 28 percent probability.[16] Contrary to general belief, older offenders, possibly due to the greater awareness of the social consequences of their act, seem to be better parole risks than younger offenders.[17] Additional

---

[12] Sellin, *op. cit.*, pp. 185–86.

[13] *California Male Prisoners Released on Parole* (Sacramento: California Director of Corrections and Adult Authority, 1953), pp. 12–14.

[14] F. P. Miller, "Parole" in William T. McGrath (ed.), *Crime and Its Treatment in Canada* (New York: St. Martin's Press, Inc., 1965), p. 332.

[15] Glaser, *op. cit.*, p. 20. Refer to Alexander van West, "Cultural Background and Treatment of the Persistent Offender," *Federal Probation*, Vol. 28. (June, 1964), pp. 17–19.

[16] *Home Office, The Sentence of the Court* (London: H. M. Stationery Office, 1964).

[17] Wilkins, *op. cit.*, p. 56.

TABLE 26-2
Summary of follow-up studies of inmates released from U.S. prisons, total systems

Prison System	Year of Release	Duration of Follow-up	Releases Covered	Researchers	Sources of Follow-up Information	Percent Returned to Prison	Percent Convicted or Accused of New Felony
Federal.........	1943–44	Approx. 5 yrs.	All releasees (25% parolees)	U.S. Bureau of Prisons	F.B.I. fingerprint record	24	(Not tabulated)
California........	1946–49	3 yrs.	The 88% who were paroled	Calif. Bd. of Corrections (Beattie)	State parole and criminal identification records	44	28
Wisconsin........	1952–56	2 yrs.	The approx. 85% who were paroled or conditionally released	Wisc. Dept. of Public Welfare (Mannering)	State parole and criminal identification records	31	14 (Convicted)
New York........	1956	Parole period or up to 5 yrs.	The 76% who were paroled	N.Y. Board of Parole (Stanton)	State parole records	44	7 (Convicted)
Federal.........	1956	Approx. 4 yrs.	Every 10th adult male releasee (31% parolees)	U. of Ill. (Glaser)	Some FBI fingerprint records; prison and probation office tracing	31	28
Washington......	1957–59	½ to 2½ yrs.	99% of all releasees	Wash. Dept. of Institutions (Babst, Suver, Kusano, Little)	State parole records	20 (Another 18% in "wanted" status)	13
Pennsylvania.....	1947–57	Parole period: Aver. 2⅓ yrs. Max. 5 yrs.	The approx. 70% who were paroled	Pa. Board of Parole (Jacks)	State parole records	31	17

Source: Daniel Glaser, *The Effectiveness of a Prison and Parole System* (Indianapolis: Bobbs-Merrill Co., Inc., 1964), p. 25.

TABLE 26-3
Summary of follow-up studies of inmates released from U.S. prisons, youthful offenders only

Youth Prisons	Year of Release	Duration of Follow-up	Releasees Covered	Researchers	Sources of Follow-up Information	Percent Returned to Prison	Percent Convicted or Accused of New Felony
Massachusetts Reformatory	1921	5 yrs. post-parole (8–10 yrs. post-release)	The 83% that could be traced (all parolees) of 510 total cases	Sheldon and Eleanor T. Glueck	Field inquiries; state and local records	31.5 (of those traced); 26.1 (of total)	36.1 during parole (of total); 43.8 post-parole (of those traced)
Minnesota Reformatory	1944–45	Approx. 5 yrs.	All releasees (53% parolees)	Zuckerman, Barron, and Whittier	FBI fingerprint and state parole records	38	23
Federal Youth Correction Act cases	1955–58	Parole period (2–4 yrs.)	Those committed 1954–55 (all parolees)	U.S. Board of Parole (Neagles)	Federal parole records	58	36 (Includes some serious misdemeanors)
Federal Youth Correction Act cases	1955–58	Parole period (2–4 yrs.)	All released 1955–58 (all parolees)	U. of Ill. (Glaser)	Federal parole records	49	34

Source: Glaser, *Effectiveness of a Prison and Parole System*, p. 26.

studies in New York State, Washington, Pennsylvania, and within the federal system disclose general recidivist rates that range as high as 58 percent (see Tables 26–2 and 26–3).

Recidivism and reformation

As a result of his study of post-release recidivism, Daniel Glaser differentiated a series of illustrative categories which covered the population. These included:

I. "Success" Cases
1. Clear Reformation
   a) Late reformation after a criminal career (last release at age 30 or more);
   b) Early reformation after a criminal career (last release before 30th birthday);
   c) Crime-facilitated reformation (crimes provided for easily shifting to non-criminal success);
   d) Reformation after crime interval (short-term crime involvement and early life reorientation);
   e) Reformation after only one felony: (lives disorderly; rehabilitated following a severe prison sentence); ·
   f) Crime-interrupted non-criminal career (lives orderly; no further crime after conviction; best prospect for probation);
2. Marginal Reformation
   a) Economic retreatism (i.e., man rejecting modest economic self-sufficiency);
   b) Juvenile retreatism (individuals "young beyond their years" maintain associations with juveniles; are not realistically oriented to achieving independence);
   c) Addictive retreatism (men who avoid felonious drug use but maintain heavy dosage of some legal drug as compensation);
   d) Crime-contacting non-criminality (maintain legitimate occupations while still maintaining extensive contacts with underworld);
   e) Non-imprisoned criminality (participants in crimes not generally prosecuted extensively, or if prosecuted, resulting commonly in fines and short jail terms);
II. "Failure" Cases
1. Marginal Failure
   a) Defective-communications cases (cases in which no violation occurred or the violation was the kind that would not ordinarily lead to revocation of Federal parole);
   b) Other non-violations (drinking, persisting in a juvenile social life, or not seeking work);
2. Clear Recidivism
   a) Deferred recidivism (i.e., men who originally pursue a non-criminal career and only later revert to crime, usually after 1 or more years);

b) Immediate recidivism (men who have no intention of avoiding crime upon release and promptly initiate felonies).[18]

Glaser's findings are that the older the man is when released from prison, the less likely he is to return to crime; that the younger a prisoner is when arrested, convicted, or confined for any length of time, the more likely he is to continue in crime; and that the extent of the offender's prior criminal record and his likelihood of becoming a recidivist are directly correlated. The highest rate of recidivism occurs in the category of felony offenses related to economic offenses not involving violence (*i.e.*, larceny, burglary, auto theft, and forgery). Intermediate recidivism rates are consistently shown in such diverse types of crime as narcotic offenses, robbery, and kidnapping. Lowest recidivism rates are associated with unusual circumstances within the offender's life, such as murder, rape, and embezzlement, rather than with offenses related to vocational pursuits.[19] The most recidivistic single felony type is auto theft.

Recidivism and employment

Prerelease job arrangements, Glaser discloses, do not necessarily result in greater parole success rates than release on parole without a prearranged job. However, the recidivism of adult male offenders, he suggests, varies inversely with their postrelease employment. The chief barrier to employment is not the inmate's criminal record, but rather his lack of extensive or skilled work experiences.[20] J. E. Baker's earlier study of 83 respondents at the Federal Correctional institution at Terminal Island (California) supports this conclusion. Fifty-five men had jobs upon release and sixteen obtained them following release. Only 22 percent of the original 55 destined for employment upon release, however, worked at the same jobs six months later. The remaining 78 percent left employment immediately after release or within five months after release. The majority of severances, Baker found, occurred within 90 days after release. Of the 71 employed at the time of reply, 87 percent indicated that they liked their jobs and intended to stay. The employer had not been told of their prison record in 38 percent of the cases. A large part of the unemployment problem for many inmates, Baker concluded, was due to their low frustration tolerance.[21]

William R. Arnold finds that recidivists do not have any more antisocial attitudes than do nonrecidivists, their friends' expectations are

---

[18] Glaser, *op. cit.*, pp. 54–85.
[19] *Ibid.*, pp. 36–53.
[20] *Ibid.*, pp. 359–61.
[21] J. E. Baker, "Preparing Prisoners for Their Return to the Community," *Federal Probation,* Vol. 30 (June, 1966), pp. 47–50.

no more antisocial than are those of nonrecidivists friends, they experience less effective antidelinquent teaching than do nonrecidivists, they are more likely than nonrecidivists to maintain interaction with groups possessing delinquent history, they have more difficulty adjusting to their peers than do nonrecidivists, and they are more likely than nonrecidivists to be in groups to which it is difficult to adjust while paroled.[22]

THE PROBLEM OF PREDICTION

The quest for prisoner rehabilitation and for a lessened recidivism rate inevitably turns to the problem of original and continuing delinquency and criminality prediction. The problem is complex, and so far the results are inconclusive. Even a simple question as to when prisoners permanently change from being interested in committing crimes reveals the major problem of the multiple variables in the treatment and prediction processes.[23] Of the 250 releases examined in the extensive study by Daniel Glaser, 4 percent replied that they had changed before sentencing, 13 percent said they had changed at the time of sentencing or between sentencing and the time of imprisonment, 52 percent indicated that the change occurred during imprisonment, 16 percent said it happened after release, 10 percent denied ever having changed, and 4 percent indicated that they did not know when they had changed. Each respondent represented a different life capacity, psychological capability, attitude, orientation, and crime commitment. Prediction methods inevitably have to deal with each of these factors. It is at this point that they frequently fail.

The scope of prediction

The original concern for prediction methods was based upon a desire to establish criteria for parole board decision making.[24] However, as Norman S. Hayner indicates, parole boards are hesitant to use prediction devices due to their sensitivity to public opinion, their desire to encourage constructive use of prison time, their firm belief in the uniqueness of each case, their recognition that legal and traditional restrictions often frustrate intelligent selection for parole, and their own reaction to the prediction tables.[25]

---

[22] William R. Arnold, "A Functional Explanation of Recidivism," *Journal of Criminal Law, Criminology, and Police Science,* Vol. 56 (June, 1965), pp. 214–17.

[23] *Ibid.,* p. 89. Consult Arthur E. Elliott, "Parole Readiness: An Institutional Dilemma," *Federal Probation,* Vol. 28 (March, 1964), pp. 26–30.

[24] Wilkins, *op. cit.,* pp. 61–62.

[25] Norman S. Hayner, "Why Do Parole Boards Lag in the Use of Predicting Scores," *Pacific Sociological Review,* Vol. 1 (Fall, 1958), pp. 73–76.

Given this goal, many researchers have attempted to develop valid prediction devices. One of the earliest, and possibly the most debated, is the Glueck Social Prediction Table which differentiates and relates delinquency to family factors, including the supervision of the boy by the mother, the discipline of the boy by the father, the affection of the mother for boys, the affection of the father for boys, and the cohesiveness of the family.[26] Since then, the attempts have been many and varied, but few have achieved much success.

Part of this failure is due to the fact that many prediction attempts only result in typological listings and tend to be oriented toward a method of analysis. Leslie T. Wilkins argues that this is not enough and maintains that prediction should more appropriately refer to influences by persons "on a basis of evidence of varying quality and type." Nevertheless, because methods in predictive situations vary, no single method can be *the* prediction method. Most studies of recidivism, he holds, do not predict but are merely estimates of the probability of recidivism. While estimates of probabilities have been and may continue to be used as predictions if desired, "some so-called prediction methods," Wilkins says, "are nothing more than crude weighting devices for items of information found to be related to recidivism."[27]

Lloyd E. Ohlin criticizes prediction techniques on the ground that they are deterministic, and he suggests that any predictions based on a fixed sequence of cause and effect in human relationships do not realistically consider elements of indeterminacy and uncertainty that operate in all personal and social life.[28] Not only do such prediction methods create a static instrument which is incapable of taking account of change and social or personal conditions but these devices rely on only a small number of personality and situational interactions and "relate them singly rather than in combination to the outcome of action."[29]

Leslie T. Wilkins maintains that probability accounts for the likely acts of the person due to free will or to chance. Additionally, although prediction tables, he argues, are static in form, they are dynamic in theory and may change as new information concerning the value of treatment and aftercare procedures for the individual and the society are conceived. Because factors are not selected or related singly to a singular outcome, the dynamic interplay of the many elements in human interaction must be accounted for. The mere fact of simplicity of predic-

---

[26] Eleanor T. Glueck, "Spotting Potential Delinquents: Can It Be Done?" *Federal Probation*, Vol. 20 (September, 1956), pp. 7–13.

[27] Wilkins, *op. cit.*, pp. 61–63.

[28] Leslie T. Wilkins, "An Essay in the General Theory of Prediction Methods," in Norman B. Johnston, Leonard Savitz, and Marvin E. Wolfgang (eds.), *The Sociology of Punishment and Correction.* (New York: John Wiley & Sons, Inc., 1962), p. 251.

[29] *Ibid.*, p. 253.

tion tables, Wilkins maintains, should not be taken as an indication of their efficiency. Because prediction in itself is dynamic, prediction methods may use any information available for consideration. "To reject classification," Wilkins argues, "is to reject the scientific method and to provide nothing in its place. The result is not a 'better' approach to human problems but an acceptance of complete defeat or an excuse for avoiding all forms of action."[30]

Predictions concerning inmate postrelease behavior, Daniel Glaser believes, are likely to be inaccurate in a large proportion of cases regardless of persons or procedures employed because a great variety of prerelease and postrelease variables and circumstances affect individual behavior. Nevertheless, the most selective prediction tables are consistently more accurate than case study prognoses. Both techniques, however, may be more fully refined in the future. Prediction tables, he concludes, may be used most effectively to establish "base expectancy" categories against which individuals receiving specific treatment may be evaluated.[31]

Hermann Mannheim and Leslie T. Wilkins note that prediction tables must fulfill the basic requirements of simplicity, efficiency, repeatability or reliability, and validity. The requirement of *simplicity* demands that no technical skills other than the ability to do simple multiplication, addition, and subtraction should be required in their application. In order to achieve *efficiency*, prediction tables must make use of the maximum information available concerning a particular individual. Because prediction is prediction only if it fits the facts of the case, any prediction table must be *reliable* in the sense that if someone else performs or evaluates the same individual or case, he will secure the same results. "No variation in the prediction derived should arise," Mannheim and Wilkins suggest, "when computed by different persons of average intelligence nor should any different results occur when the computation is carried out by quite inexperienced personnel."[32] Although prediction tables must finally be useful and valid in their ability to differentiate the likely successes from the likely failures with reasonable accuracy, *validity* must be tested in relationship to the actual tendency of evaluated persons to follow the trend predicted for their cases.

Despite the various criticisms of the prediction methods, the prediction of deviance, John P. Conrad believes, will eventually become a useful correctional tool. Because sentencing currently involves a composite of state or federal legal requirements, a judicial policy of retribution, and the professional opinions of probation or other court officials,

---

[30] *Ibid.*, p. 254.
[31] Glaser, *op. cit.*, pp. 309–10.
[32] Hermann Mannheim and Leslie T. Wilkins, *Prediction Methods in Relation to Borstal Training* (London: H. M. Stationery Office, 1955), pp. 137–42.

a comparative statement of offender prospects is as valid as the other ingredients. Through the use of prediction, the courts, Conrad contends, "could consider the statistical experience of the community in sentencing a particular class of offenders to prison, jail or probation."[33] While the responsibility of the judge in decision making would not be eliminated, prediction would assist him in making the right decision. In addition, the use of prediction capabilities will eventually offer probation supervisors an experimental foundation upon which to make discharge or probation decisions. When utilized within institutions themselves, these predictive capacities may be especially valuable in matching the particular inmate with available programs which may offer him the greatest treatment value.[34] However, an effective use of prediction depends upon the meaningful differentiation of offenders.

Prediction and prediction typologies

The more than 23 separate typologies which currently differentiate offenders fall into the five categories of prior probability, psychiatrically oriented, reference-group and social-class, behavior classification, and social perception and interaction typologies. The *prior probability* approach merely determines risk and gauges results, failing to identify the problem or to prescribe alternative solutions. Although *psychiatrically oriented* methods provide information concerning the distribution of patient caseloads in relation to clinical experience and the pattern of evident symptoms, they do little to solve the problems of individual offenders within the community. *Reference-group and social-class* typologies valuably describe criminal orientations and client groups, but they fail to suggest meaningful prevention and treatment programs. *Behavior classification* methods identify and group significant behavior symptoms and offer the promise of future insight into the effectiveness of individualized treatment. The *social perception and interaction* approaches, founded upon diverse theories of ego strength, relate the individual's difficulties to ego development, personality integration, and arrest of psychological maturation. Marguerite Q. Grant, for example, believes that several strategies leading to the social restoration of the offender can be devised through "an identification of the modes of interaction with the social environment characteristic of particular levels of personality development."[35]

---

[33] John P. Conrad, *Crime and Its Correction* (Berkeley: University of California Press, 1967), p. 191.

[34] *Ibid.*, pp. 191–92.

[35] Marguerite Q. Grant, "Interaction between Kinds of Treatment and Kinds of Delinquents," *Proceedings of the 90th Congress of Corrections* (Denver, 1960), pp. 455–65.

What can be said accurately?

Because evaluation is a challenge to current operational treatment systems, any attempt to delineate current foundations of knowledge concerning treatment, Leslie T. Wilkins believes, should be set forward in minimal terms until these foundations can be further delineated by future research. In general, current evidence suggests:

1. Humanitarian systems of treatment (*e.g.*, probation in the community and elsewhere) are *no less* effective in reducing the probability of recidivism than severe forms of punishment. This statement holds with respect to the developed countries of the Western world.
2. Because humanitarian systems usually involve less intervention on the part of the correction processes, they are normally cheaper than the methods that stress supervision or security.
3. There are many ways in which money (if not souls!) can be saved without having the penal system show any increase in the rate of recidivism.
4. There is no inconsistency between a humanitarian and a cheap and effective system of penal measures, insofar as we have any hard evidence. Harsh measures are supported by the beliefs of many experienced persons, but no known research study has shown any support for these forms of belief.
5. One of the main costs, which from research results cannot be justified, is in the construction and use of unnecessary security provisions. The public pays heavily for the marginal gains that repressive custodial apparatus systems may provide. Because the use of "cost-benefit" assessments of effectiveness does not yet present any known situations for conflict with humanitarian principles, the "cost-benefit" approach might be extended to cover concepts of public safety and thus provide a measure of the degree of security necessary under certain sets of assumptions.
6. It is generally believed that when an object is defined, the definition (attachment of a label) does not change the thing so defined. When human beings are defined (classified and so forth), the act of definition itself modifies the information setting and may thus be said to change the object (person) defined through the definition process. The self-fulfilling prophecy is a factor to be reckoned with in all aspects of criminological and penological decision making for both policy and research.
7. Many ways of solving "decision-type" problems are known, but these methods are everywhere underemployed in the penal field. A large proportion of administrative costs are incurred in ascertaining where the public money is being spent under approved budgets and accounts headings, but very little is expended in testing whether the money that is so correctly spent assisted in furthering the underlying purposes provided. It seems reasonable to allot for evaluation studies a proportion of the funds allocated for an operation carried out on behalf of the administration.
8. Evaluation methods are an essential part of a well-run system in providing

feedback, whereby the administration is informed regarding the degree of effectiveness with which its intent is being carried out. Evaluation studies are not to be confused with research. Research is needed to establish means whereby evaluation may itself be more effectively (and cheaply) carried out, as well as to establish other results. The distinction that seems operationally useful is in the time focus of the two operations: Evaluation is concerned with assessing what has been done and what currently is being done; research is concerned with what might be done and with what the position might be in the future. An analogy with industrial quality control may make this point clearer. Quality control is part of the production process to insure that the product continues to meet consumer-acceptability standards. Research will be used to establish a quality control system in the first instance, but the operation of the quality control system is not a research operation.

9. Very few if any of the substantive results of criminological and penological research can be expected to be free from cultural factors. The cultural setting is as important for the consideration of offenders and their treatment as for any other social problems. Methods for solving problems are invariant (or nearly so) with respect to different cultures; hence, a technology of problem solving is exportable. But the solutions obtained in one culture are not necessarily the solutions for another culture. It is always risky to assume the "proofs" of any treatment method or related hypotheses established in one country can be applied with the same effects in another. Pilot trials or other forms of tests are necessary to establish whether the different cultural setting is of significance.

10. Similarly, solutions that may apply at one point in time in any one culture may also continue to apply as technological change induces other changes in the social setting within a country. Sequential test procedures, systems for monitoring the operation of the solutions in practice, and similar research methods must be carefully considered.

11. No treatment today is standarized and possibly can ever be completely standardized. There are, in fact, wide variations within any one treatment (as defined by the court disposal) in the operation of the treatment process. It is not even established that variation within treatments are less than variations between treatments in terms of the operational variables which affect outcome.

12. There are different kinds of treatments and punishments, both within classifications of disposal and independent of the application of   procedures that have been termed "individualization of treatment" within institutions.

13. There are different kinds of offenders and different kinds of crimes. Various means for classification are known, but no means for selecting the best classification is available.

14. Treatment and punishment can be meaningfully considered only as an interaction between types of treatments and types of offenders. Such considerations must refer to typologies.

15. There are, within any institutional setting, forms of "subcultures" that have their own communication networks and norms of culture.

TABLE 26–4
Rough comparative modes of difference

Classical Research Designs and Criminological Philosophy Tend Toward:	*Systems Advocated by Wilkins Tend Toward:*
Concepts of truth.	Action that is assessed as rational (strategic) and in accord with an ethic that must be defended.
	Boundary conditions under which decisions are valid.
Internal criteria (e.g., use of factor analysis).	External criteria (e.g., regression analysis and decision models).
Facts.	Acts and reactions.
Absolutes.	Relatives—degrees of belief.
Certainty.	Uncertainty.
Cause and effect.	Probability.
Simple explanations.	Complex explanations.
Grand theories.	Specific theories.
Right vs. wrong (fixed values).	Variable values—situations is relevant to considerations of values.
Can ignore situation as irrelevant, since truth is universal.	Cannot ignore situation, since truth is relevant to the situation.
Assumptions simplified.	Model is simplification of situation; divergence of "map" is discussed as relevant (see below).
Consistent with a *two*-value logic and dichotomies (e.g., guilty or not guilty, responsible or not responsible, true or false, etc.).	Dichotomies may or may not provide an adequate model. Usually dichotomies are seen as a simplification of the situation which may occasionally be justified as a means to provide approximations.
Deterministic philosophy.	Not deterministic, since deterministic models are not usually as powerful as probabilistic models. Does not consider determinism as a significant question or issue at this time.
Nature of the "real" universe is important and is seen as deterministic.	Nature of *model* is important in relation to results derived from its use.
	Strategy of research is decided in terms of prior research results, not by beliefs about a "true" universe.
Reference to some ultimate (e.g., truth) outside the scientist himself.	Reference to our own concept (model) in terms of a democratic authority of the community of scientists.
Data are seen as supporting beliefs of a fairly general kind.	Data are seen as providing information relevant to such further actions as more research action or social policy decisions. However, all results are related to the situation that must be specified. No generalization is expected, although some general qualities may be found.

Hence

Since truth can be known, "our" system may be pressed upon others as being "true." (We may identify this tendency as prejudice or dogma.)	Since truth cannot be known (we discuss reasonable decisions under conditions of uncertainty), "our" system may not be the right or best system in other situations. We may not generalize without further support.

Source: Leslie T. Wilkins, *Evaluation of Penal Measures* (New York: Random House, 1969), pp. 164–66.

16. Such subcultures have an impact upon inmates and influence the interactions any single inmate may develop with the form of treatment officially operated. The influence of inmate upon or the inmate culture need not be assumed to be independent of the treatment program. Indeed, some systems of treatment attempt to utilize these influences in a positive way.

17. Combinations of different forms of treatment reveal interactions that have been discovered to be negatively related to desired outcome in specific instances. It therefore seems probable that elements within a complex treatment program may also interact, and some of these forms of interaction may be dysfunctional for the treatment programs as a whole. Clearly the assumption that two "good things" when added together into a combined whole are better than either singly is not a sound generalization. Indeed more of a "good thing" may not continuously increase the pay-off for all cases; some even seem to be less likely to succeed if given too much help. The degree of "too much" in any instance is not known, but quantitative measures should not be assumed to be linear or additive in terms of each other.

18. Pre-sentence probabilities of individual recidivism can be fairly estimated from information available at that time by use of reproducible and rigorous methods. Such rigorous methods are superior to subjective judgments of probable outcome both as regards to power of the estimation and in terms of methodology.

19. The estimates obtained (as in 18) may be used to describe the types of offenders subjected to different treatments and to provide a reasonable assessment of their relative effectiveness.

20. Taxonomic classification systems applied to offenders provide a powerful system for subdivisions of the total offender population.[36]

Wilkins suggests that future criminological research must move from classical-philosophical research designs to an operations approach, which has been generally foreign to criminological research. In order to clarify the distinction between the two, Wilkins, therefore, summarizes the essential differences between the more traditional and his point of view as shown in Table 26–4. Once the move to an operations approach has occurred, the outcome of prediction research and application will be more valuable.[37]

---

[36] Wilkins, *Evaluation*, pp. 110–13.

[37] Ibid., pp. 164–66, Also consult Robert M. Martinson, Gene G. Kassebaum, and David A. Ward, "A Critique of Research in Parole," *Federal Probation*, Vol. 28 (September, 1964), pp. 34–38.

Part EIGHT

The prevention of delinquency and crime

Chapter
27

THE PREVENTION OF DELINQUENT AND CRIMINAL CONDUCT

APPROACHES AND ASSUMPTIONS OF PREVENTION

Most attempts to prevent delinquency represent a primary emphasis upon one of three presuppositions; it is assumed that delinquency prevention: (1) is the sum total of all activities that contribute to the healthy adjustment of children; or (2) can lessen deviance through modification of environmental conditions contributing to the occurrence of delinquency; or (3) depends upon the providing of specific preventive services to individual or groups of children.[1] The first approach assumes that all positive attempts to aid adolescent adjustment and to develop healthy personalities is a form of delinquency prevention. Therefore, its proponents presume that the continuation of programs designed to reduce economic inequities, raise income levels, provide better housing, offer job tenure in more meaningful work settings, reduce discrimination, improve marital relationships, and reinforce religion automatically aid the prevention process. Preventive programs of the second type, however, attempt to overcome environmental factors restricting the growth of children through use of community organization methods, including the creation of coordinating councils, recreation programs, reduction of vice, and control of illegal and detrimental community activities. Preventive activities within the third category emphasize probation and parole services for children and adolescents, special schools and pro-

---

[1] Herbert A. Block and F. T. Flynn, *Delinquency: The Juvenile Offender in America Today* (New York: Random House, Inc., 1956), p. 512.

grams for delinquents, residential institutions, child guidance clinics, and other services designed to conserve the positive potentials of adolescent development.[2]

Although each of these programs and approaches has a certain degree of merit, they do not possess equal value. The improvement of the collective welfare will undoubtedly cause some delinquency reduction, but the relationship between delinquency and the sum total of all positive activities, as John M. Martin summarizes the appraisal, is rather obscure and much more complicated than commonly believed. Although development of better housing and work opportunities undoubtedly possess some positive effect upon delinquency prevention, people may well remain unchanged despite the upgrading of their particular environmental situation. Delinquency prevention, Martin maintains, is closely related to community reintegration and to the development of indigenous community leadership. He believes, in agreement with the earlier conclusions of Frederic M. Thrasher, that delinquency control depends upon the maintenance of community organization. Therefore, special steps must be taken to insure reorganization where community disorganization emerges. Eventually, delinquency prevention programs must be located within the community and must use the best possible methods of individual treatment and corrections while assisting in the successful assimilation of low-status groups to modern urban living.[3]

In another vein, Peter P. Lejins conceives of prevention in terms of its punitive, corrective, or mechanical aspects. *Punitive prevention* refers primarily to the threat to use punishment to forestall the criminal act. Designed as a system of social control, it emphasizes teaching the individual violator a lesson. Stressing a negative conditioning, this approach attempts to replace pleasure with punishment-pain.[4] *Corrective prevention*, however, assumes that criminal behavior has its origins in particular factors that result in a certain type of motivation which is defined as delinquent or criminal. Therefore, these causes, factors, or motivations must be eliminated before that type of negative behavior occurs. The *mechanical prevention* approach, on the other hand, refers to the attempt to constrain delinquent and criminal conduct by placing obstacles in the path of their completion. Consequently, as an approach it emphasizes the development of security measures, signal systems, bet-

---

[2] John M. Martin, "Three Approaches to Delinquency Prevention: A Critique," *Crime and Delinquency*, Vol. 7 (January, 1961), pp. 16–24.

[3] *Ibid.*, pp. 18–24. Refer to Leslie T. Wilkins, *Social Deviance: Social Policy, Action and Research* (Englewood Cliffs, N.J.: Prentice-Hall, Inc., 1965); and Israel Drapkin, *Proceedings of the Twelfth International Course in Criminology* (Jerusalem: Hebrew University, 1963).

[4] Peter P. Lejins, "The Field of Prevention," in William E. Amos and Charles F. Wellford (eds.), *Delinquency Prevention* (Englewood Cliffs, N.J.: Prentice-Hall, Inc., 1967), p. 3.

ter and more efficient police patrol, or other activities and methods used to interrupt the offender's capacity for delinquency or crime.

Although all three exist simultaneously, corrective prevention currently receives greater emphasis. However, corrective prevention, Lejins suggests, may be differentiated into three basic types of areas: (1) the manipulation of general social policies (i.e., education, employment, and defense) which affect many different aspects of life and crime and delinquency; (2) programs to detect symptoms of crime and delinquency and to prevent their active expression; and (3) preventive work upon spatial or temporal crime and delinquency concentrations which are evidenced either by exorbitant crime and delinquency rates or waves.[5]

Clyde E. Sullivan and Carrie S. Bash propose that prevention programs be classified in a different typology, which they categorize in three inclusive propositions:

1. Programs that have explicit primary functions and goals involving deliberate intervention in the lives of specifically identified individuals for the express purpose of preventing the occurrence of behavior that would label them as antisocial or as delinquent by the laws and rules of general society.
2. Programs that have explicit primary goals of planned intervention in participation in the development, employment, or organization, and interrelationship of various *social institutions,* groups, or *agencies* in the community with the intention of preventing the formation of patterns of delinquent behavior in specific individuals or groups.
3. Programs that have explicit primary goals of deliberate participation in the social processes of reviewing and developing laws, social policies, and public attitudes that have a specific and direct relevance to activities designed to prevent delinquency.[6]

Programs in accord with the individual-centered type 1, Sullivan and Bash maintain, are oriented to direct individual intervention and tend to presume biological origins of deviance, theories of temperament, pure psychological explanations, and physical sources of deviance. Often carried out through child guidance clinics or other agencies designed to bring psychological services to the child or adult, this orientation encourages the psychological readjustment of the individual violator. However, many programs go beyond this level and include elements of both type 1 and type 2 categories. The Cambridge-Sommerville Youth Study, Big Brother and Big Sister approaches, and other school-oriented pro-

---

[5] *Ibid.,* pp. 4–8.
[6] Clyde E. Sullivan and Carrie E. Bash, "Current Programs for Delinquency Prevention," in Amos and Wellford (eds.), *op cit.,* pp. 61–62.

grams generally possess both psychological and social dimensions. Many of the latter emphasize group therapy, which is more in keeping with a pure type 2 orientation. Settlement activities, the Los Angeles Youth Project, and various other programs in Chicago, Cleveland, Philadelphia, and Boston tend to emphasize aggressive group work methods through the use of detached or street club workers to reach neighborhood gangs.

Type 3 prevention efforts, on the other hand, are less focused upon the individual and the group and are more oriented to the variables which assist the development of delinquent and criminal conduct. Dealing more specifically with social strategies and questions of political organization, efforts in this area are intended to stimulate federal or state action toward delinquency prevention and to encourage individuals to undertake community action.[7]

While many of these prevention strategies are broad and inclusive, Sophia M. Robison supposes that ultimately proposals for the prevention of juvenile delinquency may for simplicity be reduced to one of two basic assumptions:

1. The individual or his parents are in complete control of their actions; therefore, they should be punished by the community, the parent, or the school when their behavior deviates from the norm set by the community.
2. The community is partly responsible, therefore, and should help prevent delinquency by creating and/or coordinating services which have been provided by the more enlightened members of the community; by providing special services; recreational opportunities and casework or group work in or out of settlement, community centers or schools; or by helping the disorganized community to pull itself up by its bootstraps.[8]

All programmic attempts are designed to operationalize one or both of these two theoretical presuppositions.

Variations in prevention methods

Many methods have been used in the attempt to prevent a continuing increase in delinquency and crime. Street club guidance projects, designed to reach the unreached, strive to bring their workers into inter-

---

[7] *Ibid.*, pp. 64–65. See Charles L. Newman, "The War on Crime," *Federal Probation*, Vol. 30 (December, 1966), pp. 35–38; and Charles Morris, "Crime Prevention and Control Around the World," *Federal Probation*, Vol. 29 (December, 1965), p. 8.

[8] Sophia M. Robison, "Why Juvenile Delinquency Prevention Programs Are Ineffective," *Federal Probation*, Vol. 25 (December, 1961), p. 41.

action with clients in their environment. After gaining the confidence of neighborhood members, the street worker, operating in a specified urban area, generally establishes contact with delinquents and nondelinquents in his assigned territory. Through such contacts he further strives to bring adolescents into constructive relationships with other juveniles in community street clubs carefully planned to appeal to youth interest levels. Although such programs are designed to establish youth and adult working relationships, many potential or actual delinquents refuse to join such clubs and periodically work to undermine their programs. Because the sheer numbers of juveniles in the area often makes it largely impossible to service their needs, the eventual success of many of these ventures depends upon the personality of the leader, a factor which may lead to the failure of the street-club when leadership changes. However, while he is engaged in the operation of the project, the street worker may intervene in the lives of youth and adults through the use of community organization, group work, or casework procedures. If he uses community organization techniques, the street worker, Irving Spergel finds, is eventually concerned for dependent-independent (authority) relationships. At this point he attempts to aid the delinquent to change his behavior.[9]

Street work with delinquents probably originated in the 19th century as charity workers and members of religious groups expressed concern for gangs and wayward boys. An organized approach to street work was not developed until 1930, when street workers were used in a Chicago area project to contact "unreached" boys on the streets and to "help them to find their way back to acceptable norms of conduct."[10] Since that time, a wide variety of area projects have been operationalized in Washington, D.C., Tokyo, Vienna, and Liverpool in order to prevent an increasing volume of juvenile delinquency. More recently, further refinements have been made. Contemporary treatment by street workers strive to modify those feelings, acts, or relationships of predelinquents and delinquents which may cause later problems with law enforcement and the community.

While the area orientation seeks the reduction of aggressive group behavior through the development of institutional opportunities for delinquents, the balanced orientation, a third alternative, actually incorporates both approaches in its emphasis upon the improvement of interpersonal relations with a consequent reduction of delinquency. Because the street worker is able to reach out to people in need by the simplest and most direct means possible, Spergel holds, he is able to provide

---

[9] Erving Spergel, *Street Gang Work* (New York: Doubleday & Co., Inc., 1967), pp. 266–67.

[10] *Ibid.*, pp. 265–66.

highly personal services of almost unlimited scope and identity.[11] Consequently, the street worker serves as a bridge between resource persons in the spiritual, psychological, economic, social, and cultural aspects of the community and its organizations and youths who need to acquire access to these resources and to use them in seeking new goals. While it is a disciplined approach, it is also a free and flexible method which emphasizes intimacy and involvement in human problems.

In the area project approach, recreational and educational opportunities are offered neighborhood youths in an area center, commonly staffed by community members. Operating upon the assumption that a large number of such youths are emotionally maladjusted, staff members seek to develop constructive juvenile relationships with other youths and adults in order to lessen adolescent contacts with delinquents and criminals. Parents are similarly encouraged to discuss parent-children problems with other community members in an attempt to seek meaningful solutions.

Utilizing another method, the Cambridge-Somerville Youth Study in Massachusetts, initiated by Richard Cabot, attempted to prevent juvenile delinquencies by the use of social work methods. Emphasizing concentrated social services in the form of counseling, psychiatric and medical care, recreation, and other forms of assistance, the program sought to reduce or eliminate juvenile deviance. However, 10 years after its 1936 beginning the study was terminated due to inadequate results. A second Cambridge-Somerville project was begun as a follow-up study in 1956. Several hundred boys who were predicted to become delinquent were examined in this study. They were randomly divided into control and treatment groups. The latter were treated on the assumption that potential delinquents may develop into law-abiding youths if they are offered adult friendship, understanding, counseling, guidance, and a maximum of community assistance. The control group merely received normal prevention services. While the program provided juvenile-adult contact, it did little to restructure social situations. Edwin Powers and Helen L. Witmer were critical of the program. They point out that it was a "professionally rather naïve program" incapable of effectively diminishing the problem of juvenile delinquency despite its ambition and treatment generosity.[12]

Still other efforts to prevent the adolescent's participation in delinquency are illustrated in the development of community center programs for the prevention of school dropouts in low-income areas of the lower east side of New York City by the Educational Alliance, a community

---

[11] *Ibid.*, p. 271. Consult Alfred J. Kahn, *Planning Community Services for Children in Trouble* (New York: Columbia University Press, 1963).

[12] Edwin Powers and Helen L. Witmer, *An Experiment in the Prevention of Delinquency* (New York: Columbia University Press, 1959), p. 577.

center–settlement house sponsoring group located in that area[13] serving 1,200 adolescents within a population of 6,500 persons. The Alliance provides clubs with lounges and game rooms, athletic activities, tutoring, and other programs under the guidance of social workers, teachers, and recreational specialists. Striving to cope with the dropout problem, the center in its early development selected from a nearby junior high school 120 children who were scholastically borderline and showed signs characteristic of school dropouts (*i.e.*, school achievement significantly below the child's intellectual capacity, truancy, poor morale, and behavior difficulties. By working intensively with these youths the staff was able to prevent their anticipated withdrawal from school. In the two years of operation of the program, only four of the 120 pupils had dropped out of school. Analyzing the reasons for such success, Louis Berkowitz and Jacob Chwast concluded tentatively that any effort to reduce the number of school dropouts seems to depend upon adequate supportive and comprehensive multiple-service programs. Success is possible, they say, only if the potential school dropout, his family, and his school—what they call the three systems of human experience—anticipate the development of an ameliorative system to deal with the stresses and pressures which are often evident in the interaction of these systems.[14]

Prevention and social institutions

Because the family is a biological, psychological, and social unit of individual and group importance, any attempt to prevent delinquency must eventually come to grips with family problems. As a *biological* unit, the family provides its members with basic hereditary characteristics which may be shaped in many different ways in relationship to environmental factors. As a *psychological* unit, the family, C. Ray Jeffery and Ina A. Jeffery emphasize, serves as a fundamental base for personality development. As a *social* unit, it relates the individual to other influences represented by such variables as place of residence, social class position, educational locus, racial responses, deviant family characteristics, and region of kinship relations. Although many analysts of deviance relate delinquency and crime to inadequate family life, most data con-

---

[13] Louis Berkowitz and Jacob Chwast, "A Community Center Program for the Prevention of School Dropouts," *Federal Probation,* Vol. 31 (December, 1967), p. 36; and William E. Amos and Marilyn A. Southwell, "Dropouts: What Can Be Done? *Federal Probation,* Vol. 28 (March, 1964), pp. 30–35.

[14] *Ibid.,* pp. 38–39. Also see *Dropout Studies: Design and Conduct* (Washington D.C.: National Educational Association, 1965); Daniel Schrieber, *Guidance and the High School Dropout* (Washington, D.C.: National Educational Association, 1964); and Daniel Schrieber, "Juvenile Delinquency and the School Dropout Problem," *Federal Probation,* Vol. 27 (September, 1963), pp. 15–19.

cerning such relationships, the Jeffreys caution, are only clinical or statistical and do not demonstrate causal connections.[15] Nevertheless, Ruth S. Tefferteller maintains that a large portion of delinquency may be prevented through the revitalization of parent-child relationships and through the creation of preadolescent groups which reinstate the influence of parents with their children.[16] But this goal is easier stated than achieved. Prevention through the family cannot be achieved without effective cooperation with the school system, inasmuch as peer relations may quickly undermine family attempts to reestablish parental influence.

The value of the peer group was recognized several decades ago with the establishment of the Hawthorne–Cedar Knolls School in Thornwood (New York) in the early 1900's by the Jewish Board of Guardians of New York. The school developed an early delinquency-prevention and treatment program for some 200 boys and 50 girls between the ages of 8 and 18 who were housed in small cottages of 20 to 25 boys or girls. The program relied upon a military type of discipline, which quickly proved unsuccessful. However, with the adoption of a new orientation which emphasized greater freedom, vocational training, and organized leisure in the form of games, walks, dances, and visits to neighboring villages, the experiment met with greater success in the mid-1920's. The Hawthorne–Cedar Knowles School expanded its social services for parents of the boys and girls of the school. While the young people were prepared to readjust to the community, these workers also assisted the parents to react to their children with greater kindness and understanding. During his average two-year stay, the juvenile was treated individually with the cooperation of the staff and his parents. The school also utilized the dynamic and social controls of the peer group to bring about new juvenile attitudes.[17]

The withdrawal of youths from the public school system and the building of an independent educational unit also lessened the number of early program weaknesses. The greater flexibility of the curriculum in the private setting permitted a greater realization of prevention and treatment goals. More emphasis could be placed upon the creative use of freedom, status, participation, and responsibility. As youths were encouraged to accept a greater degree of freedom, they inevitably accepted a level of responsibility commensurate with their evident capacities. In time, they accepted even greater responsibilities and developed "ever

---

[15] C. Ray Jeffrey and Ina A. Jeffrey, "Prevention through the Family," in Amos and Wellford (eds.), op. cit., p. 83.

[16] Ruth S. Tefferteller, "Delinquency Prevention through Revitalizing Parent-Child Relations," Annals, Vol. 322 (March, 1959), pp. 69–78; and C. Downing Tait, Jr., Delinquents, Their Families and Community (Springfield, Ill.: Charles C. Thomas, Publisher, 1962).

[17] Stephen Schafer and Richard D. Knudten, The Problem of Juvenile Delinquency (New York: Random House, Inc., 1970).

greater capacities to control their primitive impulses."[18] As they gradually identified more fully with adults and the group culture, they also developed a degree of inner control which seemed to be reinforced as they became more secure in their identification. Overall, "the basic requirement," S. R. Slavson concluded upon evaluating the effectiveness of the program, "in all education is that the adult places himself in relation to the child whereby the child accepts him and therefore accepts his social concepts and community values."[19] The controls which youths develop in such circumstances, Slavson suggests, are common denominators of their experiences and identifications with adults.

The gradual acceptance of responsibilities provided the youth with a personal and community status which he worked to maintain. The Hawthorne–Cedar Knowles School emphasized the development of individual talents and interests and encouraged self-expression. It emphasized the youth's need for self-fulfillment on the assumption that "an individual attains the highest levels of development when he merges creatively and progressively with common will and common cause."[20] Seeking to convince rather than to control the youth, the Hawthorne–Cedar Knowles staff refused to deal with such youths in a prohibitive, arbitrary, or punitive manner. The ensuing mutuality of act, relation, and respect "reoriented" and changed feelings and attitudes even among the more disturbed who participated in the more extensive treatment facet. However, when one member of the staff acted irresponsibly to a child, a chain reaction of hostility, aggression, and destructiveness quickly affected the atmosphere of the school and the attitudes of many other youths. In summarizing the many years of experience at the Hawthrone–Cedar Knowles School, S. R. Slavson concluded that "adults must possess a consistent and unified quality, attitude, and a sense of communal and individual value."[21] Only under these conditions can a truly reeducative community emerge.

Although the correct use of education holds much promise for delinquency and crime prevention, any coherent attempt to restrict juvenile delinquency through education must include programs to assist the emergence of a new value system for children in disadvantaged areas, the development of school curricula which improve student employability and the modification of the delinquency-prone child's self-concept. However, even these are not enough. Other efforts must also be taken to develop an effective scholastic program. Frequently, this goal may only be reached by providing more adequate financial support to educational

---

[18] S. R. Slavson, *Re-Educating the Delinquent* (New York: Collier Books, 1961), pp. 241–43.

[19] *Ibid.*, p. 243.

[20] *Ibid.*, p. 244.

[21] *Ibid.*, p. 246.

programs within culturally and financially deprived communities; by recruiting higher-quality teachers who understand the nature, the needs, and culture of children within their teaching community; by developing and implementing curricula that hold relevance to the student and to his community; by providing student personnel and guidance services that are sensitive to the needs of the social group; by coordinating community efforts toward delinquency control and prevention on behalf of youth under school leadership; and by creating new and more flexible administrative structures to deal with problems which existing organizations often obstruct.[22]

Recognizing the importance of the schools in prevention, the U.S. Office of Education recommends that existing school programs and structures be modified in order to prevent and to control existing delinquency-crime tendencies. Educational programs, it suggests, should be sufficient to community needs and should be related to employment opportunities. While curriculum and educational materials should be relevant to the needs of youth within a changing society, teachers interested in experimentation and innovation should be employed within the educational process in high-delinquency areas. School and school system programs should become more flexible and should provide expanded facilities for multieducational purposes or other innovations of value to the youth, adult, and the community. Special services, including guidance and counseling services, social work services, remedial reading programs, reach-out services, and job placement and health services should be expanded and coordinated for youth. Quality controls, the Office also recommended, should be established in the educational process in order to determine the adequacy and effectiveness of existing programs and operations. In order to evaluate the total context of education, a program of research and evaluation, designed to gain information concerning such diverse concerns as student and teacher attitudes, self-identification processes, social mobility, program effectiveness, preschool program value, and general educational testing should be continued.[23]

Employment and prevention

While these suggestions and remedies appear helpful, their success is neither automatic nor guaranteed. Many are unrealistic; others are rather naïve. Most lack specificity and are only generalizations which need definitive implementation. Costs of operationalizing these recommendations make their value somewhat prohibitive.

---

[22] William E. Amos, "Prevention through the School," in Amos and Wellford (eds.), op. cit., p. 148.

[23] Office of Education, "Delinquency and the Schools," Task Force Reports: Juvenile Delinquency and Youth Crime (Washington, D.C.: U.S. Government Printing Office, 1967), pp. 278–304.

Despite the fact that education is important to prevention of delinquency, education without opportunity for employment may quickly undermine many socioeducational prevention efforts. Employment, however, increasingly depends upon one's marketable skills. Far too often those who became delinquent and criminal are marginal workers with few skills or positive work attitudes. In order to overcome these limitations, some states and communities maintain various job-upgrading and training programs. Detroit, for example, supports a job upgrading program, originally inaugurated in 1949, at 11 centers operated at 10 city high schools and 1 junior high school. Sponsored by the Detroit Board of Education and the Detroit Council for Youth Services, Inc., the program offers a short-term job guidance course together with a subsidized work experience designed to prepare school dropouts for employment or return to regular school programs. Youths between 16 and 20 are enrolled in the program after referral and interview. During the 12 weeks of the program, students enroll in two related or overlapping phases. During the first six weeks of Phase One, they participate in formal job guidance classes which meet three hours each morning for five days per week with the upgrading teacher. Each pupil receives instruction and assignment in relation to his established rate of progress. He learns how to get and keep a job and receives instruction in reading, arithmetic, and other basic skills. During this period, he is also encouraged to attend one or two regular afternoon classes in such diverse topics as typing, remedial reading, welding, or the like. If he shows progress and expresses a desire to return to the regular credit subjects, they replace his former morning program. During the second six-week period of Phase Two, the student who does not return to school may continue part-time subsidized job training during afternoon hours. Working in social agencies, private industry, or city departments for a limited wage, he may participate in unskilled clerical and maintenance activities, counter sales, or stock work. After 12 weeks of such training, each youth is placed in a full-time job if available. During 1960–61, the program served nearly 1,000 youths at a cost of approximately $140,000 per year.[24]

In another prevention approach, the Hamilton County Juvenile Work Therapy Program in Cincinnati (Ohio), created in 1958, strives to rehabilitate youth through work within a "milieu-therapy" setting. Open to boys and girls between 15 and 18 who possess no serious mental or emotional difficulties which might undermine potential learning processes, the program begins with the placement of recruits in screening groups for periods of 5 to 10 weeks. The youths meet as a unit at least once a week in a public agency and engage in leaf raking, grass cutting, painting, dusting, mopping, or other tasks under the direction

---

[24] Judith G. Benjamin, Seymour Lesh, and Marsha K. Freedman, "Youth Employment Programs in Perspective," in Don R. Stratton and Robert M. Terry (eds.), *Prevention of Delinquency* (New York: Macmillan Co., 1968), pp. 240–41.

of a work counselor. Although each individual receives carfare and lunch, he is not paid a wage or salary. After evaluation, the youth enters that specific phase of the program which seems to promise him the greatest potential value.

During Phase One, the youth may continue the work he began in the screening group but at a rate of $5 per day for not more than one day per week. At the same time, a staff member may guide the youth in spending his money so that he may enhance his appearance and develop a sense of pride. Upon completion of the first phase, he may move into Phase Two where he is placed in full-time community employment within a job originally solicited by staff members. Later, the youth is hired on his own merits after interviews with potential employers. If hired, he receives the going wage. Participants in this phase who are unable to gain immediate full-time employment may engage in domestic work one day per week as an interim step to full placement in Phase Three. If the youth demonstrates aptitudes for particular community training programs, he may then enter Phase Four of the program and enroll in welding, art, modeling, or other training programs. Tuition is generally covered by the court, other agencies, or private industry. Although these phases will be sequential for some individuals, entrance to each phase is determined in relationship to the particular needs of the individual. During 1962, 288 youths were enrolled in the special summer, 45 in the afterschool dropout, and 150 in subsidized work programs. Another 75 were employed in permanent part-time or full-time jobs within the community.[25]

The Kansas City (Missouri) Work Study Program sponsored by the Kansas City Public Schools, the Kansas City Association of Trusts and Foundations, and the Ford Foundation has followed a similar approach to delinquency and crime prevention. Begun in September, 1961, as a six-year controlled experiment testing the hypothesis that boys vulnerable to delinquency will become less delinquent if they are given a systematic work experience, the program is presented in three stages to predelinquent boys who have been screened into experimental and control groups in the seventh grade. Beginning Stage One in the eighth grade, boys aged between 13 and 15 spend one-half of each school day in basic and in non-solid subject classes which are adapted to their learning capacities. During the second half of the day, they participate in "socially useful work" in the school or within city agencies or programs. Working in teams of 10 to 24, the boys share in landscaping, planting, trenching, painting, furniture repair, or similar activities under the direction of a work supervisor and assistant. During the period of

---

[25] *Ibid.*, pp. 239–40. Also see Joy Nelson, "Girls at the end of the Viaduct," *Federal Probation,* Vol. 25 (September, 1961), p. 58.

the program operation, payment for work rendered was given only 22 boys during the summer of 1962 at a rate of 50 cents per hour.

Those completing the first phase move to Stage Two, for boys between 15 and 17 years of age. During this segment of the program, the boys follow a similar approach to that noted in Phase One. However, they work three hours per day in individualized employment as an order biller, stockboy, service station helper, small-animal hospital attendant, or helper in various other projects. Paid a subminimum wage except if working in interstate commerce, workers remain under close supervision and are evaluated in regard to their progress. In Stage Three, for boys aged between 16 and 18 who were in their fifth or last year of the program, the youths leave school for a full-time job. Because the program is highly flexible, boys participating in the latter two stages are able to work with school supervisors to find the best alternative for their personal adjustment. Because the program only ended in June, 1969, the value of this approach has not yet been ascertained.[26]

Since 1960, a large variety of attempts have also been undertaken to prevent delinquency through general and special youth employment programs. Much of the leadership in this direction was taken by the federal government. Congress passed the Area Redevelopment Act in 1961, which introduced the idea of federally supported retraining programs for unemployed workers in distressed areas. It was followed by the Manpower Development and Training Act of 1962 which initiated a program to prepare and train workers for unfilled jobs either through instruction or through on-the-job training. Most of these projects concentrate on reaching functional illiterates, school dropouts, delinquents, and handicapped youths aged between 16 and 22. In addition, still other training programs have been sponsored by the Department of Labor, and the 1962 Public Works Acceleration Act increased public welfare aid to long-term unemployed, raised minimum wages, and presented new initiatives in the area of youth employment. The 1964 Economic Opportunity Act extended these beginnings even further through work-study, job corp, and neighborhood youth corps programs.[27]

Since work-study programs are still in their infancy and the tools for their evaluation have not yet reached a level of scientific precision, the value of these efforts has not been effectively documented. The Opportunities for Youth Project, which originated in 1964 in Seattle, for example, revealed few differences in work attitudes and success between the project's work and control groups. Nevertheless, some preliminary support is reported by James C. Hackler for the further testing

---

[26] *Ibid.,* pp. 237–38. See Marcia K. Freedman and Eli E. Cohen, "Delinquency, Employment and Youth Development," *Federal Probation,* Vol. 25 (December, 1962), pp. 45–49.

[27] *Ibid.,* p. 233.

of several hypotheses which suggest that a work program may have impact when combined with a teaching machine testing program, that a teaching machine testing program may have some impact by itself, that a program may have more impact on boys who have not been in trouble in school, and that Negro boys and mothers support the program to a greater degree than white boys and mothers. However, the general lack of impact of the overall program makes it largely impossible, Hackler concludes, to reach sound conclusions. While it is possible that boys may change more significantly than current research designs are able to measure, it is also possible, he concludes, that the world may not recognize any change and therefore fail to treat the boys differently, causing them to continue to react in the same deviant manner.[28]

Prevention and boy's clubs

The mixed findings regarding the effectiveness of educational and work programs in prevention of delinquency and crime are also evident when considering the ultimate impact of boy's clubs in effecting prevention. Roscoe C. Brown, Jr., and Dan W. Dotson, for example, found that delinquency rates for a club area in Louisville (Kentucky) decreased from 1 in 19 boys in 1946, when the clubs opened, to 1 in 39 in 1954. At the same time, the rate in other Louisville areas without boy's clubs increased from 1 in 29 boys in 1946 to 1 in 18 in 1954. Similarly, delinquency rates in two other Louisville areas also rose from 1 in 44 and 1 in 28 in 1946 to 1 in 16 and 1 in 21, respectively, during the same period. While other factors may have been influential in the decrease in delinquency in the boy's club area, the effective operation of clubs for adolescent boys, Roscoe C. Brown and Dan W. Dotson suggest, may have a clear impact upon delinquency prevention in a particular area.[29]

Although the Brown and Dotson data suggest a positive preventive relationship, the findings should be interpreted in relationship to the earlier work of Frederic M. Thrasher, who found between 1927 and 1931 that a New York City Boy's Club only possessed a limited effectiveness in promoting desirable behavior standards and in preventing delinquency. Although the New York City club was created to serve 4,000 boys, no more than 2,500, approximately 60 percent of capacity, participated at any one time. The club generally appealed to more older (14 and over) than younger boys. Many of the eligible boys in 30 nearby

---

[28] James C. Hackler, "Boys, Blisters and Behavior: The Impact of a Work Program in an Urban Central Area," *Journal of Research in Crime and Delinquency*, Vol. 3 (July, 1966), pp. 155–64.

[29] Roscoe C. Brown, Jr. and Dan W. Dotson, "The Effectiveness of Boy's Clubs in Reducing Delinquency," *Annals*, Vol. 322 (March, 1959), pp. 47–52.

city blocks failed to enroll or to participate. Of the 635 delinquents in that area, 298 never enrolled in the club program during the entire period of the study. Over the four-year interval one third of the club membership was replaced. Only 18 percent of the total official offenses of Boy's Club members occurred before they joined the club; 28 percent originated after they formally became members. Nevertheless, the proportion of delinquents participating in these activities increased with each year of continuing membership.[30]

Although the police have periodically utilized a club-type approach to prevention, the value of their efforts similarly remains unmeasured. They originally enacted such programs as a public relations attempt to lessen public distrust of law enforcement officers, but their activities now emphasize recreational or other group participation. The Police Athletic League of New York City (PAL), one of the best publicized of such programs, was established in 1932. It first offered recreational opportunities and later expanded its efforts in the 1950's to include arts and crafts, dances, and other juvenile-oriented programs. Acting both as authorities and as friends, police officers have often served as youth leaders with varying degrees of success.[31]

Religion and prevention

Most efforts to study the relationships of religion, the church, and other religious institutions to delinquency causation and prevention have been ineffective. Not only do such studies fail to define the concept of religion with accuracy but they also fail to measure the degree of religiosity expressed both by the deviant and the conformist. Consequently, any attempt to establish such a relationship must be hypothetical rather than actual. George E. Powers recognizes that religious activities in delinquency prevention are commonly divided into the four categories of religion centered and person based, religion centered and community based, secularly centered and person based, and secularly centered and community based (see Figure 27–1). *Religion-centered and person-based* church activities generally take the form of institutional chaplaincies, church-sponsored arts and crafts programs, YMCA and YWCA programs, Catholic Youth Organization activities, or other programs which are often foreign to the subculture of delinquency.

Religion-centered and community-based church activities, on the other hand, possess a prevention focus and frequently revolve around

[30] Frederic Thrasher, "The Boy's Club and Juvenile Delinquency," *American Journal of Sociology*, Vol. 42 (July, 1936), pp. 66–80.

[31] Schafer and Knudten, *op. cit.;* and James L. Brennan, *The Prevention and Control of Juvenile Delinquency by Police Departments* (New York: New York University, 1952).

FIGURE 27-1

Religion and prevention: Types of religious relationships

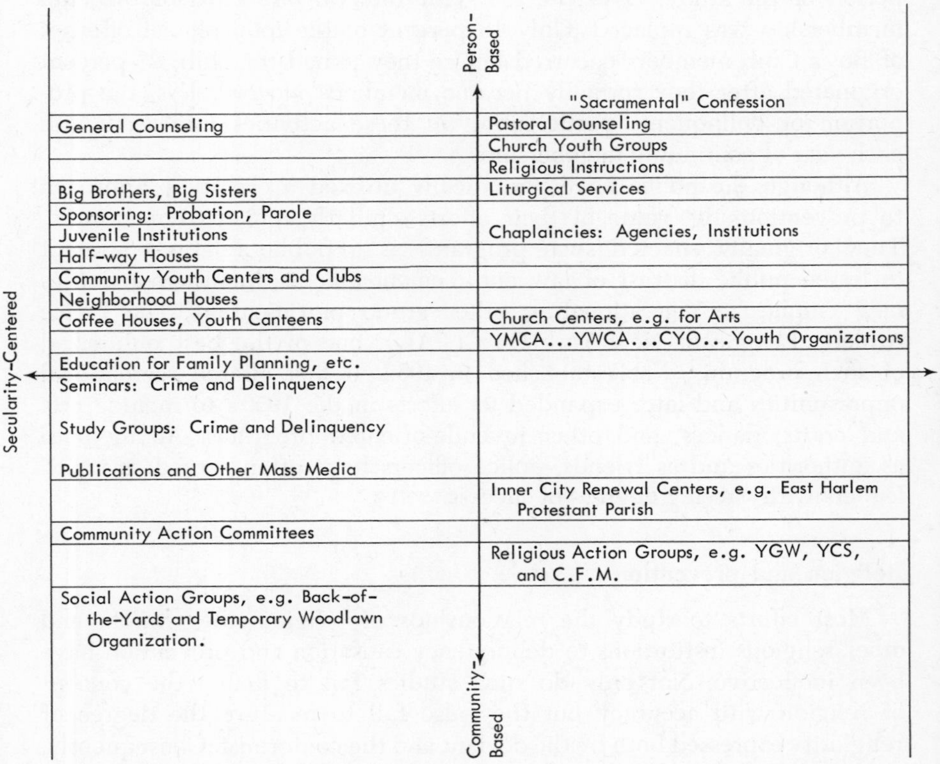

Secularity-Centered	Person-Based →	Religion-Centered
		"Sacramental" Confession
General Counseling		Pastoral Counseling
		Church Youth Groups
		Religious Instructions
Big Brothers, Big Sisters		Liturgical Services
Sponsoring: Probation, Parole		
Juvenile Institutions		Chaplaincies: Agencies, Institutions
Half-way Houses		
Community Youth Centers and Clubs		
Neighborhood Houses		
Coffee Houses, Youth Canteens		Church Centers, e.g. for Arts
		YMCA...YWCA...CYO...Youth Organizations
Education for Family Planning, etc.		
Seminars: Crime and Delinquency		
Study Groups: Crime and Delinquency		
Publications and Other Mass Media		
		Inner City Renewal Centers, e.g. East Harlem Protestant Parish
Community Action Committees		
		Religious Action Groups, e.g. YGW, YCS, and C.F.M.
Social Action Groups, e.g. Back-of-the-Yards and Temporary Woodlawn Organization.		
	Community-Based ↓	

Source: George E. Powers, "Prevention through Religion," in William E. Amos and Charles F. Wellford (eds.), *Delinquency Prevention*. (Englewood Cliffs, N.J.: Prnetice-Hall, Inc., 1967), p. 109.

an inner-city ministerial program—for example—in the form of the East Harlem Protestant Parish and such movements as the Young Christians Workers and the Christian Family. However, those church activities which are *secularity centered and person based* may minimize the religious dimension and emphasize the idea of laity in action. In this context, churches may sponsor the reentry of parolees or probationers, justify participation in Big Brother and Big Sister movements, develop hostel or other institutional programs, sponsor halfway houses, or maintain neighborhood houses, youth clubs, or other youth centers. A more recent development has been the coffee house or canteen approach to delinquency prevention. *Securally centered and community-based* church activities pass beyond this level and may include remedial education, academic counseling and guidance services, school social work and after-school services, tutoring summer and weekend after-school classes, adult literacy programs, rehabilitation and retraining of physically and mentally handicapped, and a wide diversity of other community-based improvement attempts. Focusing primarily upon environmental change through all available means, the role of religious functionaries and religious institutions has been one of acting out a social conscience and expressing religion through example rather than through evangelical proclamation.[32]

While little research has been conducted in the area of religion and delinquency, this does not mean that religious values and beliefs may not have preventive effect. Juan Cortes, for example, maintains that a sense of responsibility depends upon moral behavior, which in turn is derived from religious reality. Consequently, delinquency and crime will not be prevented until delinquents and criminals recognize their irresponsibility and perceive that their antisocial behavior is morally and socially wrong. The crime problem, Cortes maintains, is a moral problem which relates to self-esteem and self-worth.[33]

The failure of delinquency and crime prevention programs

Although the success rate of delinquency and crime prevention programs have not been effectively measured, a number of attempts have clearly failed over the years. This has been true, Albert W. Silver suggests, due to low worker morale, an emphasis upon diagnosis rather than treatment, inappropriate treatment when applied, a greater concern for rehabilitation rather than prevention, continuing staff vacancies, the limited number of ongoing staff training programs, the lack of evaluational research concerning prevention and court effectiveness, limited communication with the community, and a basic conflict between the legal and psychological approaches to the prevention and treatment problem.[34] Walter B. Miller believes that delinquency prevention programs fail because of apparent differences in conception of the etiology and the disposition of delinquency, the priority of approach, the organizational method, and the proper status of personnel. These tensions are commonly evident, Miller believes, in six major categories.

The question of *morality-pathology* is due, Miller notes, to the many

[32] George E. Powers, "Prevention through Religion," in Amos and Wellford (eds.), *op. cit.*, pp. 110–20; James Meyer, *Crime and Religion* (Chicago: Franciscan Herald Press, 1936); and William E. Albers, *Ministers Attitudes toward Juvenile Delinquency* (Washington, D.C.: General Board of Social Concerns of Methodist Church, 1962).

[33] *Ibid.*, p. 122.

[34] Albert W. Silver, "Re-Tooling for Delinquency Prevention and Rehabilitation in Juvenile Courts," *Federal Probation*, Vol. 30 (March, 1966), pp. 29–32; and Francis J. Kelly, "The Delinquent Child—Whose Responsibility?" *Federal Probation*, Vol. 25 (December, 1961), pp. 24–29.

alternative theoretical assumptions concerning the origins of juvenile delinquency and crime. Some workers conceive of delinquency and criminality in terms of morality or immorality and argue that a delinquent act is an expression of evil against the good that normally exists within society. Opponents of this view maintain that such deviancy is related to problems of sickness and inner drives over which the delinquent has little control. On the other hand, the problem of *individual locus–social locus* represents a second major problematic category. Some prevention workers attribute criminal and delinquent behavior to the individual; others relate such conduct to the social environment and its need for modification. The pressures evident in the restriction-rehabilitation conflict, Miller suggests, focuses on another dimension of the prevention problem. The restrictive approach tries to protect society through the isolation of the individual from normal social relationships and inflicts punishment to penalize the violator and to deter possible future delinquents. In contrast, the rehabilitation orientation seeks treatment of the condition through the delineation of etiological factors and the development of a sound treatment program.

In a further dimension, the problem of *action-research* underlies much of this earlier discussion. Some would-be delinquency preventors seek immediate action on this problem, as they claim that urgency demands such a response. Others who also share the problem demand that action be based upon sound knowledge and seek evaluation of the condition before action is taken to correct the situation. But the concern for *localization-centralization,* one of authority and control, compounds the problem. Some workers argue that delinquency must be solved through community organizations, inasmuch as the needs of the individual and the community can only be realized through local autonomy. Their critics persist in the view that the problem of delinquency is so pervasive that it can only be treated when a wide variety of groups and institutions seek a common goal of prevention through concerted action. Overlying even these basic issues and concerns, Miller finds, is the tension of *lay-professional* qualifications. Some proponents of prevention programs argue that laymen are best able to deal with delinquency problems because they exude a greater warmth and sympathy than found among professional workers and are more familiar with the local community. On the other hand, professionals maintain that only they have the skills and background necessary for effective treatment of the individual delinquent. Because these conflicts continue within and among agencies and institutions, general and special prevention programs are continually undermined by those seeking to prevent delinquency and criminality.[35]

---

[35] Walter B. Miller, "Inner-Institution Conflict as a Major Impediment to Delinquency," *Human Organization,* Vol. 17 (Fall, 1958), pp. 20–23.

Toward realistic prevention programs

More recent thinking concerning the prevention of delinquency and crime has tended to assume many of the following elements originally contained in a policy statement isued by the Office of Juvenile Delinquency. While open to question, they nevertheless represent new conceptualizations of the delinquency problem and of procedures to be operationalized for its solution. The Office proposes the following operational presuppositions:

1. Programs dealing with social conditions that can be conceptualized as causal to delinquency rather than programs of individual rehabilitation and control will be more effective in the long run.
2. Lower-class youths dwelling in the slums of our great cities, represent the populations of greatest risks. It is the population in which delinquency is most amenable to strategies of social change rather than psychotherapy.
3. Because youths, like other human beings, live in a variety of social situations, efforts aimed simultaneously at a variety of situations will be most effective in facilitating conforming behavior.
4. While a comprehensive program seeks to create opportunities for conforming behavior, it also must seek to increase the skills and motivation of youths to enable them to perform satisfactorily in the situations confronting them. It is the dual attempt to *raise* skills and to *create* new opportunities that will be most effective in dealing with the problem of delinquency.
5. Programs must seek to enhance the confidence and concern of local community residents so that they become a more potent influence on the lives of their children. Such confidence will lead to a diminution of the problem of delinquency in the neighborhood.[36]

Viewing these problems in England, Giles Playfair and Derrick Sington concluded that delinquency and crime prevention goals will never be realized until the prison is eliminated as an institution. Imprisonment, they contend, is the second most severe sanction available within criminal law and consequently is a form of outright retribution. The rights of the prisoners, therefore, are highly circumscribed, and this tends to undermine the attempt to secure realistic normative social responses from imprisoned criminals. In England, the prisoner possesses the right only to complain to the prison governor or to request an interview with

---

[36] Melvin B. Mogulof, "Design for Community Action," in Amos and Wellford (eds.), *op. cit.*, p. 231; and D. H. Stott, "The Prediction of Delinquency from Non-Delinquent Behavior," *British Journal of Delinquency*, Vol. 10 (January, 1960), pp. 202–10.

the prison commissioner, the assistant commissioner, or a member of the visiting committee; to attend church services on Sundays or Holy Days; to receive "proper and reasonable" visits at times acceptable to the prison staff; to obtain legal advice; to possess access to a medical officer; to have a weekly bath, daily shave, or required haircut; to share a minimum of a half-hour daily exercise in open air; to receive adequate clothing suitable to the weather and environment; to receive food of adequate nutritional value; and not to be required to work more than 10 hours in any day.[37]

These privileges, Playfair and Sington allege, do little to change personal behavior patterns. Further, they maintain that the biggest fraud within the prison system rests in the failure to conclude the bargain made at the time of imprisonment which assumes that once a man is punished for his crime he is a rehabilitated individual whose slate has been wiped clean. The failure of society to fulfill its retributive-rehabilitative bargain, Playfair and Sington hypothesize, is one fundamental reason for the need for aftercare services designed to aid the reentry and readjustment of the prison-freed individual within society, the prison can never fully resemble the free democratic community to which the offender will eventually return.[38]

On the basis of these considerations, Playfair and Sington propose that England:

1. Abolish Borstal training programs.
2. Eliminate probation in its present form.
3. Lower the age of consent to the same age as that of criminal responsibility.
4. Raise the age of criminal responsibility to the same as the school-leaving age.
5. Provide that all offenses constituting a public nuisance, including female soliciting, male importuning, and indecent exposure, not be prosecuted without evidence from a witness other than a policeman that it involved an annoyance.
6. Amend the British Official Secret Act to exclude any action that does not directly endanger the security of the state from the contents of the criminal law.
7. Modify the law of content to permit the publication of any matter other than that which can be shown to be prejudicial to a fair and impartial trial.
8. Introduce maximum and minimum fines for all remaining offenses

---

[37] Giles Playfair and Derrick Sington, *Crime, Punishment and Cure* (London: Secker & Warburg, 1965), pp. 13–17.

[38] *Ibid.,* p. 39. Consult Don C. Gibbons, *Changing the Lawbreaker* (Englewood Cliffs, N.J.: Prentice-Hall, Inc., 1965).

except premeditated murder graded to the gravity of the offense and set in relationship to the individuals' income and/or capital.

9. Establish a special police body possessing wide executive powers to enforce fines and restore stolen property.

10. Abolish a not guilty by reason of insanity defense to a criminal charge or a plea of diminished responsibility to a murder charge.

11. Withdraw the power of the court to hospitalize convicted offenders under the 1959 British Mental Health Act.

12. Provide that anyone convicted of premeditated murder shall be given over for mandatory custodial treatment.

13. Hold that any convicted recidivist who shall be judged *prima facie* unpunishable should be referred to a diagnostic clinic before sentence, such clinics also possessing the authority to conduct some reexaminations as necessary.

The court should be bound by any recommendation for treatment and freedom from such a diagnostic clinic. It should also have the discretionary power to reject a recommendation for treatment in *custody* and substitute an order for treatment in *freedom*. Consequently, probation should also be replaced by treatment in freedom, and probation officers by rehabilitation officers concerned solely with the care and guidance of convicted offenders. In order to achieve such ends, prisons and Borstals should be replaced by small, nonpunitive custodial treatment centers designed to meet the psychiatric and social needs of the offender and society. Ideally, the indeterminate Borstal sentence and the fixed prison sentence of preventive detention, so Playfair and Sington propose, should be replaced by an order for a completely indefinite treatment in custody. However, a bill of minimum rights, including the right of periodic appeal to an independent tribunal, should also be defined for those deprived of their liberty. In order to protect the community's interest in these proceedings, the freedom of the press should also be guaranteed.[39]

As these authors suggest, the problem of prevention cannot be divorced from criminal law. While many think that punishment is imposed upon the offender because of the crime he committed (*quia peccatum est*), others presume that punishment is justified in order to prevent future crimes (*ne peccetur*). Since the last third of the 19th century, new deterministic ideas have stressed the idea that delinquent and criminal acts are impelled by particular internal and external forces. Carried to its extreme, this radical approach assumes that delinquent behavior is a product of "certain characteristics or stigmata" which result in particular predetermined behavior forms when "submitted to a certain order

---

[39] *Ibid.*, pp. 333–36.

of social pressures."[40] Therefore, just as one does not punish a person who catches the flu, one does not subject another who has been a victim of varied social conditions to inconsistent threats of punishment.

As a result of his studies of delinquency prevention and control, Robert M. MacIver concludes that the prevention of delinquency is more feasible, less costly, and more promising than later efforts toward rehabilitation. However, the rescue of the delinquent or near-delinquent youth cannot be effectively undertaken unless those who are assigned to this service are properly qualified through training and experience and possess the attributes of character that permit them to understand the diverse character of the problems of troubled or disturbed youth. Officials appointed to organize or to administer public or private anti-delinquency programs should be familiar with the problems of youth and should be in the position to keep in touch with new developments in treatment and with the results of research. The overall planning of urban programs and policies regarding delinquency control and youth problems should be administered by a special advisory and planning unit located within the city government in a position, preferably within the office of the mayor, where its recommendations will carry the most weight.[41]

Educational guidance for difficult and troubled children, MacIver believes, has been most often neglected in those large city school systems where its need is greatest. If youths with emotional or mental disturbances and cultural or educational shortcomings are to be offered an adequate education, schools must provide extensive guidance services and incentive programs. Additionally, teacher training and curricular adaptations should be given greater attention so that the level of essential instruction may be elevated. Not only must problem children be identified, but programs must be created to rescue dropouts and to prepare students for work opportunities. The school system, MacIver concludes, should recognize the following recommendations:

1. Since the earlier the child's learning problems are observed, recognized, and treated, the better the chance of overcoming them, every school should establish a thoroughgoing early-identification program

[40] Sebastian Soler, "Prevention in Criminal Law," *American Criminal Law Quarterly,* Vol. 4 (1965–66), pp. 196–97; and Thomas J. Dodd, "We Know More about Crime Prevention and Control than We Put into Practice," *Federal Probation,* Vol. 25 (September, 1962), pp. 11–13.

[41] Robert M. MacIver, *The Prevention and Control of Delinquency* (New York: Atherton Press, 1966), pp. 97–103; *Juvenile Delinquency Prevention in the United States* (Washington, D.C.: U.S. Department of Health, Education, and Welfare, 1962); Helen L. Witmer and Edith Tufts, *The Effectiveness of Delinquency Prevention Programs* (Washington, D.C.: U.S. Department of Health, Education, and Welfare, 1954).

beginning with kindergarten. Such a program might indeed be extended with considerable advantage into the preschool programs that are now developing.

2. All teachers should be trained in their preparation for training or in in-service training to identify problem children and to provide preliminary help and guidance to sympathetic understanding of their needs.

3. All schools should have available specially trained guidance counselors to whom more difficult cases should be referred.

4. To make this service possible, classes should, whenever possible, be limited from 20 to 25 pupils and for particularly refractory or difficult groups to 15.

5. A far more intensive effort is essential for the proper instruction of disprivileged groups, particularly the in-migrant groups in urban centers in order to help them adjust to the conditions of city life and overcome the educational deficiencies of their background. This is of high importance for their future as citizens and directly to prevent their lapsing into delinquent habits.

6. In substandard poverty-stricken urban areas, the school cannot operate effectively as an educational agency unless it becomes a neighborhood institution, cooperating with the families of the area and the local welfare organizations and providing special services for the children in order to equip them for schooling. No less imperative is the need to anticipate the likelihood that certain pupils will become dropouts, and to give special consideration to their needs and their difficulties and to stimulate their families through friendly contacts to encourage them to remain in school.

7. For older pupils who have either no interest or too little ability to incline them to continue the regular academic curriculum, it is eminently desirable that the school have a division providing work-experience courses directly related to the types on which they have a reasonable chance of being employed.

8. The schools in this country cannot rise to the high demand and challenge involved in the education of the young, and in special and individual guidance that is the best assurance that the children will overcome their difficulties and not fall into delinquent ways, unless the community comes to their aid and enables them to raise their standards, qualifications required of teachers, the salary rates, and the whole status of the profession.[42]

Because delinquency takes many forms and is a product of a variety of adverse conditions, any prevention program must be many-sided and

---

[42] *Ibid.*, pp. 112–23.

well integrated. Central emphasis should be placed upon a well-delineated neighborhood area. Any enacted program is generally more valuable if its activities are centered in an appropriate school or community center in the neighborhood and its program is focused toward a particular goal (*i.e.*, education or employment). Such programs, MacIver believes, should be financed by government and private sources and utilize area representatives, welfare specialists, and social scientists in the gathering of data concerning the nature and development of meaningful prevention programs. These professionals, however, should not be engaged in defining and prescribing policies and methods of operation.

All policemen on the beat, MacIver further concludes, should be fully instructed in the character and scope of laws and regulations pertaining to juvenile and youthful offenders. Police bureaus or divisions staffed by young officers capable of effectively communicating with youths with problems should be created or continued. Such members should be responsible for assessing and reporting on cases involving youths who exhibit serious problems and relate to troublesome gangs. Thoroughly integrated into the totality of the neighborhood program and working in cooperation with the various agencies in the area, the police should show a friendly attitude to the public and reflect an understanding that they are the guardians of all people, including the minority or disprivileged.[43]

Juvenile court judges, MacIver maintains, should be specially qualified for their function. The intake system should also be carefully designed and equipped to investigate and to eliminate those cases which do not need to come before the court for consideration. Inadequately staffed probation departments with a limited caseload should be provided sufficient time and opportunity to attend to every probationer need. Because the judge depends in large degree upon the capabilities of the probation service, the court should have a diagnostic center available to its probation personnel. However, in order to coordinate an overarching program of treatment, a state youth authority should be empowered to utilize all available agencies in the disposition of the cases of adjudged delinquents. Because delinquency, MacIver believes, cannot be separated from a complex of family problems, the juvenile court, if it is to operate with greater efficiency, should be assimilated into an inclusive family court system and should maintain jurisdiction over adolescents up to the age of 21.[44] Despite the value of many of

[43] *Ibid.*, pp. 146–47. See William E. Amos, *Action Programs for Delinquency Prevention* (Springfield, Ill.: Charles C. Thomas, Publisher, 1965); and Kenyon Scudder and Kenneth Beam, *The Twenty Billion Dollar Challenge* (New York: G. P. Putnam's Sons, 1961).

[44] *Ibid.*, pp. 155–56.

these recommendations, MacIver's conclusions are likely to be ignored due to their high cost of implementation.

While institutionalization of juveniles is filled with many hazards, some of these limitations can be overcome by the establishment of small-scale institutions which permit closer and more informal inmate and staff relationships. However, neglected, homeless, and younger juveniles, should not be sent to training schools or other similar institutions but to householdlike shelters or foster homes. Juveniles possessing physical handicaps or mental troubles should be provided therapy as needed in special treatment centers. A special authority or agency of the state responsible for the control and prevention of delinquency, MacIver suggests, should also experiment in planning diversified institutions and in evaluating the length of residence and conditions for release. Included in this consideration should be an examination of aftercare services, the use of halfway houses or group residences for releasees, or other means of aiding the violator's transition from prison and reentry into the community. However, the effectiveness of a treatment program largely depends, MacIver holds, upon the quality of service offered those being treated. Persons assisting in prevention and treatment should be well trained, offer a wide variety of professional services and skills, possess patience, and show clear evidence of personal discretion.[45]

The basic weakness of these proposals rests with the fact that each demands funding if it is to be effective. Where the tax base is already overextended and overburdened, funds are not quickly available for these projects. Many approaches to or programs of crime control are more costly than their result justify. Consequently, evaluation of cost effectiveness should gain increasing future importance. But few economists have expressed any concern for such facets of the crime prevention problem. Then, too, the diversity of juvenile and adult interests have fragmented the community's ability to seek clear and integrated solutions to these problems. Until resources are allocated more intelligently and national priorities are restructured, the prevention of delinquency and crime will only remain a dream rather than a reality.

Prevention and the President's Commission

The President's Commission on Law Enforcement and the Administration of Justice, reporting in 1967, concluded that a significant reduction in crime is possible if a similar series of objectives are vigorously pursued. Society, the Commission proposed, must seek to prevent crime

---

[45] *Ibid.*, p. 190; and Pauline V. Young, *Social Treatment in Probation and Delinquency* (New York: McGraw-Hill Book Co., 1952); John R. Ellingston, *Protecting Our Children From Criminal Careers* (New York: McGraw-Hill Book Co., 1948).

before it happens by relating all citizens and American life to the benefits and responsibilities of crime prevention and by strengthening reinforcement and reducing criminal opportunities. However, the system of criminal justice must also develop a broader range of techniques for meeting the particular conditions and needs of the specific offender. In order to win the respect and cooperation of all citizens, the system of law enforcement must eliminate injustice and update its ideas. However, even these steps will be inadequate unless a higher grade of police officer, prosecutor, judge, defense attorney, probation and parole officer, and correction official is recruited. Research into basic administrative operations and problems must be continued by those within and without the system of criminal justice. Simultaneously, more money must be alloted to law enforcement, the courts, and correctional agencies if they are to improve their ability to control crime. However, individual citizens, religious institutions, civic and business organizations, and all levels of government must assume responsibility for planning and implementing changes within the system of criminal justice if these goals are to be achieved.

At the same time effort must be continued to strengthen family life. Select schools must be given the necessary resources to help children to move from their current environment to higher vocational and life goals. Efforts to combat school segregation, the Commission maintained, must be continued and expanded, employment opportunities must be enlarged, youths must be given more effective vocational training and job counseling, better communication systems must be developed to utilize on-duty police officer time more effectively. Court disposition of cases must become more efficient. Stricter gun controls should also be enacted to reduce particular types of crime committed by selected individuals.

Youth Service Bureaus, the Commission proposed, should be developed in order to respond to adolescent needs as juveniles are referred for counseling, work, education, or recreation and job placement programs by police, parents, schools, and social agencies. Hopefully, such bureaus would offset the inadequacies of the juvenile court and provide continuing assistance to youths which the courts have failed to provide in the past despite their acceptance of juvenile court philosophy. Greater attempts must also be made to develop community-oriented individual, group, and family counseling and group therapy.

Because community treatment programs are less expensive and more effective than institutional treatment, a new type of correctional institution located close to population centers should likewise be established. Housing as few as 50 inmates and maintaining close relations with schools, employers, and universities, such institutions should serve as classification centers, ports for community reentry, and centers for various types of local programs. Work furloughs, work release, and vocational training programs should likewise be expanded to include a greater number of institutionalized offenders. Public drunkenness should be processed as a medical rather than legal problem. Communities should develop civil detoxification centers and comprehensive aftercare programs for alcoholics. Drug addicts should also be civilly rather than criminally committed.

But even more important, assembly-line justice should be replaced by a just system of due process. When placed in lockups, juveniles should be separated from hardened offenders. Defense counsel should be made available to both juveniles and adults. In order to guarantee the integrity of the system of justice, each state should finance regular statewide assigned counsel and defender systems for the indigent. Legal aid should also be provided the probation and parole violator at the revocation hearing. Greater opportunities should be allowed for the release of charged offenders on their own recognizance, especially in misdemeanor cases. Inept, callous, and corrupt law enforcement and judicial personnel must be eliminated from the system of justice. Greater attempts must be made by the police to relate effectively to the urban poor. Because the system of justice is the product of the community, it must be responsive to all elements of the community without prejudice. In order to raise the capability level of personnel and the effectiveness of law enforcement and the administration of justice, federal support, the Commission recommends, should be given for state and local planning; the training of criminal justice personnel; surveys and supervisory services pertaining to the organization and operation of police departments, courts, prosecuting offices, and corrections agencies; development of a coordinated national information system for operational and research purposes; a limited number of demonstration programs; scientific and technological research and development; development of national and regional research centers; and grants-in-aid for operational innovations.[46] Each of these aspects is finally involved in any attempt to prevent and control delinquency and criminality.

The recommendations of the Presidents Commission, however, fall short of a solution to the problems of delinquency and crime. While opposing sin and evil, it chose to wave the flag, support motherhood, and make community reintegration dependent upon the return of the public to the higher values of past society and to expressions of personal piety—in short, a return to the communal values of the past. This is an improbable and an impractical quest. Society is no longer as it was

---

[46] The Presidents Commission on Law Enforcement and the Administration of Justice, *The Challenge of Crime in a Free Society* (Washington, D.C.: U.S. Government Printing Office, 1967). Also refer to the series of more detailed *Task Force Reports* of the Commission.

in the "past." While the Commission may be criticized for its tendency to idealize and its failure to delineate a clear path for the solution and prevention of delinquency and crime, it alone cannot carry the blame. The plain fact of the matter is that we are deficient in our knowledge concerning these deviant social expressions and only now have entered what promises to be the "golden age" of data-gathering and program development in search of solutions. Whether modern research techniques and programs will be able to meet the challenge remains to be seen. But we continue into the future with the belief that solutions will be found. The only question is: Will they be found in time? Or will they be too little and too late?

Appendix

Appendix

FIGURE A–1
Crimes by the month

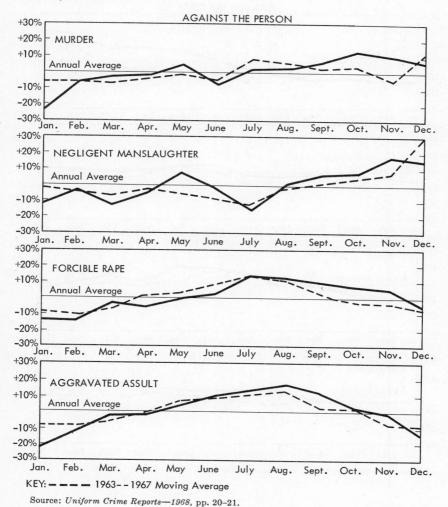

KEY: ━ ━ ━ 1963–1967 Moving Average

Source: *Uniform Crime Reports—1968*, pp. 20–21.

FIGURE A–1 (*Continued*)

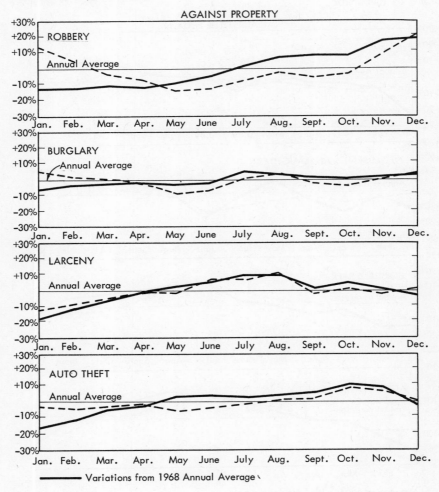

Variations from 1968 Annual Average

TABLE A–1

Disposition of persons formally charged by the police, 1968
(2,734 cities; 1968 estimated population 67,574,000)

Offense	Charged (held for prosecution)	Guilty		Acquitted or dismissed	Referred to juvenile court
		Offense charged	Lesser offense		
TOTAL.........	**2,425,732**	**64.1**	**2.6**	**15.6**	**17.8**
Criminal homicide:					
(a) Murder and nonnegligent manslaughter......	2,687	40.9	17.3	32.9	8.9
(b) Manslaughter by negligence.........	923	39.5	10.3	41.6	8.6
Forcible rape..........	3,910	31.8	12.2	33.1	22.8
Robbery..............	19,152	31.9	9.2	20.3	38.6
Aggravated assault.....	35,226	43.0	11.7	29.4	15.9
Burglary—breaking or entering.............	91,226	24.0	6.7	11.4	57.9
Larceny-theft..........	195,672	41.3	3.1	13.8	41.8
Auto theft.............	50,142	19.2	5.0	10.8	65.1
Subtotal for above offenses.	398,938	34.2	5.4	14.9	45.5
Other assaults.........	109,188	49.7	3.0	34.9	12.5
Arson................	3,017	15.1	5.1	14.0	65.8
Forgery and counterfeiting........	11,408	57.4	7.8	20.7	14.1
Fraud................	23,001	66.4	3.1	27.1	3.5
Embezzlement.........	1,885	63.5	5.8	25.0	5.6
Stolen property; buying, receiving, possessing.	13,726	38.2	5.8	19.7	36.3
Vandalism.............	34,850	24.3	1.6	19.4	54.8
Weapons; carrying, possessing, etc.......	33,724	61.0	6.2	19.5	13.3
Prostitution and commercialized vice..	10,403	72.8	2.5	22.9	1.8
Sex offenses (except rape and prostitution)	19,879	54.6	6.2	18.4	20.8
Narcotic drug laws.....	44,935	36.9	7.1	21.6	34.4
Gambling.............	26,559	62.8	4.0	31.7	1.4
Offenses against the family and children..	21,741	60.6	2.3	29.3	7.8
Driving under the influence............	136,889	78.4	12.2	8.7	.8
Liquor laws............	107,084	66.0	1.3	12.4	20.3
Drunkenness..........	834,932	86.8	.2	11.7	1.3
Disorderly conduct.....	237,552	65.7	.7	20.4	13.1
Vagrancy.............	43,080	72.5	.8	18.9	7.8
All other offenses.......	312,941	48.4	1.2	14.2	36.2

Source: *Uniform Crime Reports—1968*, p. 105.

TABLE A-2

Total arrest trends, 1960–68
(2,634 agencies; 1968 estimated population 100,029,000)[1]

	Number of persons arrested								
	Total all ages			Under 18 years of age			18 years of age and over		
Offense Charged	1960	1968	Percent Change	1960	1968	Percent Change	1960	1968	Percent Change
TOTAL	3,501,905	4,146,684	+18.4	515,422	1,032,788	+100.4	2,986,483	3,113,896	+4.1
Criminal homicide:									
(a) Murder and non-negligent manslaughter	4,970	8,310	+67.2	378	858	+127.0	4,592	7,452	+62.3
(b) Manslaughter by negligence	1,971	2,086	+5.8	147	157	+6.8	1,824	1,929	+5.8
Forcible rape	7,309	9,747	+33.4	1,303	2,025	+55.4	6,006	7,722	+28.6
Robbery	33,587	59,523	+77.2	8,238	20,104	+144.0	25,349	39,419	+55.5
Aggravated assault	55,564	82,242	+48.0	6,532	14,059	+115.2	49,032	68,183	+39.1
Burglary—breaking or entering	125,376	189,213	+50.9	59,675	101,372	+69.9	65,701	87,841	+33.7
Larceny—theft	205,686	339,165	+64.9	100,260	180,138	+79.7	105,426	159,027	+50.8
Auto theft	57,805	98,962	+71.2	35,235	59,237	+68.1	22,570	39,725	+76.0
Subtotal for above offenses	492,268	789,248	+60.3	211,768	377,950	+78.5	280,500	411,298	+46.6

Offense								
Other assaults	131,033	182,795	+39.4	13,463	32,258	+139.6	117,670	150,537	+27.9
Forgery and counterfeiting	21,618	25,946	+20.0	1,541	3,113	+102.0	20,077	22,833	+13.7
Embezzlement and fraud	35,358	46,418	+31.3	880	2,193	+149.2	34,478	44,225	+28.3
Stolen property; buying, receiving, possessing	10,139	28,773	+183.8	2,715	9,601	+253.6	7,424	19,172	+158.2
Weapons; carrying, possessing, etc.	33,289	65,463	+96.7	6,776	11,107	+63.9	26,513	54,356	+105.0
Prostitution and commercialized vice	28,033	39,469	+40.8	423	788	+86.3	27,610	38,681	+40.1
Sex offenses (except forcible rape and prostitution)	47,046	36,370	-22.7	9,891	8,016	-19.0	37,155	28,354	-23.7
Narcotic drug laws (2)	32,752	134,006	+322.0	1,688	33,091	+1860.4	30,064	100,915	+235.7
Gambling	121,117	68,247	-43.7	1,542	1,762	+14.3	119,575	66,485	-44.4
Offenses against family and children	41,048	37,459	-8.7	549	364	-33.7	40,499	37,095	-8.4
Driving under the influence	145,184	218,783	+50.7	1,145	2,186	+90.9	144,039	216,597	+50.4
Liquor laws	90,324	145,969	+61.6	18,618	43,910	+135.8	71,706	102,059	+42.3
Drunkenness	1,249,612	1,070,668	-14.3	13,023	27,337	+109.9	1,236,589	1,043,331	-15.6
Disorderly conduct	422,249	461,957	+9.4	48,227	97,856	+102.9	374,022	364,101	-2.7
Vagrancy	135,164	75,447	-44.2	7,738	8,038	+3.9	127,426	67,409	-47.1
All other offenses (except traffic)	466,571	719,666	+54.2	175,435	373,218	+112.7	291,136	346,448	+19.0
Suspicion (not included in totals)	113,948	73,067	-35.9	20,944	16,265	-22.3	93,004	56,802	-38.9

[1] Based on comparable reports from 1,944 cities representing 82,384,000 population and 690 counties representing 17,645,000 population.
[2] The trend for narcotic drug law violation is largely influenced by the large cities.
Source: Uniform Crime Reports—1968, p. 112.

TABLE A-3

Total arrests, distribution by sex, 1968
(4,812 agencies; 1968 estimated population 145,306,000)

Offense Charged	Number of Persons Arrested					Percent of Total[1]		
	Total	Male	Female	Percent Male	Percent Female	Total	Male	Female
TOTAL............	5,616,839	4,891,343	725,496	87.1	12.9	100.0	100.0	100.0
Criminal homicide:								
(a) Murder and nonnegligent manslaughter............	10,394	8,722	1,672	83.9	16.1	.2	.2	.2
(b) Manslaughter by negligence....	3,144	2,824	320	89.8	10.2	.1	.1	.....
Forcible rape.........	12,685	12,685	....	100.0	....	.2	.3	.....
Robbery............	69,115	65,241	3,874	94.4	5.6	1.2	1.3	.5
Aggravated assault.....	106,475	93,256	13,219	87.6	12.4	1.9	1.9	1.8
Burglary—breaking or entering......	256,216	245,526	10,690	95.8	4.2	4.6	5.0	1.5
Larceny—theft.........	463,928	350,818	113,110	75.6	24.4	8.3	7.2	15.6
Auto theft...........	125,263	119,088	6,175	95.1	4.9	2.2	2.4	.9
Subtotal for above offenses	1,047,220	898,160	149,060	85.8	14.2	18.6	18.4	20.5

Offense	Total						
Other assaults	**239,918**	212,484	27,434	88.6	11.4	4.3	4.3	3.8
Arson	**9,121**	8,386	735	91.9	8.1	.2	.2	.1
Forgery and counterfeiting	**34,497**	26,971	7,526	78.2	21.8	.6	.6	1.0
Fraud	**56,710**	43,113	13,597	76.0	24.0	1.0	.9	1.9
Embezzlement	**5,894**	4,736	1,158	80.4	19.6	.1	.1	.2
Stolen property; buying, receiving, possessing	**37,769**	34,847	2,922	92.3	7.7	.7	.7	.4
Vandalism	**110,182**	102,949	7,233	93.4	6.6	2.0	2.1	1.0
Weapons; carrying, possessing, etc.	**83,721**	78,428	5,293	93.7	6.3	1.5	1.6	.7
Prostitution and commercialized vice	**42,338**	9,197	33,141	21.7	78.3	.8	.2	4.6
Sex offenses (except forcible rape and prostitution)	**47,573**	41,897	5,676	88.1	11.9	.8	.9	.8
Narcotic drug laws	**162,177**	137,960	24,217	85.1	14.9	2.9	2.8	3.3
Gambling	**76,909**	70,539	6,370	91.7	8.3	1.4	1.4	.9
Offenses against family and children	**51,319**	46,802	4,517	91.2	8.8	.9	1.0	.6
Driving under the influence	**307,601**	287,601	19,630	93.6	6.4	5.5	5.9	2.7
Liquor laws	**215,376**	189,700	25,676	88.1	11.9	3.8	3.9	3.5
Drunkenness	**1,415,961**	1,316,905	99,056	93.0	7.0	25.2	26.9	13.7
Disorderly conduct	**593,104**	513,788	79,316	86.6	13.4	10.6	10.5	10.9
Vagrancy	**99,147**	89,063	10,084	89.8	10.2	1.8	1.8	1.4
All other offenses (except traffic)	**643,404**	547,397	96,007	85.1	14.9	11.5	11.2	13.2
Suspicion	**89,986**	75,792	14,194	84.2	15.8	1.6	1.5	2.0
Curfew and loitering law violations	**98,230**	79,193	19,037	80.6	19.4	1.7	1.6	2.6
Runaways	**149,052**	75,435	73,617	50.6	49.4	2.7	1.5	10.1

[1] Because of rounding, the percentages may not add to total.
Source: *Uniform Crime Reports—1968*, p. 118.

TABLE A-4

Arrests, number and rate, 1968, by population groups

(Rate per 100,000; 1968 estimated population)

		Cities		
Offense Charged	Total (4,812 agencies; Total Population 145,306,000)	Total City Arrests (3,500 Cities; Population 108,474,000)	Group I (50 Cities Over 250,000; Population 40,522,000)	Group II (90 Cities, 100,000 to 250,000; Population 13,335,000)
Total.................	5,526,853	4,807,904	2,097,940	659,986
Rate per 100,000 inhabitants.............	3,803.6	4,432.3	5,177.3	4,949.4
Criminal homicide:				
(a) Murder and nonnegligent manslaughter...	10,394	8,831	5,879	1,137
Rate per 100,000..	7.2	8.1	14.5	8.5
(b) Manslaughter by negligence.............	3,144	2,085	868	309
Rate per 100,000..	2.2	1.9	2.1	2.3
Forcible rape.............	12,685	10,018	6,025	1,158
Rate per 100,000........	8.7	9.2	14.9	8.7
Robbery.................	69,115	62,838	45,829	5,910
Rate per 100,000........	47.6	57.9	113.1	44.3
Aggravated assault........	106,475	90,508	49,840	11,149
Rate per 100,000........	73.3	83.4	123.0	83.6
Burglary—breaking or entering...............	256,216	208,046	101,135	27,021
Rate per 100,000........	176.3	191.8	249.6	202.6
Larceny—theft............	463,928	409,249	155,154	57,907
Rate per 100,000........	319.3	377.3	382.9	434.3
Auto theft................	125,263	108,545	58,323	14,023
Rate per 100,000........	86.2	100.1	143.9	105.2
Subtotal for above offenses............	1,047,220	900,120	423,053	118,614
Rate per 100,000..	720.7	829.8	1,044.0	889.5
Other assaults............	239,918	209,843	91,592	30,914
Rate per 100,000........	165.1	193.5	226.0	231.8
Arson...................	9,121	7,321	3,260	938
Rate per 100,000........	6.3	6.7	8.0	7.0
Forgery and counterfeiting.	34,497	26,803	11,394	4,277
Rate per 100,000........	23.7	24.7	28.1	32.1
Fraud...................	56,710	40,544	14,769	6,649
Rate per 100,000........	39.0	37.4	36.4	49.9
Embezzlement............	5,894	4,262	1,471	925
Rate per 100,000........	4.1	3.9	3.6	6.9
Stolen property; buying, receiving, possessing.......	37,769	31,938	16,356	3,203
Rate per 100,000........	26.0	29.4	40.4	24.0
Vandalism................	110,182	93,538	33,854	11,072
Rate per 100,000........	75.8	86.2	83.5	83.0

	Cities				Other Areas	
	Group III (232 Cities, 50,000 to 100,000; Population 16,061,000)	Group IV (396 Cities, 25,000 to 50,000; Population 14,003,000)	Group V (968 Cities, 10,000 to 25,000; Population 15,276,000)	Group VI (1,764 Cities under 10,000; Population 9,277,000)	Suburban area[1] (1,776 Agencies; Population 39,427,000)	Rural Area (1,135 agencies, Population 19,631,000)
	649,584	515,792	547,484	337,118	1,009,307	350,988
	4,044.4	3,683.5	3,583.9	3,633.8	2,560.0	1,787.3
	682	492	454	187	1,330	790
	4.2	3.5	3.0	2.0	3.4	4.0
	323	252	209	124	663	763
	2.0	1.8	1.4	1.3	1.7	3.9
	1,016	738	684	397	2,514	1,285
	6.3	5.3	4.5	4.3	6.4	6.5
	5,111	2,881	2,316	791	8,345	1,762
	31.8	20.6	15.2	8.5	21.2	9.0
	10,738	6,773	7,410	4,598	18,221	6,916
	66.9	48.4	48.5	49.6	46.2	35.2
	27,741	19,996	20,624	11,529	56,334	21,358
	172.7	142.8	135.0	124.3	142.9	108.8
	65,192	53,047	51,802	26,147	103,017	22,141
	405.9	378.8	339.1	281.8	261.3	112.8
	13,384	9,341	8,848	4,626	23,728	7,176
	83.3	66.7	57.9	49.9	60.2	36.6
	124,187	93,520	92,347	48,399	214,152	62,191
	773.2	667.9	604.5	521.7	543.2	316.8
	27,691	23,605	23,560	12,481	45,505	12,451
	172.4	168.6	154.2	134.5	115.4	63.4
	1,076	790	836	421	2,139	909
	6.7	5.6	5.5	4.5	5.4	4.6
	4,101	2,735	3,066	1,230	6,804	4,223
	25.5	19.5	20.1	13.3	17.3	21.5
	5,721	4,864	5,997	2,544	13,994	8,750
	35.6	34.7	39.3	27.4	35.5	44.6
	845	448	422	151	1,501	549
	5.3	3.2	2.8	1.6	3.8	2.8
	4,373	3,127	3,207	1,672	7,706	2,987
	27.2	22.3	21.0	18.0	19.5	15.2
	13,581	12,169	14,197	8,665	29,772	8,025
	84.6	86.9	92.9	93.4	75.5	40.9

TABLE A-4 (*Continued*)

			Cities	
Offense Charged	Total (4,812 agencies; Total Population 145,306,000)	Total City Arrests (3,500 Cities; Population 108,474,000)	Group I (50 Cities Over 250,000; Population 40,522,000)	Group II (90 Cities, 100,000 to 250,000; Population 13,335,000)
Weapons; carrying, possessing, etc..............	83,721	74,794	41,637	9,830
Rate per 100,000........	57.6	69.0	102.8	73.7
Prostitution and commercialized vice..........	42,338	40,611	37,156	2,224
Rate per 100,000........	29.1	37.4	91.7	16.7
Sex offenses (except forcible rape and prostitution).....	47,573	40,336	20,833	6,183
Rate per 100,000........	32.7	37.2	51.4	46.4
Narcotic drug laws........	162,177	139,400	83,271	13,145
Rate per 100,000........	111.6	128.5	205.5	98.6
Gambling...............	76,909	71,787	58,144	6,093
Rate per 100,000........	52.9	66.2	143.5	45.7
Offenses against family and children.................	51,319	34,771	12,186	7,246
Rate per 100,000........	35.3	32.1	30.1	54.3
Driving under the influence	307,231	246,690	96,255	24,169
Rate per 100,000........	211.4	227.4	237.5	181.3
Liquor laws...............	215,376	167,735	34,085	18,364
Rate per 100,000........	148.2	154.6	84.1	137.7
Drunkenness.............	1,415,961	1,306,261	530,633	230,618
Rate per 100,000........	974.5	1,204.2	1,309.5	1,729.5
Disorderly conduct........	593,104	548,612	270,832	60,547
Rate per 100,000........	408.2	505.8	668.4	454.1
Vagrancy................	99,147	90,241	51,161	10,983
Rate per 100,000........	68.2	83.2	126.3	82.4
All other offenses (except traffic)...................	643,404	523,888	190,270	69,573
Rate per 100,000........	442.8	483.0	469.6	521.8
Suspicion (not included in totals)..................	89,986	85,941	50,934	9,180
Rate per 100,000........	61.9	79.2	125.7	68.8
Curfew and loitering law violations................	98,230	90,335	33,520	6,056
Rate per 100,000........	67.6	83.3	82.7	45.4
Runaways................	149,052	118,074	42,208	18,363
Rate per 100,000	102.6	108.9	104.2	137.7

[1] Includes suburban, city and county police agencies within metropolitan areas. Excludes core cities. Suburban cities are also included in other city groups. Population figures rounded to the nearest thousand. All rates were calculated on the population before rounding.
Source: *Uniform Crime Reports—1968*, pp. 110–111.

	Cities			Other Areas	
Group III (232 Cities, 50,000 to 100,000; Population 16,061,000)	Group IV (396 Cities, 25,000 to 50,000, Population 14,003,000)	Group V (968 Cities, 10,000 to 25,000; Population 15,276,000)	Group VI (1,764 Cities under 10,000; Population 9,277,000)	Suburban area[1] (1,776 Agencies; Population 39,427,000)	Rural Area (1,135 agencies, Population 19,631,000)
8,077	6,152	5,858	3,240	12,105	4,271
50.3	43.9	38.3	34.9	30.7	21.8
740	263	123	105	1,579	343
4.6	1.9	.8	1.1	4.0	1.7
5,069	3,661	3,199	1,391	9,635	2,578
31.6	26.1	20.9	15.0	24.4	13.1
18,224	11,745	9,370	3,645	37,089	4,651
113.5	83.9	61.3	39.3	94.1	23.7
3,125	2,172	1,534	719	4,702	2,415
19.5	15.5	10.0	7.8	11.9	12.3
5,136	3,957	4,401	1,845	12,930	8,492
32.0	28.3	28.8	19.9	32.8	43.3
32,544	32,627	36,220	24,875	70,529	35,018
202.6	233.0	237.1	268.1	178.9	178.4
24,082	26,403	35,985	28,816	50,041	35,670
149.9	188.6	235.6	310.6	126.9	181.7
183,944	130,471	140,839	89,756	161,733	57,779
1,145.3	931.7	922.0	967.5	410.2	294.3
61,137	56,771	58,750	40,575	99,665	19,919
380.7	405.4	384.6	437.4	252.8	101.5
9,733	6,710	6,959	4,695	11,853	3,340
60.6	47.9	45.6	50.6	30.1	17.0
80,441	65,978	72,242	45,384	148,055	62,760
500.8	471.2	472.9	489.2	375.5	319.7
9,210	7,572	5,041	4,004	12,244	1,559
57.3	54.1	33.0	43.2	31.1	7.9
14,462	12,879	14,441	8,977	26,515	2,227
90.0	92.0	94.5	96.8	67.3	11.3
21,295	14,745	13,931	7,532	41,303	11,440
132.6	105.3	91.2	81.2	104.8	58.3

TABLE A-5
Total arrests by age, 1968
(4,812 agencies; 1968 estimated population 145,306,000)

Offense Charged	Grand Total	Under 15	Under 18	Number Arrested by Age								Percentage Arrested by Age		
				18 and Over	10 and Under	11-12	13-14	15	16	17	18	Under 15	Under 18	Under 21
TOTAL	5,616,839	564,343	1,457,078	4,159,761	80,600	132,420	351,323	726,402	313,524	302,809	282,708	10.0	25.9	38.8
Percent distribution	100-0	10.0	25.9	74.1	1.4	2.4	6.3	4.9	5.6	5.4	5.0			
General homicide:														
(a) Murder and non-negligent manslaughter	10,394	164	1,027	9,367	16	26	122	163	298	402	501	1.6	9.9	23.6
(b) Manslaughter by negligence	3,144	32	244	2,900	6	8	18	21	64	127	189	1.0	7.8	25.3
Forcible rape	12,685	489	2,559	10,126	24	79	386	471	715	884	1,043	3.9	20.2	43.1
Robbery	69,115	8,231	22,876	46,239	635	2,071	5,525	4,068	4,907	5,670	6,180	11.9	33.1	56.2
Aggravated assault	106,475	5,974	17,590	88,885	685	1,498	3,791	3,209	4,058	4,359	5,104	5.6	16.5	29.8
Burglary—breaking or entering	256,216	67,267	140,229	115,987	10,180	17,521	39,566	26,235	25,189	21,538	18,903	26.3	54.7	72.0
Larceny—theft	463,928	133,897	250,503	213,425	21,563	37,973	74,361	41,964	40,820	33,822	28,390	28.9	54.0	68.1
Auto theft	125,263	20,547	75,988	49,275	426	2,322	17,799	19,804	20,278	15,359	10,554	16.4	60.7	79.0
Subtotal for above offenses	1,047,220	236,601	511,016	536,204	33,535	61,498	141,568	95,935	96,319	82,161	70,864	22.6	48.8	64.8
Percent distribution	100.0	22.6	48.8	51.2	3.2	5.9	13.5	9.2	9.2	7.8	6.8			

Offense	Total												
Other assaults	239,918	16,626	197,747	2,322	4,168	10,136	7,047	8,862	9,636	10,612	6.9	17.6	30.0
Arson	9,122	3,934	3,390	1,478	1,045	1,411	692	636	469	381	43.1	62.8	72.9
Forgery and counterfeiting	34,497	816	30,372	51	157	608	678	1,113	1,518	1,994	2.4	12.0	29.9
Fraud	56,710	776	54,185	94	214	468	370	539	850	1,554	1.4	4.5	14.2
Embezzlement	5,894	58	5,647	8	15	35	25	50	114	160	1.0	4.2	14.2
Stolen property; buying, receiving, possessing	37,769	4,547	24,693	415	1,037	3,095	2,621	2,966	2,942	3,028	12.0	34.6	54.4
Vandalism	110,182	53,477	27,334	13,911	15,479	24,087	12,162	9,841	7,368	4,443	48.5	75.2	84.1
Weapons; carrying, possessing, etc.	83,721	4,211	68,841	303	821	3,087	2,784	3,661	4,224	4,818	5.0	17.8	33.3
Prostitution and commercialized vice	42,338	95	41,470	8	9	78	97	206	470	1,409	0.2	2.1	16.7
Sex offenses (except forcible rape and prostitution)	47,573	4,458	36,222	521	960	2,977	2,245	2,448	2,200	2,023	9.4	23.9	36.2
Narcotic drug laws	162,177	6,243	118,977	146	658	5,439	7,795	12,628	16,534	17,875	3.8	26.6	56.5
Gambling	76,909	333	74,894	6	56	271	341	569	772	1,044	0.4	2.6	6.8
Offenses against family and children	51,319	125	50,712	42	22	61	88	116	278	1,809	0.2	1.2	11.8
Driving under the influence	307,231	65	304,049	6	11	48	174	772	2,171	4,844	(1)	1.0	6.5
Liquor laws	215,376	5,492	146,956	66	370	5,056	9,867	21,779	31,282	38,779	2.5	31.8	75.3
Drunkenness	1,415,961	4,154	1,378,719	74	322	3,758	6,082	10,769	16,237	26,027	0.3	2.6	7.8
Disorderly conduct	593,104	49,930	464,380	6,495	12,683	30,752	23,390	25,624	29,780	36,565	8.4	21.7	37.3
Vagrancy	99,147	1,975	88,144	150	339	1,486	1,560	2,608	4,860	7,628	2.0	11.1	29.0
All other offenses (except traffic)	643,404	80,517	438,924	13,390	17,148	49,979	40,738	42,997	40,228	38,185	12.5	31.8	47.2
Suspicion	89,986	6,345	67,901	1,172	1,462	3,711	3,339	4,184	8,217	8,666	7.1	24.5	47.7
Curfew and loitering law violations	98,230	98,230	......	1,478	4,163	19,039	20,847	29,832	22,871	......	25.1	100.0	100.0
Runaways	149,052	58,885	......	4,929	9,783	44,173	37,525	35,005	17,637	......	39.5	100.0	100.0

Source: Adapted from *Uniform Crime Reports—1968*, pp. 115, 117.

TABLE A-6

Total arrests by race, 1968

(4,758 agencies; 1968 estimated population 135,545,000)

Offense Charged	Total	Total Arrests					
		White	Negro	Indian	Chinese	Japanese	All Others (Includes Races Unknown)
TOTAL	5,349,450	3,700,012	1,471,730	119,265	1,666	4,186	52,591
Criminal homicide:							
(a) Murder and nonnegligent manslaughter	9,458	3,536	5,699	93	2	2	126
(b) Manslaughter by negligence	2,965	2,184	733	18	.....	7	23
Forcible rape	11,607	5,967	5,406	84	.....	9	141
Robbery	59,424	21,550	36,862	485	3	16	508
Aggravated assault	93,972	46,039	46,198	814	24	23	874
Burglary—breaking or entering	241,455	156,196	80,627	1,582	81	194	2,775
Larceny—theft	448,392	299,304	140,406	2,976	339	605	4,762
Auto theft	116,745	72,875	40,969	943	40	141	1,777
Subtotal for above offenses	984,018	607,651	356,900	6,995	489	997	10,986

Other assaults	226,488	136,055	86,148	1,559	64	100	2,562
Arson	8,498	5,653	2,709	64	....	7	65
Forgery and counterfeiting	31,176	22,576	8,140	237	10	19	194
Fraud	54,931	42,479	11,921	234	10	22	265
Embezzlement	5,241	4,252	952	16	1	1	19
Stolen property; buying, receiving, possessing	31,398	19,231	11,739	131	8	9	280
Vandalism	101,915	79,667	20,865	489	28	59	807
Weapons; carrying, possessing, etc.	77,844	37,912	38,575	366	17	30	944
Prostitution and commercialized vice	34,418	12,267	21,737	96	14	41	263
Sex offenses (except forcible rape and prostitution)	44,853	33,796	10,130	238	17	47	625
Narcotic drug laws	137,598	105,886	29,608	270	70	218	1,546
Gambling	63,506	18,692	40,111	18	119	662	3,904
Offenses against family and children	49,956	33,704	15,529	446	9	5	263
Driving under the influence	298,664	241,899	50,586	4,250	86	249	1,594
Liquor laws	204,214	176,045	23,573	3,632	62	39	863
Drunkenness	1,393,886	1,011,138	292,596	81,465	198	442	8,047
Disorderly conduct	560,537	348,179	195,577	8,595	120	74	7,992
Vagrancy	89,472	66,827	20,516	1,168	41	90	830
All other offenses (except traffic)	617,347	450,071	153,604	6,178	190	668	6,636
Suspicion	98,006	48,188	40,318	399	5	3	93
Curfew and loitering law violations	97,540	76,282	18,656	850	47	288	1,417
Runaways	146,944	121,562	21,240	1,569	61	116	2,396

Source: *Uniform Crime Reports—1968*, p. 120.

TABLE A-7

Total arrests by race, 1968

Offense charged	Arrests under 18							Arrests 18 and over						
	Total	White	Negro	In-dian	Chi-nese	Japa-nese	All others (includes race unknown)	Total	White	Negro	In-dian	Chi-nese	Japa-nese	All others (includes race unknown)
TOTAL............	1,382,725	1,002,143	351,399	10,555	490	1,671	16,467	3,966,725	2,697,869	1,120,331	108,710	1,176	2,515	36,124
Criminal homicide:														
(a) Murder and nonnegligent manslaughter............	927	294	612	5	......	......	16	8,531	3,242	5,087	88	2	2	110
(b) Manslaughter by negligence.	226	179	44	1	......	1	1	2,739	2,005	689	17	......	6	22
Forcible rape............	2,360	967	1,351	7	......	1	34	9,247	5,000	4,055	77	......	8	107
Robbery............	18,640	5,150	13,229	69	1	5	186	40,784	16,400	23,633	416	2	11	322
Aggravated assault............	14,644	6,786	7,569	110	5	3	171	79,328	39,253	38,629	704	19	20	703
Burglary—breaking or entering....	133,482	87,463	43,224	761	47	143	1,844	107,973	68,733	37,403	821	34	51	931
Larceny—theft............	244,664	165,316	74,605	1,326	157	406	2,854	203,728	133,988	65,801	1,650	182	199	1,908
Auto theft............	71,958	46,595	23,619	430	22	109	1,183	44,787	26,280	17,350	513	18	32	594
Subtotal for above offenses..	486,901	312,750	164,253	2,709	232	668	6,289	497,117	294,901	192,647	4,286	257	329	4,697

Other assaults	40,052	22,394	16,952	179	7	18	502	186,436	113,661	69,196	1,380	57	82	2,060
Arson	5,456	3,831	1,527	49	2	6	43	3,042	1,822	1,182	15	......	1	22
Forgery and counterfeiting	3,844	2,905	893	27	......	......	17	27,332	19,671	7,247	210	8	19	177
Fraud	2,177	1,449	694	9	......	4	21	52,754	41,030	11,227	225	10	18	244
Embezzlement	210	160	49	1	......	......	......	5,031	4,092	903	15	1	1	19
Stolen property; buying, receiving, possessing	11,627	7,106	4,359	33	3	3	123	19,771	12,125	7,380	98	5	6	157
Vandalism	76,549	62,110	13,584	304	20	50	481	25,366	17,557	7,281	185	8	9	326
Weapons; carrying, possessing, etc.	14,201	8,418	5,534	47	7	7	188	63,643	29,494	33,041	319	10	23	756
Prostitution and commercialized vice	821	278	533	1	......	......	9	33,597	11,989	21,204	95	14	41	254
Sex offenses (except forcible rape and prostitution)	10,806	7,494	3,119	29	3	3	158	34,047	26,302	7,011	209	14	44	467
Narcotic drug laws	38,911	33,454	4,844	108	13	87	405	98,687	72,432	24,764	162	57	131	1,141
Gambling	1,784	505	1,118	3	......	28	130	61,722	18,187	38,993	15	119	634	3,774
Offenses against family and children	603	509	76	11	......	......	7	49,353	33,195	15,453	435	9	5	256
Driving under the influence	3,119	2,817	234	44	2	......	22	295,545	239,082	50,352	4,206	84	249	1,572
Liquor laws	65,434	62,017	2,320	848	16	12	221	138,780	114,028	21,253	2,784	46	27	642
Drunkenness	36,244	30,280	4,059	1,695	3	12	195	1,357,642	980,858	288,537	79,770	195	430	7,852
Disorderly conduct	111,195	73,670	35,893	598	17	21	996	449,342	274,509	159,684	7,997	103	53	6,996
Vagrancy	9,775	7,296	2,087	50	7	58	277	79,697	59,531	18,429	1,118	34	32	553
All other offenses (except traffic)	197,111	150,680	42,265	1,276	50	289	2,551	420,236	299,391	111,339	4,902	140	379	4,085
Suspicion	21,421	14,176	7,110	115	......	1	19	67,585	34,012	33,208	284	5	2	74
Curfew and loitering law violations	97,540	76,282	18,656	850	47	288	1,417	......	......	......	......	......	......	......
Runaways	146,944	121,562	21,240	1,569	61	116	2,396	......	......	......	......	......	......	......

Source: *Uniform Crime Reports—1968*, pp. 121–122.

TABLE A-8

Total arrest trends by sex, 1967–68
[4,216 agencies; 1968 estimated population 136,780,000]

Offense Charged	Males Arrested						Females Arrested					
	Total Number			Under 18			Total Number			Under 18		
	1967	1968	Percent Change	1967	1968	Percent Change	1967	1968	Percent Change	1967	1968	Percent Change
TOTAL	4,419,863	4,579,429	+3.6	1,023,210	1,113,572	+8.8	629,730	681,777	+8.3	220,420	251,170	+14.0
Criminal homicide:												
a) Murder and nonnegligent manslaughter	7,136	8,277	+16.0	713	907	+27.2	1,389	1,588	+14.3	78	75	−3.8
b) Manslaughter by negligence	2,532	2,645	+4.5	211	199	−5.7	294	299	+1.7	19	26	+36.8
Forcible rape	11,782	11,973	+1.6	2,378	2,448	+2.9	...	...	...	...	...	...
Robbery	54,297	63,536	+17.0	17,480	21,266	+21.7	2,969	3,793	+27.8	921	1,213	+31.7
Aggravated assault	87,034	87,798	+.9	15,465	14,933	−3.4	13,005	12,704	−2.3	2,318	2,016	−13.0
Burglary—breaking or entering	214,045	233,314	+9.0	115,239	128,426	+11.4	9,078	10,223	+12.6	4,636	5,261	+13.5
Larceny—theft	318,661	334,046	+4.8	185,054	189,655	+2.5	100,695	109,143	+8.4	48,244	50,640	+5.0
Auto theft	105,653	113,870	+7.8	65,596	69,046	+5.3	4,729	5,941	+25.6	3,082	3,751	+21.7
Subtotal for above offenses	801,140	855,459	+6.8	402,136	426,880	+6.2	132,159	143,691	+8.7	59,298	62,982	+6.2

Other assaults	189,451	203,621	+7.5	30,333	33,909	+11.8	22,980	26,543	+15.5	5,730	6,812	+18.9
Arson	6,909	7,918	+14.6	4,600	5,110	+11.1	521	700	+34.4	210	356	+69.5
Forgery and counterfeiting	23,733	25,363	+6.9	2,912	3,093	+6.2	6,289	7,182	+14.2	692	809	+16.9
Fraud	39,441	40,811	+3.5	1,876	1,980	+5.5	11,905	13,077	+9.8	423	457	+8.0
Embezzlement	4,653	4,254	−8.6	223	196	−12.1	1,125	1,012	−10.0	25	41	+64.0
Stolen property; buying, receiving, possessing	24,911	32,607	+30.9	8,875	11,422	+28.7	1,982	2,709	+36.7	568	718	+26.4
Vandalism	95,897	97,533	+1.7	74,531	73,783	−1.0	6,315	6,882	+9.0	4,196	4,519	+7.7
Weapons; carrying, possessing, etc.	62,636	75,132	+20.0	11,725	13,598	+16.0	4,418	5,103	+15.5	452	577	+27.7
Prostitution and commercialized vice	8,536	9,120	+6.8	242	271	+12.0	29,694	33,007	+11.2	565	589	+4.2
Sex offenses (except forcible rape and prostitution)	43,750	40,140	−8.3	9,247	8,407	−9.1	6,669	5,467	−18.0	3,178	2,422	−23.8
Narcotic drug laws	82,846	133,776	+61.5	17,174	33,733	+96.4	13,195	23,367	+77.1	3,219	7,884	+144.9
Gambling	74,883	69,370	−7.4	1,995	1,876	−6.0	7,082	6,267	−11.5	64	41	−35.9
Offenses against family and children	46,631	43,278	−7.2	682	400	−41.3	4,853	4,251	−12.4	308	128	−58.4
Driving under the influence	241,026	271,817	+12.8	2,531	2,806	+10.9	16,980	18,817	+10.8	120	140	+16.7
Liquor laws	173,388	175,160	+1.0	50,933	52,831	+3.7	23,220	24,132	+3.9	9,206	10,074	+9.4
Drunkenness	1,297,768	1,254,396	−3.3	29,079	31,258	+7.5	100,435	94,895	−5.5	3,404	4,059	+19.2
Disorderly conduct	451,560	491,268	+8.8	89,592	105,773	18.1	70,788	76,147	+7.6	14,880	17,450	+17.3
Vagrancy	86,442	85,420	−1.2	7,795	9,232	+18.4	9,093	9,740	+7.1	1,112	1,458	+31.1
All other offenses (except traffic)	529,069	517,315	−2.2	141,536	151,343	+6.9	85,221	90,942	+6.7	37,964	41,808	+10.1
Suspicion (not included in totals)	76,992	73,071	−5.1	18,385	18,396	+.1	16,082	13,826	−14.0	2,575	2,769	+7.5
Curfew and loitering law violations	72,715	75,082	+3.3	72,715	75,082	+3.3	15,936	17,687	+11.0	15,936	17,687	+11.0
Runaways	62,478	70,589	+13.0	62,478	70,589	+13.0	58,870	70,159	+19.2	58,870	70,159	+19.2

Source: *Uniform Crime Reports—1968*, p. 119.

Indexes

NAME INDEX

SUBJECT INDEX

This book has been set in 10 and 9 point
Caledonia, leaded 2 points. Part numbers are
in 24 point Ultra Bodoni and part titles are in
24 point Kennerly. Chapter numbers are in 18
point Ultra Bodoni and chapter titles are in 18
point Kennerly. The size of the type page is
27 × 45½ picas.